Folens

EXPLORING
psychology

for
A2 Level
AQA 'A'

Matt Jarvis and Julia Russell

awton

© 2009 Folens Limited, on behalf of the authors.

United Kingdom: Folens Publishers, Waterslade House, Thame Rd, Haddenham, Buckinghamshire HP17 8NT.

www.folens.com

Ireland: Folens Publishers, Greenhills Road, Tallaght, Dublin 24.

Email: info@folens.ie

Project development: Rick Jackman (Jackman Publishing Solutions Ltd)

Concept design: Patricia Briggs

Layout artist: GreenGate Publishing Services

Illustrations: Barking Dog Art and GreenGate Publishing Services

Cover image: P.E. Reed/Photonica

First published 2009 by Folens Limited.

Every effort has been made to contact copyright holders of material used in this publication. If any copyright holder has been overlooked, we should be pleased to make any necessary arrangements.

British Library Cataloguing in Publication Data. A catalogue record for this publication is available from the British Library.

ISBN: 978-1-85008-343-6

Contents

Introduction

Exploring Psychology for A2 is an entirely new resource for the updated AQA-A Psychology specification from the authors of the hugely successful *Exploring Psychology for AS*. If you have already encountered *Exploring Psychology for AS*, you will know that we have developed a textbook that really meets the changing needs of psychology students and their teachers. But what makes *Exploring* so special as a book?

The text is clearly written to make reading easy. It contains all the essential information required by the AQA-A specification and is enhanced by the use of much up-to-date, interesting research. Matt, Julia and Jean-Marc *enjoy* psychology and want their readers to as well. The text also includes interactive features that are designed to teach students to think psychologically – to construct their own understanding of the subject rather than echo that of the authors. These will extend students' learning, enabling them to go beyond the information provided so that they can become competent researchers. In short, it aims to produce students who not only have knowledge and understanding of psychologists but also think like psychologists.

The text contains the following features, designed to develop higher-level thinking and research skills.

To develop higher-level psychological thinking skills:

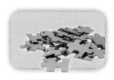

- *Thinking practically about psychology*: an interactive feature providing cues and requiring students to use psychological theory and research in a range of real-life situations.
- *Thinking critically about psychology*: an interactive feature requiring students to evaluate theories and studies in different ways, such as in terms of evidence, ethics, methodology and validity.
- *Thinking creatively about psychology*: an interactive feature requiring students to design studies to test ideas, to consider alternative ways of investigating a phenomenon and to combine explanations for psychological phenomena to come up with broader understandings.

To develop advanced secondary research skills:

- *Looking further*: an interactive feature in which students are guided through the process of researching a topic, for example making general enquiries about psychological issues, using online databases and specialist search engines to locate additional studies to add to their notes.

To develop examination skills:

- *What do I know?*: a feature based on examination-style questions to help students to practise using their newly acquired knowledge in order to develop a good understanding of the format of testing they will encounter in their module examinations.

- *Exploring issues and debates*: a new feature for the A2 text which raises general questions in each chapter to help students to apply the topic to issues and debates such as gender and cultural bias, the role of animals in research, ethical issues, the nature/nurture debate, free will and determinism and reductionism.
- *Research in action*: a feature that uses real examples of studies described in the Unit 3 chapters (9–12) to help students to understand specific ideas in research methods.

- *Your examinations*: an entire chapter devoted to developing a good examination technique. Written by an experienced AQA-A examiner, this section provides example questions, worked answers and examiner commentary.

The overall content of the book is structured closely around the AQA-A specification. As it is the product of a collaborative project with a senior examiner you can be sure that you won't waste a lot of time reading material you don't need to know. However, we have made sure that, within the demands of the specification, we have provided you with as much interesting, up-to-date and relevant to real life material as possible to study. This is because motivation is incredibly important in learning; we want you to share our love of psychology, work hard at it and do well. Happy exploring!

Acknowledgements

Matt, Julia and Jean-Marc would like to thank Rick Jackman who, as always, has been an excellent guide on this project, also the team at Folens who have provided terrific support.

Dedications

JR to Em with love

MJ to Clare with love

From JML to Mara

CHAPTER 1
Biological Rhythms and Sleep

Thinking ahead

By the end of this chapter you should be able to:

- outline different types of biological rhythms (circadian, infradian and ultradian) and describe the role of endogenous pacemakers and exogenous zeitgebers in the control of biological rhythms

- explain the effects of disrupting biological rhythms

- describe the nature of sleep

- describe and evaluate restorational theory and evolutionary explanations of sleep

- describe and explain lifespan changes in sleep

- describe and explain primary and secondary insomnia and factors that affect insomnia

- describe and explain sleep walking and narcolepsy as sleep disorders

This chapter explores the biological factors controlling our bodily rhythms, the nature of sleep, including how the patterns of sleep change over the lifespan, and explanations of why we sleep. We will also look at what happens when our biological rhythms are disrupted, by shift work and in jet lag. Finally, we will consider what happens when sleeping goes wrong – the causes of sleep loss and the nature of two other sleep disorders, sleep walking and narcolepsy.

Biological rhythms

In general, we get up in the morning and go to bed at night. Even when we're on holiday, we usually get up and go to bed each day. What causes this pattern? And what happens if it is disrupted? Why, during the holidays, do we tend to lie in? And why, if we travel to our holiday destination by air, do we find it difficult to sleep? These are some of the questions we will answer in this section. Many physiological and behavioural responses of animals, including ourselves, are controlled by a regular cycle of bodily changes. These bodily rhythms may be *endogenous*, dictated by internal events, or *exogenous*, controlled by external events. More commonly, control is exerted by interaction of the two factors.

Our bodily and cognitive functions go through cyclical changes. Some of these cycles last about one day and are called *circadian* rhythms (*circa* = about, *dies* = day). Those cycles occurring more often than daily are described as *ultradian* rhythms (*ultra* = more [often than once per], *dies* = day). Our heart beat, for instance, is an ultradian rhythm and like other functions it is affected both intrinsically, by the pacemaker, and by external factors, such as air quality. Similar rhythmicity can be seen in psychological functions, such as appetite and awareness. Cyclical changes occurring over the course of periods longer than one day are called *infradian* rhythms (they occur *infra* = less [often than], *dies* = daily).

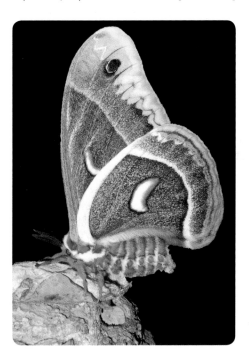

◀ **Figure 1.1** A female moth *Hyalophora cecropia* uses a circadian rhythm to avoid attracting a mate of the wrong species

Before we look at the nature and control of biological rhythms it is important to consider why they exist at all. For modern humans, time is clearly important but you may have more difficulty understanding why time-measuring systems would have evolved in animals. Consider a bee that leaves the hive for a patch of flowers that only open in the evening. Unless it can 'tell the time' it will have a wasted journey. One reason for biological rhythms therefore is to enable animals to anticipate changes and respond accordingly in advance of being able to directly see the change happening. Now imagine a female moth in search of a mate. She can release an airborne chemical (a pheromone) that males can detect but it attracts males of her own and other species. Clearly she needs to find a male of her own species with the least effort. This is exactly what happens with two closely related species of moth (*Hyalophora cecropia* and *Hyalophora promethea*). They avoid the problem by releasing their pheromones at entirely different times of day. Another reason for cycles, therefore, is to synchronise behaviours.

Circadian rhythms

Many biological cycles, including the examples of the behaviour of the moths and bees above, are circadian rhythms. Over the course of 24 hours, there are regular changes in variables such as our body temperature and the production of urine – both of which fall while we are asleep.

Our most familiar behavioural rhythm is the sleep–wake cycle, that repetitive programme that insists that we go to sleep each night and wake up the next day. Whilst we can 'lie in', we can't keep ourselves asleep indefinitely, nor can we stay endlessly awake. Our patterned sleeping and waking therefore runs on a circadian rhythm.

KEY TERMS

endogenous cues   internal control factors

exogenous cues   external control factors

circadian rhythms   bodily cycles that occur every 24 hours (*circa* = about [once a], *dies* = day)

ultradian rhythms   bodily cycles that occur several times a day (*ultra* = more [often than once per], *dies* = day)

infradian rhythms   bodily cycles that occur less frequently than daily (*infra* = less [often than], *dies* = daily)

▼ **Figure 1.2** We cannot help but sleep

▶ **Figure 1.3** Without cues about day length our biological clock free-runs

Tied to our 24-hour sleep–wake cycle is a rhythmical variation in awareness. When our body clock expects us to be asleep, our cognitive processing reaches a trough. Between 1am and 6am our sensitivity to pain, manual dexterity and reaction time bottom out, regardless of whether we are sleep-deprived. So 4am might seem a good time to visit your dentist (because your sensitivity to pain is lower) but, given cyclical changes in dexterity, will you be safe? Some important consequences of our reduced task performance during the small hours relate to safety, on the road and in the workplace. These applications are considered on pp8–10. Other circadian rhythms are exhibited in behaviours such as eating and drinking, as well as our emotions, such as cheerfulness, and physiological processes such as the metabolism of alcohol.

Our circadian rhythm regulates behaviours such as sleeping and waking. By affecting the activity of neurones in particular brain areas (including the hypothalamus and the suprachiasmatic nuclei) and neurotransmitters (such as acetylcholine, noradrenaline and serotonin) in a cyclical way, the daily pattern of sleeping and waking is precisely regulated. In the typical day, sleep onset coincides with the absence of daylight but even without this external cue the desire to sleep arises regularly. What happens to this cycle without exposure to daylight?

Studies have been conducted with participants isolated from natural light–dark schedules in caves or in more comfortable experimental rooms (where they have exposure to light on demand, are able to request food or old newspapers at any time of day and can sleep whenever they like). One such case was reported by Folkard (1996). A university student, Kate Aldcroft, was housed in a laboratory for 25 days with no access to cues about time of day. To indicate her perception of the passage of time, she was asked to play *Amazing Grace* on the bagpipes twice a day at what she believed was the same time on each occasion. The time at which she played became later over the study period. She began to sleep for longer – up to 16 hours at a time – and her sleep–wake cycle extended to 30 hours. Findings from such experiments suggest that without external cues the human biological clock maintains rhythmical activity but that the apparent day length extends.

LOOKING FURTHER Use the internet to explore biological (*body* or *circadian*) rhythms. A classic study of circadian rhythms involved a Frenchman, named Michael Siffre, spending a long time in a cave, isolated from cyclical cues. Find out about Siffre and use your knowledge of the control of circadian rhythms to explain his experiences

Experimental evidence with rats confirms the spontaneous lengthening of the circadian cycle. Groblewski *et al.* (1980) found that rats' circadian clocks advanced an hour a day if they were isolated from daylight schedules. In such isolation experiments with humans, participants maintain 'daily' activities but, as with rats, these began to *free-run*. By free-running we mean that the biological clock extends the length of its cycle to a period of about 25–30 hours instead of the normal 24. Daily exposure to bright light or to regular social cues such as a telephone call at the same time each day is sufficient to keep the human clock in time (Empson, 1993). Environmental factors other than light can also *entrain* (that is, 'set') the clocks of animals such as hamsters. They will maintain a 24-hour sleep–wake cycle without light cues in response to regular feeding (Jilge, 1991), exercise (Mistlberger, 1991) or social interaction (Mrosovsky, 1988).

Control of circadian rhythms

What controls a circadian rhythm such that it assumes a 24-hour cycle? Both internal and external factors seem to be involved. The most obvious cue to set the cycle, the *zeitgeber* (German for 'time-giver'), is day length – the sun rises and sets every 24 hours. This external cue can affect our behaviour because information about light levels is detected in the eyes and passed on to the brain and endocrine (hormonal) system. Evidence suggests that these structures are responsible for the control of circadian rhythms.

In humans, the light level is detected by the retina, and passed on to retinal ganglion cells, which also contain a light sensitive pigment (Provencio *et al.*, 2000). These cells release a neurotransmitter (called acetylcholine) and have several effects. They activate the neurones that cause dream sleep and some also connect to a part of the brain called the *suprachiasmatic nucleus* (SCN) – a clump of cells in the hypothalamus. Rats that have been blinded lose their cyclical behaviour. They sleep for the same amount of time in total but they don't have a clearly defined sleep phase. This confirms that visual information is needed to 'set' the pattern.

▼ **Figure 1.4** This MRI scan shows the suprachiasmatic nucleus, located either side of the 'cross' of the optic chiasm

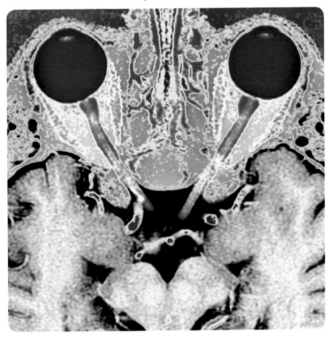

Rats are nocturnal (awake at night) so, given an activity wheel, will run at night. This activity can be automatically recorded, producing data about periodic behaviour. Groblewski *et al.* (1980) kept rats under artificial light. Initially the lights were on for 12 hours during the day and the rats ran at night. When the lighting schedule was shifted so that the 12-hour light phase occurred six hours later in the day, the rats began to run later, stabilising their active phase six hours later. Finally, the rats were exposed to continuous light, but their patterned activity persisted. When allowed to free-run, however, their clocks ran a little slow, extending their day to 25 hours instead of 24.

Miles *et al.* (1977) reported a case study of a young man who was blind from birth and had a circadian rhythm of 24.9 hours. He had problems keeping in step with a 24-hour schedule even with continual use of stimulants (in the morning) and sedatives (at night). This evidence, and that of

▶ **Figure 1.5** Hamsters with a suprachiasmatic nucleus transplanted from mutant hamsters with a 20-hour body clock changed their circadian rhythm

Groblewski *et al.*, suggests that, although light 'sets the clock', ie acts as a zeitgeber, it is not needed to maintain the cycle. This is the role of another part of the system.

Lesions of the SCN in animals abolish regularity in various behaviours such as drinking and activity (Stephan & Zucker, 1972) as well as their sleep patterns. Ralph *et al.* (1990) confirmed the role of the SCN in the sleep–wake cycle by transplanting the SCN between hamsters with different 'free-running' clocks. First they removed the SCN from foetuses of a mutant strain of hamsters with clocks that free-ran at 20 hours. These were transplanted into the brains of normal adult hamsters whose cycles had been disrupted by lesions. Instead of reverting to their old 25-hour rhythm, the adult recipients assumed a new 20-hour 'day'. Likewise a second transplant, of SCN from animals free-running at 25 hours, into ones of the mutant strain, produced individuals with a new cycle of 25 hours. This shows that the circadian rhythm is intrinsic to the SCN. Interestingly, the '20-hour' hamsters had experienced a mutation of a single gene (called *tau*), providing an example of the way in which genetics can directly affect behaviour.

The SCN responds to day length with neural messages to the *pineal gland*. This small gland is part of the endocrine system but is up inside the brain behind the hypothalamus and is insensitive to light. The cells of the pineal gland do, however, share characteristics with the rod-shaped photoreceptors of the retina, suggesting that its original role was as a light-sensitive organ. In some animals it lies closer to the surface of the head and is light-sensitive (see Figure 1.6).

▼ **Figure 1.6** The tuatara lizard has a 'third' eye on the top of its head which is sensitive to light and similar to our pineal gland

Information from the SCN about darkness causes the pineal gland to secrete the hormone *melatonin*, whilst daylight inhibits its production. The release of melatonin makes us feel sleepy. The absence of light, however, does not prevent cycling. Even in uninterrupted light or darkness, melatonin levels continue to rise and fall daily, although the rhythm does 'free-run'. Destruction of the SCN, in contrast, prevents cycling, showing that the SCN acts to control the release of melatonin through an endogenous rhythm. The SCN, therefore, is the endogenous clock or 'pacemaker'.

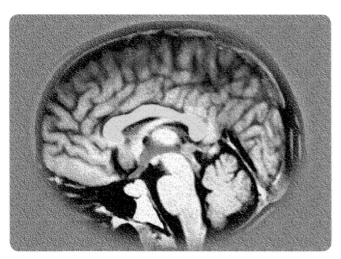

▲ **Figure 1.7** The pineal gland (coloured green above) is part of the endocrine system. It is tucked up beside the brain and releases fluctuating levels of the hormone melatonin to regulate the sleep–wake cycle

▼ **Table 1.1** Resetting the clock: the effects of melatonin and of bright light on sleep

		Time of day		
		Morning	Afternoon	Evening
Taking melatonin		sleep later (phase delay)	sleep earlier (phase advance)	little effect
Exposure to bright light		sleep earlier (phase advance)	little effect	sleep later (phase delay)

Melatonin affects our sleep cycle. If people take a 0.5mg dose of melatonin in the afternoon, they fall asleep earlier in the evening (and wake earlier the next day). This is called a 'phase advance' effect on the biological clock – we *advance* the sleep *phase*, ie make it arrive sooner. If we are exposed to bright light in the evening, the opposite occurs: we sleep and wake later. This effect is called 'phase delay' (see Table 1.1).

As you may guess from Table 1.1, not only does the SCN affect melatonin secretion, but the reverse occurs too. There are receptors for melatonin in the SCN and these may be involved in the process that allows the change in melatonin levels to help to reset the timing of the SCN clock.

Discussion of the biological control of the sleep–wake cycle

The control of our circadian rhythm is clearly complex and new processes are still being identified. It is controlled by both external (exogenous) factors such as light and endogenous (internal) factors. Detection of light may, at a cellular level, involve more than one system (the rods and cones and the retinal ganglion cells) and two or more structures – the SCN and the pineal gland – may act as 'pacemakers', being capable of maintaining the rhythm. There are likely to be other clock sites, for example daily fluctuations in body temperature (that are normally synchronised with the sleep–wake cycle) may be controlled by a separate mechanism, as destruction of the SCN does not entirely eradicate this rhythm (Thompson, 2000). Although the most important zeitgeber is light, many other rhythmic stimuli may act to entrain the biological clock, a factor that may be of use in assisting people whose daily lives are not diurnal, such as those working shifts.

Infradian rhythms

Some rhythms last longer than a day, these are the infradian rhythms. They include annual cycles (circannual rhythms), the menstrual cycle and animal activity cycles governed by the moon. Such cycles are adaptive as they enable animals to prepare, physiologically or behaviourally, in advance of changes in their environment.

M E D I A W A T C H :

Any ideas to help me get to sleep at night?

Dear Doctor Daniel,
I am having trouble getting to sleep at night. I don't want to take any drugs but just counting sheep isn't helping. Are there any natural products that work?

Doctor Daniel replies,
There are several brands of Night Time milk. These are simply fresh milk containing more melatonin that normal milk. It is a substance that helps to regulate your body clock and makes you feel sleepy. The dairies achieve the increase naturally by milking the cows at night when the melatonin in their system is at its peak.

1 What biological explanation would you give to account for the proposed effectiveness of Night Time milk?

▶ **Figure 1.8**

KEY TERM

spring tides the highest high tides each lunar month, which occur around the time of the full and new moon. The term is not related to 'spring', the season, but to the water jumping or 'springing' up the beach

A variety of sea creatures have breeding cycles that are linked to moon phases. These lunar cycles are adaptive as the highest and lowest tides are governed by the moon. For example, the grunion fish is washed on to the beach on each spring tide. The fish deposits its sperm and eggs on the beach where they are safe at least from predators in the sea. The fertilised eggs stay in the damp, warm sand where they grow. At the next spring tide the young fish are sufficiently developed to swim when they are washed back into the water.

▲ **Figure 1.9** The grunion fish *Leuresthes tenuis* comes out of the water to spawn on Californian beaches on the highest high tides, once a fortnight: an ultradian rhythm

Another infradian cycle is the human menstrual cycle. This is *not* a lunar cycle, although the average length of a woman's menstrual cycle is around 28 days (so is described as circalunar). It is controlled by hormones and, apart from controlling the release of eggs and preparation of the uterine lining for potential implantation of a fertilised egg, it also affects cognition and emotion. An example of the affect of the menstrual cycle on cognitive ability is described in the *Research Now* box.

Thinking creatively about psychology

Another factor that may vary over the menstrual cycle is mood. Design a study to investigate this.

The activity of many animals displays an annual rhythm. Breeding, aggression and migration often show cyclical variation over the year. The golden-mantled ground squirrel is a mammal that lives in North America and hibernates underground each autumn until the following spring. Pengelly & Asmundson (1974) studied the behaviour of five ground squirrels that had been born in captivity, blinded and kept in constant darkness. Their environment was kept at a constant temperature and ample food was continuously available. This ensured that the cues about the seasons available in the wild (day length, the abundance of food and temperature) were absent. Nevertheless, the ground squirrels continued to hibernate at roughly the same time each year, and emerge at about the same time as they would if they had been in the wild (see Figure 1.10). This suggests that they had an effective long-term clock.

Thinking critically about psychology

Identify the potential ethical issues in Pengelly & Asmundson's study on ground squirrels. What could the researchers have done to minimise these ethical issues in their study?

RESEARCH NOW

Celec P, Ostatnikova D, Putz Z & Kudela M (2002) The circalunar cycle of salivary testosterone and the visual-spatial performance. *Bratislavské Lekárske Listy* **103**(2), 59–69

Aim: To investigate the infradian cycles of testosterone levels and spatial ability in females.

Procedure: 31 young adult female participants provided daily saliva samples to assess for testosterone over a period of 30 days. They were tested daily with visuo-spatial tasks: mental rotation and spatial visualisation. Data about each participant's menstrual cycle was also collected.

Results: A circalunar cycle of testosterone level was found and this peaked prior to ovulation. There was a positive correlation between testosterone level and spatial task performance.

Conclusion: High testosterone levels in females are linked to better performance on spatial tasks.

▲ **Figure 1.10** Ground squirrels kept in continuous darkness still hibernate and emerge at about the right time of year

One possible explanation for the control of circannual rhythms when daily zeitgebers are present relates to the control of *circadian* ones. As day length shortens towards winter, the night-time excretion of melatonin increases. The endogenous pacemaker provided by the SCN and the pineal gland could therefore act as an annual as well as a circadian clock.

In hamsters, the breeding season begins as spring days get longer. Male hamsters begin to produce more testosterone. This is controlled by the SCN because if it is destroyed, the level of testosterone stays constant throughout the year (Rusak & Morin, 1976). This again suggests that the circadian and circannual clocks may be linked.

There are other similarities between the two types of clock. If the annual exogenous cues are changed, the rhythm changes too. Pengelly & Asmundson (1974) found that when woodchucks were moved from the USA to Australia they reversed their normal rhythm of hibernation (because the seasons were at different times). Furthermore, if blood from a hibernating ground squirrel was injected into a non-hibernating one, it triggered hibernation. This suggests that a biological factor controlling this infradian rhythm is present in the blood.

Studies have confirmed that melatonin is important in controlling seasonal changes in male sexual behaviour. By removing the pineal gland and replacing melatonin via injections Bartness *et al.* (1993) altered the timing of this behaviour in hamsters and sheep. More recent studies suggest that this biological 'calendar' is controlled by an interaction between melatonin (from the pineal gland) and another hormone, prolactin, from the pituitary gland.

Ultradian rhythms

Ultradian rhythms are ones that happen more often than daily (hence *ultra-dies*). You have probably noticed yourself occasionally feeling tired or losing concentration in even the most interesting lessons. This may be because of your basic rest and activity cycle (BRAC). Our attention and other physical and cognitive functions go through peaks and troughs approximately every 90 minutes. For example, eating, drinking, heart rate and oxygen consumption (and even nose-picking!) all rise and fall in cycles of approximately 90 minutes. However, other factors, such as fixed 'meal times', the amount of exercise we do and the behaviour of other people also affect these functions, so the BRAC is hard to see clearly in adults who are awake. It is, therefore, easier to observe in babies. Kleitman (1961) first observed this pattern in the regular feeding times of infants who are fed on demand.

Thinking practically about psychology

Kleitman (1969) suggested that the reason people like a coffee break at 10.30am is that it breaks the morning into two 90-minute halves.

If people don't stop work, but they are in a BRAC 'trough', they probably just fiddle around tidying the desk or doodling. What are the implications of this for school or college timetables?

The BRAC varies between species and is dependent on metabolic rate. Smaller animals which typically have faster metabolic rates have shorter BRACs. This ultradian rhythm in a cat, for instance, is only 20 minutes long. It can be demonstrated by observing any continuous behaviour. If a cat is observed performing a non-stop behaviour such as self-stimulation of the brain the pattern can be clearly seen. The cat's continuous activity shows a dip every 20 minutes. A similar pattern, which varies in different individuals between 40 and 85 minutes, can also be detected in rhesus monkeys (Maxim & Storrie, 1979).

Ultradian rhythms in sleep

In general, we sleep once during each 24-hour period: a circadian rhythm. This sleep phase is broken into shorter cycles with repeated psychological and physical changes during the night. This patterned activity can be traced using various physiological methods. These include:

- electroencephalogram (EEG) – this measures 'brain waves' using macroelectrodes (1cm diameter electrodes stuck to the surface of the head). They pick up, through the skull, the electrical activity of groups of active neurones
- electrooculogram (EOG) – this measures eye movements
- electromyogram (EMG) – this measures the activity of body muscles.

Tracing the type and amount of activity in the brain, eyes and muscles reveals a very consistent pattern from person to person and night to night. We all tend to fall into a light sleep which gets deeper (so we are harder to wake), then lighter again before we enter dream sleep. After some time spent dreaming, we re-enter deeper sleep. These phases of lighter and deeper sleep, alternate throughout the night, with each whole cycle taking about 90 minutes (see Figure 1.11). This is therefore an ultradian rhythm. This is just like the BRAC when we are awake, but it is easier to identify as there are fewer other factors to alter the patterns of changes. We will look at the detail of the changes in sleep on pp10–11.

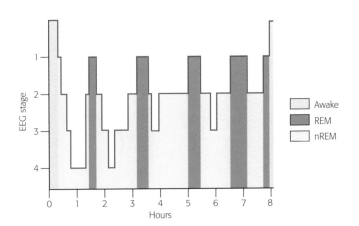

▼ Figure 1.11 The stages of sleep

Disrupting biological rhythms: shift work and jet lag

Although our sleep–wake cycle is usually in phase with the zeitgeber of sunrise and sunset so that we sleep when it is dark, this isn't always the case. In *shift work*, employees are required to work different patterns, such as starting work late in the afternoon and working until very late at night or starting at night and working through until the morning. People may also disrupt their circadian rhythm when they go on holiday. When we fly across time zones and try to adapt to a new pattern of exogenous cues we experience *jet lag*. In both cases problems can arise because it takes time for our biological clocks to adapt. During that time the endogenous and exogenous rhythms are *desynchronised*.

The endogenous clock free-runs on a longer than 24-hour cycle (see p3). Because of this, we find it easier to make changes that lengthen the day rather than shorten it. As a consequence, making a change of shift or a flight across time zones that produces phase delay is less of problem than the reverse. When problems do arise as a result of shift work or jet lag, they are very similar. Symptoms include feeling tired (but finding it hard to sleep), headaches, irritability and illness (eg stomach upsets). There are also cognitive effects such as reduced performance and poor judgement. In this section we will explore some of the problems caused by these changes to our daily schedule and some ways to reduce them.

Shift work

When we are working 'out of phase' with our biological clocks our performance is reduced, we are less attentive and are slower to respond regardless of whether we have slept. One reason for this is that we find it more difficult to fall asleep when we can. Fatigue is a possible contributory factor in many

▼ Table 1.2 Some examples of disasters caused by human error by shiftworkers

Place	Disaster	Time disaster occurred
Bhopal	Chemical plant explosion	12.40am
Chernobyl	Nuclear reactor disaster	1.23am
Three Mile Island	Nuclear reactor disaster	4.00am
Mexico City	Western Airlines crash	3.30am

disasters; consider those listed in Table 1.2, and the time of day when they occurred.

Two independent problems arise with shift work: the need to maintain a 24-hour cycle that is out of sync with the world, and the demands of a changing shift pattern. People working shifts are often sleep-deprived simply because it is difficult to sleep well when it is light and noisy outside. The social constraints of being awake when no one else is may tempt night shift workers to get up early or stay up late for company or facilities, depriving themselves of sleep. For example, Seo *et al.* (2000) found that older workers on night shifts, but not other shifts, had reduced total sleep times as they woke up early. To solve the problem of being woken up by daylight, shift workers are recommended to use thick curtains or blackout blinds. These also help to solve the second problem of circadian disruption.

To work shifts, people need to be awake during the late evening and/or early morning and sleep during the day. Unless workers succeed in resetting their biological clock, they experience sleepiness at work and insomnia when they go home. This is particularly severe if shifts change often, or if they move 'against' the body clock. After a shift change, people

▼ Figure 1.12 Assembly line production often runs 24 hours a day so employees work shifts. When they change shift, their body clocks are affected

take a week or more to adapt to the new regime, during which time they are less effective at work as they are operating during their body clock's 'night' and are restless when they should be sleeping.

Many workers on night shift are performing passive tasks such as monitoring and are often in a warm, dimly lit environment. According to Czeisler *et al.* (1990) this is counterproductive to keeping them alert. They compared the rate of adaptation of two groups of participants to an imposed 'shift change' by asking them to report to the laboratory during the night and sleep at home during the day. The control group worked during the night in ordinary indoor lighting of about 150 lux. The experimental group worked under bright illumination of 7000–12,000 lux, equivalent to early morning light. The experimental group were also asked to stay in complete darkness from 9am to 5pm, whilst the controls were given no specific instructions. The resetting of the participants' biological clocks was monitored by measuring body temperature, which varies rhythmically. After six days the experimental group had all shifted the low point of the circadian temperature rhythm by 10 hours, the controls had moved by only one hour. A similar pattern was observed in task performance. Bright lighting in the work environment seems to be a key to ensuring that workers adapt to new shifts so that they sleep well during the day and are alert during the night. Even in this situation adaptation can take up to four days, so people who change shift every week would spend most of their time desynchronised from their environment.

The hormone melatonin can play a role in helping shift workers to adjust to a new rhythm. Sharkey *et al.* (2001) found that taking melatonin could help shift workers to sleep during the afternoon (as they have to when shifts change), but only on the first day of use. It did not reduce alertness or performance during the subsequent simulated 'night shift'.

Thinking practically about psychology

Imagine a nurse working a night shift on a ward where patients are sleeping. What is the environment probably like?
Decide what changes you would put in place to make it easier for the nurse to adapt to the new shift pattern.

Sharkey & Eastman (2002) went on to investigate whether melatonin, compared to a placebo, would help shift workers to adjust their circadian rhythm. The change in circadian rhythm (indicated by the body temperature cycle and the natural release of melatonin) was greater in participants taking oral melatonin than in those taking placebos, and this effect was greater at a dose of 3mg than at 0.5mg. Again, this suggests that melatonin can be used to move the phase of the circadian rhythm.

Jet lag

Air travel has introduced another problem for our internal clocks, resulting in problems such as fatigue, reduced attention, loss of appetite and depression, which cannot be explained by sleep loss alone. When we cross time zones we have to reset our biological clock to the local zeitgeber. As with shift changes that extend the day, travelling east to west produces fewer problems as we 'gain' time. The return journey however presents problems. Pilots can be severely affected by changing time zones repeatedly, due to frequent and erratic exposure to the bright light of sunrise. This causes them to sleep poorly when they can rest, resulting in tiredness when flying.

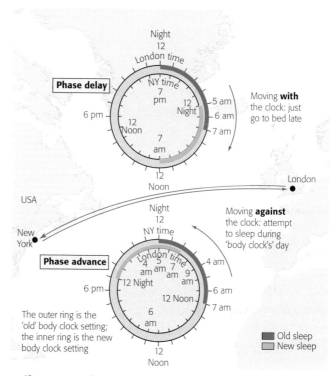

▲ Figure 1.13 Jet lag: the problem with crossing time zones quickly

Harma *et al.* (1994a,b) and Suvanto *et al.* (1993) examined the effects of a four-day flight that crossed 10 time zones on the sleep, attentiveness, body temperature and salivary melatonin levels of flight attendants. Forty female participants logged their subjective sleepiness and sleep quality each day. Their alertness, visual task performance, melatonin level and body temperature were monitored every two hours. They found that the participants became sleepier over the four days and slept less well. Their cognitive skills also varied with their endogenous rhythm. The rhythm of melatonin secretion and body temperature had delayed by almost four hours after the westward flight. Interestingly, these two measures became desynchronised from one another. Body temperature was faster to resynchronise than the melatonin secretion rhythm and their other symptoms.

▼ **Figure 1.14** Pilots cross many time zones, putting them at risk from jet lag

Research has investigated whether taking oral melatonin can combat the effects of jet lag. Herxheimer & Petrie (2001) reviewed the results of 10 studies and found that in nine of these, participants reported experiencing decreased jet lag (from flights crossing at least five time zones) when taking melatonin compared with those given placebos. When taken later in the 'day' of the destination time zone, melatonin in doses up to 5mg was effective at inducing sleep. Slow-release capsules, however, were ineffective. This suggests that a single daily dose of melatonin at the right time can help to reset the circadian rhythm.

Some evidence suggests that light may not be the only important zeitgeber in adjustment to new time zones. Amir & Stewart (1996) have shown that rats who receive a breeze before their light phase can reset their clocks just using this exogenous cue. For people, there may be many signals that help to maintain our circadian rhythm that are absent when we travel abroad, such as the time we eat or TV programmes we watch. Whereas light schedules exist everywhere, other aspects of our regulated lives may change, particularly if we are on holiday. This may contribute to the slow rate at which we adapt to new time zones. The simplest way to combat the effects of a long-haul eastbound flight is to start going to bed and getting up progressively earlier before you travel. Other factors that are important include the timing of meals and exercise.

> ↪ **Exploring issues and debates**
> ### Determinism
> *'I can't go to sleep, my brain won't let me'*
>
> Draw up a table with two columns, one for the uncontrollable (determined) aspects of the control of our circadian rhythm and one for the aspects over which we have free will. To what extent do we *really* have free will about when we sleep?

Sleep states

Sleep can be defined as a necessary state of altered consciousness experienced by animals with a central nervous system. It is characterised by rhythmical occurrence, limited sensitivity and reduced mobility. By its very nature, therefore, sleep is difficult to study. Look back to p7 at the methods used to study sleep.

Aserinsky & Kleitman (1953) recorded the EEGs of sleeping participants and found that they sometimes consisted of *alpha* waves, resembling wakefulness (see Figure 1.15). During these times the EOG was active, as it is when we are awake. Participants in this condition were hard to wake up but tended to report dreams when woken. This stage is 'paradoxical', it shares

characteristics with both very deep sleep and with wakefulness. It was identified as a separate stage of sleep by Dement & Kleitman (1957) and has been variously called *paradoxical sleep*, *dream sleep* or *REM sleep*, after the characteristic rapid eye movements (40–60 movements per minute) that occur throughout the stage. REM sleep is also identifiable by the loss of muscle tone (measured with an EMG). So while the EOG is active during REM sleep, the EMG is inactive; our bodies are effectively paralysed.

Everyone has dreams, but we only recall them if we happen to wake up, even briefly, during REM. People who 'don't dream' simply always wake up in nREM (non-REM) and may have poor visual memories.

Most of the night is spent in nREM sleep. This is not a single state but consists of four stages (see Figure 1.15).

- *Stage 1*: light sleep – the sleeper is easily woken, has a slow heart rate and an irregular EEG, with little alpha activity.
- *Stage 2*: deeper sleep – the sleeper is still fairly easy to wake. The EEG has occasional *spindles* (high frequency low amplitude waves) and *K complexes* (occasional high amplitude waves).
- *Stage 3*: deep sleep – the sleeper is unresponsive, has a slow pulse, low blood pressure and a lowered body temperature. The EEG contains some slow waves (low frequency delta waves).
- *Stage 4*: deep sleep – the EEG consists mainly of high amplitude, low frequency *delta waves*.

Figure 1.11 (p8) shows how we move from relaxed wakefulness into sleep and then through deeper sleep stages before returning through shallower nREM to reach our first REM phase. We then alternate between REM and nREM during the night. Several patterns can be seen in recordings of sleeping participants:

- the deepest sleep occurs early in the night
- REM phases increase in length during the night
- natural waking tends to occur during REM
- each 'cycle' from stage 1 back to stage 1 or REM takes about 90 minutes (an ultradian rhythm).

▼ **Figure 1.15** The four stages of non-REM sleep

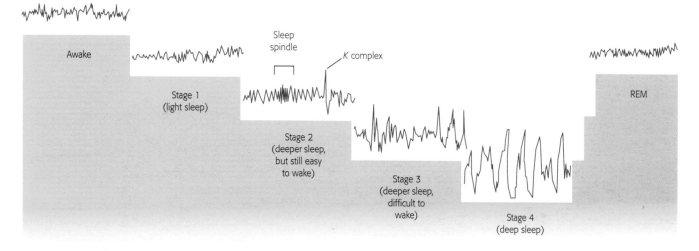

Functions of sleep

People spend a great deal of their lifetime asleep – somewhere in the region of 175,000 hours in a lifetime. This behaviour could only have evolved if the costs associated with sleeping were outweighed by its benefits. And in evolutionary terms sleep is costly. We are asleep when we could be eating or reproducing and, because of the lowered level of sensitivity, we are at greater risk from the weather, competitors or predators. There should, therefore, be potential benefits that have made sleeping an evolutionarily worthwhile investment. In this section we will explore two possible explanations – evolutionary theory and restorational theory.

Evolutionary theory

Kleitman (1963) suggested that sleep may simply serve to save energy by ensuring that an animal is inactive when it would be inefficient. This makes sense as, during sleep, animals not only save energy by being inactive but, in the case

of mammals, also by the slight lowering of body temperature. Meddis (1977) argued that sleep is an instinctive behaviour that has evolved to keep animals 'out of trouble'. For humans, being out in the dark is dangerous, so we sleep at night. Cats and owls, on the other hand, have better night vision than us and can gain an advantage over their prey in the cover of darkness. They sleep during the day when their chances of successful hunting are lower. It is beneficial for small desert mammals to avoid the intense heat so they sleep during the day. In each case, sleep occurs when the animal is least effective. Empson (1993) has described this as the 'waste of time' theory; animals are simply biding their time until the environment is more suitable, so the function of sleep is to 'waste time'! The amount of time an animal spends asleep should therefore be related to how vulnerable it is and how hard it has to work to find food. In general, predatory species that eat highly nutritious food and are at less risk sleep for longer than their prey (see Figure 1.16).

▼ Figure 1.16 Sleeping predators are safe, their prey are not. This affects how long they sleep

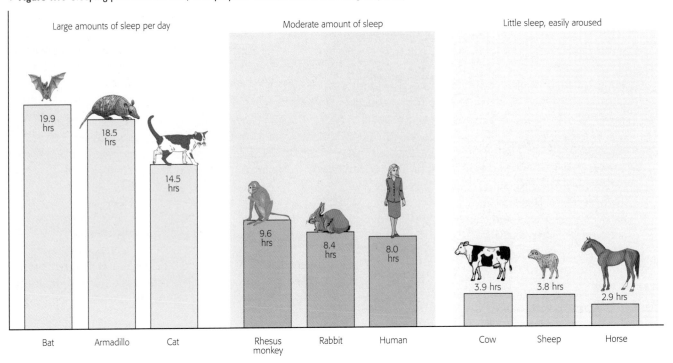

The absence of motor activity during sleep can be accounted for by evolutionary theory. Keeping still has the benefit of saving energy, but being entirely inactive is even better: a motionless animal is less likely to attract the attention of predators. This can be extended to explain the reduction in sensitivity. For animals that rely on camouflage or concealment for protection, keeping completely motionless even when a predator is very near will lower the chances of detection. Being asleep ensures that the animal won't respond and blow its cover. It could even be argued that the reduction in brain activity ensures that the hiding animal is not motivated to seek out sources of stimulation.

▼ Figure 1.17 Small mammals are at risk from predators during the daytime so tend to sleep during daylight and are active at night. In the daytime, sleeping keeps them quiet and safe from predators and still so that they use little energy

If we wish to explain the existence of sleep through evolutionary adaptation, we need to be able to demonstrate that it has a long and common evolutionary history. Reptiles, the ancestors of modern birds and mammals, show various characteristics of sleep. Most reptiles only have REM sleep. The lizards, quite advanced reptiles, have both nREM and REM sleep, with loss of muscle tone and rapid eye movements. This observation may help to explain the appearance of REM sleep before nREM sleep in the human foetus. In embryological development, characteristics generally appear in phylogenetic (ancestral) sequence. Birds and mammals, which evolved later than lizards, have very similar nREM and REM sleep.

Discussion of evolutionary theory

Evolutionary theory can explain why different species sleep at different times of day because they stay awake when they are better adapted, for example to hunt or avoid being hunted. This explanation can also account for the reduction of movement and sensitivity during sleep as it serves to keep animals still and quiet thus reducing the risk of predation.

However, evolutionary theory cannot account for the absolute necessity to sleep, even when this is apparently maladaptive. Two marine mammals, the bottle-nosed dolphin and the porpoise, which have to come to the surface to breathe, sleep with each brain hemisphere alternately. For animals with a very high metabolic rate that need to eat almost continuously, sleeping seems disadvantageous. Animals such as shrews sleep for very short periods so that they can eat frequently. These observations suggest that sleep has some purpose beyond keeping the animal out of trouble. Furthermore, the evolutionary theory cannot explain other observations about sleep, such as why we need both REM and nREM sleep.

▼ **Figure 1.18** The dolphin sleeps with one side of its brain, then the other

Restorational theory

Restorational theory, proposed by Oswald (1969), suggests that we need to sleep in order to conduct growth and repair functions. The processes of restoration and activity are mutually exclusive: we cannot 'recharge our batteries' whilst we are still running on them. Oswald (1980) reports that high levels of ATP, the energy currency of the cell, are only found during sleep because, during wakefulness, we are constantly using up the ATP. This is especially so for the brain: it represents little of our body weight but uses a great deal of energy. Sleep is much better than just rest in this respect – the energy cost of sleeping is only about two-thirds that of rest.

Bodily inactivity during REM sleep may be important for restoration of muscles. Adam (1977b) found a positive correlation between the weight of participants and the time they spent in REM sleep; heavier people spent longer in REM sleep. This is perhaps because heavier participants would expend more energy maintaining posture and moving during the day, so would need more time to restore their muscles at night. Zepelin & Rechtschaffen (1974) found a similar relationship between the activity levels of different animal species and the time they spent asleep. However, experimental evidence does not in general support a relationship between physical exertion and total sleep time. For example, resting in bed does not reduce sleep time (Ryback & Lewis, 1971) and increased exercise either has little effect or only increases nREM sleep.

One way to test the restorational function of sleep is to deprive people of sleep and observe the effects. Sleep deprivation experiments suggest that humans begin to suffer after relatively short periods of sleep deprivation. Dement (1960) deprived young volunteers of REM or nREM sleep on five successive nights. The REM sleep-deprived participants became irritable, nervous, unable to concentrate, and some reported hallucinations. When allowed uninterrupted sleep, these individuals fell straight into REM sleep and spent up to 60 per cent more time in REM sleep; this is called a *REM rebound effect*. Similar effects have been reported during total sleep deprivation, such as experienced by Peter Tripp, a disc jockey who kept himself awake for 200 hours during a charity broadcast. Luce & Segal (1966) describe the decline in his cognitive ability and emotional stability, including his experiences of hallucinations and extreme paranoia. His extreme responses have, however, been attributed to his drug misuse.

A one-time holder of *The Guinness Book of Records*' 'longest time without sleep' was 17-year-old Randy Gardener. He was closely observed by Gulevich *et al.* (1966) and showed none of the problems exhibited by other sleep-deprived participants. Although sleepy, he successfully beat William Dement at 100 straight games on a baseball machine on his first sleepless night! Following his 264-hour sleep deprivation, he slept for 15 hours and awoke feeling quite normal.

Dement (1965) concluded that the severe effects of sleep deprivation reported in early research resulted from experimenter effects. The participants were expected to suffer bizarre sensations and these were duly reported. When warned of potential side effects and offered a round-the-clock psychiatrist, to whom unusual sensations could be reported, demand characteristics alone could have accounted for the hallucinations and paranoia experienced.

▼ **Figure 1.19** Following vigorous exercise, there is little change in athletes' sleep

Thinking critically about psychology

Identify the potential ethical issues in Dement's study. What would the researchers have had to do to ensure that the study was conducted in an ethical way? To what extent could these precautions have led to demand characteristics?

Sleep deprivation in animals can be maintained for much longer periods and the physical effects are much more severe. Early experiments were hindered by the confounding variable of forced exercise; it is necessary to keep the animal moving in order to keep it awake. Rechtschaffen *et al.* (1983) overcame this difficulty by designing a piece of apparatus in which pairs of animals could be housed and would experience identical exercise demands. One of the animals would be sleep-deprived, the other not – so providing a well-matched control (see Figure 1.20). The rats lived in the apparatus and the experimental animals soon began to look ill. They stopped grooming, became weak and uncoordinated and often fell off the turntable. Several of the rats died and others had to be put down because they were suffering from stomach ulcers and internal bleeding. None lasted longer than 33 days. The rats were not infected, so the disorders must have been caused by the stress of sleep deprivation.

▼ **Figure 1.20** The apparatus used by Rechtschaffen *et al.* (1983) to deprive one rat, but not its 'yoked' partner, of sleep. Whenever the deprived rat began to sleep, it was prevented from doing so by rotating the platform, keeping it awake (by making it walk to avoid falling in the water) for at least six seconds. In between these times the non-deprived animal could take undisturbed sleep

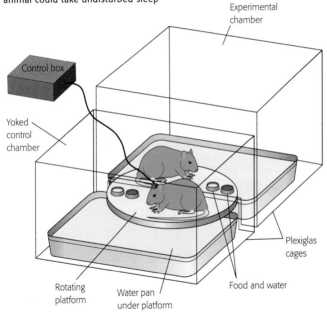

Experimental chamber

Control box

Yoked control chamber

Plexiglas cages

Rotating platform

Water pan under platform

Food and water

Maquet *et al.* (1997) studied the blood flow to different regions of the brain during sleep (using PET) as an indicator of activity. They found that the areas that were least active were the orbitofrontal cortex and the cingulate cortex, two regions involved in emotional behaviour. This provides evidence of a physiological basis for the effects of sleep deprivation on emotional stability. Studying the emotional responses of participants in experimental settings is, however, confounded by the novelty of the setting.

As well as the physical and emotional roles that sleep might fulfil, it also has cognitive functions. If sleep is important for restoring brain functions, doing without sleep should impair cognitive functioning. Rideout (1979) tested the maze learning ability of sleep-deprived mice.

Three deprivation conditions (total sleep, REM- or nREM-deprivation) were compared to non-sleep-deprived mice. Mice deprived of REM sleep, either selectively or by total sleep deprivation, were equally bad at maze learning compared with nREM or undeprived animals. This suggests that REM sleep is especially important for brain restoration.

⤷ Exploring issues and debates
Ethics

'Using animals is essential to answering questions about human behaviour.'

To what extent is this statement true? Draw up a table with two columns, one for the reasons why it *is* important to use animals and one for the reasons why we should not or it is not appropriate to.

Junior doctors who work long hospital shifts without sleep provide a real-life opportunity to investigate the effects of sleep deprivation on learning. In casualty, doctors have to listen to patients, extract relevant facts and memorise them in order to make accurate diagnoses. Deary & Tait (1987) studied emergency ward doctors who had an average of 1.5 hours sleep per night. When tested on memory tasks, doctors on duty performed significantly worse than those off duty.

Smith (1995, 1996) has conducted a series of experiments with rats and human participants investigating the effects of learning on REM sleep requirements. Rats that learned to respond to a light and avoid an electric shock spent more time than usual in REM sleep. If they were deprived of REM sleep for four hours immediately after training, they only remembered the response half as well as those that slept normally. If the sleep deprivation was delayed for more than 20 hours after training, the rats showed no decrement in learning.

Similarly, increased cognitive demands should increase the need for sleep. In research with students, Smith found that in the week after revising for exams, the requirement for REM sleep increased. In tests on REM sleep deprivation, memory for cognitive-procedural tasks was particularly affected. For instance, the learning of logical puzzles, where symbols had to be manipulated according to arbitrary rules, was impaired by REM deprivation, but the memorising of paired lists of words was not.

Herman & Roffwarg (1983) generated a novel task by asking participants to wear inverting goggles (which cause the world to appear upside down). Following this experience, the participants spent more time than usual in REM sleep. In a naturalistic rather than experimental test, Horne & Minard (1985) asked participants to come to the laboratory for an experiment to do tests on reading. When they turned up, the experimenters told them their plans had changed and they were going on an all-expenses paid day out. They were taken out on various stimulating but not stressful or physically tiring excursions including to an art gallery, the zoo and a museum. Horne & Minard found although they felt tired, the participants did not sleep for longer than normal. However, on the following night they did have more slow wave (stage 4) sleep than usual.

Discussion of restorational theory

As we have an ongoing need to recuperate both the body and brain, restorational theory accounts for our circadian rhythm of sleep as we cannot keep going without regular restoration. When additional physiological needs are placed on us, such as in illness, drug overdoses or brain damage, sleep time increases. This suggests that sleep is needed to repair damaged tissue. Furthermore, when sleep is prevented in animals they become very ill, suggesting that sleep is essential for maintaining health.

At least some evidence supports the need for more sleep when physical demands are greater, and in both animals and humans there is a need for both REM and nREM sleep in order for the brain to cope effectively with cognitive demands. However, restorational theory cannot account for our preference for sleeping at night, as the replacement or repair that happens during sleep could be conducted as effectively if we slept during the daytime.

Both REM and nREM sleep seem to be important but cases of individuals who survive happily without REM sleep, or with very little sleep at all, suggest that sleeping in order to restore is not an absolute necessity. Lavie (1996) reports two such cases, one of a man with a piece of shrapnel in his head who slept very little (about 15 minutes per night) and experienced virtually no REM sleep at all, just a few minutes a week, and another of a woman who slept for just an hour a day. Neither suffered any ill effects and both were very cognitively competent.

In reality, the evolutionary and restorational theories are not in conflict. If sleep evolved for efficiency and safety, there is no reason why it should not subsequently come to serve a recuperation function at the same time.

Lifespan changes in sleep

Sleep rhythms

In the first few months of life, babies' sleep patterns are very different from those of an adult. Although we say 'sleeping like a baby' and mean sleeping deeply, in fact – as any parent will tell you – babies wake up often. Typically, an infant wakes to be fed approximately every four hours throughout the day and night until it is about four months old. The night-time awakenings then reduce in frequency until, at about six months, it begins to sleep through the night, that is, it adapts to a circadian rhythm. This change can be clearly seen in Figure 1.21.

If you study Figure 1.21 carefully you will see diagonal patterns tracing across the top section. This shows that the infant does have a sleep–wake rhythm, it is just much shorter than 24 hours. This gradually lengthens to a circadian rhythm over time. Although this adaptation is generally reached by six months, it may take up to three years and, in a small number of individuals, it simply never happens.

The pattern of sleeping seen in newborn babies seems to follow that of the unborn child. Birnholz (1981) recorded REM sleep in foetuses as young as 23 weeks. Well defined REM sleep becomes more frequent between 24 and 35 weeks. Periods when eye movements are not detectable become more common after 36 weeks and this has been linked to periods of nREM state.

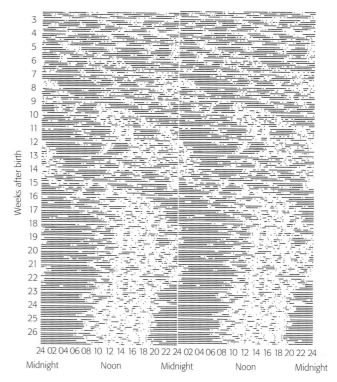

▲ **Figure 1.21** An infant slowly adapts to a 24-hour sleep–wake cycle

In premature babies, only REM sleep is seen at 30 weeks but by the time they are full term this has fallen to about 50 per cent of their sleep time. While they are dreaming they move and make facial expressions. Indeed, in full-term babies the first smiles occur during dreaming.

At the other end of the lifespan, in old age, sleep patterns change again. Night-time sleep becomes fragmented and shorter, due to a reduction in the amount of melatonin released. However, this leads to sleepiness during the day and a tendency to nap. Having fulfilled some of their need for sleep in the daytime, the older person thus feels less tired at night and cannot fall, or cannot stay, asleep. The role of melatonin can be demonstrated by giving elderly people suffering from troubled sleep melatonin tablets. They find that they fall asleep more quickly and wake less often.

The need for sleep and for REM sleep

Two other changes over the lifespan reflect the total amount of sleep and the proportion of REM and nREM sleep. The number of hours' sleep a day falls over the lifespan, with a much longer sleep requirement in childhood and a slower decline through adulthood. Babies and children also have relatively more REM sleep, reaching an adult ratio by about 10 years of age (see Figure 1.22).

The reduced amount of sleep with old age is partly accounted for by early waking. This represents a phase-advance response (see p5). This observation, and the changes in melatonin levels in old age (see above), suggest that the sleep problems of older adults might relate to changes in their circadian rhythm. This idea is further supported by evidence that older people find adjusting to new shifts

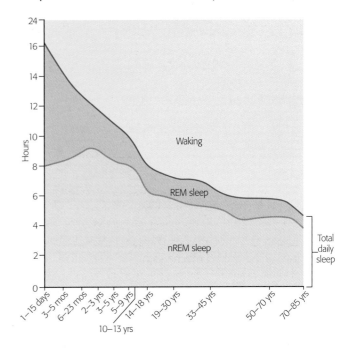

▼ **Figure 1.22** The total amount of time spent asleep and in REM both decline over the lifespan

(Campbell, 1995) and to the effect of jet lag (Moline *et al.*, 1992) more difficult than younger people.

Changes in REM sleep occur over the lifespan too. Feinberg *et al.* (1969) compared vertical eye movement in the REM sleep of younger and older adults. They found that the older adults experienced fewer vertical eye movements and concluded that this reflected a decrease in intensity of the REM sleep process.

Disorders of sleep

As we have seen, sleep is important to psychological and physical welfare. It therefore follows that almost everyone finds sleep disturbances and sleep loss distressing and debilitating. We will look now at three sleep disorders, insomnia, sleepwalking and narcolepsy.

Insomnia

Insomnia is the inability to fall asleep or to stay asleep. As a result the individual experiences daytime tiredness. Insomnia is not defined by the amount of sleep that an individual gets, because individuals vary so much. Instead it is related to whether they feel that they 'slept well'. It is based on their perception of their sleep quality and quantity.

One way to classify insomnia is into 'primary' and 'secondary' insomnia. Some people simply find it difficult to sleep, regardless of other factors. These people have *primary*

insomnia. Others experience sleeplessness as a result of an identifiable cause, such as too much noise, circadian disruption, stress or the side effects of drugs. Children may experience insomnia because their parents expect them to go too bed too early and they cannot sleep. These are examples of *secondary insomnia*.

This is not the only possible classification system for insomnia. An alternative system identifies three categories according to when the sleep problem occurs:

- *onset insomnia* – difficulty falling asleep
- *maintenance insomnia* – difficulty staying asleep
- *termination insomnia* – waking up too early and being unable to get back to sleep.

These categories can be applied to primary and secondary insomnia.

Oddly, most people who suffer from insomnia do not actually lose as much sleep as they perceive. When observed in a sleep laboratory, the amount of sleep lost is much less significant than the individual imagines. One reason for this is that the person may wake from sleep repeatedly but believe they have not slept in between the awakenings.

Primary insomnia

Primary or idiopathic insomnia is a long-term condition that appears early in life. It is probably caused by a brain abnormality. This seems likely given the effect of the brain injury experienced by the war veteran described by Lavie (see p15). The shrapnel was located in his pons, an area of the brain known to be related to the control of sleep, particularly in the onset of REM sleep. The effect of such brain disorders could cause insomnia by disrupting either the sleep onset mechanism or the waking mechanism.

People with primary insomnia often come to terms with their symptoms, simply accepting that they will spend longer awake than average. There is little point in using traditional sleep mediation (hypnotics) as this tends to have little effect in cases of primary insomnia. Since this is the case, alternative cognitive and behavioural investigations and therapies have been explored.

One common, persistent type of primary insomnia is psychophysiologic insomnia. It is characterised by learned arousal, persistence with behaviours that are incompatible with sleep and a preoccupation with sleeping. This is explained in the *Research Now* box.

Secondary insomnia

Many factors can cause secondary insomnia. These include too much noise, circadian disruption (see pp8–10), stress, food intolerance, family conflict, bereavement, stress and abuse of stimulant drugs. In any of these situations, the cause of the problem should be the focus of any therapeutic intervention. However, if the problem remains untreated the insomnia can become chronic. This occurs because the individual learns a new (maladaptive) sleep pattern.

***

KEY TERM

dot-probe task a measure of attentional bias. The participant watches a screen and fixates on a central cross. Two stimuli, a control (neutral) one and an experimental (eg sleep-related) one, are presented very briefly, randomly appearing on the left or right. A dot then appears where one of the stimuli was located and the participant has to press a key to indicate which side of the screen the dot was. The time this takes them (the latency) is measured. A shorter latency indicates greater attention.

***

▶ **Figure 1.23** Noise is often a cause of secondary insomnia

Thinking creatively about psychology

Redesign MacMahon *et al.*'s study using attention to pictorial stimuli rather than words.

***

RESEARCH NOW

MacMahon KM, Broomfield NM & Espie CA (2006) Attention bias for sleep-related stimuli in primary insomnia and delayed sleep phase syndrome using the dot-probe task. *Sleep* 29(11), 1420–7

Aim: To investigate attentional bias as a causal factor in primary insomnia.

Procedure: Three groups of approximately 20 participants each were compared in an independent groups design: good sleepers (GS), people with delayed sleep phase syndrome (DSPS) – a sleep disorder unrelated to cognitive problems – and those with primary insomnia. The participants were tested on a *dot-probe task* with sleep-related and neutral words that were balanced for frequency and length.

Results: The primary insomnia group showed greater attention than the GS and DSPS groups to the sleep-related stimuli as they were faster to respond to them.

Conclusion: This suggests that cognitive factors are important in primary insomnia. Specifically that an attentional bias to sleep-related stimuli acts to maintain the problem.

RESEARCH NOW

Kim H, Roh S, Kwon HJ, Paik KC, Rhee MY, Jeong JY, Lim MH, Koo MJ, Kim CH, Kim HY, Lim JH & Kim DH (2008) Study on the health status of the residents near military airbases in Pyeongtaek City. *Journal of Preventative Medicine and Public Health* **41(5), 307–14**

Aim: To investigate the effect of aircraft noise on the health of the residents living near military airbases in Pyeongtaek City, Korea.

Procedure: 917 residents answered a questionnaire asking about several variables including insomnia. Records were also taken of environmental noise level. There were four groups of participants:
- high exposure: those living in a village close to the fighter airbase
- intermediate exposure: those living along the course of fighter planes
- helicopter noise: those living near a helicopter airbase
- control group: not living near an airbase.

Findings: The prevalence of insomnia was higher in the exposed groups than in the control group. After adjusting the data for age, sex, agricultural noise and occupation, all groups exposed to aircraft noise were more likely to experience insomnia, especially those in the high exposure to fighter planes and helicopter noise groups (see Figure 1.24).

Conclusions: Aircraft noise has an adverse effect on sleep. There is, therefore, a need to impose controls on aircraft noise to maintain people's health.

▶ **Figure 1.24**

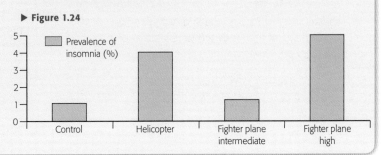

Factors affecting insomnia

In the explanations above we have identified several factors that affect insomnia. These include external factors such as noise and light, and internal ones such as attention and worry. We will now look at three factors in detail.

Noise

You have probably been woken up by a sudden sound or been kept awake by strange noises. We find it harder to sleep through loud noises and ones that are unpredictable. One common source of disturbance to sleep is aircraft noise (see *Research Now*). This is more problematic than other transport noise such as road or rail noise because it is louder and intermittent.

Terzano *et al.* (1990) investigated the effect that noise has on the ultradian rhythms in sleep. Using six healthy volunteers they made five recordings of sleep under different noise conditions of increasing apparent noise level (measured in dBA). This was achieved by playing white noise (all different frequencies, like the buzz of an out-of-tune TV) at 45, 55, 65 and 75dBA plus a baseline control. With increasing volumes they found changes in several aspects of sleep:

- **more:**
  - time awake after falling asleep the first time
  - stage 2 sleep
  - nREM sleep
- **less:**
  - stage 4 sleep
  - REM
  - total sleep.

The participants also reported lower quality sleep with louder noiser. However, they were no faster at falling asleep the night following the experimental noise.

Although noise is clearly associated with poor sleep, part of the problem is caused by the way the sleeper feels towards the noise. If it is perceived as a nuisance they are more likely to suffer disturbed sleep. It is difficult to ascertain whether their poor sleep is a result of the noise itself, of the associated annoyance, or alternatively whether individuals who sleep badly attribute this to the noises that they hear when they are lying awake.

Oddly, noise is sometimes beneficial to people with insomnia. López *et al.* (2002) report that playing white noise to both infants and adults can help to induce sleep. They suggest that this probably works by making individual sounds less obvious against the background noise so they are less likely to disturb sleep.

Thinking critically about psychology

Many parents say that their baby sleeps most easily when they do the vacuuming. Why might this be so?

Handscomb (2006) investigated a range of techniques for improving sleep in people with tinnitus (persistent 'ringing in the ears'). Thirty-nine participants were given bedside sound generators and the 35 who were followed up reported an improvement in sleep quality. The least preferred sound was white noise and the most popular were sounds of a brook and of birds. The majority of participants preferred one sound type and reported that they chose it because it was emotionally pleasant rather than because it affected their tinnitus directly.

Food

A recent study illustrates one of the major problems in identifying causes of insomnia. Lichstein *et al.* (2007) asked a random sample of 772 participants aged 22–98 years old to complete questionnaires about their sleep, keep a two-week sleep diary and report all the nutritional supplements they were using. An interesting pattern emerged. Those using vitamin supplements had poorer sleep than those who were not, and the rate of insomnia was also higher in this group. Lichstein *et al.* propose five possible explanations for these findings:

- vitamins cause disturbed sleep
- the interaction of an unknown combination of vitamins causes poor sleep
- poor sleepers use vitamins
- unidentified factors (such as anxiety or depression) cause both poor sleep and vitamin use
- the findings of the study are unreliable and unreplicable.

Although there are many possible conclusions from Lichstein *et al.*'s study, it does show that dietary intake is a potential cause of sleep problems. One obvious culprit is caffeine. This stimulant drug, found in coffee but also – to a lesser extent – in tea, colas and chocolate, is one cause of insomnia. Březinová (1974) compared the effects of pre-sleep decaffeinated coffee compared with decaf with added caffeine. Even though the participants were unaware which coffee they had received, those drinking coffee with caffeine experienced, on average, two hours less total sleep, took 66 minutes longer to fall asleep and their sleep was more broken.

You may have grown up with the belief that 'cheese causes nightmares'. For at least some individuals, this may be true. Charles Shee (1964), a doctor, wrote a letter to the *British Medical Journal* in which he reported the case of a patient on a drug for high blood pressure who reported horrifying nightmares, such as one about seeing the mutilated body of a work colleague hanging from a meat hook. The patient habitually ate about 30–60g of Cheddar cheese for his supper before going to bed. When he stopped doing this, the nightmares ceased!

▼ **Figure 1.25** Coffee: an insomniac's nightmare

A study conducted by the British Cheese Board, which involved 200 people eating 20g of cheese each night half an hour before sleeping, revealed more positive effects of cheese. The participants each kept a sleep diary and these showed that 72 per cent slept well throughout the study. However, in the absence of a non-cheese-eating control group, this finding is difficult to interpret.

Some foods and food supplements seem to have a positive effect on insomnia. Morin *et al.* (2005) compared the effect of the herb combination valerian and hops with a placebo and sleeping pill containing the drug diphenhydramine. The participants all suffered with insomnia and were recruited from sleep disorder centres. Although the effects were small, and mainly non-significant, they found that after 28 days those participants taking the valerian-hops supplement fell asleep faster than the placebo group and stayed asleep for slightly longer.

▼ **Figure 1.26** Cheese and nightmares, cause or cure?

For some individuals, their insomnia is a direct consequence of a food intolerance. For example, in children with a milk intolerance, sleep latency can be reduced and total sleep time increased by eliminating cows' milk from the diet (Kahn *et al.*, 1989).

Thinking critically about psychology

The children in Kahn *et al.*'s study were unaware of whether they were being given cows' milk or not. Furthermore, in all but one child, their sleep problems returned when cows' milk was reintroduced. Why are these observations important?

In some people milk products, conversely, help to *overcome* sleep problems. Yamamura *et al.* (2009) tested the effect of drinking milk fermented with the bacterium *Lactobacillus helveticus* on elderly people. Twenty-nine participants aged 60–81 were used in a repeated measures design experiment. One group spent three weeks taking a daily 100g drink of fermented milk and another three weeks taking a placebo milk drink instead, the other group did the same in reverse order. The fermented milk produced a shorter sleep latency (although this was non-significant), significantly greater sleep efficiency (more time asleep during the sleep period) and fewer periods of waking.

One reason why milk and cheese may affect sleep is that they contain the amino acid tryptophan. This is a precursor to the neurotransmitter serotonin, which is important in the control of sleep. Kleitman *et al.* (1937) investigated many foodstuffs and found that only a malted milk drink reduced restlessness during sleep. However, a subsequent study (Adam, 1977a) raised doubts about the value of such drinks. She recruited people to participate in a study in which they would have a malted milk drink, Horlicks, each night before going to bed. Compared with a baseline without the drink, they did indeed sleep better than those drinking nothing, milk alone or a calorie, protein, fat and carbohydrate matched equivalent. As part of the experiment she also enquired what they usually ate or drank at bedtime. This revealed that, in fact, people slept better when they did whatever they normally did, whether that was having something before they slept or not. The effect had arisen because the sample was biased – only people who liked having a snack before going to bed had volunteered!

Drug use

Somewhat ironically, one of the major causes of insomnia is the use of sleeping pills! Imagine a person who is unable to sleep well because they are sick or worried. If they are given medication to help them to sleep without solving the underlying problem, they will continue to need the medication. As tolerance is developed to many sedatives, they will need larger doses to achieve the same effect on sleep. The doses cannot be endlessly increased however, so it is found that the medication works less well and they experience insomnia. Furthermore, any attempt to cut back and reduce their dependency also results in sleeplessness (a withdrawal symptom – see p249). As a consequence, sleep medication is really only useful as a short-term solution.

Drugs that are prescribed for insomnia include the older 'sleeping pills', the barbiturates (eg sodium amytal). These, however, are highly addictive and produce a 'hangover' effect. They were largely replaced by benzodiazepine drugs including diazepam (Valium). Recently, even newer drugs, the 'z-sedatives', are being prescribed for insomnia. These include zolpidem (Stilnoct), zaleplon (Sonata) and zopiclone (Zimovane). Melatonin (Circadin) is also used in the treatment of insomnia but only in older people.

Substance abuse can also result in insomnia. Amphetamine is a stimulant drug that increases arousal and induces insomnia. Likewise nicotine is a stimulant, and although smokers may perceive that having a cigarette calms them down, this is simply satisfying the craving for the drug to which they are addicted. Since nicotine is also a stimulant, in the long term smoking inhibits sleep. Other, less obvious drugs can also reduce sleep quality. For example, alcohol initially induces sleep but as it is broken down the metabolites disrupt sleep. Abuse of alcohol can therefore lead to insomnia.

Sleepwalking

Sleepwalking, or somnambulism, is most common in children (but also occurs in adults, especially when stressed), generally happens early in the night and runs in families. It affects approximately 18 per cent of the population. Sleepwalkers behave automatically and don't respond to their environment: their eyes are open but they do not see. It may be accompanied by sleep-talking – a meaningless stream of words.

Contrary to the myth, no harm is done by waking a sleepwalker. When woken, the sleepwalker can, however, be very disoriented – unaware how they came to be in a different place from where they went to sleep. As children tend to outgrow sleepwalking, it is possible that it is caused by late maturation of the neural systems that control sleeping and waking. However, this cannot explain the increased instance of sleepwalking in adults when they are stressed.

Non-REM sleepwalking

Almost all instances of sleepwalking occur during nREM, in stages 3 or 4. In nREM sleep the body is not paralysed so it is possible for the sleeper to move around. When in a familiar environment it is possible to negotiate obstacles and open doors, although this is more difficult and more dangerous in an unfamiliar place. Rather than waking a sleepwalker, it is generally preferable to turn them around and direct them back to their bed, which they will climb into and continue to sleep. In the morning they will recall nothing of the event.

As they are in nREM sleep, sleepwalkers are not acting out a dream. The behaviours performed are simply automatic, well-rehearsed ones. Lavie (1996) provides an illustration that the behaviours that occur in sleepwalking are highly learned. He describes a six-year-old boy who was being observed in a sleep laboratory. The boy got out of bed and walked as far as the electrodes from the EEG would allow. He then stood and waved his arms in an exotic fashion. On replaying a video of the event to his parents the next day it transpired that he was acting out a practised scene from a school play in which he had been 'the sun'!

To understand how sleepwalking is passed on through families, genetic studies have been conducted. Lecendreux *et al.* (2003) compared 60 participants from families with a history of sleepwalking with a group of ethnically matched non-sleepwalkers and found a human leucoyte antigen (HLA) genetic marker that was related to the incidence of sleepwalking.

Hafeez & Kalinowski (2007) reported two cases of sleepwalking induced by the treatment of attention deficit hyperactivity disorder (ADHD) with the drug quetiapine. In discussing their observations they suggest that this might shed light on the cause of sleepwalking. One explanation suggests that sleepwalking is caused by a failure in the serotonin system in a part of the brain called the Raphé nuclei, which is involved in the control of sleeping and waking. Interestingly, ADHD is also linked to problems with serotonin, specifically with variations in the genes that control the transportation of serotonin, and enzymes that help in the conversion of the amino acid tryptophan (see p20).

REM sleep behaviour disorder

Most sleepwalkers perambulate in nREM. This makes sense as we are paralysed in REM sleep – usually. The neurotransmitter acetylcholine is important in controlling voluntary movements. During REM sleep, the activity of acetylcholine in specific parts of the body is blocked and we are paralysed. This prevents us from acting out our dreams. Since acetylcholine serves other important functions, this blocking is normally very precise. An area of the brain called the magnocellular nucleus appears to be responsible for sending signals to the spinal cord that prevent motor neurones from being activated. Sometimes, however, this system malfunctions. In the condition *REM sleep behaviour disorder*, the normal blocking of this neurotransmitter fails. As a consequence, the sleeper acts out their dreams. This condition is, for obvious reasons, dangerous for both the dreamer and their bed partner.

Like nREM sleepwalking, REM sleep behaviour disorder (RSBD) appears to be inherited. Schenck *et al.* (1996) demonstrated that men with RSBD shared a common phenotype, with 85 per cent having the HLA-DQwl markers. RSBD can also be caused by brain damage. Unsurprisingly, it is damage to the magnocellular nucleus that causes this problem (Cuelbras & Moore, 1989).

M E D I A   W A T C H : Sleepwalking

A dangerous sleep

Judith Woods, *The Daily Telegraph*, 18 October 2004

As a teenager, musician Chris Sheldrick's sleepwalking was a great source of amusement to his friends and family.

A former head musician at Eton, his disturbed sleep patterns were well known; he would often wake his fellow boarders with his blood-curdling howls, or be discovered by staff asleep in a cupboard or the laundry room. At youth hostels, he would clamber into strangers' beds in the middle of the night – to their consternation – or stroll through public areas dressed only in his underpants.

But a year ago, Sheldrick's sleepwalking took a tragic turn. One night, while staying with a friend, former BBC Musician of the Year Guy Johnston, Sheldrick, 23, severed eight tendons, a nerve and an artery in his left arm after punching a window pane. The accident was to spell the end of his promising career as a performer, as he was no longer able to play the clarinet, bassoon or piano properly.

'I couldn't remember what had happened, but by following the trail of blood, it was easy to deduce that I'd smashed the window, then wandered around the house before going outside, where I was stopped by the next-door neighbour,' says Sheldrick.

'He'd heard the glass breaking and thought I was a burglar, but the fact that I was in my boxers convinced him otherwise. He took me into his house and saved my life. Because I had lost so much blood, I was losing consciousness.'

▲ **Figure 1.27** Cruel blow: Chris Sheldrick's musical career was cut short after an accident while sleepwalking

---

1 Which neurotransmitter was faulty in Chris Sheldrick's brain when the accident occurred?

2 Would the level of this neurotransmitter be disrupted all the time, or only some of the time?

3 Which part of the brain could be responsible for the problem?

Narcolepsy

Narcolespy is a sleep disorder in which the sufferer falls instantly and involuntarily asleep. This rapid change is associated with a sudden loss of muscle tone and paralysis called cataplexy. The individual therefore collapses without warning. They sleep for only a short time, usually two to five minutes, then awaken feeling refreshed. In addition, someone with narcolepsy may experience sleep paralysis, a state in which they are awake but cannot move. This is most common when falling asleep or on waking. Although not harmful, it can be unpleasant or frightening. Whilst in this state the individual may also experience hypnagogic hallucinations. This is where the mental content of a dream is experienced while awake but paralysed – an effect that can be terrifying. Narcoleptics may also suffer from disrupted night-time sleep and insomnia. The symptoms of narcolepsy themselves are not dangerous, although the consequences may be.

The paralysis in cataplexy appears to be the same as the paralysis experienced during REM sleep. It is possible, however, for someone to experience cataplexy whilst fully conscious. This may arise in response to a sudden burst of emotion such as laughter or anger. Narcoleptic attacks in contrast tend to occur in response to monotonous situations, for example driving at night. In this respect narcolepsy can be very dangerous.

When observed in a sleep laboratory there are several characteristics that can be recognised. In a narcoleptic attack, the individual falls immediately into REM sleep. This suggests that the disorder arises from poor control of the neural mechanisms that trigger REM sleep. When they awaken they report very vivid dreams.

Like sleepwalking and REM sleep behaviour disorder, narcolepsy is a genetic disorder (and can also be triggered by brain damage). Aldrich (1992) identified two mutations responsible for the symptoms of narcolepsy, and more recently

HLA typing has identified a genetic marker for narcolepsy (Alaez *et al.*, 2008). There is a considerable difference between the incidence of narcolepsy in different ethnic groups, again supporting the belief that there is a strong genetic component. In Europe about 0.05 per cent of the population are affected, whereas it is much more common in Japan, with an incidence nearer to 2 per cent.

Further evidence for the role of genes in the control of narcolepsy comes from animal studies. It is possible to breed strains of mice, dogs and other animals that are narcoleptic. Apart from indicating that the trait must, therefore, be inherited, this provides animal models to study. Early research demonstrated that genetically modified animals could be produced that had narcoleptic symptoms caused by either an absence of hypocretin (Chemelli *et al.*, 1999) or an absence of the receptors to which the molecules attach (Lin *et al.*, 1999). Hypocretins are small molecules released by the hypothalamus that act as neurotransmitters in the brain, and the findings of these studies suggested that these molecules play a central role in controlling REM sleep and causing narcolepsy. The findings also account for why some, but not all, people with narcolepsy have low hypocretin levels. The 10 per cent of sufferers who have normal hypocretin levels probably have a fault with the hypocretin receptors.

Mishima *et al.* (2008) have found mutations to the same genes (hcrtR1 and hcrtR2) in narcoleptic mice, dogs and people. This gene is involved in the production of receptors for the hypocretins. The exact way in which this molecule is involved in the control of REM sleep is still unclear, however.

Interestingly, cataplexy appears to be the opposite of REM sleep behaviour disorder. In the former, the individual exhibits paralysis in the *absence* of REM sleep, in the latter the individual *fails* to achieve paralysis during REM sleep. It is possible, therefore, that these two disorders are controlled by different but related processes in the brain.

Chapter summary

Biological rhythms
- External (exogenous) cues set the biological clock to a 24-hour (circadian) rhythm. This is maintained by the endogenous rhythm of the suprachiasmatic nucleus (SCN). This triggers the release of melatonin from the pineal gland each night, which makes us sleepy.
- When external cues are absent the clock free-runs and perceived day length increases but rhythmical activity continues.
- Infradian rhythms are cycles that last longer than a day, such as lunar cycles, the menstrual cycle and annual breeding or hibernation. These are also controlled by endogenous cues from the SCN and melatonin, and by exogenous cues such as changes in temperature and day length. They help animals to prepare in advance for changes in their environment.

- Ultradian rhythms are cycles lasting less than a day. Humans have a 90-minute basic rest and activity cycle that affects attention and other cognitive variables when we are awake. This rhythm is also seen in the alternation of rapid eye movement (REM) and non-REM (nREM) sleep.
- Problems associated with jet lag and shift work arise because of the need to suddenly sleep and wake up in a different time frame, which desynchronises the endogenous clock from the new sleep–wake regime. This causes problems such as sleepiness but also increases the incidence of illness and accidents.

Sleep
- Sleep can be divided into five stages, REM and stages 1–4 which are nREM. Each stage is characterised by a

different pattern of brain waves. In REM sleep our body is paralysed but our eyes move rapidly and we dream.

- Sleep can be explained by the evolutionary theory that suggests that sleeping saves animals using energy inefficiently or taking risks at times of day to which they are poorly adapted. This explains why some animals sleep in the daytime and others at night and why species differ in the amount they sleep – predators sleep for longer as they are not in danger.
- Evolutionary theory cannot, however, explain why animals sleep even when it seems disadvantageous, such as marine mammals, or why we need both REM and nREM sleep.
- The restorational theory suggests that sleep is necessary to recoup energy used by the body and brain. This explains why we need to sleep every day, why we need more sleep when we have had a stimulating day, why babies need more sleep, and the detrimental effects of sleep deprivation.
- Restorational theory cannot explain our preference for sleeping at night or how some unusual individuals manage with virtually no sleep at all.
- Over the lifespan the overall need for sleep, and the need for REM sleep, reduces. Initially, babies' sleep–wake cycles are much shorter than 24 hours and in old age sleep becomes fragmented, with more daytime napping.

Sleep disorders

- Insomnia is a disorder in which the sufferer cannot get to sleep or stay asleep. It may be entirely biological in origin and arise early in life (primary insomnia) or may be the result of some other problem, such as noise or illness (secondary insomnia).
- Excessive noise, some kinds of food and some drugs can cause insomnia. However, other sources of noise, foods and drugs help to reduce insomnia.
- Sleepwalking almost always occurs during nREM sleep. It is more common in children and is harmless except for the risk of injury as the sleepwalker is unaware of their environment. If woken, the sleepwalker will be disoriented, but if they do not wake they will have no memory of the episode on waking later.
- In REM sleep behaviour disorder the usual mechanism for initiating paralysis fails and the sleeper acts out their dreams, which can be dangerous.
- In narcolepsy, the sufferer falls unpredictably into REM sleep with a corresponding loss of muscle tone due to REM paralysis. Narcoleptics may experience sleep paralysis and suffer from insomnia.
- Each of the sleep disorders has a strong genetic component.

What do I know?

1 (a) Describe what is meant by endogenous pacemakers and exogenous zeitgebers. (5 marks)
(b) Describe the biological control of either infradian or ultradian rhythms. (10 marks)
(c) Evaluate the restorational theory of sleep. (10 marks)

2 (a) Describe the nature of sleep. (9 marks)
(b) Discuss explanations of narcolepsy. (16 marks)

3 (a) Describe circadian rhythms and **one** other type of rhythm. (10 marks)
(b) Describe and evaluate explanations for insomnia. (15 marks)

4 (a) Outline **two** types of insomnia. (5 marks)
(b) Explain how insomnia is affected by **two or more** different factors. (20 marks)

5 Describe and evaluate the ecological theory of sleep. (25 marks)

CHAPTER 2
Perception

Thinking ahead

By the end of this chapter you should be able to:

- describe and critically evaluate Gregory's top-down (indirect) theory of perception and Gibson's bottom-up (direct) theory of perception

- describe and evaluate the development of perceptual abilities

- describe and critically assess the nature–nurture debate in relation to explanations of perceptual development

- describe and evaluate Bruce & Young's theory of face recognition, including explanations and case studies of prosopagnosia

Perception is a cognitive process that allows us to understand the information that constantly arrives at our sensory organs, for example the eyes and ears. This sensory information has physical properties, such as light and sound, and is detected by sensory receptors, converted into electrical impulses and sent to the central nervous system. The information is then processed and results in our perceptual experience of the world.

In this chapter we will consider Gibson's theory which suggests that we perceive directly from the sensory information around us. As an alternative explanation we will also consider Gregory's theory, which suggests that we perceive indirectly by going beyond the sensory information to infer our perceptual world.

Perceptual abilities, for example the ability to perceive depth, have been shown to develop over time. We will explore how psychologists have tried to assess whether such abilities are a result of nature (biological factors) or nurture (environmental factors) and the extent to which these factors interact.

Psychologists have also studied how it is possible for humans to recognise faces. Bruce & Young's theory suggests that we have different mechanisms to recognise familiar and unfamiliar faces. Research based on case studies of brain-damaged individuals has helped us to understand conditions such as prosopagnosia, in which the patient cannot recognise familiar faces, but can recognise familiar objects.

Perception allows us to make sense of and interact with our everyday world and in that sense it can be seen to have survival value. Through studying our perceptual abilities and their development, psychologists hope to gain a better understanding of this important cognitive process.

▲ **Figure 2.1** Is this person familiar? How do you know?

Theories of perceptual organisation

Sensation and *perception* are two separate but closely linked processes. Sensations have no meaning on their own, while perception cannot occur without sensations to make sense of. Theories of perceptual organisation have looked at the relationship between the two processes. Either our understanding of the world can be determined directly from the information detected by the sensory receptors, or this information may be used to make inferences about our perceptual world, based on prior knowledge.

Gregory's top-down (indirect) theory of perception (1972)

Richard Gregory's theory has its origins in Von Helmholtz's (1909) empiricist belief that we perceive through the experience of interacting and experimenting with our world. Gregory believes that our perception is constructed from previous knowledge gained through experience and therefore involves going beyond the sensory data that our sensory receptors provide us with. He believes that 'perception is not determined simply by stimulus patterns. Rather it is a dynamic searching for the best interpretation of the available data ... which involves going beyond the

immediately given evidence of the senses' (Gregory, 1966). Therefore Gregory sees perception as an active process where induction is used to form hypotheses from incoming sensory data. In this sense perception is an intelligent thought process similar to problem solving. We are not consciously aware of doing this and the whole process occurs within milliseconds, but it is regarded as an indirect process as we do not perceive directly from the sensory information available but instead process the information at a higher cognitive level.

KEY TERMS

perception the recognition and interpretation of sensory stimuli

sensation the awareness of a stimulus registered by sensory receptors

direct perception (bottom up) perception that arises just from the stimulus input without cognitive processing

indirect perception (top down) perception requiring cognitive processing that involves going beyond the sensory input

Gregory also believes that many sensory properties of objects cannot be understood directly through their retinal images. He thinks that as the visual input is so uninformative, perception must be an active process where we search for the best explanation of the available sensory data. As we 'construct' our perception, other factors such as previous experiences, cultural expectations, motivation and emotion can affect the process. Perception is therefore described as a 'top-down' process because information from the 'top' (such as our knowledge and experiences) works 'downwards' to influence the way sensory stimuli are interpreted.

Gregory disagrees with Gibson's idea that perception can occur directly from sensory information without any input from cognitive processes because our perception is much richer than if we were just using the information contained in the stimulus. Often sensory stimuli are incomplete or ambiguous so we need to go beyond the information given to make sense of it. Therefore the eye is not simply a camera that gives us a direct view of our world.

The reversible figure of Rubin's vase (see Figure 2.2a) shows how we use visual information to make inferences about meaning. The Rubin's vase is ambiguous: it can be seen as a white vase against a black background or as two faces looking at each other. You may find it seems to jump between the two different possibilities. Gregory would say this is because we are testing out alternative ways to understand the stimulus. These are alternative *perceptual hypotheses*.

▼ **Figure 2.2** Rubin's vase. a) Can you see a face and a vase? b) In the real world, Rubin's vase is much less ambiguous

(a)　　　　　　　　　　(b)

However, Gregory suggests that in the real world there is usually enough sensory information for us to work out which hypothesis about a given stimuli is correct (see Figure 2.2b). When we make mistakes in the process of hypothesis-generating and testing, we experience visual illusions.

The Kanizsa triangle (see Figure 2.4) appears to contain an upside down white triangle whose three points lie on top of black circles with an upright white triangle with black edges beneath it. The ultra-whiteness of the upside down triangle and its crisp edges are, however, illusory.

CLASSIC RESEARCH

Leeper RW (1935) A study of a neglected portion of the field of learning — The development of sensory organization. *Journal of Genetic Psychology* 46, 41–75

Aim: To investigate the effect of previous experience on perception.

Method: Leeper used an ambiguous picture that can be seen as either a young or an old lady (see Figure 2.3). Five groups of participants were given different experiences prior to seeing the ambiguous figure. The control group were just shown the ambiguous picture. In the experimental groups, each participant was initially either:

- given a verbal description of an old woman
- given a verbal description of a young woman
- shown a picture of the old woman
- shown a picture of the young woman.

Results: 65 per cent of the control group saw a young woman in the ambiguous figure. 100 per cent of those originally shown the young woman saw the ambiguous image as a young woman and 94 per cent of those originally shown the old woman picture, saw it as an old woman.

Conclusion: Expectation based on previous experience helps to determine our perception in an indirect manner.

▲ Figure 2.3

▼ **Figure 2.4** The Kanizsa triangle

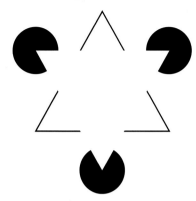

Gregory would explain our perception of this illusion as due to our going beyond the sensory information supplied. The edges and brightness are not physically present in the sensory data. We are using our previous experience of what objects look like when they are superimposed upon each other to understand a two-dimensional image. The 'hypothesis' that there are two triangles, one on top of the other, is the best interpretation of the data.

Perceptual set

The idea of *perceptual set* is important to Gregory's theory. Expectation, emotional and motivational factors and cultural influences can all affect the way we process sensory information. As perceptual set reduces the number of possible interpretations of sensory data, it can be said to improve the efficiency of perception by speeding up the process of recognition, but it may also introduce error.

Expectation

Aarts & Dijksterhuis (2002) found that they could influence estimates of a man's walking speed by creating an expectation of it being faster or slower than what it actually was by asking participants first to think about fast animals like cheetahs or slow animals like turtles. This shows how prior experience can bias perception, indicating that perception is an indirect and active process.

KEY TERMS

perceptual hypotheses possible interpretations of a stimulus that are based on sensory data and tested using prior knowledge and other stimulus information from the real world in order to understand it

perceptual set a bias in the way we interpret or respond to sensory information, eg a readiness to perceive certain features based on previous experience, motivational and emotional factors and cultural influences

perceptual defence the tendency to take longer to understand or respond to emotionally threatening words, ie we are slower to consciously perceive them than neutral words

Thinking creatively about psychology

Imagine that you are going to conduct an experiment looking at the effect of perceptual set on the 'rat-man' illusion. What possible experiences might you use to produce an effect? An alternative experiment would be to look at participants' emotions. Who would you expect to be more likely to see the rat than the man?

▲ **Figure 2.5** The rat-man

Murch (1973) was unable to replicate Leeper's findings, but thought that after 40 years the image was so well known that it may have influenced his results. The additional drawings that Leeper used were very similar to the original ambiguous woman. It is possible that the participants simply believed they were the same, so did not need to generate perceptual hypotheses at all. This would explain why the verbal priming was less effective.

CLASSIC RESEARCH

Bruner JS & Minturn AL (1955) Perceptual identification and perceptual organization. *Journal of General Psychology* 53, 21–28

Aim: To demonstrate how expectation and context affect perception.

Method: Participants were shown a figure known as the B-13 ambiguous stimulus figure, which can be seen to resemble either the letter 'B' or the number '13'. Half of the participants in the study saw the figure as either surrounded by adjoining letters (ie A and C) or by adjoining numbers (ie 12 and 14) (see Figure 2.6).

Results: Participants shown the stimulus with adjoining letters reported seeing the figure as the letter 'B', while those participants provided with adjoining numbers reported seeing the number '13'.

Conclusion: Contextual material does affect perception. This supports Gregory's belief that perception is shaped by factors other than the direct sensory information received by the sense organs.

▶ **Figure 2.6** The B–13 ambiguous stimulus figure

A
12 B 14
C

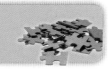

Young female participants tend to perceive the young woman in Leeper's illusion because their social world tends to consist of fellow young women. This is an example of perceptual set where there is a tendency to perceive certain features of the available sensory data and ignore others. Design a study to compare the responses of younger and older female participants to the Leeper's lady illusion.

Thinking critically about psychology

The B-13 stimulus figure presents the numbers as a horizontal row but the letters as a vertical column. Design a counterbalanced condition for this experiment to avoid possible bias from the presentation of items as lines or columns.

Motivational and emotional factors

McGinnies (1949) introduced the concept of *perceptual defence*, where emotionally threatening words take longer to consciously perceive than neutral words. Participants were given neutral words such as 'apple' and emotionally threatening words such as 'bitch'. The presentation time for each word was increased until the word was recognised. This took significantly longer for the emotionally threatening words, which seems to suggest that emotional factors affect our perception. This again lends support to Gregory's theory that perception does not occur directly from the sensory information.

Aronfreed *et al.* (1953) criticised these findings, suggesting that participants were unwilling to say such words aloud. They found that females took longer to recognise emotionally threatening words with a male than with a female researcher, presumably because they were more embarrassed. This seems likely as Bitterman & Kniffin (1953) found that if participants wrote the words down instead of speaking them, there was no difference in recognition time between neutral and emotionally threatening words.

Electric shocks cause negative emotions. Lazarus & McCleary (1951) found that pairing shocks with nonsense syllables caused participants to be anxious when they were exposed to the same nonsense at a rate so fast that they could not consciously perceive it. Unfamiliar nonsense syllables did not raise anxiety levels. The emotions they experienced affected their anxiety even though the perception was subliminal.

Motivational factors such as hunger and thirst can also indirectly affect perception by changing the way in which we interpret sensory information. Bruner & Goodman (1947) asked rich and poor children to estimate how big coins were, and poor children overestimated their size. Solley & Haigh (1948) got four- to eight-year-olds to draw pictures of Santa Claus at intervals

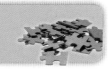

OVER TO YOU What letter is in the middle of each of the words below? 'H' and 'A'? Look at them carefully. The context surrounding the letters creates an expectation, so affects our perception. Use this illusion to test the effect of expectation on perception. You might like to put the words into a sentence to make the context more realistic.

▶ **Figure 2.7**

OVER TO YOU You can demonstrate how context affects perception on yourself with three bowls of water: one hot (not too hot as you are going to put one of your hands into it), one warm and one cold. Place the bowls in front of you – the hot one to the left, the warm one in the middle and the cold one to the right. Put your left hand into the bowl of hot water and your right hand into the bowl of cold water for about 30 seconds then move both hands simultaneously into the middle bowl.

Explain your left and right hand perception of the temperature of the middle bowl using Gregory's theory.

before and after Christmas. As Christmas grew closer, Santa was drawn larger, as was his sack of toys, but after Christmas Santa and the toy sack shrank. The findings from both studies suggests that motivational factors influenced the children's perception, as predicted by Gregory.

Balcettis & Dunning (*Research Now*) suggest that their research shows that the impact of motivation on information processing extends down into preconscious processing of stimuli and therefore shapes what the visual system presents to conscious awareness. In other words, motivation biases perception and participants are seeing what they want to see.

Thinking critically about psychology

Subsequent experiments involving different ambiguous visual stimuli confirmed Balcettis & Dunning's (2006) findings. The participants' first eye movements around the ambiguous figure (ones not under conscious control) showed that they were perceiving the desired interpretation. Reaction times also indicated that they were only seeing one interpretation (the one they wanted).

What does this tell us about whether the participants were seeing both interpretations and then consciously choosing the desired one?

RESEARCH NOW

Balcetis E & Dunning D (2006) See what you want to see: motivational influences on visual perception. *Journal of Personality & Social Psychology* 91(4), 612–625

Aim: To investigate the effect of motivation on object recognition, based on Bruner & Mintern (1955).

Method: Participants sat in front of a screen and were told that a computer would randomly select which of two drinks they would receive for an experiment on taste – either orange juice or a gelatinous, foul-smelling goo – and hoped, of course, that they would get the orange juice. The participants were told that the computer would give them either a letter or a number to indicate which drink they were to receive. This procedure was counterbalanced: for half the participants a letter meant orange juice, while for the other half a number would mean orange juice. A figure then appeared on the computer screen that could either by interpreted as a letter 'B' or a number '13'. After a very brief period (400 milliseconds) the computer appeared to crash and participants were asked if they had seen anything on the screen.

Results: When the letter would get them orange juice, 72 per cent reported seeing the letter. When the number would get them orange juice, 60.5 per cent reported seeing the number.

Conclusion: The participants' motivation to get the orange juice affected their perception of the visual stimulus, supporting Gregory's idea that perception does not occur directly from sensory information.

To test the effect of motivation on perception, collect some sports-related and non-sports-related pictures and show them to sporty people. In all pictures, hide a letter – look for the letter A in the examples below. To measure the effect of motivation, time how long the participants take to locate the letters. As they are motivated by sport they should find the hidden letters more quickly in the sports-related pictures.

▲ Figure 2.8

Cultural influences

People of different cultural backgrounds sometimes perceive sensory stimuli differently. Pettigrew *et al.* (1978) presented various South African ethnic groups with a series of different pictures to each eye. Pictures displaying a member of a particular ethnic group were shown to one eye and pictures of a different ethnic group to the other eye. Afrikaners (white South Africans of Dutch origin) tended to see the images as either European or African; they were not able to distinguish between black and mixed-race people, suggesting that the cultural influence of their racial prejudice was affecting their perception.

Gregory believes that from an early age in western cultures we learn how to read the third dimension of depth into two-dimensional (flat) images and the experience of the Müller-Lyer illusion is another example of how cultural factors affect perception (See Figure 2.9).

▶ **Figure 2.9**
The Müller-Lyer illusion. Which line is longer below? Measure them!

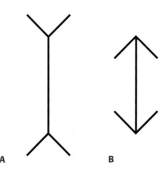

A   B

People from a western culture see line A as being longer than line B when, in fact, they are equal. However, people from some cultures do not experience the illusion, ie they see lines A and B as equal in length. This can be explained by differences in physical environment. In western cultures we tend to live in a carpentered world of buildings constructed of straight lines, edges and angles. Some other cultures have buildings made from natural materials that lack straight lines. Thus to a person of a western culture the fins on the Müller-Lyer illusion appear to offer information about distance. In Figure 2.10, the vertical line in A seems to be the farthest point, while in B the vertical line appears to be the nearest point. As experience tells us that things far away look small, we scale them up. This makes us experience the illusion of line A being longer than line B. Therefore the illusion happens because we unconsciously convert the two-dimensional images into three-dimensional objects. This supports *indirect perception* as it shows that we use prior knowledge based on our cultural experiences.

▼ **Figure 2.10** Which lines in Figure 2.9 do each of these images match?

A   B

Discussion of Gregory's theory

Gregory's theory has stimulated much research and given psychologists a deeper understanding of perception. It is supported by a large body of evidence from laboratory studies that demonstrates the role of emotional and motivational factors and cultural influences as well as explaining illusions and the importance of context. It also seems logical that we use indirect processing to extract sense in ambiguous circumstances, for example to work out whether it is the train that we are on or the adjacent one that is pulling out of the station.

▲ **Figure 2.11** When we see ourselves move in relation to the next train we have to test hypotheses to decide whether we, or the other train, are moving.

However, if we do construct our perceptual world based on our individual experiences, then why do our perceptions seem so similar, even in general across cultures? Research has shown that infants have similar perceptual views of the world, for example in the way they process information about shape (Slater & Morrison, 1985) (see also pp39–41).

Gregory's theory underestimates the richness of sensory information available in the real world – so evidence from laboratory experiments may lack validity. In real situations, retinal images are rarely seen in isolation, as they are in the artificial environment of the laboratory. Instead, there is a vast array of sensory information including other objects, background, the horizon and movement of objects in our visual field available to us, making *direct perception* possible. Gregory perhaps overemphasises the making of perceptual errors, such as with illusions. Usually, however, we perceive fairly accurately.

Laboratory studies of indirect perception often use fragmented and briefly presented stimuli, such as in Balcettis & Dunning (2006) (p29). In such artificial conditions it would be difficult to perceive directly from the sensory information available so such studies are biased in Gregory's favour.

A key criticism concerns why we see illusions even when we know why they occur. Logically this knowledge should cause us to modify our hypotheses but as we still experience the effect it would seem that we don't. Also illusions are not an everyday occurrence. Eysenck & Keane (1990) believe that Gregory's theory is better at explaining illusions than perception – illusions being unreal and simplified stimuli as opposed to real, physical objects.

Gregory's theory suggests that we would need to search through stored material to establish the best interpretation via hypothesis generation and testing. This is likely to take too long, so it seems probable that we are using processes that narrow down our search for understanding. This would seem to need further investigation. Indeed, other theories such as Marr's (1982) computational theory give more detailed accounts of the constructive (indirect) perceptual processes than Gregory's does

Gibson's bottom-up (direct) theory of perception (1950)

James Jerome Gibson's theory of direct perception can be described as 'nativist', implying that innate ideas and mechanisms are used in perception so we do not need to *learn* to understand sensory stimuli. Gibson felt that we perceive our environment directly through the stimulation of the retina. He believes that the pattern of light reaching our eyes, which he called the *optic array*, is richly structured and that the movements of a person and of surrounding objects cause some aspects of the optical array to change (variants), while others remain constant (invariants). He suggested that visual perception was due to the direct detection of invariants as they contain sufficient information to allow direct perception of features in our environment, such as spatial arrangements, depth and distance. Therefore, unlike Gregory, he believes that visual perception does not require inference or information processing.

▼ **Figure 2.12** Gibson felt that the rich optic array faced by a pilot provided enough information for direct perception

Gibson's interest in perception came from his work training pilots. The apparent rich array of sensory information available to pilots is an example of what Gibson called *optic flow patterns*. Optic flow patterns concern the movement of objects within the visual environment that provide information to the observer about spatial position and depth. Gibson investigated the sensory information available in other environmental conditions, considering the importance of features such as texture gradients, like the pattern that cobbles on a street make into the distance. He suggested that these real-world patterns were linked to similar gradients in the eye and that they allow us to experience depth. He developed his ideas into a general theory of perception, which contains several key points, such as the optic array, *texture gradients*, *optic flow patterns*, *horizon ratio* and *affordance*. The information used for perception, according to Gibson, is present in the stimulus information and unambiguous, so he is saying that we 'build up' our understanding of the visual world, that is, perception is a *bottom-up* process that does not require inference or cognitive processing.

KEY TERMS

optic array the structure of light patterns that reach the eye, which provides rich data sufficient for direct perception

optic flow patterns the apparent visual motion of the environment around us that occurs as we move towards a fixed point, which seems to stay still. This provides unambiguous sensory information about the spatial layout of objects

texture gradient information from surface patterns that indicate distance and depth, eg a surface getting smoother further away

horizon ratio the proportion of an object that is above the horizon in relationship to the proportion that is below it

affordance the attaching of meaning to sensory information through direct perception; it is the quality of an object that permits an individual to carry out an action upon it

Gibson saw perception as being an innate mechanism with a survival value that had been shaped by evolutionary forces. Gibson criticised Gregory's reliance on evidence gained from artificial laboratory conditions that only contained an unnatural 'frozen array' of a motionless observer in an uneventful world, preferring himself to work in real-world conditions and to seek practical applications of his work. He saw perception as being very accurate and believed that we experience visual illusions, which he believed have little to do with everyday life, as they are usually two dimensional and static and because we only view them momentarily.

Gibson ultimately saw the perceiver not as the brain, but rather as the person embedded in their environment. The function of perception is therefore not the production of experiences or representations, but rather the enabling of an animal to function appropriately in its environment.

Pagano (2008) investigated whether invariant sensory information is available to any senses other than vision. His research involved dynamic touch, the perception of actively manipulated objects via muscle sensitivity. Objects were hidden from sight and physically manipulated. Hand-held tools and other implements were found to be perceived by the detection of movement-produced physical invariants. This suggests that the constancy of perception is derived from the invariant nature of physical stimulation available to an observer, just as Gibson theorised.

The optic array

According to Gibson the starting point for perception is found within the optic array. The things we see either emit light (like the sun or a torch) or reflect light (like most objects). As a consequence, the optic array contains different intensities of light shining in different directions and therefore contains sensory information about the complexity of our physical world. Optic flow patterns are created when objects in our visual environment flow past a moving observer, giving information about position and depth.

There are three ways in which Gibson sees ambient light not containing information and therefore failing to be part of the optic array:

- *Ambient darkness* – occurs when the retina is not stimulated enough, resulting in an absence of stimulus information, eg when it's too dark to make out any shapes.
- The *uniform optic array* – occurs when there is light but it does not offer any stimulus information. The photoreceptive parts of the eye are stimulated, but not higher receptive units, such as the excitatory neurones. Cohen (1957) was able to produce this effect experimentally by putting the eye of an observer to the aperture of a large optical integrating sphere that had a very smooth surface.
- The *homogenous optic array* – occurs when the intensity of light is not equal in all directions, but the changes in intensity in different directions are not sufficient to provide the contrast, detail, form or structure needed to fully stimulate the visual system,

eg when we are in thick fog or in a snowstorm. It can also be created artificially with diffusing eye-caps or by the 'Ganzfeld' technique (see Chapter 12).

The optic array is composed of light and allows us to perceive structure in different ways. The structure of the optic array depends on 'intensity transitions' – that is, how areas of light and dark relate to one another. There are four possible structures:

- *Shadowy structure* – occurs when there are gradual changes of intensity within the optic array. This is not enough to give any clear impression of surface, distance or depth, but does give a basic impression of motion. This suggests that motion is a primitive type of sensory information that is not dependent on object form. Imagine an invisible hand running along the pile on a piece of velvet – you would know which way the hand was moving.
- *Spotty structure* – occurs when the optic array contains a group of points or spots, for example the stars in the night sky. This structure allows motion to be perceived as well as pattern, but not form, as it is not sufficient to allow clear impressions of objects.
- *Textured structure* – occurs when information in the optic array becomes sufficiently sharpened or discontinuous to allow the perception of the hardness of objects. Higher order forms of texture include surface colour and optical slant.
- *Contoured structure* – occurs when the optic array contains enough information about relative light and dark to permit the perception of contours (outlines). A single closed contour is sufficient to allow the perception of an object, for example if the object is against a background. It is the differences between the intensities of information, and not just the intensities themselves that form the basic properties of the optic array, that allow us to perceive form.

Thinking creatively about psychology

Which of Gibson's reasons for an absence of sensory information occurs when you can see changing light and dark patterns through the frosted glass of a bathroom window but can't make out any shapes? Think of two more examples like this.

So Gibson argues that light itself is not enough for perception to occur – we need the sensory information to have structure. This information is complex and constantly changing, because we see light from all different points in the surrounding environment. Movement is important, as even slight motion, such as the movement of eyes and the angle of our gaze, provide an ongoing updating of sensory information. Motion thus provides an essential variant – a source of information from the changes in the optic array.

The other crucial elements of the optic array are those that Gibson describes as invariant: they are unchanging regardless of the movements of an observer. We shall look at three main types of invariant information: optic flow patterns, texture gradient and the horizon ratio.

Optic flow patterns

During World War Two, Gibson was involved in the selection and testing of pilots and made training films to demonstrate the problems pilots might experience when taking off and landing. As a pilot approaches the runway to land, the point towards which they are moving appears motionless, while the rest of the visual information seemingly moves away from that point (see Figure 2.13).

▼ **Figure 2.13** Optic flow patterns as seen by a pilot

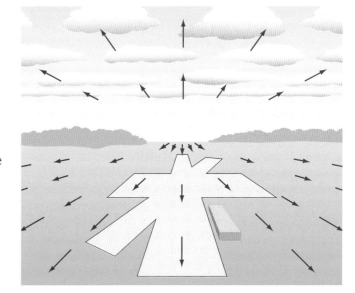

Gibson thought that optic flow patterns provided unambiguous information for pilots about their direction, speed and altitude. Information about distance is also available. As we move, objects far away, like clouds and hills, appear to move very slowly, while objects that are closer seem to move more quickly. This cue to depth is called *motion parallax*.

There is a statistical relationship between the scale of the optic flow and where an object is in relation to the observer. When your speed doubles, the optic flow you experience also doubles. If an object is brought twice as close, the optic flow will again double. The optic flow also varies according to the angle between the observer's direction of movement and the direction of the object being looked at. If you are travelling forwards, the optic flow is quickest in relation to objects at 90 degrees to your side and those directly above or below you. An object directly in front will have no optic flow, so will appear stationary. However, because the object's edges are not directly ahead they will appear to move, and so the object will appear to get bigger. This description illustrates the detailed, changing information provided by optic flow that informs direct perception.

Bardy *et al.* (1996) investigated how it is possible to maintain balance while walking. Participants had to walk on a treadmill, in the dark, in front of a large screen on which three-dimensional optic flow patterns were projected. To stay balanced while walking they had to use motion parallax to change their posture while maintaining forward motion. Bardy *et al.* concluded that optic flow patterns allow walkers to make compensatory responses. This supports Gibson's idea that optic flow patterns contain unambiguous information that aids our perception.

Johansson (1973) demonstrated the importance of motion in determining optic flow patterns using lights placed on the ankles, knees, hips etc of a black-clad actor. A film was made of the actor walking in a dark room so that only the lights were visible. A viewer can easily perceive that the lights are a person moving but cannot perceive a person if the lights are still. Kozlowski & Cutting (1977) showed that even the gender of the actor could be determined from the moving patterns of light, and Mather & West (1993) found that animal species could be recognised using this seemingly limited information source. Indeed Sumi (1984) ran the film backwards and upside down – and a human walker was still perceived! There is little doubt that movement helps in our understanding of objects and that motion is very important in determining optic flow patterns, supporting Gibson's theory that optic flow patterns are a sufficient source of sensory information for direct perception.

Texture gradient

A texture gradient is a surface pattern that provides information about the distance, depth and shape of an object. This idea is central to Gibson's theory.

The perceptual environment is made up of surfaces with different textures that give the perceptual experience of depth, distance and spatial awareness. We therefore perceive 'surface' because of the shape and material that objects are made of – this is 'visual texture', the objects within the visual environment. The texture gradient, in contrast, is the change in relative size and density of those objects. As an observer moves about in their environment, the visual textures expand as they are approached and shrink as they pass beyond

▼ **Figure 2.14** Linear perspective is a cue to depth from parallel lines appearing to converge in the distance

the observer's head. The 'flow' of these textures provides information about the sensory world. Two cues to depth help here: motion parallax and **linear perspective** – a cue to depth indicated by parallel lines appearing to converge in the distance. These help us to perceive depth in a direct manner and therefore Gibson sees the third dimension of depth as being directly available to the senses.

Horizon ratio

The horizon ratio is another example of an invariant feature of sensory information contained within the optical array, and concerns the position of an object in relation to the horizon. Objects of different sizes that are the same distance from an observer have different horizon ratios, while same-sized objects on a level surface have the same horizon ratios. If an observer approaches a building it will appear larger but the ratio of the building that is above or below the horizon remains the same and thus is a perceptual invariant. This provides another source of information for direct perception.

CLASSIC RESEARCH

Gibson & Bridgeman (1987) The visual perception of surface texture in photos. *Psychological Research* **49(1), 1–5**

Aim: To investigate the role of surface texture in perception.

Procedure: 49 students viewed photographs of rectangular samples of surface textures, for example sand, fur and rock. Participants had to respond to questions concerning the physical properties and viewing conditions of each texture.

Results: Correct identifications were usually made and participants were generally able to identify the physical state of objects, such as whether they were lying flat, what colour they were and details of incident light (the light that falls on a surface).

Conclusion: Sensory information contained within the surface texture of objects is sufficient to allow direct perception of the objects in line with Gibson's bottom-up processing theory.

Affordance

Affordance involves attaching meaning to sensory information; it is the quality of an object that permits an individual to carry out an action upon it. 'The affordances of the environment are what it offers animals, what it provides or furnishes, either for good or ill,' according to Gibson (1979). Gibson defined affordance as all the 'action possibilities' of objects in an environment, and he believed that potential uses of an object are directly perceivable, for example a flight of stairs 'affords' climbing up or down, while a bench 'affords' sitting down, and a bottle 'affords' drinking from. Therefore the affordance of an object is what it means to the observer. Action possibilities are also dependent upon a person's capabilities, for example a flight of stairs does not 'afford' the act of climbing to an infant who cannot yet crawl.

Affordances come from the invariant qualities of an environment and are affected by an individual's psychological state, but are directly perceivable. Thus the concept of affordances is crucial to rejecting Gregory's idea that meaning is stored in long-term memory. Gibson believed that evolutionary forces shaped perceptual skills and that learning is not required for accurate, meaningful perception.

Discussion of Gibson's theory

Gibson's theory has been as influential as Gregory's, creating an interest in perception that has led to further research and a better understanding of the subject area. For example, Gaver (1996) applied and extended Gibson's theory of affordances into the design of computer displays.

Further evidence suggests a biological basis for Gibson's theory. Logothetis & Pauls (1995) trained monkeys to recognise novel objects from a given viewpoint and then tested their ability to recognise the objects from other viewpoints. Recordings taken from the brain identified neurones that appeared able to perceive specific objects regardless of their orientation. This evidence suggests a physiological mechanism behind the ability to perceive in a direct fashion.

Prisidi (2008) suggested a practical application to Gibson's theory whereby robots could be built to mimic our neural structure. Other practical applications for Gibson's theory include painting road markings with parallel lines increasingly closer together as the junction nears, causing the driver to slow as the lines give a false impression of greater speed. Similarly, as pilots approach runways they are aided by lighting and landing strip markings that maximise the optic flow patterns, enabling them to land planes more safely.

Gibson's theory of direct perception can explain how we can perceive quickly and accurately. However, it cannot really explain why perception is sometimes inaccurate, for example with visual illusions. Gibson claimed that the illusions used in research are artificial, but this doesn't apply to all situations. Gibson's theory cannot account for people's tendency to overestimate vertical extents relative to horizontal ones (see *Over To You*), nor why some illusions occur naturally. For instance, if you stare at a waterfall and then at the motionless bank, it will appear to move upwards.

Gibson's theory is based on the idea that we see events under ideal viewing conditions where there is a lot of stimulus information and plenty of time to look. Tulving & Schacter (1994) used a word identification task and manipulated stimulus clarity and the amount of context. As the stimulus clarity was improved (with longer exposure times) and the amount of context was increased, perceptual accuracy improved. However, as the duration of exposure increased, so

This is an example of the horizontal–vertical illusion. Which line appears longer, the red or the green one? Check using a ruler and you may be surprised.

▼ Figure 2.15

▼ **Figure 2.16** It is unlikely that you have innate knowledge about what these are for

the impact of context was reduced, meaning that if stimulus information is high then our need to use other sources of information may be reduced. This is not what Gibson's theory would predict.

Perhaps the major problem with Gibson's work is his theory of affordances (1977). It states that the optical array not only contains information allowing perception of the environment, but also information for the perception of what the objects in the environment offer, ie 'afford'. Affordances are seen as being invariant and the 'values' and 'meanings' of objects can also be directly perceived, ie they are external to the perceiver. This seems unlikely as there are individual differences in perception.

Some theorists, like Bruce & Green (1990), have shown that the idea of affordance can explain the visually controlled behaviour of certain animals, such as insects. However, humans are likely to have a different conceptual representation of the environment from animals. Our knowledge about objects and their uses and meanings is affected by cultural influences, experience and emotional states. For example, it would be difficult to argue a pair of trainers afford that they

are for running, or that a sports shop affords buying trainers, without any prior knowledge.

It may well be that a combination of both Gregory's and Gibson's theories is needed to explain perception, where Gibson's theory explains perception under good viewing conditions and Gregory's is best when viewing occurs in less than ideal conditions. One theory that attempts to explain how top-down and bottom-up processes interact to provide the best understanding of a stimulus is Neisser's 'perceptual cycle' (1976), which demonstrates how knowledge, actions and features of the environment all interact to produce perceptions.

↻ Exploring issues and debates

The Nature versus Nurture debate

The nature–nurture debate concerns the relative contributions of genetic and environmental factors in determining characteristics and abilities.

Construct a table of points that illustrates how Gregory's theory of perception favours the nurture side of the debate, while Gibson's favours the nature side of the debate.

The development of perception

Babies and adults see the world differently. The next section explores those differences and how they arise.

The development of perceptual abilities

A baby is born with limited perceptual abilities, and most take time and experience to develop fully. Research has investigated the extent to which perceptual abilities are innate or learned: the *nature versus nurture debate*. A baby, although dependent on its carers, does need some basic perceptual abilities from birth to help it to survive and also to interact with its environment safely. Perceptual abilities will be shaped to suit each individual's needs and environmental conditions – it wouldn't make sense for all of an individual's perceptual abilities to be present and fixed at birth as they couldn't adapt to changing environmental conditions. It is likely that the development of perceptual abilities has evolved to aid survival and reproduction.

To understand the influence of nature and nurture on perception, psychologists have performed research into abilities such as depth and distance perception and *visual constancies*. There are several ways to do this including studies on *neonates* (newborns) and cross-cultural studies.

Depth and distance perception

Depth perception is the ability to detect *three-dimensional (3D)* space and to be able to judge distances between objects and ourselves, and each other. Depth perception aids survival – we need to move around and function in our environment. Without depth perception we couldn't judge the distances of

KEY TERMS

nature the influence of biological factors such as genes on development

nurture the influence of the environment and experience on development

2D (two-dimensional) appearing to have length and breadth, but no depth

3D (three-dimensional) appearing to have length, breadth and depth

neonate a newborn baby (with no learning experiences)

visual constancies the tendency for objects to be perceived as similar despite variations in the conditions of observation

objects and therefore how far we need to move to grasp or avoid them, and we wouldn't be able to tell the difference in distance between stepping down the rung of a ladder or walking off a cliff.

Depth perception involves space perception, the ability to understand the distances of objects from each other in space. This results mainly from two types of visual information:

- *monocular cues* – apparent to one eye (eg accommodation, interposition, texture gradient, retinal size, motion parallax, aerial perspective, elevation, linear perspective)
- *binocular cues* – apparent only when using both eyes (eg retinal disparity and convergence).

Depth cues can also be divided according to whether they require learning:

- *primary cues* – are not dependent on learning
- *secondary cues* – are dependent on learning.

Young infants usually use primary rather than secondary cues, because they are innate.

We will consider three primary cues:

- *Retinal disparity* – our two eyes are set apart from each other, so we receive two different, but overlapping views of the environment. The brain combines these images (stereopsis) to produce an impression of depth. The greater the difference (disparity) between the two views of an object, the closer we judge it to be. This is a binocular cue.
- *Convergence* – our eyes rotate inward towards each other (converge) in a co-ordinated way that allows us to focus clearly on nearby objects. When we look at objects that are far away, our eyes rotate away from each other so the two lines of vision approach parallel. Feedback from muscles during convergence provides us with sensory information about depth and distance.
- *Accommodation* – this occurs when the lens of the eye changes shape to focus images of objects nearby and far away. This is controlled by the ciliary muscles and feedback from them provides sensory information about the distance of objects.

▼ **Figure 2.17** Binocular convergence is a cue to depth

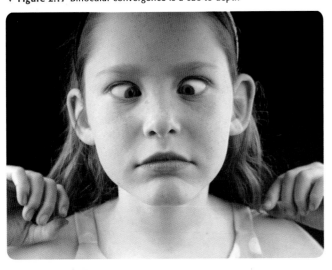

Research evidence indicates that neonates (newborn infants), have innate abilities to perceive depth and distance, that is tend to focus on primary cues, because they are not dependent on learning. However, infants can use some secondary cues from quite an early age too.

- *Interposition* – occurs when objects seem to partially block out or overlap each other. The fully visible object is seen as being nearer.
- *Texture gradient* – objects reflect light differently because they vary in complexity and density. As the size of elements making up surface texture appears smaller,

they are perceived to be further away. Sudden changes in texture gradients usually indicate a change in the direction of an object's surface and its distance from the observer.

- *Retinal size* – as an object's distance from us increases, the size of its retinal image becomes smaller. In the absence of other cues, larger objects appear closer than smaller objects.
- *Motion parallax* – as we move, more distant objects appear to move more slowly than closer ones (see also p32).
- *Aerial perspective* – objects with sharp, clear images appear nearer than objects with blurry, unclear ones.
- *Elevation* – for objects below the horizon, nearby objects appear further from the horizon than more distant ones (the reverse is true above the horizon).
- *Linear perspective* – parallel lines (and the space between them) appear to converge in the distance (see also p33).

▼ **Figure 2.18** Monocular depth cues

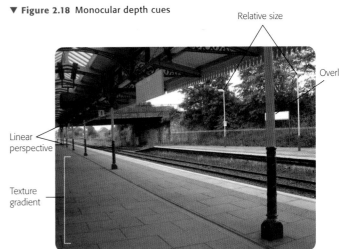

Visual constancies

We can never see all of an object at once – there will always be parts of it hidden to us. Also, we often see objects from viewpoints that don't reveal their real shape and size in the retinal image, yet we perceive them as unchanging. If somebody walks towards you, the image on the retina will get larger but they don't seem to grow. This is a result of *visual constancies*.

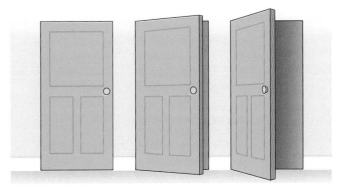

▲ **Figure 2.19** As a door is opened the retinal image of its shape changes and yet we still perceive it as a rectangular door

Visual constancies allow our perception of objects to be more constant and stable than our retinal images. As we move and as light conditions change, our retinal images alter. If we relied only on retinal images for perception, our world would consist of things getting bigger as they approached us, colours changing with lighting conditions, and objects appearing to change shape as we moved about. What we actually experience is an ordered world where objects seem constant in our consciousness. This would have adaptive value as a predictable world is safer.

The main visual constancies are size, shape, brightness and colour.

- *Size constancy* – if two same-sized objects are seen, one twice as far away as the other, the retinal image of the further object will be half the size of the retinal image of the nearer one. However, they do not appear to differ in size. This occurs because of perceptual interpretation of the retinal image.
- *Shape constancy* – an object's shape appears to remain constant regardless of any changes in the viewing angle. A rectangular door face-on presents a rectangular image to our eyes. As the door opens the shape the door makes on our retina becomes trapezoidal, but we do not perceive the door as changing shape. Our perceptual system solves the problem by combining information from the retinal image with information from the viewing angle to create a conscious perception of the door's real shape, allowing us to perceive objects accurately.
- *Brightness constancy* – when the illumination of a visual scene alters, the amount of light reflected from an object changes. However, the perceived brightness of the object generally remains constant. This helps us to recognise objects as being familiar.
- *Colour constancy* – objects retain their colour regardless of the lighting conditions (eg under coloured lights) as long as there is enough contrast and shadow, for example several objects of different colours.

 OVER TO YOU You can see brightness constancy in action. Take a piece of white paper and turn all the lights full on and note the whiteness of the paper. Next, reduce the lighting a bit (by turning off a light or using a dimmer switch) and note that the paper still appears to be the same shade of white. Reduce the lighting more and more, without making it totally dark, and the paper will retain its apparent whiteness regardless of the amount of light energy that is actually entering your eye.

Investigating perceptual development

What psychologists have tried to find out is whether visual constancies are innate or learned. As with depth and distance perception, neonate studies and cross-cultural studies are often used to investigate this area.

Methods used in neonate studies

The basic idea behind neonate studies is that because the participants (babies) have not had learning experiences through interaction with their environment, then any perceptual abilities they possess must be innate.

However, there are problems with this methodology. Neonates are too young to communicate so we must infer what they can perceive and cannot be sure that our inferences are correct. Also, neonates have short attention spans so tests must be quick or else the infant loses interest. There are ethical issues too – such as the risk of psychological or physiological harm and the need for informed consent.

Even if a neonate doesn't exhibit a certain perceptual ability we cannot conclude that this ability is not innate. The ability may simply emerge later, with maturation but without the need for external influences. However, this creates another problem as it is difficult to work out whether a perceptual ability that emerges some time after birth is the result of maturation or of learning, although the earlier a perceptual ability is exhibited the more likely it is to be innate.

When researching the development of perception it is important to note that it is a *group* of abilities not a single skill. Visual perception is made up of separate skills: the perception of colour, shape, movement etc, and some of these may have a greater genetic basis, while others require more learning.

In order to construct useful and valid research psychologists use a range of approaches. There are two key forms of research methodology, looking at:

- the *physical structure* of neonates' sensory equipment
- the *behaviour* of neonates towards sensory stimuli.

Common methods of study include:

- *Preference* – two stimuli are presented and if the infant looks at one more than the other it is presumed to be able to discriminate between the two.
- *Light reflection* – reflected light from an infant's eye is filmed to determine what the infant is looking at.

▶ **Figure 2.20** Are babies born knowing how to see?

- *Habituation* – a sensory stimulus is continually presented until the infant loses interest. A new stimulus is then introduced, and if the infant pays attention to it it is inferred that the infant can differentiate between the two stimuli.
- *Sucking rate* – the amount the infant sucks a dummy connected to a recorder is measured. This changes when a stimulus is presented but returns to the norm as the baby loses interest. Then a new stimulus is presented to see if the sucking rate again changes. If so, this indicates that the infant can differentiate between the two stimuli.
- *Conditioned rotation* – an infant is conditioned to respond to a stimulus by being reinforced every time it alters its gaze to look in the right direction. The stimulus is then presented alongside other non-reinforced stimuli and if the infant shows a preference for the conditioned stimulus, it must be able to recognise it.
- *Heart and breathing rate* – baseline heart and breathing rates are established and then a stimulus is introduced, which changes the rates. They return to the norm as the infant loses interest. A new stimulus is introduced, and if the rates change this indicates that the two stimuli can be distinguished.
- *Focus change* – a dummy is connected to audio-visual equipment and the baby learns that by sucking it can change the focus of an image projected onto a screen, indicating its awareness of and interest in the image.
- *Brain scanning* – PET and MRI scans (which you learned about at AS) are conducted during presentation of stimuli to see what, if any, brain areas are activated. These are then related to specific perceptual abilities.

▲ **Figure 2.21** A baby's sucking rate changes when it recognises different visual stimuli

Neonate research into the development of perceptual abilities

The physical structure of a neonate's visual system is not well developed at birth. Courage & Adams (1996) found that neonates do not perceive visual detail well. Infants have to view an object at 7 metres to see as well as an adult would at 250 metres.

CLASSIC RESEARCH

Gibson & Walk (1960) The visual cliff. *Scientific American* 202, 64–71

Aim: To see if babies would attempt to crawl over an apparent cliff to indicate they had no innate depth perception.

Procedure: A glass-topped table was built with a chequerboard design and a plate of non-reflective glass covering a vertical drop each side of the 'bridge'. This 'visual cliff' had a deep and a shallow side (see Figure 2.22). Neonates could not be used as they cannot crawl so 6–14-month-old babies were used. Thirty-six babies were each placed individually on the apparently shallow side of the equipment and called by their mother to crawl towards her over the apparent cliff.

Findings: Even though they were encouraged to do so by their mothers, 92 per cent of babies refused to cross over the cliff even if they wore an-eye patch over one eye. The few who partially did were thought to have done so accidentally. Research with a variety of animal species (whose young were mobile soon after birth so definitely had no prior learning experiences) also refused to cross the cliff.

Conclusions: Depth perception seems to be an innate perceptual skill. As neonates with one eye-patch wouldn't cross the deep side, they must have been able to use monocular cues to perceive depth.

The conduction of visual information along the optic nerve in infants is less effective than in adults and the visual cortex cannot process sensory information as well as it too lacks maturation. Jacobs & Blakemore (1988) believe that the immature physical development of the eye, especially the retina, at birth is the main constraint on a neonate's visual ability, while Bronson (1974) believes instead that it is due to the immaturity of the central nervous system. However, physical development of the visual system occurs fairly rapidly after birth.

▼ **Figure 2.22** Child on the visual cliff

Thinking creatively about psychology

On the basis of Gibson & Walk's findings, what advice might be given to parents about letting babies crawl around at the top of the stairs? How might such advice be contradicted?

Depth and distance perception

Gibson & Walk's study can be criticised because neonates could not be used and the older infants used may have learned about depth from experiences, which would explain their reluctance to cross the cliff. However, the fact that neonate animals also refuse to cross weakens this criticism.

There is an ethical concern with asking mothers to call babies over the cliff as it may have caused psychological distress to the infants.

Campos et al. (1970) backed up Gibson & Walk's findings using two-month-old infants on the visual cliff. As the infants were too young to crawl their heart rate was measured. This decreased when the infant was moved across the deep drop, indicating an awareness of depth. Interestingly, infants of nine months of age showed an *increase* in heart rate when moved across, indicating anxiety. This suggests that depth perception is innate, but associating danger with depth is learned.

However, Schwarz et al. (1973) found no change in the heart rates of five-month-old babies when placed on a visual cliff, although there was in nine-month-olds. This suggests that depth perception emerges somewhere between five and nine months of age.

Bower et al. (1970) tested very young babies, aged 6–20 days old, on their response to an approaching object and found that they held their hands out and even cried, supporting the idea that depth perception is innate. The findings were the same when only one eye was used, suggesting that monocular cues (such as motion parallax) are important cues to depth. The study did, however, raise an ethical concern; it was stopped early due to the distress it was causing.

Stereopsis is an important binocular depth cue. The use of stereopsis in infants is tested by presenting them with two slightly different stimuli, one to each eye using special goggles. Some pairs of stimuli can be fused to form an image, others cannot. If an infant can use stereopsis then they will prefer stimuli that allow them to perceive a 3D shape. Held (1985), using this technique, found that stereopsis appears at four months of age and approaches an adult level within a few weeks.

Slater et al. (1984) found that neonates will fix their gaze on a 3D stimulus in preference to a photograph of the same stimulus, even when restricted to just monocular viewing, with the major depth cue here seeming to be motion parallax. This suggests that some ability to perceive depth is apparent at a very early age.

Yonas et al. (1978) used apparatus known as the 'Ames window', where a 2D trapezoidal window is rotated around its vertical axis. When adults view it using monocular vision, they perceive an illusion of a slanted window with the larger side appearing nearer than the smaller one. The researchers found six-month-old infants were twice as likely to reach for the large side (which appears nearest) than the small side, indicating that they could detect when the edge appeared closest to them.

▶ **Figure 2.23** An Ames window seen face on. Imagine what it would look like as it rotated

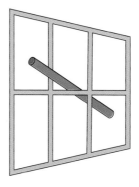

LOOKING FURTHER Watch the video on this website with Richard Gregory explaining the Ames window:

http://www.richardgregory.org/experiments/video/ames_window.htm

RESEARCH NOW

Sen *et al.* (2001) Development of infants' sensitivity to surface contour information for spatial layout. *Perception* **30, 167–76**

Aim: To find the age at which infants are able to use monocular cues to judge depth.

Method: Using a visual illusion viewed by monocular vision (see Figure 2.24), infants were tested for depth perception by looking to see whether they chose to reach for the apparently closer end of the cylinder.

Results: Seven-month-old infants reached for the nearer end of the cylinder, but not 5.5-month-olds.

Conclusion: The ability to perceive monocular depth cues appears at about six months of age.

▶ Figure 2.24
The cylinder illusion

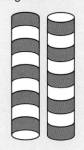

Imura *et al.* (2008) tested infants' sensitivity to shading and line junction cues to decide whether they had shape constancy. The infants, aged five to eight months, were shown computer-generated images. First they were presented with a pair of displays: one that alternated between 2D and 3D images, and one that alternated between two 2D images. The 3D images gave the impression of a 3D folded surface, the 2D ones did not. The seven- to eight-month-old infants had a looking preference for the alternating 2D–3D display, while five- to six-month-old infants did not show a looking preference. The results suggest that the depth cues from shading and line junctions change between six and seven months of age.

▲ Figure 2.25
Shading is a monocular cue to depth

CLASSIC RESEARCH

Bower T (1966) The visual world of infants. *Scientific American* **215, 80–92**

Aim: To see if young children have size constancy.

Method: Nine infants aged six to eight weeks were conditioned by being rewarded (an adult smiled, tickled them and played peek-a-boo) every time they turned their heads towards a 30cm cube 1m away. Various other cubes at varying distances were then presented. These were:

1. 30cm cube at 3m – produces a smaller retinal image than the original stimulus
2. 90cm cube at 1m – produces a retinal image three times larger than the original
3. 90cm cube at 3m – produces a retinal image the same size as the original.

The number of times an infant turned its head to each cube was recorded. If the infant showed a preference for option 1 this would be evidence for size constancy, as it would be reacting to the actual size of the cube. If, however, an infant preferred option 3 this would be evidence against size constancy, as the infant would be reacting to the size of the retinal image without taking distance into account.

Results: Option 3 was the least preferred (22 head turns) and option 1 the most preferred (58 head turns). Option 2 produced 54 head turns. The infants were mainly responding to the same-sized cube, regardless of its distance away, and to the cube at the same distance away as the original.

Conclusion: The ability to perceive size constancy develops very early.

Visual constancies

Research has also investigated whether visual constancies are innate or learned (see *Classic Research*).

Following on from the study described in *Classic Research*, Bower investigated which cues were being used by the infants. He produced three variations of his procedure to provide:

a texture gradient and motion parallax cues
b just texture gradient cues
c texture gradient and stereopsis cues.

With variation **b**, the infants appeared unable to judge size or distance, which suggests that texture gradient is not being used as a cue to determine size constancy. Option **a** produced results similar to the original study, suggesting that motion parallax is most important. Stereopsis was, to a lesser extent, also used.

Support for Bower's findings came from Slater *et al.* (1990), who used the habituation method (see p38) to find that infants as young as 18 weeks of age could perceive the real size of a stimulus, as did Granrud (2006) with four-month-old infants.

Bower (1966) also investigated the development of shape constancy. Two-month-old infants were trained to turn their heads to look at a tilted rectangle (which makes a wedge-shape on the retina, ie a trapezoidal image). They also reacted to a 'face-on' rectangle but not to an actual trapezoidal stimulus when face on or tilted. This confirms that even at two months infants have a sense of shape constancy.

Kaye & Bower (1994) found that one-day-old infants could recognise a visual image of an object they knew by touch. By training babies to suck a dummy to make a picture of it appear on a screen in front of them, they found that, when given a choice of pictures, they preferred to look at a familiar dummy. This suggested that a neonate can determine the shape of an object in its mouth and recognise this shape, visually supporting the idea that shape constancy is an innate perceptual ability.

Expanding on this research, Sann & Steri (2007) found that neonates could visually recognise an object they had previously held, but could not recognise by touch an object they had previously seen. This suggests that neonates gather information differently in visual and tactile (touch) modes. The sensory modes used to perceive shape constancy must therefore differ in terms of the input of innate factors and learning.

Adults can readily judge the relative brightness of an object and its surroundings and use this to maintain brightness constancy. Chien *et al.* (2003) found that four-month-old infants performed a novelty-preference task based on brightness in the same way an adult would, showing that brightness constancy is present very early in life. Using paper smiley faces as stimuli, Chien *et al.* (2006) investigated this further and found that the infants showed brightness constancy even when the level of illumination changed, so their perceptual ability in this respect is well developed.

Dannemiller & Hanko (1987) tested 45 four-month-old infants for colour constancy under two conditions, one where there was a change in the lighting conditions between familiarisation with the stimuli and the test, and one with no change in lighting. The infants could recognise familiar colour under some conditions, but not all, suggesting that they have some colour constancy but that at four months this perceptual ability is still developing.

To confirm the presence of some colour constancy, Pereverzeva & Teller (2004) tested four-month-old infants with stimuli of various colours, embedded in either a dark or a white surround. It was found that infants' looking preferences changed with alterations in the surround colour. The infants preferred those stimuli where the difference in colour between the stimulus and the surround was greatest, showing that they did indeed have colour constancy.

↪ Exploring issues and debates
Ethical issues

Researching into the origins of perceptual skills often involves conducting neonate studies. However, before such research can be undertaken, there are a number of sensitive ethical issues that must be considered.

Construct a table that illustrates the ethical issues concerned with perceptual research that involves using small children. You should include details of how these issues can be dealt with.

Cross-cultural studies

Cross-cultural studies into perception involve comparing people from different cultures with the same test materials to look for similarities and differences in their perceptual abilities.

Basically, if people of different cultures have similar abilities this is evidence for genetic origins for perceptual abilities. This evidence is especially so if there are similarities even when people live in very different environments. Conversely, if people of different cultures differ in their perception, these abilities are more likely to be learned.

One source of evidence comes from comparing the responses of people from very different physical environments to visual illusions.

▼ **Figure 2.26**

CLASSIC RESEARCH

Turnbull C (1961) *The Forest People*. **New York: Simon & Schuster**

Aim: To investigate the effect of growing up without experience of long-distance vision on size constancy.

Method: The researcher befriended members of the Bambuti pygmies who are of relatively short stature and live in the dense Ituni forest with no open spaces. One of the pygmies, Kenge, acted as a guide and Turnbull observed his reactions to seeing animals far away on the grasslands and asked him questions.

Results: Kenge showed little reaction to a herd of distant buffalo on the savannah. When asked what he could see, Kenge replied 'strange insects'. He would not believe they were actually large animals a long way off and when Turnbull drove towards them and they grew in size the pygmy accused Turnbull of sorcery.

Conclusion: Living without open spaces provides little experience of depth cues or need for size constancy. The absence of this ability in Kenge suggests that these perceptual abilities are learned.

Thinking critically about psychology

To what extent is it possible to generalise from Turnbull's study?

Western children, exposed from an early age to 2D images, can readily recognise objects' depth and distance relationships within them. To find out whether these abilities are learned, Hudson (1960) tested over 500 people from varied ethnic groups (Bantu, Indian and European South Africans and Ghanaians). He showed them 2D pictures of a hunting scene that contained several depth cues, such as overlap and relative size (see Figure 2.27). They were asked what the hunter was doing and what was close to the hunter.

At the start of primary education, children from all the different cultures had trouble perceiving the pictures in 3D, but by the end of primary education nearly all the European children could do so. However, some Bantu and Ghanaian children still saw the images in 2D, as did non-literate adults from all cultures. The critical factor wasn't schooling but constant exposure to pictures, so understanding the information that represents depth in such images appears to be a learned skill.

Deregowski (1972) used a pre-test to divide Zambian children into '2D perceivers' and '3D perceivers'. The children were then asked to copy the ambiguous picture in Figure 2.28 or a non-ambiguous control picture. The drawing produces an illusion of three prongs due to trying to perceive the 2D image as a 3D object.

The '3D perceivers' spent longer looking at the ambiguous image than at the control trident that actually portrayed three prongs. The '2D perceivers' spent equal time viewing the two images. This suggests that the 3D perceivers could interpret depth cues in pictures whilst the 2D perceivers could not. This again seems to indicate that such a perceptual ability is learned.

▼ Figure 2.27 Hunting scenes like this one were used by Hudson (1960).

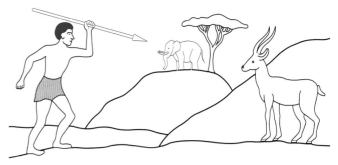

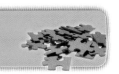

Thinking practically about psychology

Decide which depth cues are provided by the card in Figure 2.27, then design two more pairs of scenes that could be used in a similar experiment.

▼ Figure 2.28 The ambiguous trident

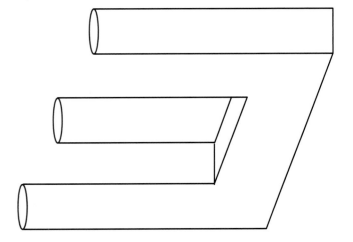

Jahoda & McGurk (1974) compared 227 African, Chinese and European children aged 4–10 years on their pictorial depth discrimination. They were asked to build 3D models of objects in three pictures. Their models were used to assess perception of size and spatial relationships in the 2D pictures. The results were similar across cultures: size accuracy was quite good in younger participants and increased with age and the number of depth cues available. Spatial accuracy also improved with age but was worse when more depth information was available. The lack of cultural differences points towards this ability being more innate in nature.

There is an argument that drawings do not relate directly to the actual world but are cultural representations that we learn. Cox (1992) showed how Australian Aborigines use a semi-circle to represent people and a group of semi-circles around a circle to represent a family. Such cultural representations in Aboriginal art cannot be readily understood by people of other cultures, showing that to relate drawings to the actual world we need to understanding the social 'coding' behind them.

Montello (2006) meta-analysed cross-cultural studies of depth/distance perception and found that cultural differences are generally small. This supports an evolutionary explanation for such perceptual abilities being primarily innate This suggests that depth perception has survival value so is present at birth but has some capacity to change with experience.

▼ **Figure 2.29** Aboriginal art uses cultural coding

Cross-cultural research into perceptual abilities has also investigated whether visual illusions are universal to all cultures. The Müller-Lyer illusion (see p29) is often used in such research.

Segall *et al.* (1963) showed various illusions to 1878 children and adults from 14 non-European cultural groups, mainly from Africa and some European ones. The Europeans were more likely to experience the Müller-Lyer illusion than non-Europeans. Segall believed that the illusion was only perceived by people who lived in a carpentered environment (a world of straight lines and angles). People such as the Zulus, who live in a world of round natural shapes, are less likely to experience the illusion because their physical environment provides less experience of the perspective cues that cause the illusion to arise.

Thinking creatively about psychology

Segall (1990) comments: 'People perceive in ways that are shaped by the inferences they have learned to make in order to function most effectively in the particular ecological settings where they live'. How might an alien who lives in a world of circles and rounded tunnels perceive the Müller-Lyer illusion?

Further support for the 'carpentered world' idea came from Stewart (1973). Black and white children from urban Illinois and black children in urban and rural Zambia were shown the Müller-Lyer and Sander illusions (see Figures 2.9 and 2.30). The urban American children, both black and white, were equally susceptible, more so than the rural Zambians.

▼ **Figure 2.30** The Sander illusion: which line looks longer, the blue or the green?

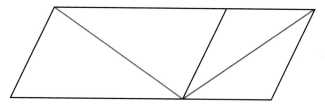

Allport & Pettigrew (1957) used the Ames window (see p39) in a cross-cultural study. Participants from a western culture perceive a rectangle that rotates to and fro, rather than what it actually is, a rotating trapezoid. As the illusion occurs for people who interpret it as a window, so are expecting it to be rectangular, the researchers showed it to Europeans, urban Zulus and rural Zulus. The rural Zulus, whose environment does not include rectangular windows, were less likely to see the illusion. This supports the idea that our environment determines our perceptual abilities, in line with Segall's concept of the carpentered world.

However, the view that environment determines perception has been criticised. Gregor & McPherson (1965) gave the Müller-Lyer illusion to Australian Aborigines who lived in an urban carpentered world and to rural Aborigines who did not. No differences in seeing the illusion were found, suggesting that the perception of illusions may be due to education rather than environment.

Pollack (1963) found that susceptibility to the Müller-Lyer illusion decreases with age. He believed this to be due to the lesser ability to detect contour as you grow older. Following this, Pollack & Silva (1967) found that Europeans are more susceptible to the illusion than other ethnic groups because a difference in the structure of their retinas means they can detect contours better. This is evidence against the carpentered hypothesis because it suggests a biological reason for cultural differences in perception of the illusion.

Animal studies

Animal studies typically use sensory deprivation to investigate its effects on perceptual abilities. The aim of such studies is to explore what early sensory experiences are required for normal perceptual development. Procedures can be conducted on animals that could not, ethically, be performed on humans, providing access to a different source of information about development.

However, there are two problems with such studies. Firstly we should be cautious about generalising from animals to humans, and secondly such studies raise ethical questions regarding the psychological and physical harm caused to the animals used. Such studies may be justified by the argument that the knowledge gained may have practical applications, such as treatments for visual impairments. This is an example of a cost-benefit analysis where, if the benefits outweigh its costs, then it can be argued that is to justifiable to conduct the research.

Hubel & Wiesel (1962) tested pattern recognition in cats by surgically planting microelectrodes in various parts of the visual cortex. They detected neurones called 'simple cells' that only fired (sent an impulse) when the cat viewed a line of unique orientation in a certain part of its visual field. Different simple cells fired only in the presence of other characteristics, such as a moving dot, and 'complex cells' responded to input from several simple cells. The researchers also found evidence of hypercomplex cells that responded to the presence of patterns

Thinking critically about psychology

Consider the effect of testing on cultural groups who are anxious about being tested on illusions. How would this affect their attentional focus and what effect would this have on their perception? Think about the implications of these conclusions for the validity of cross-cultural studies of perception.

and shapes. Such cells are organised into functional columns that prompt the brain to make comparisons, like the ones used in depth perception. This suggests that the perceptual ability of pattern recognition has a biological basis and is therefore innate, favouring the nature argument.

However, Wiesel & Hubel (1982) also provided evidence that favoured nurture. When a cat's eye was sewn shut for long enough and from an early enough age, then the eye became permanently blind. Irreversible changes occured in the visual area of the cat's brain. This indicates that innate mechanisms for perception require visual experience in order to become fully functioning.

Riesen (1965) fitted see-through goggles to the eyes of cats, chimpanzees and monkeys for the first three months of their lives that allowed them to see light, but not patterns within that light. Some perceptual abilities, such as distinguishing between colours, were preserved, while others, such as tracking a moving object, did not develop properly. This suggests that light is necessary for the visual system to develop normally and that patterned light is needed for more complex perceptual skills to develop

Perceptual readjustment studies

The basic idea behind readjustment studies is to see if it is possible to adapt to a perceptually different world. If this were possible, it would provide evidence that perceptual abilities are learned, supporting the nurture idea.

Some animal species seem unable to adapt. Sperry (1943) rotated salamanders' eyes through 180 degrees and found that they could not learn to interpret their new

RESEARCH NOW

Al-Ansari BM & Baroun KA (2005) Impact of anxiety and gender on perceiving the Müller-Lyer illusion. *Social Behavior and Personality* 33(1), 33–42

Aim: To investigate the relationship between anxiety and gender and perception of the Müller-Lyer and horizontal–vertical illusions.

Method: 66 male and 176 female Kuwaiti university students were divided into three groups according to their anxiety level (high, medium and low). They were shown the Müller-Lyer and horizontal–vertical illusions.

Results: There were no differences between genders but more anxious males and females were more susceptible.

Conclusion: Anxiety causes attentional focus, increasing susceptibility to illusions.

perceptual world. Hess (1956) fitted prisms to chickens' eyes that shifted images to the left or right of the visual field. Again they seemed unable to readjust, which suggests their perceptual abilities were innate.

However, human studies have provided different results. Snyder & Pronko (1952) found that motor adaptations to wearing inverting-reversing goggles (which make the world appear upside-down and back-to-front) were long lasting. After wearing the goggles for 30 days participants had adapted successfully to their new perceptual world. Two years later they were instantly able to readjust if they put the goggles on again.

Kitazaki & Shimizu (2005) investigated visual stability, the tendency for our perceptual world to remain stable even as retinal images change drastically with the movement of heads and eyes. They created a virtual reality environment using a head-mounted display. When the visual world altered using the virtual reality gear, visual stability adapted to present a still predictable world. These results back up the conclusions of the earlier, simpler experiments that humans can adapt their motor functions to novel perceptual worlds.

Thinking critically about psychology

Why might Stratton have had some visual distortion after taking the telescope off?

OVER TO YOU See if your college physics department has any inverting prisms. *Making sure that you aren't facing towards the sun*, look through the different sides of the prism to see if you can observe an 'upside-down' world. **Do not try to walk around.** Instead, point at something fixed while looking through the prism and check whether you were right.

Cataract patients: regained sight

Case studies of people who have had cataracts removed from their eyes to restore their sight are another source of evidence for the development of perceptual abilities.

Gregory & Wallace (1963) reported on a patient (SB) who had cataracts from birth that were not surgically removed until he was 52 years old. SB could visually recognise objects already familiar by touch but could not learn to recognise unfamiliar objects by sight alone. Neither could he learn to judge distances using vision or interpret facial expressions. SB's inability to adjust his perceptual abilities supports the nature side of the debate.

Von Senden (1960) reported on 65 cases of cataract patients with restored sight. Generally patients experienced some visual confusion at first, though they were able to distinguish objects against a background and track moving objects with their eyes. The patients could not recognise faces visually and, in contrast to the experience of SB, even objects familiar by touch were not recognised by vision alone.

Case studies of readjustment and regained sight suggest that the ability to perceive simple objects is an innate skill as it doesn't require previous experience to develop. More complex perceptual abilities, however, seem to rely more heavily on nurture. However, it should be considered that adults differ from neonates in important ways, such as having more advanced alternative sensory systems to compensate for their lack of vision.

The nature–nurture debate in perceptual development

The nature versus nurture debate (also known as the heredity versus environment debate) concerns whether the qualities we possess develop through biological factors (nature) or are learned from interactions with the environment (nurture). The nature argument suggests that we are born with our perceptual abilities and that these develop over time through a process of biologically controlled maturation. Those who favour the nurture side of the argument believe that our perceptual abilities develop due to environmental factors.

CLASSIC RESEARCH

Stratton G (1896) Some preliminary experiments on vision. *Psychological Review* **3, 611–17**

Aim: To investigate the effect on human perception of inverting the visual world.

Method: Having blindfolded one eye, Stratton fitted a telescope to his other eye that inverted visual images. Over eight days he wore the inverting telescope for 87 hours, wearing a blindfold at all other times. He then removed both telescope and blindfold.

Results: At first he found his inverted world very difficult to interact with, but by the fourth day was showing signs of readjustment, imagining unseen parts of his world as being inverted too. He tended to forget he was wearing the telescope and could interact with his environment quite easily, for example not colliding with things.

On taking the telescope off he recognised his visual world from before, but had some short-lived problems interacting with it. He did not, however, experience any inverted after-images.

Conclusion: Rather than learning to see his new perceptual world as being inverted, Stratton had instead learned to adapt his motor responses to a seemingly inverted world.

Psychologists in the behaviourist tradition, such as Skinner, favour the nurture side of the debate, as they believe in environmental determinism, which sees all behaviour, including perception, as being created by learning experiences. Bio-psychologists on the other hand, favour the nature side of the argument, as they believe it is innate biological mechanisms that create our attributes, including perceptual abilities.

However, the debate is difficult to resolve. As we have seen, perception is not a single ability but rather a collection of different, and sometimes inter-related, skills. It is likely that some of these abilities are more genetic in origin while others are more environmental.

Also, many would consider the debate to be redundant, as genes cannot determine anything on their own; they need an environment in which to express themselves. Take the example of someone with genes to be tall: this does not mean they will be tall, just that they have genetic potential to be so. It will require a certain environment, such as good diet, for them to actually grow up to be tall. A more realistic view is that of the interactionists who would argue that our perceptual abilities arise from a combination of genetic and learned factors. This would certainly assist survival: basic skills apparent from birth would have immediate survival value and give us something for environmental experiences to shape. As the environment would shape each individual's perceptual abilities differently it would allow perception to be adaptive to changing environmental conditions.

The research we have considered in this section provides evidence for both innate and learned aspects in the development of perceptual abilities. Very little perceptual ability – as opposed to sensation – is present at birth. There is some shape detection and ability to use depth cues but much of this, and the understanding of visual constancies, develops over time. Evidence from cross-cultural studies suggests that this may be the result of experience rather than simply maturation.

Evidence from neonate studies seems convincing but researchers may be subjective in their interpretation because the infants themselves cannot report their perceptions directly to us. There is also a risk of experimenter bias, where the experimenter's behaviour can affect the outcome. Although many methods try to reduce such risks, techniques such as 'preferential looking' are especially prone to biased interpretation.

Research involving neonate and cross-cultural studies tends to be laboratory based and therefore artificial. Visual illusions and 2D drawings are often used, which may not fairly reflect the perceptual abilities that participants have. A further complication is that some perceptual abilities may begin to develop in the womb, for instance it is well known that unborn babies respond to external light and noise. It is therefore difficult to decide whether abilities present at birth are actually innate.

Clearly a neonate's visual abilities are poor compared with an adult's, but many abilities approach adult levels by three or four months of age and there is no real evidence that infants are handicapped by their 'lesser' abilities, as their main focus is on stimuli that are nearby. Hainline (1998) comments that 'visually normal infants have the level of visual functioning that is required for the things that infants need to do'.

Visual perception in any meaningful sense relies on the visual cortex. Bronson (1974) believes that the visual cortex is not fully functional at birth so infants' vision is limited for the first two months of life. One role of the visual cortex is to process information about orientation (whether lines are upright or slanting). Slater *et al.* (1988) habituated neonates to a sloping black and white striped pattern and found that they preferred the same pattern in a novel orientation. This shows that at least some parts of the visual cortex are functioning from birth.

The findings from cross-cultural studies have been criticised, as early studies were very anecdotal and not conducted under controlled conditions. Even in later studies there is a risk of experimenter bias and ambiguous or even conflicting evidence has been found, making it difficult to assess the relative contributions to perception of innate and learned factors. A problem with cross-cultural studies is that they often use pictures as stimulus material and, as there are cultural differences in interpretation of pictorial stimuli, differences may not be due to perception. For instance some cultures portray animals with all their features showing (split style) rather than in the western side-on or plan views (see Figure 2.31). For people with no experience of western-style art, the perceptual cues in the stimuli would be hard to use.

▶ **Figure 2.31** Split style and plan view drawings of elephants

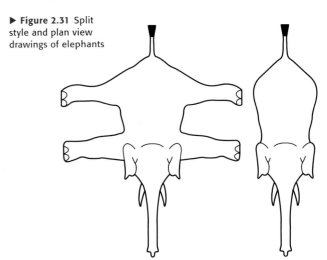

Overall, neonate and cross-cultural studies indicate that humans have some basic perceptual abilities at birth and that these need to be refined through experience with the environment. Also, because perception is not a single ability, there may be a greater influence of innate or learned factors on some perceptual skills than others.

Thinking critically about psychology

On pp25–30 we looked at Gregory's indirect (top-down) model and Gibson's direct (bottom-up) models of perception. Consider their viewpoints and decide whether each would support the nature or the nurture side of the debate. You should be able to provide reasons for your answer.

In conclusion, it seems that we cannot resolve the nature–nurture debate in perception as research from different methodologies produces different conclusions. For example, Bower's studies on neonates found that size and shape constancy are innate, while Von Senden's work on cataract patients suggests otherwise. These apparent contradictions may arise because perception isn't a single entity so each perceptual ability should be considered separately. Some are more innate in origin, for example the ability to perceive movement, while others need more experience, such as the ability to perceive depth in pictures.

Also, each methodology can be criticised, for example the extent to which we can generalise from animal studies to humans, or the problem of knowing exactly what neonates perceive.

The best way to understand the debate is probably through interaction: learning modifies innate perceptual abilities. We are born with simple abilities, which require experience to develop.

Recognising faces

Recognising faces is important for humans from an early age. Fantz (1961) showed that young infants have an innate interest in and preference for human faces. This matters as it allows us to build relationships and distinguish between known people and strangers, which helps survival. The value of recognising and remembering individuals is important for animals too. Pascalis & Bachevalier (1997) found that monkeys recognise faces, though this is limited to members of their own species – a skill that helps in maintaining relationships such as dominance.

Faces contain many similarities, for example eyes and ears, but each has unique features – even between identical twins. We can recognise those faces that are familiar and differentiate between them because we have experience of them, including viewing them from different angles, which brings a richness of information. However, this ability seems to decline over time. Seamon & Travis (1993) found that teachers were able to name 28 per cent of photographs of former students six months after they had last seen them, while Bahrick (1984) found that this had dropped to 8 per cent after one year and to almost nil after eight years.

Faces are ever-changing sources of information; during social interactions we extract interpretations from them. A face is the most reliable means of identifying a known person, but we also seem able to get useful information from unknown faces, such as age, gender, intelligence and mood. We make decisions based upon these inferences, for example whether to go and ask a person for directions. Movements of the face also help us to comprehend what someone is truly saying, such as whether they are being serious or joking.

We seem to have some ability to determine gender and age in faces. Davidenko et al. (2007) gave participants silhouettes of face profiles and found that 83.3 per cent of male silhouettes and 55.7 per cent of female silhouettes were correctly determined and 68 per cent of participants placed silhouettes in the correct age category. This indicates that it is not just facial features that are important in *face recognition*, but also facial shape.

One key question is whether our ability to recognise faces is a specialised ability different from our ability to recognise other types of objects. Wojciulik et al. (1998) found evidence to suggest that faces undergo specialised processing in the primate visual system. Using functional magnetic resonance imaging (fMRI), objects and faces were presented to participants and it was found that faces seemed to be processed in a separate brain area, the fusiform gyrus.

However, Righi & Tarr (2004) performed research on people who were expert chess players and could readily recognise chess game situations. They found that the fusiform gyrus was also active when they were processing such items. This suggests that there isn't a specialised brain area that deals solely with face recognition.

Theories of face recognition use key evidence from *visual agnosia*, a condition where people are not blind, but cannot make sense of normal visual stimuli such as faces.

KEY TERMS

face recognition   the process by which the human face is interpreted and understood

visual agnosia   the inability to make sense of normal visual stimuli such as faces whilst other aspects of vision are unimpaired

holistic processes   systems for dealing with information where elements, such as facial features, are used collectively rather than as separate factors

Thinking critically about psychology

Evidence from studies such as Wojciulik et al. (1998) and Righi & Tarr (2004) suggests that we have a specialised system for recognising highly salient stimuli such as faces. What factors in evolution could have made recognising faces particularly important for animals and humans?

▼ **Figure 2.32** Bruce & Young's face recognition theory (1986)

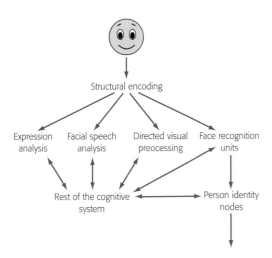

Bruce & Young describe a stage theory of face recognition. In order for a face to become familiar, it has to be seen on several occasions and in different contexts so that a firm representation of a face is stored. As more memory traces are created, the more familiar the face becomes. The structural description improves as memory traces with differing viewpoints, expression and lighting conditions are added, so the face can be recognised in different settings and contexts.

This influential theory states that the perception of faces is a holistic process where facial features are processed collectively rather than as separate factors. It involves eight independent sub-processes working together, some of which are linked together sequentially (one at a time) and others in parallel (simultaneously). To understand a face involves several stages, from extracting basic data (eg age and gender) from sensory material to remembering meaningful facts such as name and previous experiences of that person. Bruce & Young believe that different processing 'modules' are used to make sense of information from faces, for example that expression analysis works independently from face identification.

▼ **Table 2.1 The subcomponents of face recognition**

Type of component	Description of component
Structural encoding	The creation of descriptions and representations of faces
Expression analysis	Analysing facial characteristics to infer emotional state
Facial speech analysis	Analysis of facial movements to comprehend speech, for example lips
Directed visual processing	Specific facial data is selectively processed, eg shape of nose
Facial recognition nodes	Stored structural descriptions of known faces
Person identity nodes	Information that is stored about familiar people, eg hobbies and interests
Name generation	Separate storage for names
Cognitive storage	Provides extra information to aid the recognition process, such as where you would normally meet the person

Structural encoding involves the creation of a pictorial code that is transformed into a more abstract (structural) representation. Sometimes person recognition can occur with just pictorial information but in general representations are inadequate as they cannot cope with changes in hairstyle, age, changes in lighting conditions etc.

The theory explains how we know different types of information about a person, for example:

- *visually derived semantic code* – details related to physical aspects of the person such as age, gender, race, attributions about how we feel towards the person and any similarities to other people
- *identity-specific semantic code* – biographic or semantic information that has no relationship to physical aspects of a person, such as the fact they used to play in your school netball team.

It is the retrieval of information from the identity-specific semantic code that gives us the idea that recognition has occurred.

The model says there are two kinds of nodes:

- *facial recognition nodes* (FRN) – contain structural information about each known face
- *person identity nodes* (PIN) – provide identity-specific semantic information, containing details about familiar people, such as their occupation, interests and friends.

There is also a separate name generation subcomponent for familiar faces.

Structural encoding, face recognition nodes, person identity nodes and name generation are used mainly to recognise familiar faces, while structural encoding, expression analysis, facial speech analysis and directed visual processing are used mainly in the recognition of unfamiliar faces.

The model is not just a description but attempts to explain how some types of information from faces are processed. Structural encoding processes are used to analyse facial aspects of speech, expression and face recognition. Recognising familiar faces involves matching the outcomes of structural encoding and stored structural codes that describe the appearance of familiar faces, which are contained within face recognition nodes. Following this, identity-specific semantic codes are then gained from person identity nodes, so name codes can be found. We then make an active cognitive decision about whether the initial match is very close – recognition – or just similar – resemblance.

This functional model is based on information from sources including case studies of people with brain damage, experiments and research into everyday errors. The model is also used to illuminate similarities and differences in processes for word, object and face recognition.

Face identification

Bruce & Young believe that both facial features and the configuration of those features help us to recognise individuals. Even though faces are dynamic, research tends to use photographs and photo identikit faces.

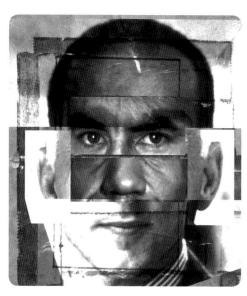

◀ **Figure 2.33**
Example of photo
identikit face

Sergent (1984) presented participants with two identikit faces that either differed on one facial dimension or two. The facial dimensions tested were: type of eye, placement of internal facial features, and shape of chin. The participants could decide whether the two faces were different more quickly when they differed on two dimensions rather than one. This suggests that the dimensions of variation are processed together rather than independently (configural processing). This was supported by Young *et al.* (1987) who constructed 'composite faces' from the bottom and top halves of different famous faces. When the new face was made up of very misaligned halves, participants identified the top half much more quickly than when the two halves of the new face were closely aligned halves. This suggests that the composite faces produce a new configural identity, from which it is difficult to recognise familiar features.

Facial recognition needs to be more than just sensitivity to the configuration of facial features such as eyes, mouth and nose but to the overall configuration of the face. Diamond & Carey (1986) found that expert dog breeders were worse at identifying individual members of a familiar breed if the image of the dog was upside down. This suggests that the breeders were sensitive to the overall configuration of the dog rather than just its individual features. This explains how we can tell a face from a simple line drawing – the overall configuration is still there even though individual facial features are not.

However, there is evidence to suggest that we do also use individual facial features in face recognition. Shepherd *et al.* (1981) asked participants to describe briefly presented familiar and unfamiliar faces. The participants tended to describe individual features – hair, followed by eyes, nose, mouth, eyebrows, chin and forehead – rather than overall shape. However, as participants were asked to *describe* rather than identify faces, it may be that describing features is a simpler task and does not relate to the usual method of face recognition.

Some facial features seem more important in the recognition of unfamiliar faces than familiar ones. Ellis *et al.* (1979) found that external features such as hairstyle and the outline of the face matter more with unfamiliar faces, while internal features such as the eyes are used more when recognising familiar ones. Such studies typically use static images, however, so may not relate to how faces are recognised in real life. For example, could we recognise eyes if they constantly changed shape? We concentrate on the more static aspects of faces (invariants) and ignore the changeable ones. This would explain why Ellis *et al.* found that hairstyle and facial outline were important in recognising unfamiliar faces as they are relatively invariant facial features.

Bruce & Valentine (1988) investigated whether expressive movement in facial expressions could provide invariant information. They used films of familiar people showing expressive movement, such as smiling, and rigid movement, such as nodding. Patterns of expressive movement seemed to transmit little variant information to aid identification, suggesting that we tend to ignore variant information and concentrate on the invariants to perform face recognition.

CLASSIC RESEARCH

Malone D, Morris H, Kay M & Levin H (1982) Prosopagnosia: a double dissociation between the recognition of familiar and unfamiliar faces. *Journal of Neurology, Neurosurgery and Psychiatry* **45, 820–22**

Aim: To look for differences in the processing of familiar and unfamiliar faces.

Method: Two case studies of prosopagnosia were used, one of a 64-year-old with visual blurring, and a second of a 26-year-old man reporting problems with vision following surgery.

Results: When the first man's vision improved he could not recognise familiar people, including his wife, by sight though he could by voice alone. He subsequently regained the ability to recognise familiar people, either known ones or famous ones (he successfully identified 14 out of 17 famous faces), but he could not match up photographs of unfamiliar faces. The second man also improved but was unable to recognise known people such as relatives or famous people (he could only identify five out of 22 famous faces). However his ability to match up photographs of unknown people was normal.

Conclusion: As the two cases produced different results this suggests that known and unknown faces are processed differently.

Another important study that backs up Bruce & Young's theory is that of Tanaka & Farah (1993). They asked participants to learn names for faces, some of which were normal and some of which were scrambled (see Figure 2.34).

They were asked to identify:

- a single feature (eg nose) when seen in isolation
- the face from two normal faces that differed in nose only
- the face from two scrambled faces differing in nose only.

Scrambling the position of the features impaired face recognition, suggesting that configural processing, where all parts are processed collectively, is occurring. This processing relies on information from the whole face being matched to a stored representation of an upright face. These findings have been confirmed for representations of same-race faces in a more recent study (see *Research Now*).

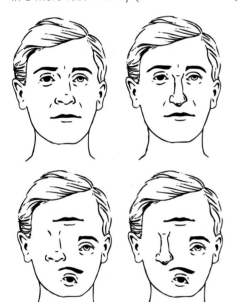

◀ **Figure 2.34**
Tanaka & Farah (1993) used stimuli like these

Thinking creatively about psychology

Devise a study similar to Tanaka *et al.*'s to test whether there is a difference in the holistic processing of same and opposite-gender individuals by males and females.

Experimental support for the idea of a unique face processor comes from Thompson (1980) who demonstrated the 'Thatcher effect' (see Figure 2.35). Participants found it difficult to detect changes in facial features in an upside-down face but could do so in an upright face. In inverted faces it is not possible for configural (overall) processing to occur, as predicted by Bruce & Young's theory of face recognition.

The theory also predicts that, as they are separate stores, if an FRN is activated, but not the PIN, then we should feel the person is familiar but be unable to provide any relevant information about them. Young *et al.* (1985) asked participants to keep a diary of specific problems with recognising faces. A total of 233 cases of 'I feel I know them, but I cannot say how or why' were reported, supporting the prediction. There were also 190 incidents of recognition and semantic information only, where a participant could remember a good deal of information about a person, but could not name them (showing that person identity nodes and name generation have different stores). There were no incidents of naming faces without any other accompanying information.

Evaluating Bruce & Young's model of face recognition

The model can account for the processes involved in face recognition and makes several predictions that can be tested – and which are generally supported by evidence. The model is also consistent with the findings from studies of patients with visual agnosias (see p51).

RESEARCH NOW

Tanaka W, Kiefer M & Bukach C (2004) A holistic account of the own-race effect in face recognition: evidence from a cross-cultural study. *Cognition* **93(1), B1–B9**

Aim: To test a holistic explanation of the 'own race effect' where people's memories for faces of members of their own ethnic group are more easily remembered than for faces of other groups.

Method: Caucasian and Asian facial features were presented in isolation and in the whole face.

Findings: Caucasian participants recognised own-ethnic group faces more holistically than Asian faces, whereas Asian participants demonstrated holistic recognition for both own and other ethnic group faces. This difference mirrored differences in experience with own and other ethnic group faces.

Conclusions: The 'own race effect' arises from the holistic recognition of faces from a highly familiar ethnic group. This supports the central concept in Bruce & Young's theory that facial features are processed collectively, rather than independently.

▼ **Figure 2.35** The Thatcher effect

The central concept of face recognition occurring in a holistic fashion is generally accepted, as is the idea that a series of independent stages occur. For example, being able to put a name to a face in the absence of other information about them indicates that the name generation sub-component is separate. People do seem to have person recognition nodes, because we can tell whether faces are familiar or not.

Bruce & Young's belief that familiar and unfamiliar faces are processed differently is supported by evidence from patients with brain damage. If Malone *et al.*'s (1992) patients had damage to different brain areas with differing roles this would explain the differences in their face recognition problems.

Another idea central to the theory is that name generation arises from sequential processing. Young *et al.*'s (1985) diary study confirms that this occurs. Furthermore, Young *et al.* (1986) found that people could decide if a face was familiar (using the FRN) faster than if the face was that of a politician (using the PIN). This indicates that processing was indeed following a sequence. They also found that placing a face in a certain category (eg 'politician') was quicker than face-naming. This again suggests that processing is sequential.

The theory also has useful applications. Computerised security systems can use facial recognition techniques. The Aurora system, used in 940 sites in the UK and the United Arab Emirates, uses facial data that is compared with stored information to confirm identity. The Australian customs service uses a similar system that scans faces and compares them with information stored on a microchip in a person's passport. Similar systems could be used for cash machine security. However, such systems are not without their problems, for example being able to discriminate between twins, and they raise concerns about infringement of civil liberties.

Although well supported and useful, Bruce & Young's theory cannot really explain unfamiliar face recognition and does not specify how familiarity is determined or achieved. It is not clear whether a PIN stores information or merely allows access to it. Another valid criticism is that although many aspects of the theory are clearly explained and well supported by research, for some components, especially the cognitive system, it is not clear how they help to determine face recognition.

Finally, not all of the theory's predictions are supported: there is an assumption that names can only be accessed via relevant autobiographical information stored in the PINs.

However, De Haan & Campbell (1991) reported on a case study of a patient (ME) for whom this was not true.

One remaining question is the relationship between face recognition and other forms of object recognition. This is explored in the next section.

Thinking practically about psychology

Bruce & Young's theory has practical applications such as helping the police to develop better methods of creating identikit pictures of suspects. In what two ways could this help in arresting the correct individual?

Visual agnosia

A visual agnosia occurs when the brain is unable to make sense of or use normal visual stimuli such as familiar objects or faces. It does not involve blindness or damage to the eye or early stages of impairment of the visual system, but tends to be caused by damage to the posterior occipital and/or temporal lobes of the brain, often from a stroke. Sufferers can usually describe objects or faces they can see, including details of colour, texture and shape, but cannot recognise them even if they are familiar. There are two main types of visual agnosias:

- *apperceptive* – failure to recognise familiar objects despite having normal visual abilities. Sufferers cannot copy drawings
- *associative* – failure to recognise familiar objects due to impaired access to stored semantic information resulting from disruption of neural connections between visual perception and verbal systems.

Moscovitch *et al.* (1997) reported on a patient, CK, who had poor recognition for objects but normal recognition of faces. This challenged the original idea that perception of stimuli such as objects and faces shared a common neural substrate and suggested instead that there may be a specific processing mechanism for face recognition.

Prosopagnosia (face blindness)

Prosopagnosia is a form of visual agnosia where the sufferer can generally recognise objects but cannot recognise faces. There are different forms and levels of prosopagnosia and case studies of the condition have tended to generate evidence that supports Bruce & Young's idea that face perception involves a sequence of stages, because they show that each stage can be impaired independently (see also p54). A sufferer can recognise a face as a face, but will be unable to recall any other details, such as the person's name or hobbies. The condition has been linked to brain damage in the fusiform gyrus. Sufferers find it hard to conduct normal social relationships and there is no fully effective treatment, although some improvements are possible.

Bidders offer thousands for Madonna of the cheese

The Times, **17 November 2004**

The Lord may move in mysterious ways but his mother, it is claimed, has chosen a rather ordinary piece of cheese on toast to make herself known to the world.

Diana Duyser, 52, of Hollywood, Florida, screamed and almost fainted as she chomped into a grilled cheese sandwich ten years ago because she saw the face of the Virgin Mary staring back at her. The toasted likeness sits, a bite out of its bottom lefthand corner, surrounded in cotton wool in a plastic box. But now, after a decade of watching over the Duysers from her crusty caryatid, Mary is being sold to the highest bidder on eBay, the internet auction website.

▼ **Figure 2.36** Diana Duyer

Indeed the toastie went on to receive 1.7 million hits and eventually sold for $28,000. This interest in objects that appear to contain faces, such as the rock man of Holy Island, discovered in 1997, or the face on Mars photographed by Viking 1 in 1976, might appear to be a rather recent media phenomenon, but the apparent perception of faces in objects has actually been occurring for a very long time. The 'man in the moon' is probably the most well known and may be even the oldest example. But why should humans so readily perceive faces in objects? Indeed can psychology help to provide an answer?

1 Read through the section in this chapter concerning the recognition of faces. Why do you think face recognition should be so important to us?

2 Consider the evidence that supports the idea that recognising faces is a specialised ability different from that which enables us to recognise other types of objects. Does this suggest a possible reason to you why we so easily perceive faces in an object like a piece of toast?

▼ **Figure 2.37a** A 1976 image of Mars: the shadows on this rock formation give the illusion of eyes, nose and mouth

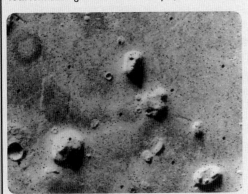

▼ **Figure 2.37b** A close-up of the 'man on Mars'

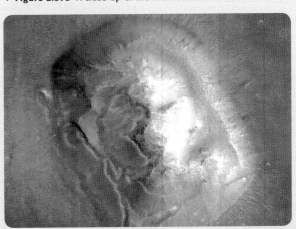

KEY TERM

prosopagnosia a type of visual agnosia, where sufferers can describe objects in their visual field, but are unable to recognise the objects

The term prosopagnosia was first used by Bodamer (1947) reporting on three cases, including that of a 24-year-old man with a bullet wound to the head, who was unable to recognise family members, friends and even himself in a mirror. He could, however, recognise people via other senses, such as their smell and physical mannerisms.

Brunsdon *et al.* (2006) described an eight-year-old boy, AL, who could not recognise familiar or unfamiliar faces, indicating that the deficit was at the level of structural encoding. He appeared to have some internal representation of facial features and this ability was used to provide treatment focusing on training him in the perception and analysis of facial features. This enabled AL to name familiar faces and avoid mistakenly identifying unfamiliar people as family members.

Case studies of prosopagnosia have provided evidence that facial speech analysis is a separate component of face analysis as predicted by Bruce & Young's theory. Campbell *et al.* (1986) described a prosopagnosic who was unable to identify familiar faces or comprehend their facial expressions, but was able to perform speech analysis.

Another case demonstrated a specific impairment but to a different component of the face recognition process. Lucchelli & De Renzi (1992) reported on a male patient who could not put a name to known faces, or from verbal descriptions, but was able to provide detailed and precise semantic information about the people he could not name. McKenna & Warrington (1980) reported on a similar case of a patient who could give biographical information on about 90 per cent of famous faces, but could only name 15 per cent of them. Neither patient had a problem naming objects or geographical names, thus supporting Bruce & Young's idea that face recognition occurs via separate components and that facial processing is separate from the processing of other perceptual information.

Evidence that facial expression analysis is a separate component of face recognition, as proposed by Bruce & Young's theory, comes from Kurucz & Feldmar (1979), who found prosopagnosia sufferers who could successfully name known faces, but could not identify their facial expression. Similarly Bruyer *et al.* (1983) found cases where known people's facial expressions could be understood, but the patient could not name them.

The idea of specific processing mechanisms existing for face recognition has been further supported by neurological evidence. Kanwisher *et al.* (1997) compared brain activity when presented with images of faces, scrambled faces, houses and hands using fMRI scans. A greater role was played by the fusiform gyrus in face recognition than object recognition. However, Righi & Tarr (2004) have found evidence that this brain area is not just involved with face recognition (see p47).

Case studies of prosopagnosia indicate that object and face recognition are separate processes, possibly involving different neural pathways and brain areas, but there are ways in which prosopagnosia could indicate damage to a general purpose recognition system. For example, Humphreys & Riddoch (1987) have suggested that face recognition may simply be more difficult than other forms of recognition. Slight damage to a general purpose recognition system would therefore affect face recognition more than non-face object recognition. Indeed, prosopagnosic patients do tend to have some impairment of object recognition, for example response time, as well as problems with face recognition.

Gauthier *et al.* (2000) also thinks that faces are merely complex objects that, through practice, we become skilled at recognising – just like any other complex stimuli. They found that the fusiform gyrus is not only active when face recognition occurs but also when participants discriminate between differing types of birds and cars. This suggests that the fusiform gyrus does not deal exclusively with face processing.

CLASSIC RESEARCH

Brédart S & Schweich M (1995). *Journal of the International Neuropsychological Society* 1, 589–95

Aim: To interpret a case of prosopagnosia within the framework of Bruce & Young's model.	**Method**: A case study of GB, a 31-year-old agricultural engineer who was trying to understand and overcome his inability to recognise people. He could say if a person was familiar or not and whether they were related to his profession from their clothes. He could not, however, remember names, under what circumstances he had met someone before or retrieve any biographical information about them. He often confused identities and had problems recognising images of famous people.	**Results:** There was no evidence of cerebral disease and GB's long-term memory and object naming was normal. He had no impairment in his structural encoding – he could recognise that faces were faces and say if a picture of a face was incomplete or not. He could also decode facial expressions.	**Conclusion:** His impairment was interpreted in terms of Bruce & Young's model. It suggested processing of facial information occurs in separate stages because GB had a specific impairment where he demonstrated no particular problems in early visual processing, but had difficulty accessing PINs from FRNs and with accessing the name codes from PINs.

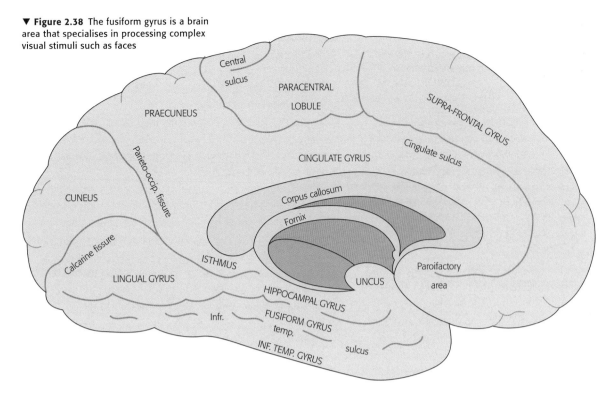

▼ **Figure 2.38** The fusiform gyrus is a brain area that specialises in processing complex visual stimuli such as faces

Further evidence suggesting that face recognition is a separate process from object recognition comes from Gauthier *et al.* (1999). They found that not all prosopagnosic patients have selective problems with face recognition, but general problems with complex object recognition regardless of whether faces are involved. However, this applies only to a minority of cases.

Although patients with prosopagnosia appear unable to name familiar faces, if the person's occupation or other biographical details are given they may be able to do so. Bauer (1984) studied a patient, LF, who appeared to lack face recognition abilities. However, when five names were read out while LF looked at a familiar face, the patient's galvanic skin resistance (an indicator of emotional arousal) changed significantly more to the presentation of the real name than the others. Although conscious face recognition did not occur, it appears that, in some patients at least, there can be unconscious recognition. Similarly, Bruyer (1991) described prosopagnosic patients who lacked face recognition skills but could match familiar faces significantly better than unfamiliar ones.

Dailey & Cottrell (1999) have explained how a separate face processing mechanism could arise. Evidence from prosopagnosia case studies indicates that face processing in the brain is localised, with face and object recognition being served by partially independent neural mechanisms. From their work with computer models they believe that face processing specialisation can be attributed to three factors.

- A simple selection mechanism that, during development, devotes neural resources to the tasks a person is best at performing.
- The fact that developing infants need to identify faces from an early age.
- The fact that infants have low visual acuity at birth.

These factors bias the visual system to develop a processing sub-system that is useful for face recognition, and this seems to suggest that something resembling a face processing module arises as a natural consequence of an infant's developmental environment.

Chapter summary

Perceptual organisation
- Perception is a cognitive process that enables us to understand sensory information.
- Gibson's bottom-up theory sees perception occurring directly from sensory information, while Gregory's top-down theory sees it as occurring indirectly by inferring beyond sensory information.

- Gregory believes we use knowledge gained from previous experience to actively shape our perception, with factors such as expectation, motivation, cultural influences and emotion playing an important role.
- Gibson thinks that sensory information is such an ever-changing and rich source of data that perception needs no information processing and we use invariant features of this data to perceive indirectly.

- There are strengths and weaknesses to both theories and it may well be that a combination of the two best explains perception, Gibson's theory being best under ideal viewing conditions and Gregory's best under less than ideal conditions.

Development of perception

- The development of perceptual abilities concerns the nature versus nurture debate as to whether such skills are innate or learned.
- One popular method of study looks at neonates, as any perceptual talents evident at birth are deemed to be innate. However, there are problems communicating with neonates and difficulties in assessing which skills are maturational, as well as ethical concerns.
- Another method of research is cross-cultural studies, as similar perceptual abilities found in different cultures are seen as evidence for them being learned. There are problems though with possible biased interpretations of results.
- Animal and perceptual readjustment studies plus research on cataract patients have also been used to investigate the development of perceptual abilities.
- Overall, simple perceptual skills generally appear to be innate in origin, while more complex ones rely more on nurture. The interactionist viewpoint explains that we are born with simple abilities and experience develops them in more complex ways.

Recognising faces

- Faces contain a wealth of ever-changing information and the recognition of faces is important for humans to establish and conduct social relationships.
- Bruce & Young's theory states that face recognition is a holistic process comprising eight independent components working in unison.
- The theory is supported by research evidence and has practical applications such as the development of computerised facial recognition techniques. However, some aspects of the theory, such as how familiarity is determined, are not fully explained.
- Research into a type of visual agnosia known as prosopagnosia, where generally objects but not faces can be recognised, tends to lend support to the notion that face recognition occurs through a separate processing system.
- Case studies of prosopagnosic patients indicate that brain damage can affect different components of the face recognition process, which supports Bruce & Young's theory.
- There are difficulties generalising results from case studies and some evidence is contradictory. It is possible that face recognition may actually just be part of a general purpose recognition system, or alternatively develops as a processing sub-system as a consequence of the developmental environment.

What do I know?

1 Compare Gregory's top-down (indirect) and Gibson's bottom-up (direct) theories of perception. (25 marks)

2 (a) Outline the development of perceptual abilities. (9 marks)
 (b) Evaluate infant studies in the development of perceptual abilities in terms of their strengths and weaknesses. (16 marks)

3 (a) Outline **one** case study of prosopagnosia. (5 marks)
 (b) Outline and evaluate Bruce & Young's theory of face recognition. (20 marks)

4 (a) Explain what is meant by the nature–nurture debate in relation to perceptual development. (5 marks)
 (b) Outline and evaluate cross-cultural studies of the development of perceptual abilities. (20 marks)

5 Outline and evaluate explanations of prosopagnosia. (25 marks)

CHAPTER 3
Relationships

Thinking ahead

By the end of this chapter you should be able to:

- describe and evaluate theories of relationship formation, for example the mere exposure effect, matching hypothesis and ideal choice hypothesis

- describe and evaluate theories of relationship maintenance and dissolution, including social exchange theory and needs satisfaction

- understand the relationship between sexual selection and human reproductive behaviour

- outline and evaluate evolutionary explanations of parental investment, in particular sex differences and parent–offspring conflict

- outline research into the relationship between relationships in childhood and adolescence, in particular with parents and peers, and romantic relationships in adulthood

- outline cultural differences in relationships

I n this chapter we are concerned with explaining human relationships, in particular those of a romantic nature. Romantic relationships are profoundly important to us. Being in a successful romantic relationship is one of the most important factors to adult happiness. From an evolutionary perspective, relationships are important in conceiving and rearing children and are therefore essential for the survival of the species. We begin by looking at what influences the formation of relationships.

Theories of relationship formation

We are concerned here with the factors that affect whether people get together and form relationships. Common sense tells us that for a relationship to be possible, two people first have to come into contact and must find each other attractive. We can look at three hypotheses (technically they aren't elaborate enough to be called theories) based on these simple ideas.

The mere exposure effect

People tend to feel more favourably about things as they become more familiar with them. This effect is not confined to people; Zajonc (1968) presented participants with a range of stimuli including words and faces and asked them to rate them. Each stimulus was rated more positively as people became familiar with it. This *mere exposure effect* seems to apply to romantic attraction. We find familiar people more attractive than strangers. Rhodes *et al.* (2005) demonstrated this effect by showing participants pictures of male and female faces and asking them to rate each face for attractiveness. They repeated faces in the sequence and also put in new composite faces created by combining features of the faces already seen and rated. As faces were seen more than once, ratings of their attractiveness increased. However, composite

faces were not rated as more attractive when they were made up of faces already seen. This suggests that it is whole faces rather than particular features with which we become familiar.

So what about familiarity breeding contempt? Norton *et al.* (2007) suggest an answer. They distinguish between being familiar with someone and knowing a lot about them. They propose that people are attractive when they are familiar but we don't know a great deal about them. Too much information about people makes them less attractive. The researchers tested this idea using members of an online dating service. We can look at this study in detail in *Research Now*.

▲ **Figure 3.1** Office romances are common because of the mere exposure effect

RESEARCH NOW

Norton MI, Frost JH & Ariely D (2007) Less is more: the lure of ambiguity, or why familiarity breeds contempt. *Journal of Personality & Social Psychology* **92**, 97–10

Aim:
To investigate whether knowing more about potential dates makes them more or less attractive.

Procedure: 294 users of an online dating site followed a link to complete a survey. This asked them whether they believed they would find someone more attractive if they knew more about them. The same question was then asked of 49 students on a university campus. To establish whether in fact greater knowledge led to greater attraction, the researchers again surveyed 76 students on campus and 120 volunteers from a dating website. This time they gave participants varying amounts of information about potential dates (up to 10 characteristics randomly drawn from a list of 28) and asked them to rate their attractiveness. Participants were also asked to rate how similar they were to potential dates based on the information they were given about them.

Findings: In the initial surveys, respondents overwhelmingly believed that they would prefer to date someone about whom they knew a lot. However, when actually presented with the information, a negative correlation emerged between the number of traits they were told about and liking (−0.23 on campus, −0.12 online). The reason appeared to be dissimilarity. The more traits the participants knew about, the more differences they discovered with themselves (−0.18).

Conclusion:
As we learn more about people we discover more ways in which they differ from us. This makes them less attractive to us.

Thinking critically about psychology

Suggest a reason why the authors might have been cautious about using only the online sample and why they ran the study on campus as well as online.

The results of this study suggest that although familiarity can make people more attractive to us, this is mediated by another factor, similarity. We respond very negatively to information that suggests we are dissimilar to a potential date. This has a clear practical application: if you fancy someone make sure they see you around a lot but keep yourself a bit of mystery!

▲ **Figure 3.2** The more similar you are, the more familiarity is likely to lead to love

OVER TO YOU

Investigating attractiveness is an ethical minefield and you should not carry out practical work that involves rating people you know for attractiveness. However, you can investigate the relationship between similarity and attractiveness. Find a photograph of a person and ask participants to rate on a scale how similar they consider themselves to that person. Also ask them to rate how likeable they believe the person to be. If you are carrying this out in a school or college, it is likely that some of your sample will be gay but not out. To avoid making them feel awkward, talk about likeability or attractiveness in very general terms rather than how much they fancy the person. Calculate the correlation between similarity and likeability (see p330 for help with this).

Attractiveness: realistic versus ideal choice hypotheses

Clearly, how physically attractive we find someone is going to make a difference to whether we try to get it together with them. However, before this starts to sound like the psychology of the blindingly obvious, stop and consider two predictions we might make from common sense that can't both be true. First, we try to form a relationship with the most attractive person possible. Second, we aim for someone of similar attractiveness to ourselves. We can call the first of these the *ideal choice hypothesis* and the second the *realistic choice* or *matching hypothesis*. Both these possibilities were tested in a classic study by Walster *et al.* (1966).

Thinking critically about psychology

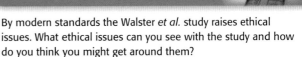

By modern standards the Walster *et al.* study raises ethical issues. What ethical issues can you see with the study and how do you think you might get around them?

CLASSIC RESEARCH

Walster E, Aronson V, Abrahams D & Rottmann L (1966) Importance of physical attractiveness in dating behaviour. *Journal of Personality & Social Psychology* 4, 508–16

Aim: To test whether ideal choice or matching hypothesis better predicted how randomly matched blind dates would respond to each other.

Procedure: 376 male and 376 female students were invited to a dance at the end of Freshers' week at an American university. The students were told they had been matched to a date by a computer. In fact they were randomly paired. Stooges sold students the tickets and secretly rated them for attractiveness. The students then completed questionnaires about their own popularity, self-esteem and nervousness. They also completed personality tests. During an interval in the dance participants were asked to rate their partners for attractiveness and how much they would like to date them again. Four to six months later they were followed up to find out whether they had in fact dated after the dance.

Findings: The initial findings strongly supported ideal choice hypothesis. The only factor predicting how much participants liked their dates and wanted to see them again was attractiveness. However, when followed up later, those rated as similar in attractiveness were the most likely to have continued to date after the dance.

Conclusion: Initial attraction is based mostly on physical attractiveness, supporting the ideal choice hypothesis. However, actual dating was most common where couples had similar levels of attractiveness, supporting matching hypothesis.

Support for matching hypothesis over ideal choice hypothesis comes from a follow-up to this study. Walster & Walster (1969) replicated the original study with one key difference: the couples spent time getting to know each other before the dance. This time the results firmly supported matching hypothesis. Participants were more likely to find partners attractive and wished to see them again when they were rated as similar in attractiveness by the stooges.

Fiore & Donath (2005) tested whether matching hypothesis holds true in online dating. They were allowed access to an online dating service for eight months so they could see information about users' profiles and their ratings of themselves and other users. Forty-seven per cent of contacts made and 49 per cent of those responded to were with someone with the same physical appearance rating. Chance would have predicted this to be true 37 per cent of the time. This finding supports matching hypothesis.

Of course, not all couples meet in purpose-built dating scenarios like dances or dating websites. Where people have an opportunity to get to know each other before pairing up, the first impression impact of physical attractiveness is lessened. Research

in this area has over-represented formal blind date scenarios of one sort or another and largely neglected the range of ways in which real-life couples meet. Take for example what happens when people are introduced by mutual friends. Typically they have some time to get to know each other in a much more relaxed situation before committing to going out together than is the case on a dating website or at a dance. Information about each other is filtered through the friends, who tend to emphasise positive features and common interests. By the time a rapport is built up the first impression of physical attractiveness may fade in importance. A meta-analysis of studies rating the attractiveness of partners (Feingold, 1988) concluded that the average correlation is +0.49. This means that other factors are more important in affecting attraction leading to the formation of a relationship.

▶ **Figure 3.3** There is a fairly strong correlation between attractiveness of partners in relationships

Theories of relationship maintenance and dissolution

Romantic films generally end with the formation of a relationship and the happy couple disappearing off into the sunset. The implication is that once you find and secure a relationship with the right person all will go smoothly from there on in. In reality, most romantic relationships break down, or *dissolve*, to use the technical term. Precise figures are impossible to obtain because many people separate but never divorce, but it seems that at least 40 per cent of marriages break down. Amongst long-term *dating* and *cohabiting*

couples, the rates of dissolution are probably considerably higher. We can consider two theories that aim to explain why some relationships are maintained and others dissolve.

Social exchange theory

Thibaut & Kelley (1959) propose that we can understand the stability of relationships in terms of costs and rewards. Social exchange theory (or SET) assumes that we can calculate the costs and rewards of the relationship and arrive at a positive or negative figure called the *outcome*. A positive outcome indicates that rewards outweigh the costs and a negative outcome indicates the reverse. We can also compare the costs and rewards associated with the current situation with a theoretical default position and actual alternatives. Our default level of cost and reward is called the *comparison level*. Alternatives such as being single or ditching the partner in favour of someone else have their own *comparison level for alternatives*.

▲ **Figure 3.4** Most relationships break down

Where the outcome is positive and the comparison level for alternatives low, relationships are stable. They may also appear stable where the outcome is negative if the comparison level and comparison level for alternatives are lower still. However, such relationships are unlikely to be happy and can easily be destabilised if a new and attractive alternative presents itself. Thibaut & Kelley offer the example of a battered wife whose current outcome is negative, but who perceives her situation as normal and the comparison level for the alternative of living alone in poverty as worse. Six qualities of relationship based on social exchange theory are shown in Table 3.1.

▼ **Table 3.1 Six types of relationship according to social exchange theory. From Thibaut & Kelley (1959)**

Relative value of outcome, CI, CI$_{alt}$	State of the relationship
outcome > CI > CI$_{alt}$	satisfying stable dependent
outcome > CI$_{alt}$ > CI	satisfying stable non-dependent
CI$_{alt}$ > CI > outcome	satisfying break relationship happy elsewhere
CI$_{alt}$ > outcome > CI	satisfying unstable happier elsewhere
CI > CI$_{alt}$ > outcome	non-satisfying break relationship continue unhappy
CI > outcome > CI$_{alt}$	highly unsatisfying can't break away dependent and unhappy

SET has good face validity, ie it makes sense at first glance. It also has good explanatory power. SET can be used to explain a range of situations where relationships endure despite common sense suggesting they should not. One such example is in domestic violence, where a victim might perceive the comparison level for alternatives as very low and so remain in the relationship. Another such example is forced marriage. A wife might remain in a forced marriage because the comparison level, ie her perception of the norm in marriage, is so low.

SET also has practical applications in couples therapy. The behavioural marital therapy (BMT) model of couples therapy (Jacobsen & Margolin, 1979) is based on SET. Its aim is to increase the ratio of positive to negative interactions between couples so that each reassesses the rewards of the relationship as higher than the costs. Outcome research suggests that this approach is as effective as other forms of couples therapy (Christensen *et al.*, 2004).

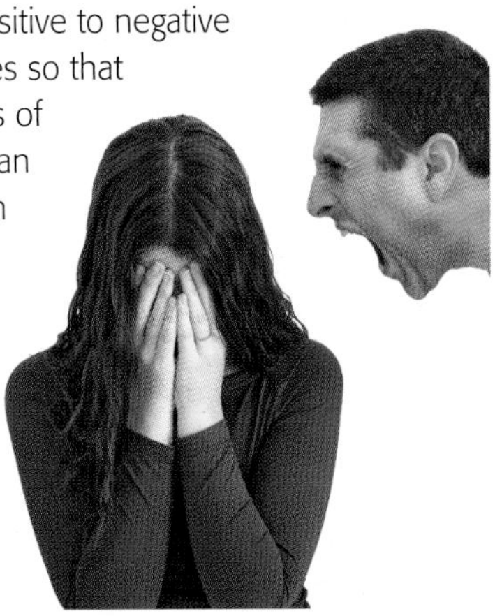

▶ **Figure 3.5** Social exchange theory can explain why people tolerate domestic violence

There are, however, important criticisms of SET. Sociologist Milan Zafirovski (2005) accuses social exchange theorists of psychological reductionism because SET explains relationships only in terms of the individual. Relationships also have a cultural aspect, and we cannot understand institutions like marriage just in terms of costs and rewards. We have to look as well at the whole situation; religious faith might, for example, compel someone to remain in an unhappy relationship and prevent someone even considering alternatives in terms of their costs and rewards. Nakonezny & Denton (2008) points out that there is no way to measure the costs and rewards of a relationship and no way to know when or how partners in a relationship go about measuring them themselves. This makes the theory untestable.

Thinking practically about psychology

You friend has confided in you that she is not enjoying her relationship with her boyfriend and does not know what to do. She has low expectations of relationships and is afraid she will be isolated and lonely if she is single. Explain her situation using SET.

Thinking critically about psychology

Consider the strengths of SET (face validity, explanatory power and practical application) against its weaknesses (reductionism, testability). How good a theory is it?

Needs satisfaction

A different approach to explaining the maintenance and dissolution of relationships is to examine human needs and see whether these are satisfied by romantic relationships. There are a range of possible needs that can be addressed by romantic relationships, but the basic idea behind the approach remains the same. If our current romantic relationship satisfies our needs it is likely to be maintained, and if it does not meet our needs it is likely to be dissolved.

Maslow (1950) suggested that all human behaviour is based on satisfaction of needs. So what needs are we talking about when we consider relationships? Schutz (1966) identifies three interpersonal needs that we all seek to satisfy through our relationships:

- *Inclusion* – we need to feel that others give us attention and interest.
- *Control* – we need a healthy balance between influencing and being influenced by others.
- *Affection* – we need to be loved and have love demonstrated to us.

◀ **Figure 3.6** A good relationship is associated with good quality of life because it fulfils many of our needs

Schutz's framework is intended to apply to relationships as a whole, not simply to our romantic relationship. However, it serves as a good starting point to understanding what might leave us satisfied or unsatisfied with our relationships. Ickes (1985) suggests that what we really mean when we talk about compatibility in romantic relationships is the extent to which we meet each other's interpersonal needs. This is quite hard to investigate because we don't usually think about compatibility or needs satisfaction until our relationships break down.

Osborne (2009) investigated the relationship between satisfaction of Schutz's interpersonal needs and relationship satisfaction. Ninety-one students who identified themselves as being in a long-term monogamous relationship completed questionnaires measuring loneliness, life satisfaction and interpersonal needs. Overall, the satisfaction of needs correlated significantly with life satisfaction, supporting the needs satisfaction model. Interestingly satisfaction of the need for affection was the least strongly correlated of the three interpersonal needs with life satisfaction.

Modern research suggests other needs that may be satisfied by romantic relationships. Drigotas & Rusbult (1992) looked at the satisfaction of students in their relationships in relation to their needs for intimacy, sex, emotional involvement, intellectual stimulation and companionship. Those whose needs in any of these areas were not being met by the current relationship were more likely to terminate the relationship. Interestingly, this was true regardless of whether those needs were being met by other people. This is important because it suggests that a partner needs to provide the whole package; if we leave even one need such as intellectual stimulation to friends to provide instead of us, we reduce the chances that the relationship will last.

Thinking creatively about psychology

Research into needs satisfaction in relationships requires a measure of how satisfied people are with their relationships. Put together a questionnaire to measure relationship satisfaction.

Human reproductive behaviour

Up to now in this chapter we have taken a social psychological approach to understanding human relationships. In this section we take an evolutionary psychology approach. We are interested in explaining human sexual behaviour from the point of view of how it might have evolved. Evolutionary psychology is based on the idea that our behaviour is influenced by instincts left over from our evolutionary past when they were adaptive, ie they increased our chances of surviving or reproducing.

Sexual selection and human reproductive behaviour

First let us understand what sexual selection is. Natural selection, the most basic process in evolution, is the tendency of individuals who are best adapted to their environment to survive and pass on their genes. Sexual selection is a slightly different mechanism by which evolution takes place. The probability of our passing on our genes depends partly on our chances of survival but also on our ability to attract a mate. Sexual selection is the process by which a species changes over time as a result of the passing on of the genes that make one individual more attractive than another. It happens because members of a species compete with other members of the same sex for a mate. Those with genes for features that make them attractive are more likely to reproduce and pass all their genes on, including those for the attractive features, which become more and more pronounced over generations. Sexual selection is important in the evolution of a species because it means that some of the characteristics of that species are present not for survival but for attracting a mate. It is also important in explaining why males and females of some species look so different.

Charles Darwin, who first proposed the theory of evolution in the nineteenth century, suggested that the purpose of peacocks' bright colouring was to attract peahens. He went on to suggest that sexual selection is important in human evolution, and that some of our physical characteristics are for the purpose of attracting the opposite sex. Thus our hair and eye colour and distribution of muscle and fat may thus have developed not for their survival value but to make us sexually attractive. It is possible that our sexual *behaviours* are similarly influenced by evolution. If sexual selection is important in affecting human reproductive behaviour, then we would expect that sex differences in reproductive behaviour are reasonably consistent across different cultures. We would also expect that the same physical characteristics are attractive to most people, and that these characteristics signal fertility or some other variable directly relevant to successful reproduction.

◄ **Figure 3.7** This peacock's display is likely to have evolved to attract a mate

Sex differences in human reproductive behaviour

Ridley (2000) points out that in the past 100,000 years, the human species has hardly evolved at all and therefore our psychology is very much as it would have been when we were all hunter-gatherers. To Ridley, men are driven to

behave in ways that will maximise the probability that they will reproduce. This means looking to gain power and resources that will allow them to lure women to mate with and mating with as many women as possible. Women, on the other hand, are driven by a desire to secure the best genes possible for their children and to be protected by a powerful man in order to maximise the chances of those children surviving. Thornhill & Palmer (2000) go further and propose that rape has evolved as a mechanism to allow sexually unsuccessful men to reproduce. This has proved a hugely controversial idea. Rose & Rose (2000) believe that this amounts to justifying rape as a good thing for a species. A number of studies have tested the idea that reproductive behaviour is similar across a range of cultures. Buss (1989) carried out the classic study.

More recent research supports Buss's idea that there are broad sex differences in mating priorities. A key idea is that men are motivated to seek sex with a range of women in order to maximise the chances of reproducing, while women are choosier, seeking sex with a smaller number of men carefully chosen for their good genes and ability to support a mother and child. Schmitt (2003) tested this idea, surveying 16,288 people from 53 countries. In every country represented in the survey, men reported wanting to have sex with more people than did women. Most research in this area has used a survey methodology, although there have been occasional ingenious experiments to test actual sexual selection behaviour. We can look at an example of such an experiment in *Research Now*.

CLASSIC RESEARCH

Buss D (1989) Sex differences in human mate preferences. *Behavioural & Brain Sciences* **12, 1–49**

Aim: To test the hypothesis that the factors affecting mate choice in men and women are consistent across a range of cultures.

Procedure: 37 samples were obtained from 33 countries from six continents. The sampling method varied but was either by opportunity or self-selection. In total, 10,047 people participated, 4601 male and 5446 female. Participants were given a questionnaire in their native language measuring the importance of factors affecting mate choice. Eighteen characteristics were assessed for importance. The variables of age, physical attractiveness, healthy finances, chastity, ambition, industriousness and virginity were directly relevant to the study. Participants rated the importance of each factor on a 0–3 scale, where 0 was irrelevant and 3 was essential. Participants were also asked to rank 13 factors affecting mate choice in order of importance. Within the 13 factors were 'good earning capacity' and 'physical attractiveness'.

Findings: Men and women prioritised different features in a mate. In 36 out of 37 samples, women emphasised good financial prospects in a mate than did men. The exception was Spain; here women placed only fractionally more importance than men on money. In 29 of the 37 cultures, women placed significantly more emphasis on ambition and industriousness than did men, and in a further five they placed fractionally more. In all 37 cultures men rated the ideal age of a mate as younger than did women. Looks were more important to men than women in all 37 cultures.

Conclusion: Although there were some anomalies, most findings supported the idea that men and women differ consistently in the characteristics they find attractive in a potential mate.

▲ **Figure 3.8** Fortunately, women place more emphasis on ambition and industry and less on looks than do men

RESEARCH NOW

Griskevicius V, Cialdini R & Kenrick DT (2006) Peacocks, Picasso and parental investment: the effects of romantic motives on creativity. *Journal of Personality & Social Psychology* **91, 63–76**

Aim: To test the idea that creative displays such as art, music and literature have developed in order to attract mates. If this is the case, then we would expect male creativity to increase in response to any mating cue because males want to reproduce with large numbers of females. We would not expect women's creativity to be stimulated in the same way because females are driven to seek a single high-status mate.

Procedure: 91 psychology students, 35 men and 56 women, took part. They were invited into a laboratory in small groups and asked to write a short story. This established a baseline of creativity for each person. They were then primed to respond sexually by being shown six photographs of highly attractive people taken from a dating website. They were then asked to write a story about their perfect first date with one of the people in the photographs (of their choice). In a control condition, participants in another group were asked to write about their general perfect first date without seeing the photograph. Independent judges then rated the creativity of the stories on a 1–9 scale.

Findings: In the control condition, short stories from the female students were rated as slightly more creative. However, following the mating cue the creativity of male stories shot up to 4.5 as opposed to 3.7 in the control condition. Women's creativity ratings remained the same at 3.8.

Conclusion: Men but not women are inspired to displays of creativity in response to simple sexual cues. This is in line with the idea of sexual selection because it suggests that men show off in response to any sexual stimulation, as we would expect as men are motivated to mate almost indiscriminately where women are not.

Thinking critically about psychology

Critically consider the Buss (1989) study. In particular, consider his sample. What are the strengths and weaknesses of the sample used in this study?

▶ **Figure 3.9** Griskevicius *et al.* (2006) suggest that Pablo Picasso's tremendous creativity was inspired by his large number of girlfriends

Universal features of attractiveness

The idea that sexual selection has led to the development of human characteristics only really holds up if we broadly agree on what makes someone physically attractive. This is because these physical characteristics are biological and directly controlled by our genetic make-up. If there is no evidence for sexual selection in the development of physical characteristics, then it becomes much less likely that it is a factor in reproductive *behaviour*. In fact, most research has found quite a lot of agreement on attractive physical characteristics.

Waist–hip ratio seems to be a particularly reliable indicator of how attractive people will be rated as. This is particularly interesting from the perspective of sexual selection because waist–hip ratio is a fairly reliable indicator of fertility (Wass *et al.*, 1997). Streeter & Burney (2003) showed male participants 'Photoshopped' photographs of women in which the waist–hip ratio had been manipulated so that the same woman could be evaluated for attractiveness with the entire spectrum of possible waist–hip ratios. There was general agreement amongst participants that a waist–hip ratio of 0.7 was particularly attractive. This suggests that we use waist–hip ratio as an indicator of fertility in sexual selection.

Thinking creatively about psychology

There are cultural differences in attractiveness including the preferred waist–hip ratio. Suggest a reason for this based on evolutionary principles and a non-evolutionary alternative explanation.

Science puts the sexiness in Jessica Alba's stride

Academics from Cambridge claim that the film star's perfect waist–hip ratio is the key to her sexy stride.

A study was carried out to determine which famous figure had the sexiest womanly walk, revealing that it's all in the waist–hip ratio: the closer to 7.0, the sexier the sway. According to the study, this ratio provides the perfect balance of upper body strength and swing of the hips to put a sexy spring in your step.

Scoring exactly 7.0, Jessica Alba's perfect proportions topped those of fellow celebrities Kate Moss and Angelina Jolie, even beating Marilyn Monroe, whose curvaceous figure scored an almost perfect 6.9.

▶ **Figure 3.10** Jessica Alba's waist–hip ratio gives her a sexy walk

Parental investment

Trivers (1971) defines parental investment as any investment in an individual offspring that reduces the parent's ability to invest in other offspring. Parental investment begins at gametogenesis (egg and sperm production). It also includes behaviours after the birth of the offspring that increase their survival chances, for example defence against predators, feeding, and teaching skills like hunting. Parental investment benefits the parents because it increases the probability of passing on their genes to future generations.

▲ **Figure 3.11** This lioness is investing time and energy in teaching her cubs to hunt

Sex differences in investment

Studies across many species have found that mothers invest more in their young than fathers. It takes more energy to produce an egg than a sperm, so this sex difference begins even before conception. In birds and mammals, sex differences in parental investment are particularly large because the young require extensive rearing. Having made considerable investment in producing an egg and nurturing it to hatching or birth, the mother is then obliged to put in the additional effort to produce milk to feed her young as well as to protect them. Otherwise her initial investment will be wasted. Males, on the other hand, have just invested a few sperm and the physical energy needed to get jiggy with the mother for a few minutes. They are therefore rather freer to leave their offspring to it and move on. This is because males are typically biologically adapted to invest time and energy in impregnating lots of females rather than concentrating on nurturing a few offspring.

Thinking critically about psychology

What do you think feminists might have to say about this argument applied to humans?

◀ Figure 3.13
Men get very upset by sexual infidelity. Women are more bothered by emotional infidelity

KEY TERMS

r-selected species that produce large numbers of offspring but provide little parental care

K-selected species that produce fewer young and invest more energy in caring from them.

fidelity faithfulness

sexual infidelity having sex with someone other than the partner

emotional infidelity falling in love with someone other than the partner

Of course different species vary a lot in terms of how much care their young need and how well adapted adults are to provide it. Some species, known as *r-selected*, produce large numbers of young and provide little care. Few of these young survive to adulthood, but the numbers are great enough for this not to threaten the survival of the species. K-selected species by contrast produce few young and invest considerable effort in keeping them alive to adulthood. Part of the process of sexual selection in K-selected species may involve the males demonstrating their skills as a carer. This can be seen in male birds who may feed their mate or show off their nest-building skills as part of their courtship rituals. Humans are K-selected, and we can interpret some human behaviour in the same way – see Figure 3.12.

▲ Figure 3.12 There's nothing like evolutionary theory to kill romance. From a parental investment perspective this male is simply demonstrating his ability to bring food and make fire!

One source of evidence for the role of parental investment in human sexual behaviour comes from partners' responses to being cheated on. Buss (1992) looked at both physiological responses and verbal reports from men and women about how they would feel if their partner slept with someone else. Both reports and physiological measures showed that men were more upset by sexual infidelity, ie it was the act of sex with someone else that upset them. Women, on the other hand, were more upset by *emotional* infidelity, ie their partner feeling love for someone else. This fits neatly with the idea of sex differences in parental investment; from this perspective men are getting upset that offspring might not carry their genes, whereas women are concerned they might lose their long-term support. Another approach to examining sex differences in parental investment is to look at men's and women's responses to suspicion that a child is not biologically theirs.

Men invest considerably more time in child-rearing than males in any other species (Bjorklund & Shackleford, 1999). However, in every culture studied, fathers average less time in childcare than mothers (Geary, 1998). Wherever we find a universal like this in human behaviour, it is a clue that it may be the product of evolution rather than social custom – we would expect different groups of people to vary considerably in behaviours rooted in society and culture.

Parent–offspring conflict

Parents are motivated to invest energy and resources in reproducing, and in K-selected species like humans this extends to nurturing and protecting offspring. However, the interests of parents and offspring are not exactly the same. Parents have to balance the needs of any child against those of their other children, who are all of roughly equal importance, and against their own survival. Offspring are simply concerned with their own well-being, and so they tend to demand more resources than parents are willing to give. This gives rise to conflict (Trivers, 1974).

Parent–offspring conflict begins in the womb. Pregnancy is physically demanding, and the mother needs to keep some resources to maintain her own health, in order both to care for older children and to maintain her ability to bear more children in the future. The foetus, however, is developing rapidly and needs all the resources it can get. Human foetuses can release hormones that cause the mother's blood pressure to increase and so increase the supply of blood to the placenta. This benefits the foetus, which can extract more nutrition from this blood. It is bad news for the mother, however, and in extreme cases can even be fatal.

Parent–offspring conflict continues in early childhood. Babies and young children signal needs by crying and parents respond to this. Although some needs (like food and warmth) are urgent, others may not be, and children tend to use strategies like crying and temper tantrums to obtain more resources from parents than they need or parents wish to provide. Weaning may be a time of particular conflict. Children can derive benefits from breast milk for some years after birth, although milk production requires a lot of energy on the mother's part. Conflict around potty training can be explained in a similar way; Badcock (1994) suggests that by refusing to poo, children are signalling that they are not being fed enough!

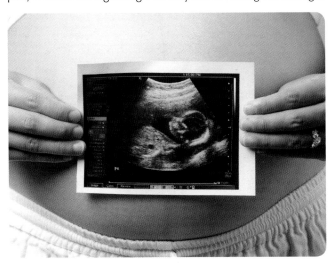

▲ **Figure 3.14** Parent–offspring competition begins in the womb

Parent–offspring conflict can continue into adulthood. In particular, parents and children argue about the child's mate choice. Parental investment would suggest that parents are primarily interested in the ability of their in-laws to support their child whereas their grown-up children are more interested in finding a partner with good genes to reproduce with. Both these ideas were tested by Apostolou (2008). We can look at this in *Research Now*.

Thinking critically about psychology

The Apostolou (2008) study used a repeated measures design, where common sense suggests it would make more sense to compare the attitudes to potential mates in children and their parents. Identify the strengths and weaknesses of using repeated and independent measures designs in a study like this.

↻ Exploring issues and debates in psychology – Determinism

'Evolutionary ideas about human reproductive behaviour suggest our decisions about our sex life and child-rearing are largely instinctive'.

Draw up a two-column table. In one column list examples from this chapter of how our behaviour might be biologically determined. In the other column list arguments against this.

RESEARCH NOW

Apostolou M (2008) Parent–child conflict over mating: the case of beauty. *Evolutionary Psychology* 6, 303–15

Aim: To test the idea that parents rank looks as less important in potential partners for their children than in partners for themselves.

Procedure: 292 parents with a mean age of 40 were obtained by a specialist research company and asked to complete an online questionnaire. The questionnaire asked them to consider two scenarios.

1 'You have two children, one male and one female, and you live in a society where marriages are arranged. It is your duty as a parent, through negotiations with other parents, to find an appropriate spouse for both your daughter and son'.

2 'You live in a society where marriages are not arranged and it is up to you to find a husband or a wife. You are not married yet but you think that the time has come for you to do so.'

In each scenario the participants were asked to rate a number of characteristics of potential mates for importance.

Findings: Most characteristics were rated as of roughly the same importance in the two scenarios. However, participants rated looks as significantly more important in scenario 2, where they were looking for a mate for themselves. They also rated health as more important than personality for their children's mates but personality as the more important in a mate for themselves.

Conclusion: Parents rate looks and personality as less important in a mate for their children than in a mate for themselves and health as more important. This supports the idea of parent–offspring conflict as it suggests they were motivated to prioritise a mate for their children that would free them up from looking after them.

The influence of early experience on adult relationships

Not everyone has romantic relationships of equal quality. It seems likely that the major factor affecting how well we manage romantic relationships is the quality of our previous relationships. We look first at attachment theory and how infant attachment might be related to adult romantic attachment. We also look at adolescence and the role then of both parents and peers.

A quick recap on attachment theory

Recall attachment theory from your AS level. John Bowlby and Mary Ainsworth proposed that our first relationship with our primary carer is extremely important in determining the quality of all our future relationships, including romantic ones. Bowlby (1969) proposed that we take from our primary relationship an internal working model of how relationships are. The better the quality of the first relationship the better the relationships

◀ **Figure 3.15** A good early relationship with your mother makes it more likely that you will have successful romantic relationships

we will be capable of later. Neglectful or abusive relationships in childhood will predispose a person to end up in such relationships as an adult.

Ainsworth introduced the idea of attachment types. A type B (secure) attachment is the product of sensitive parenting in infancy. This means that the primary carer has successfully spotted and responded to the child's signals that it is hungry, cold, lonely etc. Type B infants explore their environment but are wary of strangers and regularly visit the primary carer. They are moderately distressed when left alone but easy to comfort when reunited with the primary carer. In Ainsworth's framework, type As (avoidant) have not had the benefit of sensitive parenting and have adopted the coping strategy of emotional withdrawal. As infants they explore environments without visiting their primary carer and are not distressed at being separated from her. Type C (resistant) people have also had insensitive parenting but have adopted a different coping strategy. Rather than withdrawing from emotional relationships they are angry and controlling. These are clingy babies, becoming extremely distressed on separation and are very hard to comfort when reunited with their primary carer.

Attachment and adult relationships

Ainsworth believed that the patterns of relating to other people established in infancy as type A, B and C behaviour stay the same as the child grows up. We would therefore expect that type Bs would form the most successful relationships whilst type As would avoid close relationships and type Cs would engage in controlling relationships. This was tested in a classic study by Hazan & Shaver (1987).

CLASSIC RESEARCH

Hazan C & Shaver P (1987) Romantic love conceptualised as an attachment process. *Journal of Personality & Social Psychology 52, 511–24*

Aim: To investigate whether attachment theory could be used to understand romantic love. Specifically whether adults could be classified into types based on attachment theory and to see how these types differed in their experience of romantic love.

Procedure: A 'love quiz' was published in a local American newspaper. The replies received within a week of publication (n=620) were analysed. The first 56 items were statements about the respondent's current or recent relationship. They measured aspects of the relationship including friendship (a type B characteristic), jealousy (a type C characteristic) and fear of closeness (a type A characteristic). Respondents agreed or disagreed with each on a 4-point scale. Part 2 of the love quiz asked for details about respondents' love lives, for example how often they had been in love and how long it had been since their last relationship. Part 3 was a measure of attachment type.

Findings: 56 per cent of the sample were classified as secure, 25 per cent as avoidant and 19 per cent as ambivalent. This was very similar to the distribution of infant attachment types in the USA. The secure group reported longer relationships (mean=10.02 years compared with 4.86 for ambivalents and 5.97 for avoidants). The avoidants were most likely to report fear of getting close to someone, whereas the ambivalents were most likely to report extreme crushes and jealousy. Security was strongly associated with the quality of relationship with parents.

Conclusion: We can use attachment theory to understand romantic relationships in adulthood. The quality of relationship with parents influences adult attachment type. Secure adult attachment is associated with longer and happier relationships. Problems experienced by people with insecure adult attachments are those we would expect given the behaviour of those attachment types in infancy.

Hazan & Shaver's classic study opened the door to a whole new way of thinking about adult relationships. Later studies have consistently shown that securely attached adults are advantaged in their friendships as well as romantic relationships. McCarthy (1999) followed up 40 women aged 25 to 44, who had previously been assessed for attachment type as children. They were given a questionnaire designed to assess their current attachment type and an interview to assess the state of their adult friendships and romantic relationships. Type Bs were found to have the best friendships and romantic relationships. Type Cs had particular trouble maintaining friendships, whilst Type As found the intimacy of romantic relationships particularly difficult.

More recently Banse (2004) looked at the relationship between attachment type and marital satisfaction in 333 German couples. Satisfaction in each partner was associated with type B attachment in themselves and their partner. In other words, where both partners were secure, satisfaction was greatest. Scores of secure attachment correlated strongly (coefficients of 0.43 for wives and 0.37 for husbands) with marital satisfaction. Scores for each of the insecure attachment types correlated negatively with satisfaction.

► **Figure 3.16** Insecure attachment is associated with low marital satisfaction

Parental relationships in adolescence

It is well established that the quality of infant attachment impacts on later romantic relationships. However, although infancy is clearly a key time in our social development, it is not the only important period. Another period linked to adult romantic relationships is adolescence. Adolescence is a time when relationships start to become important. It is also a key time when the quality of relationships with parents is particularly delicate and peers are of growing importance. We would thus expect some relationship between parental relations and the development of romantic relationships.

One aspect of parenting that becomes important in adolescence is the promotion of autonomy (independence). As adolescents develop, parents can either promote or inhibit their autonomy. McElhaney & Insabella (2000) studied the link between the promotion of autonomy at age 16 and romantic relationships at 18. One hundred and fifty adolescents and

their parents were interviewed to establish the parental promotion of autonomy. Two years later the adolescents and their partners were interviewed again. Participants whose parents inhibited autonomy at 16 tended to be more dependent on their romantic relationships at 18, and to have lower levels of trust and communication.

Peer relations and later romantic attachments

During adolescence, peer groups shift from same sex to mixed. This provides an environment where adolescents can experiment with early romantic relationships while keeping the security of a stable and supportive group of friends. Kuttler & La Greca (2004) assessed quality of same-sex friendship and heterosexual dating in 446 girls aged 15–19. Girls who dated seriously tended to have worse quality friendships than those who did not date or dated casually. This may be because the dating affected the friendship or it might have been because poor friendships led girls to seek companionship through dating. There was a shift with age, as girls began to rely for support more on boyfriends and less on friends.

◄ **Figure 3.17** The relationship between quality of teenage friendships and later romantic relationships is unclear

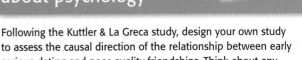

Thinking creatively about psychology

Following the Kuttler & La Greca study, design your own study to assess the causal direction of the relationship between early serious dating and poor quality friendships. Think about any additional factors that might affect both variables.

Seiffge-Krenke *et al.* (2001) carried out a longitudinal study of 72 adolescents for six years, beginning at age 14. The quality of their relationships with peers and parents was assessed annually. At age 20, the quality of their romantic relationships was assessed. There was no correlation between the quality of relationships with friends and the quality of romantic relationships. However, the quality of relationship with parents and the quality of relationship between parents was related. Those with better parental relationships tended to have better romantic relationships.

Passionate friendships

Most research into adolescence has concerned heterosexuals. Because close friendships in heterosexual adolescents are usually with the same sex there is a very clear demarcation between friendship and romance. Diamond (2002) suggests that this is not quite the same for lesbians. Diamond interviewed 80 lesbian adolescents and found that many had best-friendships that combined many of the qualities of friendship and romance. Whilst it was rare for young lesbians to have sexual contact with heterosexual friends they often held hands and cuddled, physical intimacies that are more common in romantic relationships than between friends. Interviewees made the point strongly that although they felt very strongly about their best friends they were not sexually attracted to them. This is important because the stereotype of this sort of 'passionate friendship' is of repressed sexuality or one-sided love. Diamond suggests that this is misleading and that passionate friendships in adolescent lesbians are a unique and understudied type of relationship.

◀ **Figure 3.18** Young lesbians often have physically intimate but non-sexual relationships with best friends

Thinking critically about psychology

1 The study by Seiffge-Krenke *et al.* (2001) and that by Kuttler & La Greca (2004) came to different conclusions about the relationship between the quality of friendship and that of romantic relationships. What differences between the two studies might have contributed to this?
2 How might an attachment research interpret the correlation between quality of parental relationships and quality of romantic relationships?

Cultural differences in romantic relationships

Culture is a system of beliefs and practices that are shared by a group of people. This group can be as large as a country or as small as a family. Usually when we talk about cultural differences we are thinking on a fairly large scale. Cross-cultural psychologists compare the cultures of people from different countries, ethnic groups and religions. There are cultural differences in several aspects of relationships, ranging from what characteristics make an individual attractive to what leads to relationship breakdown.

Cultural differences in attraction

Some things appear to be universally physically attractive. For example, people generally prefer the appearance of those with symmetrical faces (Fiore & Donath, 2004). However, there are some cultural differences in what is considered attractive, in particular with regard to body type. Anderson *et al.* (1992) investigated the idea that tastes in body type vary according to availability of food. Although in contemporary European and American culture stereotypically attractive women are slim, this may be because we have no problems with food supply. Evolutionary theory would suggest that women with more fat reserves represent a better prospect in environments where food is less reliably available. Anderson *et al.* divided 54 cultural groups into four categories according to the availability of food, then looked at the preferred body type in each. The results are shown in Table 3.2.

▼ **Table 3.2** Preferred body type varies with reliability of food supply

Preferred body type	Very unreliable food supply	Moderately unreliable food supply	Moderately reliable food supply	Very reliable food supply
Heavy	71%	50%	39%	40%
Medium	29%	33%	39%	20%
Slender	0%	17%	22%	40%

As Table 3.2 shows, in the majority of cultures where food supply was unreliable, heavily-built women were rated as most attractive. No cultures rated slender women as the preferred body type where food supply was very unreliable, and few did so even where it was even moderately unreliable. These findings support evolutionary theory.

▶ **Figure 3.19** Larger women are seen as more attractive in societies where food supplies are unreliable

Cultural differences in the formation of relationships

The norm in mainstream western culture is for a couple to find each other attractive, flirt, date and perhaps go on to form a stable romantic relationship, which may or may not be permanent. However, this pattern is far from universal. Many cultures have a tradition of arranged marriage. Arranged marriage takes place where families make the choice of who their children will marry. The families of the bride and groom make the arrangements together, and this may involve payment.

Arranged marriage is largely misunderstood, and receives a bad press in the twenty-first century UK. Uddin (2006) points out that the system of arranged marriage has operated successfully in Asian cultures, but has run into trouble in the UK because many young people no longer see it as an acceptable alternative to free individual choice of a partner. This clash between generations has led to an increase in the practice of forced marriage, in which young people are made to marry someone against their will. Don't get confused, however, between arranged and forced marriage. The vast majority of arranged marriages take place with the full and free consent of both parties.

So what happens about attraction and flirting in a culture where marriage is arranged? It is *not* the case that people in cultures where there is arranged marriage do not fancy people and fall in love (Goodwin, 2005). The difference lies in the extent to which other people are involved in the decision-making that comes between initial attraction and marriage. Nor is it usually the case that parents don't take their children's feelings into account when arranging marriages. Studies of the process of marriage arrangement (eg De Munck, 1996) have shown that parents often go to considerable effort to arrange marriages with partners their children find attractive or have fallen in love with.

Another cultural variation concerns the popularity of marriage as an institution. Marriage in the UK has been on the decline for some time. In 1972, just over 0.8 per cent of the UK population got married. In 2007, this was around 0.5 per cent. This pattern matches that in the majority of economically developed countries (see Figure 3.20). The alternative to marriage is cohabiting. Surveys (eg Diener *et al.*, 1999) suggest that in individualist cultures such as the UK, cohabiting couples are happier than married couples or single people. However, this is not the case in more collectivist countries, in which people define themselves more in terms of their family and community than as individuals.

Cultural differences in the maintenance and dissolution of relationships

There are massive cultural differences in the number of relationships that break down. Some people, particularly those from conservative political and religious groups, have suggested that the current high divorce rates in Europe and the USA mean that modern dating and partner selection practices are unsuccessful compared with those in other more traditional countries and previous generations. However, there is an alternative interpretation; national divorce rates may reflect not so much the number of failed relationships as the freedom to leave a failed marriage. First of all, what does the data tell us? Figure 3.21 shows comparative change in divorce rates between 1970 and 2007.

The social acceptability of divorce and separation varies from one culture to another. There seems little doubt that where it is socially unacceptable to leave a marriage, unhappy marriages persist. Honour-cultures are those in which the term 'honour' refers to status and reputation as well as a code of conduct (Pitt-Rivers, 1966). Typically in honour-cultures, male honour represents toughness whereas female honour is gained through fidelity and submissiveness. Vandello & Cohen (2003) suggest that women in honour-cultures have less power than do other women relative to men, and that they are expected to remain in relationships even when those relationships are abusive. For a woman to leave a marriage in an honour-culture is hugely socially unacceptable and may be dangerous.

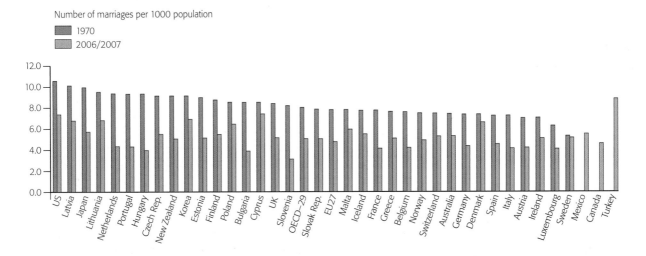

▲ **Figure 3.20** The fall in marriage rates across a range of countries

Number of divorces per 1000 population

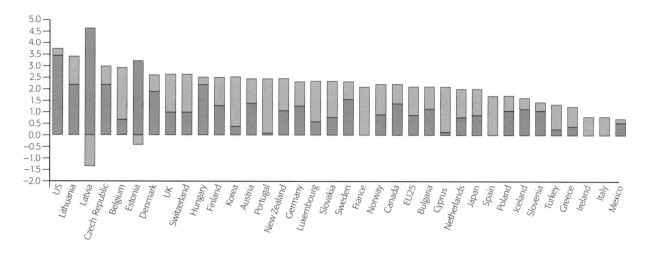

▲ **Figure 3.21** Divorce rates across a range of countries since 1970

Needs satisfaction also appears to be an important factor in maintaining relationships. There is some evidence to suggest that satisfaction of some needs may vary between cultures. De Munck & Korotayev (2007) proposed that intimacy, identified in previous research as a need, is greater in cultures where men and women have more equal status. They tested this in a cross-cultural study, correlating measures of gender status in a culture, such as witch-hunting and equal burial rights, with measures of intimacy such as whether husbands and wives shared a bed. Cultures with greater gender equality tended to be those where husbands and wives shared greater physical intimacy. This suggests that married women in some cultures are doubly disadvantaged in relationships, lacking both power and intimacy.

Thinking critically about psychology

Use social exchange theory to explain why women in some cultures who have low status and low intimacy in marriage might remain in the marriage.

Chapter summary

Formation, maintenance and breakdown of relationships

- One factor in the formation of relationships is the mere exposure effect. The more often we are exposed to someone the more attractive we tend to find them.
- We are sensitive to information suggesting we are dissimilar to someone we find attractive. If we learn more about someone and decide they are not like us, then we cease to find them attractive.
- Physical attractiveness is important in affecting who we are attracted to. There is a large body of evidence supporting matching hypothesis: the idea that we choose people of similar attractiveness to ourselves.
- Social exchange theory is the idea that we judge our relationships based on their costs and rewards

as opposed to those of alternatives like leaving the relationship.
- Social exchange theory has good explanatory power and practical applications in therapy. However, it is reductionist, looking just at individuals and ignoring the wider cultural influences on the relationship.
- Needs satisfaction is an alternative approach to explaining why relationships survive or dissolve. It involves looking at the human needs that can be met by relationships.
- In line with the needs satisfaction approach, there is evidence to show that satisfaction is highest in relationships that meet the needs of partners.

Human reproductive behaviour

- Sexual selection may explain some human reproductive behaviour. In particular, men and women behave differently in terms of reproduction.
- There is evidence to support the idea of universal sex differences in reproductive behaviour.
- One way males and females of most species differ is in terms of parental investment. Men put less energy than women into conceiving and bringing young to term, therefore there is little incentive for them to protect their investment by looking after offspring.
- Parent–offspring conflict occurs because parents and their children have slightly different interests. Conflict begins in pregnancy and continues throughout childhood and adolescence.
- Our relationships with parents during childhood and adolescence impact on the quality of our adult romantic relationships. We can understand this effect in terms of attachment theory.

Effects of early experience and culture

- The impact of peer relationships on romantic relationships is more complex and evidence is contradictory. Some studies show that good quality peer relations are associated with good quality early romantic relationships, but other studies show the reverse.
- There are cultural differences in relationships. This begins with which features people find attractive. Relationships can form by different mechanisms as some cultures have arranged marriages whilst others do not.
- Culture affects the likelihood of relationships breaking down. However, this may be simply because women find it harder to leave unhappy relationships in some cultures. 'Honour-cultures' are associated with both poor status and treatment of women and particular difficulty in leaving a relationship.

What do I know?

1 (a) Outline **one** theory that explains the formation of relationships. (10 marks)
 (b) Outline and evaluate research into sexual selection in humans. (15 marks)

2 (a) Explain what is meant by sexual selection. (5 marks)
 (b) Outline and evaluate research into parent–offspring conflict. (10 marks)
 (c) Explain criticisms of **one** theory of maintenance/dissolution of relationships. (10 marks)

3 (a) Outline **one** theory of the maintenance of relationships. (10 marks)
 (b) Outline and evaluate research into cultural differences in relationships. (15 marks)

4 (a) Explain what is meant by parental investment. (5 marks)
 (b) Explain how early experience can affect adult relationships. (10 marks)
 (c) Evaluate research into the effect of adolescent experience on adult relationships. (10 marks)

5 Describe and evaluate research into cultural differences in relationships. (25 marks)

CHAPTER 4
Aggression

Thinking ahead

By the end of this chapter you should be able to:

- describe, evaluate and apply explanations of aggression from social psychology including social learning theory and deindividuation
- describe and evaluate explanations of institutional aggression
- describe and analyse biological explanations of aggression including the roles of genes, hormones and neural mechanisms
- describe and evaluate explanations that suggest that aggression is an adaptive response, including evolutionary explanations and group display in humans

In this chapter we look at a range of explanations for aggressive behaviour. Aggression can be defined as any behaviour that is intended to cause harm to another person or persons. More often than not, when we talk about aggression we mean direct physical aggression or violence. However, there are many ways we can act to harm others and so there are different forms of aggression. Direct verbal aggression involves teasing, criticism and insult directed towards the person to whom harm is intended. We can also harm people indirectly without attacking them physically or even speaking to them. This indirect aggression might involve spreading rumours or encouraging others to exclude them.

There are a number of factors affecting aggression and we can explain aggression in a range of ways. Social-psychological explanations focus on the role of other individuals and groups. Biological explanations focus instead on the possible roles played by evolution, hormones, brain mechanisms and our individual genetic make-up.

Social psychology and the explanation of aggression

Social learning theory

Social learning theory proposes that learning can occur when one individual (the learner) observes and imitates another, the model. For example, a young girl may watch an older one putting on make-up and try to copy her. According to Bandura (1977), modelling will occur when the observer pays attention, is able to remember and reproduce what they have observed and when they are motivated to do so. This motivation may be an external reward or some inner drive. Internal motivation may be generated by the model, and this can explain why there are differences in the effectiveness of models.

Unlike classical or operant conditioning, where we can see the process of learning directly as the individual performs the behaviour, this is not always the case in social learning. When a model is observed and a new behavioural potential gained, it is not necessarily demonstrated. A young child may listen to his parents swearing, but may not utter the newly acquired words until he has an audience! Such examples help to illustrate another difference between conditioning and social learning. In modelling, there is no requirement for reinforcement, at least not to learn. Reinforcement can, however, play a part in the performance of the behaviour. Children who imitate the offensive language of others may learn to demonstrate their behaviour only in situations where it will be rewarded, such as to impress friends or annoy parents.

MEDIA WATCH : TV and behaviour

Call to turn off *South Park*

Times Educational Supplement, **11 February 2000**

Parents at a North Yorkshire primary school have been urged to stop their children watching the cult TV cartoon *South Park* after an increase in swearing and bad behaviour in the playground.

Glyn Hopper, head of Sowerby County Primary School, near Thirsk, wrote to parents after children raised the issue in her school council.

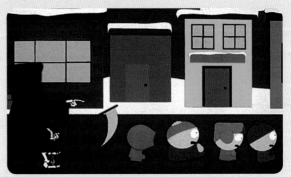

▲ Figure 4.1 South Park has been cited as a source of undesirable role models

1 Explain, using social learning theory, how the children might have acquired antisocial behaviour from watching *South Park*.

2 How important do you think the media is as an influence on children's behaviour?

CLASSIC RESEARCH

Bandura A, Ross D & Ross SA (1961) Transmission of aggression through imitation of aggressive models. *Journal of Abnormal & Social Psychology* **63, 575–82**

Aim: To investigate whether aggression could be acquired through modelling and to see whether children were more likely to imitate same-sex role models.

Procedure: Children aged three to six years (36 boys and 36 girls) were assigned to three groups. Two groups were exposed to adult models who behaved in either aggressive or non-aggressive ways, with half seeing a same-sex model, the others an opposite-sex model. A control group did not see any model. In the non-aggressive condition, the model assembled Tinker toys for 10 minutes; in the aggressive condition this lasted only one minute, after which the model attacked a Bobo doll. The doll was sat on, punched, picked up and hit on the head with a mallet. This sequence was performed three times over nine minutes accompanied by aggressive comments such as 'kick him' and 'pow'.

All participants were then deliberately annoyed. They were shown to a room with attractive toys such as a fire engine and a doll with a wardrobe (remember, this is the 1960s), but after a short time to play the children were told that these toys were for other children and were moved to another room containing a Bobo doll. The children were observed playing here for 20 minutes, using a one-way mirror.

Findings: Children exposed to violent models imitated their exact behaviours and were significantly more aggressive – both physically and verbally – than those children who did not receive aggressive modelling. This effect was greater for boys than girls, although girls were more likely to imitate verbal, and boys physical, aggression. Boys were also more likely to imitate a same-sex model, as, to a lesser extent, were girls.

Conclusion: Observation and imitation can account for the learning of specific acts without reinforcement of either the model or observer. Observers have a greater tendency to imitate same-sex models.

◀ Figure 4.2
The Bobo doll study

Pennington (1986) identifies three categories of variable that affect imitation:

- characteristics of the model
- characteristics of the observer
- the consequences of the behaviour for the model.

Bandura *et al.* (1961) indicated one important characteristic of the model, their sex. Others include age and status. A model who is of similar age and high in status is more likely to be imitated. For example, a young person who perceives a gang leader to be high in status may be drawn into violent behaviour because the sight of high status people being threatening to others is more influential than other, pro-social, models such as their parents.

For observers, their own level of self-esteem is an important determinant of imitation. Individuals with lower self-esteem are more likely to imitate the behaviour of models. One important consequence for models is whether they are reinforced. If observers see models receiving positive reinforcement for their actions, they are more likely to imitate them. This effect is called *vicarious reinforcement*. Aggressive behaviours may be seen to be successful – a child who bullies others for their pocket money is seen to reap rewards.

There may also be direct positive reinforcement for imitated violence. Children who are aggressive may be rewarded for their behaviour by obtaining benefits through

Thinking practically about psychology

To allocate the children to conditions, Bandura *et al.* (1961) assessed them for aggressiveness before the experiment and ensured that the three groups contained a similar spread of children. Why was this important?

threatening others, such as taking their sweets. Positive reinforcement may also be experienced through the feeling of power over others, or via increased status. Simply being able to imitate the voice or actions of a popular TV character may increase a child's popularity. Any of these examples would act as reinforcers and could increase the frequency with which the aggressive behaviours are performed. Bandura (1965) demonstrated that a child was more likely to copy an aggressive adult model if the child was reinforced, and less likely to if he or she was punished. In this sense, as well as in the provision of models, the social environment influences the likelihood of aggressive behaviour.

LOOKING FURTHER Try searching YouTube for segments of the footage from Bandura *et al.*'s original experiment. There are several versions, for example this one which includes Bandura giving a description of the study:

http://uk.youtube.com/watch?v=IK4NPc7HCnY&feature=PlayList&p=F7CFA1F23349B6C6&playnext=1&index=4

Media violence

A different aspect of the social environment, the media – eg television – is often claimed to be a cause of children's aggression. Children certainly see a lot of media violence and they pay attention to what they see, even when very young. Troseth (2003) showed that children as young as two years old could use information they had seen on a video. For two weeks, some children were allowed to watch themselves 'live' on the family television. They later saw, on video, a toy being hidden in another room and were asked to find it. Children of this age generally find tasks like this very difficult. These children, however, were successful, suggesting that they had learned to reproduce behaviours they had viewed on TV.

▼ **Figure 4.3** The latest Rambo film has 236 killings – an average of 2.59 per minute

We have seen from Bandura *et al.* (1961) that people in real life can be important as role models for aggression, but media role models may also be important. When characters on TV use violence they are modelling aggression. Recall that, for behaviour to be acquired by social learning, four processes take place: attention, retention, reproduction and reinforcement. By watching TV and following a storyline, we are paying attention. If the violence seen is distinctive and arousing this means it is likely to be retained. Children may be impressed by the violence used, motivating them to reproduce it later. This is particularly true if the model is rewarded for their actions (vicarious reinforcement).

TV heroes are designed to have the precise features that make them effective models. They have high social status, are likeable and powerful. Take the on-screen persona of Jean-Claude Van Damme or Vin Diesel. These are just the sort of characters that young males aspire to be like, therefore they identify with them. This identification makes imitation more likely.

If we accept that there is a link between media violence and aggressive behaviour, then learning theory provides an effective explanation. However, we need to think a little critically about whether this link is causal. If individuals who are exposed to an aggressive social environment are subsequently aggressive this may be a causal effect, or there may be other influences such as genetics or personality.

OVER TO YOU If possible, try to work in a group for this activity. Each individual needs to choose a time and television channel to watch and the group needs to agree definitions for aggressive behaviour. Your aim is to compare aspects of television programmes with regard to violence. Plan and conduct an observation. In your planning you might consider: when the programmes are shown; whether the aggression is verbal, physical or both; whether it is perpetrated and/or directed towards males, females or inanimate objects; whether the perpetrator is a powerful character etc. If you have more than one person viewing the same programme, you can assess the records for inter-observer reliability.

Eron *et al.* (1972) measured the level of violence in TV programmes watched by seven- to eight-year-olds and measured their aggressiveness. They found a positive correlation between the two. By their teenage years, Eron *et al.* (1972) found an even stronger positive correlation of violence viewed and aggressiveness in boys (though not girls). And the more violence the boys had watched on television as children, the more likely they were to be violent criminals as adults (Eron & Huesmann, 1986). Of course, these findings are based on data from several decades ago and not all of the sample were available for the follow-up work, so the results may not be generalisable. This study was also correlational, raising doubts about cause and effect. The level of aggression may not be caused by the individuals' viewing habits – it is possible that both the watching of violence and the aggressive behaviour may have been caused by some other variable such as harsh parental punishment.

MEDIA WATCH: Games and violence

Video games warp brain

Jerome Starkey, *The Sun*, 9 January 2006

Violent computer games alter your brain to make you aggressive, experts say. New research shows gory games interfere with natural reactions to real-life violence.

Brain specialists found games such as *Mortal Kombat* and *Grand Theft Auto*, which include killings and street crime, desensitise players to genuine images of violence.

It is the first research to show that violent games could CAUSE violent behaviour.

Studies have shown that people who play violent video games are more aggressive.

But critics claim this just means that naturally violent people enjoy playing violent games.

US psychologist Bruce Bartholow has shown that people who play violent video games have diminished responses to images involving violence.

◀ **Figure 4.4** Game aggro... dulls reaction

But they have normal responses to other distressing pictures, such as images involving sick children or dead animals.

Scientists from the University of Missouri-Columbia carried out their research with the help of 39 experienced gamers.

1 How does this evidence help to separate the effects of cause and effect in viewing violence?

2 Comment on the sample used by Bartholow. To what extent would his findings be generalisable?

This can be countered, however, by experimental evidence. Bandura *et al.* (1963) also demonstrated the influence of televised models. They compared the effect of an aggressive adult model and a film of the same adult, performing the same behaviours, dressed as a cartoon cat. Using a procedure similar to Bandura *et al.* (1961), they found that aggressive behaviour modelled by the cartoon cat produced the highest levels of imitated aggression in children.

Some studies, however, have failed to find a link between aggression and TV viewing. Hagell & Newbury (1994) found that young offenders watched no more violent television than a school control group. The delinquents were also less focused on television viewing, being less able to name favourite programmes or television characters they imitated and were more likely to be on the streets getting into trouble than indoors watching television. In a natural experiment, Charlton *et al.* (2000) showed that media violence does not necessarily lead to aggression (see *Research Now*).

▲ **Figure 4.5** Aggressive cartoons affect children's behaviour

RESEARCH NOW

Charlton T, Panting C, Davie R, Coles D & Whitmarsh L (2000) Children's playground behaviour across five years of broadcast television: A naturalistic study in a remote community. *Emotional & Behavioural Difficulties* 5, 4–12

Aim: To investigate the effect of the introduction of satellite TV on the aggressive behaviour of children.

Procedure: A naturalistic experiment was conducted using three- to eight-year-olds on the island of St Helena who had not previously seen transmitted TV. Their aggressive behaviour was analysed in 1994 prior to the introduction of transmitted television in 1995. They were filmed in the playground, and their parents and teachers were given questionnaires to assess the children's behaviour. Their behaviour was assessed again after satellite TV became available. Aggressive behaviours such as pushing, hitting and kicking were recorded (as well as pro-social behaviours such as turn-taking and affection). They also measured the amount of television the children watched and the aggressive content of the programmes.

Findings: The initial level of aggressive behaviour displayed by the children was very low and remained so following the change in viewing opportunities. The children displayed almost twice as much pro-social behaviour as antisocial behaviour both before and after the introduction of broadcast television. Some increases and some decreases in aggressive behaviour were found, but the only two significant differences were *decreases* in incidence.

Conclusion: Exposure to more violent TV does not necessarily result in an increase in aggressive behaviour.

Thinking critically about psychology

St Helena is an isolated island and the population is very small and cohesive. The children's parents and other members of the community are very watchful and supportive. For example, in another study (of secondary age children on St Helena) Charlton & O'Bey (1997) report a child saying: 'Because everyone watches you… everyone knows you… you've just got to behave' (p134). How would this affect the impact of television on the children?

The procedure used by Charlton et al. was clearly highly valid in that, unlike studies such as those of Bandura et al., it used children in a real-life setting and pre- and post-experience to aggressive models to which the children were genuinely (rather than artificially) exposed. Their method was also rigorous, with good inter-observer reliability and efforts to ensure that the children's behaviour was unaffected by the presence of the video cameras. However, St Helena is a very isolated, unusual environment and the findings may be unrepresentative of other western communities. Williams (1981) conducted a similar study looking at the effect of the introduction of broadcast television to a remote community in Canada. The aggressiveness of children in a town (nicknamed 'Notel') that initially had no television was compared, over the same time span, with children in two other towns (one with just one TV channel and the other with many channels). Following the introduction of broadcast television, the level of physical and verbal aggression in the children in Notel almost doubled. Although levels of aggression in the other towns also increased over the same period, the change was less marked.

Thinking critically about psychology

Williams (1981) reports that the children's TV viewing patterns and level of aggression in 'Notel' were not correlated. How could this observation be explained?

Thinking creatively about psychology

Williams also found that gender differences in the children's behaviour increased following the introduction of television to 'Notel'. Design a study to investigate whether there are gender differences in the aggression shown by TV models and whether this relates to the behaviour of boys and girls.

LOOKING FURTHER Use the internet to find out more about Charlton et al. (2000) and Williams (1981). Compare their methods and findings. To what extent do the differences in results relate to differences in the populations studied and what does that tell us about the importance of the social environment to levels of aggression?

MEDIA WATCH : internet control

Clamp down on net's violent videos

Graeme Wilson, *The Sun*, 27 March 2008 [edited]

▶ Figure 4.6 Reforms… TV's Dr Tanya Byron

A powerful internet watchdog to guard kids from porn and violence will be demanded today.

Cinema-style ratings for video games will also be called for in a major report by TV child guru Dr Tanya Byron. PM Gordon Brown summoned the star of *House of Tiny Tearaways* and *Little Angels* last autumn to investigate the online menace. And her final report today offers the most detailed analysis yet of the risks our kids face.

Dr Byron will argue that parents, Ministers, internet firms and game producers must all do more to protect youngsters.

She wants cinema-style U, PG, 12, 15 or 18 ratings – with parents told if a game shows violence or sex scenes. And she will urge families to ban computers from kids' bedrooms – and put them in the lounge or kitchen.

A Whitehall insider said: 'She is not lecturing parents but is saying it's probably a good idea to keep an eye on what they're up to.'

And the TV doctor wants the sites to be monitored to check they are not showing 'happy slap' attacks or street fights.

1 How do the findings of Charlton et al. (2000) and Williams (1981) help to justify Dr Byron's comments about parents?

2 Describe two other pieces of evidence that suggest such measures are necessary.

Deindividuation

As far back as the nineteenth century, psychologists were interested in the factors underlying mob violence. Why do normally peaceful non-aggressive people sometimes become so aggressive when in large groups? After studying French rioters, Le Bon (1895) concluded that people in large groups feel themselves to be primarily part of the group rather than an individual. This leads to the removal of their usual inhibitions. Le Bon believed that in large groups the individual mind became submerged into a collective mind that functioned in a primitive and instinctive way. Aggression in crowds was thus a result of unleashed instinctive behaviour.

The term 'deindividuation' was first used by Festinger (1952). He disagreed with Le Bon about the existence of a collective mind but agreed that people in groups are anonymous and that this anonymity reduces their inhibitions, causing them to act differently from how they tend to when alone. Zimbardo (1970) carried out a classic study of deindividuation, demonstrating its role in aggression.

► Figure 4.7 According to Le Bon's analysis, this rioter is functioning in a primitive and instinctive way

 LOOKING FURTHER You can read the original research paper here: http://www.prisonexp.org/pdf/ijcp1973.pdf. You can also read a simplified account by Zimbardo, complete with film footage (requires RealPlayer).

CLASSIC RESEARCH

Haney C, Banks C & Zimbardo P (1973) Interpersonal dynamics in a simulated prison. *International Journal of Criminology and Penology* **1, 69–97**

Aim: To investigate the psychological effect of becoming a prisoner or prison guard.

Procedure: 70 people answered an advert in a local newspaper asking for volunteers in a study of prison life. After being given a battery of psychometric tests to eliminate people with criminal histories, drug problems, psychological or medical problems, 24 white male college students were selected to take part. Eighteen were randomly assigned to be prisoners or guards. The rest served as reserves. The prisoners were arrested at home and taken to the basement of a university psychology department that had been converted into a prison. Each prisoner was strip-searched and de-loused on arrival. They were then made to wear a uniform, a stocking cap to cover their hair and an ankle chain. They were only allowed to refer to themselves and others by a prisoner number. Guards, although given uniforms, were not trained and were allowed to make up the prison rules. Unknown to the participants, the prison area was bugged and monitored 24 hours a day. The lead experimenter, Philip Zimbardo, took the role of Prison Warden.

Findings: Guards initiated a programme of 'counts' in which prisoners were assembled and ordered to repeat their prisoner number. At first the prisoners did not take this seriously, but the guards began to use press-ups as punishment. One guard in particular stood on prisoners' backs to make press-ups harder and more painful. For the first day, prisoners conformed, but on the morning of the second day they rebelled, barricading themselves in their cells. The guards forced their way into each cell and stripped the prisoners. They put the ringleaders in solitary confinement. They then tried to divide the prisoners by establishing a 'privilege' cell where those least involved in the rebellion were allowed to live and have privileges like washing. By the third day, the guards had become more brutal, refusing to let prisoners leave their cells to go to the toilet. One prisoner started to show extreme anxiety symptoms, although he was not allowed to leave until day four. On day five, the guards' aggression increased, making prisoners clean toilets with their bare hands. At night, when they thought researchers were not looking, they subjected prisoners to sexual humiliation. By day six, their power was almost total and prisoners obeyed without question. A visiting researcher objected strongly and convinced the experimenters to end the study.

Conclusion: Prisoners and guards adopted their roles and soon lost touch with the fact that they were taking part in an experiment. Deindividuation appeared to have been a factor in this, both groups being made anonymous by their uniforms and group membership.

Thinking critically about psychology

Consider the ethical implications of the prison study. In particular:

1 Was sufficient care taken not to threaten the participants' safety and dignity?
2 To what extent was 'real' consent possible and to what extent did participants have the means to withdraw from the study?
3 In what ways was privacy breached?
4 Was it wise for the experimenter to have a role in the prison?

▲ Figure 4.8 A guard intimidates a prisoner

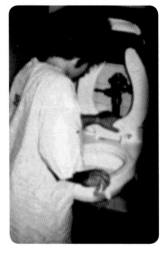

▶ Figure 4.9 A prisoner is made to clean a toilet with his bare hands

Once the study had ended, Zimbardo realised that he had lost perspective and fallen too completely into the role of prison warden. The participants were debriefed. Interestingly some of the guards were angry during the debrief that the study had been stopped. Christina Maslach, the visitor who persuaded Zimbardo to stop the study, married him and became a famous psychologist in her own right. The prisoner who left early went on to become a prison psychologist. Craig Haney, participant

and co-author when the study was published, became a successful lawyer specialising in prisoners' rights. The most brutal guard, known as 'John Wayne' by the prisoners, became an estate agent.

So how does deindividuation lead to aggression of the sort shown by the guards in Zimbardo's prison experiment? Influenced by Le Bon, Zimbardo (1969) suggested that in groups we lose a degree of our personal identity; the larger the group, the greater this effect. An alternative explanation, from Diener (1980), suggests that deindividuation leads to the following four changes:

- reduced ability to monitor one's own behaviour
- reduced ability to inhibit impulsive behaviour
- reduced ability to respond or think clearly
- reduced concern about the social judgements of others.

All these effects can contribute to aggression. Aggressive behaviour is often carried out on impulse. If we are not thinking clearly or monitoring the social acceptability of our behaviour then we are more likely to act on aggressive impulses which, under different circumstances, we would be able to analyse and inhibit.

▼Figure 4.10 These rioters may not be aggressive under other circumstances, but we tend to be more impulsive and less able to analyse and inhibit our own behaviour in a large group

Discussion of deindividuation

There is evidence to support the idea that people are more aggressive when deindividuated. Zimbardo's prison study is consistent with this, although the study was not designed specifically to test the effect of deindividuation. He did, however, carry out such a direct test. Zimbardo (1970) asked female participants to give electric shocks to other women in a procedure similar to that used by Stanley Milgram (1963). (You should recall that one from your AS level.) In one condition, participants wore hoods and were addressed as a group rather than individually. They gave on average twice the voltage of participants in the control condition.

The major problem with linking deindividuation in its original form with aggression is that not all crowds become aggressive. Serious violence is uncommon even in crowds engaged in angry protest. Moreover, even when protests do become violent, the majority of protesters do not participate.

Postmes & Spears (1998) have suggested a modern analysis of deindividuation that takes account of this in two ways.

1 Deindividuation also leads to an increase in conformity. We are thus more likely to display the behaviour of people around us. This explains why crowds are generally peaceful – if people around us are not behaving aggressively then we tend not to. However, if a crowd does become aggressive, we may conform to that new norm and join in.

2 Deindividuation leads to a reduced focus on the self as an individual but not its disappearance altogether. This means that individuals in a crowd are affected by what is happening around them to differing degrees; some conform more than others with the behaviour around them. This explains why even in the most extreme crowd violence many people do not join in.

Institutional aggression

All aggression involves an attempt to harm another person or persons. Sometimes this takes place in an institution. In this context an 'institution' can be any organisation to which people can belong and which influences their behaviour. It can be as small as a school or psychiatric hospital or as large as a country's armed forces. Institutional aggression can be defined as any aggression that is influenced by the institution in which it takes place. It includes both aggression within the same group, for example *bullying* in a school or workplace, or aggression by one group towards another, for example by psychiatric patients towards staff and by prison guards towards inmates. We can apply social learning and deindividuation to explain *institutional aggression*. We can also look at the sort of social processes that take place alongside deindividuation and question whether the media can affect attitudes to institutional aggression.

Social learning of institutional aggression

We have already looked at social learning and deindividuation as explanations for aggression in general. So can we use them to explain institutional aggression? Social learning theory (SLT) is based on the idea that we tend to imitate high status successful role models. Randall (1997) has applied this idea to explain bullying, an example of institutional aggression. When we join an institution we usually begin with a low social status. According to SLT, we then seek models within our group with high status to imitate. If those models are aggressive, it follows that we will adopt their aggressive ways. Rigby & Slee (1993) found evidence to support the idea that school bullies can be role models. They found that Australian boys rated class bullies as highly popular and admired. These are precisely the characteristics that we would expect in effective role models.

Twemlow *et al.* (1996) suggest that schools with bullying problems are ones in which aggressive role models dominate, and that making non-bullies the dominant role models can dramatically reduce institutional aggression in the form of school bullying.

Institutional aggression in the form of bullying is not limited to schools. Archer (1999) examined institutional bullying in the US Fire Service. He suggested that harsh treatment of new recruits is a tradition passed on from one generation to the next. It is interpreted – even by victims – simply as a custom rather than acts of hostility. Role models are seen as having been through the same aggression themselves so victims are strongly motivated to tolerate it in order to live up to their example.

Randle (2003) conducted in-depth interviews with student nurses at the beginning and end of their training. Nurses early in their training experienced considerable institutional aggression at the hands of more experienced students and qualified nurses. By the end of their course, nurses tended to have adopted this behaviour from their role models and displayed their own institutional aggression.

▲ **Figure 4.11** Where experienced workers serve as role models for young recruits, the recruits may tolerate institutionalised aggression from them

---

KEY TERMS

institutional aggression aggression that takes place as a result of being in an institutional setting

bullying sustained and deliberate behaviour aimed at harming an individual

Evaluation

Although social learning probably does contribute to institutional aggression, it is certainly not the only factor. It is hard when carrying out research into institutional bullying to separate out role modelling from more general institutional culture. For example, it is difficult to know whether victims of institutional aggression are reluctant to rebel or inform because they want to be like the aggressor, or whether other factors – such as working in close-knit teams that depend on one another – make it hard to avoid conforming with the group norm. All occupational groups have their role models and operate within institutions of some sort, yet some are more associated with institutional aggression than others. In particular, note that the three examples we have looked at so far – school children, nurses and fire-fighters – are all uniformed. This may suggest that deindividuation also has a role and it is to this that we now turn.

Deindividuation and institutional aggression

Much of the research into institutional aggression has focused on uniformed occupations. Zimbardo believed that wearing a uniform contributed to deindividuation. This is why in his classic prison study (p79) he ensured that both guards and prisoners were uniformed at all times. Recall the basic idea of deindividuation: that when in groups we are more impulsive, less able to monitor our own behaviour and perhaps that we lose a degree of our personal identity, seeing ourselves as part of the group rather than an individual. It is quite possible that the deindividuation we experience when we are part of a close-knit, uniformed group makes us more likely to take part in institutional aggression.

Zimbardo (2004) has named deindividuation as one of a number of social processes that contributed to the abuse of Iraqi prisoners at Abu Ghraib, one of the greatest recent scandals of institutional aggression. The Abu Ghraib case came to light in 2004 following the occupation of Iraq. Abu Ghraib is a jail in Baghdad, the capital of Iraq. Following the American takeover of Baghdad, Abu Ghraib was used as a military prison for Iraqi insurgents and suspects. It was later estimated that 90 per cent of detainees were innocent. Insufficiently trained, unsupervised and stressed by their proximity to battle, some US military police and CIA officers subjected prisoners to torture and humiliation. There were striking parallels between some of the abuses

◀ **Figure 4.12**
Lynndie England, who was convicted and imprisoned for committing prisoner abuse at Abu Ghraib

committed at Abu Ghraib and those seen in the Zimbardo prison experiment. For example, guards in both situations tended to sexually humiliate prisoners at night.

Evaluation

Evidence for the role of deindividuation in institutional aggression comes from a cross-cultural study by Watson (1973). He identified 37 societies characterised by high aggression and 47 as low in aggression, as defined by willingness to kill, torture and maim in battle. Watson then looked at the deindividuation practices of each society, for example painting faces or wearing masks to disguise features in battle. Those cultures that deindividuated in battle were significantly more aggressive.

As Zimbardo says, however, deindividuation is just one of the social processes that leads to institutional aggression such as that seen at Abu Ghraib. Others include conformity, role-modelling, role-playing and dehumanisation. In addition, there may be individual differences as well as social processes at work; why, for example, if all the guards at Abu Ghraib were subjected to the same social situation did many not participate in prisoner abuse?

▼ **Figure 4.13** Cross-cultural studies suggest that masked or painted warriors tend to be more aggressive

Other social processes in institutional aggression

Zimbardo is clear that he places the blame for institutional aggression of the type seen in his prison experiment and at Abu Ghraib on the situation not the individual. He describes himself as a *situationalist* because he believes that most human behaviour can be explained by the social situation rather than the character of the individual. Zimbardo served as an expert witness in the trial of Sergeant Chip Frederick, one of the Abu Ghraib guards. His argument was that people influenced by powerful systems like the military lose some of their free will and therefore have diminished responsibility for their actions in the same way as does someone who commits a crime as a result of a serious mental health problem.

Zimbardo suggests that role-modelling, role-taking, conformity and dehumanisation are also important. We have already looked at role-modelling. Recall your work on conformity from your AS level. Conformity takes place when we adopt the behaviour of those around us. This may be due to informational influence, in which we trust that the majority must be right, and normative influence, in which we fear social rejection if we do not conform. *Dehumanisation* takes place when we portray a group as less than human. In the run-up to the Holocaust the Nazis dehumanised Jews by portraying them as animals in cartoons and as monsters in children's fairy tales. Once a group is thought of as not quite human, it becomes easier to deny the people in it what we normally think of as human rights.

Thinking practically about psychology

Read the following extracts from an interview with Lynndie England from *Stern* magazine, Germany. What evidence of role-modelling and conformity influences can you see? Does the conformity seem to be more about normative or informational influence?

Extract 1 I just wanted to serve my country and be a patriot, I guess. As a child I mainly grew up on military gung-ho movies so that's where I got the idea. Old Chuck Norris movies, '*Delta Force*', '*Rambo*', '*Missing in Action*', '*Platoon*'.

Extract 2 Of course it was wrong. I know that now. But when you show the people from the CIA, the FBI and the MI the pictures and they say, 'Hey, this is a great job. Keep it up,' you think it must be right. They were all there and they didn't say a word. They didn't wear uniforms, and if they did they had their nametags covered.

KEY TERMS

situationalism the belief that human behaviour has more to do with the social situation than the personality of the actor

dehumanisation the strategy of making a group appear less than human

LOOKING FURTHER You can read an interview with Zimbardo about Abu Ghraib here: http://www.wired.com/science/discoveries/news/2008/02/ted_zimbardo?currentPage=1 and watch a video of Zimbardo commenting on footage of Abu Ghraib here: http://www.wired.com/video/abu-ghraib-how-good-people-turn-evil/9472299001. Contains disturbing scenes.

Exploring issues and debates
Free will and determination

'The Abu Ghraib case raises the issue of free will vs determinism because we need to judge the guilt of guards who committed abuses under extreme pressure from the situation.'

Construct a table. In one column list the social pressures the guards were under. In the other, list the arguments for saying they were still responsible.

Biological explanations of aggression

Studies into the development of aggression often find that aggressive children have aggressive parents. One explanation for this is the role of social factors. However, this is not the only possible cause. Individuals may be more aggressive than average due to some biological difference. If this difference is heritable, then it would be possible for parents to pass on their aggressive tendencies to their children and we should be able to identify patterns using twin or adoption studies.

For genes to have an effect on behaviour they must act through a biological mechanism such as hormones or the brain. If this is the case, it should be possible to investigate 'biological correlates of behaviour', that is to find hormone levels or brain areas that are linked to the control of aggressive behaviour.

It is unlikely that a simple set of factors controls all kinds of aggression. In animals, two kinds of attack can be observed. Imagine a tom cat fighting an intruder – all bristling fur and highly aroused. The same cat killing a mouse will hardly be aroused at all. This contrast can also

be seen in human aggressive behaviour. Consider the difference between a child who bites and kicks another out of anger, and one who deliberately hides someone else's homework to get them into trouble. These two kinds of 'attack', called *affective* (the emotional kind) and *non-affective* (the cold, calculating kind) are unlikely to be controlled by identical biological systems. However, it is possible that individuals may inherit a genetic predisposition to become more aggressive under certain situations, and that there are some of the same biological systems controlling such aggression.

The roles of genes

Lagerspetz (1979) bred 25 generations of mice. In each generation, she chose the least aggressive individuals to breed together and the most aggressive ones to breed together. The result was two very different strains. One group of mice were super-aggressive, the other very docile. This showed that there is, at least in animals, a genetic component to aggressive behaviour. To be certain that this difference was not due to social influences, Lagerspetz & Wuorinen (1965) cross-fostered offspring from the seventh generation. Even when raised by non-aggressive mothers, the mice from the 'aggressive' strain still demonstrated more aggressive behaviour.

Nobody is suggesting, however, that there is a single 'gene for aggression' in humans or animals. Nor is it likely that aggressiveness is simply the product of a combination of genes; the environment is clearly important too. Even so, how much genes matter and which genes are important is of great interest. Many investigations of aggression, criminality and antisocial behaviour have shown that there is a significant genetic contribution. In a meta-analysis of twin and adoption studies, Mason & Frick (1994) estimated a mean heritability of 0.48 for such behaviours.

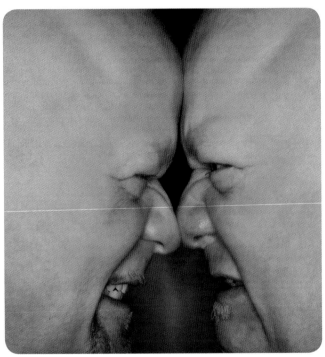

▲ **Figure 4.14** The aggression in these twins is likely to be influenced by their genes

It is possible to see that genes and the environment must be interacting in the development of aggressive behaviour from the combined findings of twin and adoption studies. If the aggression levels in monozygotic twins are not a lot more similar than in dizygotic twins, this suggests that the environment is important. This was what Lyons et al. (1995) found when they investigated misbehaviour and juvenile crime in thousands of twins. However, records of criminal and aggressive behaviour in *adult* twins showed that monozygotic twins were indeed more similar. This suggests that genetic factors are more important in adulthood than in childhood. One explanation for this is that, in childhood, individuals' environment is controlled, for example their exposure to violent television or being made to play with 'sensible' friends. As adults, however, individuals with aggressive tendencies can make choices that increase the risk of behaving aggressively.

Thinking creatively about psychology

If you were asked to suggest ways to reduce adult aggressive behaviour, what advice would you give on the basis of the findings of Lyons et al. (1995)?

KEY TERMS

NOS a gene with many variants that has been linked to aggression. It is involved in the production of an enzyme with a role in the control of nitric oxide which, among other things, acts as a neurotransmitter

knock-out a term used to refer to animals that have a particular gene deleted

Cadoret et al. (1995) found that adopted children were somewhat more likely to show aggressive behaviours and have conduct disorders either if their adoptive home was disrupted by, for example, marital disputes or drug problems, or if their biological parents had criminal records. However, when they were exposed to *both* of these factors, the risk was much greater. This illustrates how genes and the environment can interact.

As evidence suggests there is a role for genes in human aggression, it should be possible to identify some of the genes involved. Research in this area has already identified genes in animals that are associated with aggression. The NOS gene has several variants that are involved in aggressive behaviour in rodents. Demas et al. (1999) found that deleting the eNOS2/2 gene eliminated aggression in male mice – even though they had extra-strong front legs! Conversely, Nelson RJ et al. (1995) found that male mice with the nNOS2/2 gene deleted were *more* aggressive than normal.

In a review of such experiments, Nelson RJ et al. (2006) questioned whether these changes in behaviour could be due to changes in pain sensitivity or anxiety. They suggest that increased aggression in male mice with a different deletion (nNOS-1-/- knock-out mice) might be because they are also less sensitive to pain and less anxious. This shows that genetic influences on aggressive behaviour are complex, with many behavioural systems involved, as well as the interaction with environmental factors.

Few studies have investigated the roles of specific genes in the control of aggressive behaviour in humans in the same detail as those studied in animals. In a study of 153 men attending psychiatric assessments in relation to criminal behaviour, Retz et al. (2004) looked at the relationship between violent behaviour and a variant gene called 5-HTTLPR. They found an association between a particular form of the gene and violent behaviour when the individuals had symptoms like ADHD in childhood, but not when they had symptoms of personality disorder or impulsivity. Retz et al. concluded that this gene (which controls aspects of the neurotransmitter serotonin) is associated with violent behaviour in male criminals. Another study linking a gene to human aggression is described in the *Research Now* box.

RESEARCH NOW

Reif A, Jacob CP, Rujescu D, Herterich S, Lang S, Gutknecht L, Baehne CG, Strobel A, Freitag CM, Giegling I, Romanos M, Hartmann A, Rösler M, Renner TJ, Fallgatter AJ, Retz W, Ehlis AC & Lesch KP (2009) Influence of functional variant of neuronal nitric oxide synthase on impulsive behaviors in humans. *Archives of General Psychiatry* **66**(1), 41–50

Aim: To investigate links between impulsivity (which could be a factor in aggression) and variants of the NOS1 gene in humans.

Procedure: One part of the study looked for an association between impulsivity and the gene variant NOS1 Ex1f VNTR using over 3200 participants from German psychiatric clinics (1954 controls, 403 with personality disorder, 383 with ADHD, 151 with ADHD in their family, 189 who had attempted suicide and 182 criminals). Other parts of the study used molecular and imaging techniques to see how the gene variant affected the brain.

Findings: The gene variant was more frequent in adults with ADHD, some personality disorders, and aggressive behaviour to the self and other people. In terms of brain activity, the gene variant reduced activity in the anterior cingulate cortex, a brain area involved in controlling behaviour which processes information about emotion and reward.

Conclusion: The gene variant appears to affect a brain system with control of impulsive behaviour that is associated with aggression.

Thinking critically about psychology

Compare the findings of Reif *et al.* (2009) and Retz *et al.* (2004) with regard to impulsivity and aggression. What can you conclude about the two genes?

Hormones and aggression

Studies of cultural differences (see p132) suggest that males are typically more aggressive than females. Of course, this difference could be environmental – they are affected by aggressive models or reinforcement – but it is likely that there are also biological differences. One important difference is in the levels of the hormone testosterone (see also p129). The hormone is found in both sexes, but adult males produce about 10 times more than adult females. In males, the testes produce testosterone from birth, the levels escalating at puberty – and males aged 15–25, with the highest levels of testosterone, are also the most likely group to commit violent crimes. The effect of testosterone on aggression is also well known from its role in animal behaviour. A castrated cat or dog is much less aggressive than an entire one.

Roman emperors employed eunuchs – castrated males – to make them unlikely to rebel. Investigating the role of testosterone in human aggression using castration is not, however, an option! Instead, investigations rely on animal studies or on measuring testosterone levels and correlating this with reported or observed indicators of aggression.

Olweus *et al.* (1980) measured blood testosterone levels in 16-year-old boys and assessed aggression using a questionnaire. Higher levels of self-reported physical and verbal aggression were associated with higher levels of testosterone. Whilst such differences are well documented, there are exceptions to this pattern. People with high levels of testosterone are not exclusively driven towards aggression. Their energy and drive may alternatively be directed towards sport or success in their chosen career. If testosterone were the major force behind aggression, we would expect all men to be aggressive and women not to be. This obviously isn't the case: there are aggressive women and non-aggressive men. This suggests that the relationship between testosterone and aggression is not a simple one; other factors must clearly be involved. Since the relationship between testosterone and aggression is correlational, we cannot be sure that high testosterone levels are even *causing* aggressive behaviour, or whether both high testosterone and high levels of aggression are the consequence of some other factor.

◀ **Figure 4.15** Reducing testosterone levels by castration is often used to reduce aggression in pet, farm and zoo animals

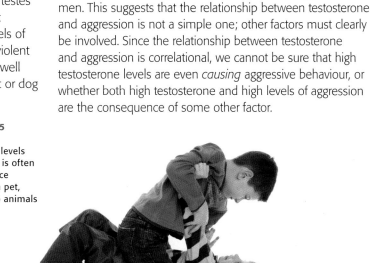

◀ **Figure 4.16** Are boys biologically destined to be aggressive?

Experiments with male animals have shown that castration reduces aggression and that injecting testosterone reinstates aggressive behaviour (Beeman, 1947). Early castration generally has the lasting effect of reducing aggression, apparently changing the animal's predisposition permanently. If, however, testosterone is repeatedly administered to castrated animals they will eventually become aggressive. These findings suggest that testosterone has two roles, firstly to prime the individual for behaving aggressively (eg by changing its nervous system), and secondly to initiate aggressive responses. This interpretation is supported by evidence showing that injected testosterone also increases aggression between females (van de Poll *et al.*, 1988).

Thinking creatively about psychology

Some zoo and farm animals cannot be castrated to reduce their aggression as it affects other aspects of their development. For example, castrated fallow deer grow less muscle and more fat. Wilson *et al.* (2002) investigated the effect of two drugs that inhibit the action of testosterone, and looked at several variables including aggressive behaviour and growth of antlers. Design a method that Wilson *et al.* could have used.

◀ **Figure 4.17** Fallow deer fighting

There is usually, but not always, a direct link between testosterone level and aggression in animals. Is this the case in humans? Although men are typically more aggressive than women, and more likely to pick a fight with no apparent reason (Bettencourt & Miller, 1996), women do demonstrate as much aggression as men when they are seriously provoked. Unsurprisingly, Dabbs *et al.* (1995) found that male prison inmates who had committed violent crimes had higher levels of testosterone than those committing non-violent crimes (see Figure 4.18). Interestingly, Dabbs & Hargrove (1997) found the same relationship in female prisoners. These patterns, however, were not strong, indicating that other factors are also at work – the control of behaviour, including aggressive behaviour, is simply more complex in humans than in animals. In a series of experimental studies with students, Dabbs *et al.* (2001) demonstrated that individuals with high testosterone levels were more assertive, direct and confident in their interactions

with other people. This finding could explain the prevalence of the most cold-hearted and premeditated murderers among the prisoners with the highest testosterone levels.

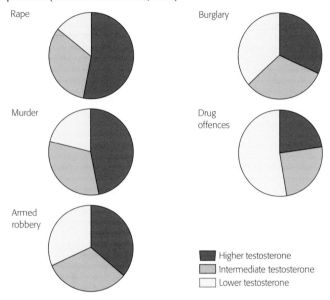

▼ **Figure 4.18** Testosterone levels in violent and non-violent male prisoners (based on Dabbs *et al.*, 1995)

Neural mechanisms in aggression

The findings from van de Poll *et al.* (1988) (see above) suggest that testosterone affects early development and influences the tendency of an animal to become aggressive later. One way in which such an effect might operate is through the 'priming' of neural systems. Testosterone may influence brain development such that the individual is more inclined towards aggressive responses. A range of experimental evidence confirms that there are indeed specific brain areas involved in aggressive responses and that these may be sensitive to testosterone levels during development.

Early research into the control of aggressive behaviour indicated that the hypothalamus was important. Bard (1929) showed that decorticate cats (ones with their cortex removed) were overly aggressive, responding to the slightest provocation with arched backs, growling, hissing and bared teeth. This 'sham rage' could not, however, be elicited if the hypothalamus had also been removed. More recent research has shown that stimulation of the ventromedial hypothalamus leads to the spontaneous production of aggressive responses (Siegel & Pott, 1988). These findings suggested that the hypothalamus plays a role in the expression of aggressive behaviours.

↻ Exploring issues and debates
Reductionism

The hypothalamus: an all-purpose brain area

If you are also studying the psychopathology of eating disorders (Chapter 9) or eating behaviour (Chapter 5) you will encounter another role for the hypothalamus – in satiation. Think about why basic behaviours such as aggression and eating might be controlled by the same brain area and why, although this neural control system is present in both animals and humans, it appears to be less important in humans.

The amygdala, an area of the brain close to the hypothalamus, is also involved in aggression. Direct stimulation of an area of the amygdala in hamsters produces aggressive behaviour (Potegal *et al.*, 1996). This area is also involved in real aggression. When an animal attacks another (eg a hamster defending its territory) it stays on 'red alert' for about half an hour and is more likely to attack than it would be normally.

Potegal *et al.* (1996) found that the same area of the amygdala – that produces aggression when stimulated – was more active during this period of 'red alert'. People seem to respond in a similar way. We too are 'armed' to be more aggressive for 5–20 minutes after being provoked (Potegal, 1994).

CLASSIC RESEARCH

Raine A, Buchsbaum M & LaCasse L (1997) Brain abnormalities in murderers indicated by positron emission tomography. *Biological Psychiatry* **42, 495–508**

Aim: To investigate patterns of brain activity in murderers compared with a matched sample of non-murderers using positron emission tomography (PET) to see whether there are differences in areas of the prefrontal cortex thought to be involved in violent behaviour.

Procedure: An experimental group consisted of 41 participants charged with murder or manslaughter who had pleaded 'not guilty by reasons of insanity' but had been convicted (referred to as 'murderers'). Their mean age was 34.3 years and there were 39 men and two women. A control group was matched for sex and age. Six of the murderers had a diagnosis of schizophrenia and were matched to controls who were also diagnosed schizophrenics. No participants took any medication for at least two weeks prior to testing. Following a practice task, participants were injected with a radioactive glucose tracer, then did a 'continuous performance task' – a visual task that increases brain activity in the frontal lobes of normal participants – for 32 minutes. A PET scan was performed immediately after this, taking 10 horizontal images through the brain at 10mm intervals. These scans were then used to indicate the level of activity in many different brain areas.

Findings: Significant differences in activity levels in many areas were found between murderers and controls. In areas such as the lateral and medial prefrontal cortex the murderers showed much less activity (see Figures 4.20a and b). Other areas showing differences included the amygdala, thalamus and hippocampus. In some areas, such as the thalamus and the area surrounding the hippocampus, there was a difference in lateralisation. In both cases the murderers' brains were more active on the right than the left. In the control participants' brains there was equal activity in both sides of the thalamus and in the hippocampus the pattern was opposite to that of the murderers, ie there was more activity on the left.

Conclusion: The areas identified as having abnormal activity are associated with a lack of fear, lowered self-control, increased aggression and impulsive behaviours and problems with controlling and expressing emotions. All of these could lead to an increased risk of committing acts of extreme violence. They are also linked to problems with learning conditioned emotional responses and failure to learn from experiences, which could account for the type of violent offences committed. Finally, effects on areas associated with learning could lower IQ, which links to lower chances of employment and a higher risk of criminality.

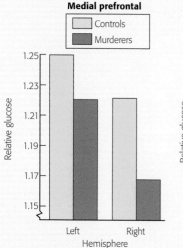

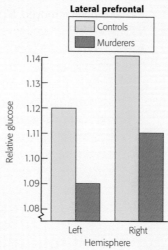

▲ **Figure 4.19** The level of brain activity indicated by the rate of use of glucose in murderers compared with controls

▼ **Figure 4.20** Do serial killers – like those depicted in the film *Natural Born Killers* – have different brains?

Thinking critically about psychology

Why are studies such as Raine *et al.*'s more useful than those looking at the effects of brain lesions on human aggression?

Lesioning the amygdala in animals reduces aggressive behaviour. This finding led to attempts to control severe cases of human aggressive behaviour with a surgical procedure to remove the amygdala (amygdalectomy). Although the operation was moderately successful in reducing aggressive behaviour, Aggleton (1993) questions whether surgery can be justified since it is not always effective and leaves patients so emotionally unreactive that they can appear sedated.

Thinking practically about psychology

You may have been told to 'count to 10' before responding if you are angry. Do you think 10 is enough?

As you will recall from your AS level, communication between neurones is achieved by neurotransmitters and particular groups of neurones often operate using the same neurotransmitter. One neurotransmitter, serotonin, is associated with aggressive behaviour. Specifically, low levels of serotonin turnover (how quickly it is recycled after use) are linked with higher aggression. In a laboratory experiment with mice, Valzelli (1973) showed that males with lower serotonin levels were more likely to fight when put together. Furthermore, Valzelli & Bernasconi (1979) demonstrated differences in serotonin levels between more and less aggressive strains of mice. In a natural environment study of rhesus monkeys, Higley *et al.* (1996) found that those males with the lowest serotonin levels were most likely to fight, had the most scars and wounds and were more likely to be dead by age six years than those with the highest serotonin levels. The aggressive monkeys were more likely to pick fights with opponents they could not possibly beat and to take other risks such as jumping from trees higher than 7 metres!

◄ **Figure 4.21** Rhesus monkeys with low serotonin levels take risks like jumping from great heights and picking more fights

'It's not my fault, it's my serotonin.'

To what extent do you think it would be useful and appropriate for courts to use evidence from serotonin turnover to decide whether to give violent prisoners parole?

Serotonin seems to be important in people too. For example, Virkkunen *et al.* (1987) found that violent offenders had a lower than average serotonin turnover. They were also more likely to commit further violent crimes after their release from prison (Virkkunen *et al.*, 1989). Such findings link to genetic research. For example, Chen *et al.* (1994) found that mice with a mutation that caused reduced release of serotonin were more aggressive. However, the relationship is not a simple one. Brunner *et al.* (1993) studied a Dutch family, many of whom were aggressive. The antisocial behaviour of members of this family was linked to a mutation of the gene for monoamine oxidase type-A (MAO-A), the enzyme that breaks down serotonin. Since the mutation cased a *lack* of this enzyme, logically it should have produced a *reduction* in aggression as it would be more difficult for the body to dispose of serotonin.

Thinking practically about psychology

Serotonin levels can be altered by dietary control. Serotonin is manufactured in the body from the amino acid tryptophan, but high levels of another amino acid, phenylalanine, make it difficult for the body to obtain tryptophan as they share a 'transporter'. Moeller *et al.* (1996) showed that young men on an unbalanced diet like this became more aggressive within hours of eating. The artificial sweetener aspartame (Nutrasweet) is high in phenylalanine and low in tryptophan. What would you recommend about suitable diets for people with aggressive tendencies?

Discussion of biological explanations of aggression

Early evidence suggested a role for genes in the control of aggressive behaviour, and subsequent research has confirmed this. However, this does not mean that genes *control* aggression but that there is a genetic influence on aggressive behaviour. We have neither identified all the genes involved in aggressive responses nor concluded that genetic influences alone are the cause of aggressive behaviour – even in animals.

Whilst evidence relating to some of the probable routes through which genes may act, such as priming brain development or altering neurotransmitter levels has been found, this is incomplete. Furthermore, some evidence, such as that relating to the role of genes controlling serotonin levels, is contradictory. Similarly, although testosterone undoubtedly influences aggressive behaviour, its relationship to levels of aggression is unclear. Finally, many brain areas have been identified that play a role in the expression of aggression, but the extent to which any one is responsible for aggressive behaviour is difficult to establish. This is especially so because there are different types of aggressive behaviour in both animals and humans and these are controlled in different ways.

Aggression as an adaptive response

There are several levels at which biological explanations can try to account for aggressive behaviour. The approaches we have seen explain aggression at 'proximal' and 'ontogenic' levels. The proximate causes are the immediate triggers for aggressive behaviours. The ontogenic explanations account for how aggressive responses develop, for example under the influence of genes. An alternative approach looks at the 'ultimate' reasons for aggressive behaviour. Aggression may have been an effective solution to a problem facing our evolutionary ancestors – the 'ultimate' reason for aggression would therefore be that it was a behaviour that increased survival and reproduction.

Evolutionary explanations of aggression

Evolution by natural selection operates because the physical and/or social environment places pressures on individuals that make it hard to survive. As individuals vary, for example in how aggressive they are, there may be differences in their survival and reproduction as a result. If aggressive individuals tended to be more likely to survive, *and* if this behavioural difference was at least in part genetically controlled, they would pass their aggressiveness on to their offspring. More aggressive individuals would therefore be born and the population would progressively contain more aggressive individuals. This would suggest that aggression was an *adaptive* response. However, imagine an alternative scenario. Some individuals are highly aggressive and frequently kill each other. What sorts of individuals are more likely to survive and reproduce now? Those who are non-aggressive and successfully avoid conflict. We can explore the extent to which these explanations applied to humans during their early evolution, and in the modern world.

Recall the study of rhesus monkeys by Higley *et al.* (p88). Many monkeys were highly aggressive and most of them died. If aggression were always a 'bad idea', highly aggressive individuals would be less likely to survive and aggressive behaviour would, eventually, be infrequent. However, the existence of aggressive behaviour within animal populations indicates that it does have survival value – for example for defending territory, food, mates or offspring.

Since actual aggression is clearly detrimental, it is relatively infrequent. Humans evolved from ape-like animals. Modern non-human apes are large, strong animals with powerful limbs and jaws. Within groups of apes such as gorillas and chimpanzees, it is not uncommon for animals to be harmed in fights, although the general level of aggression is quite low. This is made possible by the use of aggressive displays, which have evolved precisely because it is safer for an individual to indicate that it is strong than to have to risk injury demonstrating their strength. Look at Figure 4.17 of fallow deer fighting. This is typical of males in competition for status and therefore for access to females to mate with. One deer could easily kill the other with a prong on its antler, but their aggressive behaviour has evolved to minimise the risk of death but still enable individuals to assess who is stronger.

Sexual aggression in humans

As you may discover in Chapter 6 (on gender), there are evolutionary explanations for the differences between the behaviour of men and women with respect to their choice of mates and their behaviour. One important idea is that although a woman can be certain whether a child is her own, a man cannot. Evolutionary theory would predict that men would have developed strategies for avoiding *cuckoldry* (unknowingly raising a child that is not their own), ie behaviours that would ensure paternity certainty. There are two possible options, mate-guarding and sanctions against infidelity by women.

K E Y   T E R M

cuckoldry   when a male is tricked by a female into raising the offspring of another male

---

Mate-guarding is seen in animals and is a strategy to ensure that the male who invests in the offspring is indeed their father. In evolutionary terms, a male who jealously defends his mate against alternative potential mates would be more successful. Males would therefore need to be able and be prepared to fight over females. In humans, the institution of marriage serves to formalise the mate-guarding function, thus, at least theoretically, reducing the need for actual aggression. Daly & Wilson (1994) suggest that, in the course of evolution, young men would have had to display aggressive behaviour in warfare and hunting in order to win mates and that they are physically and psychologically adapted to take risks and be confrontational. For example, young male drivers have a high incidence of accidents as they behave dangerously. Young males in every society studied also have the highest rates of same-sex homicide (Daly & Wilson, 1988) and these are usually the consequence of disputes over status compared with other males or directly about women. It is interesting to note that, in Britain, one of the three defences that a man can use to reduce the charge of murder to manslaughter is sexual contact with his wife.

▼ **Figure 4.22** Can male aggression be explained by evolutionary theory?

Both males and females experience sexual jealousy, but for different reasons and with different consequences. Females need to protect the resources offered by their partner (see Chapter 3). Males on the other hand need to ensure their partner's fidelity. Buss *et al.* (1992) asked male and female students the question: 'What would distress you more? (a) imagining your mate having sexual intercourse with someone else or (b) imagining your mate forming a deep emotional attachment to someone else? Response (a) represents a threat to paternity certainty and (b) represents a threat to domestic security. Sixty per cent of the men chose (a) and 85 per cent of the women chose (b), supporting the idea of male sexual jealousy. Interestingly, of the 40 per cent of males who did not choose (a), most had never had a committed sexual relationship so were unlikely to have experienced sexual jealousy. This suggested that, even if there is an underlying evolutionary mechanism behind male sexual aggression, it is modified by experience.

An alternative male strategy is to attempt to prevent infidelity by controlling the female partner. Some actions, such as coming home at unpredictable times, are non-violent but other strategies may explain aggression towards *women* rather than towards other men. Daly & Wilson (1992) report that in every culture studied, adultery by a woman is considered to be an offence against her husband and is likely to precipitate violence. Furthermore, a cuckolded husband has the legal right to murder his wife in many societies (Daly *et al.*, 1982). Indeed, men are more likely to kill their estranged wives than vice versa, and jealousy appears to be the main motive in the killing of a spouse (Daly & Wilson, 1988). Wife-killing seems counterproductive in terms of reproductive success. However, if a husband suspects that his wife may bear the child of another man, he faces both a reduction in his own reproductive success and an increase in that of his rival. In evolutionary terms, killing his wife is therefore adaptive. Note that arguments such as this above do not justify aggression. Humans, unlike animals, are rational and can choose to control their behaviour.

It has been claimed that some historical aids to beauty may in fact have been strategies employed by males to ensure the fidelity of their wives. The neck rings worn by some women in Myanmar stretch the neck and cause the neck muscles to weaken. If the woman commits adultery, her husband can remove the rings with very painful and potentially fatal results. Without some other means of support, she would be unable to breathe.

▶ **Figure 4.23** The neck rings still worn by some women in Myanmar can be interpreted as an act of aggression by men against women to guarantee their fidelity

Shackelford *et al.* (2005) conducted an investigation of men and women in relationships, looking at their reports of mate-guarding behaviour and violence towards females. Four types of behaviour by males were particularly associated with a risk of female-directed violence. These were:

- *vigilance* – eg 'He dropped by unexpectedly to see what she was doing'
- *emotional manipulation* – eg 'He told her he would *die* if she ever left' and 'He pleaded that he could not live without her'
- *monopolisation of time* – eg 'He monopolised her time at the social gathering'
- *possessive ornamentation* – eg 'He hung up a picture of her so others would know she was taken'

When these behaviours were frequent, especially vigilance, the women were more likely to report violent behaviour. This is clearly an important finding as it may help to identify women who are at risk. However, it is also difficult to determine causality since it was not a longitudinal study.

▲ **Figure 4.24** Many pressure groups campaign against violence towards women. Most of this violence is perpetrated by men

Free will and determinism

'I had to kill him, he stole my wife.'

To what extent can evolutionary theory be used as a defence against committing acts of violence?

Mize *et al.* (2009) used a database of information about 50,000 intimate partner homicides. They found that men are likely to kill their partner by beating and are more likely to do so if dating or cohabiting rather than if they are married. They concluded that the lack of commitment in non-marital relationships produces greater jealousy in men. This drives them to kill the victim in a more violent manner compared with men who kill their wives.

Aggressive group displays in humans

In this section we are concerned with explaining displays of aggression between groups. There are many examples of such aggression, but two notable examples are sporting events and lynch mobs. Let us give a little background to these situations, then look at possible explanations.

Aggression at sporting events

Sporting events involve two (or more) teams and their spectators. Sometimes groups of rival spectators can be extremely aggressive to one another. Much of this aggression is simply in the form of a group display, as terraces full of fans chant, taunt each other and throw occasional missiles. Most such displays do not lead to serious violence, although it is debatable whether this would be true without skilled policing and stewarding. Football clubs frequently also have a *'firm'* associated with them. Firms of football hooligans are highly organised and discrete, meeting rivals for fights away from football grounds. Sometimes sports fans not involved in firms do become involved in serious violence. One of the worst incidents in recent years took place in 2000 when two Leeds fans were killed in a fight with Turkish fans of the Galatasaray team.

Violence associated with sport is nothing new. A few hundred years ago across Europe, football matches were not played by a picked team but by whole towns – some games had over a thousand players and there was no distinction between players and spectators. Games were largely just drunken fights between towns. This led to football being banned at various times, including famously by Henry VIII.

Lynch mobs

Lynching takes place when a mob administers the death penalty independently of the law. Most of the literature looking at the actions of lynch mobs has concerned the hanging of black Americans in the nineteenth and early twentieth centuries. Lynching became common after the abolition of slavery and became so common after the First World War that in 1922 the US Senate considered an anti-lynching bill that would have set a minimum of five years in jail for anyone taking part in a lynch mob. It never became law and it was only in 2005 that the Senate formally apologised for this. Although lynching ends in murder, it is often associated with a much larger group display of aggression. Some of the lynchings of black Americans attracted crowds of several thousand people and were held in a party atmosphere.

▶ **Figure 4.26** Laura Nelson and her son were lynched in 1911 after her son shot a deputy who was searching their house for stolen meat

▲ **Figure 4.25** Leeds and Galatasaray fans clash in Istanbul

KEY TERMS

firm an organised group of football hooligans associated with a particular club

necklacing a current way of killing by lynch mobs. It involves burning the victim to death with a petrol-filled tyre

Lynching is not just an American phenomenon and it still goes on today. In 2004 at Tlahuac, Mexico, three undercover federal agents investigating drug trafficking were mistaken for paedophiles and beaten for several hours before being burned by an angry crowd. In South Africa under the Apartheid regime, those convicted by 'people's courts' were *necklaced*. Necklacing involves forcing a tyre filled with petrol over the arms and chest then setting it alight, killing the victim in around 20 minutes. Currently in South Africa, Zimbabwean immigrants suspected of crimes are sometimes subjected to necklacing.

Explaining group displays of human aggression

Deindividuation

We have already looked at deindividuation as an explanation for aggression in general and for institutional aggression. To recap, deindividuation takes place when we are in a crowd and we focus less on our personal identity and more on our group identity. This leaves us more conformist to the norms of the group and less able to monitor and regulate our behaviour. Deindividuation does not always lead to aggression, but where the group is behaving aggressively then we tend to conform to this new norm and fail to monitor the social acceptability of our actions.

Contrary to popular stereotypes, football crowds are not usually aggressive. The behaviour of football fans is highly ritualised (Marsh, 1978), so although huge chanting crowds might appear intimidating they do not routinely adopt a norm of physical aggression. However, when trouble starts it can be dramatic because of the sheer numbers involved. Large crowds are likely to produce more deindividuation than smaller groups, so deindividuation is likely to be a factor in crowd trouble. The idea that crowds have a collective identity is important in understanding aggression at sporting events. Group identity tends to be strengthened by the presence of opposing forces (Postmes & Spears, 1998). The presence of an opposing crowd at a match therefore pushes football fans into an even closer and more deindividuated group than they were initially.

▼ **Figure 4.27** A Portsmouth fan in an aggressive display to Southampton supporters

Thinking creatively about psychology

Design a study to investigate the link between deindividuation and violence in football crowds. You will need a way to assess deindividuation and a measure of violence.

Postmes (2005) points out how policing practices at football matches have developed in order to take account of our understanding of deindividuation. Traditional crowd control strategies treat everyone in a crowd as equally responsible for individual acts of aggression within the crowd. It follows that action against the crowd will target innocent individuals, which in turn will make the whole crowd more cohesive and aggressive. Modern policing strategies aim to target individuals while being careful not to antagonise the whole crowd. Club stewards also have a key role in modern crowd control. Stewards, who are known by fans to be supporters of the same club, are perceived by crowds as part of the same group rather than an opposing force. As part of the crowd, they can directly influence the norms of its behaviour.

Deindividuation may also be a factor in the behaviour of lynch mobs. Again, collective identity seems to be important because mobs generally kill members of out-groups. In the classic US lynchings, white crowds lynched members of the minority black community. In the current South African lynchings, the minority Zimbabwean community are usually those necklaced. Another reason why deindividuation is likely to be important in lynching is the sheer social unacceptability of the behaviour. People acting as identifiable and accountable individuals with normal capacity to judge their own behaviour against what is socially acceptable do not generally commit cold-blooded murder. Deindividuation explains neatly how people can become capable of such extreme behaviour.

Social dominance theory

Social dominance theory (or SDT) begins with the idea that human societies are organised into groups, each of which has a different status. Groups make up a hierarchy in which some have higher and some lower positions. Sidanius & Pratto (1994) propose three types of hierarchy:

- *gender* – men have more status and power than women
- *age* – adults have more status and power than children and adolescents
- *arbitrary set* – there are also status differences between socially constructed groups such as races, nationalities, social classes or religious groups.

Each society has a range of mechanisms to keep hierarchies in place. Particularly important are *legitimising myths*. These are common beliefs used to justify social hierarchies. For example a society might hold the belief that women are not intelligent, responsible or moral enough to hold positions of authority. A common legitimising myth is that minority ethnic groups are less intelligent than the dominant group.

According to SDT, the group tendency to form hierarchies is evolutionary in origin. Historically, societies where adult males are firmly in control have tended to be more efficient in combat, therefore more likely to survive wars and pass on the tendency to maintain rigid hierarchies. Gender and age hierarchies exist in all cultures. The arbitrary set, however, does not exist in hunter-gatherer societies but it emerges whenever a society has more resources than it needs for survival. All aggression between groups can be traced to the instinct to form group hierarchies.

As individuals we differ in our social dominance orientation (SDO). This is the extent to which we desire and support the dominance of groups at the top of the hierarchy over those lower down. Generally, men have a higher SDO than women. Those in high status groups and those low in empathy also tend to be highly socially dominant in their orientation. The standard measure of social dominance orientation is the SDO scale, shown in Table 4.1.

So what can social dominance theory bring to our understanding of group displays of aggression that deindividuation cannot? To take lynch mobs first, lynchings are virtually always carried out by a dominant group against another group that is lower in the hierarchy. This is neatly explained by STD because dominant groups can use lynching as a display of their social power. Such displays become particularly important when the dominance of the highest status group is challenged. This would predict that lynching becomes particularly common when social change in favour of the lower status group occurs. In the case of black Americans, lynching became well established after slavery was abolished, and increased dramatically after the First World War when campaigners challenged the practice of having separate black and white army units. More famous cases took place in response to the 1960s Civil Rights Movement. This is precisely what we would expect from a social dominance perspective.

The existence of legitimising myths being used to maintain the dominance of white Americans over the black community is also well documented. Morton LG (2007) reminds us that sexual threat is a powerful way of maintaining prejudice against a group. In the USA, the myth that black men had an insatiable desire for white women was used to whip up resentment against black men. Even those not actively hostile to black Americans bought into legitimising myths to keep them 'in their place'. Following the lynching of Laura Nelson in 1911 (Figure 4.26), the district judge who investigated the case concluded: 'The more then does the duty devolve upon us of superior race and of greater intelligence to protect this weaker race from unjustifiable and lawless attacks'. This may seem a bizarre statement by modern standards, but from an SDT perspective it served to maintain legitimising myths about black people and so maintain white dominance.

▶ **Figure 4.28** Protests by black American soldiers that they had earned equality by fighting in the First World War resulted in a wave of lynchings

▼**Table 4.1** The social dominance orientation scale

		Strongly disagree				Strongly agree		
1	Some groups of people are simply inferior to other groups	1	2	3	4	5	6	7
2	In getting what you want, it is sometimes necessary to use force against other groups	1	2	3	4	5	6	7
3	It's OK if some groups have more of a chance in life than others	1	2	3	4	5	6	7
4	To get ahead in life, it is sometimes necessary to step on other groups	1	2	3	4	5	6	7
5	If certain groups stayed in their place, we would have fewer problems	1	2	3	4	5	6	7
6	It's probably a good thing that certain groups are at the top and other groups are at the bottom	1	2	3	4	5	6	7
7	Inferior groups should stay in their place	1	2	3	4	5	6	7
8	Sometimes other groups must be kept in their place	1	2	3	4	5	6	7
9	It would be good if groups could be equal	1	2	3	4	5	6	7
10	Group equality should be our ideal	1	2	3	4	5	6	7
11	All groups should be given an equal chance in life	1	2	3	4	5	6	7
12	We should do what we can to equalise conditions for different groups	1	2	3	4	5	6	7
13	Increased social equality	1	2	3	4	5	6	7
14	We would have fewer problems if we treated people more equally	1	2	3	4	5	6	7
15	We should strive to make incomes as equal as possible	1	2	3	4	5	6	7
16	No group should dominate in society	1	2	3	4	5	6	7

SDT can also be used to explain football violence. There are, of course, key differences between the two situations. Unlike football crowds, lynch mobs gather in response to a crime (real or imagined), and their shared purpose is explicitly aggressive. However, the two situations have one very important characteristic in common. They are highly public *displays* of aggression. Lynching has often attracted large crowds and takes place in a party atmosphere. This is easy to explain using SDT because the real purpose of the lynching is for the dominant group to assert their position at the top of the group hierarchy. Football violence, by contrast, can be explained by SDT as an attempt to achieve this dominance in a situation where there is no clear hierarchy.

According to SDT we have an instinct to form group hierarchies based on gender, age and more arbitrary divisions like race. SDT would predict that the greater the visible difference between two football teams and their supporters, the more they will be seen to be different groups with different status and so the more violence. Now that most UK football clubs are multi-ethnic we would expect less violence than in international matches where the division between teams and supporters is along ethnic lines. This is, in fact, the case. Evans & Rowe (2002) analysed the 40 matches played in Europe by English teams. Far more crowd trouble was recorded in internationals, ie when the England team played other national teams, than when English club teams played European clubs.

Thinking creatively about psychology

Deindividuation and social dominance both seem to explain aspects of group displays of aggression. See if you can put them together and produce a new theory that combines both ideas.

Chapter summary

Social learning and deindividuation

- Social learning theory explains aggression as learnt by imitation of models and reinforcement of aggressive behaviour.
- Social learning has proved particularly important in understanding the possible impact of media violence on aggression.
- Deindividuation is important in explaining aggression in groups. A modern understanding of deindividuation sees it as a process in which we conform to the norms of a crowd, lose some of our ability to self-monitor and adopt the identity of a group.
- Institutional aggression can be partly explained by both social learning theory and deindividuation. Social learning theory explains that when we enter an institutional setting we tend to imitate those who have status in that environment. Deindividuation explains why we become capable of highly aggressive acts when part of a group, particularly a cohesive uniformed group.

Biological explanations

- It seems likely that our tendency for aggression is genetically influenced. Genes have been isolated that appear to influence aggression in humans and animals.
- A major hormonal influence on aggression is testosterone. It primes the individual for aggressive behaviour during development and increases aggressive behaviour in adults. However, the effects of testosterone on aggression are complex.
- Various brain areas including the hypothalamus, amygdala and parts of the cortex have all been associated with aggressive responses. None individually acts as an 'aggression centre'.

Evolutionary explanations

- Evolutionary theory can help to explain male aggression. Sexual jealousy can explain aggression towards other males as it helps to raise status and guard the female partner. Threatened or actual violence towards the female partner by males can also be explained by evolutionary theory as a way to reduce the risk of infidelity. Both of these strategies reduce the risk of cuckoldry.
- It has suggested that aggression is adaptive, ie it increases an individual's chances of survival. The truth may be slightly more complex: under some circumstances aggression may be adaptive, but note that some species have evolved aggressive displays to reduce the extent of real aggression.
- Humans have group displays of aggression, for example in lynchings and by crowds at sporting events. Deindividuation is likely to be a partial explanation for crowd behaviour in both these situations.
- Social dominance theory is also useful in explaining both these situations. SDT suggests that we have an instinct to organise societies into groups of different status. Lynching can be seen as a way of asserting the dominance of the high status group over others, whereas football violence can be seen as an attempt to establish such dominance.

What do I know?

1 (a) Describe social learning theory as an explanation of aggression. (9 marks)

  (b) Evaluate social learning theory as an explanation of aggression. (16 marks)

2 (a) Outline what is meant by deindividuation. (5 marks)

  (b) Describe and evaluate explanations of group displays of aggression in humans. (20 marks)

3 (a) Describe genetic and hormonal explanations of aggression. (10 marks)

  (b) Evaluate **one** of these biological explanations. (15 marks)

4 (a) Outline evolutionary explanations of aggression. (5 marks)

  (b) Compare the evolutionary explanation to **one** other explanation of aggression. (10 marks)

  (c) Evaluate the biological influence of neural mechanisms on aggression. (10 marks)

5 Describe and evaluate explanations of institutional aggression. (25 marks)

CHAPTER 5
Eating Behaviour

Thinking ahead

By the end of this chapter you should be able to:

- describe factors influencing attitudes to food and eating behaviour
- give explanations for the success or failure of dieting
- outline and evaluate the role of neural mechanisms involved in controlling eating and satiation
- outline and evaluate evolutionary explanations of food preference
- outline and evaluate psychological explanations of one eating disorder
- outline and evaluate biological explanations, including neural and evolutionary explanations, of one eating disorder, *either* obesity *or* anorexia *or* bulimia

E ating is a requirement necessary to ensure healthy development and
maintenance of energy levels for normal day-to-day living; eating
therefore has a fundamental survival value. At birth we are dependent
upon our carers for all our nutritional needs, but as we age we increasingly
develop our own eating habits and behaviour. In this chapter we will examine
the various biological and psychological explanations and factors that influence
these habits, such as neural mechanisms and cultural factors, as well as
evolutionary explanations.

Although the majority of the population will attain and maintain normal,
healthy eating patterns and body weight levels, a minority of individuals do not
and can be seen as suffering from an eating disorder, such as obesity, anorexia
nervosa and bulimia nervosa. Explanations of such eating disorders again
centre on biological and psychological factors. There is a wealth of research
evidence to support these explanations, though they are not without their
criticisms, and no one explanation can cover all cases of eating disorders.

▲ **Figure 5.1** Eating is a necessary and
generally pleasurable experience

Factors influencing attitudes to food and eating behaviour

A lot of the focus on eating behaviour has tended to be
on abnormal eating patterns that give rise to pathological
disorders such as obesity, but psychologists have also
become increasingly interested in examining the reasons
underpinning normal eating behaviour, as this may give insight
into abnormal eating patterns. The influences that shape our
food preferences and eating behaviour involve biological,
psychological and other factors, such as economics, and these
combine to shape, maintain and alter eating habits. In this
chapter we are particularly concerned with cultural influences,
mood and health concerns.

Mood

Emotional states influence eating behaviour. Wansink *et
al.* (2008) recorded the food choices of 38 participants,
who were offered either hot buttered popcorn or grapes as
they watched either an upbeat comedy or a sad film. Those
watching the sad film consumed 36 per cent more popcorn,
while those watching the comedy consumed more grapes.
The researchers concluded that people who are in a sad mood
want to jolt themselves out of their gloom by eating a quick,
indulgent, nice-tasting snack, while those in a happy mood try
to extend their mood in the long term by eating comfort food
with a nutritional value.

▶ **Figure 5.2** People
watching sad films
eat more popcorn

KEY TERMS

innate food preferences the idea that humans are born
with an attraction to certain foods

learned food preferences the idea that some food
preferences are learned through experience

binge-eating disorder a mental disorder in which people
periodically eat large quantities of food

The researchers then tested to see if nutritional information
influences comfort-food consumption. They offered popcorn
to volunteers who completed several assignments, including
irrelevant mental tasks, describing things that made them
happy or sad and reading happy or sad stories. One group
of participants also reviewed nutritional information about
popcorn, while the other group didn't. Participants in a
sad mood, who did not have nutritional information about
popcorn, ate twice as much as those feeling happy. However,
in the participants who were given nutritional information
about popcorn, the happy people ate about the same amount,
while the sad people curtailed their consumption, eating less
than the happy people. The researchers concluded that people
eat more comfort food when they are sad, but that giving
people in a sad mood nutritional information checks their
consumption. They recommend that comfort foods should
display prominent nutritional information to curb people
with depressed moods from indulging in bad eating habits,
because such people who eat to comfort their mood can
become bulimic, overeating and then purging.

Another approach to investigating the link between mood
and eating is to look at *binge-eating disorder*, which can
be seen as comfort eating taken to an extreme. Wolff *et al.*
(2000), investigated differences between 20 female binge

eaters and 20 female normal eaters. Daily measures of mood, coping and eating behaviour were self-recorded for a three-week period. The binge group reported more stress and negative moods, but stress levels were similar on their binge and non-binge days, which suggests that it was negative mood states that were responsible for binging, especially as negative mood states were more apparent on binge days. The research findings suggest that negative mood states are related to abnormal eating practices such as binge eating.

Health concerns

Another factor that influences people's eating behaviour is the desire to eat foods that are regarded as nutritious and to avoid ones that have been labelled unhealthy. Monneuse *et al.* (1991) found that participants who through taste tests had demonstrated preferences for medium to high sugar content in dairy products, actually consumed items with a lower content, presumably due to health concerns.

Kähkönen & Tuorila (1998) found that information-based expectations can affect food preferences in both a negative or a positive manner. They got young men to rate the expected and actual pleasantness of two types of sausage (normal or reduced fat) either with or without prior information concerning fat content. Unrealistically high expectations created a contrast effect with actual ratings. If the actual quality of the food tasted is a lot lower than expected, then food liking is rated lower than a blind tasting, ie without being given prior information.

▲ **Figure 5.3** People eat more healthily than their food preferences would suggest

Evidence has also been found which suggests that liking based on the sensory qualities of food was a better predictor of consumption than health beliefs. Tuorila & Pangborn (1988) obtained questionnaire data about women's intended and actual consumption of milk, cheese, ice cream and high-fat foods and found that actual consumption was based more on liking than health concerns. Steptoe *et al.* (1995) put into rank order the factors taken into account by participants when choosing food to eat; at the top was sensory appeal, followed by health, convenience and then price.

Cultural factors

Different cultures and subcultures have different eating practices and attitudes that they transmit to group members. Chrisler (1997) reports that culture can influence eating behaviour directly, but more often plays a moderating role on other variables to determine individual eating practices. Learning plays a role in our food preferences and children growing up in different cultures and subcultures will have different experiences and therefore learn different tastes. For example, vegetarians are rewarded by positive responses from other vegetarians whenever they eat vegetarian food and more negative responses if they sample meat.

Not all societies like the same flavours. Stefansson, the famous Arctic explorer, reports (1960) that the Copper Inuits, who lived in isolation from other human groups, had no experience of tea, salt or sugar and lived exclusively on flesh foods and a few roots. In 1910 visiting traders gave them their first taste of sugar, which disgusted them. Although somewhat anecdotal this evidence goes against the idea of a preference for sweetness being universally innate.

Cultural attitudes also vary towards the health concerns associated with eating. McFarlane & Pliner (1987) found that only people who consider nutrition to be important have preferences for healthy foods. This is affected by socio-economic factors: if nutritious foods, such as organic foodstuffs, are too expensive for those on low incomes, then the attitudes of those groups are unlikely to shift in favour of healthy foodstuffs.

▲ **Figure 5.4** Stefansson reported that the Copper Inuits did not like sugar

Thinking practically about psychology

The Japanese fugu (blow-fish) is exceedingly dangerous to eat as it contains deadly toxins. It is a delicacy, but if not prepared exactly correctly can kill. Hundreds of people have died eating this fish, but can you think of an explanation based on personality factors (see earlier) that would explain why people might try it?

KEY TERMS

dieting a form of restrained eating

calories the amount of energy in food

Explanations for the success or failure of dieting

Although not everyone on a diet needs to be, statistics from the USA suggest that *dieting* may be a good move towards being healthier for many people. Bartlett (2003) reports that over 50 per cent of Americans can be classed as overweight or obese and that weight-related conditions are second only to smoking as being preventable causes of morbidity. Three hundred thousand deaths a year can be attributed to such weight-related conditions as increased risk of diabetes, cardiovascular disease, strokes, cancer and lung conditions.

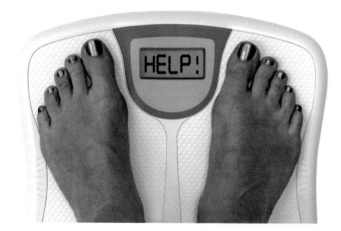

▲ **Figure 5.5** Over 50 per cent of Americans are overweight or obese

Dieting can be classified as a form of restrained eating. There are many reasons why people should indulge in such behaviour and dieters also differ in the extent to which they restrain their eating and for how long. These factors, plus individual differences and social factors, all combine to affect success and failure rates. What an individual classifies as success or failure will also play a determining role.

Technically, dieting itself does not 'fail' as long as it leads to weight loss, because dieting is merely a method of losing weight. What people usually mean when they say a diet failed is that they put the weight back on later. Most diets fail in this

sense because they are unsustainable: the more restrictive a diet is, the less likely it is that people will stick with it. Another reason for failure is that diets generally don't teach people new eating habits that will help them to maintain weight loss. Most overweight people got that way by eating more *calories* than was necessary. Dieting incurs a period of restricting calories, but as the diet is regarded as temporary with a definite end to it, dieters then return to their old eating habits and regain the weight lost. So diets don't fail: it's dieters who fail to learn how to eat properly to prevent weight regain.

Thinking creatively about psychology

Often diets are evaluated by non-scientists and it is wise not to take claims at face value. Design a study to test the effectiveness of a new diet. Consider the following:

1   What sort of design will you use?
2   What controls will you put in place to ensure that any change in dieters is due to the diet?
3   What measures of success will you use?
4   How long will you follow up participants?

Polivy & Herman (1999) see dieting as a voluntary restriction of food intake and believe it may have adaptive benefits, but only when food has a limited availability, therefore dieting may not be a modern behaviour at all. When there is no shortage of food, as in the modern world, then there is no need to diet and that's why it's hard to diet surrounded by food. Therefore dieting is the worst response to plenty, resulting in maladaptive eating behaviours.

Wing & Hill (2001) defined dieting success as 'successful long-term weight loss maintenance, involving the intentional loss of at least 10 per cent of initial body weight and keeping it off for at least one year'. Using their definition they reported that 20 per cent of overweight people meet the criteria for success. They also found that those who did successfully maintain long-term weight loss shared common behaviours that promoted weight loss and its maintenance. These behavioural strategies included a low-fat diet, frequent self-monitoring of weight and food intake, and high levels of physical activity. They also found that once weight loss had been maintained for two years, then the chances of long-term success increased dramatically.

Making dieting more effective

Jeffery (2000) noted that dieting among obese people creates initial rapid weight loss which then slows down. After six months weight regain begins and it was concluded that failure to maintain the behavioural changes of dieting was the main factor for this pattern. This was due to loss of knowledge and skills, loss of motivation and unpleasant side effects such as hunger, stress or social pressure to eat. Jeffery proposed that teaching skills useful for weight maintenance, rather than just weight loss, is important. Focus should be on maintaining a stable energy balance around a lower weight and this can be achieved by *relapse prevention*, which involves teaching people to identify situations in which lapses are likely to occur. Then strategies are created in advance to prevent such lapses, or to get back on track if they do occur. The prime component here is not to treat 'breaking the rules' as failure, as that would lead to negative psychological reactions and a return to pre-weight loss behaviours.

Motivation is an important factor in dieting and several areas have been focused upon including financial incentives and improved social networks. Thomas & Stern (1995) found that modest payments as a reward for weight loss do not enhance initial weight loss, nor do they slow the rate of weight regain. The researchers also reported that strategies to improve social networks have focused on teaching spouses or significant others to provide social support during the weight-loss process and modest success rates have been achieved. Strategies of drawing up contracts in which groups aim for individual or group weight loss targets have also been successful.

WeightWatchers is a very well known and generally successful dieting organisation. Its success is attributable in no small amount to the support its members provide each other. The social support offered here includes the provision of successful role models, vicarious reinforcement and a positive social identity for each member which empowers them to try and succeed. Miller-Kovach *et al.* (2001) reported that being on a WeightWatchers programme was much more successful than using a self-help method over a period of two years. Lowe *et al.* (2004) found that weight losses acheived through being a member of WeightWatchers were reasonably maintained over a five-year period and that an average of 71.6 per cent of people maintained a loss of 5 per cent of body weight or more.

Another important factor in creating motivation and maximising the possibility of dieting success is *goal-setting*. Bartlett (2003) found this is best achieved when goals set are realistic and are objectively defined. Optimal level targets centre around reducing calorific intake by about 500 to 1000 calories a day for a period of about six months; this will generally result in the loss of around one to two pounds of body weight a week. Targets should be open-ended rather than over-specific to maximise chances of success. The goal-setting should include short-, medium- and long-term goals; indeed long-term goals (product orientated) should be best regarded as achievable by a series of short-term goals (process orientated). Progress should be monitored and regular feedback given, with adjustments made to targets if necessary. The dieter should be involved in setting the goals: though utilising expert advice is a good idea, under no circumstances should the targets be imposed upon the dieter as this will reduce the chances of success. Another good practice in goal-setting is to make initial targets easy so that they will be achieved: this increases confidence and motivation levels to succeed towards the next target. This is a form of *operant conditioning*, where the initial success acts as a reinforcer and encourages the dieter to continue towards more success.

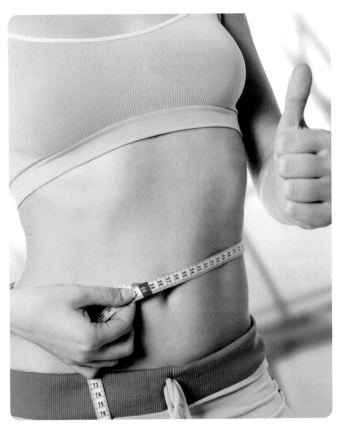

▲ **Figure 5.6** Setting regular goals can make dieting more effective

Factors leading to diet failure

A biological factor that may contribute to diets not succeeding is that of *hormones*. Cummings *et al.* (2002) found that the hormone ghrelin, which is produced in the stomach, stimulates appetite and that being on a low-calorie diet increases ghrelin levels by 24 per cent, thus making hungry people feel even hungrier. This is probably the body's natural response to having restrictions placed upon energy intake; however, it can reduce the chance of dieters losing weight. The success of stomach reduction surgery in achieving weight loss may be attributable to the fact that reduced stomachs produce less ghrelin which therefore does not stimulate the appetite as much.

Cognitive factors have also been associated with dieting failure. Williams *et al.* (2002) used the Dutch Eating Behaviour Questionnaire to measure eating behaviour and attention and found that people who have problems with maintaining concentration were less successful with their diets, presumably because they lose focus on the targets and behavioural strategies they should be undertaking. However D'Anci *et al.* (2008, see below) may be able to explain this finding.

There is other evidence to suggest that low-fat diets can also lead to cognitive impairments, negative moods and even mental health problems. Nolen-Hoeksema (2002) found that many females attempt to address their negative moods by overeating and that 80 per cent of these go on to develop clinical depression within five years. Therefore it is possible that low-fat diets are not only at a high risk of failing to bring about weight loss, but are also bringing about serious mental health problems.

D'Anci *et al.* (2008) investigated the effect of different types of diet upon concentration. Participants regularly completed a battery of cognitive tests during their dieting and the researchers found that losses of concentration among women dieters occurred more to those on a low-carbohydrate diet than a reduced-calorie diet. Those on the low-carbohydrate diet were also deficient in memory performance and scored highly for confusion. When carbohydrates were reintroduced the effects lessened. It does not seem that differences in preoccupation with food were responsible for the results as both groups reported equal measures of hunger ratings. More probable was that the low-carbohydrate diet led to reduced glycogen levels leading to confusion, reduced concentration and impaired memory. The results suggest that different weight-loss regimes may explain the impaired cognitive functioning.

Thinking creatively about psychology

Based on what you have learned about in this chapter, put together a leaflet or web page giving advice on successful dieting.

Biological explanations of eating behaviour

The role of neural mechanisms involved in controlling eating and satiation

The role of the ob gene

Ingalis *et al.* (1950) found the first evidence of a circulating factor involved in the control of appetite when a strain of mice deficient in a gene called 'ob' were discovered. These mice were obese, insulin-resistant and lethargic.

◀ **Figure 5.7** Mouse with deficient 'ob' gene next to normal mouse

KEY TERMS

satiety   the condition of being full or satisfied

hypothalamus   brain area associated with food regulation

ventromedial hypothalamus   brian area linked to satiation

lateral hypothalamus   brain area linked to appetite

lesion   the surgical damaging of brain tissue

This theory was confirmed by Coleman (1973) who discovered an obese type of mouse 'db' that was a different genetic mutation from the 'ob' mouse. He used *parabiosis*, a technique that unites two individual animals anatomically and physiologically, to pair up different genetic strains of mice. When an 'ob' mouse was paired with a normal wild mouse, the obese mouse lost weight. When the normal mouse was paired with a 'db' mouse, the normal mouse starved to death. When an 'ob' mouse was paired with a 'db' mouse they co-existed happily with the 'ob' mouse losing weight. Coleman concluded that the 'db' mice had a circulating factor that caused the cessation of eating in the 'ob' and normal mice, but that the 'db' mice were resistant to it. If an 'ob' mouse was paired with a normal mouse, then the 'ob' mouse got the circulating factor from the normal mouse and lost weight due to a decrease in hunger, but the 'ob' mice seemed not to have enough of the factor to affect the normal mice. Therefore the 'db' mice were circulating a factor that their *satiety* centre (in the *ventromedial hypothalamus*) did not respond to, while the 'ob' mice had a normal satiety centre, but were producing insufficient levels of the satiety signal. This research provided evidence for a circulating lipostatic factor and showed that complex molecular mechanisms were involved in the regulation of hunger. However, it wasn't until 1994 that Friedman, using the 'ob' strain of mice, isolated the satiety molecule leptin, which is secreted from the adipocyte, thus revealing the adipocyte to be involved in controlling energy levels.

London & Baicy (2007) gave leptin replacement to three adults with the 'ob' gene mutation and found that it normalised body weight and feeding behaviour. Functional magnetic resonance imaging (fMRI) was paired with presentation of food cues and during viewing of food-related stimuli, leptin replacement lowered brain activity in areas associated with appetite, while enhancing activity in areas associated with satiety. Therefore leptin seems to adjust eating behaviour through these circuits, which suggests a practical application in helping to reduce obesity.

The role of the hypothalamus

The *hypothalamus* (see Figure 5.8), often refered to as the body's 'control centre', is a cone-shaped brain structure situated above the pituitary gland in the midbrain, which plays a critical role in the regulation of eating, acting like a thermostat to initiate or stop eating behaviour. The hypothalamus regulates *homeostasis*, receiving information about the state of the body to make compensatory changes. It has regulatory areas for body temperature, water balance and blood pressure as well as hunger and thirst. It also links the nervous system to the endocrine system.

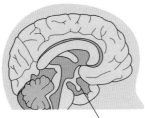

▼ **Figure 5.8**
The hypothalamus

hypothalamus

Dual control theory

The *dual control theory of eating* centred on the idea of a homeostatic perception of hunger and satiety, whereby a decline in glucose triggers the *lateral hypothalamus* (LH), giving rise to the sensation of hunger that motivates a search for food. When eaten, the food releases glucose, which activates the ventromedial hypothalamus (VMH), giving rise to the sensation of satiety, which stops any further eating.

▼ **Figure 5.9** The dual control theory

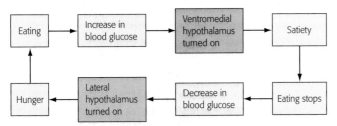

Early support for the idea of the hypothalamus having a central role in feeding came from Hetherington & Ranson (1940) who found that *lesions* of the VMH led to *hyperphagia* (overeating) and obesity, while Anad & Brobeck (1951) found that lesions of the LH led to decreased eating and weight loss. It was Stellar (1954) who originated the idea of the LH being the feeding centre and the VMH being the satiety centre. When these brain areas were electrically stimulated the VMH seemed to decrease eating, but when lesioned it appeared to increase eating, while the LH when stimulated seemed to increase eating, but when lesioned appeared to decrease eating. This was taken as clear evidence for the two brain areas being the feeding and satiety centres. What wasn't considered at the time was that the effects of the lesions might actually have been due to the peripheral damage they caused, rather than the destruction of one particular hypothalamic area.

The effect on eating behaviour when lesions are made to the VMH of rats is that they indulge in hyperphagia and gain weight. These affects are temporary and body weight eventually stabilises. What is clear is that dual control theory cannot explain the results as the VMH rats can attain satiety even though their satiety centre is not present.

With the effect on hunger, the dual control theory would predict that lesions to the VMH of rats would result in increased appetite (motivation to eat) as well as increased food intake. Indeed the rats do eat more, in line with the theory, but the findings do not clearly support the idea of an increased motivation to eat. Teitalbaum (1957) performed an experiment where rats had to push a bar an increasing number of times to get a pellet of food, indeed up to 256 presses. The theory predicts that lesioned VMH rats should have increased motivation to obtain food and will therefore work harder to get a pellet of food. The results showed that control rats with no VMH lesioning work harder as more presses are required to get a food pellet. The VMH lesioned rats did indeed initially press the bar more often than the control rats, but strangely became increasingly lazy and less willing to work hard when more presses were required to receive a food pellet. Also VMH lesioned rats can be choosy eaters and will eat less than normal control rats if quinine is added to food making it taste bitter or when the food tastes stale. These results therefore do not fit the predictions of the theory.

The effect on eating when LH lesions are performed on rats is that they won't eat (*aphagia*) or drink (*adipsia*) and thus they lose a lot of weight. However, these effects are temporary and the LH lesioned rats recover their ability to eat despite having lost their eating centre. Again, dual control theory cannot explain these results.

Thinking critically about psychology

Summarise the evidence for and against dual control theory, using two columns, for and against. What conclusions could you reach based on this?

Set point theory

One solution to the inability of the dual control theory to explain the long-term effects of lesions to the LH and the VMH was the idea that they control body weight by a *set point* mechanism.

Set point theory states that lesions to the LH will lower the set point for body weight and therefore lesioned LH rats should maintain body weight, but at a lower level than before. Similarly, lesions to the VMH will heighten the set point for body weight, and therefore lesioned rats should maintain body weight, but at a higher level than before. Starving rats so that they lost weight before LH lesions were performed tested the theory. If set point theory was correct the lesions should have no effect, as the starved rats would have slimmed their body weight down to a new set point before the lesions were made. The results showed this to be true: LH lesions did not produce further losses in body weight.

Another type of experiment that lends support to set point theory is taking rats that have become obese through having VMH lesions and then force-feeding them to increase body weight even more. These rats were then allowed to feed freely and they lost weight, returning to the weight they were before force-feeding, ie back to their new increased set point. Marshall *et al.* (1971) experimented with different types of LH lesions in rats and found a range of motor and sensory damage, such as being unresponsive to sensory stimuli, not moving unless disturbed and not righting themselves when placed on their sides. He called these effects *sensory neglect*.

Ungerstedt (1971) performed research that showed that the sensory neglect that occurs following LH lesions seems to be a result of peripheral damage to the nucleus of the tractus solitarius (NST). A nerve poison was injected into the NST, which lies outside of the LH – any effect of this chemical lesion could not therefore be due to LH damage. A second group of rats received conventional electrical lesions to the LH. The result was that initial aphagia and adipsia followed by a gradual and complete recovery of food and water intake were produced by both types of lesions, suggesting that it is indeed peripheral damage to the NST that produces sensory neglect.

Experiments involving electrical lesions therefore failed to show what the role of the LH is in feeding, while experiments involving chemical lesions were able to resolve the matter of sensory neglect. Winn *et al.* (1984) used chemical lesions that didn't affect the NST but did destroy cells in the LH. The result was a lasting decline in eating and body weight, but no sensory neglect.

Contemporary research into the role of the hypothalamus

Overall we can see that perceiving the LH as a 'feeding centre' oversimplifies matters, because it is possible to recover from LH lesions and LH lesions also produce disruptions in aggression levels, sexual behaviour and reinforcement behaviour; moreover, lesions to the NST alone produce aphagia and adipsia. Schneider & Tarshis (1995) believe that the LH has a role in the control of insulin, as stimulating the LH causes the release of insulin from the pancreas allowing glucose to be broken down to provide energy. If the LH is lesioned then insulin production declines and our body compensates by breaking down stored body fat to provide fuel and this leads to a fall in body weight. However, the blood stream is full of energy-rich free fatty acids, which cause a failure to eat as the body is sending signals to the brain areas that control feeding that we require no more energy.

Pinel (2000) has given a corresponding explanation to account for the role of the VMH in eating. Rats with VMH lesions have increased insulin levels in their blood, which triggers the conversion of glucose into fat (*lipogenesis*). Any food eaten is therefore quickly converted into fat and so the rats incur an energy shortfall, causing them to eat even more in a futile attempt to address the shortage of glucose in their bloodstream.

Morton G (2007) states that the current view is that food intake, energy output and glucose production are regulated by hypothalamic areas that respond to a variety of peripheral signals. So when there is a reduction of energy stores, the brain initiates responses that promote restoration and maintenance of energy stores and glucose homeostasis. Also when there is excess energy storage, then key hypothalamic areas initiate responses that reduce food intake and increase the expenditure of energy as well as reducing glucose production.

One general problem with research into hunger and eating is that it has tended to consist of artificial laboratory-based experiments. The animals in such experiments were not allowed to eat freely, food intake being controlled by the researchers and whole cycles of hunger, satiety and then hunger again were not really studied. However, a recent more naturalistic experiment has addressed this criticism with interesting results (see *Research Now*).

Thinking critically about psychology

1 How reasonable is it to generalise from studies of eating in rats to eating in humans?
2 What ethical issues are raised by studies of eating in rats?

RESEARCH NOW

De Araujo IE, Oliveira-Maia AJ, Sotnikoa TD, Gainetdinov RR, Caron MG, Nicolelis MG & Simon SA (2008) No such thing as a sweet tooth. *Neuron* 6, 930–41

Aim: To look at rats' brain activity in a more natural setting with the rats being able to choose when to start and finish eating.

Procedure: Brain function was analysed throughout whole hunger–satiety–hunger cycles. Neural activity was measured in brain areas known to be associated with eating motivation, such as the LH, throughout a full eating cycle, in which the rats were hungry and then fed on sugary water until satiated and then became hungry again. The activity of individual neurones within the brain areas was analysed and levels of glucose and insulin in the blood were also measured.

Findings: Different stages of the feeding cycle were correlated with brain activity and it was found that most individual neurones responded only to a particular metabolic state, for instance to low or high glucose levels, but not to both, throughout the whole eating cycle. The brain activity in the areas analysed increased consistently during hunger episodes and decreased during satiety. It was also found that of the brain areas studied, the LH appeared to be the most important for eating motivation, because its neural activity had the biggest correlation with the changes within the eating cycle.

Conclusions: The results suggest that the mechanism that regulates eating motivation is distributed across the different brain areas to form a connected circuit that shares information on sensory and motivational elements of eating, gathered from a huge number of individual neurones. The lateral hypothalamus is a particularly important part of this circuit.

Evolutionary explanations of food preference

What is evolutionary theory?

Evolutionary theory proposes that there is *genetic variability* within every species, and if certain variations suit environmental conditions they will be favoured by the process of natural selection, ie those individuals are more likely to reproduce and pass that genetic make-up on to the next generation. Such individuals are said to have high 'fitness'. For example, the ability to detect poisonous food is likely to be passed on to future generations, as individuals with that genetic make-up are more likely not to be poisoned before they have a chance to reproduce. Over time, genetic characteristics such as the ability to detect poison become part of the species.

Evolutionary psychology attempts to explain the workings of the mind from an evolutionary perspective, with the central belief being that the process of natural selection has shaped the mind. So our mental behaviour reflects the evolutionary history of our species, especially with regard to how we have dealt with adaptive problems, such as avoiding predators and finding and eating the right kind of food. The *Pleistocene era*, between 10,000 and 2 million years ago (also known as the Environment of Evolutionary Adaptiveness or EEA) is seen as the time when most evolutionary adaptations took place in response to environmental demands.

Badcock (2000) believes that the EEA was a time of hunter-gatherer nomadic peoples, living in small kin-related groups. There was low population density, high infant mortality and low life expectancy. Simple technologies were used, such as basic tools, and people were vulnerable to predators and disease. This era ended with the introduction of agriculture about 10,000 years ago and the development of static populations living in towns and cities.

So *evolution* tends to produce adaptations that increase inclusive fitness — an individual's indirect reproductive ability (the process of *kin selection*). Such individuals contribute genes to the next generation through the offspring of relatives as well as through their own offspring. However, we do not behave in a way that maximises fitness, instead we carry out adaptations that in the past increased fitness. Therefore natural selection designed our minds to exist in an environment not that dissimilar from the African savannah in which our hunter-gatherer ancestors lived for 99 per cent of our evolutionary history. So in the EEA we lived in an environment in which food was only periodically available and therefore we had a strong desire for fatty foods, as they were energy rich, therefore it became desirable for natural selection to favour an adaptation whereby people stored fat. Therefore we still have a strong desire to consume fatty foods, even though it is no longer necessary. This is seen as the reason why people overeat fatty foods today – because they are always available – even though, unlike in the EEA, we are not going to experience periods of food being scarce. This therefore is an evolutionary explanation of obesity. We can look now at how preferences for and against particular flavours might have evolved.

▲ **Figure 5.10** Evolutionary psychologists see human behaviour as rooted in our evolutionary past

KEY TERMS

evolution   the process of adaptation through natural selection

the Pleistocene era   time period where the majority of human evolution occurred

▲ **Figure 5.11** Before Tesco and McDonald's we didn't know where the next meal was coming from, so fatty food was a good thing

Sweet tastes

Many of us are accused of having a 'sweet tooth', and sweet-tasting foods are usually an indication of high calorifie content. They are also generally not poisonous, making them doubly valuable to a primitive food gatherer. So, a preference for such a taste would have been adaptive at one time, and may be an evolved mechanism. This idea is supported by the widespread fondness for sweetness throughout much of the animal kingdom; however, remember that not everyone has a sweet tooth.

De Araujo *et al.* (2008) conducted a study that questioned the notion that a preference for sugary foods is based on the ability to taste sweetness. A sample of mice was genetically modified to lack the ability to taste sweetness and was then given a sugar solution and a solution containing sucralose (a non-calorific sweetener). The 'sweet-blind' mice had a preference for the sugar solution, the preference appearing to be based not on sweetness, but on calorie content. This suggests that a preference for calorie-rich foods is an adaptive trait and that the calorie-rich sugar solution raised dopamine levels, leading to stimulation of neurones in the *nucleus accumbens*, a brain area associated with the reinforcement of rewarding experiences, thus consolidating the experience of eating sweet foods. The findings may help to explain high obesity levels as being due to over-consumption of high-calorie food additives such as high fructose corn.

Bitter and sour tastes

Evolutionary theory sees bitter and sour tastes as indicative of poison and therefore there should be a tendency to avoid them. Plants are much more likely than animals to contain toxins and, because avoiding bitter plants would severely limit their food sources, strict herbivores have fewer bitter taste genes than omnivores or carnivores. Instead, animals that graze on plants have a high tolerance to toxins. Grazers have large livers that are able to break down toxic compounds. In the EEA, the ability to discern bitter tastes developed as an evolutionary mechanism to protect early humans from eating poisonous plants. Plants produce a variety of toxic compounds in order to protect themselves from being eaten, and the ability to discern bitter tastes evolved as a mechanism to prevent early humans from eating poisonous plants. Humans have about 30 genes that code for bitter taste receptors and each receptor can interact with several compounds, allowing people to taste a wide variety of bitter substances.

Mennella (2008) suggests that children reject the bitter taste of medicine due to basic biology, because many toxic substances are bitter and distasteful. Children appear to be 'hard-wired' by evolution to do so. Menella identified a variation of a taste gene called TAS2R38, which can make children very sensitive to bitter tastes. '*Our basic biology is telling us to reject bitter; that it's poison. We're designed to reject this stuff.*' Nine hundred people aged between five and 50 years of age were tested and it was found that children were more sensitive to bitter tastes than adults. Childhood would seem to be a time of heightened sensitivity and as we get older learned preferences seem to overtake innate ones. Mennella also believes this is why many children do not like vegetables such as broccoli as they are bitter tasting and therefore indicative of containing toxins.

There are 27 taste receptors for bitter tastes, but only two for sweet tastes. Simmen & Hladik (1998) propose that this asymmetrical difference between sweet and bitter taste discrimination reflects different evolutionary trends for meeting energy requirements (sweet tasting) and for avoiding noxious substances (bitter tasting). This seems to indicate the evolutionary importance of being able to detect potentially harmful foodstuffs in our diet.

▼ **Figure 5.12** Our dislike of bitter flavours may be an evolutionary mechanism to avoid poison

Salty tastes

Having salt in our diet is essential for survival (though it is toxic to most land plants). Salt contains *sodium chloride*, without which we dehydrate and die. Too much salt, though, can lead to high blood pressure and associated health risks, but we do not crave other minerals like we do salt. Animals' need for salt stems from the high sodium concentrations needed to maintain the body's nerve and muscle activity and water balance. Animal blood and fluids, including those of humans, are 100 to 1000 times saltier than the average salt concentration — 1 milligram of sodium per kilogram of weight — in terrestrial plants.

Dudley *et al.* (2008) found that ants prefer salty snacks to sugary ones in inland areas that tend to be salt-poor. Ant populations at varying distances from the ocean were tested for taste preferences and ants that lived 60 miles inland preferred a 1 per cent salt solution to a sugar solution 10 times more concentrated. Carnivorous ants did not exhibit this difference as they get sufficient salt from their prey. This is why grazing animals like deer seek out salt licks to complement their salt-poor diet, while carnivores like lions don't as they get sufficient salt from raw meat. The salt preferences of inland ants are seen as an adaptive response to maintain their competitiveness and the researchers believe this may be true for all animals, including humans.

Thinking practically about psychology

Recently the young daughter one of the authors was very ill, but refused point blank to take her bitter medicine. The author insisted it would make her feel better, but after swallowing it she vomited it straight back up. Nothing he could do would persuade her to try it again. How can evolutionary theory explain this?

▼ **Figure 5.13** Many people love salty food

Salt preferences differ widely across individuals and this is puzzling from an evolutionary point of view, because as salt is so essential it would be expected that humans would have a uniform preference for salty foods and that natural selection would have removed these differences in salt preference. Fessler (2003) says these differences can be explained by reference to the fact that high salt intake protects against sudden dehydration, a benefit that outweighs potential costs. Fessler believes that an adaptive mechanism calculates salt preferences as a function of the risk of dehydration as indicated by past experience of dehydration and maternal salt intake.

Thinking practically about psychology

The Scottish Highlands comprise a rugged wilderness of rocky mountains and nutrient-poor vegetation. The roads in wintertime are especially treacherous due to large deposits of snow and ice. These roads are regularly gritted with rock salt to reduce traffic accidents, but a dangerous new phenomenon has emerged in the last few winters, that of large herds of deer congregating on the roads. Many accidents, including fatal ones, have occurred involving collisions with deer.

Can you think of an explanation that refers to evolutionary taste preferences that can account for the winter gathering of deer upon Scottish Highland roads?

▼ **Figure 5.14** Why do deer like roads ready salted?

Zinner (2002) tested a large group of babies for salt taste preference by presenting various salt solutions and measuring sucking rates on a dummy as an incident of preference. For health reasons the babies were not directly fed salt, instead they were exposed to small stimuli placed upon the tongue. It was found that within three days of birth, 67 out of 234 babies tested showed a high preference for salty tastes and had higher blood pressure than the other babies and that also they tended to have at least one grandparent with hypertension, a medical condition often linked to high salt consumption. These findings indicate a genetic base to salt taste preferences and seem to fit in with Fessler's belief that high salt intake protects against sudden dehydration and that this benefit outweighs any potential costs, bestowing an adaptive advantage for such individuals.

Meat

Humans are omnivores, capable of eating both vegetable- and meat-based diets. Some other primates, such as chimpanzees, do include meat in their diet. Meat is generally rich in protein, but Smil (2003) believes that it is the presence of animal fat and its high energy content that makes meat palatable to many and provides the feeling of satiety after consumption. He believes that it was this that prompted humans to spend large amounts of time and effort in the EEA hunting large animals as a food source, a very risky venture at the best of times.

Archaeological evidence suggests that meat-eating was occurring at least 1.5 million years ago, though of a lot of this was possibly scavenged meat following a kill by lions etc. Goudsblom (1992) believes that the use of controlled fires allowed greater meat consumption, as roasting and searing it made meat more palatable and smoking it preserved it for later eating. Smil (2003) points out that the human gastrointestinal tract is about 40 per cent smaller than that in similar-sized primates, and he believes this reduction resulted from eating meat, which has a high energy density and is more easily digested. But it has been hypothesised that meat-eating did more than provide a high-quality substitute for plant foods. Standford (1999) concluded, on the basis of research done with chimpanzees, that the origins of human intelligence are related to meat-eating, not because of its nutritional value, but because the development of intellect required for the social sharing of meat led to the expansion of the human brain. Foley & Lee (1991) think that human meat-eating directly energised the process of encephalisation. But the downside of meat-eating, aside from the risks incurred while hunting, is that meat-eating can be dangerous as it can quite easily contain life-threatening microbes and lead to transmittable diseases, hence the current worries about 'bird flu' causing an epidemic among humans. There is even some suspicion that AIDS originated from humans eating the meat of monkeys infected with a form of HIV.

Kendrick (1980) provides support for the idea of meat-eating being associated with a shorter life span. He studied groups of people around the world who were noted for their general longevity and found that a common factor was a vegetarian diet. Finch & Standford (2004), however, believe that humans gained a selective advantage by adapting to eat diverse foodstuffs, including meat, which allowed them to thrive in different environments. The move towards consumption of fatty animal tissues is seen as being mediated by selective evolutionary pressure towards 'meat-adaptive' genes, which would have produced a protective effect by favouring resistance to the harmful effects of fat, toxins and pathogens.

▲ **Figure 5.15** Vegetarians live longer!

Prado-Lima *et al.* (2006) believe instead that there is a genetic basis to food preferences, which affects the choice of meat in the human diet. They conducted a study to see if a variant of the serotonin 5-HT 2A receptor gene, which has been linked with the regulation of energy balance and food intake, is associated with choice of food in an elderly population who ate a stable diet.

Two hundred and forty participants of mixed European descent living in Brazil had their genotypes and their diet patterns recorded and the results suggested that genes were influencing food choice and that the consumption of meat can be determined in part by genetic factors. This would seem to indicate that a preference for meat-eating has been determined by evolutionary factors. However, the population studied was elderly (because elderly people tend to have a more stable diet) and this means that their meat preference could have been learned; it tells us nothing about the taste preferences of babies.

Eating disorders: obesity

Obesity is a condition in which excess fat accumulates to such an extent that the body mass index (BMI) is $30\,\text{kg/m}^2$ or higher (compared with being overweight, which is defined as $25\,\text{kg/m}^2$ or higher). The World Health Organization (1998) reports that 1.1 billion people are overweight and there has been a shift in disease patterns from infectious diseases associated with nutrient deficiencies, to chronic degenerative diseases associated with an excessive and unbalanced intake of energy and nutrients. In England, government figures (Health Survey for England, 2008) have revealed that obesity levels have nearly doubled in the past 14 years, with 24 per cent of people now being obese compared with 14 per cent in 1993, and an analysis of age groups showing obesity becoming more prevalent with age. It is estimated that by 2010, 12.5 million people in Great Britain will be obese. The situation is even worse in the USA, where obesity levels among adolescents trebled between 1980 and 2000 and obesity is now the second highest cause of preventable death, after smoking. Obesity rates have risen in most other developed countries, too. The highest obesity levels are to be found among South Pacific Islanders, with Nauru having the highest incidence of all with an obesity level of 80 per cent.

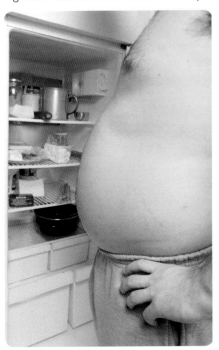

◀ **Figure 5.16**
There are high levels of obesity in many countries

Obesity is linked to cardiovascular diseases, diabetes, sleep apnoea, types of cancer, liver disease and osteoarthritis; it therefore reduces life expectancy. It can be treated with a combination of dieting and exercise or drugs or even surgery. Obesity and its health effects generate huge financial costs. In the USA in 1998, the medical costs attributed to obesity were 78.5 billion dollars, or 9.1 per cent of all medical expenditure. Obese people also create more costs due to their high absenteeism from work.

Although seen in a negative light in modern-day western culture, obesity was historically regarded as a sign of wealth and fertility and certain cultures, such as in Africa, still regard it in this manner. However, interestingly, unlike anorexia nervosa and bulimia nervosa, obesity is not classed as a psychiatric condition.

Various factors have been associated with rising levels of obesity, such as increased food intake and lack of exercise. However, if this rising trend is to be positively addressed, we need to understand fully the factors at play. We shall now consider the psychological and biological explanations of obesity.

KEY TERM

obesity a medical condition of being grossly overweight to the point of endangering health

Thinking critically about psychology

To what extent is obesity normal? How strong is the case for classifying it as a mental disorder in the same way as anorexia and bulimia?

Psychological explanations of obesity

Behavioural explanations

Behavioural explanations focus on the idea that obesity is a maladaptive learned behaviour occurring through overeating. It should therefore also be possible to reverse the procedure and replace the maladaptive behaviour by the use of similar behavioural techniques. There are two main ways in which behaviourism sees obesity as occurring.

Classical conditioning

Obesity occurs because food is naturally associated with pleasure and food cues come to be associated with the pleasure response. This idea is backed up by evidence that classical conditioning can be used to treat obesity and develop normal eating patterns. Foster (2006) reports that overeating is often prompted by cues that become strongly linked to food intake and that treatments based on classical conditioning help patients to identify the cues that trigger inappropriate eating and then learn new responses to them. The treatment has the benefit of creating specific goals that can be easily measured and it identifies clearly what is required. By examining the cues that lead to overeating it is possible to identify areas where modifications in behaviour can be made and thus prevent future overeating.

This then is a tool that can be used to extinguish conditioned responses. For example, if it has been identified that watching television is part of the sequence of events that leads to overeating, then the solution is to limit eating to a room without a television. The more often the patient refrains from eating in front of the television, the less likely it is that television will automatically trigger overeating. Wing *et al.* (2002) reviewed several weight-loss studies from 1996 to 1999 based on this idea and found an average weight loss of 15.6 kg in 18 months. Although it seems clear that classical conditioning may be involved in the development of obesity, there are many other explanations to consider as well.

Operant conditioning

Obesity is seen as occurring due to food being used as a reinforcer (reward) for desirable behaviour, for example, being

◀ **Figure 5.17** Eating junk food can become associated with television-watching

rewarded with ice cream for tidying up your toys. Food is used by people as one of their prime reinforcers, such as going out for a slap-up meal to celebrate special occasions like getting a promotion. So it can be seen that there are plenty of opportunities for operant conditioning using food as a reinforcer to lead to obesity, especially if we are constantly using food to reward each other and ourselves. It may well be that the widely varying rates of obesity in different countries could be due to differential rates of reinforcement, which occur because of different social norms. This explanation may also explain gender differences in obesity levels, though of course cultural and gender differences could also be explained by biological factors.

Jackson (2008) suggests that the roots of obesity, which she calls the 'food monster', lie in operant conditioning during childhood. She likens overeating leading to obesity to a kind of compulsion that occurs because children are encouraged to believe that clearing their plate makes them a good child. This behaviour is constantly reinforced and, coupled with the increase in food portion sizes, leads to people being overweight from a very early age.

Operant conditioning has also been successfully used to tackle the problem of obesity, on the basis that all maladaptive behaviours, such as overeating, can be unlearned and replaced with adaptive behaviours. Devlin & Yanovski (1995) have reported how operant conditioning techniques have been successfully used to reinforce more healthy eating behaviours and also to incorporate strategies such as regular exercise regimes. After five months such a programme resulted in an average weight loss of between 15 and 20 pounds. However, the downside was that weight loss was not maintained. After one year, 35–50 per cent of weight loss had been regained, rising to 100 per cent in most patients after five years. This seems to suggest that although operant conditioning is successfully addressing the effects of obedience, it is not addressing the causes of obesity, hence the weight regain.

Cognitive theory

This explanation is based on the notion that obesity occurs as a result of maladaptive thought processes. The general idea behind this is that information processing has an elevated focus for food-related stimuli. This can trigger strong emotional responses that might affect eating behaviour.

RESEARCH NOW

Barthomeuf, Droit-Volet and Rousset (2009) Obesity and emotions: Differentiation in emotions felt towards food in obese, overweight and normal-weight adolescents. *Food quality and preference* **20, 62–68**

Aim: To look for a relationship between body mass index and the strength of emotion directed towards food.

Procedure: 111 adolescent participants were asked to imagine eating 30 food products in a picture and rate their emotions on a five-point scale. Their body mass index was also recorded.

Findings: Obese participants, defined as having a body mass index of 30 or more, had stronger negative emotions towards palatable foods than did normal weight participants. They also showed lower levels of negative emotion than normal weight participants in response to non-palatable foods.

Conclusion: Emotional factors play a part in the development of obesity.

Braet & Crombez (2001) investigated information-processing biases for food-relevant stimuli in 34 children in a residential treatment centre for obesity, compared with a control group of 40 normal weight children. Participants completed a modified Stroop task, which included food words, negative emotion words and control words. The results showed that the obese children were more hypersensitive to food words and this suggests that such hypersensitivity can initiate and maintain maladaptive eating behaviour.

Cserjesi *et al.* (2007) compared the cognitive profiles of 12 obese schoolboys with peers of normal weight. Memory, intelligence, verbal fluency and attention endurance were measured and the results indicated that the obese boys were deficient in their attention abilities. This suggests that childhood obesity involves cognitive deficits in attention capabilities. However, the attention deficit could actually be an effect of being obese. Indeed Elias (2003) has found evidence from the well-respected Framingham Heart Study to indicate that early-onset, long-term obesity leads to a decline in cognitive functioning. However, there was only a significant effect in men and the researchers believe that this may be due to the different distributions of fat on men's and women's bodies.

The obese personality

One proposed explanation for obesity is that such individuals share common personality characteristics. Cloninger (2007) has suggested that the trait of novelty-seeking may be involved in obesity and difficulties in losing weight, because high novelty-seeking indicates a strong appetite drive. The Temperament and Character Inventory (TCI) personality measurement test was given to 264 lean and 239 obese people. The obese participants scored significantly higher on novelty-seeking and lower on persistence and self-directedness. Interestingly, obese people who managed to lose more than 10 per cent of their body weight scored significantly less on novelty seeking than those who didn't. Therefore it was concluded that personality traits are involved in the development of obesity.

Cloninger offers a biological explanation because he believes that individual variations in the novelty-seeking trait are mediated by genetic variability in dopamine transmission. Wiesbeck *et al.* (1995) provided neuroendocrine-based evidence for this idea, finding that novelty-seeking was related to dopaminergic activity, though in brain areas not directly associated with personality traits. One suggested practical application of Cloninger's research was that weight-loss programmes should be designed to take personality traits into consideration.

KEY TERMS

gene a region of DNA that controls a hereditary characteristic

hormones chemicals released by cells that affect cells in other parts of the body

neural factors biological mechanisms associated with the nervous system

meta-analysis a mathematical technique for combining the results of several studies

Biological explanations of obesity

In addition to the possible psychological influences upon obesity, several genetic, hormonal and *neural factors* are currently under investigation. Some of these seem to have a long-term influence on the control of energy intake, for instance leptin, while others seem to have more of a short-term impact, for example insulin.

Genetic factors

Can obesity be explained by reference to genetics? Although rare, obesity syndromes caused by mutations in single *genes* do exist and this suggests that genes can play a role in the development of obesity. Bardet-Biedl syndrome is one such condition and is characterised by excessive eating and weight gain. However, it seems that the greatest proportion of obesity in humans is not due to mutations in single genes. Genes alone do not predict future health; they need an environment in which to express themselves. Some people do seem to be more at risk of becoming obese and there can tend to be a family tendency

▲ **Figure 5.18** Obese people may be reproducing more

RESEARCH NOW

Wardle, Carnell, Haworth and Plomin (2008) Evidence for a strong genetic influence on childhood adiposity despite the force of the obesogenic environment. *American Journal of Clinical Nutrition* **87, 398–404**

Aim: To look at the relative importance of genetic and environmental influences on BMI and body fat deposits.

Procedure: 5092 British pairs of twins aged between eight and 11 years were assessed for BMI and waist circumference. A mathematical technique called quantitative genetic modelling was employed. This involved looking at the similarity of BMI and waist size in identical and fraternal twins.

Results: BMI and waist size were much more similar in identical than fraternal twins. Quantitative genetic model fitting found a heritability figure of 77 per cent with only a small environmental input.

Conclusions: Obesity is primarily genetic in origin, with environmental factors playing a much smaller role than common sense would suggest.

to be overweight, but it is more likely that people have different levels of genetic risk of obesity, with multiple genes increasing an individual's susceptibility to obesity. It is environmental factors that ultimately decide whether this obesity develops. Genetic factors are also beginning to be implicated in the degree of effectiveness of diet and physical activity interventions for weight reduction. Another possibility, as suggested by Musani *et al.* (2008), is that genes may be changing, and overweight people may be more fertile, therefore reproducing more and ultimately increasing genes that favour obesity.

Twin studies have provided evidence linking genetics to obesity, because the body weights of identical (MZ) twins tend to be similar. The problem with such studies is that genetically similar people tend to also have similar environments. However, Stunkard *et al.* (1990) tested 311 pairs of twins reared apart and 362 pairs reared together. The results indicated that a shared childhood environment had little if any influence on obesity.

Another way of untangling genetic from environmental factors is by adoption studies. Stunkard & Sorensen (1986) performed one such study that compared the degree of obesity of participants who had been adopted, with the degree of obesity in their biological relatives and members of their adoptive family. The results indicated genetics to be the main factor as an individual's body weight was more correlated with that of biological relatives than adoptive ones.

Thinking critically about psychology

Consider the Willer *et al.* study.

1 Why is *meta-analysis* so potentially useful?
2 What is the risk in studies using meta-analysis?

Thinking creatively about psychology

Devise an adoption study to validate Wardle *et al.*'s findings.

RESEARCH NOW

Willer CJ, Speliotes EK, Loos RJF et al. (2008). Six new loci associated with body mass index highlight a neuronal influence on body weight regulation. *Nature Genetics* **41, 25–34**

Aim: To see whether particular genes are associated with BMI, and to see whether these genes act on the brain.

Procedure: A meta-analysis that provided data from 32,387 participants of European descent from 15 *genome-wide analyses* (GWA) was conducted. The GWAs looked at small genetic variations called *single nucleotide polymorphisms* (SNP) scattered throughout DNA, to isolate the SNPs that are more common in people with a high BMI. The 35 variants that had the highest effect were selected and these were tested on a further 59,082 participants to identify the variants that still showed an association with a high BMI.

Findings: Variations in eight genes increased the chances of being overweight by between 3 per cent and 14 per cent, and of being obese by between 3 per cent and 25 per cent. Seven of the eight were found to be active in the brain.

Conclusions: Particular genes are important in obesity. Most of these act on the brain, suggesting that they work by affecting eating behaviour.

Neurological factors

The hypothalamus is known to regulate hunger and feeding, with the VMH and the LH playing important roles (see p102). Friedman (2005) has argued that two types of neurones found in the hypothalamus are the key regulators of appetite. The *neuropeptide* (NPY) neurone seems to stimulate hunger and the *proopiomelanocortin* (POMC) neurone appears to suppress appetite. The activity of these neurones is 'turned up' or 'turned down' as chemicals wash over them, and Friedman believes that a dominant factor in controlling weight is this basic neural circuit.

The main chemical involved is leptin, a hormone produced by fat cells in the stomach. Leptin is produced in proportion to the level of body fat and thus informs the brain of the fat store level. As people gain weight, fat cells increase the levels of leptin and as leptin washes over the POMC neurone, appetite is decreased. When people start to lose weight, body fat is reduced, which decreases the levels of leptin. Less leptin means the POMC turns down and activity in the NPY neurones predominates, which increases appetite. This seems to indicate that leptin deficiency is not a primary cause of obesity, but rather a decreased response to leptin. Other chemicals, fats, sugars and neural transmitters also influence the actions of these neurones, but leptin seems to be the key.

It was hoped that leptin might prove an effective treatment for obesity, but injections of leptin are only effective for a few people. The majority of obese people do produce leptin, but their bodies resist its effects by blocking its ability to turn up the appetite-suppressing action of the POMC neurone. Therefore their appetite stays high as does their eating and they gain weight up to a point at which the resistance stops; Friedman believes that this point is genetically determined. This would explain why appetite suppressants have little effect.

⤷ Exploring issues and debates
The biological model

The biological approach to psychology sees all behaviour and mental processes as having a physical basis to them.

Construct a table that illustrates points showing the biological approach to explaining eating behaviour.

Dopamine is a neurotransmitter, and obese people are known to have fewer dopamine receptors in the brain. However, as only correlational research had been performed, it was not clear if this is a cause or an effect of being obese. Stice *et al.* (2008) have now provided evidence that indicates dopamine as a cause of obesity. The researchers used fMRI scans and studied a genetic variation, TaqIA A1 allele, which leads to a lesser number of dopamine receptors, to see if activation of the *dorsal striatum* in response to eating is related to current and future increases in body mass. The results indicated that obese individuals overeat to compensate for having a poorly performing dorsal striatum, which leads to lessened dopamine signalling in the brain.

Hormonal factors

Insulin is important as it directs the storage and utilisation of energy. Kahn & Flier (2000) report that a link has been found between insulin resistance and obesity. Insulin resistance occurs mainly due to genetic factors, but certain carbohydrates seem to worsen insulin sensitivity when eaten to excess. Insulin does not therefore seem to be a sole or major cause of obesity, but insulin resistance coupled with a large consumption of high-glycaemic-value foods (often found in fast foods) does seem to be a potential cause of obesity. However, the relationship between insulin and obesity is not yet fully understood.

Cortisol is a *glucocorticoid* with powerful metabolic effects. Epel *et al.* (2001) found that women with high cortisol secretions overate, especially sweet foods, which suggests that a high level of cortisol leads to an increase in stored abdominal fat and obesity. Bjorntorp & Rosmond (2000) believe this is related to dysfunction in the hypothalamus, which suggests a neural explanation. However, it is still unclear whether cortisol abnormalities are a cause or merely a result of obesity.

Ghrelin (see p100) is a growth hormone that is highly concentrated in the stomach. Fasting increases its secretion, which in turn stimulates eating. Obese people have reduced concentrations of ghrelin. Shintani *et al.* (2001) found that its action is mediated through the production of leptin, rather than a direct blood-flow effect into the hypothalamus, and that this action in turn is mediated through increased action of NPY (see Neurological factors).

Evolutionary explanations of obesity

Can the obesity phenomenon be explained by evolutionary theory? Lieberman (2003) states that it takes little effort to obtain food in the modern world and that therefore we are vulnerable to overeating and obesity; we have evolved to find high calorific foods very palatable. You might think we would be designed to eat what is good for us now, but we are not adapted to life in the modern world, rather to life in the EEA, a kind of 'evolutionary time lag'. The system would work fine if we lived on the African savannah in the time of our distant ancestors, because then fat, salt and sugar were in such short supply that when found, the most sensible response was to eat them. Fat has twice as many calories as carbohydrates, and sugar is associated with ripe fruits, so seeking them out was beneficial to us. Now that we can choose our foods, we prefer to eat what was in short supply on the African savannah. We also choose levels of exercise that minimise energy expenditure and this would have been sensible in the EEA when wasting calories could bring death. This evolutionary tendency for humans to be sedentary, coupled with our evolutionary preference for big portions of high-calorie, high-fat-content foods may have caused the explosion in obesity rates.

There is no adaptive benefit to patience or waiting for better foods, therefore humans have evolved to eat more than their immediate nutritional needs require. The behaviour was once adaptive in the EEA, an environment of food scarcity, but has now become maladaptive in the modern environment where high calorific foods are always available. Natural selection has shaped our appetite regulation mechanisms to ensure that we survived periods of food scarcity. In the Pleistocene era, eating required walking for hours each day to get food, with a calorific cost that made it difficult for most people to accumulate surplus as fat. Periodic food shortages activated a mechanism that prepared for famine by increasing appetite and basal weight above the starting point. Dieting activates the same system, so weight can rebound to above what it was when the diet began. When people try to lose weight by using willpower to drastically limit their food intake, their regulation mechanisms react with a response that is adaptive: they often gorge themselves.

The biological systems involved in human weight regulation promote levels of consumption that maintain the energy levels well above the levels required to meet immediate needs so that excess energy can be stored to meet future needs. So our eating behaviour has not evolved to cope with continuous exposure to chips and burgers. Food consumption is driven by the availability of food; so modern humans continue to behave as if food supplies are uncertain, resulting in dysfunctional overeating. It seems as if the eating regulation system is overwhelmed by the food-replete world in which we now live. Bray (1998) notes: *'Genes load the gun, environment pulls the triggers.'*

Bray *et al.* (2004) think otherwise and believe it is our consumption of liquid calorie-rich snacks that makes us obese, because liquid calories were not part of the mammalian diet in our evolutionary past. In the USA, high fructose corn syrup (HFCS) is commonly used to sweeten drinks and consumption increased by 1000 per cent between 1970 and 1990. The researchers see HFCS as explaining obesity, because its digestion, absorption and metabolism differ from glucose, as it does not stimulate the secretion of insulin or leptin production. Insulin and leptin act as key signals in the regulation of food intake and body weight, therefore HFCS may be leading to increased energy intake and weight gain. DiMeglio & Mates (2000) conducted research that compared liquid versus solid carbohydrate effects on food intake and body weight. They gave a daily calorie load of 450 calories, in the form of a sweetened drink, to 15 participants for four weeks and found that they gained significantly more weight than when the calorie load was a solid food in the form of jelly beans. This provides evidence to back up the idea that it is the consumption of liquid calories that has caused the huge increase in obesity. Monsivais *et al.* (2007) have cast some doubt on this idea. They point out that obesity has also increased sharply in countries where beverage consumption is lower than in the USA and HFCS is not a common sweetener.

The thrifty gene model

Jorgensen (2003) put forward the *thrifty gene model*, which believes there may, in the past, have been a selective advantage for people with insulin resistance. Bindon & Baker (1997) provided support for this by finding that certain populations were under selective pressure to maximise energy due to cyclical patterns of feast, famine and energetic balance. Beta cells in the pancreas secrete insulin, which transports glucose into cells. High insulin levels over a period of time may improve the metabolic efficiency of individuals with the thrifty gene by increasing glycogen production. Increased levels of insulin lead to excessive production of fat in two ways:

- increased insulin levels break down triglycerides in the blood and store the material as fat
- insulin suppresses the enzyme lipase, keeping it from breaking down triglycerides as fat.

KEY TERM

thrifty gene model   the idea that some ethnic groups may be more prone to obesity due to a gene that predisposes them to be so

Unfavourable outcomes from the genotype, such as diabetes and obesity, would historically have been stopped by occasional famine and exercise, which reduce insulin secretion. A person with the thrifty gene would have increased sensitivity to insulin that would improve their metabolic efficiency, which meant they were more likely to survive and reproduce. Anyone in the modern world with abundant food, little exercise and the thrifty gene would put on excess weight and suffer from insulin resistance, leading to obesity and diabetes, so it would not be obesity that caused diabetes, but rather that they were both caused by increased efficiency of metabolic processes.

Lieberman (2003) found another version of the thrifty gene in Inuit people living on a diet rich in protein and fat, but with little carbohydrate. Natural selection here favoured metabolic efficiency for production of glucose from fat and protein, rather than carbohydrate. Therefore different versions of the thrifty gene can explain the prevalence of different metabolisms in different populations and the biological heritage of our ancestors may have led to dysfunctional responses to the modern eating environment.

Further evidence for the thrifty gene hypothesis has been found by Rowe *et al.* (2007) who studied the genetics of modern day Pima Indians. These people have an unusually high level of obesity and the researchers linked this to a thrifty metabolism that allows them to metabolise food more efficiently. This would have been advantageous when food was less abundant, but now leads to obesity.

In 1994, Friedman and a team of molecular biologists arrived on the Polynesian island of Kosrae, a volcanic outcrop with one of the highest levels of obesity in the world. The aim, though, was to find out why not everyone on the island was obese. Before World War II the population were generally slender and lived a subsistence existence off mainly fruit, fish and taro (a plant). There were frequent storms and droughts that led to periods of food scarcity. After WWII their diet changed radically and there was a never ending abundance of tinned and processed foods. The majority of the population became overweight, but not everyone, even though eating habits were very similar.

◀ **Figure 5.19** Researchers have looked at the genetic make-up of people on the Polynesian island of Kosrae, which has a very high rate of obesity

The isolated population consists of just 7600 people descended from a few families and everyone shares a genetic make-up that is far more similar than would be the case in most parts of the world. Friedman and his colleagues believe that the thrifty gene hypothesis explains why most, but not everyone, on the island is prone to obesity. The gene was well represented among the islanders and gave an adaptive advantage in times of food scarcity, as the gene predisposes them to store excess nutrition as fat to help them through the lean times. This has now become their liability, condemning them with their new eating patterns to high levels of obesity. The small percentage who remain lean are individuals who don't have the gene. Friedman also believes that people in early agricultural societies, such as the Fertile Crescent in the Middle East, had a steady supply of abundant food and thus didn't need to store fat. These people are therefore much less at risk of becoming obese.

Friedman also believes that leptin resistance, which has been associated with obesity, may be a relic of the thrifty gene response, increasing appetite in those whose ancestors had lacked regular food supplies, and indeed leptin resistance levels among the islanders are high. It may well be that each person has a genetically determined 'set point' of hunger and satiation that we have inherited from our ancestors and we are motivated to keep on eating until we reach it. It would seem that the islanders had a much higher set point than is usual due to the high occurrence of the thrifty gene among their population.

The evolutionary view of obesity offers a plausible explanation for modern obesity levels by explaining that we are adapted to meet the harsh environment of the EEA rather than the food-plenty modern world. Evolutionary theory also explains why so many people find dieting difficult and the fact that they tend to put back on any weight lost; our bodies are just designed to consume as much as possible and lay down fat stores up to a set point. Through the thrifty gene hypothesis the evolutionary viewpoint can explain why some individuals, and indeed groups of people, seem more vulnerable to becoming obese through varying levels of insulin resistance. This would also explain why some people can consume relatively large amounts of food and remain lean, while other people can consume a lot less and become easily overweight.

The evolutionary approach is not one of 'genetic determinism' where other influences play no part and our behaviour lacks free will. Instead it is an interactionist viewpoint that sees our eating behaviour as being determined by a mixture of genetic and environmental influences one cannot occur without the other. The evolutionary explanation has also been accused of being reductionist in that it reduces eating behaviour down to a single factor, but referring to the previous point, this is not strictly true as other influences are acknowledged too.

Thinking critically about psychology

One of the criteria for a good scientific theory is that it can be tested. Evolutionary psychology theories are sometimes criticised on the basis that they are not easily testable. After having read this section how true do you think this is in this case?

Anorexia and bulimia nervosa

Anorexia and bulimia are classified as mental disorders under the major systems for classifying and diagnosing mental health problems like the *DSM-IV* (see p190). Anorexia has been recognised as a mental disorder since the nineteenth century, and there are records suggesting that it existed considerably earlier than this. No such records exist for bulimia and this has only been recognised since the 1970s. It is a matter of debate whether bulimia existed unrecognised prior to this or whether it is actually quite a new disorder.

Both anorexia and bulimia involve a preoccupation with body size and shape and a fear of gaining weight, leading sufferers to reduce food intake to a dangerously low level. Anorexia is diagnosed when the individual refuses to maintain a normal body weight for their age and height, has an irrational fear of becoming fat and perceives themselves as fat, although in reality they are likely to be dangerously thin. These psychological effects are accompanied by the physical effects of starvation, such as insomnia and low blood pressure.

Females, who make up the majority of anorexic patients, stop menstruating.

Whereas patients with anorexia stop eating normally and may also exercise excessively in order to control their weight, bulimia is associated with a different set of behaviours. Bulimic patients eat large quantities of high calorie food in short periods known as binges. Binges are followed by depressed mood and self-criticism. Patients then attempt to lose weight by vomiting or purging. This leads to fluctuations in weight.

⟳ Exploring issues and debates
Ethical issues

Conducting studies that involve using participants with eating disorders poses a lot of ethical problems for researchers.

Construct a table that lists the ethical issues involved with research into obesity, anorexia and bulimia nervosa. You should include details of how each issue could possibly be dealt with.

Psychological explanations for anorexia and bulimia

Psychodynamic theory

Recall from your AS level that the psychodynamic approach focuses on unconscious influences on symptoms, resulting from largely forgotten childhood experiences. Bruch (1982) proposed a psychodynamic theory to explain anorexia and bulimia. She distinguishes between effective parents, who pick up correctly on their babies' signals, feeding them when they are hungry etc, and ineffective parents, who impose their own interpretations on infant signals, for example feeding a tired child or comforting a hungry one. Bruch believes that a child only develops normal awareness of their physical states, such as hunger, if they internalise it during interactions with effective parents. Along with this awareness goes a normal sense of self. Without a normal sense of self children can feel out of control of their bodies.

Children of ineffective parents develop neither a healthy sense of self nor an accurate perception of hunger or satiety. In adolescence the children of ineffective parents can become desperate to feel in control of their bodies. This can lead them to take control of their bodies by extreme measures like restricting eating. Where this attempt is successful and the adolescent gains complete control over food intake, anorexia results. Where it is unsuccessful and only partial control over food intake is achieved, the symptoms are those of bulimia.

There is some evidence to support Bruch's explanation of eating disorders. Leon *et al.* (1993) compared awareness of physical states such as hunger in patients with anorexia and bulimia and with a control group. Not only was perception of hunger less accurate on average in the patients, but also poor perception in the healthy controls made it more likely that they would go on to develop an eating disorder. There is also evidence to support the idea that insensitive parenting is linked to eating disorders. Recall from your AS level research into attachment theory and the idea that insensitive parenting (what Bruch calls ineffective parenting) is associated with later problems in development. We can look at one study of this in *Classic Research*.

Thinking critically about psychology

What ethical issues does research such as Salzman's raise?

Although Bruch's ideas have some support it is important to remember that not all people who experience eating problems have insensitive or controlling parents. It seems likely that ineffective parenting is a risk factor for anorexia and bulimia but it is not the only or main cause in most cases.

Cognitive theory

One of the main features of both anorexia and bulimia is a distorted perception of one's body shape, accompanied by the irrational belief that one is fat when one is not. There therefore seems to be a cognitive bias in the way that information about the body is processed in patients with eating disorders. Slade & Russell (1973) had anorexic patients estimate their own body size and found overestimates ranging from 25 per cent to 55 per cent. There were, however, methodological flaws with the Slade & Russell study; most of us overestimate our body size to some extent and we get better at self-estimation with age. Slade & Russell's control group were significantly older than their anorexic group so we would expect them to overestimate to a lesser degree.

The emphasis of cognitive research into eating disorders has shifted away from body-size perception to a more general view of beliefs about the self. In other words, people with eating problems don't so much perceive their size incorrectly as have a set of false beliefs about and emotional responses to their body. Cooper & Turner (2000) looked at the emotional aspects of body self-perception in anorexic patients using a standard questionnaire, the Eating Disorder Belief Questionnaire. Anorexic patients reported more negative beliefs about themselves than dieters or a control group with no unusual eating behaviour. They were more likely to believe that acceptance from others was conditional on their body type, and more likely to base their own self-esteem on their body type.

CLASSIC RESEARCH

Salzman JP (1997) Ambivalent attachment in female adolescents: association with affective instability and eating disorders. *International Journal of Eating Disorders* 21, 251–9

Aim: To investigate the adolescent experiences of children classified as having a type C attachment, associated with insensitive and controlling parenting.

Procedure: 28 female undergraduates had two-hour interviews designed to assess their current mental health and history of mental health problems. Eleven had been previously assessed as having a type C attachment to their primary carer. Ten were classified as securely attached (type B) and seven as avoidant (type A).

Findings: 7 of the 11 students with a type C attachment had a history of anorexia and/ or bulimia. None of the students with other attachment types had a history of eating problems.

Conclusion: Children with type C attachments are most likely to suffer eating disorders. Because type C attachment is associated with insensitive and controlling parenting, results suggest that this parenting type is linked to development of eating disorders.

One way of evaluating the usefulness of the cognitive model of eating disorders is to assess whether therapies that aim to change cognitions succeed in removing the symptoms. Recall cognitive behaviour therapy (CBT) from your AS level. CBT involves changing the way people think. If CBT can alter the poor cognitions people have when suffering eating disorders, and if this in turn relieves their symptoms, this supports the idea that faulty cognitions lead to eating disorders. Wilson (2005) reviewed treatments for bulimia and concluded that CBT is the most effective treatment but that it is still limited in its effectiveness. Other studies have shown that anorexia is even harder to treat, by CBT or any other means. This all means that studies of CBT do not paint a clear picture of the usefulness of the cognitive approach for explaining eating disorders.

The major problem with explanations of eating disorders is the direction of causality. Clearly, patients with anorexia and bulimia have distinctive and abnormal cognitions associated with the disorder. However, this does not necessarily mean that the cognitions *cause* the disorder. They could be a bi-product of the physical symptoms or of upbringing as Bruch suggested. Cognitive approaches may ultimately be of more use in understanding the experience of having an eating disorder than its origins.

Biological explanations for anorexia and bulimia

Genetic factors

There is some evidence that some people may be more vulnerable than others to developing an eating disorder as a result of their genetic make-up. Kortegaard *et al.* (2001) surveyed 34,000 twins, asking them whether they had ever experienced anorexia or bulimia. Identical twins were more likely to share both disorders than fraternal twins. Their results are shown in Table 5.1.

▼ Table 5.1 Identical and fraternal twins sharing eating disorders

Disorder	% identical twins sharing the disorder	% fraternal twins sharing the disorder
Anorexia	0.18	0.07
Bulimia	0.25	0.13

The low percentages in Table 5.1 suggest that eating disorders are not primarily genetic in origin. However, the fact that identical twins share eating disorders more commonly than fraternal twins does strongly suggest that there is some role for genes in making people vulnerable. However, this sort of data can be analysed and interpreted in different ways. Fairburn & Harrison (2003) reanalysed the data of Kortegaard *et al.* and concluded that anorexia, though not bulimia, is mostly genetic in origin. Given that the data on heritability of eating disorders can be interpreted in such radically different ways, we would have to conclude that it remains an open question.

Biochemical factors

A number of hormones are present in abnormal levels in eating disorders, and some researchers have suggested these may be involved in causing eating disorders. However, bear in mind that eating disorders cause malnutrition, which may in turn be responsible for the abnormal hormone levels. A classic study in the 1980s set out to test whether simple starvation led to the same hormonal changes as are seen in anorexia. If they are the same then it is more likely that they are a bi-product of malnutrition and not a cause of the eating disorder.

 LOOKING FURTHER You can read a good general review of the characteristics and origins of eating disorders here:

http://www.ama-med.org.ar/obesidad/Eating-disorders-Lancet-2003.pdf

CLASSIC RESEARCH

Fichter MM & Pirke KM (1986) Effects of experimental and pathological weight loss on the hypothalamo-pituitary-adrenal axis. *Psychoneuroendocrinology* 11, 295–305

Aim: To starve participants and compare the resulting changes in hormone levels with those in anorexia.

Procedure: 5 male volunteers were studied over four phases. In the first phase, the levels of several hormones in the blood including cortisol, growth hormone and thyroid-stimulating hormone were measured every 30 minutes for 24 hours. This established the normal hormone levels for each participant. In the next phase of the study participants were deprived of all food for three weeks. Their hormone levels were then measured again over a 24-hour period. In the third phase, the weight of the volunteers was restored to normal and their hormone levels were measured again. Finally, participants were monitored for a time as normal body weight was maintained. The results were compared with those of prior studies looking at hormone changes in anorexia.

Findings: In the starvation phase, growth hormone levels and cortisol levels increased, while thyroid-stimulating hormone levels decreased. When weight was restored to normal, all hormone levels returned to normal. This is exactly what has been observed in studies of hormone change in anorexia.

Conclusion: There is no evidence to suggest that eating disorders are caused by abnormal hormone levels. The changes in hormone levels in anorexia are the same as occur in starvation and are therefore probably a result of the restricted food intake in anorexia.

Thinking critically about psychology

Consider the kinds of people who would volunteer for a study that included phase two of Fichter & Pirke's investigation. Why might the findings be unrepresentative?

Another biochemical explanation for eating disorders involves the neurotransmitter serotonin. We know serotonin is lower in patients with depression and OCD (see Chapter 9 for a discussion of both of these). Depression and OCD often occur with eating disorders, so it makes sense that the serotonin levels are involved in all three. There is also evidence to suggest that drugs like Prozac ,which lead to higher levels of serotonin in the brain, relieve the symptoms of eating disorders.

There is further support for the idea that serotonin levels are lower in patients with eating disorders from metabolite studies. Metabolites are the chemicals produced when biochemicals are broken down. We can get an idea about levels of serotonin by looking at the levels of serotonin metabolites in urine or spinal fluid. Jimerson *et al.* (1992) drew spinal fluid from bulimic patients and a control group and measured levels of serotonin metabolites. Metabolites were lower in the bulimic patients than in the control group and lower in the most severe cases.

There is thus strong evidence linking serotonin to eating disorders. However, this still leaves us with the problem of causality. Low serotonin levels are probably not the cause, certainly not the *only* cause of eating disorders. The relationship between biology and psychology is complex and it is possible that the serotonin levels are a result rather than a cause of the psychological symptoms of eating disorders.

Chapter summary

Factors influencing eating and dieting behaviour

- Eating is essential to maintain energy levels and ensure healthy development and therefore has a fundamental survival value.
- There are several factors that influence attitudes to food and eating behaviour, which shape our food preferences and dietary habits. Cultural influences, mood and health concerns are especially important.
- Dieting is a form of restrained eating and success is dependent upon the extent and duration of dieting, combined with social factors and individual differences.
- Most diets fail as they are unsustainable and therefore weight lost tends to be regained. Diets generally don't teach people sustainable new eating practices.

Neural and evolutionary explanations for eating behaviour and food preferences

- Various neural mechanisms have been associated with the control of eating. The hypothalamus has especially been seen as having a central role.
- The lateral hypothalamus and ventromedial hypothalamus have been closely associated with the idea of a homeostatic perception of hunger and satiety

(dual control theory) and control of body weight by a set point mechanism (set point theory).
- Evolutionary theory sees eating preferences as having been shaped by natural selection during the Pleistocene era when food was often only periodically available. Therefore preferences have evolved for sweet, fatty and salty foodstuffs, plus a tendency to avoid bitter tastes indicative of toxins.
- Meat-eating is a contentious area. Meat is rich in fatty tissues and has been linked with the development of human intelligence, but there are short- and long-term health risks associated with its consumption.

Explanations of eating disorders

- Obesity is an epidemic and life-threatening modern phenomenon. Its increase has been linked with overeating and a lack of exercise, but various psychological and biological factors have also been put forward as possible explanations, with evolutionary theories such as the thrifty gene hypothesis being especially favoured.
- Anorexia and bulimia nervosa are two other important eating disorders characterised by a preoccupation with body size and abnormally reduced food intake. Psychological and biological explanations have both attracted a lot of research attention.

What do I know?

1 Compare psychological and biological explanations of **one** eating disorder. (25 marks)

2 (a) Outline **one** factor that influences attitudes to food and eating behaviour. (5 marks)
(b) Outline and evaluate explanations for the success and failure of dieting. (20 marks)

3 (a) Outline **one or more** biological explanations of **one** eating disorder. (9 marks)
(b) Evaluate evolutionary explanations of food preference. (20 marks)

4 Discuss the role of neural mechanisms involved in controlling eating and satiation. (25 marks)

5 (a) Outline **two** evolutionary explanations of food preference. (9 marks)
(b) Evaluate psychological explanations of **one** eating disorder. (16 marks)

CHAPTER 6
Gender

Thinking ahead

By the end of this chapter you should be able to:

- describe and evaluate psychological explanations of gender development including Kohlberg's cognitive developmental theory and gender schema theory

- describe and evaluate, using relevant research, explanations for psychological androgyny and gender dysphoria

- describe and analyse biological influences on gender development including the role of genes and hormones

- describe and evaluate evolutionary explanations of gender roles

- describe and evaluate the biosocial approach to gender development

- describe your understanding of social influences on gender role, such as from parents, peers, schools and the media, and evaluate this knowledge

- describe and evaluate cross-cultural studies of gender role

This chapter looks at a range of explanations of our gender development in terms of the influences on our physical sex and our psychological gender identity. This is an important distinction and one that we don't usually make in everyday speech: we tend to use 'sex' and 'gender' interchangeably but to psychologists they mean different things. *Sex* refers to the physical, biological differences between men and women whereas *gender* relates to the social and psychological differences. One key way in which men and women differ is in the individual's experience of being the male or female; this is their *gender identity*. From these definitions you will see that biological, psychological and social factors all have a part to play in our gender development. We will explore the roles played by each of these factors.

Psychological explanations of gender development

Adults and older children understand that they are male or female, very young children do not. In this section we will discuss explanations of how children acquire their understanding of their own gender and that of others.

There are several different things that a child has to learn. They need to understand that each individual belongs to a category 'male' or 'female'. Allied to this is the idea that gender is a permanent characteristic – 'maleness' or 'femaleness' doesn't depend on what clothes you wear and cannot change over time. These cognitive steps are separate from the social aspects of gender – such as the understanding of the way males and females behave in society. This is the concept of *gender role* and is dependent upon cultural expectations.

Although biological sex, the influences children have from society, and their cognitions are different factors, they all contribute to the development of a child's gender-related beliefs. Understanding these beliefs can help us to explain the changes in a child's behaviour, such as the ability of two-year-olds to classify actions and objects by gender, such as food and vacuum cleaners with women but hammers and cars with men. Kohlberg's cognitive developmental theory and gender schema theory are two explanations that we will explore.

Kohlberg's cognitive developmental theory

The theory of gender development proposed by Kohlberg was based on earlier ideas about cognitive development which said that children went through stages of understanding. Specifically, Kohlberg suggested that children's knowledge of their social world, which includes the concept of gender, is limited by their cognitive capabilities; as these become more sophisticated over time, so does their understanding of gender. He observed that children's understanding of sex – in terms of anatomy, birth, relationships etc, is very different from that of adults. These differences, Kohlberg felt, are due to differences in *thinking*.

Kohlberg divided the changes in the way children think about gender into three stages (see Table 6.1). Importantly, he said that a child's progress was determined not by reinforcement but by their cognitive capacity – children literally *understand* gender in different ways as they grow older. The child's concepts about gender develop as he or she actively

structures experiences with themselves and their social world. They are not simply passively acquired by observation or instruction.

The stages proposed by Kohlberg were:

- *gender identity* – knowing who to call a 'girl' or a 'boy', including an understanding of the individual's own gender; this is also called 'self-labelling'
- *gender stability* – knowing that an individual's gender stays the same over time; girls grow up to be women and boys grow up to be men
- *gender constancy* – knowing that an individual's gender is consistent whatever they do; for example, dressing or cutting their hair differently cannot change somebody's gender.

◀ **Figure 6.1** Children progressively develop knowledge about gender so they understand that differences in appearance don't change someone's gender

KEY TERMS

sex the physical, biological differences between men and women

gender the social and psychological differences between men and women

gender identity an individual's personal, internal perception of being male or female, eg for a child, whether they 'feel like' a boy or a girl

gender role the behaviours of males and females expected by a culture

Although Kohlberg believed that learning processes were not the driving force in gender development, he nevertheless accepted that social experiences were important. For instance a child's culture provides examples from which they derive their knowledge. A child's social interactions provide information about the expectations of each gender role. Furthermore, when the child understands his or her own gender, and what society expects from that gender, they can behave accordingly. Kohlberg (1966, p89) neatly summarised this idea: 'I am a boy, therefore I want to do boy things, therefore the opportunity to do boy things (and to gain approval for doing them) is rewarding'. We can see from this that children must first be able to reliably categorise themselves in order to value gender-consistent actions and objects. Hence Kohlberg's theory predicts that children will only begin to deliberately seek out and engage in behaviours that are consistent with their gender identity when they have achieved full gender constancy (at around age seven).

▼ Table 6.1 **Kohlberg's stages of gender development**

Stage name	Age (years)	Description of child's understanding of gender
Gender identity	2–3	Learning to identify boys and girls correctly, and correctly labelling themselves
Gender stability	4–5	Understanding that an individual's gender stays the same throughout their life
Gender constancy	5–7	Knowing that gender is consistent even when behaviour or appearance change or are different

Rabban (1950) asked children about gender. The children's responses showed that their thinking does change as Kohlberg suggests. Rabban asked 60 children (aged 30–41 months, with an average age of three years) the questions 'Which doll looks most like you?' and 'Is it a boy or a girl?' Two-thirds of the children could answer these questions correctly but only half could correctly label all six dolls they were shown (a mother, father, two girl and two boy dolls). By four years old, almost all the children could do both tasks. This illustrates the acquisition of gender identity. However, the majority of the three-year-olds could not correctly answer the question 'When you grow up would you like to be a mummy or a daddy?' In contrast, 97 per cent of five-year-olds replied correctly. This illustrates that older but not younger children understand gender stability – that they cannot change gender as they grow up.

Thinking practically about psychology

Kohlberg (1966) (p95) gives an illustration of a conversation between two young children. Which stage is each boy in and why?

Johnny	I'm going to be an airplane builder when I grow up.
Jimmy	When I grow up, I'll be a mommy.
Johnny	No, you can't be a mommy, you have to be a daddy.
Jimmy	No, I'm going to be a mommy.
Johnny	No, you're not a girl, you can't be a mommy.
Jimmy	Yes I can.

Kohlberg's theory has implications for children's own behaviour. When children develop a gender identity they know their own gender ('self-labelling') and they can identify the gender of others. Thompson (1975) found that, by age two years, most children could correctly select a same-sex picture when shown pictures of boys and girls. Once children can accurately label themselves and others, they have a basis for preference – for example choosing to play with children of the same gender. Weinraub *et al.* (1984) found that as early as three years, children selected gender-typed toys. Those choices, in turn, reinforce the children's understanding of gender differences – little girls play 'little girl games' with other little girls, and vice versa for boys.

▲ **Figure 6.2** According to Kohlberg (1966) children first understand their gender, then choose gender-consistent activities

Until the stage of gender stability, children are unclear whether their future roles are fixed. As Slaby & Frey (1975) showed (see *Classic Research*) children under four years old cannot reliably answer questions such as 'When you grow up will you be a mummy or a daddy?' correctly.

KEY TERMS

gender stereotype beliefs about maleness and femaleness with regard to appearance, behaviour, attitudes, occupations etc

sex-typed behaviour activities performed by males and females that fit with the *gender stereotype*

CLASSIC RESEARCH

Slaby RG & Frey KS (1975) Development of gender constancy and selective attention to same-sex models. *Child development* 46, 849–56

Aim: To investigate gender constancy.

Procedure: 55 children aged two to five years were interviewed to assess their gender constancy using 14 question pairs, eg:

testing gender identity:
- [Showing a boy- or girl-doll] 'Is this a boy or girl?'
- 'Are you a boy or girl?'

testing gender stability:
- 'When you were a little baby were you a little girl or a little boy?'
- 'When you grow up will you be a mummy or a daddy?'

testing gender constancy:
- 'If you wore boys'/girls' [opposite sex] clothes, would you be a boy or a girl?'
- 'Could you be a boy/girl [opposite sex] if you wanted?'

On the basis of their gender-constancy answers, children were then classified as 'low gender constancy' if they answered the identity or stability questions incorrectly; otherwise they were put into the 'high gender constancy' group. Several weeks later they were shown a film in which a man and a woman, on opposite sides of the screen, performed the same activities. The time each child spent watching the same-gender adult was recorded.

Results: High gender constancy children spent more time looking at the same-gender adult than low gender constancy children. However, unlike boys, girls spent more time attending to the male than the female model on the film.

▼ Table 6.2 **Mean percentage of time spent watching the male model**

	High gender constancy	Low gender constancy
Boys	61.4	47.9
Girls	50.8	57.8

Conclusion: As predicted by Kohlberg's theory, higher gender constancy children are more likely to attend to a same-gender model than are children with low gender constancy, suggesting that cognition does affect gender-related behaviour. However, social factors also appear to be important as even high gender constancy girls still attend fractionally more to male than to female models.

Thinking creatively about psychology

Slaby & Frey's results show that even the girls preferred male models. Why might this be so? If Slaby & Frey's research were replicated now, do you think the results might be different? If so, why?

When children reach gender constancy, they are highly motivated to behave in a gender-consistent manner. This means their behaviour becomes more sex-typed – they are more likely to follow their culturally dictated gender role stereotypes. Kohlberg says that changes in cognition *cause* differences in behaviour, such as playing with or imitating same-sex peers. Learning theories, which we will discuss later in the chapter, say the opposite.

In support of Kohlberg, Frey & Ruble (1992) gave children a choice between attractive and unattractive toys, which they had been primed to believe were 'boys'' or 'girls'' toys by a televised child model. Frey & Ruble found that boys with gender constancy were more likely to choose a sex-typed toy even when it was uninteresting and that girls, although more strongly affected by the attractiveness of a toy, were also affected by gender stereotypes.

There are, however, several problems with Kohlberg's theory. One issue surrounds the age at which children begin to show gender-stereotyped choices. Although the exact ages of events is not especially important, children typically demonstrate preferences such as for copying same-sex models and rewarding gender-appropriate behaviour in peers (Bussey & Bandura, 1984, 1992) *before* they have attained gender constancy.

Campbell *et al.* (2000) measured the time infants spent attending to same or opposite-sex toys. For boys at nine months and girls at 18 months the preference was for sex-typed toys, but the infants' choices were not related to their ability to identify their own gender correctly. Such findings suggest that, although gender differences do develop over time, they may not be driven purely by cognitive factors.

Gender schema theory

An alternative to Kohlberg's theory is gender schema theory. It was developed from Kohlberg's theory and has been expanded since (eg Bem, 1981; Martin & Halverson, 1981). These theories suggest that children develop the various concepts about gender by processing information from their social world. This cognitive process allows them to develop *schemas*, that is frameworks for knowledge, about gender.

One important difference between Kohlberg's theory and that of Martin & Halverson is that, rather than gender constancy being required for developing gender consistent behaviours, this is dependent only on having gender identity. Thus children can develop gender schema once they can label themselves and others as male or female. The gender schema then expands to include a wide range of applications, such as behaviours, personality and social attributes. The consequences of this schema are to direct the child's attention towards same-sex activities and to motivate gender-consistent behaviour.

Gender schema theory predicts that alongside the development of an understanding of gender we should see an increase in *sex-typed behaviour*. Martin & Halverson (1981) illustrate this in an example in which a little girl is presented with toys. When offered a doll she uses her gender schema to recognise that dolls are for girls and that she is a girl so concludes that 'dolls are for me'. When given a truck instead, she thinks 'trucks are for boys' and since she also knows 'I am a girl', she doesn't play with the truck. So, for example, children whose gender schema leads them to believe that all car mechanics are men are likely to take up different hobbies and choose different courses at school depending on whether they are a boy or a girl.

KEY TERMS

schema   a framework for knowledge and attitudes about an aspect of the world (such as gender) that can be adapted and expanded with experience. A schema can affect the way subsequent information is attended to, interpreted or remembered and how the individual interacts with others

◀ **Figure 6.3** According to gender schema theory, children use their understanding of gender to choose gender-consistent activities

A major advantage of gender schema theory over Kohlberg's stage theory is that development is not dependent upon gender stability – a child can build on a gender schema before appreciating that gender is a fixed state. It is therefore easier to understand why children demonstrate gender-based preferences as early as they do. For example, Martin & Little (1990) found that children as young as 30 months preferred same-sex playmates and gender-stereotyped activities. This alone does not tell us whether these changes in behaviour are related to the development of schema. Serbin *et al.* (1993) demonstrated this relationship using a range of sex-typed activities and occupations by showing that children with greater knowledge about gender also demonstrated stronger preferences. Aubry *et al.* (1999) followed up the same children for three years, looking at their beliefs about gender-related things and their liking for them. They showed that an awareness that an item was meant for the opposite sex in one year led to a reduced preference for it in the subsequent year. Again this suggests that the gender schema affects behaviour.

▼ **Figure 6.4** Some evidence suggests that children with advanced gender schemas are more likely to engage in sex-typed play

However, gender schema theory has problems too. As children's gender schemas develop, they should (at least initially) demonstrate greater sex-typing as they conform to their own conception of maleness or femaleness – but not all evidence confirms this pattern.

In direct contradiction of Martin & Little's findings, Campbell *et al.* (2002) found no evidence of greater preference for gender-consistent toys in two-year-old boys and girls who showed more gender knowledge. Children who preferred to play with sex-typed toys were no more likely to be able to identify 'boys' toys' and 'girls' toys' than those who showed no play preference.

Although Weinraub *et al.* (1984) found differences in 26–36-month-old children's selection of gender-typed toys (p119), most were unaware of the sex differences in those toys. Furthermore, those who were aware of sex-role differences in toys were no more likely to be aware of sex-role differences in adults. The children's understanding of sex roles was, however, predicted by social factors such as the mother's employment and sex-typed activities in the home.

The findings of Fagot & Leinbach (1989) also suggest that parental activities are important in the development of gender-related knowledge. They observed 18-month-old children in their homes. None could gender-label and there were no differences in their sex-typed behaviour. At 27 months, the children were divided into those who could and those who could not apply gender labels, and the researchers looked back at the parental behaviour at 18 months. Parents of 'early labellers' had given more positive and negative responses to sex-typed play with toys. At 27 months, these children showed more traditional sex-role behaviour and, at age four years, they demonstrated more sex-role discrimination.

Of course, even if gender knowledge, such as the ability correctly to apply gender labels, *is* linked to sex-typed preferences in terms of toys or other behaviours, this does not necessarily mean that the schema is the cause of the behaviour. It is possible that both of these variables (behaviour and thinking) are the consequence of some other influence, such as the role of parenting. Parents who emphasise gender differences may both increase knowledge and change behaviour, for example.

Another problem for gender schema theory is that if children *do* engage in a non-stereotypical activity for their gender, they tend to adjust their thinking to accept this new activity as within the bounds of acceptability. So, a girl who likes to play football re-evaluates football as an activity for girls or at least for girls and boys rather than one just for boys. This suggests that behaviour can influence thinking, rather than vice versa, as predicted by the theory.

▲ Figure 6.5

A final limitation of gender schema theory is that it cannot readily account for the differences in development of gender knowledge between boys and girls. For example, boys develop their preference for play with gender-consistent toys earlier and it becomes stronger than that of girls (La Freniere *et al.*, 1984 – see Figure 6.6). They also differ in their tendencies to copy same-gender models and play with same-gender peers, yet it is difficult to demonstrate consistent differences between the knowledge of gender stereotypes.

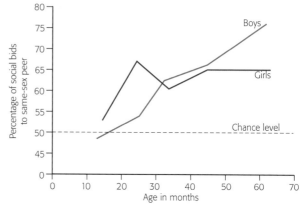

▲ **Figure 6.6** Children prefer same-sex playmates but although this starts earlier in girls, it becomes stronger in boys

Source: La Freniere *et al.* (1984). By permission of the Society for Research in Child Development

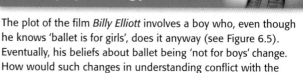

Thinking critically about psychology

The plot of the film *Billy Elliott* involves a boy who, even though he knows 'ballet is for girls', does it anyway (see Figure 6.5). Eventually, his beliefs about ballet being 'not for boys' change. How would such changes in understanding conflict with the ideas of gender schema theory?

Gender identity issues: beyond 'male' and 'female'

So far we have assumed that developing a stable male gender identity for males, and a stable female gender identity for females, is inevitable. In reality, people differ in the extent to which they develop identities that conform to simplistic 'male' and 'female' extremes, and in the extent to which they are happy with their identity. In the following sections we discuss these outcomes.

KEY TERMS

androgyny having psychological characteristics of both males and females in one individual

hermaphroditism having gonads of both sexes (testes and ovaries) in one individual

Psychological androgyny

The word '*androgyny*' is made up of '*andro*' meaning male and '*gyn*' meaning female. Psychological androgyny does not refer to sexual orientation, to sexual equality or to *hermaphroditism* (having biologically both male and female body parts). Someone who is psychologically androgynous has, to a greater or lesser extent, characteristics that their culture associates with both males *and* females. Rather than being opposites, the traits associated with males and females can co-exist in one individual. This is androgyny.

The different gender traits may appear one at a time or together. For example, a woman may behave in a stereotypically aggressive male way at work but be submissive and demonstrate more typically female traits at home. Alternatively, an androgynous person may blend masculinity and femininity, such as being assertive and confident but using that power to be supportive and caring. Of course, androgyny is not necessarily positive. An individual may combine the stereotypically negative traits of both genders – being insensitive but weak or dominant and nagging.

The Bem Sex Role Inventory (BSRI) used to measure androgyny was developed by Bem (1974). It consists of 60 items which are rated on a seven-point scale. Twenty of them relate to stereotypically feminine characteristics and 20 to stereotypically masculine characteristics. The remainder are gender-neutral filler items. Masculinity and femininity can be represented as two separate dimensions, so individuals' scores can be plotted to illustrate their overall personality (see Figure 6.7).

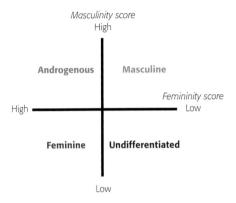

▲ **Figure 6.7** Masculinity, femininity and androgyny

 You can try the Bem Sex Role Inventory for yourself here:

> http://faculty.sunydutchess.edu/andrews/bem_sex.htm

Alternatively, a shortened version here works out your score for you:

http://www.okcupid.com/quizzy/take

▼ **Figure 6.8** Androgynous personalities may have advantages in the workplace

Since society places such emphasis on maleness and femaleness, androgyny would appear, at least superficially, to be a disadvantage. For example, pre-teenage children who do not conform to gender stereotypes are less popular with their peers than those who do (Sroufe *et al.*, 1993). Children, and adults, refer negatively to those who cross gender boundaries: boys can be sissies, girls tomboys. You might recognise, however, that the former is more critical than the latter – society finds the appearance of masculine traits in girls more acceptable than feminine ones in boys.

Clearly, there could be situations in which having positive characteristics associated with each gender would be beneficial. In fact, Bem suggested that androgynous people would be more mentally healthy than people who were either predominantly masculine or feminine. Some research has supported this view. Peters & Cantrell (1993) investigated various aspects of satisfaction with social relationships (with partners, co-workers, daughters etc) of feminists. They found that, regardless of whether the women were heterosexual or lesbian, androgynous individuals had the best quality of relationships. In an investigation of factors affecting satisfaction in employment, Arkkelin & O'Connor (1992) found that androgynous characteristics were the most desirable. Kurdek & Siesky (1980) found that androgynous individuals had higher self-esteem and social competence and were more behaviourally flexible than masculine, feminine or undifferentiated sex types.

With regard to mental health, the evidence is somewhat mixed. Although studies such as Steenbarger & Greenberg's (1990) found that androgynous nurses were less depressed and experienced lower levels of work stress than those identified as undifferentiated, masculinity was also associated with low levels of depression and femininity was associated with the best vocational adjustment. Similarly, Burchardt & Serbin (1982) found that androgynous individuals scored lower on depression and social introversion than feminine and undifferentiated individuals – but masculine types were also well adjusted.

Thinking creatively about psychology

Employers and employees stand to benefit from androgynous colleagues. Produce a list of possible masculine and feminine characteristics and identify how each could be advantageous in the workplace.

Some more specific problems have also been identified. Cook (1985) found that some androgynous people found that their sex type led to social pressures which had negative consequences such as anxiety and moodiness. Others found balancing their masculine and feminine traits difficult so were unable to direct their behaviour effectively.

The BSRI is a very reliable measure but questions have been raised about its validity. For example, Bem suggested that by comparing females to a male 'standard', androgyny was biased, defining the 'perfect *man*'; that androgyny, by being gender-neutral, failed to acknowledge the reality of historical gender inequalities; and, by focusing on male/female relationships it implies that heterosexuality is a 'norm'.

The BSRI was based on the opinions of 100 American students in the 1970s. The extent to which this is valid is questionable in terms of both historical changes and cultural differences in what is considered to be masculine and feminine. A further challenge suggests that reducing the differences to two constructs — of masculinity and femininity — is too simplistic. Golombok & Fivush (1994) observe that few men or women have all the personality traits theoretically associated with their gender, which implies that there must be narrower or more specific dimensions, for example gender-related behaviours, abilities, interests and social relationships.

Consider the extent to which society values traits (from the BSRI) such as being ambitious or gullible — the former is masculine and positive, the second feminine and negative. This issue is overcome by an alternative measure of androgyny, the Personal Attributes Questionnaire, which identifies positive attributes associated with each gender (Spence *et al.*, 1973).

▼ Table 6.3 **Items from the Personal Attributes Questionnaire**

Male	Female
active	emotional
adventurous	kind
outspoken	considerate
intellectual	creative

Gender dysphoria

So far we have assumed that people with male bodies 'feel like males' and people with female bodies 'feel like females'. This, however, is not always the case. In cases of gender dysphoria (gender identity disorder) the individual feels that they are trapped in a body of the wrong sex — they are *transsexuals*. This results in uncertainty, anxiety and distress, which can lead to depression and suicide. This is worsened by the prejudice and misunderstanding that such individuals face from society. Although the condition is relatively rare, with an estimated 4000 people in the UK receiving medical help, there are probably many people who are undiagnosed. Many more men are affected (ie have male bodies but feel that they are female) than women. For example, Wilson *et al.* (1999) surveyed all general practices in Scotland and found that gender dysphoria was reported in approximately eight in 100,000 patients and a ratio of 4:1 males to females.

▼ Table 6.4 *DSM-IV-TR* **criteria for diagnosing gender identity disorder**

1	Evidence of a strong and persistent cross-gender identification.
2	This cross-gender identification must not simply be a desire for any perceived cultural advantages of being the other sex.
3	Evidence of persistent discomfort about one's sex or feeling inappropriate in the gender role of that sex.
4	No physical intersex condition (eg androgen insensitivity syndrome).
5	Evidence of significant distress or impairment in social, occupational or other important areas of functioning.

LOOKING FURTHER Gender roles in society are less fixed than they were 50 or even 20 years ago. David Beckham has been described as a 'metrosexual icon'. Investigate what this means in terms of androgyny and the extent to which a metrosexual individual benefits from this image.

▲ Figure 6.9

The symptoms may become apparent early in childhood, with a reluctance to wear clothes typical of the child's own gender – such as boys wanting to wear dresses rather than trousers — or to engage in sex-typed games. Such behaviour is often a normal part of growing up, but where these feelings persist through adolescence and into adulthood, they may indicate gender dysphoria. Wallien & Cohen-Kettenis (2008) followed up a group of children who were gender dysphoric. Their study is discussed in *Research Now*.

Other symptoms include children insisting they the opposite sex, expressing a hope of 'becoming' the opposite sex or refusing to urinate in the manner typical for their sex — such as a girl wanting to stand up. For many individuals with gender dysphoria, puberty is extremely distressing, although for others symptoms do not become apparent until adulthood.

The distress people with gender dysphoria experience is associated with the physical signs of their bodily sex, especially their genitalia. Trans-women (men with a female gender identity) may want to hide or get rid of their muscular male shape and facial or body hair. Trans-men may want to remove their breasts. These feelings may be lessened by taking on the gender role of the preferred sex, such as dressing or living as the preferred gender does.

KEY TERM

transsexual an individual with gender identity disorder (gender dysphoria). They have an absolute conviction that they are trapped in a body of the wrong gender

RESEARCH NOW

Wallien MS & Cohen-Kettenis PT (2008) Psychosexual outcome of gender-dysphoric children. *Journal of the American Academy of Child and Adolescent Psychiatry* **47**(12), 1413–23

Aim: to find out whether children who are gender-dysphoric retain their gender identity.

Method: 77 children with gender dysphoria (59 boys, 18 girls; mean age 8.4 years, aged 5–12 years) were assessed for cross-gender identification and discomfort with their own sex and gender roles. Fifty-four children were followed up approximately seven to 13 years later (at about age 19, range 16–25 years) and were again assessed for gender dysphoria and for sexual orientation.

Findings: 27 per cent (12 boys and nine girls) were still gender dysphoric (GD group) and 43 per cent (28 boys and five girls) were not (non-GD group). Both boys and girls in the GD group were more extremely cross-gendered in their behaviour and feelings and were more likely to satisfy the criteria for a diagnosis of gender identity disorder than the other children. At follow-up, most male and female participants in the GD group were homosexual or bisexual. In the non-GD group, all of the girls and half of the boys were heterosexual.

Conclusions: Most children with gender dysphoria do not remain gender dysphoric after puberty. However, those with persistent gender identity problems have more extreme symptoms in childhood than children who do not become gender dysphoric. Childhood gender dysphoria is also associated with a homosexual or bisexual gender orientation.

Thinking creatively about psychology

Imagine that you are a parent of a child with gender dysphoria. What advice would you give? Think carefully about the possible outcomes for the individual child. You may want to read to the end of this section before coming to firm conclusions about your advice.

▶ **Figure 6.10** Cross-dressing may help to relieve the feelings of distress associated with gender dysphoria

Gender dysphoria is classified as a psychiatric condition although recent evidence suggests there may be a range of physical causes, suggesting it is not purely psychological. As we will see later, the sexual development of a baby is determined by the chromosomes it inherits and the effect they have on the release of hormones. This means that there are several stages at which the biological impact on the development of gender identity can be influenced.

✎ Exploring issues and debates
Ethics

Psychologists have a responsibility to respect and assist individuals and to act in the best interests of society.

Draw a mind map to illustrate the issues confronting psychologists conducting research with transsexual individuals.

To help individuals with gender dysphoria, several routes are possible. The least drastic is to enable the individual to become more content by living as their preferred gender either some or all of the time.

Thinking creatively about psychology

People approaching transition are offered guidance not just on dress, but on deportment – so individuals can carry themselves and adopt the posture and behaviour associated with their gender identity – and help with speech and with hair removal. Think about why these aspects might be important to the transsexual person's sense of self.

Some individuals are unable to live with the feelings of being trapped in the wrong sex body. Under medical supervision these individuals can take hormones to change their physical appearance. These differ according to the individual's gender identity:

- trans-men take androgen therapy – this has masculinising effects such as enlarging muscles, enhancing growth of facial and body hair and lowering the voice
- trans-women take anti-androgen therapy – this has feminising effects such as reducing muscle volume and body hair and inducing breast growth.

For some transsexual individuals only full transition to the sex of their gender identity enables them to feel appropriate, so they undergo surgery to change their anatomical gender permanently. This is called gender reassignment, gender confirmation surgery or simply 'transitioning'. Prior to this irreversible step, individuals needs to have experienced living in their preferred gender identity to be certain that they are making the right decision. In the UK, this requires them to have lived in the desired gender role 24 hours a day for at least a year before they are considered. The treatment received is performed in stages and includes:

- for trans-men – mastectomy (breast removal), hysterectomy (removal of the womb), removal of the fallopian tubes and ovaries, and the construction of a penis (enabling the individual to urinate standing up and retain sexual sensation)
- for trans-women – mammoplasty (cosmetic breast surgery), removal of the testes and penis, and the construction of a vagina and labia (from the leftover tissue of the penis and scrotum).

Some, but not all, transsexuals who undergo transition experience a change of sexual orientation, but it is important to realise that for a transsexual, it is the mismatch between their physical sex and their gender identity that is problematic, not their sexual orientation. Thus it is unsurprising that in a review of 20 years of treatment of transsexuals in Serbia, Vujovic *et al.* (2008) report that, although 10 per cent of those applying for sex reassignment chose not to undergo the surgery, of those who did, none regretted their decision.

Thinking critically about psychology

Children over 16 years of age with gender dysphoria may be treated with hormone blockers to arrest development. Why do you think this treatment is not available for younger children and that full hormone therapy is only available to over-18s?

Where sexual ambiguity is evident in the chromosomes or genitalia, gender dysphoria is not diagnosed (although it is understandable). For those individuals where biologically they appear to be one sex but psychologically another, the explanation is more complex and, as yet, not fully understood. Evidence suggests that during the development of the foetus, hormones affect the masculinisation or feminisation of the brain. It is likely that disruption to this process is one cause of gender dysphoria. Kula & Słowikowska-Hilczer (2000) reviewed findings in relation to the causes of gender dysphoria and identified several key issues including:

- experimental studies on animals show that sex hormones prior to birth have a key influence on sexual behaviour in adulthood
- in patients with abnormal external genitalia caused by hormone imbalances, genetic and physical sex and gender identity may not correspond again, suggesting that hormones are vital in the development of an individual's gender identity.

Some of this evidence is explored in more detail in the next section. One recent source of evidence suggesting that transsexualism is not, as it has been accused of being, a 'lifestyle choice' but a matter of biology comes from a genetic study of the cell-surface receptors for androgens (male hormones) – see *Research Now*.

Thinking critically about psychology

Consider the ethical issues raised in research such as Hare *et al.*'s. What issues would the researchers need to consider for both the transsexual and control participants?

RESEARCH NOW

Hare L, Bernard P, Sánchez FJ, Baird PN, Vilain E, Kennedy T & Harley VR (2009) Androgen receptor repeat length polymorphism associated with male-to-female transsexualism. *Biological Psychiatry* 65(1), 93–6

Aim: To demonstrate a genetic component to transsexualism by investigating gene variants of the androgen receptor (AR) which affects the action of testosterone, and two other genes including one for an oestrogen receptor.

Method: 112 male-to-female transsexuals and 258 non-transsexual males were used to obtain samples of the three genes.

Results: A significant association was found between transsexualism and the AR gene, with transsexuals having longer AR genes than non-transsexual male controls. (Transsexualism was not associated with patterns in the other genes.)

Conclusion: Gender identity may be affected by the androgen receptor. In transsexual males it would fail to masculinise the brain during foetal development as the long version of the gene results in weaker testosterone signals.

Genetic differences that affect hormones could produce effects on gender identity in different ways. One likely route is through changing brain structure. Zhou *et al.* (1995) studied a brain area known to differ in size between men and women (the central subdivision of the bed nucleus of the stria terminals or BSTc). This area, essential for sexual behaviour, is normally larger in men than women. Their study of trans-females showed that they had female-sized BSTcs – and that this difference was independent of sexual orientation or the effect of sex hormones in adulthood. This therefore provided good evidence that gender identity develops as a result of an interaction between the developing brain and sex hormones. In a study to check the findings of this research, Kruijver *et al.* (2000) investigated the number of neurones present in the BSTc region. Again men (regardless of sexual orientation) were found to have almost twice as many neurones in this area as women, but the number in trans-females was significantly more similar to that for females. Furthermore, the number for trans-males was

in the male range. The validity of this evidence for a biological basis for gender identity is supported by the observation that these differences were unaffected by hormone treatment or sex hormone variations in adulthood – the transsexuals' brains and gender identity are clearly in conflict.

Studies conducted on individuals with physical disorders that cause early disruptions to sex hormone levels have confirmed that these differences early in development do affect gender identity (Cohen-Bendahan *et al.*, 2005). However, it is also important to show that this, in turn, affects cognition in transsexuals. Cohen-Kettenis *et al.* (1998) used tests of cognitive abilities such as verbal memory that illustrate differences between males and females. When early-onset but hormonally untreated transsexuals were tested, differences were also found. The scores of trans-males and trans-females were intermediate between those of the control males and females, showing that, in cognitive style, the transsexual individuals performed unlike members of their biological sex.

It's all in the genes for a transsexual

The Daily Mirror, 27 October 2008

Transsexual men who 'feel' female have an unusual version of a gene that affects the male sex hormone, a study shows. The discovery was made by scientists who examined DNA from 112 male-to-female transsexuals.

In many cases there was a longer version of a gene known to modify the action of testosterone. This may 'under-masculinise' the brain's development in the womb.

The Australian study leader, Dr Vincent Harley, said: 'There is a social stigma that transsexualism

is simply a lifestyle choice. However, our findings support a biological basis of how gender identity develops.'

1 Consider Dr Harley's comment. Why do you think this research is so important for people who are transsexual?

2 What scientifically crucial part of the procedure of the study is omitted from this report that was essential for the researchers to be sure about the role of the gene?

R E S E A R C H   N O W

Garcia-Falgueras A & Swaab DF (2008) A sex difference in the hypothalamic uncinate nucleus: relationship to gender identity. *Brain* 131(12), 3132–46

Aim: To investigate the role of part of the brain called the interstitial nucleus of the anterior hypothalamus (INAH) area 3 in gender dysphoria.

Method: 42 post-mortem brains were examined from 14 control males, 11 control females, 11 trans-females, one trans-male and five non-transsexual males who were castrated because of prostate cancer. The volume and number of neurones in the INAH3 was measured.

Results: The INAH3 was almost twice as big in control males as females and contained 2.3 times as many cells. The volume and number of neurones in the INAH3 of trans-females was similar to that of control females. The trans-male had an INAH3 volume and number of neurones within the male control range, even though testosterone treatment had stopped three years before death. The castrated men had an INAH3 volume and neurone number between that of males and females. There was no difference in INAH3 between pre-and post-menopausal women, showing that the feminisation of the INAH3 in trans-females was not due to oestrogen treatment.

Conclusion: The differences suggest that the INAH3 in transsexual people indicates an early change in sexual differentiation of the brain that is related to (though not necessarily the cause of) gender identity.

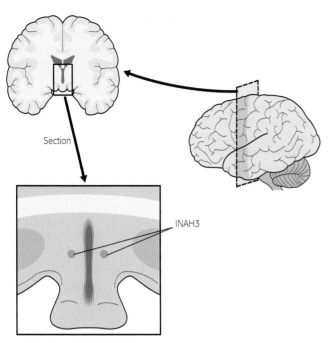

▲ **Figure 6.11** The INAH3 lies on either side of the midline of the brain, just above the optic chiasm (where information from the left and right eyes crosses over)

Studies into the causes of gender dysphoria are both practically and ethically difficult. Garcia-Falgueras & Swaab's (2008) study is particularly good because there were so many groups to compare offering good controls. Using these ideas, design an ethical study that investigates the cognitive styles of transsexuals.

Although the evidence for the influence of genetics and hormones is very strong, it is not simple. There are many interacting factors contributing to the development of gender identity and this can explain why not all research findings demonstrate clear patterns. For example, Hunt *et al.* (1981), like Cohen-Kettenis *et al.* (1998), found that, on intelligence tests, the conceptual style used by transsexuals matched their gender identity. However, they also found that their overall performance more closely resembled that of their biological sex.

Biological influences on gender

Men and women look and sound different and there are behavioural differences too. At least some of these are purely biological. This section looks at the role our biology plays in controlling sex differences in development.

▼ **Figure 6.12** The X and Y chromosomes

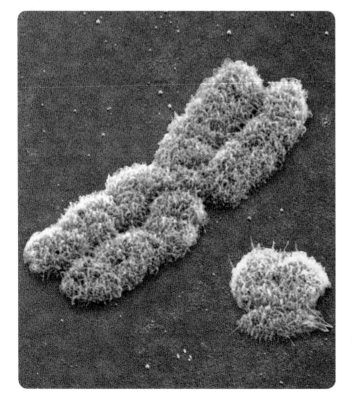

The role of genes and hormones in gender development

The genetic control of sex

A person's genetic sex is determined at conception by the *sex chromosomes* (called X and Y) they inherit from each parent (see Figure 6.12). Each egg cell (from the mother) contains an X chromosome. Each sperm (from the father) can contain either an X chromosome or a Y chromosome. If the combination is XX, the child will be female. If there is one X and one Y chromosome (making XY) the child will be male (see Table 6.5). This combination of chromosomes, XX or XY, is called the *genotype*. The resulting characteristic, in this case the genetic sex, is called the *phenotype* – it is the physical expression of the *genes* that have been inherited.

KEY TERMS

genotype   the genes an individual has for a particular characteristic

phenotype   the characteristics an individual displays; these may be physical, behavioural or psychological

sex chromosome   the X and Y chromosomes that are responsible for determining biological sex in humans and other mammals

genes   units of information that are inherited from our parents. They control, or influence, characteristics such as risk of mental health disorders, personality and sexual development

Chromosomes contain the genetic material that controls the biology of development. The X and Y chromosomes are responsible for guiding the development of an embryo into a male or female baby. This biological influence is very complex and is controlled by many genes. However, some aspects of it are quite clear. One of the key effects of the sex chromosomes is to trigger the development of glands that produce sex hormones, which control whether a foetus grows into a male or a female.

▼ Table 6.5 **Genetic sex determination**

		Sex chromosomes from the father	
		X	Y
Sex chromosomes from the mother	X	XX	XY
	X	XX	XY
Children inheriting XX will be female, those inheriting XY will be male			

Hormones and gender development

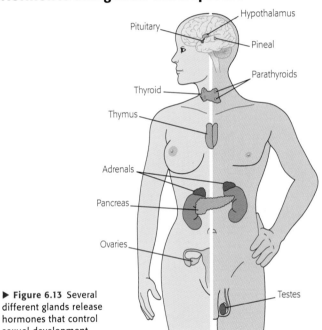

▶ **Figure 6.13** Several different glands release hormones that control sexual development

Hormones are chemicals in the blood that are released from glands. Together, these glands and their hormones form the *endocrine system*. Each hormone has 'target organs' — the parts of the body which the hormone affects. Sex hormones, such as oestrogen and testosterone, are released by the *gonads* (sex organs). Oestrogen is produced by the ovaries in sexually mature females and testosterone is produced by the testes in sexually mature males (although a little of each is produced by both sexes). These hormones are responsible for the changes that occur around puberty, such as the deepening of the voice in males and the onset of menstruation in females. These changes are specific to certain parts of the body because these are the target organs, eg the breasts in females or facial hair follicles in males. The changes caused by hormones have psychological as well as physical consequences.

Early in the development of the embryo, gonads begin to develop which produce both sex cells (gametes) and hormones. Until about eight weeks, all embryos are the same in terms of their physical sex. A single gene on the Y chromosome, called *SRY*, dictates whether the gonads become ovaries or testes. If *SRY* is present, it produces an enzyme called testes-determining factor

and the undeveloped gonads develop into testes. If the *SRY* gene is absent the foetus will remain female. If a genetically female mouse embryo, which lacks the *SRY* gene, has it implanted, it will develop into a male mouse (Koopman *et al.*, 1991).

▼ Table 6.6 **Hormones in puberty**

Hypothalamus gonadotropin-releasing hormone	
Anterior pituitary gland gonadotropic hormones	
Testes testosterone (male)	**Ovaries** oestrogen (female)

Without the *SRY* gene, the 'default mode' of a foetus is to be a female, so female sex organs such as the uterus and vagina develop. In male embryos the testes produce hormones called androgens that change this developmental sequence. Firstly, the hormones prevent foetal development into a female and secondly they trigger development into a male. One important androgen is testosterone, which makes the foetus into a male, for example causing the development of the external male sex organs such as the penis.

⟳ Exploring issues and debates
Animal research

Many experiments investigating the biology of gender development, both historical and contemporary, have been conducted on animals.

Draw a two-column table listing the strengths and limitations of such research. Try to distinguish between practical and ethical issues.

In normal sexual development, the testes and ovaries are also important after birth. After approximately a decade they become active again during puberty to control the development of secondary sexual characteristics. These are the physical features that distinguish women from girls and men from boys (see Figure 6.13). These changes, although caused by hormones from the *gonads*, are triggered by via a sequence of hormones from other glands (see Table 6.6). In males, androgens are again important. Both males and females are capable of producing testosterone and oestrogen but produce the 'opposite sex' hormone in only very small quantities. However, there are some important effects, for example testosterone in girls is responsible for the development of underarm and pubic hair at puberty (see Table 6.7).

▼ Table 6.7 **Secondary sexual characteristics**

Males (triggered by testosterone)	Females (triggered by oestrogen)
• production of sperm • growth of facial hair (and hair in armpits and pubic hair) • enlargement of the larynx (so deepening the voice) • increased muscle growth	• growth of breasts • development of fatty tissues, eg on hips • development of the lining of the uterus (part of the control system of the cycle that releases eggs and causes menstruation)

Androgen insensitivity syndrome is a disorder of sexual development. As the name implies, the individual's body does not respond to the masculinising effects of androgen. As the 'default' development of a foetus is to become female, a genetic male (XY) foetus that is insensitive to androgens grows testes under the influence of the *SRY* gene but then no further masculine

KEY TERMS

hormone a chemical that is released from a gland, travels in the blood and affects target organs (eg muscles, sex organs or other glands)

endocrine system all the hormones and the glands that produce them

gonads sex organs, the testes in males (which produce sperm and release testosterone) and ovaries in females (which produce eggs and release oestrogen)

Thinking practically about psychology

The inheritance of sex chromosomes is sometimes disrupted. In Turner's syndrome, the individual inherits only one sex chromosome, an X. Which sex would you expect people with Turner's syndrome to be? Why?

In Klinefelter's syndrome, the individual inherits two X chromosomes and a Y chromosome. Which sex would you expect people with Klinefelter's syndrome to be? Why?

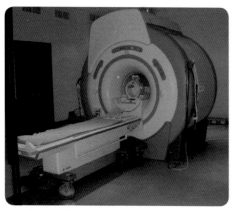

◄ **Figure 6.14** Rossell *et al.* (2002) used fMRI scanning to detect differences in brain activity between men and women

development occurs. The foetus develops female external genitalia, with the testes still inside the body, and the internal female genitalia do not form. At puberty, female secondary sexual characteristics appear, such as breasts and widening of the hips. This shows that both genes and hormones are important.

Genetic and hormonal differences might account for differences in structure between the brains of men and women, such as we saw on p127–8. Brain lateralisation is the idea that there are differences between the left and right sides (hemispheres) of the brain. Some of these patterns are more apparent in one sex than the other. Language is typically lateralised, with most comprehension and speech functions being controlled by the left hemisphere. Visuo-spatial skills, in contrast, are typically lateralised to the right. However, this pattern is more noticeable in men than in women.

Rossell *et al.* (2002) found both behavioural and brain differences in a task where participants were asked to judge whether a real word or a pseudoword had appeared on one side of a screen. A pseudoword is legally spelled and pronounceable, such as *cloom*. Men were faster if the stimulus was seen on the right, whereas women were faster if it appeared on the left. Brain scans showed that in men the response mainly generated activity in the left hemisphere, whereas in women both sides of the brain were activated.

Evolutionary explanations of gender roles

Natural selection and sexual selection

Many of the differences in brain and behaviour that we see between men and women can also be identified in animals. This suggests that, at least in part, these differences may be evolutionary in origin. Evolutionary explanations suggest that, for animals or the early humans we have descended from, there must have been advantages to certain abilities or ways of thinking. Their responses must have been, at least in part, under genetic control so that those individuals with advantageous behaviours would be more likely to survive and breed, and thus could pass their beneficial genes on to their offspring. This is the process of natural selection.

To account for sex differences, evolutionary explanations suggest that the selective pressures – the challenges in the environment – must have acted differently on males and females. Think about the evolution of humans in a hunter-gatherer society. Women needed to remember the locations of scattered plants for food. In terms of genes, women with any genetic advantage for remembering the location of widespread items would be more likely to pass on these genes to their well-fed offspring. Men who were aggressive and able to fight or hunt would be more likely to survive and protect their offspring. If these differences were due to genetic predispositions, they would be passed on, so females who remembered specific locations and males with aggressive tendencies would predominate.

Evolutionary theory and mate choice

Evolutionary explanations can also account for differences in men's and women's choice of sexual partner. Trivers (1972) proposed the idea of parental investment – the amount of effort an individual spends on having surviving offspring. In humans, females are committed by their biology to invest time and energy in pregnancy and breast-feeding. They therefore commit much more to each child than does the male – whose minimum provision is a single sperm. Trivers' theory suggests that, on the basis of this difference, women should be more fussy about their choice of partner than men. Women should prefer an individual who is likely to contribute to child-rearing – a man who is ambitious, rich and likely to look after them and their children!

▶ **Figure 6.15** According to evolutionary theory, men and women should look for different things in a potential mate!

Men, according to evolutionary theory, should look for signs of fertility in women since the selective pressure is to maximise the opportunities to father offspring. Males would therefore look for signs of youthfulness (indicating fertility) such as facial attractiveness.

Within a partnership, a woman can be certain that any offspring is her own. The same is not guaranteed for a man. Therefore, another characteristic that evolutionary theory would predict men should look for is chastity. On the basis of these predictions from evolutionary theory, women should seek rich, ambitious, industrious partners and men should seek chaste, young, attractive ones. Evidence supporting this pattern comes from Buss (1989) – see *Classic Research*.

Thinking critically about psychology

One problem with Buss's (1989) study was that the samples were selected in different ways in different counties and most were opportunity samples. Identify some of the strengths of the study and consider why this weakness may have been problematic.

Thinking creatively about psychology

If evolutionary pressures have contributed to the factors that affect mate choice, then it should be possible to see this in the way people describe themselves, and their desired partners, in 'lonely hearts' columns. Design a study to test evolutionary predictions in this context.

Increasingly, research is showing that the pattern of mate choice predicted by Trivers and demonstrated by Buss is not inevitable. Simpson & Gangestad (1991) developed a scale to measure sociosexuality – an indicator of sexual unrestrictedness (the Sociosexual Orientation Inventory). In a subsequent study they found that, although men rated attractiveness highly and women rated financial resources highly (as Buss had), they also found both men and women who were sexually unrestricted. Regardless of gender, these individuals rated attractiveness as important, whereas restricted individuals focused on personal and parenting qualities (Simpson & Gangestad, 1992). So, for example, unrestricted women emphasised physical attractiveness and sex appeal over financial resources or social status. These findings were based on a student population – and their views might not remain the same. The student populations may be more diverse and changeable in their social and sexual relationships than adult populations, which means that the findings may not generalise to adults.

Evolutionary theory and gender roles

Differences based on mate choice are not the only possible evolutionary causes of gender differences. Most cultures divide activities between the genders, be the society based on hunter-gatherer, agricultural or industrial labour. Wood & Eagly (2002) suggest that division of labour arises in pre-industrial societies as a product of biology. Women are constrained by the biological demands of motherhood and men are physically bigger, stronger and faster. The roles women take in this situation must be flexible and facilitate child care (eg not requiring distant travel or uninterrupted activity) and men can more efficiently perform tasks requiring physical strength (such as hunting and fighting in competition for resources). The actual behaviours performed by each gender would depend on the environment in which they lived.

CLASSIC RESEARCH

Buss, D (1989) Sex differences in humam mate preferences. *Behavioural & Brain Sciences* **12, 1–49**

Aim: To test the predictions of evolutionary psychology that men would prefer young, attractive and chaste women whilst women would favour industrious, ambitious and high-earning men, using a cross-cultural comparison.

Method: A survey asked 4601 males and 5446 females from 33 countries and 37 cultural groups about their preferred mate characteristics.

Results: In 36 of 37 samples women placed more emphasis than men on financial prospects and in 34 samples they placed more emphasis on industriousness and ambition. In all samples men emphasised attractiveness more than women and in all samples men gave a younger ideal age for a partner than women did. Attitudes to chastity were more variable. Only 23 of the 37 cultures revealed a gender difference, although where a difference existed, men placed more importance on chastity than women.

Conclusion: All of the predictions of evolutionary theory were supported, with men valuing indicators of fertility and certainty of being the father and women valuing the potential to look after children, ie ambition, industriousness and earning capacity.

If gender roles are the product of an evolutionary impact on the efficiency with which each gender can perform activities, patterns of division of labour should be consistent across cultures. Furthermore, the socialisation provided for girls and boys in a culture would be expected to enable them to perform the roles for which they are best adapted. If, however, gender roles are cultural constructions, they *might* (although would not necessarily) differ betwen cultures. Wood & Eagly made comparisons using several standard sources, detailing a range of aspects of many hundreds of different societies. This provided strong evidence that a sex-typed division of labour is characteristic of non-industrial societies, with men killing animals for food and working with metal, wood and stone, and non-hunters (primarily women) cooking vegetables, gathering food and fuel and caring for children.

▼ **Figure 6.16** Are gender roles rooted in our evolutionary past?

The findings from non-industrialised societies suggest that there is an evolutionary origin to sex roles. However, some evidence raises issues with this conclusion. According to Zeller (1987), much child care is conducted by older children in a society, as well as food gathering and preparation, so women could have been freed for other roles. Although some activities were always or almost always performed by men or by women in non-industrialised societies, there were also a larger number assigned to either sex – such as milking, planting, harvesting, weaving and making pottery. Nevertheless, within any one society, almost all tasks were performed primarily by one sex or the other.

In some non-industrialised societies women contribute a substantial amount to subsistence (eg Aronoff & Crano, 1975, estimated 44 per cent). In the majority, however, men are the primary providers. According to Wood & Eagly, this accounts for the relative status of men in such societies as they are at the centre of commerce, are readily able to access transportation and are more likely to engage in warfare. This means that, compared with women with specialised domestic roles, men have access to more senior public positions. Nevertheless, the existence of many exceptions to this rule presents a challenge for the evolutionary explanation.

Schmitt (2005) examined the findings of the Sociosexual Orientation Inventory (see p 131) given to over 14,000 participants across 48 nations. As expected on the basis of evolutionary theory, he demonstrated a cross-cultural universality in the pattern of sociosexuality, with males being much more promiscuous than females. However, two factors affected the extent of sex differences. Firstly, in cultures with greater political and economic gender equality, sociosexuality was more similar, supporting the view of Wood & Eagly. When reproductive environments were demanding, however, eg in harsh physical conditions, and with monogamy important to ensure the survival of children, the sociosexuality of women was lower. This again supports an evolutionary argument, though in this case the differences in mate choice between men and women were the product of an environmental rather than a cultural constraint.

LOOKING FURTHER You can read the whole of Schmitt's report as an ipaper at:

http://bradley.academia.edu/DavidSchmitt/ Papers/75078/ISDP-Sociosexuality

Clearly, many of the primarily male roles do require considerable strength, supporting the evolutionary view. However, some typically female tasks, such as carrying water and fuel, are also physically demanding and, according to Ember & Levinson (1991), there is little evidence to suggest that the predominantly 'male' tasks are, in fact, significantly more energetic. Thus, the most important evolutionary force may well have been the impact of pregnancy and lactation, leading women to specialise in those activities that could be performed simultaneously with these biological necessities.

The biosocial approach to gender development

As we have seen in the discussion of psychological androgyny and gender dysphoria, biological factors are very important but gender identity is not simply a matter of biological sex. The biosocial theory suggests that gender identity arises from the interaction of environmental and biological influences. Evidence for the early and spontaneous sex-segregated actions of boys and girls suggests that innate, biological factors are at work. For example, babies as young as 10 months will preferentially look at same-gender children in photographs or on film. Kujawski & Bower (1993) found that 10–14-month-old infants even preferred to watch another girl or another boy running and walking when all they could see were points of light attached to their limbs.

CLASSIC RESEARCH

Money J (1975) Ablatio penis: normal male infant sex-reassignment as a girl. *Archives of Sexual Behavior* **4(1), 65–71**

Aim: To use a surgical accident to investigate whether gender could be reassigned or whether it is biologically determined at birth.

Procedure: 45 males were followed up after gender reassignment. One in particular was of interest. This was because he had an identical twin, a natural control. Bruce and Brian were normal twin boys. At age seven months it was decided that the twins would be circumcised for health reasons. The operation on Bruce went wrong and, instead of simply severing the foreskin, burned across the penis. It was impossible to repair the damage surgically. Dr Money, a specialist in sex research, believed the best course of action was to surgically change Bruce's external genitalia to appear female and to raise the child as a girl. This decision was based on previous successes with sex-assignment of children born with ambiguous genitalia which suggested that children were 'gender neutral' at birth. Aged just under two years, Bruce was castrated, received oestrogen treatment and was renamed Brenda. Her family treated her like a little girl, for example letting her hair grow long and buying her dolls. She was seen at regular intervals by Dr Money. She also received further reconstructive surgery and hormone treatment to achieve the transition into a female appearance.

Findings: Money reported that at nine years old, Brenda had a female gender identity and predicted that in adulthood she would have a female sexual life. Although some tomboyish behaviours were seen, these were explained as the result of imitating her brother.

Conclusion: The evidence reported suggested that it was possible to reassign physical appearance through surgery and hormone therapy, and gender identity through rearing experiences. This implies that gender identity is undifferentiated at birth, ie that, in psychological terms, we are born 'gender neutral'.

▶ **Figure 6.17** Bruce during his adulthood as David. He was known during his childhood as Brenda

Thinking critically about psychology

Why, from a scientific viewpoint, was Money particularly interested in the case of Bruce?

John Money (see *Classic Research*) continued to report the success of Brenda's gender reassignment and vigorously opposed conflicting opinions. However, the reality of 'Brenda's' experience was very different from that which was implied in his reports. From the outset, she rejected her treatment as a girl and found both her childhood feelings and the expectations of others increasingly difficult to cope with. She was ultimately told about her early life and chose, with relief but many painful operations, to revert to a male identity and assumed the name 'David'. The evidence of the failure of the gender reassignment conducted by Money was reported by Diamond & Sigmundson (1997). The subsequent reports suggest that Money's conclusion was incorrect and that, in the case of sexually unambiguous individuals, gender identity is biologically determined.

LOOKING FURTHER Use the internet to search for information about David Reimer and other similar cases. Some interesting reports include:

- http://www.guardian.co.uk/print/0,,4921671-103680,00.html
- http://infocirc.org/rollston.htm
- http://slate.com/toolbar.aspx?action=print&id=2101678
- http://www.cbc.ca/news/background/reimer/
- http://www.ukia.co.uk/diamond/ped_eth.htm

Remember, however, to think critically — not everything that you will read can be substantiated.

Although the initial evidence from Money (1975) supported the biosocial explanation of gender identity, the subsequent evidence from the case of David Reimer did not. However, more recent evidence based on another case of ablatio penis suggests otherwise. Bradley *et al.* (1998) report on a similar situation to David Reimer's. After damage to a normal male infant's penis at two months, his gender reassignment began early. At seven months the decision was made to raise the child as a girl. When interviewed aged 16 and again at 26 years, the individual – whilst aware of her history – felt unquestionably female. Although she recalled being quite tomboyish as a child, she also preferred girls as friends. In adulthood, she was bisexual in sexual orientation (unlike David Reimer, who was heterosexual). Whilst again only a single case, this does suggest that controlling biological factors such as hormones and the home environment can change gender identity. In the next section we will consider exactly how social factors can influence gender development.

Social contexts and gender role

Kohlberg and gender schema theory focused on the child's understanding of gender but neither considered the way in which this understanding is acquired or translated to sex-typed behaviour. We have also considered how genes and hormones determine sex but have seen that neither biological sex nor gender identity are clear cut, such as in cases of androgen insensitivity or gender dysphoria. One way that we characterise maleness and femaleness is through behaviour and social roles. In this section we look at the importance of social contexts to the acquisition of gender identity and sex-typed behaviours.

One way in which social context may provide a route for the acquisition of gender stereotyped behaviour is through observing role models. Social learning theory proposes that learning can occur when one individual observes and imitates another – called the model. For example, a young girl may watch an older one putting on make-up and try to copy her. According to Bandura (1977) this will occur when the observer pays attention, is able to remember and reproduce what has been observed and when they are motivated to do so. This motivation may be an external reward or some inner drive. Internal motivation may be generated by the model and this can explain why there are differences in the effectiveness of different models.

One key feature of models is their gender. The findings of Bandura *et al.* (1961) (see p75) suggest that same-sex models are more effective than opposite-sex models for increasing aggressive behaviour in children. Is the same pattern found in the acquisition of other gender-stereotyped behaviours? Before we can answer this question, we need to know a little about what the stereotyped expectations might be.

Williams & Best (1990) have shown that beliefs about maleness and femaleness are fairly consistent across cultures. Golombok & Fivush (1994) suggest the essence of these stereotypes are:

- male: being instrumental, ie acting on things in the world to make things happen
- female: being relational, ie having a concern for interactions between people and how they feel.

These differences are then reflected in identifiable beliefs and expectations in society, for example that:

- males: will be aggressive, active and competitive
- females: will be nurturing, passive and co-operative.

Note that just because these stereotypes are widely believed does not mean that they represent real differences between the sexes. One difference is clear, however, namely that, in general, traits associated with maleness are more highly valued in society.

A child will be exposed to models of both sexes. As Bandura has shown, they are more likely to imitate same-sex models. However, there are factors other than the role model to consider. When children copy gender-matching behaviour they are likely to be reinforced, for example by parents or by same-gender peers. Girls may be encouraged when playing with dolls but ignored, laughed at or told off for playing with guns. The reverse is often the case for boys. This selective reward or 'reinforcement' shapes their behaviour to conform to gender stereotypes. Because they are reinforced more for same-sex activities than opposite-sex ones, children learn to value sex-typed behaviours for their own gender more than those for the opposite gender. This effect is also evident in the way children treat one another – children who engage in counter-stereotyped behaviour are less popular than ones who are

◀ **Figure 6.18**
Children are motivated to imitate adult models as they are seen as powerful. However, same-sex models are preferred, and we may acquire sex-typed behaviours by observing and imitating them

more stereotypical. Even in adulthood such influences are still powerful. An assertive woman may be described as 'pushy', a caring man as a 'wimp'. These represent significant pressures to behave in what society dictates to be 'gender-appropriate' ways.

Social influences: parents, peers, schools and the media

Evidence suggests that both imitation and reinforcement do occur. Lytton & Romney (1991) reviewed studies of how parents treat male and female children. They found that

sex-typed behaviour was encouraged in both genders, for example shaping children's choices of activities and interests. However, there were also many similarities in the ways that boys and girls were raised and they concluded that it was unlikely that differences in reinforcement could account for the acquisition of sex-typed behaviour.

In a review of studies, Tenenbaum & Leaper (2002) found a weak relationship between the gender-related self-concept and attitudes held by children and their parents – children of parents with stereotyped beliefs were stereotyped themselves. There may be many ways in which such a pattern could arise.

M E D I A   W A T C H : DIY mental health check

Pink toys create generation of 'princesses'

John Bingham, *The Daily Telegraph,* **January 2009**

http://www.telegraph.co.uk/family/4074374/Pink-plague-on-the-High-Street-widening-gender-gap.html [edited]

Experts have claimed that the so-called 'pink plague' on the High Street is brainwashing girls and reinforcing gender stereotypes. They claim that girls are already becoming 'hooked' on the colour before the age of three and soon reject toys and clothes if they are not pink.

The apparent increase in pink in products for girls has incited heated debate on parents' internet discussion forums and educationalists believe that it is widening the gender gap.

'You can't find girls past the age of three who aren't obsessed with the colour,' said Sue Palmer, an author who wrote the book *Toxic Childhood.* 'You can't seem to get anything that's not pink for girls, whether it's clothes, books or toys. To me, the real danger is the extent to which marketers influence and infiltrate young children's minds.'

The subject has attracted hundreds of postings on the mothers' website, Mumsnet. 'I cannot believe how sexist toys are.'

Scientists are divided over why exactly young girls seem to have such a strong attraction to the colour pink. Many point to social conditioning, with girls developing a love for the colour after being surrounded by it from the moment they are first laid down to sleep in their pink-walled nursery wrapped in pink blankets.

Others believe the attraction could be somehow 'hard-wired' with one recent study showing a marked preference for pink among girls and women in different cultures.

In a study published last year by Anya Hurlbert and Yazhu Ling of Newcastle University, volunteers were shown various combinations of colours and asked to indicate their favourites within a split

▲ Figure 6.19

second. Female participants showed a marked preference for pink or red shades while men were more likely to opt for blue, suggesting a possible inbred preference.

1 Find examples from this article which relate to ideas about gender schema, evolutionary theory and social context.

2 To what extent do you agree with the conclusion from Hurlbert & Ling's study?

Parents with stronger stereotypes may be more gender-typical models, offer toys or opportunities that are gender-biased or may reinforce sex-typed behaviour.

Parents, of course, can begin to influence children very early in development. Lindsey & Mize (2001) investigated parents' play with their pre-school children. They found that parents, especially mothers, engaged in more pretend play with their daughters than their sons. Fathers also engaged in more physical play with their sons than they did with their daughters. This suggests that pretend play may provide an early context for gender-role differentiated behaviour, especially as Lindsey & Mize also found that the children themselves replicated the pattern in their own play. Girls were more likely than boys to engage peers in pretend play, while boys were more likely to play physically.

Not only do parents' behaviours affect their children but their beliefs do too. Friedman *et al.* (2007) found that mothers' gender attitudes predicted the gender stereotyping of their younger children (aged three to five) though not their older ones.

Schools provide another source of adult role models. Bigler (1995) conducted a field experiment in which classroom teachers were asked to use gender as a category in the classroom, for example to divide children into working groups. Control class teachers were asked to divide children into 'colour' groups (red/green) or were given no explicit instructions about groupings. Four weeks later, the children in the experimental group demonstrated more gender stereotyping views compared with their pre-test scores.

The materials used in schools may also promote gender stereotyping. Calvert *et al.* (2003) used an internet game to ask children aged eight to 12 about their favourite educational and informational television programmes. The children's reports were stereotyped (reflecting the content of the programmes), containing more male than female characters, pronouns and behaviours – this was especially true for boys. The pattern was eliminated, however, for boys who chose a programme with an adventurous female lead character and, although males were usually portrayed in masculine roles, females were equally likely to be described in masculine as in feminine roles. As girls grew older, their preferences changed towards programmes featuring female lead characters and their written reports changed accordingly. Calvert *et al.* concluded that it is characters' actions, rather than their gender, that matter to children. The design of educational material is therefore important to ensure that the quality as well as the quantity of male and female role models is balanced.

The models to which children are exposed are not simply the people they encounter in life, such as their parents, peers or teachers. The media provides a range of very powerful models as they are often high in status, likeable and seen to be reinforced. All of these factors increase the likelihood that they will be imitated. Ceulemans & Fauconnier (1979) conducted an extensive review of the representation of women in mass media, eg in advertising, television, film and radio. Their findings showed an overwhelmingly stereotypical representation. Research into a range of media suggests that the sexes are still represented in biased ways.

Thinking critically about psychology

David Bell, chief executive of school inspection service Ofsted, suggested that it was important for girls to have strong fictional female characters such as Buffy the Vampire Slayer. Explain why Buffy would be an excellent role model for girls.

▲ **Figure 6.20**

LOOKING FURTHER Use the internet to search for recent research into gender stereotypes in the media. You might compare the findings to those reported three decades ago by Ceulemans & Fauconnier available at: http://unesdoc.unesco.org/images/0003/000370/037077eo.pdf

▼ **Table 6.8 Source: Evans & Davies (2000)**

Trait	Males	Females
Aggressive	24	5
Competitive	36	11
Emotionally expressive	14	33
Passive	8	30

One focus of research has been on gender representation in children's books. Although books are much less stereotyped than they were, significant differences in representation still exist. Evans & Davies (2000) looked at the books published in 1997 for children in the first, third and fifth grade at school. They found that, although there were approximately equal numbers of males and females represented (54 per cent and 46 per cent respectively), the characters were still somewhat stereotypical (see Table 6.8). Similarly, Milburn *et al.* (2001), in an analysis of males and females in computer clip art, found that males are more often portrayed as active and non-nurturing than females.

Thinking practically
about psychology

▼ **Figure 6.21** What proportion of readily available images of men and women are gender-stereotyped?

You could replicate Milburn *et al.*'s study using actual clip art or other sources such as magazine images. Think carefully about what search terms to use if you look for clip art and how you will classify images as gender-stereotyped or gender-neutral. If you work in a group, consider the reliability of individuals' rating the images.

We have seen that children copy real and media same-sex models and that they experience selective reinforcement. Evidence appears to confirm that for media sources such as television, observing stereotyped models in programmes does lead to more stereotyped views and more sex-typed behaviour. Several studies (eg Morgan, 1982 — see also p137) have demonstrated that when children watch more television they hold more stereotypical views about sex roles. Children who are heavier TV viewers also choose more sex-typed toys (Frueh & McGhee, 1975). However, these findings tend to be difficult to interpret as other variables such as IQ are also important, and it is generally difficult to separate the effects of TV viewing itself and of family environment or the child's own selection of sex-typed programmes.

Evidence does not only suggest that there is a relationship between TV viewing and gender stereotypes in children. Ross *et al.* (1982) found that both adults and elderly people were more likely to hold stereotypical views if they watched more hours of television. However, research also shows that exposure to counter-stereotypical examples in real life can reduce these views.

▲ **Figure 6.22** Children's gender stereotypes are affected by their experiences of gender consistent examples and counter-stereotypes

Cordua *et al.* (1979) were interested in whether young children's gender stereotypes affect their memories. In their study, 128 children aged five to seven years were shown films illustrating each of the possible combinations of female and male doctors and nurses. The children's memory for gender-consistent illustrations of occupations was good. However, when faced with counter-stereotypes, the children tended to mis-recall them as male doctors and/or female nurses. Only 22 per cent of the children who saw a male nurse and a female doctor correctly remembered both roles. The tendency to re-label the male nurse was stronger than for the female doctor. This suggests that the children's gender schema (see p121) affected their recall. Neither sex, age nor number of recent visits to a doctor affected their accuracy. The participants' mothers' jobs, and whether they had encountered male nurses in real life, did however affect correct identification, suggesting that real-life models matter.

▲ **Figure 6.23** For girls, fathers are still important role models as men are more powerful in society. It is more acceptable for a girl to be a tomboy than for a boy to be a sissy

As evidence shows that television affects children's gender stereotypes, so programmes with a balanced outlook should have a positive effect. Johnston & Ettema (1982) compared nine to 12-year-olds before and after watching 26 episodes of a drama, *Freestyle*, which was designed to challenge gender stereotypes. They reported a significant reduction in stereotyping after watching the programmes. For example, their questionnaire responses showed that girls became more interested in sports and in roles that were traditionally male, such as being a mechanic or an engineer. Likewise, boys were more accepting of girls' participation in these activities. These effects were, however, very small unless viewing was backed up by classroom discussion.

It is not only dramas that contribute to gender stereotyping. Leaper *et al.* (2002) found that some cartoons were biased in their representation of men and women. In adventure cartoons there were more male than female characters and the former were more likely to be aggressive. Females in all types of cartoon were more likely than male characters to show fear, act romantically, be polite and act supportively.

M E D I A   W A T C H : a modern hero

Dad, lad, gay icon, player – why Beckham is Britain's model man

Dennis Campbell, *The Observer,* **2 February 2003**

David Beckham has overcome the hostility and endless jokes he inspires to emerge as the most influential man in Britain, according to a new academic study. An analysis of the effects of the England captain's global fame portrays him as a bold crusader who is making the world a better place by single-handedly transforming men's attitudes towards sex, love, babies, nights out with the lads and even homosexuality.

▼ **Figure 6.24** A potent role model

'David Beckham is a hugely important figure in popular culture and now probably the most influential male figure for anyone in Britain aged five to 60,' said Dr Andrew Parker of Warwick University, co-author of the research. 'By defying expectations in areas such as what clothes men are allowed to wear, he has helped create a complex new concept of masculinity. That has already begun to change male behaviour and has the potential to encourage a whole generation of young men who admire him to act more like him.'

The academics praise Beckham as a trailblazer for subverting male stereotypes by showing an interest in ballet and fashion, publicly confessing his love for his wife Victoria and daring to acknowledge his large gay following. 'He has broken so many strict traditional working class masculine codes of behaviour that he has the potential to influence lots of boys and young men to do the same, for example accepting homosexuality as part of life.'

1 What characteristics might make Beckham such a powerful role model?

2 Explain, using social learning theory, the process by which a young man might be influenced by David Beckham.

Thinking about social contexts can clearly help us to understand some aspects of the acquisition of gender stereotypes. There is considerable evidence to suggest that gender stereotyped models exist and that children are responsive to them. This evidence is, however, somewhat conflicting with many studies demonstrating fairly small effects and indicating that other factors, such as IQ and socio-economic status, are important in stereotyping. One interesting finding from Morgan (1982) was that girls with the heaviest TV viewing had the highest expectations of themselves. This is counter to expectations based on the negative effects of gender-stereotyped viewing, but was predicted by Morgan on the basis that female role models with professional status are well represented on television.

Although much evidence does support the sex-typed portrayal of males and females, this appears to be changing. Yanowitz & Weathers (2004) used content analysis to investigate the representation of males and females in undergraduate-level educational textbooks. They looked at the way real and fictitious males and females were represented in scenarios. Like previous researchers, they found some evidence of a bias in the way men and women are portrayed but they also found many similarities. They concluded that there was a very positive representation of both genders, for example in illustrating both genders acting bravely and being caring. This too suggests that modelling is important, but that it can have positive as well as negative influences.

↪ Exploring issues and debates

Nature–nurture

Our gender identity is fixed at birth.

Draw a two-column table to present evidence to support this idea on one side and evidence against it on the other.

Cross-cultural studies of gender role

Whilst much of the research we have looked at in this chapter was conducted in the UK or the USA we have also seen examples of the continuity of gender stereotypes across cultures such as in many of the findings from Buss (1989) and Schmitt (2005). In addition, we have looked at specific examples of studies carried out around the world that illustrate commonalities, such as in the findings of Vujovic *et al.* (2008) in relation to gender identity in transsexuals (from Serbia) and Cohen-Kettenis *et al.* (1998) in relation to cognitive styles in transsexuals in Holland.

Cross-cultural studies also find differences between cultures. These help to illustrate that evolutionary explanations alone are unlikely to be sufficient to explain differences in the attitudes, personality and behaviour assumed to represent males and females.

Some studies collect the same information from different cultures so that findings can be usefully compared, whilst others deliberately seek to compare cultures. In the former category, investigations of gender stereotyping in the media conducted in India provide a useful example. Behera (1989) reported that gender role biases in Indian television reinforced gender stereotypes that degraded women. Looking at news, fictional programmes and advertisements, Behera found women were commonly portrayed as victims, caretakers and sex objects, whilst men were presented as masters, doers and intellectuals. In news coverage, men featured in 71 per cent of items and women in only 10 per cent, in which they were often reported as needing welfare, as victims or in their role as a wife. In dramas, men were illustrated as decisive, assertive and career-oriented, whilst women were emotionally dependent, sentimental, concerned with family relationships and engaged in household chores. This bias, Behera concluded, impeded the struggle of women in India to achieve economic and political autonomy.

Thinking critically about psychology

How do Behera's findings compare to similar research in other countries?

Brown & Cody (1991) investigated the influence of a pro-social soap opera, *Hum Log*, on attitudes to women in India. Although the programme enjoyed good viewing figures and promoted a positive image of equality for women, it had little effect on the views of those who watched it, even when they were engaged with the characters. One reason for this may have been the way the women were presented. Often self-sufficient, career-focused women experienced negative consequences whilst those in more traditional female roles were rewarded. This suggests that, as we have seen before, it is the actions of the characters and the consequences of those actions that influence gender stereotypes.

Thinking critically about psychology

How do Brown & Cody's findings compare with similar research in other countries?

In a direct comparison of masculine and feminine traits measured in participants in Germany and the USA, Runge *et al.* (1981) used the Personal Attributes Questionnaire (PAQ — see p124). They found very similar stereotyped gender differences in both cultural groups. Research into the success of women in the traditionally male career domain of medicine provides an interesting example. Men and women enter medical school in approximately equal numbers and women are equally successful in the early stages of their medical careers (Alexander *et al.*, 2000). In both Germany and Switzerland, however, the proportion of men achieving a certificate in a medical specialty, particularly a prestigious one such as surgery, is much greater. Buddeberg-Fischera *et al.*

(2003) investigated why this difference might arise. Assessing students prior to graduation using various tests such as the PAQ, they found that women scored higher on traits such as helpfulness, empathy and family responsibility, but men scored more on traits such as independence, self-confidence, prestige and income. The women made career decisions earlier and preferred fields with more patient contact, whereas men opted for different areas including high-technology medicine.

LOOKING FURTHER If you want to look at a complete Personal Attributes Questionnaire, the first website below provides the questionnaire and the second gives the scoring system:

www.ewi-psy.fu-berlin.de/einrichtungen/arbeitsbereiche/arbpsych/media/lehre/ss08/12736/personal_attributes_questionnaire.pdf

www.yorku.ca/rokada/psyctest/paq.pdf

◀ **Figure 6.25** Although roughly as many women as men enter medical school and qualify, men have more prestigious careers

Chapter summary

Psychological explanations of gender

- Psychological explanations of gender development account for how children develop a sense of gender identity and engage in gender role behaviours.
- Kohlberg's cognitive developmental theory suggests that the complexity of children's gender identity is limited by their understanding. As their cognition develops, their gender identity matures too.
- According to Kohlberg, children engage in activities that are appropriate for their gender because when they know what gender they are and what society expects of that gender, they are rewarded by doing what other people expect of them.
- Evidence shows that children are more likely to make sex-appropriate choices once they can reliably identify their own gender, which supports Kohlberg.
- However, some evidence suggests that children make stereotyped choices before their gender identity is fully developed.
- Gender schema theory suggests that children develop a gender identity from information in their social world. As soon as they know their own gender their 'gender schema' directs their attention to same-gender information and motivates them to behave in gender-consistent ways.

- This accounts for why very young children show gender stereotyped preferences and behaviours — although they do not always do so. With less gender-stereotyped parenting, children are slower to develop sex-typed behaviours. Another problem is that boys and girls differ in the pattern of their gender development, with girls starting off more stereotyped than boys but ending up less so.
- Bem suggested that psychological androgyny, having both traditionally male and female characteristics, such as personality traits, was psychologically healthy. Although some evidence supports this, both Bem's measure of androgyny and the possible benefits have been criticised.
- Gender dysphoria is a serious mismatch between gender identity and biological sex. Children with strong feelings of gender dysphoria are the most likely to be transsexual as adults.
- The decision to have irreversible gender reassignment surgery is a difficult one but enables transsexuals to overcome their distress.

Biological influences on gender

- Biological studies have found genetic, neural and hormonal influences are important in the control of gender identity. Transsexuals' brains also seem to function more like those of the gender that they feel they are.
- Genes and hormones affect biological sex. Both XX (female) and XY (male) foetuses start off developing like females. In males, the *SRY* gene changes this to the male developmental pattern. These different developmental patterns are controlled in the foetus and at puberty by hormones such as oestrogen (female) and testosterone (male). These differences also produce gender differences in brain structure and function.
- As their biology commits female mammals to more parental care, evolutionary theory predicts that they would choose males who could provide help with child-rearing and, in modern terms, money. Evolutionary theory predicts a different strategy for male mammals, who should seek out young mates who are not already pregnant. In general terms these predictions hold across many cultures.
- Evolutionary theory also explains gender role differences. For early human societies child-care demands would have restricted the distance women could travel. This and the greater size and strength of males would have determined the division of labour.

- Although evidence from non-industrialised societies roughly supports this idea, the extent of the distinction between the roles of men and women and the necessity for women (rather than the younger or the older members of a society) to have responsibility for child care is variable.
- The biosocial approach to gender development suggests that both biology and social factors affect gender identity. Although biology is clearly important, changing biological factors such as hormones alone is not sufficient to change gender identity.

Social contexts of gender role

- Social learning theory suggests that children acquire gender role behaviours by observing and imitating same-sex models. These may be present in their social environment (eg parents and peers or at school) or in the media. Evidence suggests that all of these sources typically do provide gender-stereotyped models.
- Being selectively rewarded for gender-appropriate behaviour makes the acquisition of gender role behaviour more likely. This happens because children (and, to a lesser extent, adults) tend to prefer individuals who conform to gender stereotypes.
- Counter-stereotyped examples are, however, very important as gender stereotypes are limiting and inaccurate. Providing such models helps to reduce gender stereotyping.

What do I know?

1 (a) Outline psychological androgyny. (5 marks)
 (b) Describe biological influences on gender. (10 marks)
 (c) Evaluate biological influences on gender. (10 marks)

2 (a) Outline gender dysphoria and discuss research relevant to this issue. (9 marks)
 (b) Describe and evaluate the biosocial approach to gender development. (16 marks)

3 (a) Discuss **two** social influences on gender role other than culture. (10 marks)
 (b) Describe and evaluate cross-cultural studies of gender role. (15 marks)

4 (a) Outline evolutionary explanations of gender roles. (5 marks)
 (b) Compare the evolutionary explanation with **one** other explanation of gender roles. (20 marks)

5 Describe and evaluate **one** cognitive developmental theory of gender development. (25 marks)

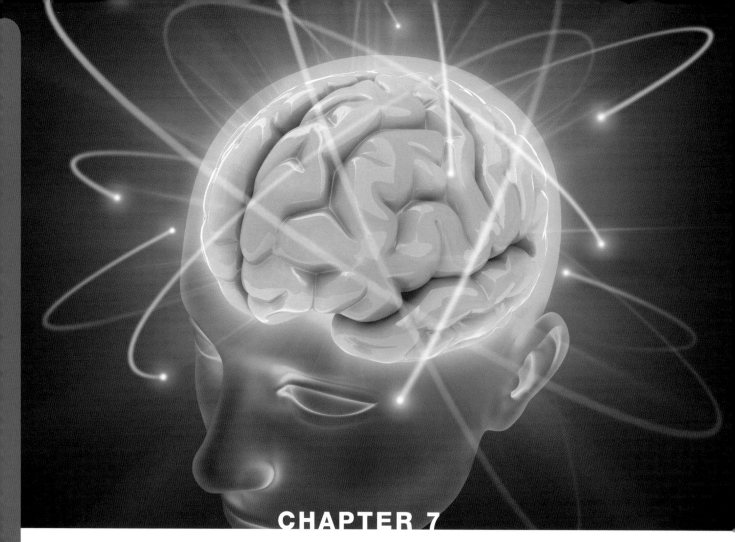

CHAPTER 7
Intelligence and Learning

Thinking ahead

By the end of this chapter you should be able to:

- define and describe concepts of intelligence

- describe and evaluate psychometric, information processing and learning approaches to intelligence

- describe and evaluate Gardner's theory of multiple intelligence

- describe and evaluate the nature of simple learning and its role in the behaviour of non-human animals

- describe and evaluate evidence for intelligence in non-human animals

- describe and evaluate evolutionary factors in the development of human intelligence

- describe and evaluate the role of genetic and environmental factors associated with intelligence test performance, including the influence of culture

Theories of intelligence

The concept of intelligence

There has been a huge interest in trying to measure *intelligence*, however it is hard to find a definition of intelligence that all psychologists agree with. If we cannot agree what we are supposed to be measuring, then measuring it is a challenge. As the whole subject of intelligence has been affected by the practical uses that have been made of intelligence test scores, and by the widely varying political viewpoints associated with the area, it has become a particularly difficult topic to study without bias.

There are different schools of thought as to what intelligence is. *Psychometric theories* define intelligence in terms of its measurement in order to show the intellectual differences between individuals, whilst *information processing theories* define intelligence in terms of the processes that individuals use in order to find solutions to problems. Each of these approaches has provided theories of intelligence.

▲ **Figure 7.1** Albert Einstein's insights into physics changed the way we see the world yet he was not identified as intelligent as a child. This illustrates how difficult intelligence is to define

Psychometric theories of intelligence

Psychometrics is a branch of psychology that tries to quantify our knowledge, abilities, characteristics and attitudes. Underlying the psychometric theories is an assumption that intelligence is a combination of abilities that can be measured by mental tests, such as questionnaires and paper and pencil tests. These theories differ in the number of basic factors that are believed to be associated with the concept of intelligence. We will explore two psychometric theories of intelligence.

Spearman's two-factor theory (1904)

Spearman observed that individuals who achieve a certain level on a test of one mental ability tend to score similarly on tests of other abilities. He reasoned that there must be a common factor that was producing this positive correlation. Spearman used the statistical method of *factor analysis* to identify the two basic factors measured by intelligence tests.

1 A general intelligence factor 'g' that underlies all intellectual tasks and mental abilities. This 'g' factor represented what all the mental tests had in common.
2 The measurement of specific abilities 's', such as verbal, mathematical and artistic skills, which are related to whatever unique abilities a particular test requires.

It was Spearman's belief that any intellectual activity had both a general and a specific factor and he placed more importance on general intelligence, as he believed that differences between individuals were mainly differences in 'g'. Spearman argued that 'g' was what scientists should mean by intelligence. His work became the major theoretical justification for intelligence testing.

In response to the criticism that he had not explained what caused general intelligence, in the 1920s Spearman suggested that it was a mental 'power' or 'energy'. It has even been suggested that 'g' may relate to neural efficiency or neural speed. Spearman saw general intelligence as being an entirely innate ability and believed that his theory would allow psychology to become a real scientific discipline.

▲ **Figure 7.2** Spearman suggested that people who were good at mathematical tasks were particularly skilled in that precise ability

KEY TERMS

intelligence the capability to comprehend our surroundings, to make sense of things and figure out what to do. Intelligence therefore involves the ability to apply knowledge in order to perform better in a given environment

psychometrics a branch of psychology that attempts to measure mental abilities such as intelligence. This is usually achieved by the formation and application of mental tests, for example IQ tests

factor analysis a statistical technique that reduces measurements down to the basic number of items (factors). This is done by finding out which items do not correlate with each other

information processing approach a cognitive psychological approach that sees the mind as a system that processes sensory information through the application of logical rules and strategies, rather like a computer

Discussion of Spearman's two-factor theory

Spearman's work stimulated interest and research into the study of intelligence and led to the use of factor analysis in psychology, but Spearman's two-factor theory was never widely accepted, and by the 1930s it was being replaced by multi-factor theories of intelligence. Although there are those who still work in the psychometric tradition, Kitcher (1985) stated that many scientists are convinced there is no single measure of intellectual ability and that the concept of general intelligence is a myth.

Although the idea of general intelligence has its opponents, there is evidence to suggest it does indeed exist. Johnson & Bouchard (2005) conducted an investigation into the structure of mental ability. They gave 42 wide-ranging tests of mental ability to 436 adults. Using factor analysis they claimed to have found a clear, single higher order factor, 'g'. They concluded that their results pointed towards the existence of a general intelligence factor that contributes substantively to all aspects of intelligence.

Guilford's structure of intellect theory (1967)

Guilford's theory is at the opposite end of the psychometric spectrum from Spearman's. Rather than Spearman's two factors, Guilford proposed 120! Unlike other psychometric theorists working in the intelligence field, Guilford rejects the notion of a general intelligence factor. A psychologist in the US Air Force in the mid-1900s, Guilford created his assessment tool to help the Air Force find pilots who would succeed in the field. From the use of factor analysis, Guilford argued that intellectual abilities could be divided into five types of *operation* (what kind of thinking an individual is being asked to perform), four types of *contents* (what an individual must think about) and six kinds of *products* (what kind of answer is required). These multiply together to produce 120 separate abilities.

A major impetus for Guilford's theory was his interest in creativity (Guilford, 1950). The divergent production operation identifies a number of different types of creative abilities. Guilford set out to devise tests to measure each mental ability. By 1985, 70 had been devised, but the scores people gained on these tests often correlated with each other, suggesting that the tests might be measuring the same thing and that therefore there may be rather fewer than 120 abilities.

Discussion of Guilford's theory

The multi-factor approach of Guilford offers an important alternative viewpoint to the more narrow psychometric theories, such as that of Spearman. Meeker (1969), a student of Guilford's, saw the potential of his work for use in the educational field, and modified the model to become an assessment and remedial teaching tool for students. The success of this model has proven it. Structure of Intellect (SOI), a teaching method that provides individual assessments based on identification of strengths and weaknesses, followed by a personalised learning programme, is currently being used in schools and learning clinics in North America to diagnose and help students with learning disabilities, as well as for enrichment of gifted students. Manning (1975), working with 490 gifted students, found that SOI is an effective tool that assists highly intelligent children to use their minds more creatively. Bradfield & Slocumb (1997) found that using the SOI teaching programme made students better critical thinkers. Parents expressed that the programme made their children better readers and, generally, more thoughtful children.

▲ **Figure 7.3** Some research has found that children taught in a style based on Guilford's SOI make better readers

 Using Google Scholar, update your notes on structure of intellect, looking in particular at how it has been applied in education.

▼ **Table 7.1 Guilford's structure of intellect model**

Content		Operations		Products	
Figural	*Sensory properties, eg smell*	Cognition	*Recognition and discovery*	Units	*A single letter, word or number*
Symbolic	*Numbers, letters etc*	Memory	*Retention and recall of thoughts*	Classes	*Higher order concepts, eg lion + tiger = cats*
Semantic	*The meaning of words and ideas*	Divergent production	*Producing solutions to problems*	Relations	*Connections between concepts*
Behavioural	*The actions of others*	Convergent production	*Producing one best solution*	Systems	*The ordering of relations*
		Evaluation	*Deciding whether intellectual content is good or bad*	Transformation	*Alteration of intellectual contents*
				Implication	*Inferring from separate pieces of information*

Evaluation of psychometric theories of intelligence

Although the factor-analysis-based psychometric theories made an important contribution to the area of study and stimulated research that led to useful practical applications, it had become apparent that there were serious problems with such theories. For one thing, the number of abilities seemed to be getting out of hand; a movement that began by theorising the existence of just one important ability had come to theorising over a hundred. This is because there are several ways to factor-analyse data, each of which produces a very different pattern of factors. Also an important methodological concern here is that different researchers used different types of participants in their studies. British theorists like Spearman used schoolchildren, who tend to have more diverse levels of intelligence than the college students used by American theorists such as Guilford. This might have contributed to the differing results and conclusions reached.

Most importantly, psychometric theories didn't seem to have anything substantial to say about the processes underlying intelligence. It is one thing to talk about 'general ability' and 'specific ability', but quite another to describe exactly what is happening in the mind when an individual is using the ability in question. The information processing approach proposed a solution to these problems, which was to study directly the mental processes underlying intelligence and then perhaps relate them to the factors of intelligence proposed by the psychometric approach.

Information processing approaches to intelligence

Rather than seeing intelligence as mental structures made up of factors, as the psychometric approach does, cognitive psychology believes instead that intelligence is made up of a set of mental representations of information and the set of processes that acts upon them, for example paying attention, encoding information, retrieving information and speed of processing. Therefore a more intelligent person will be able to represent information more clearly and act upon it more quickly. Researchers in this field therefore assume that intelligence is dependent upon the steps an individual goes through in order to solve a problem.

Sternberg's triarchic theory of intelligence (1977)

Sternberg believed that psychometric theories of intelligence were too narrow in that they focused solely on measurable mental abilities and identified only 'school smart' individuals as being intelligent. Sternberg stated that there were individuals who did poorly on IQ tests, but who were highly creative and had an advanced ability to adapt and shape their environment; such people he labelled 'street smart'.

Sternberg's theory can be regarded as radical in that it was the first theory to challenge the more established psychometric theories and propose a cognitive theory of intelligence. He defined intelligence as being how well individuals could deal with environmental changes throughout their lifetime. His triarchic theory consists of three subtheories or facets: analytical, creative and practical.

Analytical intelligence

Analytical intelligence is similar to the psychometric definition, which sees intelligence as that measured by academic problems and involving a series of components. He called these *metacomponents*, *performance components* and *knowledge-acquisition components*.

- *Metacomponents* are executive, higher-order control processes used in planning. They allow an individual to solve problems and make decisions and therefore are greatly involved in the managing of an individual's mind. Metacomponents are sometimes known as a *homunculus*, which is a kind of hypothetical person inside an individual's mind that controls their actions as they strive to solve problems and make decisions. For example, metacomponents are used to analyse a problem and pick the best strategy for solving it and they then oversee the performance components in carrying out the actions required.
- *Performance components* are the processes that carry out the actions required by the metacomponents in order to make decisions and solve problems. Such processes allow individuals to perceive problems and the relationships between objects by using long-term memory and then applying these relationships to decision-making and problem-solving. For example, performance components could involve making mental calculations based on knowledge stored in long-term memory in order to carry out the actions required to solve a problem, such as calculating which numbers to aim at in a game of darts.
- *Knowledge-acquisition components* are the processes used to learn new information. They permit the completion of tasks that involve selectively choosing information from seemingly irrelevant information. Knowledge-acquisition components also permit the selective combination of new information that has been collected. Highly intelligent individuals are seen as those who are gifted in using these components as they are able to acquire new information at a faster speed. For example, knowledge-acquisition components could involve the strategies used to memorise new information such as 'chunking' where a common meaning is found to bind several items together to be memorised. The strategies you use to help memorise things exemplify the processes that fall into this category.

Consider the problem below:

Ruaridh wishes to show the depth of his affection to his girlfriend Myfanwy by buying her a nice gift. He is in the jewellers and has given £100 to the shopkeeper to purchase a jet necklace when his ex-girlfriend Siobahn enters the shop with her mother. The jeweller hands him his purchase and £20 in change. How much did the necklace cost?

The solution involves using *metacomponents* that set up the structures to answer the question and monitor the progress of solving the problem (which involves subtracting £20 from £100). *Knowledge-acquisition components* are used to make decisions as to what information is relevant and what is not and *performance components* are used to actually calculate the sum involved by using knowledge about subtraction equations, stored in long-term memory.

Thinking practically about psychology

Read through the following scenario and see if you can identify the three components *(metacomponents, performance components* and *knowledge-acquisition components).*

Joe is playing a game of darts against his friend Louis. Joe has two darts left to throw and still requires 35 points and is also aware that he must finish on a double. He aims at 19, but misses and hits the 17 instead. His favourite number to finish on is double 8, while Louis always tries to go for double 20. What number must Joe throw to win the game?

Whilst Sternberg saw the components used as being the same for all individuals, he did recognise that people of different cultures would perceive the types of problems that needed solving in different ways, because of different contexts.

The creative/experential subtheory

The creative subtheory explains the relationship between intelligence and experience. This subcomponent is associated with how well a task is done with regard to how experienced an individual is with it. Sternberg divided experience into two parts, *novelty* and *automation.*

▲ **Figure 7.4** Driving can become largely automatic, allowing us to talk at the same time

- *Novel situations* are ones that have not been experienced before, and some individuals are seen as being especially skilled at dealing with such situations — for example, transferring skills and strategies learned from playing a familiar sport, such as tennis, to an unfamiliar one, such as badminton.
- *Automated situations* are ones that have been experienced many times before and can now be dealt with without extra thought being required. Such processes can be performed simultaneously with other processes *(parallel processing)* — for example, an experienced driver being able to drive a car safely, whilst being able to take part in a conversation at the same time.

An individual who is gifted in dealing with novel situations is not necessarily one who is gifted in dealing with automated situations and vice versa. The experiential subtheory is also associated with *synthetic giftedness*, the ability to create new ideas and solve novel problems — for example, recycling rubbish to make compressed bricks for housebuilding, not materials normally associated with construction. Such individuals do not necessarily score highly on IQ tests, as such tests do not measure this talent.

The practical/contextual subtheory

This explains the relationship between intelligence and the external world of an individual. Individuals use the three processes of *adaptation, shaping* and *selection* to manufacture an ideal fit between themselves and their environment. Individuals gifted with this subcomponent of intelligence were labelled 'street smart' by Sternberg.

- *Adaptation* happens when individuals change within themselves to adjust to their environment — for instance, keeping in the shade when temperatures soar.
- *Shaping* happens when individuals change their environment to fit their needs. For instance, a teacher may insist that students may make points only when directly asked, in order that disruption to a lesson does not occur.
- *Selection* occurs when an entirely new environment is chosen in preference to an inferior environment, in order to achieve an individual's needs — for instance, moving to a larger house as one's family grows in number.

Thinking creatively about psychology

You may have noticed our Thinking Critically, Thinking Creatively and Thinking Practically boxes throughout this book. We got the idea from Sternberg's theory. Sternberg suggests that psychology can be taught by putting exercises involving these three types of intelligence together. Put together a lesson for your class based on using all three types of intelligence.

More intelligent individuals are seen as those who are able to adapt their environment effectively to deal with situations encountered. The practical subtheory is also associated with *practical giftedness*, the ability to apply synthetic and analytical talents to everyday scenarios. Such individuals are able to adapt to any environment; they may not be especially gifted in analytical or synthetic skills, but are adept at working out what is needed to succeed in a given context — for example, someone very experienced as a footballer using their experience to devise a defensive game plan to use against a team that is more skilful. Sternberg acknowledged that individuals are not confined to being intelligent in only one of the three subcomponents, but can have a high degree of intelligence across the subcomponents.

◀ **Figure 7.5** Truly gifted footballers demonstrate practical intelligence as they respond to situations that develop during a game

Discussion of Sternberg's theory

Gottfredson (2003) has criticised the triarchic theory for not being scientific and claims it is absurd to believe that traditional IQ tests do not measure practical intelligence. As evidence for this she states how IQ tests can even predict the ability of high scorers to have high occupational prestige, live longer and even stay out of jail, all of which qualify as 'street smart'. She also claims that what Sternberg calls practical intelligence is not a broad aspect of cognition, but simply a specific set of skills people learn to cope with a specific environment — ie task-specific knowledge.

Merrick (1992) produced support for the triarchic theory by operationalising Sternberg's theory and thus making it testable. The Cognitive Abilities Self-Evaluative Questionnaire (CASE-Q) was given to 268 Dutch high-school students and the data produced was subjected to factor analysis. The results supported the components of Sternberg's theory, as individuals with of each of the three types of intelligence were found, and it was concluded that theory-driven measures of intelligence could be produced

The triarchic theory has practical applications as an educational tool. Grigorenko *et al.* (2001) conducted three studies on 1303 students at high- and middle-school level that assessed triarchically based instruction and assessment, emphasising analytical, creative and practical thinking and learning skills, as well as memory-orientated skills. In all the studies, triarchic instruction was superior to conventional teaching in improving student reading achievement.

Case's information processing theory (1985)

Case's theory of intelligence demonstrated how intellectual abilities develop and was built on Piaget's theory of cognitive development. The main focus of Case's theory, an individual's information processing ability, was related to the amount of *mental space* (M–space) they possessed.

Case explained that an individual's information processing ability developed with age due to three factors.

1 *Brain maturity* — faster neural transmission rates develop due to changes in the myelin sheath, the fatty insulating layer that lies around nerve fibres.
2 *Development of cognitive strategies* — the amount of M–space required to process tasks that have been mastered through practice reduces as children grow older. This frees up spare processing space that can be used for other cognitive tasks.
3 *Metacognitive skills* — these are mental abilities that allow individuals to concentrate on what they are thinking about. Their usage is crucial to the efficient use of M–space. This involves having a mental representation of the 'problem situation' and the 'solution situation' and then getting from one to the other by using the 'problem-solving process'. This involves moving through a set of operations that transforms the problem situation into the solution situation — for example, crossing a river using a series of stepping stones.

Evaluation of Case's information processing theory

Case's theory is able to explain the qualitative changes that occur in children's intellectual development as they age. Since it perceives intelligence in objective terms because the capacity of M–space can be determined, it should therefore be possible to measure intelligence as psychometric theories attempted to do.

It is possible to test Case's idea of M–space in an empirical way. Chi (1978) conducted research where the ability of child chess players to recall the positions of chess players on a board was compared with the ability of adult non-chess players. Because the children had learned strategies to do this they were able to recall significantly more positions than the adults. This lends support to Case's theory.

▲ **Figure 7.6** Child chess experts recall more details of board positions than adult non-experts

As with Sternberg's theory, Case's theory also lends itself to practical applications in the field of education, by the formation of relevant teaching methods for children of different ages. For example, it is possible to develop metacognitive skills through tuition. The Neuhaus Education Centre (2008) gave high-school students vocabulary word webs to use while undertaking comprehension lessons. This involved talking about the material they were learning and recording word relationships in their word webs. When tested, the students showed a 20 per cent increase in spelling ability and a 40 per cent increase in vocabulary usage.

Gardner's theory of multiple intelligences (1983)

Gardner proposed a radical theory of intelligence. He challenged the traditional views of intelligence on the basis that they failed to take account of the sheer range of human mental ability. He argued that a child who is weak at maths might actually be very able in other intellectual areas, but that if we do not recognise these areas as 'intelligence' then we risk undervaluing the child.

Gardner proposed that every individual has a *cognitive profile*, that is to say varying levels of different types of intelligence. Therefore the theory is best seen as an educational theory, in that it proposed that educational institutions, such as schools and colleges, should offer individually tailored educational programmes, ones that suit each individual's cognitive profile, rather than the more traditional uniform teaching methods where all students are taught in the same manner. Such a teaching method, Gardner argued, would help students to develop in areas where they were weakest.

An individual's unique cognitive profile was originally based upon seven core intelligences, but an eighth, *naturalistic intelligence*, was added in 1999.

1 **Bodily kinaesthetic** Concerns bodily movements. Individuals with this form of intelligence learn best by physically doing something rather than reading or hearing about it. They tend to have strong muscle memories, where things are remembered through physical actions and fine motor movements rather than visual or verbal memory. Suits dancers, sportspeople, surgeons etc.

2 **Interpersonal** Concerns interactions with others. Individuals with this form of intelligence tend to learn best by working with others via discussion and debate because they are sensitive to others' moods and feelings and work well as part of a group. Such individuals communicate well and are generally extrovert in nature. Suits managers, leaders and teachers.

3 **Intrapersonal** Concerns self-awareness. Individuals with this form of intelligence learn best by concentrating on a subject alone, as they are capable of comprehending their own emotions and motivations via introspection. They are often introverted and seek perfectionism in everything they do, for example working alone to make a wall poster. Suits scientists, analysts and theologians.

4 **Linguistic** Concerns spoken and written words. Individuals with this form of intelligence tend to learn best by reading, note-taking and discussing issues as they are good with and have an advanced memory for words and languages. Such individuals are adept at explaining and being persuasive through manipulation of language. Suits writers, lawyers and politicians.

5 **Logical–mathematical** Concerns logic and reasoning capabilities. Individuals with this type of intelligence learn best by reasoning and the use of numbers through scientific thinking and investigation. Suits mathematicians, doctors and engineers.

6 **Musical** Concerns sensitivity to sound and music. Individuals with this type of intelligence tend to learn best by auditory forms, such as lectures and by using song forms to memorise information. Such individuals are generally able to sing, compose and play music and indeed often work best with music playing in the background. Suits musicians, conductors and disc jockeys.

7 **Spatial** Concerns vision and spatial judgement. Individuals with this type of intelligence tend to learn best by visualising and mentally manipulating objects, as they have strong visual memories and artistic talents involving hand–eye co-ordination and directional sense. Suits artists and architects.

8 **Naturalistic** Not originally part of the theory, this form of intelligence was added in 1999. Concerns nature, nurturing and the relation of information to one's natural surroundings. Individuals with this form of intelligence tend to learn best by collecting and analysing information related to the natural world, as they are sensitive to nature and their place within it. Such individuals have an ability to grow and care for things and interact with animals. Suits naturalists, conservationists, horticulturalists and farmers.

Thinking creatively about psychology

Choose a topic that is taught in schools, for example learning about dinosaurs or chemical reactions. Then try to think of the different ways in which this topic might be taught to students with different kinds of intelligence.

Gardner used various criteria to determine the existence of specific forms of intelligence — for example, the existence of gifted individuals, ie people with a talent in one area, but not others — neurological evidence to indicate specialised areas of the brain for each type, the existence of *symbolic notation*, such as written language, musical notation etc, and also the presence of a distinct developmental trend, where each type of intelligence showed its own unique, stage by stage, predictable steps of development.

Claims have been made for additional types of multiple intelligences, for instance existential intelligence (the ability to think in a philosophical manner) and moral intelligence (wisdom of character). Moral intelligence has not been added, as the criteria above do not indicate it to be a separate type, and existential intelligence does not appear to be linked to a specific brain area.

⟲ **Exploring issues and debates**
Reductionism

Psychometric theories use the statistical technique of factor analysis to try to understand intelligence by reducing it down to its basic components.

Construct a table that illustrates the advantages and disadvantages of using reductionism to understand intelligence.

Discussion of Gardner's theory

The idea of naturalistic intelligence is often criticised, as it is seen as being an interest rather than a type of intelligence. However, it might have been a valuable form of intelligence in prehistoric times when humans lived closer to nature, and could be more valid for people in cultures that still live close to nature. Some of the proposed types of intelligence have also been criticised on the grounds that they are talents rather than types of intelligence that can adapt to life changes, for instance musical and bodily kinaesthetic intelligences.

A common criticism is that the theory is merely an intuitive creation of Gardner's rather than a theory based on empirical evidence and that therefore Gardner's forms of intelligences are in reality just personality types. It is true to say that there does not currently exist a set of tests that can identify and measure the types of intelligence he proposes. Gardner believes it is possible to devise such tests, but has not done so himself, as he is worried about labelling and stigmatising individuals.

Kornhaber (2001) states that the theory validates educators' everyday experience: students think and learn in many different ways. It also provides educators with a conceptual framework for organising and reflecting on curriculum assessment and teaching practices. In turn, this reflection has led many educators to develop new approaches that better meet the needs of the range of learners in their classrooms. Many individual teachers incorporate some or all of the theory into their methodology. Turner (2008) reports on the success of teachers using memorable tunes combined with lyrics that reflect the content to be learned. A song was used that had 'And what do you think he saw?' at the end of each verse. Facts to be learned were added, such as 'George Washington, the first president'. Those with high levels of musical intelligence did well, retaining a lot of the taught material. This evidence fits in with Gardner's notion of a separate musical type of intelligence.

◀ **Figure 7.7** To Gardner, musical ability is a form of intelligence

Animal learning and intelligence

There are two forms of simple learning that apply to animals: classical (or Pavlovian) conditioning and *operant conditioning*. Both of these are from the behaviourist tradition of psychology, which sees learning as occurring as a result of experience through the process of association. In *classical conditioning*, one *stimulus* becomes associated with another so that they lead to the same *response*. Operant conditioning involves acquiring a behaviour because of its consequences.

Classical conditioning

In 1927 Pavlov, a Russian biologist, was researching the salivation reflex of dogs, an automatic and involuntary process that is triggered by the presence of food. He noticed that the dogs were salivating before the presentation of food. They were able to predict its arrival because of other environmental features that coincided with their feeding, for example the sight of their food bowl.

▼ Figure 7.8
Pavlov's dogs

Pavlov realised that the dogs had learned to produce the innate salivation reflex to a stimulus that did not naturally produce that response. In a famous series of experiments, Pavlov began to study the conditioning of stimuli to reflex responses. In possibly his most famous study, he got dogs to salivate at the sound of a bell. At the start of the study the dogs salivated (unconditioned response – **UCR**) at the presence of the food (unconditioned stimulus – **UCS**). Pavlov then presented the food (**UCS**) several times whilst simultaneously ringing a bell (a neutral stimulus – **NS**). Eventually just the ringing of the bell (conditioned stimulus – **CS**) produced the salivation reflex (conditioned response – **CR**).

Before learning UCS (food)	⟶	**UCR** (salivation)
NS (bell)	⟶	no response
During learning UCS (food) + **NS** (bell)	⟶	**UCR** (salivation)
After learning CS (bell)	⟶	**CR** (salivation)

▲ Figure 7.9 The process of learning via classical conditioning

LOOKING FURTHER You can watch video of a recreation of Pavlov's experiments at:

http://uk.youtube.com/watch?v=yRLfRRNoZzI

Watch an animation at:

http://www.brainviews.com/abFiles/AniPavlov.htm

And run a simulation at:

http://nobelprize.org/educational_games/medicine/pavlov/

One trial learning

Pavlov found that usually several pairings of the UCS and the CS have to occur to produce a CR. However, it is sometimes possible for just one pairing to occur to produce the CR, for example being involved in one serious car crash can lead to a lifelong fear of cars.

First order and second order conditioning

In *first order* classical conditioning, learning occurs by pairing a CS, such as a bell, with a UCS that satisfies a biological urge, for instance food. In *second order* conditioning, the same CS,

KEY TERMS

behaviourism a school of thought in psychology that believes all attributes (skills, knowledge etc) are learned through experience

classical conditioning a process of behaviour change where one comes to respond in a certain manner to a previously neutral stimulus that has been repeatedly presented alongside an unconditioned stimulus that elicits the response

operant conditioning the use of consequences to modify the occurrence and form of behaviour through the use of reinforcements

reinforcement the presentation of a stimulus that follows a response, which increases the likelihood and frequency of subsequent responses

the bell, is used as a basis for learning a new stimulus that has motivational value that is learned rather than intrinsic, for example a light. It is possible to carry on the process with subsequent order conditionings by adding in new stimuli, but the response produced becomes weaker.

Generalisation

In subsequent experiments Pavlov found that he could *generalise* the conditioning process by slightly varying the CS. For example, using a bell with a different tone would still produce the CR. However, as stimuli become more removed from the original CS, for example bells with progressively different tones, they produced an increasingly weaker CR.

Discrimination

Pavlov also discovered that he could get his dogs to produce the CR (salivation) at one particular CS (a bell of a certain tone), but not at variations of that CS (for example bells of different tones). This was achieved by giving the dogs food when a bell of a certain tone was rung, but not giving them food when bells of other tones were rung. The dogs had learned to *discriminate* between the different sounding bells.

Extinction

Conditioned responses that are produced by the process of classical conditioning are not permanent. If the CS is given without the presentation of the UCS, then the CR becomes weaker and weaker until it ceases altogether. Therefore after the dogs had learned to salivate to a bell, Pavlov found that if subsequent episodes of ringing of the bell occurred without the dogs being fed, then the salivation reflex became increasingly weaker and eventually became *extinct*.

Spontaneous recovery

With extinction, the conditioned response appears eventually to have become unlearned. However, the CR can be revived. Pavlov discovered that if after extinction of the salivation reflex he gave his dogs a rest from the experimental procedure and then rang the bell again, the salivation reflex *spontaneously recovered* and reappeared once more. Getting spontaneous recovery to occur is dependent on when exactly the CS is re-presented following apparent extinction of the behaviour.

Operant conditioning

Edward Thorndike (1911) investigated how cats escaped from puzzle-boxes and found that gradually, by a process of trial and error, they took less and less time to release a latch and escape. The actual escape from the box created a pleasant outcome for the cat (access to food). From this research he formed his *law of effect*, which states that any behaviour that results in a pleasant outcome becomes more likely to be repeated in similar situations. Also the reverse is true, in that any behaviour resulting in an unpleasant outcome becomes less likely to be repeated in similar situations.

▼ **Figure 7.10**
Thorndike's
puzzle-box

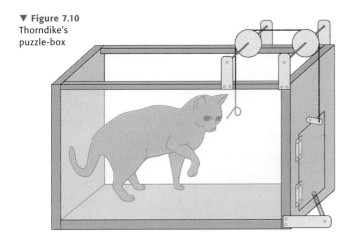

Skinner (1938) built upon Thorndike's work using a testing device now known as a *Skinner box*, where animals such as rats and pigeons were rewarded with food pellets for exhibiting desired behaviour. Initially an animal placed in the box would, as in Thorndike's puzzle-boxes, run around and seek to escape; in the course of so doing the animal would, in the fullness of time, accidentally press a lever or peck a disc that released a food pellet. Over time the animal would exhibit the food-releasing behaviour more often as it gradually learned to associate the behaviour with the reward of a food pellet. Eventually the animal would exhibit this behaviour every time and it could be said to have become a learned behaviour. The food pellet was a form of *reinforcement*, because it strengthened the likelihood of the behaviour occurring again.

▶ **Figure 7.11**
A Skinner box

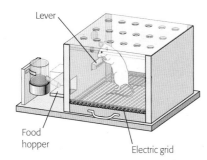

Lever

Food
hopper

Electric grid

The beauty of the Skinner box was that it not only offered the researcher a controlled environment within which to investigate behaviour, but also a simple means of measuring such behaviour. Skinner went on to produce variations in the testing regime to see what impact it had upon behaviour.

Operant conditioning can be understood using an **ABC** terminology:

- **A**ntecedents – the situation before learning occurs, eg the Skinner box and the lever/disc
- **B**ehaviour – what the animal does, eg presses the lever/pecks the disc
- **C**onsequences – what occurs after the behaviour has occurred, eg *reinforcement* is given.

One difference between classical and operant conditioning is that classical conditioning is associated with involuntary behaviour, whilst operant conditioning is associated with voluntary behaviour.

Positive reinforcement

A positive reinforcement is the receipt of something pleasurable for exhibiting a certain behaviour, for example being praised for working hard. This increases (reinforces) the chances that the behaviour will be repeated.

Negative reinforcement

A negative reinforcement involves having an unpleasant state removed in response to exhibiting a certain behaviour, for example taking a painkiller to stop a thumping headache. This also increases the chances that the behaviour will be repeated – if the painkiller works, you are likely to use it again if you have a headache in the future.

▼ **Figure 7.12** A visit to the dentist is not particularly pleasant in itself but if it results in stopping a toothache then negative reinforcement means that visits are likely to be repeated

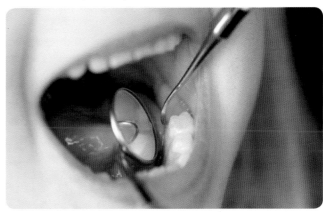

Punishment

The common factor between positive and negative reinforcements is that they both strengthen behaviour, that is to say they increase the chances of the reinforced behaviour being exhibited again. However, punishment has the opposite effect in that it decreases (weakens) the chances of behaviour occurring again. As in reinforcement, there are two forms of punishment: positive and negative. A positive punishment involves the receipt of something unpleasant for exhibiting an undesired behaviour, for example being given detention for being late to class. A negative punishment involves the removal of something pleasurable for exhibiting an undesired behaviour, for example children not being allowed out to play if they have not completed their chores.

Reinforcement schedules

Skinner began by rewarding an animal every time it exhibited a desired behaviour, for example a pigeon pecking a disc. He subsequently found, by varying the ways animals were rewarded for such actions, that the manner in which the animals were reinforced was the most important factor in determining their behaviour. Skinner discovered that there are five *reinforcement schedules*.

- *Continuous reinforcement* — reinforcement is given after every desired response. With this schedule the animal responds in a regular, but infrequent manner. Once the reinforcement, for example a food pellet, ceases, then the behaviour swiftly becomes extinct.
- *Fixed ratio* — reinforcement is given after a certain number of desired responses, for example after pecking the disc five times. With this schedule the animal responds in a very rapid manner with a pause after each reinforcement. Once the reinforcement ceases, then the behaviour swiftly becomes extinct.
- *Fixed interval* — reinforcement is given after a fixed period of time has elapsed as long as one desired response occurs within that time period, for example after every two minutes. With this schedule the animal responds in an infrequent manner, but more frequently towards the end of the time period. Once the reinforcement ceases, then the behaviour swiftly becomes extinct.
- *Variable ratio* — reinforcement is given after a certain mean number of desired responses, for example after pecking a disc every 10 times on average. This means that the food pellet may be given after only five pecks on one occasion, but then subsequently after another 15 pecks. With this schedule the animal responds very steadily and frequently. Once the reinforcement ceases, extinction is very slow to occur.
- *Variable interval* — reinforcement is given after a mean amount of time has elapsed as long as one desired response occurs within the time period, for example after every four minutes on average. This means that a food pellet may be given after only three minutes on one occasion, but then subsequently after another five minutes. With this schedule the animal responds in a fairly steady manner, with a noticeable quickening in response rate as the amount of time since the last reinforcement increases. Once the reinforcement ceases, extinction is slow to occur.

Primary and secondary reinforcers

Primary reinforcers are innate, occur naturally and therefore are *unconditioned*. They satisfy biological needs such as food. Secondary reinforcers on the other hand have to be learned

◀ **Figure 7.13** Money is a secondary reinforcer

by becoming associated with a primary reinforcer and are therefore *conditioned*. For example money can be a secondary reinforcer, not because it is a natural (primary) reinforcer itself, but because it can become associated with a primary reinforcer, for example money can be used to buy food.

Behaviour shaping

The central idea behind behaviour shaping is that an animal learns a desired behaviour gradually, by being reinforced for behaviours that become nearer and nearer to the desired behaviour. Circus animals that can perform unusual routines, such as a dog riding a bike, are trained in this manner. The first part of the behaviour, such as the dog standing on the pedals, is created by reinforcement and then the additional parts of the behaviour, for example getting the dog to steer the bike, are added on separately, again by a process of reinforcement. However, subjecting animals to such a process can often be ethically questionable.

Thinking practically about psychology

Taking into account the ideas of reinforcement schedules and shaping, how might you go about teaching your hamster to dance? (Please don't actually do it!)

The role of learning in non-human animals

Classical and operant conditioning allow animals to survive and thrive. Through conditioning, they are able to learn about their environment and adapt their behaviour when environmental changes occur. Research in both laboratory and natural settings has shown that classical conditioning enables animals to learn whether food sources are safe or not. Laboratory-based research by Garcia and Koelling (1966) showed how classical conditioning helps rats to learn about taste aversion. The researchers were looking at the effects of radiation on rats and found that the rats were nauseated (UCR) by the radiation they were exposed to (UCS). The taste of water from a plastic feeding bottle (CS) became accidentally paired with the radiation and so the rats developed taste aversion (CR) for the water. The rats did drink water though from glass feeding bottles that didn't have the plastic taste. Such experiences could help animals to learn which foods are safe to eat and so have a survival value.

CLASSIC RESEARCH

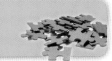

Gustavson CR, Garcia J, Hankins WG & Rusiniak KW (1974) Coyote predation control by aversive conditioning. *Science* **184, 581–3**

Aim: To find a humane way of putting wolves and coyotes off attacking sheep without having to kill them. This involved the predators learning to associate sheep with a noxious stimulus.

Procedure: Wild coyotes and wolves were fed chopped mutton wrapped in raw sheep hides, laced with lithium chloride. Lithium chloride is known to induce severe nausea and vomiting. This procedure was carried out once. The animals were then allowed to approach live sheep.

Findings: The predators ate the mutton then vomited in response to the lithium chloride. When allowed to approach sheep they were observed to retch. They then turned away and did not attack the sheep. Instead they exhibited submissive behaviour towards them, rolling over and exposing their bellies.

Conclusion: The wolves and coyotes learnt to associate the sheep with a noxious chemical. This required only a single pairing of the NS and UCS, so it is an example of one-trial learning.

Thinking practically about psychology

Identify the following terms in the Gustavson *et al.* study: neutral stimulus, unconditioned stimulus, unconditioned response, conditioned stimulus, and conditioned response.

▼ **Figure 7.14** Sheep can be made safer by conditioning the local wolf population

Seligman (1970) proposed the concept of *biological preparedness*, suggesting that the ease with which learned associations could be formed is dependent upon biological predispositions. Some learned associations are acquired quickly as an animal is biologically prepared by evolution to learn them because such behaviours have a survival value. Garcia & Koelling (1966) showed that rats quickly learned not to eat a sweet-tasting liquid that was paired with an injection of something that made them ill. This is a natural adaptive behaviour. However, when the sweet tasting liquid was paired with an electric shock, the rats did not develop taste aversion to the sweet-tasting liquid because, it was argued, there is not an innate, biological tendency for rats to avoid things linked to electric shocks.

Operant conditioning allows animals to learn from interaction with their environment by using reinforcement and punishment processes to shape their behaviour. Therefore new behaviours can be learned that have a survival value, for example finding food and avoiding danger. Operant conditioning can be seen to be at work when animals use *trial and error learning* to adapt to their environment. When an animal performs behaviours that do not result in a pleasurable outcome, eg errors, they act as a form of punishment and therefore decrease the chances of those behaviours occurring again. Over a period of time the animal learns to perform the correct behaviour, for example in the wild a bear learns in this way which methods are best for catching salmon.

Animals tend to learn behaviours that resemble innate behaviours. Fisher & Hinde (1949) reported on how the habit of blue tits feeding on cream by pecking at the foil tops of milk bottles had spread as if by imitation through the blue tit population after first being witnessed in Southampton in 1921. However, it was likely that the blue tits were easily able to learn this seemingly artificial behaviour because it closely resembled their innate tendency to strip tree bark to find grubs to eat. Attempts to condition animals with behaviours far removed from those which occur naturally within a species are less successful. Breland & Breland (1961) tried to teach a pig to place wooden tokens into a piggy bank in order to get a reward, but the pigs tended to revert to more natural pig behaviour and tossed the tokens around and rooted in the ground with them. This phenomenon is known as *instinctive drift*.

▼ **Figure 7.15** Bears learn to fish by trial and error, receiving reinforcement when a strategy works

↪ Exploring issues and debates
Ethical issues

Conducting research into animal learning and intelligence invariably involves the study of animals in both laboratory and naturalistic environments.

Construct a table that illustrates the ethical concerns with regard to the study of animals. Your table should include any strategies necessary to address the ethical issues raised.

There is evidence to suggest that homing pigeons use a variety of methods to navigate, including an innate navigational sense, but Baker (1984) argued that they also, by trial and error learning, learn to use landmarks to find their way around. Guilford (2004) showed that pigeons have learned to navigate by using motorways, however this may be possible because it resembles their natural behaviour of navigating using rivers and coastlines.

▼ **Figure 7.16** Pigeons can navigate using man-made landmarks like motorways

Discussion of animal learning

Early behavioural psychologists believed that all learning took place by classical conditioning. Although there is no controversy about the existence of classical conditioning, the theory is quite limited in what it can explain. Classical conditioning cannot explain how totally new behaviours can be learned, only how existing behaviours can be adopted in response to new situations. Classical conditioning also works best for explaining simple reflex behaviours, like the vomiting in Gustavson *et al.*'s wolves and coyotes. It cannot easily explain more complex sequences of behaviour. However, operant conditioning can explain how both new and complex behaviours develop.

Simple explanations of learning like classical and operant conditioning do not acknowledge the important role that emotional and cognitive factors play in determining behaviour. Kohler (1925) suggested that chimps use *insight learning* to solve previously non-experienced problems. Food that was out of reach of the chimps was secured by using a stick. This skill had not been conditioned in the chimps, nor witnessed from other chimps, but involved the chimp thinking about the problem to develop a novel solution. The existence of this sort of complex learning leads us neatly into the next section: intelligence in non-human species.

Thinking critically about psychology

Humans as well as animals can learn through classical and operant conditioning. To what extent are humans different? What sort of things should we take into account when studying human learning?

Evidence for intelligence in non-human animals

It is as difficult to arrive at a definition of intelligence in non-human animals as it is in humans. It can be understood in terms of a hierarchy of learning processes, with animal species differing in the amount of their behaviour that is learned. Animals lower down on the phylogenetic scale are less affected by learning, because more of their behaviour is innate and this suits their biological needs. Animals higher up the phylogenetic scale can alter their behaviour in response to a changing environment and this is seen as a sign of intelligence. However, it is often difficult to assess how much of an adapted behaviour is due to the animal's biology and how much is due to learning. Also, if intelligence in an animal species were seen simply in terms of the ability to survive and breed within their environment, then all species would be deemed of equal intelligence.

Other explanations of animal intelligence have concentrated more on the capacity of animals to learn, as well as their ability to process information. Research has tended to focus upon *social learning*, *self-recognition*, *theory of mind* and *Machiavellian intelligence*.

Social learning

There are several factors that can affect an animal's learning in a social context. Some species are *social animals* in that they live, either permanently or periodically, in social groups. Such animals have demonstrated social learning that aids their ability to form and interact within large social groupings. Social learning involves copying others' behaviour and the advantage of this is that it does not have the pitfalls associated with trial and error learning. Several types of social learning have been identified that collectively focus upon animals' abilities to solve social problems.

KEY TERMS

social learning   the acquisition of knowledge and skills that occurs through observing and imitating others

theory of mind   the ability to attribute mental states (beliefs, desires etc) to oneself and others

self-recognition   the ability to recognise one's own image, implying the possession of a self-concept

Machiavellian intelligence   the ability to allow individuals to serve their own best interest by interacting with others, either co-operatively or manipulatively, without upsetting the social cohesion of a group

Research has looked at animals' ability to observe and imitate others' behaviour. Kawai (1965) reported on the behaviour of Japanese snow monkeys living on a small island. One monkey named Imo was seen to be washing sand off sweet potatoes that had been left by the researchers on the beach. Other monkeys adopted this behaviour and it was passed on to subsequent generations of the monkeys. The obvious explanation for this was that the monkeys were imitating the beneficial behaviour. However, Nagell *et al.* (1993) offers the different explanation of stimulus enhancement, whereby when Imo was observed washing the potato this caused the other monkeys to pay more attention to the potatoes and the seawater. Therefore this enhanced the opportunities for a monkey to acquire the skill by trial and error. Evidence drawn from population-specific behaviours has, however, lent support to the idea that social learning by imitation can occur.

▼ **Figure 7.17** Chimps easily pick up behaviour from humans, but is it imitation or stimulus enhancement?

So it would seem that animals could learn from others either by direct *imitation* of a behaviour or by *enhancement* where an animal learns to direct its attention to a particular feature of the environment in order to solve a problem. However, Tomasello *et al.* (1987) reported on chimps that had apparently learned by imitation to use a rake to obtain food. However, the chimps were not seen to actually imitate the particular actions of the observed chimp, instead they developed their own techniques of rake use. It was concluded that the chimps weren't so much copying the behaviour, but rather were trying to create the consequences of the behaviour. He termed this behaviour *emulation*.

Imitation, *enhancement* and *emulation* are all passive in that the model doesn't deliberately perform a behaviour for it to be observed and imitated. Tutoring, on the other hand, is an active process, whereby a model encourages or punishes pupils or provides them with examples of behaviour, so that the pupils acquire skills more quickly than they would have done, usually at a cost to the model. There are few plausible examples and even these are hotly debated.

Rendell & Whitehead (2001) have suggested that orcas teach youngsters to hunt by delaying their own killing and eating of seals in order to provide their young with incapacitated prey to practise on. The fact that this behaviour has been rarely seen casts doubts upon such an interpretation, which is entirely subjective: the orcas could merely be entertaining themselves.

▼ **Figure 7.18** Adult orcas appear to tutor youngsters, but are they just entertaining themselves?

Thinking critically about psychology

One area of disagreement amongst researchers into social intelligence is the best form of methodology to use. Is evidence gathered in the field or the laboratory most suitable for determining whether animals can imitate? Some believe that only the highly controlled world of the laboratory can reveal the mechanisms behind apparent acts of imitation. Others argue that the laboratory is an artificial and sterile environment that will result in underestimating the imitative skills of complex animals like chimpanzees. What methods of study should researchers use to investigate social intelligence in animals?

Self-recognition

Humans are deemed to be intelligent as they are self-aware – they realise that they are a separate being from all others. It has been proposed that certain animals possess the ability to self-recognise and therefore have intelligence, because if an animal can recognise itself, this implies the possession of a self-concept necessary for higher levels of mental ability.

Research has centred on the 'rouge' (or 'mirror') test devised by Gallup (1971). An animal is anaesthetised and has an odourless red dot painted on its forehead. The amount of touching of the red dot that an animal indulges in is then recorded without and with a mirror. All the great apes have passed this test; bonobos, chimpanzees, orang-utans and gorillas and also dolphins, orcas, elephants and European magpies. Epstein *et al.* (1981) also put forward a case for pigeons being able to self-recognise, which has cast doubts on whether the test really does demonstrate self-recognition as pigeons are not generally considered to be animals capable of higher cognitive skills.

There has been a great deal of debate about whether the mirror test does determine self-recognition. The test may be of little value with animals that depend mainly on senses other than vision. Dogs have relatively poor vision and stand little chance of recognising themselves in a mirror; they can however recognise their own scent. Other species of mammals, such as rabbits and deer, do not possess stereoscopic vision. So maybe the mirror test only measures self-recognition abilities that are similar to those of humans, and cannot therefore be perceived as a test of *consciousness*.

Even if some species of animals can self-recognise in mirrors, it is not universally accepted that this illustrates self-awareness. Nefian & Hayes (1998) have argued instead that such behaviours are only evidence for a *body concept*, which would allow an animal to tell the difference between itself and other external stimuli. Animals that have successfully completed the mirror test are seen as ones that have learned to associate information from a mirror with information from their own body. Therefore this ability would not require self-awareness.

Machiavellian intelligence

Whiten & Byrne (1988) developed several theories that saw the demands of the social world as the main determinant of intelligence into the *Machiavellian intelligence hypothesis*. The central idea is that an intelligent individual best looks after its own interests by interacting with others, either co-operatively or manipulatively, but without disturbing the social cohesion of the group. This often involves the use of deception and the formation of coalitions.

The researchers showed how baboons use deceit. A young baboon watched an adult dig up a root. The youngster then

▶ Figure 7.19 Contestants on *Big Brother* have been tested for Machiavellian intelligence

looked around and screamed and this had the effect of getting the young baboon's mother, a dominant female, to chase the other adult away, allowing her child to then eat the root. This could be seen as the youngster deliberately deceiving its mother to incite her attack. However, this is somewhat of a subjective interpretation: the behaviour could also be that of a conditioned response. If the youngster had previously been threatened by an adult who was eating, causing it to scream, the response of the mother would be to chase the adult away, leaving the young baboon to eat the food. This would result in reinforcement of the screaming behaviour in similar circumstances.

↪ Exploring issues and debates
Animal learning and intelligence

Behaviourism is a type of psychology that believes all attributes are learned through experience.

Construct a table that lists the strengths and weaknesses of using behaviourism to explain animal learning.

RESEARCH NOW

Prior H, Schwarz A & Güntürkün O (2008) Mirror-induced behaviour in the magpie (*Pica pica*). Evidence of self-recognition. *PloS Biology* 6(8), e202

Aim: To test whether magpies can recognise themselves in a mirror.

Procedure: Magpies' feathers were marked with either a bright colour (yellow or red) or a black 'sham' mark, that was not noticeable on the bird's black feathers. In half the trials the magpies were presented with a reflective mirror pointing towards them. In half the trials a non-reflective plate of the same dimensions as the mirror was used. The birds were tested when marked brightly, marked with the 'sham' colouring and when not marked at all.

Findings: Mark-directed behaviour only significantly increased when a mirror was present and the bird was marked with a bright colour. As soon as the coloured mark was removed, the mark-directed behaviour ceased.

Conclusion: This evidence suggests that magpies do have a clear ability to self-recognise.

▶ Figure 7.20 A marked magpie

Maestripieri (2007) has shown that rhesus macaques constantly compete for social status and power by using nepotism (favouritism to relatives) and political manoeuvring. Rhesus macaques live in complex social groups with long-lasting social bonds and strong dominance hierarchies, and use Machiavellian intelligence to increase and maintain their influence within the group. Mothers indulge in nepotism by favouring and helping daughters to attain a similar status to themselves. Females also use Machiavellian intelligence when it comes to reproduction: they ensure they have lots of sex with the alpha (dominant) male to increase the chances he will protect the newborn

infant from other monkeys. Meanwhile they also have lots of sex with other males without the alpha male's knowledge. They do this in case the alpha male is sterile, dies or loses his status before the baby is born.

Empirical support for Machiavellian intelligence in primates is strong. It is most prevalent among those who live in large social groups with a social complexity that requires a good memory for socially relevant information, as well as evidence of neocortical enlargement (big brains). However, the evolution of such advanced cognitive abilities that allow planning and the ability to understand others' intentions has not been well explained as yet.

The evolution of intelligence

▲ **Figure 7.21** This 2 million-year-old *Homo Rhodesiensis* had a much smaller brain than modern humans

Evolutionary factors in the development of human intelligence

Fossil evidence tells us that our primitive relatives did not have the brain capacity and function that modern-day humans have. It is therefore to be presumed that these have evolved. The demands of our ever-changing environment created selective pressure for higher intelligence in our ancestors. The *ecological demands* that foraging for food creates, the need to deal with social problems and the need for a more complex brain are all examples of such evolutionary pressures, which we will now look at in more detail.

Ecological demands

A successful individual needs to be able to thrive within a given environment and this requires intelligence. Ash & Gallup (2007) explain how early humans adapted to global cooling and were able to exploit areas away from the equator through increasingly more complex cognitive and intellectual adaptations, such as more intricate patterns of co-operative hunting and the invention of more effective weapons and tools. Improved clothing and shelter accelerated the cognitive and intellectual skills needed to live in and exploit colder climates. Plants often die or become dormant in the winter, so hunting and meat-eating became necessary to survival. Foraging is time-consuming and hunters of

meat have a distinct advantage as a kill provides abundant food and has more calories, freeing up more time for other activities (see also evolutionary explanations of food preferences, p104). Good foraging and huntng skills – which require intelligence – would have led to increased survival and therefore been selected for through *evolution*.

Hunting and finding food require memory, strategy, co-ordination and use of tools, all of which involve high levels of intelligence. Also a good forager has increased chances of being selected as a mate, which increases the chances of such intelligent genes becoming more widespread in the population.

Foraging hypotheses

Milton (1988) has explained increases in intelligence as due to the demands of foraging. She describes how the development of detailed spatiotemporal cognitive maps (mental maps) could assist foraging amongst *frugivores* (fruit-eaters) as their food types are widely distributed and are seasonal in nature as opposed to those of *foliovores* (leaf-eaters). A good forager would need to be able to remember where and when to search, so selection for memory and efficient foraging techniques would be advantageous. Larger brains reflect a cognitive demand on frugivores to monitor the availability of their widely dispersed food supply.

▼ **Figure 7.22**
Fruit-eaters have to search for their food so are typically more intelligent than leaf-eaters

Dunbar (1992) tested this and found that there was no significant relationship between the percentage of fruit in an animal's diet and neocortex size in the brain. This seems to cast doubt on Milton's theory, as a large neocortex would presumably be necessary in animals with complex mental maps. However, the percentage of fruit eaten may not accurately represent its importance in an animal's diet; some fruits may supply essential nutrients, and thus be vitally important, even if they do not make up a large part of the diet. However, Dunbar's research does question the validity of the explanation given for differences in brain size between frugivores and foliovores. Also, memory of stored food items is prevalent throughout the animal kingdom and so it would be difficult to support the claim that complex mental maps would drive cognitive evolution. Nor does the hypothesis explain why frugivores specialise to a high-quality diet. Did they need the energy to support a larger brain, or did the brain develop to keep track of fruit-based resources?

The food extraction hypothesis was put forward by Gibson (1987). She stated that it is the extraction of embedded resources (hidden foods) that provided the drive for the evolution of intelligence. Extractive resources, foods hidden from sight and difficult to access, require cognitive processing, manipulative skills and tool use to obtain successfully. Many of these resources provide rich nutrition during times of scarcity and this itself may have had a role in increasing cognitive capacity. If food that required extraction was an important resource, cortex-mediated co-ordination would be strongly selected for, presumably reflected by a larger cortex. But the levels of difficulty involved in food extraction are not well defined and so the hypothesis is difficult to evaluate.

Whether extractive foraging is a cause or a consequence of intelligence is difficult to decide. Parker and Gibson (1979) believe that animals that concentrate on extracting just one type of food resource available all year round only need to use tools in a relatively unintelligent way. Animals that extract many types of foods, however, need more intelligent tool use. Therefore they see tool use as a consequence of intelligence, because intelligent animals adapt to the ecological pressures of extracting different food types by developing specifically suitable tools.

⤴ Exploring issues and debates
Theories of intelligence

Psychometrics is a scientific type of psychology that attempts to measure mental abilities such as intelligence. This is usually achieved by the formation and application of mental tests.

Construct a table that illustrates the strengths and weaknesses of attempting to study intelligence in a scientific manner.

Social complexity

There are advantages to social living, for instance in foraging, predation and sexual reproduction. The main disadvantage concerns the social problems that arise from group living, such as the inevitable conflicts. Therefore an intelligent individual is one who can survive and prosper, because they can find solutions to such social problems.

The *social complexity hypothesis* states that the driving force for the development of the brain was the need to anticipate, respond to and manipulate the social behavior of other group members. The theory suggests that large brains reflect the cognitive demands of complex social systems. In other words, the demands of social living are the main reason for the evolution of intelligence.

A secondary part to the hypothesis is that the very structure of intelligence has been moulded to be 'social' in character, an idea that presents a challenge to traditional views of intelligence as a general-purpose capacity. It is more in keeping with Gardner's ideas of multiple intelligences (see p148).

The social complexity hypothesis predicts that mammals living in large, complex groups should display advanced abilities in social cognition. Evidence for this may be seen in the expansion of the frontal cortex in the brain. The frontal cortex of the brain is heavily associated with social decision-making and the hypothesis suggests the demands of society have led to the evolution of the large frontal cortex in the human brain. Most research has focused on primates, although the theory has been tested on other social animals.

Holekamp & Engh (2004) tested the hypothesis that intelligence and large brain size in primates has been favoured by living in intricate social worlds. They did this by predicting that spotted hyenas would display the same cognitive abilities as primates, because both live in social groups of similar size and complexity. Firstly the researchers looked at the size of hyena brains, especially the frontal cortex. As complete hyena skulls are difficult to obtain, computer topography was used to create an artificial hyena brain. The results were compared with those of other carnivores that live in more or less complex social groups and a strong positive correlation was found between size of brain structures and complexity of social living, which supports the hypothesis.

Secondly the researchers looked at whether hyenas can recognise third-party relationships, those in which an individual is not directly involved. This was done by direct observation of the hyenas over a long period, to see if they could make inferences about other individuals' dominance rankings. It was deduced from evidence concerning which particular individuals formed coalitions that they indeed could do so. This finding offers strong support for the notion that cognitive abilities are shaped by the demands of life in complex societies.

▼ **Figure 7.23** Hyenas, which live in complex social groups, have large brains

LOOKING FURTHER

Do you want to know more about Kay Holekamp's ongoing research into hyena behaviour?

Then go to the two websites that she maintains for this purpose:

http://www.hyaenidae.org/

http://hyenas.zoology.msu.edu/

Dunbar *et al.* (2005) looked at the relationship between group size and relative size of the neocortex of the brain, on the assumption that neocortical increases should be seen in large groups, as when group size increases so does the complexity of the social dynamics among group members. The results showed this was so, lending support to the social complexity explanation for the evolution of human intelligence.

The social complexity hypothesis predicts that species living in large social groups should be able to track each other's individual relationships and ranks better than closely related species living in small family groups. This was investigated by Bond *et al.* (2003) – see *Research Now*.

Brain size

One possible explanation for the difference in brain size is that large brains have evolved because larger animals need to co-ordinate their larger bodies; also, having a large brain allows an individual to deal with the demands that social complexity, Machiavellian intelligence, ecological pressures etc, place upon it.

There is an evolutionary cost to having a large brain, as giving birth to big-brained infants is difficult. Also, plenty of good food is required, because large brains need more energy; indeed the brain only accounts for 2 per cent of human body weight but consumes 35 per cent of our daily calorific intake. As having a large brain carries costs, this indicates that big brains have an adaptive advantage, therefore supporting the idea that intelligence has indeed evolved.

Thinking critically about psychology

Why were the two species used in Bond *et al.*'s study well suited to the aim of the study?

▼ **Figure 7.24** There is an evolutionary cost to having a large brain as it makes human childbirth a more painful and dangerous process than in other species

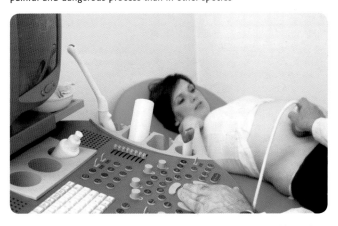

RESEARCH NOW

Bond A, Kamil A & Balda R (2003) Social complexity and transitive inference in corvids. *Animal Behaviour* 65, 479–87.

Aim: To compare the intelligence of two species of jay, one of which is social (the pinyon) and the other solitary (the Western). If the social species is more intelligent, this would support the social complexity hypothesis.

Procedure: The birds were tested on their ability to make *transitive inferences,* to recognise that if A is superior to B and B is superior to C, then A must be superior to C. The birds were given two coloured discs to peck at, A and B. By operant conditioning the birds learned to peck A to get a reward. They were then given disc B along with a new disc C, and were trained to peck disc B to get a reward. Would the jays be now able to recognise that disc A was superior to disc C, not a combination that they had experienced before?

Findings: The sociable pinyon jays were significantly more able to do this, especially as more information was added, eg disc C was superior to disc D, which was superior to disc E etc.

Conclusion: The sociable jays are more intelligent than the solitary species. This seems to indicate that social complexity and intelligence are linked.

Lynn (1989) has shown that brain size has increased three-fold during the evolution of hominids, from *Australopithecus* through to *Homo sapiens*, probably because larger brains brought greater intelligence and a selective advantage, but human brains contain no highly conspicuous characteristics that might account for the species' cleverness. Having a large brain does not guarantee higher intelligence – monkeys possess brains smaller than sheep, whilst elephants and some ceteceans, for example dolphins, have larger brains than humans. If we look at brain size relative to body weight, humans do indeed have the biggest brain among large mammals, 2 per cent of body weight, but with small mammals the shrew weighs in with a brain of 10 per cent of its body weight. This evidence therefore seems inconclusive.

Jerison (1978) developed the *encephalisation quotient* (EQ), where the actual brain mass of a species is divided by its expected brain size for that body size. Cats are used as the 'standard' for mammals, with an EQ score of 1.0; humans have the highest EQ score, 7.6, of any animal. This means that humans have a brain seven to eight times larger than expected, dolphins score next highest at 5.0. The snag with this measuring scale is that capuchin monkeys score higher than chimpanzees and gorillas, despite their apparently lower intelligence. EQ is therefore not the best predictor for intelligence.

▼ **Figure 7.25** Crows are extremely bright, casting doubt on the link between brain size and intelligence

Corvid birds (crow family) have intellectual capacities that are overturning conventional wisdom about the brain, as they have demonstrated astonishing intelligence in tool use, planning and cognitive flexibility. They have, in absolute terms, small brains in comparison with other birds, but a relatively large cortex. Data is needed on the neurone density of these birds to see if this is an indicator of their intelligence. If they have a large neurone density then this would back up such an indicator of human intelligence.

Another approach to the brain size question is to look at the relationship between brain size and IQ in humans. Willerman *et al.* (1991) performed a meta-analysis of the relationship between brain volume and IQ scores. Using data from 1530 participants drawn from 37 samples, a significant positive correlation of 0.33 was found, suggesting that brain size is associated with intelligence. Narr *et al.* (2006) investigated the relationship between cortical thickness and IQ:

65 mentally healthy participants were administered a standard IQ test (Wechsler) and had their cortical thickness measured by magnetic resonance imagery (MRI). In line with established findings, a significant positive correlation of 0.36 was found, suggesting that larger brain volumes are associated with greater intellectual ability.

The role of genetic and environmental factors associated with intelligence test performance

KEY TERMS

genetic factors influences (eg on intelligence) that are based upon heredity

environmental factors influences (eg on intelligence) that are acquired through experience

cultural influences factors affecting development (eg of intelligence) that originate from the characteristics associated with a defined group of people

The first intelligence test was devised by Binet (1905) to assess intelligence levels so as to identify children who needed help to boost their abilites to those required in the modern industrialised world. However, the test swiftly became used as a general intelligence test. By 1916 the Stanford–Binet test was being used to test normal and subnormal levels of intelligence in individuals. The other main intelligence test is the Wechsler Adult Intelligence Scale. IQ tests were used to allocate troops to different roles in World War I, but have mainly been used in education in assessment and selection roles.

The creation and application of IQ tests is controversial. They are based upon the idea that general intelligence 'g' (see p143) actually does exist and can be measured in an objective way. However, there are many who would argue against this belief and see IQ tests as actually tests of attainment (what you have learned), rather than aptitude (natural talent).

Even if IQ scores are valid measures of intelligence, there is still the nature versus nurture debate concerning the origins of intelligence. Are the differences found between individuals and different groups of people attributable to biological factors (nature), or to *environmental factors* (nurture)? This debate is highly controversial, for instance those who see intelligence as a product of our biology, use differences in IQ scores between black and white people to support the idea that white people in general have superior intelligence levels.

If differences in IQ levels are largely genetic, then people with close genetic relationships, for example identical twins, should have similar IQ scores. Also, IQ levels should not be affected by experience and should therefore remain constant throughout an individual's lifetime. Any attempts to increase IQ levels by enrichment should have no effect.

Twin studies

There are two types of twins, MZ (monozygotic), who are genetically identical, and DZ (dizygotic), who only share

50 per cent genetic similarity. If the IQ levels of MZ twins are more similar than those of DZ twins, then that would be evidence that intelligence is more genetic in nature. Bouchard & McGue (1981) reviewed 111 studies of IQ correlations between family members and found a concordance rate of 0.86 for MZ twins reared together. However, the big drawback is that MZ twins reared together not only share the same genes, but they also often share identical environments. So psychologists turned instead to looking at MZ twins who had been reared apart. Shields (1962) studied a volunteer sample of 44 pairs of MZ twins reared apart and found a concordance rate of 0.77. As this was very similar to that found for MZ twins reared together (0.76) and the concordance rate for DZ twins reared together was only 0.51, it would seem to support the idea that intelligence is mainly genetic in nature. These findings were backed up by similar findings from other researchers (see Table 7.2).

▼ **Table 7.2 IQ correlations between twins**

Study	MZ twins reared together	MZ twins reared apart	DZ twins reared together (same sex)
Newman et al. (1937)	0.91	0.67	0.64
Burt (1955)	0.944	0.771	0.552
Shields (1962)	0.76	0.77	0.51

▼ **Figure 7.26** These identical twins are likely to grow up similar in IQ

However, such studies also have their criticisms:

- So-called 'separated' twins were actually often separated after several years and therefore had shared a similar environment. Even when separated, twins were often raised by branches of the same family, or placed with families with similar backgrounds. In the Shields (1962) study the concordance rate for separated MZ twins raised within the family was 0.83, whilst for separated MZ twins raised in unrelated families it dropped to just 0.51, which casts doubts on the genetic argument.
- MZ twins that were reared apart in dissimilar family backgrounds had the widest differences in IQ scores, a fact that seems to support the notion that intelligence is more environmental in nature.
- Burt's research influenced other psychologists, but would appear to a large extent to have been fabricated.

He invented fictitious co-workers and the overall concordance rates that he found remained very much the same even though different numbers of MZ twins had been used. He was stripped of the knighthood he had been awarded.

- There is an argument over just how identical some twins are, as well as how similar the environments are of twins with a shared upbringing.

More recent twin studies have also tended to conclude that intelligence is more genetic than environmental in nature. Bouchard et al. (1990) gained data from over 100 sets of reared-apart twins and triplets and found that about 70 per cent of the variance in IQ was found to be associated with genetic variation. Thompson et al. (2001) used MRI to scan the brains of 10 sets of MZ twins and 10 sets of DZ twins and performed many tests on them to measure 17 different intellectual activities. MZ twins had more similar brain structures in areas associated with intellect and similar scores on the tests administered. Although this seems to show that intelligence is genetic in origin and, as Plomin (2003) has claimed, is based on brain biology, this view has been criticised. Kosslyn (2006) has questioned whether what was being measured was just the type of intelligence needed to do well in school and not necessarily that which is needed to do well in life.

What is apparent is that if intelligence were entirely genetically determined, then concordance rates for MZ twins on IQ would be 100 per cent, which they clearly are not. Therefore, environmental factors must play some part in determining intelligence. Genes can achieve nothing on their own; they need an environment in which to express themselves.

Adoption studies

The rationale behind adoption studies is quite simple: they allow the IQ rates of adoptive children and adoptive parents (low genetic similarity) to be compared, as well as the comparison of the adoptive children and their biological parents. It is especially interesting to see if over time the IQ levels of adoptive children move away from those of their biological parents towards those of their adoptive parents; such a move would lend support to the environmental (nurture) argument.

Horn (1983) conducted a study of 300 adoptive families and the biological parents of the adopted children. He concluded that the adopted children more closely resembled their biological mothers in IQ terms. He also found that adopted children with higher-IQ biological mothers had better IQ scores than adopted children with lower-IQ biological mothers, even though the children had been raised in similar intellectual environments. This lends support to the idea of intelligence being predominately genetically based.

Petrill & Deater-Deckard (2004) looked at families with biological and adopted children. Parents and children were given the Stanford–Binet IQ test and it was found that mothers were significantly correlated with their biological, but not their adoptive, children suggesting that *genetic factors* are important in determining intelligence. However, the adopted children's level of cognitive ability was made predictable by reference to their age of placement and number of years spent in the adoptive home, suggesting that other environmental factors were also operating. Overall then, as with twin studies, adoption studies do not provide any clear-cut answers as to the origins of intelligence.

▼ **Figure 7.27** Adopted children resemble both biological and adoptive parents, suggesting a role for genes and environment in the development of intelligence

Gene identification

Recently attempts have been made to try to identify the specific genes responsible for the heritability of intelligence. Plomin *et al.* (1998) compared 50 children whose IQ scores were above 160 points, with children of average IQ by comparing their DNA on a small part of the human genome, the long arm of chromosome six. He found that a particular variant of the I.G.F.2 receptor gene was twice as common in the high-IQ children than the average-IQ children, though the gene has a very small effect, accounting for about 2 per cent of the variance — around four IQ points.

Plomin thinks that such slight genetic influences are to be expected, as he believes intelligence to be influenced by as many as 50 genes, including at least one on each of the 23 pairs of human chromosomes, which collectively would have a much greater influence. An intelligent person is therefore one with favourable versions of these genes. Plomin believes that his and similar research will help us to understand not only intelligence, but also learning disabilities and intellectual decay such as Alzheimer's disease. However, only half the high-IQ children had the intelligence-promoting form of the gene. So this particular gene alone cannot explain where these children's superior intelligence came from.

Kihlstrom (1998) was concerned that the research would lead to the setting up of genetic centres testing parents for this gene and the idea that selective breeding could create more intelligent people. Plomin recognised that his research could be abused and be mistakenly seen as providing evidence that genes determine

intelligence on their own, but thought it would be a mistake to stop such research just to avoid confronting such issues.

Gosso *et al.* (2007) found that the *CHRM2* gene on the long arm of chromosome seven was associated with intelligence. IQ data from a sample of 762 Dutch children and adults was collected along with *CHRM2* expression levels in the participants' brains. The researchers found specific variants of the gene were linked to higher intelligence, providing support for Plomin's claim that intelligence may be affected by many different genes.

Lahn *et al.* (2004) have identified a gene, *ASPM*, that appears to be linked with the expansion of the human brain's cerebral cortex. The gene was compared in a range of primates and non-primates, and the fastest changes seemed to have arisen relatively recently in evolution, after humans parted from chimpanzees. It is thought that *ASPM* produces proteins that regulate the number of neurones produced by cell division in the cerebral cortex. This study therefore provides a possible explanation of the influence of genes on intelligence.

Environmental factors

Twin studies, familial studies and adoption studies have all suggested that environmental as well as genetic factors influence intelligence.

Family influences

Children's IQ levels appear to be affected by the degree of individual social stimulation that they are given. Saltz (1973) investigated the influence a foster-grandparent programme (FGP) had on children's intellectual development. The participants were 81 children in two similar children's homes that provided top quality physical and intellectual stimulation. The FGP was introduced into one of the homes. Forty-eight elderly people were employed part-time to provide personal relationships with the children for at least four years. If individual social relationships are necessary for intellectual development, then the children on the FGP should have outscored those not on the programme. A significant difference in IQ in favour of the FGP children was found and they attained normal levels of intellectual progress, despite the long period of institutionalisation. This research indicates that individual social stimulation is necessary for normal intellectual development. It also suggests a practical application to help raise the IQ levels of socially impoverished children. There have also been a small number of experimental studies that have set out to provide children with an unstimulating environment to see the effects. We can look at one such study in *Classic Research*.

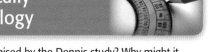

Thinking critically about psychology

What ethical issues are raised by the Dennis study? Why might it have been considered ethically acceptable at the time?

CLASSIC RESEARCH

Dennis W (1941) Infant development under conditions of restricted and minimum social stimulation. *Genetic Psychology Monographs* **23, 143–89**

Aim: To deprive children of normal levels of stimulation under controlled conditions and observe the effects on their intellectual development.

Procedure: Two female fraternal twins were removed from an institution when they were one month old and cared for in the home of a husband and wife research team, the Dennises. They were kept in a clean and warm but bare room without furniture or decoration. Social interaction with adults was kept to an absolute minimum. The time spent with adults was limited to around two hours per day. The children's development was regularly assessed using a selection of special tests to measure their early intellectual development. From 14 months they were given an intensive programme of stimulation in an attempt to make up for the poor start.

Findings: From one to seven months of age scores of intellectual development remained slightly below average. From seven to 14 months, scores declined severely. At 14 months the participants were classified as seriously retarded. After a few months of intense stimulation their developmental measures returned to normal.

Conclusion: Understimulation has serious effects on children's intellectual development. However it is reversible, at least in young children.

Birth order has also been associated with IQ levels. First-born children tend to score better on IQ than second children, who in turn outscore third children and so on, because the amount of parental attention decreases and resources may be less. Zajonc & Markus (1975) developed the *conference model*, a mathematical model of the effect of birth order and family size on IQ scores. As families grew in size, the average IQ levels of family members dropped, supporting the idea that birth order and family size affect intelligence. The last child in a family is especially affected, because as well as incurring the usual reduction in IQ seen in subsequent children, this child is also denied the experience of tutoring younger children. The differences found, though, were quite small, a range of about three IQ points. The researchers did use their evidence, however, to suggest that the drop in American high-school intelligence levels was due to the trend towards larger, closer-spaced families since World War II.

▼ **Figure 7.28** Children with lots of older siblings have lower IQ on average

Melican & Feldt (1980) tested out Zajonc & Markus's claim on children in Iowa and found that the size of the interval between children was found in selected instances to be related to IQ levels in families of three or more children, but the results were not consistent for every family size, nor from child to child in a birth sequence. Therefore the results cast doubt on the idea that population trends in child spacing can explain the decline in IQ scores.

Enrichment

If intelligence is predominantly genetic in nature, then any attempts to increase IQ levels by providing supplementary enrichment should have little or no effects on intelligence levels. *Operation Headstart* was a famous American initiative that began in 1965. The central idea was to provide a pre-school boost to disadvantaged children's intellectual levels; it involved a mixture of intervention by social services, improved diet and medical care as well as educational stimulation that involved the whole family. The early results were discouraging, with initial increases in IQ being short-lived. The programme was criticised by Hunt (1972), who said it was inappropriate, as it didn't provide the skills that middle-class children developed pre-school. However, Lazar & Darlington (1982) found that there was a long-term positive effect: those who had been on the programme were shown years later to have better reading and mathematical skills, felt more competent and were more likely to continue into higher education. There was also less involvement with crime and even a reduced level of teenage pregnancies. Atkinson (1990) reviewed several similar programmes to Headstart and concluded that the central factor was parental involvment, presumably because it led to a more stimulating home environment.

Another major interventionist enrichment programme was the *Milwaukee Project*. Heber (1972) studied the effects of intellectual stimulation on children from deprived environments by selecting 40 newborn black children from the most depressed area of Milwaukee. All the mothers had IQ scores below 80. Twenty of the children were put onto a special programme where their mothers received not only education, but also job training and home-making and child-care tuition. The children themselves received personalised enrichment in their own homes on a regular basis. The other 20 children formed the control group and had no such enrichment.

By the age of six the enriched children were far superior on all test measurements including problem-solving ability and language skills. Their average IQ score was 120.7 compared with the control group's 87.2. By the time the children were 10 years old, the enriched group's average IQ score had fallen to 105, whilst the control group was roughly the same at 85. The reason for the large decline in the enriched children's IQ may be because, from the age of six, they attended the local school where the schooling was geared up for duller children, meaning the brighter children weren't stimulated properly and fell back. Also prior to age six, the enriched children received three nutritious meals a day; this stopped when they began school.

Generally, enrichment programmes do seem able to boost intellectual performance, but improvements decline once the enrichment stops. Parental involvment and diet seem to be key factors, as is the boosting of confidence and motivation to do well.

Cultural influences on IQ scores

Typically, white middle-class people (and until fairly recently men) get the highest scores on standard IQ tests. In the past it was widely believed that this showed that the white middle classes were more intelligent than others. Only a tiny minority of (pretty unpopular!) psychologists still believe this. There is a particular problem with speaking of 'race' in relation to IQ scores because race is clearly genetic. The very term 'racial differences in intelligence' presumes that any differences in the scores obtained from different ethnic groups are genetic, and that some races are more intelligent than others as a function of their genetic make-up.

It is quite possible, however, to explore differences in IQ scores in relation to culture. Intelligence means different things in different cultures, and one reason people from cultural backgrounds other than Western white middle classes tend to do badly on IQ tests is because the tests have been designed by people from a Western culture. This means that the sort of knowledge and skills assessed in IQ tests is based upon the sort of things that are taught in the schools in dominant Western culture. Tests are thus inevitably biased towards those who have grown up in that culture.

There have been attempts to design *culture-free tests*, usually consisting of non-verbal questions, as language

ability has been seen as an obvious source of bias in intelligence testing. Probably the most famous of these is *Raven's Progressive Matrices* (1936), which consist of multiple-choice questions of abstract reasoning that become increasingly harder to solve. Candidates have to identify a missing segment from a larger pattern. The idea is that the skills needed to answer the questions are ones that are not culturally based and the tests are therefore fair for all, allowing comparison of all individuals. However, critics argue that such tests are still culturally biased because a culturally based familiarity with the whole idea of testing is required to do well on them. Metcalf (2007) goes further when he says 'using such tests, devised in the West, on semi-literate at best individuals in Africa, to "prove" that such people are retarded is laughable'. There are those who believe any attempt to create a culture-free IQ test is doomed to failure because intelligence is a cultural concept that will therefore vary from culture to culture. Vernon (1969) summed up this viewpoint by claiming that intelligence was not something that everybody, from all cultures, had in differing amounts and which determined their potential.

Williams (1972) devised the *Black Intelligence Test for Cultural Homogeneity* (BITCH). This was an IQ test that was deliberately based on black culture of the time, with the idea being that black people, who normally score poorly on IQ tests, would do well, but people from the white culture would conversely score poorly. This indeed proved to be the case and is good evidence towards the viewpoint that IQ tests are indeed culturally biased.

▼ **Table 7.3 Items from the BITCH test**

	Question 1	Question 2	Question 3
	An alley apple is?	'I know you shame' means?	'Main squeeze' means?
a	A piece of fruit	You don't hear well	To prepare for battle
b	A brick	You are a racist	A favourite toy
c	A dog	You don't mean that	A best girlfriend
d	A horse	You are guilty	To hold up someone

Another factor affecting different IQ scores in different ethnic and socio-economic groups is poverty. In Europe and the USA, minority ethnic groups are more likely to live in poverty, and this poverty leads to difficulties in providing an optimum early environment. Brooks-Gunn *et al.* (1996) reviewed longitudinal data on 800 black and white children from birth to age five. As well as IQ scores, family economic status, neighbourhood conditions, family structure and home environment were also considered. It was found that poverty accounted for over half of the difference in IQ, and that was before taking into account other social problems that are associated with poverty.

Chapter summary

Theories of intelligence
- Intelligence has proven difficult to define and there have been controversies over attempts to measure it.
- Psychometric theories have attempted to measure intelligence, but there have been disagreements as to how many basic factors there are. Indeed, it isn't certain if such a thing as general, innate intelligence actually exists.
- Information processing approaches see intelligence differently, as a set of cognitive steps an individual goes through to reach a solution to a problem.

Animal learning and intelligence
- Animals use both classical and operant conditioning to learn from environmental experiences by a process of association. With classical conditioning one stimulus becomes associated with another to create the same response, while operant conditioning involves acquiring behaviour due to its consequences.
- Animal intelligence is generally seen in terms of the ability to alter behaviour in response to changing environments, though difficulties arise in assessing how much of an adapted behaviour is due to biology or to learning.
- Other explanations of animal learning focus on learning abilities and the capacity to process information. Research here has centred upon *social learning*, where behavioural processes allowing social interactions affect what animals learn, how able animals are to *self-recognise* and have a self-concept, whether they have a *theory of mind* that permits the attribution of mental states to themselves and others, and the concept of *Machiavellian intelligence*, where individual interests are best served by co-operative and manipulative interactions that don't upset the social cohesion of a group.

Evolution of intelligence
- Human intelligence has been placed into an evolutionary framework by the notion that an ever-changing environment creates selective pressure for increased intellect.
- Humans are seen as having adapted to global cooling in the Paleolithic era by exploiting environments away from the equator due to the development of complex cognitive abilities.
- The evolution of human intelligence has especially been linked to increased social complexity and better hunting and foraging strategies.
- The evolution of increased brain size has been associated with the demands of group living, Machiavellian intelligence and ecological demands.
- Although there are costs to having a larger brain, it seems to bestow an adaptive advantage, indicating that intelligence has indeed evolved.
- Both genetic and environmental influences upon intelligence test performance have been investigated, using methods such as twin and adoption studies. Attempts to identify actual genes have been made, though such research is still in its infancy. Alternative methods have involved looking at the effects of social stimulation and enrichment upon intelligence levels.
- Conclusions drawn from such research methodologies have not produced clear conclusions and have often become bogged down in controversy.
- The effect of cultural influences on IQ has proven especially controversial and attempts to devise culture-free tests have not met with universal approval.

What do I know?

1 Outline and evaluate Gardner's theory of multiple intelligences. (25 marks)

2 (a) Outline the role of genetic factors associated with intelligence test performance. (5 marks)
  (b) Discuss the influence of culture on intelligence test performance. (20 marks)

3 Discuss the role of evolutionary factors in the development of human intelligence. (25 marks)

4 (a) Outline the role of simple learning (classical and operant conditioning) in the behaviour of non-human animals. (9 marks)
  (b) Evaluate information processing theories of intelligence. (16 marks)

5 (a) Describe **one** psychometric theory of intelligence. (9 marks)
  (b) Evaluate the role of environmental factors associated with intelligence test performance. (16 marks)

CHAPTER 8
Cognition and Development

Thinking ahead

By the end of this chapter you should be able to:

- outline and evaluate theories of cognitive development, including those of Piaget, Vygotsky and Bruner

- apply these theories to understanding and improving education

- understand theories of moral and pro-social development with particular regard to the theories of Kohlberg and Eisenberg

- explain the development of a child's sense of self, with particular reference to theory of mind

- outline and evaluate research into children's understanding of others with particular reference to Selman's work on perspective-taking

- explain biological explanations of social cognition with particular reference to the role of mirror neurones

In your AS level you will have studied some aspects of children's emotional development, including attachment and the effects of day care, institutionalisation and privation. Although there is some overlap between emotional and cognitive development, we are more concerned in this chapter with the latter. The term 'cognitive' refers to mental abilities, so cognitive development is the study of how mental abilities develop throughout life. In this chapter we are particularly interested in the development of children's reasoning, their understanding of morality and of their own and others' minds.

Theories of cognitive development

Historically, three general theories of cognitive development have been particularly important in psychology. They are those of Jean Piaget, Lev Vygotsky and Jerome Bruner.

Piaget's theory of cognitive development

Piaget produced perhaps the best known and most influential theory of cognitive development. Piaget realised that children do not simply know less than adults but think in entirely different ways. Based on this understanding he divided childhood into stages, each of which sees the development of new ways of reasoning. Piaget also looked at children's learning, in particular the role of motivation to learn.

How and why children learn

Piaget believed in *agency*, our motivation to actively pursue knowledge. To Piaget, then, we are all agents of our own cognitive development. Learning is thus an active process in which we explore the world and construct our own mental representation of reality. As we get older, we construct more and more detailed and sophisticated representations of the world. These representations are stored as schemas. A *schema* is a mental structure containing all the information we have about one aspect of the world. As adults we have schemas for people, objects, actions and abstract concepts. Children are born with a few innate schemas, which enable us to interact with others. During our first year we construct other schemas.

We learn when our existing schemas do not allow us to make sense of something new. We are motivated to understand because when we do not we experience the unpleasant sensation of *disequilibrium*. To escape this we have to equilibrate by adapting to the new situation by exploring and discovering what we need to know. Piaget identified two processes by which *adaptation* takes place, called *assimilation* and *accommodation*. Assimilation takes place when we can understand a new experience by adding (or assimilating) information into an existing schema. For example, a child in a family with dogs can adapt to the existence of different breeds by assimilating them into their dog schema. Accommodation takes place in response to more dramatically new experiences, as the child has to accommodate their existence. Thus the child whose family keeps dogs may initially think of cats as dogs but then be forced to accommodate to the existence of a separate species.

▲ **Figure 8.1** Children used to dogs may initially assimilate their first cat into their dog schema but later accommodate to the existence of cats by forming a new cat schema

KEY TERMS

agency   motivation to learn about the world

schema   a unit of knowledge holding all the information we have about one thing

disequilibrium   the uncomfortable sensation of not understanding something

adaptation   changing one's mental representation of the world in response to new information

assimilation   making a minor change to a schema in response to new information

accommodation   making a major change to a schema or forming a new schema in response to new information

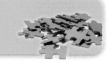

Thinking practically about psychology

Explain the following scenario using Piaget's terms, for example disequilibrium, assimilation, accommodation, adaptation, schema and agency.

A three-year-old girl is taken on holiday. When she sees an aeroplane for the first time she calls it a car. When it takes off she is curious and a little distressed. However her parents explain that aeroplanes fly and she calms down and draws aeroplanes for much of the flight.

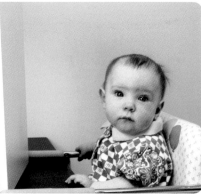

▲ **Figure 8.2** This baby has not acquired object permanence as it looks away from the toy as soon as it is covered

Operations and the four stages of development

Operations are the rules by which the world functions – or *operates*. Piaget believed that the reason that children think in different ways at different stages of their development is because the operations they are capable of change with age. Very young children have no understanding of how the world operates and they are said to be *pre-operational*. The first operations to appear are *concrete*. This means that children can understand the rules governing something as long as they can see it. Later, rules governing abstract concepts are understood.. Piaget identified four stages of development. He believed that we all pass through all four stages in the same order, hence he referred to them as *invariant*. We vary quite a lot, however, in the age at which we arrive at each stage, and the ages attached to each stage are just broad averages.

The sensorimotor stage (0–2 years)

This lasts for approximately the first two years of life. The child's main focus at this point is on physical sensation and on learning a degree of physical co-ordination. Children learn by trial and error that actions have particular effects. Babies are thus fascinated when they realise that they can move their body and eventually other objects. At around eight months the child develops an understanding of *object permanence*. This is the understanding that objects exist permanently even when they are no longer visible. Piaget watched babies looking at an attractive object as it was removed from their sight. Prior to around eight months, children immediately switched their attention away from the object once it had disappeared from view. However, from around eight months they would actively look for it. If it were placed behind a screen the child would push the screen aside. Piaget concluded from this that at around eight months children began to understand that the object still existed even though they could not see it. By the end of the sensorimotor stage the infant is aware of other people as separate beings, has some grasp of language and can begin to think using symbols such as words.

The pre-operational stage (2–7 years)

By the end of the second year, children have reasonable language, however they do not understand logical rules or operations (hence the term *pre-operational*). The child can thus be said to be *semilogical*, dealing with the world very much as it appears rather than as it is. Pre-operational children display some distinctive errors in logic. They are, for example, highly egocentric. This means that they tend to see the world only from their own point of view. This was demonstrated in Piaget & Inhelder's (1952) 'three mountains' experiment. Children were presented with three papier-mâché mountains, each of which had a different marker on the top, a cross, a house or a covering of snow (see Figure 8.3).

▼ **Figure 8.3** Piaget & Inhelder's three mountains procedure

A doll was positioned to the side of the three mountains so that it faced them from a different angle to that of the child. The child's task was to select from a choice of pictures the scene that best matched what the doll could 'see.' Piaget noted that under-sevens struggled with this task and tended to choose the picture of the scene from their own point of view.

Piaget also observed that children under seven years found conservation tasks difficult. Conservation is the understanding that objects remain the same in quantity even when their appearance changes. Piaget demonstrated this in a number of situations, including number and volume.

In his number conservation procedures, Piaget laid out two rows of counters side by side, with the same number of counters spaced the same distance apart. Even young children were able to identify that there were the same number of

---

KEY TERM

object permanence the understanding that objects still exist when they are out of sight

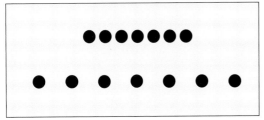

▲ **Figure 8.4** Pre-operational children tended to say there were more counters in the longer row

▲ **Figure 8.6** In the pendulum task, children have to work out whether the mass of the weight or the length of the string affect the speed of the swing

counters in each row. However, when the counters in one of the rows were pushed closer together, pre-operational children typically said there were now fewer counters in that row

In his liquid conservation procedure Piaget found that if two glasses are placed together with liquid coming up to the same height, in each most children can correctly identify that they contain the same amount. However if liquid was poured from a short, wide glass to a taller, thinner container, younger children typically believed there was now more liquid in the taller container.

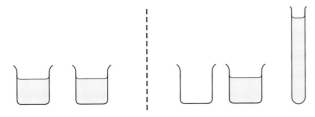

▲ **Figure 8.5** Pre-operational children tended to say there was more liquid in the taller container

The concrete operational stage (7–11 years)
By the age of around seven years children's minds are mature enough to use logical thought or operations. They can therefore generally carry out conservation tasks successfully. However, children can only apply logic to objects and situations that are present and physical (hence the term *concrete* operational). They also become gradually less egocentric.

Formal operational stage (11 years+)
Piaget believed that from about 11 years of age, children become capable of formal reasoning. This means that children become able to focus on the *form* of an argument and not be distracted by its content. Formal reasoning can be tested by means of syllogisms. For example: 'All yellow cats have two heads. I have a yellow cat called Charlie. How many heads does Charlie have?' The correct answer is 'two' (Smith *et al.*, 1998). Piaget found that younger children became distracted by the content and answered that cats do not really have two heads.

Piaget believed that once children can reason formally they are capable of scientific reasoning. A classic test of scientific reasoning is Inhelder & Piaget's (1958) pendulum task. In this test children are given pendulums of different weights and string of different lengths. Their task is to find out whether the speed of the pendulum's swing depends on the mass of the weight or the length of the string. Piaget found that most 11–15-year-olds were capable of setting up and carrying out this and similar tasks.

 Gather some participants and try them out with the pendulum task. The correct answer is that the length of the string but not the mass of the weight affects the speed of swing. They may find it quite tricky considering Piaget's 11-year-olds could do it! What do your findings suggest about Piaget's ideas? What ethical issues do you have to consider as you give feedback on participants' performance?

Discussion of Piaget's stages

Modern psychologists are generally in agreement with Piaget's principle that the nature of children's reasoning changes with age. However, modern studies tend to find that younger children do rather better in reasoning tasks than Piaget's younger participants did. On the other hand, teenagers tend to do worse than Piaget believed on formal and scientific reasoning tasks. Overall, then, we believe that although reasoning ability does change during childhood it does so slightly less dramatically than Piaget suggested. Researchers from Edinburgh University in the 1970s experimented with procedures to test egocentrism and conservation in children, taking particular care to communicate effectively with children and not to give them cues suggesting what they expected the children to say. These studies found that pre-operational children generally performed better on egocentrism and conservation tests than Piaget found. We can look at one of these studies in *Classic Research*.

CLASSIC RESEARCH

McGarrigle J & Donaldson M (1974) Conservation accidents. *Cognition* **3, 341–350**

Aim: To test whether children of pre-operational age would do better in a number conservation task if the counters appeared to move accidentally rather than be deliberately moved by the experimenter.

Procedure: 80 children aged 4–6 years took part in one of two conditions. In a control condition, they undertook the standard Piaget task. This involved the experimenter presenting them with two rows of counters, asking them about the number in each row, then pushing the counters in one row closer and asking them again. In an experimental condition, instead of the experimenter moving them closer together, 'naughty teddy' ran across the table and 'accidentally' knocked the counters in one row closer together. Participants were then asked whether there were the same number of counters in each row.

Findings: In the control condition, 13 of the 80 children (16 per cent) correctly said that there were the same number of counters in the two rows. In the experimental condition, the children did much better, with 50 of the children (62 per cent) answering correctly.

Conclusion: Most children aged 4–6 are capable of number conservation as long as they are not influenced by seeing the experimenter deliberately move counters.

Thinking critically about psychology

This experiment used an independent measures design. Why was this necessary here and what are the likely disadvantages of this sort of design?

Similar results were found in tests of egocentrism. These results suggest two possibilities: either children pass from the pre-operational stage to the concrete operations stage earlier than Piaget believed, or it may be that there is no pre-operational stage. More radically, some recent research has begun to suggest that even toddlers have some understanding of number conservation. Langer, Gillette & Ariaga (2003) showed 21-month-olds one object being added to another then hidden. When only one object was then produced the children actively searched for the other, suggesting that they had some understanding that one and one always equal two.

Piaget believed that all children achieve formal reasoning at some point, although with some variation in age. However, modern studies suggest that in fact many people are not capable of formal thinking. In one study, Bradmetz (1999) followed the cognitive development of 62 children from the age of seven to 15 years, regularly giving them a battery of tests, including the pendulum task, designed to measure formal and scientific thinking. By 15, only one of the young people could reliably carry out the tasks. This and similar studies suggest that actually Piaget overestimated the cognitive abilities of teenagers.

Although it seems that Piaget overestimated the formal thinking capabilities of teenagers, this does not mean that the concept does not have its uses. Lewis & Lewis (2007) assessed formal thinking and general academic success in

3000 students studying for the American Chemistry Society's general exam. Difficulty in formal reasoning was highly predictive of failure in the exam, and this was independent of general academic success. This shows that the ability to reason formally affects academic success.

Vygotsky's theory of cognitive development

Lev Vygotsky was a Russian psychologist writing at the same time as Piaget. Vygotsky was influenced by Piaget and agreed with him on many points. For example, both believed that cognitive development takes place in stages, each of which is characterised by different styles of thinking. However, Vygotsky disagreed with Piaget's view of the child as exploring the world and learning through motivation to understand. Instead, Vygotsky saw children as primarily social beings, with learning taking place through social interaction with more knowledgeable others. He also saw language as central to cognitive development.

▼ **Figure 8.7** According to Vygotsky children learn from each other and from adults

Culture and cognitive development

Not all children develop the same cognitive abilities. Vygotsky believed that all children are born with similar basic mental functions, such as the ability to focus their attention on particular objects. However, he also believed that higher mental functions, such as thinking and problem-solving have to be learned from others. He described these higher mental functions as 'mental tools' of the culture in which the child lives. Tools are transmitted to children by older members of the culture through a series of guided learning experiences. Guided learning experiences can be formal (such as lessons in school) or more informal, for example during play. Cultural tools include language, art and mathematics. Interactions with other people gradually become internalised to form the child's internal representation of the world. This is quite different from Piaget's view in which children's *individual* explorations form their mental representation of the world. To Vygotsky, the way each child thinks and perceives the world is shared with other members of the culture.

▼ **Figure 8.8** Computer skills are an example of a cultural tool transmitted from expert to learner

The ZPD

Vygotsky put tremendous emphasis on the role of social interaction in learning. He believed that children can develop their understanding of a situation more quickly through interacting with others than they can through individual discovery. Development of higher mental functions, such as formal and scientific reasoning, cannot be acquired just through discovery but requires learning from others. The gap between what children can understand alone and what they have the potential to understand after interaction with others is known as the *Zone of Proximal Development* (or ZPD). Instruction by an expert allows children to cross the ZPD and understand as much of a subject or situation as they are capable of doing.

The importance of language

Piaget placed very little emphasis on the role of language in cognitive development. It simply appeared when children had reached a certain point in their development. For Vygotsky, however, language was an important cultural tool. Vygotsky believed that language and reasoning develop separately and that at first language is just for communication. Later, however, children internalise language and begin to use it as a tool of thinking. In the pre-operational stage, as children are learning to use language to reason, they often think aloud. By the concrete operational stage, however, thinking in speech has been internalised and becomes silent.

Discussion of Vygotsky's theory

The most important of Vygotsky's ideas is the central role of social interaction in learning. Many studies have supported this principle by showing that children receiving help from others pick up skills that they probably could not have mastered on their own. In one such study, Roazzi & Bryant (1997) asked four- and five-year-old children to work out how many sweets there were in a box. They worked either alone or with the help of an older child. In the help condition, the older children gave prompts until the younger children worked out how to perform the task. Most children receiving help in this condition mastered the task whilst those working alone generally did not.

Slightly more controversial is the idea of speech as an aid to thinking. Vygotsky's theory would predict that younger (pre-operational) children would understand material better having read it aloud, whereas this should be of no such benefit in concrete operational children. Prior & Welling (2001) tested this, giving Canadian five- to eight-year-olds passages to read, either silently or aloud, followed by a comprehension test. In contrast to what Vygotsky's theory would predict, the seven- to eight-year-olds did better in comprehension after reading aloud whereas the five- to six-year-olds did not.

Thinking critically about psychology

How well does Vygotsky's theory fare against the following criteria?

- supporting evidence
- contradictory evidence
- practical application (look ahead to p173).

Bruner's theory of cognitive development

Some aspects of Jerome Bruner's ideas about cognitive development and learning were strongly influenced by Vygotsky, so that they are sometimes known collectively as the Vygotsky–Bruner model. However, Bruner departed from some of the ideas of Vygotsky and Piaget. For example he abandoned the idea of stages of development and replaced them with modes of representation.

Representation and cognitive development

Bruner (1974) rejected the stages of cognitive development proposed by Piaget and Vygotsky. Instead he proposed that cognitive development involves the mastery of three forms or modes in which information can be represented in the child's mind. The first mode is known as *enactive* representation: events are represented by the actions they lead to. There is thus no distinction in the mind of babies between their building blocks and the act of piling them up. Without words for or mental images of building blocks they can only think about building blocks by means of making block-piling hand movements. For the first two years or so, children have only the enactive mode of representation. This period with only enactive representation is equivalent to Piaget's sensorimotor stage.

◀ **Figure 8.9** According to Bruner's theory, babies represent objects like building blocks by the actions that accompany them, in this case building

The second mode of representation to be mastered between two and six years is *iconic* representation. This involves using mental images to represent information. The period in which this takes place is equivalent to Piaget's pre-operational stage and is an alternative explanation for the semilogical nature of young children's reasoning. Although by six years children have quite well-developed language, words are used for communication rather than mental representation. By six or seven years, however, children become capable of *symbolic* representation, using symbols like words to represent ideas.

As adults we use all three modes of representation. Bruner (1974) gives the example of tying a knot: we can imagine what it looks like (iconic), know the name for that particular type of knot (symbolic) and we know how to tie it (enactive). As this example illustrates, we use the three modes of representation together; however, symbolic representation is particularly important as this allows us to 'go beyond the information given', as Bruner put it, to manipulate ideas, developing and evaluating them.

KEY TERMS

enactive representing an object by an action associated with it

iconic representing an object with a mental image

symbolic representing an object or idea by an arbitrary symbol such as a word

scaffolding assisting a learner through the ZPD

Scaffolding

Whilst Vygotsky developed the idea of the ZPD (see p171), the gap between what a child can understand alone and with guidance from an expert, he did not go into much detail about just how the expert helps. Bruner developed this line of theory with the concept of *scaffolding*. The term 'scaffolding' refers collectively to all the ways in which someone with more expertise in a task can help a learner cross the ZPD. Generally as a learner crosses the ZPD, the level of help declines. We can see an example of this in Table 8.1, in which a mother scaffolds a child's learning to pile building bricks.

▼ **Table 8.1 An example of scaffolding through a ZPD (from Wood *et al.*, 1991)**

Level of help	Nature of prompt	Example
5	Demonstration	Mother assembles two blocks
4	Preparation for child	Mother positions blocks for child to push together
3	Indication of materials	Mother points to blocks
2	Specific verbal instructions	Mother says 'get four big blocks'
1	General prompts	Mother says 'now you make something'

Wood, Bruner & Ross (1976) identify five aspects of scaffolding:

- *recruitment* – engaging the child's interest
- *reduction of degrees of freedom* – simplifying the task
- *direction maintenance* – encouragement to maintain motivation
- *marking critical features* – highlighting the critical aspects of the task
- *demonstration* – showing the child how to do aspects of the task.

Discussion of Bruner's theory

There is ample evidence for the existence and importance of scaffolding. Conner & Cross (2003) followed up 45 children, observing them taking part in problem-solving tasks with the help of their mothers at 16, 26, 44 and 54 months. Mothers clearly helped the children with the tasks and used less intervention as age increased. They also moved from non-contingent intervention with toddlers (ie helping regardless of the difficulty children experienced) to more contingent scaffolding, in which they provided help as it was required, with older children.

▼ **Figure 8.10** As children get older, parents start to offer help only as it is needed

The existence of enactive, iconic and symbolic representation is not controversial. However, it remains unclear whether representation is purely enactive for the first couple of years as Bruner said, and whether symbolic representation really does not appear until six years. This would explain children's improved reasoning ability from around six years, but so do stage theories. It has proved tricky to design studies to tell us which approach is correct. That said, there are many practical applications that make use of alternative modes of representation. For example, some doctors are beginning to use a language of icons called VCM (from the French *Visualisation des Connaissances Médicales*) to quickly and easily represent medical terms such as drugs and medical conditions. A study by Lamy *et al.* (2008) found that doctors tested in VCM scored an average of 94 per cent correct answers as opposed to 88 per cent correct for written questions. This shows that using iconic representation for something we normally represent symbolically can improve the efficiency of information processing.

Thinking critically about psychology

Draw up a list of as many similarities and differences as you can find between the theories of Piaget, Vygotsky and Bruner.

Thinking creatively about psychology

Try to combine the ideas of Piaget, Vygotsky and Bruner into one theory. Summarise this theory in around 250 words (half a side of A4 typed).

Applying theories of cognitive development to education

Theories of cognitive development are directly concerned with children's learning, so as psychologists have looked to help make education more effective, many of the weapons in their arsenal have been inspired by the ideas of Piaget, Vygotsky and Bruner. Particularly since the 1960s, cognitive developmental theory has influenced education policy.

Prior to the 1960s, schoolchildren typically sat silently in rows, copying material from the board. They then rote-learnt it. Those unable to keep up with the majority were often punished. The Plowden Committee was set up to look at ways to improve primary education, and their 1967 report made a number of recommendations based on Piaget's ideas:

▲ **Figure 8.11** Traditional classrooms like this were the norm before the influence of cognitive developmental theory

- Children require individual attention and have different needs.
- Children should be taught things when they have developed sufficiently to understand them.
- Children mature at different rates. Teachers need to be aware of each child's level of development and treat them accordingly.

Applying Piaget's theory

Piaget's ideas have been applied to education in a number of ways, not least in the ways teachers talk to children. Traditionally it was the responsibility of the child to keep up with and make sense of their teacher. However if, as Piaget said, children think differently and less logically than adults do, it makes more sense for teachers to adapt to these ways of thinking. For example, teachers should expect some egocentrism in younger children. Donaldson (1978) illustrates this point with an account of how novelist Laurie Lee had his first day at school spoiled by a misunderstanding between himself and his teacher (Box 8.1).

■ **Box 8.1**

An example of egocentrism in the classroom. After Donaldson (1978)

I spent the first day picking holes in paper and went home in a smouldering temper.

'What's the matter love? Didn't he like it at school then?'

'They never gave me the present.'

'Present. What present?'

'They said they'd give me a present.'

'Well now, I'm sure they didn't.'

'They did! They said: "You're Laurie Lee, aren't you. Just you sit there for the present." I sat there all day but I never got it.'

A related issue concerns how teachers give feedback to children. If the aim of education is to advance children's thinking rather than just increase their knowledge, it follows that children need positive feedback when they have made a good attempt at solving a problem but have arrived at the wrong answer.

Piaget's stages have also influenced when particular ideas are taught. This is the idea behind the National Curriculum — that children should encounter ideas when they are ready to cope with them. For example, tasks requiring formal thinking would become appropriate only after the children had achieved formal operations. This means that the primary curriculum, which ends with Piaget's concrete operational stage at age 11, should contain relatively little material that requires formal thinking, although it *should* contain opportunities for more advanced individuals to practise advanced thinking.

Piaget's idea of children as actively exploring and forming their own mental representation of the world also has important applications. Learning is an active process, and

cannot be achieved in the traditional classroom situation where children are passive receivers of information. According to Piaget, children learn best by discovery. In effective discovery-learning the teacher presents children with tasks designed to lead them to discover things for themselves.

▼ **Figure 8.12** Modern primary classrooms contain opportunities for children to explore a range of activities

Thinking practically about psychology

Devise your own discovery-learning psychology lesson for AS students. It will need to pose a challenge and motivate students to find information.

Applying the Vygotsky–Bruner model

Vygotsky and Bruner shared the belief that learning is a social process that requires interaction with one or more other people. From this point of view the key to effective learning is to maximise the opportunities for productive interaction during learning experiences. This can be achieved in several ways. One way is for teachers to actively assist children who are actively engaged in learning tasks. Thus the children are working within a ZPD and teachers provide the scaffolding. This works best when the teacher sets a task that pupils can work on independently then moves around the class providing help and advice as needed. Learning support assistants (LSAs) also have a very important role in providing scaffolding.

Peers as well as teachers can provide social interaction during learning. Jarvis (2005) identifies three ways in which this is commonly achieved.

- *Co-operative group work* — children can work together in small groups. This works best either when tasks require discussion, or when they can be broken down with each child taking on a particular job.

RESEARCH NOW

Oley N (2002) Extra credit and peer tutoring: impact on the quality of writing in introductory psychology in an open admissions college. In RA Griggs (ed.) *Handbook for Teaching Introductory Psychology Vol 3.* Mahwah, NJ: LEA.

Aim: To test whether peer tutoring improves marks in a psychology essay.

Procedure: 65 students aged 17-plus at an American open admissions college (the equivalent to a British further education college) took part. They were set a five-page essay on a topic they had not studied, meaning extensive research was required. All were given basic instructions on how to use the library to locate the necessary information. Each student took part in one of three conditions. In a control condition students had no assistance. In two experimental conditions they either volunteered to have a peer tutor from the year above or were given one without any option. The completed essays were graded on a four-point scale.

Findings: Both experimental groups with peer tutoring scored significantly higher essay grades than those who worked alone. This was irrespective of whether the decision to use tutors was voluntary or forced. A positive correlation emerged between the number of consultations with a peer tutor and final grade.

Conclusion: Peer tutoring is effective in helping psychology students achieve higher essay grades.

- *Reciprocal teaching* — each child takes responsibility for finding out particular information and teaching the rest of a group.
- *Peer tutoring* — more advanced learners teach material to less advanced individuals.

In each of these strategies children or older learners provide scaffolding to one another and so help them through the ZPD.

Bruner (1966) challenged Piaget's belief that ideas can only be taught when a child reaches a particular stage of development. Instead he suggested that any subject can be taught to any age group provided it is done in the right way. Bruner proposed the spiral curriculum, which introduces ideas in a basic form then revisits them in increasingly advanced versions as children get older.

The success of cognitive developmental models of education

The large scale adoption of discovery learning in primary schools after the Plowden Report was extensively researched and the conclusion reached by most researchers was that it made little or no impact on learning. Jarvis (2005) suggests two reasons for this. First, many teachers misinterpreted Piaget's ideas and, rather than providing challenging tasks of discovery, largely left children to their own devices. Second, basing teaching on Piagetian ideas alone led to inadequate social interaction in the classroom.

Since the 1980s, the Vygotsky–Bruner model of education has become more influential, and research has clearly shown the benefits of group work, reciprocal teaching and peer tutoring. We can look at one particularly relevant study of peer tutoring in *Research Now*.

Bruner's ideas about using different modes of representation to teach have also had success. Enactive representation strategies are effective in boosting children's reading and comprehension. Glenberg, Brown & Levin (2006)

Thinking critically about psychology

What ethical issues does Oley's study raise?

▼ Figure 8.13
Second-year psychology students can make good peer tutors for first years

tested a procedure in which children reading aloud held and manipulated objects directly relevant to what they were reading. They did significantly better than controls in a comprehension test. Research has also demonstrated the success of strategies like *Jolly Phonics* (Lloyd, 1994), in which children learn their letters by matching each letter sound with an action, giving the child an enactive representation of the sound. Hatcher *et al.* (2006) divided children randomly into two groups and gave an experimental group 20 minutes of *Jolly Phonics* a day for 20 weeks. A control group waited for 10 weeks then had 10 weeks of *Jolly Phonics*. After 10 weeks the experimental group were well ahead on recognising letters and reading single words. After the second 10 weeks the control group caught up. This strongly supports the effectiveness of using enactive representation strategies like *Jolly Phonics* to teach reading.

The development of moral understanding

Every society requires children to understand a set of standards by which they can make judgements about what is right and wrong. Children need to be able not just to behave morally but also to undertake moral reasoning so that they can judge the morally correct decisions in new situations. Moral reasoning develops with age, so it is most commonly studied as an aspect of cognitive development.

Kohlberg's theory of moral development

Lawrence Kohlberg (1958) produced an influential theory of the development of moral reasoning. He investigated moral reasoning in 10–16-year-old boys using stories involving moral dilemmas. The best known of these is that of Heinz and the pharmacist. This is shown in Box 8.2.

> ■ Box 8.2
>
> ### Kohlberg's Heinz dilemma
>
> Heinz's wife was very ill with cancer, and Heinz feared she would shortly die. A local chemist had manufactured a drug that might save her, however he was charging $2000 a dose, ten times what it cost him to produce it. Heinz managed to put together $1000 and begged the chemist to sell him a dose for that or let him pay in instalments. The pharmacist refused so Heinz broke in to the pharmacy one night and stole the drug.

Kohlberg set boys the moral reasoning task of deciding whether Heinz was right to steal the drug and explaining why. He then classified the answers into three levels of morality.

- **Preconventional morality** (approximately 5–12 years) Morality is based entirely on the consequences of actions. At the start of this period the emphasis is on avoiding punishment but this shifts towards realisation that conforming to moral norms leads to rewards.
- **Conventional morality** (approximately 13–15 years) The consequences of actions are still important but are now seen in terms of approval rather than reward or punishment. By the end of the conventional level, children's morality is *internalised*, ie they make moral decisions based on their own judgement rather than the responses of others. The law is very important at this stage.
- **Postconventional morality** (approximately 16–20 years) By this stage there is an awareness that people have a variety of values and opinions and that rules are not sacred. A minority of around 10–15 per cent of people shift during this period towards the highest moral state of *universal ethical principles*, ie equality and respect for individual dignity. At this point rules become secondary and should be disobeyed where they conflict with ethical principles.

Thinking practically about psychology

What might a child at each stage say in response to the Heinz dilemma?

◀ **Figure 8.14** Is it morally right to commit burglary to save a life?

Discussion of Kohlberg's theory

Research on boys in Western individualist cultures has broadly supported Kohlberg's stages. However, many cultures do not place the same value on the freedom to make individual moral choices, so the idea of postconventional morality may be culture-bound, suitable only for explaining moral development in a limited range of cultures. Okwonko (1997) demonstrated the problems in trying to apply the theory in Nigeria. She gave Kohlberg moral dilemmas to Igbo children and found that they produced very sophisticated answers showing advanced reasoning, but their answers could not be fitted into Kohlberg's classification. For example, they placed more emphasis on the importance of community and less on the individual and so did not adopt the typical Western 'advanced' position that ultimately the individual should make personal moral choices.

Carol Gilligan (1982) has criticised Kohlberg for his reliance on boys as participants, and suggested that moral reasoning in girls develops quite differently from that in boys. Gilligan investigated moral reasoning in women, and developed a theory of how their reasoning differed from that of men. We can look at her original study in detail in *Classic Research*.

Based on this study, Gilligan (1982) proposed that men and women have different approaches to making moral decisions, using different criteria when making moral judgements. Men's moral reasoning is based more on their understanding of justice, therefore they make decisions based on their response to rules. Women on the other hand tend to base their responses more on their attitude to caring for others. Gilligan called these different ways of thinking the *justice orientation* and the *caring orientation*.

Thinking critically about psychology

Consider Gilligan's 1977 study.

1 Why was it an advantage to use participants facing a real-life moral dilemma rather than a hypothetical situation?
2 What is the potential problem with highly informal interviews?
3 What is the potential problem with small opportunity samples?
4 What ethical considerations must be taken into account in studies like this?

Gather some students into a mixed-gender group and discuss a moral issue or hypothetical decision of your choice, but not one as sensitive as the one Gilligan used. When you get consent from your participants, make sure they know the subject of the discussion in advance and that they are aware of their right to withdraw at any time. Record or make a note of what each person says. At the end of the discussion compare the views of males and females. Do the males talk more about rules and the females more about care as Gilligan suggested?

CLASSIC RESEARCH

Gilligan C (1977) In a different voice: women's conceptions of self and morality. *Harvard Educational Review* 47, 481–517

Aim: To explore how adolescent girls and young women responded to a real-life moral dilemma.

Method: An opportunity sample of 29 girls and women aged between 15 and 33 years were recruited from pregnancy and or abortion counselling services. They were currently facing the dilemma of whether to continue with an unplanned pregnancy. They were given informal interviews about what factors might underlie their decision as to whether to continue with their pregnancy. When the interviews were complete the responses were divided into classifications, based on the sophistication of the moral reasoning underlying the decision about whether to continue with the pregnancy.

Results: Three levels of moral reasoning were identified based on the interviews.
Level 1 – decisions were governed by self-interest.
Level 2 – decisions depended on self-sacrifice. This might involve keeping an unwanted baby because of the belief that its rights outweighed her own, or aborting a foetus to please a partner.
Level 3 – decisions were based on the principle of 'universal care', balancing participants' own needs with those of the child.

Conclusion: Three distinct levels of moral reasoning based on care rather than rules emerged. These may be more appropriate than Kohlberg's classification for understanding the development of moral reasoning in girls.

Eisenberg's theory of pro-social development

Nancy Eisenberg (1986) experimented with the concept of pro-social development. This is related to but distinct from moral development. Pro-social development is the development of social responsibility and altruism as distinct from moral reasoning. According to Eisenberg, pro-social development takes place alongside children's understanding of moral reasoning but is separate. Eisenberg believed that underlying pro-social development is empathy, the capacity to perceive and respond to the emotional states of other people. Eisenberg investigated children's responses to pro-social dilemmas. In some ways her scenarios were like those used by Kohlberg, but they were designed so that responses were based on empathy rather than understanding of rules. An example of Eisenberg's dilemmas is the story of Eric.

■ **Box 8.3**

An example of a pro-social dilemma

Eric is on his way to a friend's birthday party when he sees a boy who has fallen and hurt his leg. The boy asks if he can come back to Eric's house so he can call his parents and ask them to pick him up. If Eric agrees to this he will be late for the party and miss the food.

▲ **Figure 8.15** We can classify pro-social development by children's responses to a boy who has fallen off his bike

On the basis of responses to dilemmas like this one Eisenberg classified children into one of five levels of pro-social development.

- *Level 1 hedonistic* (pre-school) — children's decisions are based on consequences to themselves.
- *Level 2 needs-oriented* (pre- and primary school) — decisions are influenced by a blend of self-interest and concern for others.
- *Level 3 approval-oriented* (primary, middle and secondary school) — decisions are based on stereotyped good and bad behaviours and awareness of approval for 'good' behaviour.
- *Level 4 empathic* (secondary school) — decisions are based on empathic responses to the feelings of others. By this stage the child has a set of personal values and social responsibilities but difficulty in describing them.
- *Level 5 internalised values* (a small minority of secondary school children) — personal values and social responsibilities are clearly understood.

Discussion of Eisenberg's theory

To the non-specialist the distinction between development of moral reasoning and pro-social development is a very subtle one. However Eisenberg (1986) showed that moral and pro-social development are separate in a study in which she gave children dilemmas of both sorts. Only a moderate correlation emerged between scores of moral development and pro-social development. If many children are significantly more advanced in either moral or pro-social development than the other, then logically they must be two different things.

The concept of pro-social behaviour has proved generally useful in understanding child development. Children scoring highly in tests of pro-social behaviour have been found, for example, to go on to have better mental health (Zahn-Waxler *et al.*, 2000) and be unlikely to be involved in bullying, either as bully or victim (Warden & Mackinnon, 2003). Interestingly though, as studies have begun to look at what children and adolescents think of as pro-social behaviour, it has emerged that Eisenberg's measures were limited. Bergin, Talley & Hamer (2003) carried out focus groups with 53 children aged 11–13 on what behaviour they saw as pro-social. A wide range of behaviours emerged as pro-social, including sticking up for peers, including peers in activities and the use of humour. These have not been addressed in traditional pro-social behaviour research.

▼ **Figure 8.16** Children rate funny and supportive behaviour as pro-social

The development of social cognition

The term 'social cognition' refers to the cognitive (mental) processes by which information about the self and other people are managed. Every time we interact with others or even think about ourselves we process new information from our senses and draw on existing information from our memory. Based on this information we constantly make social judgements and decisions, for example how do I feel about this? What is she thinking now? How should I respond to that?

The development of sense of self

Before the existence of psychology, philosophers talked about the nature of the self. Philosopher and early psychologist William James (1892) made the distinction between 'I' and 'me.' 'I' am the 'self-as-knower' whereas 'me' is the 'self-as-known'. If that makes your head hurt you'll see why it's the sort of issue philosophers like to get their teeth into! Put a bit more simply (we hope), 'me' is all the information I have about myself whereas 'I' am the entity that is aware of that information. James explored the self-as-knower and self-as-known in more detail. He described four aspects to the self-as-knower:

- awareness of one's power to act
- awareness of one's uniqueness
- awareness of the continuity of one's existence
- awareness of one's own awareness.

James also described the 'me', the self-as-known, in more detail. This includes three elements:

- the *material self* – knowledge of our physical characteristics, possessions etc
- the *social self* – knowledge of our social behaviour and the way others see us
- the *spiritual self* – knowledge of our own cognition, for example our knowledge, thinking and memory.

Modern psychologists have kept James' distinction between self-as-knower and self-as-known. They are more commonly referred to now as the *existential self* (the knower) and the categorical self (the known) (Lewis, 1990).

The development of the existential self

Miell (1995) suggests that the first task in the development of children's self-concept is realising that they do in fact exist. Once this existential self is established, children start to place themselves in categories, eg gender, name, size. The number and sophistication of these categories increases with maturity and experience. It is extremely difficult to conduct scientific research into the existential self. We simply can't ask young children about philosophical issues like these and it just isn't the sort of thing we can make judgements about based on observable behaviour. There are, however, theoretical accounts of the emergence of the existential self.

▼ **Figure 8.17** At what point will this baby realise it is a separate being?

Freud (1921) proposed we begin life in a state of *autoeroticism* in which we do not differentiate at all between the self and the outside world. This is where Piaget got his idea of egocentrism, and he agreed with Freud that early in the sensorimotor period a child is completely egocentric, making no distinction between the self and the outside world. According to Freud, we progress from autoeroticism to the state of *narcissism*. Narcissistic children are aware of themselves as separate beings but do not have a realistic understanding of their relationship to the outside world and see themselves as omnipotent, or all-powerful. Narcissistic children also do not make a clear distinction between themselves and their primary carer. This is the earliest state of self-awareness. In time, normally developing children differentiate themselves from the mother to develop a full categorical self. However, a minority remain fixated at this stage, going on to develop a *narcissistic personality*. Narcissistic personality disorder is characterised by the inability to appreciate others except for what they can do for the individual.

KEY TERMS

existential self the I that is aware that I am a separate person

autoeroticism the state in which we are born, in which we are unaware we are separate from the rest of the world

narcissism a primitive state of self-awareness in which we see ourselves as a separate being but as all-powerful

The development of the categorical self

It has proved a lot easier to research the categorical self than the existential self. An important aspect of our developing self-concept is our self-esteem, ie the extent to which we like what we know of our categorical self. Carl Rogers (1961) developed a theory to explain the development of self-esteem. Rogers suggests that we hold an image of ourselves as we are, the *self-image*, and an image of our *ideal self*, ie how we would like to be. If the two images are the same, we will develop good self-esteem. Developing and maintaining really good self-esteem requires that two conditions are met:

- *unconditional positive regard* in the form of love and affection from others
- *self-actualisation* — fulfilling our potential.

These two factors are closely related because, without unconditional positive regard, we cannot self-actualise. Harsh, inattentive parenting or parenting characterised by conditional love — love which is only available if the child conforms to certain conditions — lead to low self-esteem.

There seems to be little doubt that, as Rogers believed, parenting is the single most important factor in the development of children's self-concept. However, once children spend time in school, other factors become important as well. Studies have shown that children who do well at school tend to have more positive self-concepts than those who find school difficult. In addition, athletic children who have a positive perception of their physical development also tend to have better self-esteem than others.

▼ **Figure 8.18** Unconditional positive regard from parents is important in developing a positive self-concept

LOOKING FURTHER Using PubMed or Google Scholar find some contemporary studies of self-esteem. How important does it seem to be?

Theory of mind

Theory of mind is a slightly confusing term. It is *not* a theory itself, but refers to our ability to 'mind-read', ie to understand what other people think, feel and know. We have a theory of mind when we have a belief (ie a theory) about what is in someone else's mind. Children become capable of some theory of mind tasks at around four years. This has led some researchers to propose that theory of mind appears suddenly at this age. Other researchers have pointed out that younger children are successful in other theory of mind tasks and instead see theory of mind developing more gradually.

False belief tasks and the four-year shift

It appears that a big improvement in children's theory of mind takes place at around four years of age. Evidence for this comes from *false belief tasks*. The first false belief task was devised by Wimmer & Perner (1983). They showed children a story in which a boy called Maxi left his chocolate in a green container in the kitchen. When Maxi was out his mother used some of the chocolate for cooking and put what was left in a blue container. The child's task was to say whether Maxi would look in the blue or green container when he got back. The correct answer is the green container because Maxi wouldn't know the chocolate had been moved. Understanding this requires an understanding of Maxi's mind, specifically his false belief about where the chocolate would be. Very few of Wimmer & Perner's three-year-olds gave the correct answer, but the majority of four-year-olds did so.

Baron-Cohen *et al.* (1985) (see *Classic Research*) developed a similar false belief task known as the Sally-Anne task. In this procedure, children are told a story about two dolls called Sally and Anne. Sally has a basket and Anne has a box. Sally puts a marble in her basket, but later when Sally is not looking Anne takes the marble and puts it in her box. The child's task is to identify where Sally will look for her marble. The correct response is in her basket — understanding this means understanding that Sally has a false belief about its whereabouts. The results in this procedure were similar to those in the Wimmer & Perner study. Most four-year-olds realised that Sally would look in her own basket, but most three-year-olds did not. Baron-Cohen *et al.* (1985) demonstrated in a classic study that children on the *autistic* spectrum find false belief tasks very difficult.

KEY TERMS

autism a disorder normally diagnosed in childhood, characterised by difficulty with language, social interaction and theory of mind

false belief tasks tasks in which children are required to understand that other people sometimes believe things that are not true

CLASSIC RESEARCH

Baron-Cohen S, Leslie AM & Frith U (1985) Does the autistic child have a theory of mind? *Cognition* **21, 37–46**

Aim: To test the idea that children on the autistic spectrum have a problem with theory of mind, specifically that they will find false belief tasks harder than other children.

Procedure: 20 high-functioning children with a diagnosis of autism, aged between six and 16 years, formed an experimental group. Fourteen children with Down's syndrome of similar age distribution and 27 children without any diagnosis made up a control group. All children were given the Sally-Anne task. To ensure that all participants understood the story they were asked where the marble was really as well as where Sally would look for it.

Findings: 85 per cent of the control group including those with Down's syndrome answered correctly that Sally would look in her basket; 100 per cent identified correctly where the marble actually was. In the autism group, 100 per cent identified correctly where the marble really was, but only 20 per cent correctly identified where Sally would look for it.

Conclusion: Children on the autistic spectrum find false belief tasks very difficult, suggesting they do not develop normal theory of mind abilities as most children do.

▼ **Figure 8.19** The Sally-Anne task

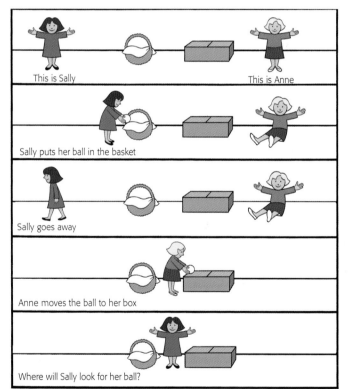

This is Sally · This is Anne

Sally puts her ball in the basket

Sally goes away

Anne moves the ball to her box

Where will Sally look for her ball?

Thinking critically about psychology

Consider the studies of theory of mind you have looked at so far.

1 What is the advantage of the Sally-Anne procedure over the Maxi story?

2 What was the purpose of including children with Down's syndrome in the control group in the Baron-Cohen *et al.* study?

Intentional reasoning in toddlers

Judging theory of mind by means of false belief studies alone would lead us to believe that theory of mind appears suddenly at age four. However on other theory of mind tasks surprisingly young child show an understanding of why adults behave as they do, suggesting that they have an understanding of their intentions, an aspect of their mind. This form of theory of mind is known as *intentional reasoning*.

Meltzoff (1988) demonstrated that 18-month-olds can make judgements about what adults intend to achieve when they act. Toddler-participants observed adults perform tasks including placing beads in a container. In a control condition the adult succeeded in the task, but in an experimental condition the adult failed, for example dropping the beads. The toddlers were then given a chance to enact the procedure. No difference emerged in the actions of the children in the two conditions – they all attempted to carry out the tasks they had seen the adults try to perform. They must have understood what the adult was *intending* to achieve rather than just imitating what they actually did otherwise those in the experimental condition would not have known what to do – they would have dropped the beads rather than put them in the container.

▶ **Figure 8.20** Toddlers will put beads in a container even when they witness an adult failing to do so

Explaining the development of theory of mind

We can apply the theories of Piaget and Vygotsky to explain the development of theory of mind. In addition we can look at a newer approach to cognitive development, *innatist modular theory*. To Piaget, cognitive development was a single process in which each cognitive ability appeared when the mind had achieved a certain general level of understanding. Perner *et al.* (2002) point out that if theory of mind appears in line with a general cognitive development, then other unrelated cognitive abilities should appear at around the same time They tested this by giving 48 children aged three to five years a false belief task similar to Wimmer & Perner's and tasks of identifying pairs of words with the same meaning. Children became capable of false belief tasks and matching words for meaning at very similar ages, supporting the Piagetian explanation for theory of mind.

Vygotsky emphasised the importance of interaction with other people in cognitive development. Astington (1998) has applied this idea to theory of mind, suggesting children internalise a theory of mind during their early social contact with other people, in particular the primary carer. The main evidence for this explanation of theory of mind comes from studies showing that children with a history of good quality interactions with their primary carer have better theory of mind than others. Symons & Clark (2000) assessed maternal sensitivity and security of attachment in two-year-old children, then tested them on false belief tasks at age five. Those who had been assessed as securely attached and those whose mothers were rated as the most sensitive at two years generally did better at false belief tasks.

A modern alternative to the ideas of Piaget and Vygotsky comes from Leslie (1994). Leslie has applied the *innatist modular approach* to explaining the development of theory of mind. The innatist modular approach is a radical departure from traditional views of cognitive development. The idea is that every mental ability depends on a brain system or module. Each module becomes active at a particular age. Leslie (1994) suggested that at least two different modules may be important for theory of mind. The first is present from an early age and allows intentional reasoning. The second becomes active at around four years, allowing the child to understand false beliefs. The main evidence for this approach comes from the study of autism, in which children may develop some advanced cognitive abilities but *not* theory of mind. The idea of a theory of mind module that fails to activate is the neatest explanation for the theory of mind problems experienced by children on the autistic spectrum.

Thinking creatively about psychology

Try to put together a theory of your own to explain the development of theory of mind that draws on the ideas of Piaget, Vygotsky and Leslie. You will need to start by picking out the key points from each, then look at how they could be made to fit together.

Exploring issues and debates
The nature–nurture debate

The factors affecting cognitive development form part of the nature–nurture debate in psychology.

Draw up a three-column table. Each column is for one explanation of theory of mind. For each theory say where it falls in the nature–nurture debate.

Developing an understanding of others

Throughout childhood we develop an increasingly sophisticated understanding of other people. In this time various changes take place. Children become better able to see things from other people's perspectives, they become more empathic and they become better able to mind read. Perhaps the most basic development is in the attention children give to the mental characteristics of others. Flapan (1968) asked children to describe people in extracts from films. Up to around six years of age, children tended to describe their physical characteristics but, by eight, most focused mainly on the intentions and personality of the characters.

We have already explored several perspectives on cognitive development that offer explanations of how children's perception of other people develops. Before going on to look at a theory that directly aims to address this, let us first review what some of the major approaches to cognitive development have had to say.

▶ **Figure 8.21** As children get older they focus more on the personal characteristics of TV characters

Piaget's perspective

Piaget introduced the concept of egocentrism. Literally this means self-centredness. To Piaget, children are initially unable to understand that others may have a different perspective from their own. He illustrated this with the famous three mountains study (see p168), in which under-sevens found it difficult to identify what a mountain scene looked like from a position other than the one they could see. To Piaget, perspective-taking was very much a single cognitive ability whether we are talking about physical position as illustrated in the three mountains study, or position in more abstract situations like disagreement. The child who cannot visualise what the doll could see in the three mountains study can also not appreciate why another child's point of view might be different when they argue. Children gradually decentre, ie become less egocentric throughout childhood in line with their general cognitive development.

Eisenberg's perspective

Eisenberg was concerned with the role of empathy in the development of prosocial behaviour. Empathy is the ability to appreciate the feelings of others. This is a different, though probably related aspect of the child's understanding of others. To Eisenberg, children as young as pre-schoolers display empathy although they are also concerned with their own needs. However, through most of childhood social decision-making is influenced more by approval from others than by empathy. This becomes more important later, and by the time they reach their teens young people will typically be basing their behaviour towards others on an understanding of their feelings.

Theory of mind

Theory of mind is very much about the understanding of others. The 'theory' in theory of mind refers to our personal understanding of what others are thinking or feeling. In the Sally-Anne task, for example (p181), children have to understand that Sally will not know that Anne has moved her marble. Children typically develop this understanding that others can have false beliefs at around four years. However, there is evidence that children acquire simpler understandings of others by toddlerhood. They can, for example, make judgements about what adults are trying to achieve when they watch adults fail to do something (p181).

Selman's theory of perspective-taking

Robert Selman (1976) adapted the method used by Kohlberg and Eisenberg to investigate moral and pro-social development to the study of perspective-taking. He presented children with scenarios in which they have to look at a decision from more than one person's point of view. An example is shown in Box 8.4.

▲ **Figure 8.22** Children's perspective-taking can be assessed using a dilemma faced by a child banned from tree-climbing whose friend's kitten is stuck up a tree

Children were asked questions that required that they take others' perspectives rather than just evaluate the situation from their own viewpoint. For example they were asked: 'Does Holly know how her friend feels about his kitten?' and 'How will Holly's father feel if he finds out she climbed the tree?'

Based on children's responses, Selman (1976) developed a stage theory to explain the way in which children develop their ability to take the perspective of other people. Selman proposes five stages:

- *Stage 0 Egocentric viewpoint* (3–6 years) – children cannot clearly distinguish between their own thoughts and feelings and those of others. They can identify emotional states in others but do not link these to the social behaviour that might have caused them.
- *Stage 1 Social information role-taking* (6–8 years) – children can now identify the perspective of others as different from their own, but they tend to focus on only one of these perspectives.
- *Stage 2 Self-reflective role-taking* (8–10 years) – by this stage children can put themselves in the position of another person and appreciate their point of view. They can, however, only take one point of view at a time.
- *Stage 3 Mutual role-taking* (10–12 years) – children are now able to look at a situation from their own and another's point of view at the same time.
- *Stage 4 Social and conventional system role-taking* (12–plus) – young people become able to see that sometimes understanding others' viewpoints is not sufficient to reach agreement, and that this is why agreed social conventions are needed to keep order.

■ **Box 8.4**

A perspective-taking dilemma

Holly has promised her worried father that she will never climb a dangerous tree again. However her friend's kitten is stuck in a tree. Both the kitten and her friend are distressed. Holly has to choose between keeping her promise and rescuing the kitten.

You can watch videos of Robert Selman talking about and applying his work here: http://www.uknow.gse.harvard.edu/teaching/TC7-1-107.html

How useful do you think his approach is?

Thinking practically about psychology

Suggest which stages the following responses to the question 'How will Holly's father feel if he finds out she climbed the tree?' fit into.

- (a) 'I want Holly to save the kitten.'
- (b) 'She mustn't do it. He will be cross.'
- (c) 'He will be cross, but if she doesn't do it the kitten will get more and more scared.'

Discussion of Selman's theory

In a comprehensive review, Durkin (1995) concluded that evidence broadly supports Selman's theory. A large number of studies have found that children's ability to take the perspective of others develops with age in the sequence Selman suggested. Selman's work also has important applications, for example in understanding and controlling aggression in children. Boxer *et al.* (2005) point out that one reason for children's aggression is that they may misinterpret others' behaviour because they are unable to take their perspective. Prior to Selman's stage 2, children find it very hard to understand that two people can make different judgements based on the same information. They therefore find it hard to accept the explanation from a child who knocked into them that it was an accident. Children *can*, however, be taught this by means of showing filmed incidents and explaining the perspectives of each person in the film.

This can form the basis of anti-violence strategies with primary school children. Perspective-taking also informs consumer psychologists' understanding of children's attempts to persuade their parents to buy them things. Selman's theory predicts that children will use coercive strategies (ie force!) to persuade parents to buy them toys when they are at an age associated with inability to see the parents' perspective. We can look at a study of this in *Research Now*.

▶ **Figure 8.23** Don't mess with the five-year-old shopper!

Thinking critically about psychology

What ethical issues are raised by naturalistic observations? How well were these dealt with in the Buijzen & Valkenburg study?

RESEARCH NOW

Buijzen M & Valkenburg PM (2008) Communication in retail environments: a developmental and socialisation perspective. *Human Communication Research* **34, 50–69**

Aim: To test the hypothesis that attempts by children to force parents to buy them products peak at pre-school age where children are verbal and aware of toys but have little ability to see parents' perspective.

Procedure: A naturalistic observation was carried out in 10 supermarkets and five toy shops in the Netherlands. A total of 269 parent–child pairs were observed, the children ranging from 0–12 years. The average time in the shop was 12.32 minutes. Their interactions were coded for coerciveness, defined as the forceful and persistent attempt by the child to persuade the parent to buy them a particular product. Observers then approached the parents and asked for consent to use the data: 100 per cent agreed and 69 per cent of these agreed to complete a questionnaire.

Findings: Overall, 69 per cent of purchase-related communications were started by the child. Twelve per cent of these were coercive. Coercive interactions were most common in three- to five-year-olds. A negative correlation (–0.12) was found between coerciveness and probability of purchase. No differences in coercion emerged between children's behaviour in supermarkets and toy shops.

Conclusion: As predicted by Selman's theory, children's attempts to coerce parents into buying them things peaked in the egocentric viewpoint stage, in which they were fully aware of products but could only see the situation from their own perspective.

Biological explanations for social cognition

Over the last decade exciting new technology has allowed us to study the brain mechanisms underlying social cognition. A new field in psychology, known as social neuroscience (Decety & Keenan, 2006) or social cognitive neuroscience (Lieberman, 2007), has thus opened up. Decety & Keenan have defined social neuroscience as 'the exploration of the neural underpinnings of the processes traditionally examined by, but not limited to, social psychology' (2006, p1). Social neuroscience is not limited to studying social cognition but it does shed new light on a number of the issues we have discussed in this chapter.

Cortical circuitry and 'self' and 'other' perception

In several sections in this chapter we have touched on the development of a child's understanding of the relationship between the self and other people. Piaget talked about the gradual decline of egocentrism as children become able to distinguish their point of view from that of others. Eisenberg talked of the development of empathy, which allows children to appreciate the feelings of others. It seems that children's brain do not permit an adult understanding of self and others. When adults think about themselves or other people, two areas of the brain become particularly active, the medial prefrontal cortex (the middle of the front bit of the brain) and the medial posterior parietal cortex (the middle of the top-back bit of the brain). Pfeiffer *et al.* (2007) had children (average age 10) and adults (average age 26) listen to phrases such as 'I get left out at school' and 'teachers think my grammar is bad' and say whether they referred to themselves or Harry Potter. They monitored brain activity with a functional MRI scanner. In both groups, the medial prefrontal cortex became more active when referring to self, and the medial posterior parietal cortex when thinking of Harry Potter. However, the difference was much more marked in children. This suggests that, on a neurological level, children's perception of themselves and others are more different processes than in adults. It seems likely that as developing individuals use more of the same brain circuitry to perceive themselves and others they become less egocentric and more empathic.

The role of mirror neurones

The existence of mirror neurones was discovered accidentally by Rizzolatti *et al.* (1996). They were studying motor activity in monkeys, recording brain activity when the monkeys reached for food. One day a researcher reached for a sandwich in front of a monkey whose motor cortex was being scanned and observed that the monkey's motor cortex activated just like it did when it reached for food itself. They went on to place electrodes in the monkey's brains to record the activity of individual neurones. It emerged that the same cells activated both when the monkey reached for food itself and when it observed a human doing the same. Rizzolatti and colleagues called these cells mirror neurones. We cannot safely do this in humans so human research generally involves brain scanning. Even the most sensitive scans cannot measure individual neurone activity (they measure a field down to about 3mm^2). Therefore, although we believe humans have mirror neurones, they have only actually been found in monkeys.

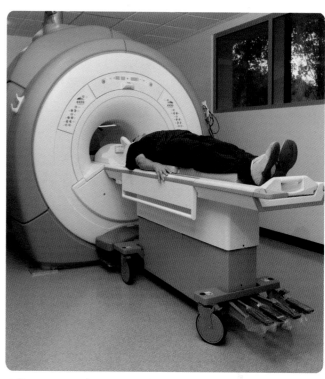

▲ **Figure 8.24** An fMRI scanner, the equipment usually used to study mirror neurone activity in humans

Mirror neurones and understanding intention

Early research into mirror neurones showed that they represent actions in both self and others. Perhaps the most exciting discovery, however, is that they also appear to represent people's intentions. This was suggested by Gallese & Goldman (1998), but it is only much more recently that solid evidence has been found. We can look at a study of mirror neurones and intention in *Research Now*.

Thinking practically about psychology

A number of children's films include robots as main characters. Examples include *Robots* and *Wall-E*. Using your knowledge of mirror neurones, suggest why children can enjoy films about robotic characters.

RESEARCH NOW

Iacoboni M, Molnar-Szakacs I, Gallese V, Buccino G, Mazziotta JC & Rizzolatti G (2005) Grasping the intentions of others with one's own mirror neurones. *PLoS Biology* **3, 530–35**

Aim: To test whether activity in the mirror neurone system associated with drinking is greater in response to seeing someone reach for a cup after cues that it is to drink or to clear up. If mirror neurone activity in the premotor system (which activates before an action) simply responds to actions, then the intention signalled for the action should make no difference to its activity.

Procedure: 23 participants watched video of someone reaching for and grasping a cup. In one condition this was done in isolation. In two other conditions the video showed background information suggesting that the intention was either to drink from the cup or to clear it away (see Figure 8.25). While they watched this, the participants underwent a functional MRI scan, which shows the relative activity of each brain region.

Findings: Activity in mirror neurones in the areas of the premotor system associated with hand movements was significantly greater when the intention of the person reaching for and grasping the cup was signalled (see Figure 8.26).

Conclusion: Mirror neurones respond not just to actions but to intentions.

▲ **Figure 8.25** Stills from the videos shown to Iacoboni *et al.*'s participants

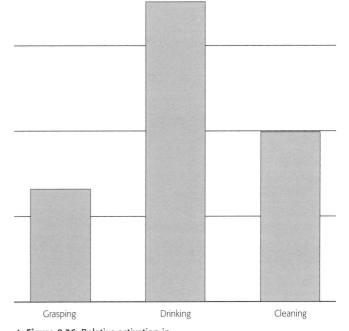

▲ **Figure 8.26** Relative activation in premotor areas in Iacoboni *et al*'s three conditions

The findings of the Iacoboni *et al.* study are fascinating because they suggest that our common sense view of how we understand others – that we draw on our memory and cognitively interpret their feelings and intentions – is wrong. Instead it seems that we understand others' intentions by simulating them and experiencing them using our mirror neurones. Further evidence for the role of mirror neurones in understanding intention comes from Gazzola *et al.* (2007). They had participants observe human and robotic arms attempting to grasp objects. Although the appearance of the human and robot arms was quite different, and although they moved quite differently, brain scans of observers revealed that their mirror neurones responded in exactly the same way, suggesting they were responding to intention rather than to action.

Mirror neurones and perspective-taking

It has been suggested that mirror neurones are important not just in understanding intention, but also in empathy, theory of mind and the ability to take others' perspective. A major source of evidence comes from the study of mirror neurones in children suffering from autistic spectrum disorders. Autism is associated with problems with all these social-cognitive abilities. If children on the autistic spectrum can be shown to have a faulty mirror neurone system, then this may not only go a long way to explaining autism, but also show how these social-cognitive abilities work in the normal brain.

Oberman *et al.* (2005) compared mirror neurone activity in 10 high-functioning participants with a diagnosis of an autistic spectrum disorder (average age 16 years) with a control group with no diagnosis. They measured mirror neurone activity by mu suppression. When neurones are inactive they produce an electrical signal at a frequency of 8–13Hz, known as mu. Mirror neurones typically reduce their mu output in response to acting and observing the actions of others. Participants had their mu monitored while they watched video of a moving hand, a moving ball or they moved their own hand. There was no difference between the groups in mu output in response to moving their own hand or watching a moving ball. However, when watching someone else's hand move, mu declined sharply in the control group but not in the autism group. This suggests that mirror neurones are not activated in response to other people's movement in autism.

LOOKING FURTHER Check out this video on YouTube: http://uk.youtube.com/watch?v=_8WV1zAh9zU You can hear about the role of mirror neurones in social cognition with particular regard to autism.

Another unlikely source of evidence links mirror neurones to perspective-taking. Mouras *et al.* (2008) suggested that enjoying pornography (at least watching couples in the act as opposed to just looking at their bits) requires the ability to take the perspective of one of the actors. They showed eight men a fishing documentary, *Mr Bean* and some heterosexual pornographic video. They measured brain activity with a functional MRI scanner and arousal with a penile plethysmograph throughout. When watching sex an area of the brain called the pars opercularis, believed to have lots of mirror neurones, was shown by the MRI to be particularly active. Pars opercularis activity came immediately before participants' erections, suggesting that it led to the arousal, and that it is the ability to take someone else's perspective that makes pornography arousing.

Exploring issues and debates
Ethics

It is always important to consider the consequences for your participants when conducting research.

Draw up a two-column table. In the left column suggest the potential ethical problems of showing participants pornography. In the right, suggest the reasons why psychologists do occasionally use it in their research.

Draw up a list of safeguards to try to ensure psychologists do not harm participants by exposing them to pornography.

Thinking creatively about psychology

For ethical reasons you may not under any circumstances carry out research using pornography. However, think in principle about how pornography **could** be used by appropriately qualified persons to further investigate mirror neurones and perspective-taking.

Thinking critically about psychology

It appears that mirror neurones are extremely important in social cognition. However, they have never been directly observed in humans. How credible do you think their existence is? How strong is the evidence and what other evidence would you like to see?

Chapter summary

Theories of cognitive development

- Historically the most influential theory of intellectual development in children comes from Jean Piaget. Piaget suggested that we act as agents of own learning and cognitive development, seeking knowledge in order to get rid of the unpleasant sensation of not understanding.
- Piaget also proposed that cognitive development takes place in stages, each of which is characterised by particular types of thinking. Logic becomes more advanced with each developmental stage.
- Most modern research supports Piaget's idea that children become more logical with age, although most current researchers would say that Piaget underestimated younger children and overestimated adolescents.
- Lev Vygotsky suggested an alternative to Piaget's theory, suggesting that cognitive development is internalised through interaction with members of the same culture, and that this makes cognitive development a cultural process. Vygotsky also saw language as important in cognitive development.
- Although the idea of cultural differences in cognitive development is socially sensitive, and although research into the relationship between language and cognitive development is ongoing, Vygotsky is tremendously influential in education because of his emphasis on interaction in learning.
- Jerome Bruner developed Vygotsky's ideas about the role of interaction in learning with the concept of scaffolding. He also replaced stages of development with three modes in which information can be represented in the mind.

- There is support for Bruner's ideas about scaffolding from observational studies of children working with adult help.
- These three theories of cognitive development have important applications in school. The school curriculum is influenced by Piaget's idea that children become capable of understanding particular ideas at different ages. From Vygotsky we get the idea of maximising interaction in learning through group work, peer tutoring and reciprocal learning. From Bruner we get scaffolding in the classroom and schemes like *Jolly Phonics* that make use of different modes of representation.

Moral development

- Kohlberg's theory has dominated the field of moral development. He suggests a stage theory in which children's understanding of moral issues becomes more sophisticated in line with cognitive development. Kohlberg has been challenged on the basis of how well his theory applies in a range of cultures and to girls.
- Eisenberg suggests that prosocial development runs parallel to moral development, depending more on empathy as well as cognitive development.

Social cognition

- A rather philosophical aspect of child psychology concerns the development of the sense of self. We know a lot more of the development of the categorical self – self-knowledge – than about the existential self – the sense of being an individual.
- An important aspect of social development is theory of mind, our understanding of what other people are thinking and feeling. People on the autistic spectrum are believed to have quite poor theory of mind.
- Piaget's and Vygotsky's theories have been applied to explain the development of theory of mind. A more recent explanation, the innatist modular theory, suggests that theory of mind depends on the activation at particular ages of systems within the brain.
- We can apply a range of theories to explaining the development of the ability to take others' perspectives throughout childhood. However, a particularly influential theory comes from Selman, who proposes four stages to the development of perspective. According to Selman, children move from being unable to take the perspective of others, through being able to see two perspectives but only one at a time, to being able to see alternative perspectives at the same time.
- The recent discovery of mirror neurones has revolutionised our understanding of social cognition. Mirror neurones activate both when we do or experience something and when we see others doing or experiencing the same thing. This probably underlies our ability to take perspective, feel empathy and understand the minds of others.

What do I know?

1 (a) Outline **two** of Piaget's stages. (10 marks)
  (b) Explain how theories of cognitive development have been applied in education. (15 marks)

2 (a) Explain what is meant by the development of a sense of self. (5 marks)
  (b) Outline and evaluate research into theory of mind. (10 marks)
  (c) Explain criticisms that have been levelled at Kohlberg's theory of moral development. (10 marks)

3 (a) Outline Vygotsky's theory of cognitive development. (10 marks)
  (b) Outline and evaluate research into the role of mirror neurones in cognitive development. (15 marks)

4 (a) What is meant by the term 'pro-social development?' (5 marks)
  (b) Outline research into the biological basis of social cognition. (10 marks)
  (c) Evaluate research into perspective-taking. (10 marks)

5 Outline and evaluate Selman's theory of the development of perspective-taking. (25 marks)

CHAPTER 9
Psychopathology

Thinking ahead

By the end of this chapter you should be able to:

- outline what is meant by the classification and diagnosis of mental disorder
- understand the issues of reliability and validity in classification and diagnosis
- recall from your AS level biological and psychological models of mental disorder
- explain how *either* schizophrenia *or* depression *or* anxiety disorders including phobias *and* OCD are classified, diagnosed and explained by biological and psychological models
- for your chosen mental disorder(s), consider the appropriateness and effectiveness of biological and psychological treatments

I n your AS level you will have studied psychological abnormality. In this chapter we aim to develop your understanding of mental disorder further by introducing you to its classification and diagnosis. We will also revisit the biological and psychological models of abnormality and apply them to explaining some mental disorders. Note that in this chapter we use the term 'psychopathology' interchangeably with 'mental disorder'. Psychopathology is a general term used to mean mental disorder or the study of mental disorder. We will be looking here at three forms of psychopathology: schizophrenia, depression and anxiety.

A brief introduction to classification and diagnosis

The focus in this chapter is on particular mental disorders. For your chosen disorder, which can be schizophrenia, depression or anxiety, you need to understand how it is classified and diagnosed. We begin this chapter therefore with an explanation of what *classification* and *diagnosis* are and a brief account of how they operate in the mental health system.

Classification

The classification of mental disorder involves taking sets of symptoms and putting them into categories. For example, symptoms of depressed mood – feeling hopeless, having low self-esteem, eating too much or little, sleeping too much or little and having difficulty in concentration – often occur together. We can therefore say that someone showing these symptoms has a particular disorder. We can go on to classify that disorder as part of a wider class of disorders. Table 9.1 shows the 14 major classes of mental disorder identified by the *Diagnostic and Statistical Manual of Mental Disorder* (DSM), one of the major systems for classification and diagnosis.

▼ Table 9.1 **The major categories of mental disorder according to**
DSM-IV-TR

1	Disorders usually first diagnosed in infancy, childhood or adolescence
2	Delirium, dementia, amnesic and other cognitive disorders
3	Substance-related disorders
4	Schizophrenia and other psychotic disorders
5	Mood disorders
6	Anxiety disorders
7	Somatoform disorders
8	Factitious disorders
9	Dissociative disorders
10	Sexual and gender identity disorders
11	Eating disorders
12	Sleep disorders
13	Impulse control disorders
14	Adjustment disorders

Reprinted with permission from the *Diagnostic and Statistical Manual of Mental Disorders, Text Revision, Fourth Edition.* (© 2000). American Psychiatric Association.

The symptoms of depressed mood listed earlier are in fact those used to diagnose *dysthymia*, a form of depression. Looking at the 14 classes of mental disorder in Table 9.1, you can probably guess that dysthymia is classified as a mood disorder.

KEY TERMS

classification categorising groups of symptoms into mental disorders and those disorders into classes of disorder

diagnosis the process of deciding what if any mental disorder a patient is suffering from based on their symptoms

Diagnosis

Once we have sets of abnormal symptoms classified into disorders we can diagnose individuals according to their symptoms. Diagnosis involves assessing a patient's symptoms and deciding whether they meet the criteria for one or more mental disorders. Typically a diagnosis requires that a certain number of symptoms are present for a particular period of time. It may also require the non-presence of factors that are known to produce similar symptoms. For example, to return to our example of dysthymia, diagnosis requires that depressed mood and two other symptoms are present for two years (or one year in children), and that the symptoms are not the result of medication or a medical condition.

The *DSM* system for classification and diagnosis

There are several systems with which we can classify abnormal patterns of thinking, behaviour and emotion into mental disorders. These systems are highly detailed; they both classify abnormality into many different disorders, and give guidelines on how to diagnose them, in some cases including standard interview questions to help make the diagnosis. The most widely used system of classification and diagnosis is the *DSM*, produced by the American Psychiatric Association. The original *DSM* was published in 1952. Since 2000, it is in its fourth edition with text revisions (that is, revisions to the wording rather than the disorders). This is usually shortened to *DSM-IV-TR*. It includes standard interview procedures called SCIDs (structured clinical interviews for *DSM*).

The rationale for classifying and diagnosing mental disorder

In this chapter we will look quite critically at the success with which mental health professionals diagnose and treat particular mental disorders. Given the limitations of our success in this area it is perhaps worth explaining at the outset just why most professionals believe it is worth classifying and diagnosing. The major reason to classify mental disorder is so that we can provide individuals with a diagnosis. The major reason to give people a diagnosis is so that we can target appropriate treatments and services towards them.

There are also spin-off benefits to classifying and diagnosing mental disorder. First, patients and their families may be able to take a degree of comfort in understanding that their symptoms can be understood and to some extent treated. Second, researchers have something solid to work with in order better to understand the origins of and effective treatment for sets of symptoms. For example, once we have the classification of dysthymia and a procedure for diagnosing it, we can take a group of people with dysthymia and test the effectiveness of a range of treatments. Without the classification of dysthymia it would be much harder to establish what sort of treatments are likely to be helpful for people with these symptoms.

Reliability and validity

For a system like *DSM-IV-TR* to work effectively it should be capable of accurately diagnosing individuals. However, we meet a logical problem here: when we talk about accuracy in many situations we make the assumption that there is an absolute value to compare against. A watch is accurate if it keeps approximately the same time as our most accurate clocks. When it comes to diagnosis, however, there is no 'most accurate clock' to compare diagnostic systems against. We therefore cannot measure true accuracy and we must rely on two approximations of accuracy. These are *reliability* and *validity*.

Reliability means consistency. A system can be said to be reliable if people using it consistently arrive at the same diagnosis. One way of seeing how reliable a diagnosis is is by testing whether different clinicians agree on the same diagnosis for the same patient. Technically this is called inter-rater reliability. Another way of assessing reliability is to assess the same patients two or more times and see whether they consistently receive the same diagnosis. This is called test-retest reliability. Test-retest reliability is the most common way of judging the consistency of diagnosis. Reliability is often presented numerically. If you're not a lover of maths try not to be too put off; there is a simple explanation in Box 9.1.

> ■ Box 9.1
>
> ## Making sense of reliability figures
>
> Reliability is calculated mathematically and presented as a figure, usually either a percentage or a number between 0 and 1. You will come across two common measures of reliability; both measure test-retest reliability.
>
> 1 **The PPV (positive predictive value)**: this is simply the proportion of people that keep the same diagnosis over time. It is usually expressed as a percentage. If depression has a PPV of 80, this means that 80 per cent of people with a diagnosis of depression received a subsequent diagnosis of depression when re-assessed.
> 2 **Cohen's Kappa**: this is a slightly more complex statistic. It is the correlation between the results of two rounds of diagnosis in a group of patients. Like all correlation coefficients it is a number between 0 and 1. A Kappa of 1 would indicate complete agreement in two rounds of diagnosis of the same patients – that is, excellent reliability. A Kappa of 0 would indicate no agreement and very poor reliability.

A way of measuring a psychological variable can be called valid if it successfully measures what it sets out to measure. A diagnostic system is valid if the diagnosis successfully identifies a condition. But what does 'successful' mean here? Actually we can answer this in several ways and hence there are several ways of defining validity. It could be that our system identifies a condition that will respond a particular way to a treatment. This is known as predictive validity. It may be that our diagnosis agrees with a diagnosis made a different way. This is known as criterion validity. We can also step back and be a bit more philosophical: construct validity is the extent to which a category of mental disorder really exists. This might be called into question if symptoms are very similar to those of another condition or if two conditions regularly occur together. As we shall see, the diagnosis of different conditions varies according to their reliability and validity. This has led to some serious criticism of the practice of diagnosis.

KEY TERMS

reliability   the consistency with which a measure of a psychological variable like mental disorder identifies the same thing

validity   the extent to which a measure of a psychological variable measures what it sets out to measure

Depression

Depression is a relatively common mental disorder. Estimates vary, but up to 10 per cent of us are likely to be depressed at any one time, and perhaps 20 per cent of us will suffer depression during our lifetime. Women are at least twice as likely to suffer it than men. Many of the most severe cases begin in adolescence. The defining symptom of depression is disruption to our mood. Technically, this type of disorder is classified in *DSM-IV-TR* as a mood disorder. The *DSM* system recognises a number of different mood disorders, each of which has a distinct set of clinical characteristics.

Clinical characteristics of depression

Because we all vary in our moods and feel 'down' sometimes, it is important to have a clear cut-off point where ordinary variation in mood ends and clinical depression begins. This is achieved by requiring that a certain number of symptoms are present for a certain length of time. All the major systems of classification and diagnosis distinguish between major depressive disorder, dysthymia and bipolar disorder.

Major depressive disorder

The distinguishing feature of major depression is that it is cyclical; in other words symptoms come and go. When present, symptoms can be very severe and typically last from four to six months, although in exceptional cases over a year. Over the course of a case, the average patient with major depressive disorder is depressed 27.5 per cent of the time (Thornicroft & Sartorius, 1993). The criteria for diagnosis of a major depressive episode according to the *DSM-IV-TR* are shown in Box 9.2.

▲ **Figure 9.1** Some of the most severe cases of depression begin in the teens

---

■ **Box 9.2**

Criteria for major depressive episode (cautionary statement)

A Five (or more) of the following symptoms have been present during the same two-week period and represent a change from previous functioning; at least one of the symptoms is either
(1) depressed mood or
(2) loss of interest or pleasure.
Note: do not include symptoms that are clearly due to a general medical condition, or mood-incongruent delusions or hallucinations.
(1) Depressed mood most of the day, nearly every day, as indicated by either subjective report (eg, feels sad or empty) or observation made by others (eg, appears tearful). Note: in children and adolescents, can be irritable mood.
(2) Markedly diminished interest or pleasure in all, or almost all, activities most of the day, nearly every day (as indicated by either subjective account or observation made by others).
(3) Significant weight loss when not dieting or weight gain (eg, a change of more than 5% of body weight in a month), or decrease or increase in appetite nearly every day. Note: in children, consider failure to make expected weight gains.
(4) Insomnia or hypersomnia nearly every day.
(5) Psychomotor agitation or retardation nearly every day (observable by others, not merely subjective feelings of restlessness or being slowed down).
(6) Fatigue or loss of energy nearly every day.
(7) Feelings of worthlessness or excessive or inappropriate guilt (which may be delusional) nearly every day (not merely self-reproach or guilt about being sick).
(8) Diminished ability to think or concentrate, or indecisiveness, nearly every day (either by subjective account or as observed by others).
(9) Recurrent thoughts of death (not just fear of dying), recurrent suicidal ideation without a specific plan, or a suicide attempt or a specific plan for committing suicide.
B The symptoms do not meet criteria for a Mixed Episode.
C The symptoms cause clinically significant distress or impairment in social, occupational, or other important areas of functioning.
D The symptoms are not due to the direct physiological effects of a substance (eg, a drug of abuse, a medication) or a general medical condition (eg, hypothyroidism).
E The symptoms are not better accounted for by bereavement, ie, after the loss of a loved one, the symptoms persist for longer than two months or are characterised by marked functional impairment, morbid preoccupation with worthlessness, suicidal ideation, psychotic symptoms, or psychomotor retardation.

Reprinted with permission from the *Diagnostic and Statistical Manual of Mental Disorders, Text Revision, Fourth Edition.* (© 2000). American Psychiatric Association.

Dysthymia

Whilst major depression involves severe symptoms but also breaks, dysthymia is characterised by constant although usually less severe symptoms. Depression must last for longer than two years for a formal diagnosis, although treatment can begin earlier. Diagnostic criteria for dysthymia according to the *DSM-IV-TR* are shown in Box 9.3.

Box 9.3

Diagnostic criteria for dysthymic disorder (cautionary statement)

A Depressed mood for most of the day, for more days than not, as indicated either by subjective account or observation by others, for at least two years. Note: in children and adolescents, mood can be irritable and duration must be at least one year.

B Presence, while depressed, of two (or more) of the following:
 (1) poor appetite or overeating
 (2) insomnia or hypersomnia
 (3) low energy or fatigue
 (4) low self-esteem
 (5) poor concentration or difficulty making decisions
 (6) feelings of hopelessness.

C During the two-year period (one year for children or adolescents) of the disturbance, the person has never been without the symptoms in criteria A and B for more than two months at a time.

D No Major Depressive Episode has been present during the first two years of the disturbance (one year for children and adolescents), ie, the disturbance is not better accounted for by chronic Major Depressive Disorder, or Major Depressive Disorder in Partial Remission.
 Note: there may have been a previous Major Depressive Episode provided there was a full remission (no significant signs or symptoms for two months) before development of the Dysthymic Disorder. In addition, after the initial two years (one year in children or adolescents) of Dysthymic Disorder, there may be superimposed episodes of Major Depressive Disorder, in which case both diagnoses may be given when the criteria are met for a Major Depressive Episode.

E There has never been a Manic Episode, a Mixed Episode, or a Hypomanic Episode, and criteria have never been met for Cyclothymic Disorder.

F The disturbance does not occur exclusively during the course of a chronic Psychotic Disorder, such as Schizophrenia or Delusional Disorder.

G The symptoms are not due to the direct physiological effects of a substance (eg, a drug of abuse, a medication) or a general medical condition (eg, hypothyroidism).

H The symptoms cause clinically significant distress or impairment in social, occupational, or other important areas of functioning.

Reprinted with permission from the *Diagnostic and Statistical Manual of Mental Disorders, Text Revision, Fourth Edition.* (© 2000). American Psychiatric Association.

Bipolar disorder

Bipolar disorder is sometimes called manic depression. It is diagnosed when patients suffer from mania – that is, high arousal accompanied by irritable or excited mood. Manic individuals tend to feel highly energetic and either happy or irritable. Typically they need little sleep and they may have a stronger than usual sex drive. Manic patients can often be highly impulsive and their judgement may be impaired. This can lead to overspending and over-ambitious business plans. Most people who suffer manic episodes also suffer depression; however, bipolar disorder can be diagnosed with or without depressive episodes. Bipolar disorder occurs in around 1 per cent of the population. Box 9.4 shows the criteria according to *DSM-IV-TR* for a manic episode.

Box 9.4

Diagnostic criteria for a manic episode

A A distinct period of abnormally and persistently elevated, expansive or irritable mood, lasting at least one week (or any duration if hospitalisation is necessary).

B During the period of mood disturbance, three (or more) of the following symptoms have persisted (four if the mood is only irritable) and have been present to a significant degree:
 (1) inflated self-esteem or grandiosity
 (2) decreased need for sleep (eg, feels rested after only three hours of sleep)
 (3) more talkative than usual or pressure to keep talking
 (4) flight of ideas or subjective experience that thoughts are racing
 (5) distractibility (ie, attention too easily drawn to unimportant or irrelevant external stimuli)
 (6) increase in goal-directed activity (at work, at school, or sexually) or psychomotor agitation
 (7) excessive involvement in pleasurable activities that have a high potential for painful consequences (eg, engaging in unrestrained buying sprees, sexual indiscretions, or foolish business investments).

C The symptoms do not meet criteria for a Mixed Episode.

D The mood disturbance is sufficiently severe to cause marked impairment in occupational functioning or in usual social activities or relationships with others, or to necessitate hospitalisation to prevent harm to self or others, or there are psychotic features.

E The symptoms are not due to the direct physiological effects of a substance (eg, a drug of abuse, a medication or other treatment) or a general medical condition (eg, hyperthyroidism).

Reprinted with permission from the *Diagnostic and Statistical Manual of Mental Disorders, Text Revision, Fourth Edition.* (© 2000). American Psychiatric Association.

Thinking practically about psychology

Kirsty's mood has suddenly dropped alarmingly. She will not get out of bed or eat. She reports having hallucinations and suicidal thoughts.

Dorothy has been feeling down for the past year. In that time she has slept 12 hours a night and put on two stone. She reports that she no longer likes herself.

Following a few weeks of depressed mood, Tammy has just acquired a lot of energy, although she is very irritable. She resigns her job and remortgages her flat in order to raise money for a business, the details of which she has not yet worked out.

1 Suggest what disorder each of the three women might be suffering.

2 What factors would you need to consider before any were given a diagnosis?

Thinking creatively about psychology

Although the best tests for depression involve standard interviews, these are long and complex and require specialist training to carry out. A quick alternative is to use questionnaires.

1 Based on the *DSM-IV-TR* symptoms, devise a short questionnaire to assess depression.

2 Design a study to test the reliability and validity of your questionnaire.

You can look at the standard interview questions for diagnosing depression according to *DSM-IV-TR* here: http://cpmcnet.columbia.edu/dept/scid/revisions/pdf/module_a.pdf You'll get an idea of how complex it would be to carry out such an interview. Don't try it at home!

Issues in the diagnosis of depression

Our everyday experience tells us that moods vary and that we all experience some symptoms of depression sometimes. We would expect therefore that to reliably distinguish clinical depression from ordinary variations in mood is a tricky business. Modern procedures for diagnosing depression have better reliability and validity than older ones because they require several symptoms to be present for some time. Generally, depression has moderately good test-retest reliability figures. Pontizovsky *et al.* (2006) looked at the agreement between diagnosis on admission and on release for the 1013 patients admitted to Israeli psychiatric hospitals in 2003 suffering from mood disorders. The PPV for this group was 83.8 per cent – that is, 83.8 per cent of patients had the same diagnosis when released from hospital as they had when admitted. The Kappa figure, which represents the statistical relationship between diagnosis on admission and diagnosis on release, was 0.62.

However, studies that have looked at long-term reliability of diagnosis of mood disorders have found rather worse results. Baca-Garcia *et al.* (2007) looked at 2322 patients assessed at a Spanish psychiatric hospital between 1992 and 2004 with a range of mood disorders. All patients in this study were assessed at least 10 times. The PPV for all mood disorders was a less impressive 54.9 per cent (Kappa = 0.4). In other words, just over half the depressed patients retained the same diagnosis. For bipolar depression the PPV was worrying low at 35.4 per cent (Kappa = 0.3).

▲ **Figure 9.2** The most reliable and valid diagnosis of depression involves standard interviews

Thinking critically about psychology

Consider the studies of Pontizovsky & Baca-Garcia *et al.* The former suggests rather better reliability than the latter for the diagnosis of depression.

1 What are the strengths of each study?
2 What additional information does the Baca-Garcia *et al.* study provide about reliability of diagnosis?
3 Suggest a limitation of the Baca-Garcia *et al.* study.

The criterion validity of the diagnosis of depression is also moderately good. Sanchez-Villegas *et al.* (2008) administered the standard interview from *DSM-IV-TR* to 62 participants with a current diagnosis of depression and 42 without any diagnosis. Forty-two of the 62 (74 per cent) who had been previously diagnosed with depression were correctly identified as depressed. Thirty-four of the 42 (81 per cent) without a previous diagnosis were confirmed as not depressed. Of course we need to be careful about interpreting these results. It may be that previously depressed patients were doing better or just having a 'good day' when Sanchez's team failed to diagnose them. Similarly, the 19 per cent who were identified by *DSM-IV-TR* criteria as depressed and who had not had a previous diagnosis might simply have never been picked up previously. This shows us just how difficult validity is to establish.

Explanations for depression

Historically, depression has been something of a battlefield between those who see it as a biological condition and those who see it as psychological. In fact there is strong evidence for the role of both biological and psychological factors.

Thinking critically about psychology

Hammen (1997) has suggested four reasons why we might think depression is biological in origin:

● some symptoms are biological – for example, disruption to sleep and appetite
● depression is more common in some families than others
● antidepressant drugs reduce symptoms of depression
● some medical conditions lead to depression.

How strong are these arguments? Suggest a counter-argument to each.

Biological explanations and treatments

Genetic vulnerability to depression

Children of depressed parents are much more likely than their peers to suffer depression themselves. However, this is just circumstantial evidence for a genetic link. Recall from your AS level the difference between genotype and phenotype. Our genotype is our genetic make-up whilst our phenotype is our characteristics, which are a product of both our genes and environment. Families provide much of our environment as well as our genotype, and it may be this family environment that causes depression to run in families.

That said, there is stronger evidence from twin studies to show that there is some genetic element to depression. In one study McGuffin *et al.* (1996) studied 214 pairs of twins, of whom one or both was being treated for major depressive disorder. Of the identical twins, 46 per cent shared major depressive disorder. Twenty per cent of fraternal twins shared major depression. This greater sharing of depression in identical as opposed to fraternal twins suggests some genetic influence on major depression.

In recent years the emphasis in genetics research has shifted somewhat. Rather than just looking at whether there appears to be a genetic influence on variables like depression, modern research looks in particular at the influence of particular genes and how those genes may interact with the environment, together influencing symptoms. Researchers have been particularly interested in the serotonin transporter gene, which is responsible for producing serotonin in the brain. This gene comes in three forms, varying in the length of its two strands: long-long, long-short and short-short. It is believed that the short form leads to inefficient serotonin production.

▲ **Figure 9.3** If one of these identical twins develops depression there is a high probability that the other will also do so

Thinking practically about psychology

Why should trainee teachers be such a good group to follow in a prospective study of depression?

▶ **Figure 9.4** The long and short forms of the serotonin transporter gene

RESEARCH NOW

Wilhelm K, Mitchell PB, Niven H, Finch A, Wedgewood L, Scimone A, Blair IP, Parker G & Schofield P (2006) Life events, first depression onset and the serotonin transporter gene. *British Journal of Psychiatry* **188**, 210–15

Aim: To examine the relationship between major depression and negative life events and variations in the serotonin transporter gene, which is responsible for producing the neurotransmitter serotonin.

Procedure: 165 participants were recruited from an Australian teacher-training programme and followed up for 25 years. Every five years they were interviewed about positive and negative life events (such as bereavement, unemployment and marital break-up) and assessed for major depression using several standard interviews. By the end of the study, 149 participants were still alive, well and contactable. Of these, 127 consented to have genetic material taken by blood test or mouth swab. The associations between major depression, life events and serotonin transporter gene type were calculated.

Findings: 53 of the 127 participants who completed the research (42 per cent) were diagnosed with major depression at some point during the 25 years. Negative life events were strongly associated with major depression, with 68 per cent of those suffering depression reporting at least one major negative event prior to becoming depressed. Variations in the serotonin transporter gene alone were not associated with depression; however, where there were negative life events and the short-short form of the gene, participants were particularly vulnerable to depression.

Conclusion: Variations in the serotonin transporter gene do not directly lead to major depression; however, they do appear to affect the individual's response to negative life events. People with the short-short version of the gene appear to be the most sensitive to negative life events.

M E D I A   W A T C H : DIY mental health check

Internet gene tests provoke alarm

Robin Mckie, Science Editor, *The Observer*, 3 Feb 2008

Plans to sell genetic tests over the internet so people can find out if they are at risk of developing mental illnesses have been denounced by leading UK psychiatrists. They say the technology is still primitive and is only likely to worsen individuals' emotional and mental problems.

The tests, which biotechnology companies will begin selling in a few months, will allow people to find out, by sending off a spittle sample, if they possess gene variants that increase their chances of suffering bipolar depression or schizophrenia. The information will help both patients and doctors, it is claimed.

But scientists argue that selling these tests on the internet is dangerous. The technology is still in its infancy and cannot yet help make helpful diagnoses. 'These tests will only worry, confuse and mislead the public and patients,' said psychiatrist Professor Nick Craddock, of Cardiff University. 'There is a long way to go before we have genetic tests that may be helpful to patients. Using tests at the moment is only likely to cause harm.'

But the usefulness of such tests was disputed by Dr Cathryn Lewis, of the Institute of Psychiatry.

'The general risk of developing bipolar depression is around 1 per cent. If you possess the worst set of gene variants, then your risk rises to 3 per cent. That means you are three times more likely than average to get bipolar depression. That may seem worrying but it is still a very low risk. It is still 97 per cent likely that you won't get depression. People are not likely to realise that, however.'

Another test – to be marketed by NeuroMark, first in the US and later this year in Europe – is based on genes that predispose people to react badly to stress. If a person inherits this gene section from both parents, he or she has an increased chance of suffering from severe depression after stressful situations. 'About 20 per cent of people have this combination,' said Kim Bechthold, chief executive of the biotechnology company. 'It is useful information to know.'

1 What gene do you think the tests might identify in relation to depression?

2 Given that the risk of depression is still small even when the genetic test identifies the target gene, are tests like this a good idea?

Thinking critically about psychology

Consider the strengths and weaknesses of the Wilhelm *et al.* study. In particular, think about the following.

1 How representative is the sample, particularly at the end of the study? Why, on the other hand, might this be a good group on which to base a prospective study?

2 What are the advantages of a prospective study over a retrospective one – that is, one that looks back at life events in a group of depressed people?

3 Why was it a strength of the study to use a range of standard interviews to assess depression?

4 Does this study have practical applications?

Biochemical factors in depression

It is widely believed that a group of neurotransmitters called the *monoamines*, which include noradrenaline, dopamine and serotonin, exist in lower levels in the brains of depressed patients. This belief is based primarily on the action of antidepressant drugs, each of which increase the levels of one or more monoamines and ease the symptoms of depression. Some newer antidepressants such as Reboxetine work by increasing the action of noradrenaline. It thus appears that noradrenaline also has a role in depression.

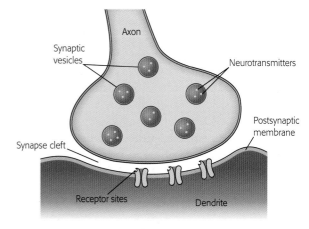

▲ **Figure 9.5** A synapse like those crossed by noradrenaline and serotonin. Depression appears to be associated with reduced levels of these neurotransmitters

There is further evidence for a role for the monoamines in depression from metabolite studies. Typically, patients suffering depression show lower levels of a chemical called 5-H1AA (which is formed when serotonin is broken down) in *cerebrospinal fluid* compared with non-depressed people. This suggests that depressed people have lower serotonin levels (McNeal & Cimbolic, 1986). An additional source of evidence for the role of noradrenaline comes from post-mortem studies showing either lower levels of noradrenaline in the dead brain or abnormalities in the locus coeruleus, an area of the brain that produces noradrenaline. Klimek *et al.* (1997) compared the locus coeruleus of 15 dead patients with major depression with that of 15 non-depressed people and found significant differences in structure. Studies like this suggest that depression may result from abnormality in brain structure that affects the production of neurotransmitters.

It is clear then that depression is associated with abnormal monoamine levels, but be a little wary about assuming that there is a simple relationship between brain chemistry and symptoms. Common sense suggests that brain chemistry affects symptoms rather than the reverse, although this is not necessarily the case. It could well be that psychological factors affect both biochemistry and symptoms of depression.

KEY TERMS

cerebrospinal fluid salty fluid that surrounds the brain and spinal cord

monoamines a group of neurotransmitters including serotonin and noradrenaline, which are believed to help regulate mood

Thinking practically about psychology

Before you read the next section, consider: if depression might be the result of abnormal brain chemistry, what sort of treatment does this suggest could be effective?

Biological treatments for depression

Depression can be treated biologically using drugs and/or electroconvulsive therapy. We have already considered these at AS level, so many of the following details should look familiar.

Antidepressant drugs

Traditionally, most people approaching their GP with symptoms of depression have been prescribed antidepressant drugs. There is a number of different antidepressant drugs and these work in slightly different ways. Generally, though, antidepressants work by raising the levels of monoamine neurotransmitters in the brain. Monoamine oxidase inhibitors (MAOIs) prevent the breakdown of serotonin, noradrenaline and dopamine, so that levels of all three monoamines

build up. Tricyclics prevent serotonin and noradrenaline being reabsorbed after it has crossed a synapse, again increasing their levels. Although these now old-fashioned antidepressants are effective in reducing symptoms, they can have serious side effects, because they interfere with a number of neurotransmitters. Tricyclics, for example, can cause drowsiness, dry mouth and constipation.

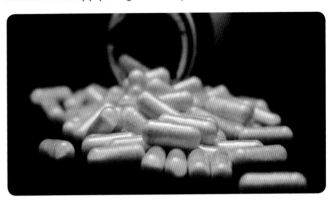

▼ **Figure 9.6** Antidepressant drugs are reasonably effective but many psychologists feel they are overused

Newer antidepressants tend to work on one monoamine only. Selective serotonin reuptake inhibitors (SSRIs) such as Prozac and Seroxat stop serotonin being reabsorbed and broken down after it has crossed a synapse, and noradrenaline reuptake inhibitors (NRIs) do the same with noradrenaline. It is important to have a number of antidepressants available because individual patients vary quite a lot in how they respond to each drug, both in terms of effects on their symptoms and side effects. Different people also show variations in their symptoms, and this can influence the choice of drug. NRIs, for example, may be particularly useful for motivating patients whose depression has left them very inactive.

Evaluation of antidepressants

Recall from your AS level that the standard procedure for testing the effectiveness of drugs is the random control trial with a *placebo* condition. A *random control trial* is an experimental procedure in which participants are randomly divided into two groups (or more than two if more than one treatment is being tested). One group is given the treatment and the other a placebo. In the case of drugs this is an inactive chemical. Arroll *et al.* (2005) reviewed random control trials with placebo conditions that investigated the effectiveness of antidepressants prescribed by GPs. Ten studies were found that compared tricyclics with placebos, three comparing SSRIs with placebos and two comparing both with placebos. Overall, 56–60 per cent of patients treated with antidepressants improved, as opposed to 42–47 per cent of people given the placebo. SSRIs took longer to work but had fewer side effects. This study suggests that both tricyclics and SSRIs are moderately effective when prescribed by GPs.

There is some debate about when antidepressants are an appropriate treatment. The problem is that there are alternative treatments that may be more effective. Pinquart *et al.* (2006) reviewed studies of antidepressants and psychological therapies used to treat depression. They concluded that psychological

KEY TERMS

random control trial a procedure in which patients are randomly allocated to a treatment or control condition and the outcomes are compared

double blind a procedure in which researchers who meet participants do not know which condition they are in

placebo a substitute for a real treatment that is given as a control condition in a study of medical or psychological treatment

NICE the National Institute for Health and Clinical Excellence (formally National Institute for Clinical Excellence). A publicly funded body attached to the NHS that is responsible for recommending safe and effective treatments for all physical and mental health problems based on research findings

therapies were overall more effective. Drugs, however, are cheaper and can be provided immediately, whereas there is usually a waiting list for psychological therapies. In an ideal world these would not be considerations and drugs would be used less often and psychological therapies more often. Many psychologists feel strongly that in spite of the cost, more psychological therapy should be made available to patients, and that we should rely less on cheap and easy drug treatment. Antidepressants are perhaps most appropriate when patients just want their symptoms relieved as quickly as possible and have no interest in psychological treatments.

Clinicians also need to consider the appropriateness of different types of antidepressant in different circumstances. Gender is an issue here: women suffer more side effects than men from tricyclic antidepressants so the latter are perhaps more appropriate for men. Women generally tolerate MAOIs well; however, these are highly toxic drugs so they are perhaps not appropriate when the patient is considered to be at high risk of suicide (National Institute for Health and Clinical Excellence, 2004).

Electroconvulsive therapy (ECT)

ECT is an alternative medical procedure for treating depression. The procedure involves administering an electric shock for a fraction of a second to the head, inducing a seizure similar to that experienced in epilepsy. This seizure generally lasts between 15 and 60 seconds. In most cases the shock is bilateral – that is, given to both sides of the head. This is generally considered to be more effective than unilateral ECT (given to one side of the head), although also more likely to lead to side effects. In a typical course of treatment, ECT is repeated between six and 12 times, usually two to three times per week.

ECT has a dodgy reputation, largely as a result of its early use when the shock was relatively large and given without anaesthetic or muscle relaxants. The resulting fits sometimes resulted in broken bones and occasionally burns to the brain. Modern ECT involves small shocks given for short periods (typically 800 milliamps for one second), given under anaesthetic and using drugs like succinylcholine to paralyse muscles and so prevent broken bones.

▼ **Figure 9.7** ECT

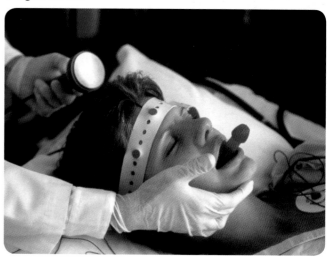

Evaluation of ECT

Eranti *et al.* (2007) evaluated the effectiveness of ECT. Forty-six patients with major depression were randomly allocated to either ECT or a control condition in which they were exposed to powerful magnetic fields, which are also believed to benefit depressed patients. Depression was assessed immediately, after one month and after six months using standard depression scales. Fifty-nine per cent of the ECT patients went into remission, experiencing no symptoms immediately after treatment and at one-month follow-up. Only 17 per cent of the control group experienced similar remission. However, at six months follow-up most of the patients were suffering major depression again. This suggests that ECT is effective in the short term but not the long term. This pattern of good short-term gains but poor long-term effectiveness is typical of ECT research.

There are ethical issues to consider in the use of ECT. One concerns side effects. The major side effect is memory loss. This is usually temporary and a single treatment does not result in serious memory impairment. However, memory problems are cumulative – that is, they get worse over a course of treatment. Lisanby *et al.* (2000) randomly assigned 55 patients with major depression to either bilateral or unilateral ECT conditions. A standard memory test called the Personal and Impersonal Memory Test was administered before and in the week after ECT and two months later. A control group without ECT were also assessed for memory. In the week after ECT the patients forgot significant personal (relating to their own lives) and impersonal memories (of events not directly connected to themselves). At two months follow-up they had recovered most but not all personal memories. Generally memory loss is not permanent but neither is the remission from the symptoms of depression.

So when is ECT an appropriate treatment? The National Institute for Clinical Excellence (NICE) (2003) suggests that ECT is appropriate when other treatments have failed or if the patient's depression is considered to be life-threatening. NICE also notes that the risks associated with ECT are worse for children, adolescents, older people and pregnant women, and that particular care should be taken when choosing ECT for patients in any of these categories.

Psychological explanations for depression

Recall your AS level when we looked at psychological models of abnormality, including psychodynamic, behavioural and cognitive approaches. All of these can be applied to explaining and treating depression. Particularly important are the cognitive and psychodynamic models.

The cognitive model of depression

In modern applied psychology, the cognitive model is the dominant one for explaining and treating depression. The cognitive model owes a lot to the work of Aaron Beck. Beck (1976) saw depression as the result of patterns of negative thinking. He identified three types of negative thinking that are particularly common in people suffering from depression:

- negative automatic thinking
- selective attention to the negative
- negative self-schemas.

Let us explain each of these a little, starting with negative automatic thinking. The cognitive triad of negative automatic thoughts consists of a negative view of the self, a negative view of the world and a negative view of the future. The cognitive triad is shown in Figure 9.8.

▼ **Figure 9.8** Beck's cognitive triad

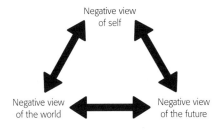

Beck's second form of negative thinking involves attending to the negative aspects of a situation and ignoring the positive aspects. This causes us to overestimate the 'downside' of any situation and reach the most negative conclusions possible. To most people half a glass of drink is half full. A depressed person will typically see it as half empty instead.

The third form of negative thinking identified by Beck involves negative self-schemas. Our self-schema contains all our information about ourselves, including beliefs, feelings, and so on. We acquire this negative set of beliefs about ourselves through criticism from our parents. When we meet a new situation we interpret it using any relevant schemas including our self-schema. If our beliefs about and feelings towards ourselves are negative, then so will be any interpretation we make about ourselves in a new situation. Say, for example, we meet someone we fancy and they are nice to us. If our self-schema contains the information that we are unattractive and unlovable, then we will not interpret the person being nice to us as meaning they fancy us. We might think instead that they feel sorry for us.

There is plenty of evidence to support a role for cognitive vulnerability in understanding depression. Studies have for

▲ **Figure 9.9** A depressed person is likely to see a half-full glass as half empty

example shown that depressed people selectively attend to negative stimuli. We can look at one such study in *Research Now*.

Mezulis *et al.* (2006) examined the origins of cognitive vulnerability. Recall that Beck believed that negative thinking was acquired from parental criticism. They followed up 289 American children from infancy to 11 years. Cognitive style, life events and parenting style were measured by standard questionnaires. In addition, 120 of the children were filmed receiving feedback on a task from parents. As we would expect if Beck were correct about the origins of depression, negative cognitive style was strongly associated with maternal anger during the feedback task in conjunction with negative life events in childhood. Interestingly, paternal behaviour was not associated with negative cognitive style.

The psychodynamic model of depression

Freud (1917) believed that many cases of depression were due to 'constitutional' factors. He was writing before we had a modern understanding of genetics, but essentially he meant that some people are genetically very vulnerable to depression. However, Freud suggested that at least some cases of depression could be linked to childhood experiences of loss or rejection in the family. He saw adult depression as a type of delayed mourning for this

RESEARCH NOW

Koster EH, De Raedt R, Goeleven E, Franck E & Crombez G (2005) Mood-congruent attentional bias in dysphoria: maintained attention to and impaired disengagement from negative information. *Emotion* **5, 446–55**

Aim: To test the idea that depressed people are more likely to attend to negative stimuli than non-depressed individuals.

Procedure: 57 student volunteers were assessed for symptoms of depression using a questionnaire called the Beck Depression Inventory. Fifteen who scored over nine, the cut-off for depression, and 15 who scored less than five took part in the study. Participants took part in a selective attention task. They were presented with positive words (eg successful, powerful), negative words (eg loser, failure) or neutral words (eg crane, paper) for 1.5 seconds each on a computer screen. Half a second after each word they saw a square on either the left or right of the screen. Their task was to press q if the square was on the left and 5 if it was on the right. How long they took to identify the location of the square was a measure of their attention to the words. The rationale was that the longer people took to locate the square, the harder they must have found it to disengage their attention from the word.

Findings: The depressed participants took an average of 12 milliseconds to disengage from negative words like 'loser' whereas the non-depressed group took only 2 milliseconds. Differences for the positive words were much smaller, with the depressed group disengaging slightly faster from words like 'successful' than negative words.

Conclusion: People suffering symptoms of depression struggle to disengage their attention from negative stimuli. This supports Beck's idea of a cognitive bias to attend to the negative in depression.

Thinking creatively about psychology

Although the results of the Koster *et al.* study provide impressive support for Beck's theory of depression, the study was carried out in artificial conditions and used a procedure quite far removed from people's everyday experiences. Design a study to test whether depressed people selectively attend to negative aspects of a situation in real life surroundings.

▼ **Figure 9.10** Depressed people find it hard to look away from words like 'loser' on a computer screen

▲ **Figure 9.11** Children who lose parents may be more vulnerable to depression

childhood loss. Freud emphasised the role of anger in both adult mourning and depression. The child's anger at being separated from or rejected by their loved one was not easily expressed at the time so it was repressed. Freud's theory covers the physical symptoms of depression as well the psychological. Lack of energy is caused by the amount of energy needed to keep anger repressed. Appetite suffers because eating is associated with nurture from the lost childhood figure. Their loss affects the ability to accept nurture and so to enjoy food.

Although Freud was writing before much of our current understanding of depression was developed, there are important strengths to his approach in that it links depression to both loss and anger (Champion & Power 2000). Modern cognitive theories of cognitive vulnerability can equally well explain the link with loss experiences, but perhaps not that with anger. Although it is methodologically difficult to test Freud's explanation for depression directly, there is support for the idea of a strong link between depression and unexpressed anger. For example, when Swaffer & Hollin (2001) gave 100 young offenders questionnaires to assess anger and health, it emerged that those who suppressed their anger had a significantly greater risk of developing depression.

It is interesting to look at some aspects of modern studies of cognitive vulnerability in the light of psychodynamic theory.

Note for example the Mezulis *et al.* study (p199). Maternal but not paternal parenting was associated with later risk of depression. This is more neatly understood from a psychodynamic perspective because the mother is usually the primary carer and has a more emotionally intense relationship with the child. We would thus expect rejecting behaviour by the mother to have more emotional impact than that by the father.

Thinking creatively about psychology

It is notoriously hard to study Freud's ideas scientifically, but it can be done, as long as you carefully select one aspect of the theory. Focus on one aspect of Freud's explanation for depression and design a study to test it.

Psychological treatments for depression

Cognitive behavioural therapies (CBT)

We introduced cognitive behavioural therapies or CBT in your AS level. In this section we are specifically concerned with the use of CBT to treat depression. CBT is now the most commonly used form of psychological therapy, in particular amongst clinical psychologists. It usually takes place once a week or fortnight for between five and 20 sessions. CBT involves helping patients to identify irrational and unhelpful thoughts and trying to change them. This may involve drawing diagrams for patients to show them the links between their thinking, behaviour and emotions. The rationale of CBT is that our thoughts affect our feelings

▲ **Figure 9.12** In CBT, therapists may use diagrams to show patients the links between their thinking, behaviour and emotions

and behaviour, so by changing our thoughts we can make ourselves feel better. Some forms of CBT also focus on directly encouraging changes in behaviour.

According to the British Association for Behavioural and Cognitive Psychotherapies (BABCP) (2002), the aims of CBT in treating depression are:

- to re-establish previous levels of activity
- to re-establish a social life
- to challenge patterns of negative thinking
- to learn to spot the early signs of recurring depression.

Therapy is collaborative: the therapist and patient will agree on what the patient wants to change. The therapist may then ask the patient to express their negative beliefs, for example in relation to their social life. A depressed patient might believe that there is no point in going out as they won't enjoy it. The therapist might respond to this by vigorous argument to convince the patient that they will in fact enjoy going out. The therapist might also employ reality testing in which the patient might be encouraged to go out and record in a diary that they enjoyed it.

Evaluation of CBT for depression

There is an impressive body of research supporting the effectiveness of CBT. Butler *et al.* (2006) reviewed studies of CBT and found 16 published meta-analyses, each of which included the results of several smaller studies. Based on this very large body of evidence they concluded that CBT was very effective for treating depression. The Royal College of Psychiatrists and NICE recommend CBT as the most effective psychological treatment for moderate and severe depression.

Although CBT is strongly supported by research and is increasingly dominating clinical psychology, there are some grounds for caution. Holmes (2002) has identified a number of limitations of the evidence to support such wholehearted support for CBT.

- The single largest study into effective treatments for depression (carried out by the *National Institute for Mental Health*, 1994) showed that CBT was less effective than antidepressant drugs and other psychological therapies.
- There is insufficient evidence for the long-term effectiveness of CBT (or other treatments).
- The evidence for the effectiveness of CBT comes mainly from trials of highly selected patients with only depression and no additional symptoms. There is far less evidence of effectiveness in real patient populations where the majority have more complex problems.

LOOKING FURTHER You can read Holmes' paper in full and the responses of various pro-CBT commentators here: http://www.bmj.com/cgi/reprint/324/7332/288. CBT practitioners can certainly cite a large volume of research in support of CBT but Holmes concludes that this simply makes them superior at marketing. Where do you stand in this debate?

Holmes' critique aside, the majority of current commentators recommend CBT as the most appropriate first line of psychological treatment for depression. There is considerable evidence for its effectiveness and little evidence of side effects. However, not all patients benefit from CBT, and NICE (2004) recommends psychodynamic therapies for more complex cases of depression.

Psychodynamic therapies

Psychodynamic therapies originated with the work of Freud. The original form, classical psychoanalysis, is very intensive, taking place four to five times per week and lasting for several years. Psychoanalytic psychotherapy is slightly less intensive and long term, typically one to three times per week for one to five years. Traditionally, patients in psychoanalysis lie on a couch, and patient and analyst do not face each other. Nowadays, particularly in psychotherapy as opposed to psychoanalysis, patient and therapist are more likely to face each other on comfortable chairs.

▲ **Figure 9.13**
Traditionally, patients in psychoanalysis lie on a couch

In psychoanalysis or psychoanalytic psychotherapy there is no attempt to teach the patient more constructive patterns of thinking or behaviour. Instead, the emphasis is on exploring the patient's past and linking it to their current symptoms. Early experiences of loss or rejection are particularly important in depression so these in particular may be explored. Patients may vividly recall these experiences (this is called *abreaction*) and 'discharge' the associated emotion (this is called *catharsis*). They may thus become very angry or upset. Often these negative emotions can become *transferred* on to the

therapist, who can be treated as if they were the absent or rejecting parent. The therapist can feed this back to the patient, who can thus gain insight into the way they transfer their anger on to other people. From a psychodynamic perspective, the relationship difficulties often associated with depression are often the result of transferring anger from early losses. In the more modern brief dynamic therapy (BDT), rather than wait for negative emotions to be transferred on to the therapist, patients are educated about the links between their current functioning and past experiences.

Evaluation of psychodynamic therapies for depression

There is a much smaller body of research into the effectiveness of psychodynamic therapies than for CBT. This reflects the fact that many more CBT practitioners are psychologists and therefore trained researchers. That said, the research that does exist is highly supportive of psychodynamic therapies for depression. Leichsenring *et al.* (2004) reviewed random control trials of BDT for specific disorders and found three studies of depression. On the basis of these studies they concluded that BDT is as effective as CBT for treating depression.

Publicly funded psychodynamic therapies are controversial because of the relatively small body of evidence supporting their effectiveness and because some varieties are so expensive. NICE (2004) recommends BDT as appropriate for complex cases where patients suffer a range of symptoms alongside depression. Psychodynamic therapies may also be appropriate where patients are aware of childhood events and have a strong desire to explore them. Psychodynamic therapies are probably inappropriate in cases of depression where patients are primarily seeking quick relief for their symptoms.

Thinking creatively about psychology

Various attempts have been made over the years to combine CBT with psychodynamic techniques. Therapies put together from others are described as integrative. If you were to integrate CBT with psychodynamic therapy in an attempt to treat depression, what would your therapy look like? Think about the following:

1 What would you assume about the causes of depression?
2 What would you explore with your patients?
3 What techniques might you use to help your patients feel better?

 NICE has a searchable website where you can look up advice about the appropriateness of particular treatments or the range of treatments, both biological and psychological, for particular disorders. Go to http://www.nice.org.uk/ and enter 'depression' as a search term.

KEY TERMS

abreaction recalling and re-experiencing painful memories

catharsis discharge of accumulated emotion

transference transferring emotions from one relationship to another, eg from parent to therapist

Schizophrenia

Around 1 per cent of the population suffers from schizophrenia. It is equally common in men and women, although symptoms typically start rather earlier in men than women. Schizophrenia is more common in lower socio-economic groups and in urban rather than rural areas. The symptoms of schizophrenia can interfere severely with everyday tasks, to the extent that a number of people with schizophrenia end up homeless.

It is commonly believed that the long-term prospects for someone with a diagnosis of schizophrenia are very poor. Actually, whilst that was once true, tremendous advances have been made in treating schizophrenia and nowadays prospects are much better. In a recent review Hopper *et al.* (2007) concluded that more than half of patients become free of symptoms and go on to lead normal lives.

▲ **Figure 9.14** People with schizophrenia sometimes struggle with day-to-day living to the extent of becoming homeless

Clinical characteristics

Unlike the other disorders in this chapter, depression and anxiety, schizophrenia does not have a single defining characteristic. It is instead a cluster of symptoms, some of which appear at first glance to be unrelated to others. If you have no personal or professional experience of mental disorder and you call to mind your perception of what 'madness' looks like it is probably something close to schizophrenia. Box 9.5 shows the symptoms required for diagnosis according to *DSM-IV-TR*.

Positive and negative symptoms

Some psychiatrists and psychologists make a distinction between positive and negative symptoms of schizophrenia.

Positive symptoms are unusual experiences such as hallucinations and delusions. Hallucinations are distortions to perception. These are most often auditory in nature, for example patients often report hearing voices. Delusions (or paranoia) are irrational beliefs, for example that the patient is someone else or is being controlled by someone else. These are called 'positive' symptoms because they are in addition to our everyday experience. Negative symptoms on the other hand involve the loss of normal functioning, for example reduced emotional responsiveness and reduced richness of speech.

Thinking practically about psychology

Explain how both positive and negative symptoms of schizophrenia might make it so hard to go about everyday tasks such as shopping and working.

LOOKING FURTHER You can look at the standard interview questions for diagnosing depression according to *DSM-IV-TR* here: http://cpmcnet.columbia.edu/dept/scid/revisions/pdf/module_b.pdf. You'll get an idea of how complex it would be to carry out such an interview. Don't try it at home!

It is very difficult for anyone not suffering from schizophrenia to appreciate the experience. However, there is a video here that attempts to recreate the perceptual distortions of schizophrenia: http://www.schizophrenia.com/sznews/archives/005976.html. Consider how difficult everyday living would be with this sort of visual and auditory experience.

■ **Box 9.5**

Diagnostic criteria for schizophrenia

A Two characteristic symptoms for at least one month. Characteristic symptoms must include:
 (1) delusions
 (2) hallucinations
 (3) disorganised speech
 (4) grossly disorganised or catatonic behaviour
 (5) negative symptoms (eg affective flattening)
 OR one characteristic symptom if delusions are bizarre or hallucinations consist of a voice keeping up a running commentary on the person's behaviour or thoughts, or two or more voices conversing with each other.
B Social/occupational functioning below levels prior to onset.
C Continuous signs of the disturbance for at least six months.
D No major changes in mood (depression or elation).
E No evidence of organic factors (eg drugs) or medical conditions.
F If there is history of a developmental disorder (eg autism), prominent delusions or hallucinations must be present for a month.

Reprinted with permission from the *Diagnostic and Statistical Manual of Mental Disorders, Text Revision, Fourth Edition.* (© 2000). American Psychiatric Association.

CLASSIC RESEARCH

Rosenhan DL (1973) On being sane in insane places. *Science* **179, 250–258**

Aim: To test the validity of the diagnosis of schizophrenia under the DSM-II system. Specifically, to test whether psychiatrists and nurses could distinguish real patients from 'pseudopatients' who reported a single symptom then acted normally.

Procedure: Rosenhan and seven volunteers (three women and five men in total) presented themselves at different American hospitals. They reported a single symptom, that they heard voices saying 'empty,' 'hollow' and 'thud'. All were admitted to the hospitals. They then acted normally. The time taken to be released and the responses of doctors and nurses when the pseudopatients spoke to them were recorded.

Findings: All the pseudopatients were admitted to their respective hospitals where they remained for between seven and 52 days (mean 19 days). All were eventually released with a diagnosis of schizophrenia in remission. In no case did doctors or nurses notice that there was nothing wrong with them. In fact some normal behaviour such as keeping a diary was interpreted as symptoms of schizophrenia. However, on several occasions real patients did make remarks suggesting they realised there was nothing wrong with the pseudopatients.

Conclusions: The diagnostic procedures of DSM-II for schizophrenia lacked validity because they failed to distinguish between real patients and pseudopatients.

Issues in the diagnosis of schizophrenia

Because the symptoms of schizophrenia are quite distinctive we would expect reliability of diagnosis to be quite good. This is very different to say depression, where we all experience some symptoms sometimes. In fact studies do show good test-retest reliability, better than for most mental disorders. Pontizovsky *et al.* (2006) looked at the agreement between diagnosis on admission and on release for the 998 patients admitted to Israeli psychiatric hospitals in 2003 suffering from mood disorders. The PPV for this group was 94.2 per cent – that is, 94.2 per cent of patients had the same diagnosis when released from hospital as they had when admitted. The Kappa figure, which represents the statistical relationship between diagnosis on admission and diagnosis on release, was 0.68.

However, studies that have looked at long-term reliability of diagnosis of schizophrenia have found slightly less impressive reliability. Baca-Garcia *et al.* (2007) looked at 2322 patients assessed at a Spanish psychiatric hospital between 1992 and

Thinking critically about psychology

Consider the studies of Pontizovsky *et al.* and Baca-Garcia *et al.* The former suggests rather better reliability than the latter for the diagnosis of schizophrenia.

1 What are the strengths of each study?
2 What additional information does the Baca-Garcia *et al.* study provide about reliability of diagnosis?
3 Suggest a limitation of the Baca-Garcia *et al.* study.

2004 initially assessed as having schizophrenia. All patients in this study were assessed at least 10 times. The PPV for schizophrenia was 69.6 per cent (Kappa = 0.6). In other words, around two-thirds of the patients retained the same diagnosis. This study shows better reliability for the diagnosis of schizophrenia than is the case for other mental disorders but it is far from perfect. Although the diagnosis of schizophrenia has reasonable test-retest reliability, its validity is another matter altogether. A classic study by David Rosenhan cast doubt on the ability of mental health professionals to recognise schizophrenia.

This can be seen as a study of criterion validity because it evaluates diagnosis against the criterion of knowing that none of the pseudopatients had a diagnosis or any real symptoms of schizophrenia. If Rosenhan's procedure were carried out today we can be reasonably assured that the results would be rather different. However, there are still concerns over the construct validity (see p191) of schizophrenia. Allardyce *et al.* (2007) suggest the following problems:

1 Although delusions and hallucinations are bizarre experiences, actually they occur fairly commonly amongst the general population. There is thus no clear cut-off point beyond which we can say someone is suffering from schizophrenia.

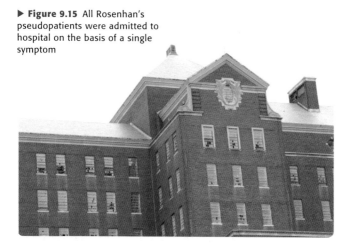

▶ **Figure 9.15** All Rosenhan's pseudopatients were admitted to hospital on the basis of a single symptom

2 Schizophrenia has a range of symptoms that occur in different combinations, thus individual patients with the diagnosis may appear very different from one another. Meanwhile there is overlap between the symptoms of schizophrenia and those of other serious mental disorders. This means that one patient with a diagnosis of schizophrenia may appear more similar to someone with a different diagnosis (or none) than to another person with the same diagnosis.

3 It is unclear whether patients suffering predominantly from negative symptoms have the same condition as those suffering mostly positive symptoms.

 LOOKING FURTHER You can read highly critical perspectives on the diagnosis of schizophrenia here: http://www.asylumonline.net/. At first reading, how impressed are you with this critical approach?

Biological explanations

Genetic vulnerability

It has long been observed that schizophrenia tends to run in families. However, this is only circumstantial evidence for a genetic link because families share an environment as well as genes. There is, however, strong evidence for a genetic element to schizophrenia from family studies. Family studies look at the degree of genetic similarity between different relatives and the likelihood of their sharing schizophrenia. For example, we share 100 per cent of our genes with an identical twin, 50 per cent with a parent etc. A classic family study of schizophrenia was carried out by Gottesman (1991).

 **Thinking critically about psychology**

Looking at the Rosenhan study, answer the following questions.

1 Looking at the *DSM-IV-TR* criteria for diagnosing schizophrenia, identify two changes that must have been made since Rosenhan's study.

2 What was the inter-rater reliability for the diagnosis of schizophrenia in this study?

3 To what extent should we see this study as a critique of modern diagnosis?

Explanations for schizophrenia

There is believed to be a number of factors underlying schizophrenia, including both the biological and psychological. With the rapid developments in our understanding of genetics and brain functioning over the past decade, the emphasis in recent research has been on biological factors. However, although it seems certain that schizophrenia has some biological basis, there is also evidence suggesting that psychological factors can be important.

▲ **Figure 9.16** If this man has schizophrenia there is around a 5 per cent probability that his grandson will go on to develop it

---

CLASSIC RESEARCH

Gottesman I (1991) *Schizophrenia Genesis: The Origins of Madness.* **New York: Freeman**

Aim: To examine the likelihood of a genetic element to schizophrenia by seeing whether most genetically similar family members are most likely to share a diagnosis of schizophrenia.

Procedure: The results of 40 family and twin studies conducted in Germany, Switzerland, Scandinavia and the UK were combined. Studies were chosen on the basis that they were by researchers unbiased on the issue of genetics and schizophrenia and they used standard procedures for diagnosis. European countries were favoured over the USA because researchers in Europe have access to national health records and because populations are more stable. The pool of information was large, including a study of 4000 relatives and another of 3000.

Findings: The greater the genetic similarity of relatives, the more likely they were both to have a diagnosis of schizophrenia. For an identical twin of a patient suffering schizophrenia the risk was 48 per cent, whilst for a non-identical twin this was 17 per cent. For a child of one parent with a diagnosis the risk was 6 per cent; if both parents had a diagnosis this rose to 46 per cent. Percentage risks are shown in Figure 9.17.

Conclusion: There was a very strong association between genetic similarity to a relative with schizophrenia and likelihood of developing the condition. This suggests that schizophrenia is partly genetic in origin. However, the risks were nowhere near as high as we would expect if the condition were entirely genetic. There is thus a role for the environment as well as genes in developing schizophrenia.

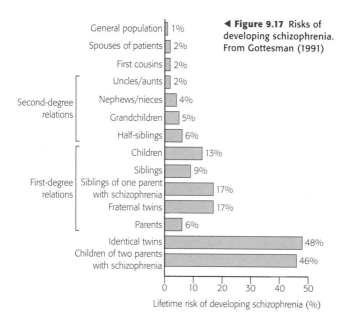

◀ **Figure 9.17** Risks of developing schizophrenia. From Gottesman (1991)

General population 1%
Spouses of patients 2%
First cousins 2%
Uncles/aunts 2% — Second-degree relations
Nephews/nieces 4%
Grandchildren 5%
Half-siblings 6%
Children 13% — First-degree relations
Siblings 9%
Siblings of one parent with schizophrenia 17%
Fraternal twins 17%
Parents 6%
Identical twins 48%
Children of two parents with schizophrenia 46%

Lifetime risk of developing schizophrenia (%)

Biochemical factors in schizophrenia

Several chemical processes appear to work somewhat differently in the brains of people with schizophrenia. In particular it has been believed for some decades that a neurotransmitter called dopamine (or DA) may be involved. Specifically, dopamine is present in higher levels in the brain and this leads to the symptoms of schizophrenia. Evidence for this *dopamine hypothesis* comes mainly from studies of drugs, in particular amphetamines (speed), which are dopamine agonists (that is, they prevent the breakdown of dopamine and so lead to an increase in levels). When amphetamines are given in large quantities they lead to delusions and hallucinations similar to those in schizophrenia. When they are given to patients suffering from schizophrenia their symptoms get worse.

▼ **Figure 9.19** A dopamine molecule. High levels of dopamine may be linked to the symptoms of schizophrenia

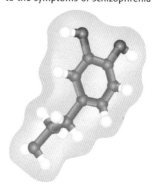

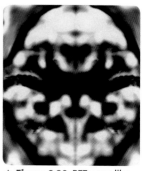

▲ **Figure 9.20** PET scans like this show that chemicals needed to produce dopamine are used more quickly by the brains of people with schizophrenia

Interestingly, genetic factors may still be important in schizophrenia when there is no family history of the condition. This may occur because of mutation. Mutations are changes to genes, resulting from copying errors during cell division or exposure to radiation, poison or viruses. Xu *et al.* (2008) examined the genetic make-up of 1077 people including 152 with schizophrenia and their parents. A total of 10 per cent of the patients but only 2 per cent of a control group had a mutation that distinguished their DNA from that of their parents. This suggests that around 10 per cent of cases of schizophrenia with no family history can be explained by mutation. The risk of mutation increases with parental age. Brown *et al.* (2002) showed that the risk of a child going on to develop schizophrenia increases with the age of their father when they were conceived. Results are shown in Figure 9.18.

Evidence for the dopamine hypothesis is mixed. There is certainly evidence to suggest that dopamine levels are higher in the brains of people with schizophrenia. In one study Lindstroem *et al.* (1999) radioactively labelled a chemical called L-DOPA, which is used by the brain to produce dopamine. They administered the L-DOPA to 10 untreated patients with schizophrenia and a control group of 10 people with no diagnosis. Using a brain-scanning technique called PET scanning they were able to trace what happened to the L-DOPA. The L-DOPA was taken up more quickly in the patients with schizophrenia, suggesting that they were producing more dopamine than the control group.

There are problems, however, with the dopamine hypothesis, at least in its original form. Raised dopamine levels only explain the positive symptoms of schizophrenia. Negative symptoms are not neatly explained – in fact we would expect negative symptoms to be associated with low rather than high levels of dopamine. Moreover, some drugs that are known to be dopamine agonists do not induce the symptoms of schizophrenia (Depatie & Lal, 2001). Clearly then there is more to schizophrenia than simply raised dopamine levels.

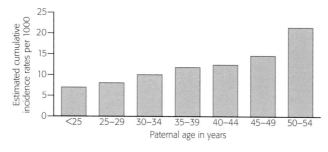

Estimated cumulative incidence rates per 1000

<25 25–29 30–34 35–39 40–44 45–49 50–54
Paternal age in years

▲ **Figure 9.18** Paternal age and the risk of developing schizophrenia. Adapted from Brown *et al.* (2002)

There is thus strong support from family and mutation studies for the idea that genes are involved in the development of schizophrenia. However, there are only fairly small statistical relationships between variations in particular genes and the development of schizophrenia. This suggests that either several genes are involved or that genes work in conjunction with particular environmental conditions to make some individuals particularly vulnerable to schizophrenia.

LOOKING FURTHER There is now a modern version of the dopamine hypothesis, involving other brain chemicals. Using the search terms 'NMDA' and 'glutamate' as well as 'schizophrenia' and 'dopamine' find out about this modern version of the dopamine hypothesis.

Biological treatments for schizophrenia

By convention, the first line of treatment for schizophrenia is biological. Antipsychotic drugs are the usual treatment, although ECT is also used on occasion.

Antipsychotics

The standard treatment for schizophrenia involves the use of antipsychotic drugs. Antipsychotics can be divided into traditional and newer, or first- and second-generation drugs. The first antipsychotics were the phenothiazines, including chlorpromazine. These work by blocking the receptors in synapses that absorb dopamine. Effectively they reduce the action of dopamine. Second-generation antipsychotics such as clozapine have fewer side effects. Each drug in this class is quite distinct in its chemistry and in some cases we have no idea how they act on the brain to reduce psychotic symptoms.

Antipsychotics can be taken in tablet or syrup form. For patients at high risk of failing to take their drugs regularly injections are available. Some people can take a course of antipsychotics and stop without their symptoms returning. Others require antipsychotics for life in order to avoid suffering the symptoms of schizophrenia.

Evaluation of antipsychotics

There is strong evidence to suggest that antipsychotic drugs are effective at reducing the symptoms of schizophrenia. There are, however, controversies over their use. Many patients suffer relapses, either through failing to take their medication or in spite of doing so. There are also potentially serious side effects. Key aims of the second-generation antipsychotics were to reduce side effects and prevent relapse. A number of studies have compared these in first- and second-generation antipsychotics. We can look at one such study by Schooler *et al.* here.

Transmitting
(presynaptic dopamine neurone)

Dopamine produces its effects by activating dopamine receptors on postsynaptic neurones. Many antipsychotics appear to act by blocking *dopamine receptors*

Synapse

Dopamine receptors

Receiving
(postsynaptic neurone)

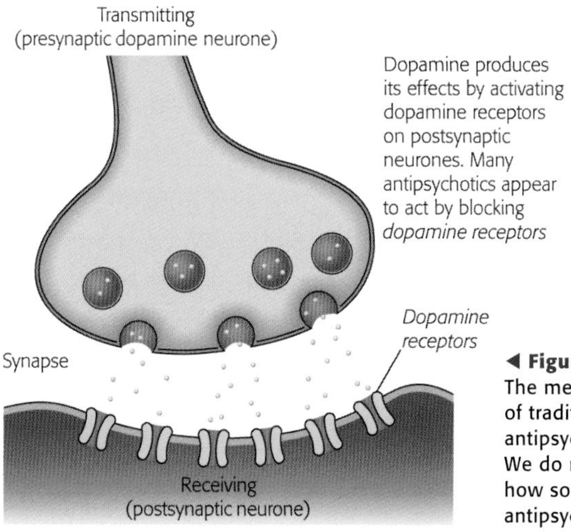

◀ **Figure 9.21**
The mechanism of traditional antipsychotics. We do not know how some newer antipsychotics work

Thinking critically about psychology

Consider the study of Schooler *et al.* (below)

1 Why was it important to randomly allocate patients to the two conditions?
2 Why was a *double blind* procedure used?
3 Why was it important to use standard measures like PaNSS to evaluate the patients?
4 The study was sponsored by a drug manufacturer. This is a very common practice, but it makes some psychologists uncomfortable. Why do you think this might be?

RESEARCH NOW

Schooler N, Rabinowitz J, Davidson M, Emsley R, Harvey PD, Kopala L, McGorry PD, Van Hove I, Eerdekens M, Swyzen W & De Smedt G (2005) Risperidone and haloperidol in first-episode psychosis: a long-term randomized trial. *American Journal of Psychiatry* 162, 947–53

Aim: To evaluate the initial effectiveness, relapse rate and side effects of first- and second-generation antipsychotics in the treatment of schizophrenia.

Procedure: 555 patients with an average age of 25.4 years took part in the study. All were suffering their first episode of schizophrenia. They were randomly allocated to two conditions. One group were administered haloperidol, a first-generation antipsychotic. The other group were given risperidone, a second-generation drug. A double blind procedure was used: those who gave the patients the drugs were not aware of which drug they were giving. Initial effectiveness and relapse were measured by changes in score on the Positive and Negative Symptoms Scale (PaNSS). Further standard tests were used to measure side effects. Patients were followed up until the last had completed treatment after two years.

Findings: In both groups there was significant initial improvement, 75 per cent of patients achieving at least 20 per cent reduction in symptoms as measured by the PaNSS. Forty-two per cent of the risperidone group as opposed to 55 per cent of the haloperidol group suffered relapses and those had a longer period before relapse (mean of 466 days as opposed to 205 in the haloperidol group). There were fewer side effects in the risperidone group.

Conclusion: Antipsychotics are effective in reducing symptoms of schizophrenia. Second-generation antipsychotics lead to lower relapse rates and have fewer side effects.

KEY TERMS

neuroleptic malignant syndrome a rare complication of antipsychotic drugs. This can be a serious neurological problem that can be fatal or lead to permanent brain damage

NICE the National Institute for Health and Clinical Excellence (formally National Institute for Clinical Excellence). A publicly funded body attached to the NHS that is responsible for recommending safe and effective treatments for all physical and mental health problems based on research findings

tardive dyskinesia neurological damage from antipsychotic drugs, leading to uncontrollable limb and facial movement

Antipsychotics are thus reasonably effective. However, there has been concern over their appropriateness due to their side effects. Common side effects include constipation and weight gain. In a minority of cases there can be more serious damage to the nervous system. In 0.05 per cent of patients antipsychotics can lead to *neuroleptic malignant syndrome*. This is a serious neurological condition the symptoms of which include nausea, high blood pressure, confusion, coma and death. Up to 10 per cent of cases lead to serious long-term neurological problems (Adityanjee *et al.*, 2005).

Neuroleptic malignant syndrome is extreme and unusual, however more common is *tardive dyskinesia*, repetitive involuntary movements of the face and limbs. These risks are lower where second-generation antipsychotics are used, and NICE (2002) recommends second-generation antipsychotics as the most appropriate treatment for schizophrenia.

▲ **Figure 9.22** Involuntary facial movements are a disabling feature of tardive dyskinesia

LOOKING FURTHER

Figure 9.22 gives an idea of the facial distortions that characterise tardive dyskinesia. You can see this rather more vividly on video. Several films about tardive dyskinesia can be seen at www.youtube.com. Consider how these symptoms might interfere with everyday social interaction.

ECT

ECT, or electroconvulsive therapy, is most commonly used for treating depression. However, it was first developed for the treatment of schizophrenia and recently psychiatrists have returned to this idea. The procedure involves administering an electric shock for a fraction of a second to the head, inducing a seizure similar to that experienced in epilepsy. This seizure generally lasts between 15 and 60 seconds. In most cases the shock is bilateral – that is, given to both sides of the head. This is generally considered to be more effective than unilateral ECT (given to one side of the head), although also more likely to lead to side effects. In a typical course of treatment, ECT is repeated between six and 12 times, usually two to three times per week.

ECT has a fearsome reputation, largely as a result of its early use when the shock was relatively large and given without anaesthetic or muscle relaxants. The resulting fits sometimes resulted in broken bones and occasionally burns to the brain. Modern ECT involves small shocks given for short periods (typically 800 milliamps for one second), given under anaesthetic and using drugs like succinylcholine to paralyse muscles and so prevent broken bones.

Evaluation of ECT for schizophrenia

There is considerable controversy surrounding the effectiveness and appropriateness of ECT in the treatment of schizophrenia. Tharyan & Adams (2005) reviewed 26 studies into the effectiveness of ECT, either alone or combined with antipsychotic drugs. They concluded that ECT was more successful than no treatment in the initial reduction of symptoms and in prevention of relapse. Overall ECT alone emerged as less effective than antipsychotics, although when used in addition to drugs it enhanced their effectiveness.

There are ethical issues to consider in judging the appropriateness of ECT. One concerns side effects. The major side effect is memory loss. This is usually temporary and a single treatment does not result in serious memory impairment. However, memory problems are cumulative – that is, they get worse over a course of treatment. NICE (2003) has concluded that there is insufficient evidence to recommend ECT as an appropriate treatment for schizophrenia.

Psychological explanations

The cognitive model

A number of cognitive factors have been proposed to explain schizophrenia. Frith (1992) set out to explain the symptoms of schizophrenia in terms of difficulties in information processing. Specifically Frith was interested in difficulties in two cognitive abilities.

- *Metarepresentation* is the ability to reflect on our thoughts, behaviour and experience. It is the mental ability that allows us self-awareness of our own intentions and goals. It also allows us to interpret the actions of others. Problems in our metarepresentation would seriously disrupt our ability to recognise one's own actions and thoughts as being carried out by 'me' rather than someone else.
- *Central control* is the ability to suppress our automatic responses to stimuli while we perform actions that reflect our wishes or intentions.

Positive symptoms of schizophrenia such as delusions and hallucinations can be neatly explained by metarepresentation problems. Many patients report hearing voices, for example. Frith suggests that the failure of metarepresentation means that patients are unable to distinguish speech heard externally from thoughts generated in their own minds. They therefore think something and cannot tell accurately whether they or someone else said it. The common delusion of thought insertion, in which patients believe their thoughts come from someone else, can be explained in exactly the same way. Another common delusion, that of being persecuted, could also be neatly explained by metarepresentation failure because we require metarepresentation to make judgements about other people's intentions.

Frith (1992) also explained negative symptoms in terms of problems with central control. According to Frith, all behaviour is either willed or stimulus-driven. In other words, we either choose to carry out an action because we have an internally generated wish to do it, or we do it in response to an external stimulus. Whenever we want to achieve something we suppress the brain systems responsible for *stimulus-driven behaviour* and activate those responsible for *willed behaviour*. The disorganised thinking and behaviour that characterise schizophrenia result from a failure to regulate willed and stimulus-driven behaviour. For example, speech in schizophrenia sometimes includes '*clanging*', in which the patient takes one word in a sentence and drifts from the sentence into words associated (for example by rhyming) with that word. For example, the sentence 'the boy went to school' might be clanged to 'the boy toy went to school scam scum'. According to Frith's model, the rhyming word 'toy' and the alliterations 'scam' and 'scum' are driven by the stimulus words 'boy' and 'school'. They are spoken because of the failure to suppress stimulus-driven behaviour.

There is supporting evidence for Frith's model. Bentall *et al*. (1991) carried out a study where participants were asked either to read out category words (eg plants beginning with the letter C) or think of category items themselves. One group had a diagnosis of schizophrenia whilst a control group had no diagnosis. A week later they were given a list of words and asked to identify which words they had read, which were new and which they had thought of themselves. The schizophrenia group did significantly worse, suggesting that they struggled to distinguish between words they had come up with themselves and those they heard. This supports Frith's idea that people with schizophrenia have metarepresentation problems; presumably participants with normal metarepresentation would be able to spot which words they had thought of themselves. A recent study by Baker *et al*. (2006) supports the idea of a central control problem and helps explain why patients with schizophrenia often have difficulty taking medication – see *Research Now*.

KEY TERMS

willed behaviour behaviour initiated in order to satisfy an intention or motive

stimulus-driven behaviour behaviour produced in response to a change in the environment

clanging a pattern of speech common in schizophrenia, in which sentences are interrupted as the patient fixes on words and identifies other words associated with it

▶ **Figure 9.23** It is hard to trust people unless you have a fully functioning metarepresentation system

You should not attempt any research with people suffering any psychological condition. You are not qualified and your teacher is probably not qualified to supervise you. However, you can investigate metarepresentation. Try Bentall's procedure for yourself. How hard is it to remember after a week which words you thought of?

RESEARCH NOW

Baker EK, Kurtz MM & Astur RS (2006) Virtual reality assessment of medication compliance in patients with schizophrenia. *Cyberpsychology and Behaviour* **9**, 224–9

Aim: To test whether patients with schizophrenia have more difficulty than others in a task of administering three drugs in a short period in virtual reality.

Procedure: 25 patients with schizophrenia and a control group of 16 adults without a diagnosis carried out a task in virtual reality. Their avatar was given a prescription for three drugs and told to take the correct dose of each drug in 15 minutes. Success in this task was measured by accuracy in the time at which the drugs were taken and the dose of each taken.

Findings: The schizophrenia group found the task harder than the control group. They made significantly more errors than the control group in both the timing and dose of the medication administered to their avatar.

Conclusion: Difficulty in taking medication is not just a long-term problem for patients with schizophrenia, but a cognitive difficulty in willed behaviour.

The psychodynamic model

The basic assumption of the psychodynamic model is that our adult characteristics, including psychopathology, are rooted in our childhood experiences. Of particular importance are the quality of our early relationships and early traumatic experiences. There are several theories within the psychodynamic model seeking to explain the development of schizophrenia. What they have in common is the belief that early experience can drastically affect the way the developing child perceives and interacts with the world.

One influential theory comes from Melanie Klein and Wilfred Bion. Klein (1946) and Bion (1967) proposed that all children go through a stage in the first few months of life characterised by feelings of persecution and omnipotence (being all-powerful). Klein and Bion called this the paranoid-schizoid position. A poor relationship with the primary carer in this critical period can prevent the child growing out of their sense of being omnipotent and persecuted. Bion (1967) described such individuals as having a 'schizophrenic core of personality'. Those with a schizophrenic core are likely as adults to respond to stress by reverting to their early mental state characterised by feelings of paranoia and omnipotence – classic symptoms of schizophrenia.

▲ **Figure**
9.24 According to Fromm-Reichmann, cold domineering mothers can cause schizophrenia

Another influential psychodynamic explanation for schizophrenia came from Fromm-Reichmann (1948). Based on the stories her patients told her about their childhoods, she suggested the existence of a particular type of parent, the schizophrenogenic mother. The word 'schizophrenogenic' literally means 'generating schizophrenia'. The schizophrenogenic mother is cold and controlling, and creates a family climate characterised by tension and secrecy.

There is ample evidence to suggest links between early experience and later development of schizophrenia. This should not strike us as odd; remember (p206) that even identical twins do not usually share schizophrenia so we would expect some aspects of the environment to be associated with the condition. In particular, childhood neglect and abuse increase the risk of developing schizophrenia. In a major Scandinavian review, Read *et al.* (2005) looked at studies linking adult schizophrenia to physical and sexual abuse in childhood published between 1984 and 2005. They found that schizophrenia was the most likely mental disorder to be associated with child abuse. The actual percentages of adult patients who reported child abuse varied according to the population and the method of measuring abuse but averaged 68.8 per cent for women and 59.1 per cent for men.

There is thus evidence suggesting that early family relations may be important in explaining some cases of schizophrenia (although bear in mind the limitations of retrospectively gathered data). It may be that some of the environmental influence on schizophrenia is due to family interactions in childhood. However almost no contemporary psychologists believe that schizophrenia is the direct result of upbringing alone. The evidence for genetic influence is simply too strong. Moreover, studies like that of Read *et al.* (2005) only support the psychodynamic principle that early experience impacts on later mental health; they do not directly support the details of particular theories like those of Bion or Fromm-Reichmann.

It is important for ethical reasons to be cautious and sensitive in how we respond to research linking schizophrenia to child abuse. On the one hand, it seems likely that, in conjunction with genetic vulnerability, child abuse increases the risk of developing schizophrenia. On the other hand, most patients have probably not been abused, and there is a real risk of blaming families without good reason when people develop schizophrenia. Given the stress associated with caring for a relative with a serious mental disorder, this is the last thing families of sufferers need.

▲ **Figure 9.25** Families can suffer extra stress if they feel blamed for schizophrenia

Psychological treatments for schizophrenia

Cognitive behavioural therapy

We introduced cognitive behavioural therapies or CBT in your AS level. In this section we are specifically concerned with the use of CBT to treat schizophrenia. CBT is now the most commonly used form of psychological therapy, in particular amongst clinical psychologists. It usually takes place once a week or fortnight for between five and 20 sessions. CBT involves helping patients to identify irrational and unhelpful thoughts and trying to change them. This may involve drawing diagrams for patients to show them the links between their thinking, behaviour and emotions.

CBT cannot completely eliminate the symptoms of schizophrenia but it can make patients much better able to cope with them. According to Turkington *et al.* (2004), the purpose of CBT for schizophrenia is to help patients make sense of how their environment, including delusions and hallucinations, impacts on their feelings and behaviour. Understanding where symptoms originate can be crucial for some patients. If, for example, a patient hears voices and believes they are demons they will naturally be very afraid. Offering a range of psychological explanations for the existence of hallucinations and delusions can help reduce this anxiety. An example of this sort of dialogue occurs in the extract from a session of CBT with a patient with schizophrenia (Turkington *et al.*, 2004) in Box 9.6.

■ **Box 9.6**

CBT for schizophrenia involves helping patients identify rational explanations for their delusions and hallucinations

Paranoid patient:	The Mafia are observing me to decide how to kill me.
Therapist:	You are obviously very frightened … there must be a good reason for this.
Paranoid patient:	Do you think it's the Mafia?
Therapist:	It's a possibility, but there could be other explanations. How do you know that it's the Mafia?
Paranoid patient:	Who else would persecute someone like this?
Therapist:	Well, for us to find out together, we need to examine the evidence, although it might feel frightening to do this. I will help you to look into this a bit more.

CBT can also help normalise the experience of schizophrenia. Patients may, for example, benefit from hearing about how common hallucinations and delusions are amongst people without a diagnosis. CBT may also focus on the patient's beliefs about schizophrenia itself. Therapists may share the results of recent studies showing good long-term prospects for sufferers.

Evaluation of CBT for schizophrenia

There is a reasonable body of evidence to support the effectiveness of CBT in the treatment of schizophrenia. Pilling *et al.* (2002) reviewed eight random control trials that varied in how and for how long CBT was delivered and how outcome was measured. Overall, CBT came out as superior to standard care, particularly in long-term outcomes. Whereas patients in standard care tend to lose some of the benefits of treatment when it finishes, CBT patients maintain their gains over longer periods. Even studies that have not supported the initial effectiveness of CBT have supported this long-term benefit (Rathod & Turkington, 2005).

NICE (2002) suggests that CBT is an appropriate treatment for schizophrenia and should be made available to patients. CBT may be particularly appropriate for new patients. Morrison *et al.* (2004) administered six months of CBT to patients showing early signs of schizophrenia. Twelve months later significantly fewer had a full diagnosis than was the case in a control group. CBT may also be particularly appropriate for patients at high risk of not taking medication. Turkington *et al.* (2002) found that CBT was effective in increasing patients' insight into their psychopathology and their awareness of the importance of taking medication. There was, however, a downside: with insight into how serious a condition they were suffering, patients became increasingly depressed.

Psychodynamic therapies

Psychodynamic therapies originated with the work of Freud. The original form, classical psychoanalysis, is very intensive, taking place four to five times per week and lasting for several years. Psychoanalytic psychotherapy is slightly less intensive and long term, typically one to three times per week for one to five years. Traditionally patients in psychoanalysis lie on a couch, and patient and analyst do not face each other. Nowadays, particularly in psychotherapy as opposed to psychoanalysis, patient and therapist are more likely to face each other on comfortable chairs.

◄ **Figure 9.26** CBT for schizophrenia involves helping patients identify rational explanations for their delusions and hallucinations

To a psychodynamic therapist the symptoms of schizophrenia, like those of other mental disorders, are rooted in early relationships. One aim of therapy for schizophrenia is to give patients insight into these links between symptoms and early life. For example, Benedetti (1987) proposed that our sense of self develops in childhood through relationships with others. Failed early relationships can lead to a poor sense of self, which can explain why people with schizophrenia have poor metarepresentation and find it hard to distinguish between their own thoughts and external sights and sounds. At the same time, therapists offer themselves as a model substitute relationship, providing a kind of substitute parenting that in turn allows the patient to undergo normal personality development and become fully aware of the distinction between themselves and others.

Evaluation of psychodynamic therapies for schizophrenia

The theoretical basis for treating schizophrenia psychodynamically is weak, with many competing theories on the origins of the condition and hence different aims for treatment. Furthermore, even Freud questioned whether psychoanalysis would ever be capable of tackling schizophrenia. However, in spite of these problems, there is actually quite good evidence for the effectiveness of psychodynamic therapies for schizophrenia. Gottdiener & Haslam (2002) carried out a meta-analysis of studies into psychodynamic therapies, CBT and assorted supportive therapies. CBT and psychodynamic therapies emerged as equally effective, with 67 per cent of patients improving significantly as opposed to 34 per cent of untreated controls. Controversially, this meta-analysis suggests that psychodynamic therapies are effective without accompanying antipsychotic medication.

Gottdiener (2006) argues that the evidence supporting psychodynamic treatment is strong enough to see it as generally appropriate for use with schizophrenia. This is, however, controversial, both because of the weak theoretical basis for therapies and because of the relatively small body of supporting evidence. NICE guidelines for the treatment of schizophrenia (2002) comment that it is appropriate to make use of psychodynamic principles to understand the experience of patients within their families but do not mention the use of psychodynamic therapies.

Thinking creatively about psychology

Various attempts have been made over the years to combine CBT with psychodynamic techniques. Therapies put together from others are known as integrative. If you were to integrate CBT with psychodynamic therapy in an attempt to treat schizophrenia, what would your therapy look like? Think about the following:

1 What would you assume about the causes of schizophrenia?
2 What would you explore with your patients?
3 What techniques might you use to help your patients feel better?

Thinking creatively about psychology

The use of psychodynamic therapies with schizophrenia is an area that cries out for further research. Design an outcome study to test the effectiveness of a psychodynamic therapy with schizophrenia. Consider in particular the following:

- Who will be your target population?
- How many conditions will you have and how will you allocate patients to them?
- What ethical issues will you consider and what safeguards will you put in place?
- What measures of outcome will you use?

Anxiety disorders

Rather like depression, anxiety disorders are extensions of the very normal experience of anxiety. A certain amount of anxiety is good for us in many situations. It can boost exam performance, for example, and make us more alert in dangerous situations. However, extreme anxiety can be disabling. Estimates vary, but probably between 15 and 20 per cent of the population suffer from some form of pathological anxiety.

Clinical characteristics of anxiety

There is a number of anxiety disorders, each of which has a distinctive set of symptoms. What all anxiety disorders share is the experience of fear. In the case of phobias this fear is directed

▲ **Figure 9.27 The common feature of anxiety disorders is fear**

towards a particular object or situation. There are also more generalised forms of anxiety in which patients experience severe anxiety in a much wider range of situations. Post-traumatic stress disorder is characterised by its appearance in response to a traumatic event. Obsessive-compulsive disorder is characterised by particular responses to anxiety. In this chapter we are concerned with phobias and obsessive-compulsive disorder.

Phobias

Phobias come in different forms. Best known are the specific phobias. These involve fear of a single stimulus, such as spiders or snakes. Around 13 per cent of us experience a specific phobia at some time. Most phobias begin in childhood and their intensity usually declines throughout adulthood. The criteria for a diagnosis of a simple phobia in the *DSM-IV* system are shown in Box 9.7.

> ■ **Box 9.7**
>
> ## Diagnostic criteria for 300.29 specific phobia (cautionary statement)
>
> A Marked and persistent fear that is excessive or unreasonable, cued by the presence or anticipation of a specific object or situation (eg, flying, heights, animals, receiving an injection, seeing blood).
> B Exposure to the phobic stimulus almost invariably provokes an immediate anxiety response, which may take the form of a situationally bound or situationally predisposed Panic Attack. Note: in children, the anxiety may be expressed by crying, tantrums, freezing, or clinging.
> C The person recognises that the fear is excessive or unreasonable. Note: in children, this feature may be absent.
> D The phobic situation(s) is avoided or else is endured with intense anxiety or distress.
> E The avoidance, anxious anticipation, or distress in the feared situation(s) interferes significantly with the person's normal routine, occupational (or academic) functioning, or social activities or relationships, or there is marked distress about having the phobia.
> F In individuals under age 18 years, the duration is at least six months.
> G The anxiety, Panic Attacks, or phobic avoidance associated with the specific object or situation are not better accounted for by another mental disorder, such as Obsessive-Compulsive Disorder (eg, fear of dirt in someone with an obsession about contamination), Post-traumatic Stress Disorder (eg, avoidance of stimuli associated with a severe stressor), Separation Anxiety Disorder (eg, avoidance of school), Social Phobia (eg, avoidance of social situations because of fear of embarrassment), Panic Disorder with Agoraphobia, or Agoraphobia Without History of Panic Disorder.
> Specify type:
> • Animal type
> • Natural environment type (eg, heights, storms, water)
> • Blood-injection-injury type
> • Situational type (eg, airplanes, elevators, enclosed places)
> • Other type (eg, phobic avoidance of situations that may lead to choking, vomiting, or contracting an illness; in children, avoidance of loud sounds or costumed characters).
>

There are other forms of phobia. Social phobias are related to other people. Common examples include fear of public speaking and of using public toilets. Some anxiety before social situations is quite common, reported by about 40 per cent of the population. It becomes a clinical condition in around 2 per cent of people when it interferes with their daily lives. Agoraphobia is the fear of public places, occurring in 2–3 per cent of people. It differs from the other anxiety disorders in appearing rather later, typically in the mid-20s.

 Ever wondered how many different phobias there are? Go to http://phobialist.com/. You may be surprised!

Obsessive-compulsive disorder (OCD)

Obsessive-compulsive disorder, or OCD as it is more commonly called, is a response to anxiety characterised by persistent and intrusive thoughts. These thoughts can be in the form of obsessions, compulsions or both.

- Obsessions are thoughts in the form of doubts, fears, images or imagined future events. They invade the consciousness of patients, dominating their lives.
- Compulsions are desires to carry out a task repeatedly, often washing or cleaning.

▶ **Figure 9.28** Compulsive hand-washing is a classic symptom of OCD

Although OCD sounds like an extreme and odd set of symptoms, actually, like other anxiety disorders, it can be seen as an extension of normal experience. We have all had the experience of not being able to get a catchy song out of our head and few of us walk on the cracks in the pavement or under ladders. When obsessions or compulsions cause significant distress or start to interfere with the patient's everyday life, they can be classed as a mental disorder. Around 1.5 per cent of the population suffer from OCD. The diagnostic criteria according to *DSM-IV* are shown in Box 9.8. Skoog & Skoog (1999) carried out a 40-year follow-up of 122 patients with OCD, giving us good quality statistics about the long-term prospects of patients. Eighty-three per cent of the Skoog & Skoog sample improved significantly during the 40-year period, with 20 per cent being completely cured. Forty-eight per cent had symptoms for 30 years or longer.

Thinking creatively about psychology

Although the best tests for anxiety involve standard interviews, these are long and complex and require specialist training to carry out. A quick alternative is to use questionnaires.

1 Based on the *DSM-IV-TR* symptoms, devise a short questionnaire to assess whether someone has a phobia.

2 Design a study to test the reliability and validity of your questionnaire.

■ Box 9.8

Diagnostic criteria for Obsessive-Compulsive Disorder (cautionary statement)

A Either obsessions or compulsions:
   Obsessions as defined by (1), (2), (3), and (4):
   (1) recurrent and persistent thoughts, impulses, or images that are experienced, at some time during the disturbance, as intrusive and inappropriate and that cause marked anxiety or distress
   (2) the thoughts, impulses, or images are not simply excessive worries about real-life problems
   (3) the person attempts to ignore or suppress such thoughts, impulses, or images, or to neutralise them with some other thought or action
   (4) the person recognises that the obsessional thoughts, impulses, or images are a product of his or her own mind (not imposed from without as in thought insertion).
   Compulsions as defined by (1) and (2):
   (1) repetitive behaviors (eg, hand washing, ordering, checking) or mental acts (eg, praying, counting, repeating words silently) that the person feels driven to perform in response to an obsession, or according to rules that must be applied rigidly
   (2) the behaviors or mental acts are aimed at preventing or reducing distress or preventing some dreaded event or situation; however, these behaviors or mental acts either are not connected in a realistic way with what they are designed to neutralise or prevent or are clearly excessive

B At some point during the course of the disorder, the person has recognised that the obsessions or compulsions are excessive or unreasonable. Note: this does not apply to children.

C The obsessions or compulsions cause marked distress, are time consuming (take more than one hour a day), or significantly interfere with the person's normal routine, occupational (or academic) functioning, or usual social activities or relationships.

D If another Axis I disorder is present, the content of the obsessions or compulsions is not restricted to it (eg, preoccupation with food in the presence of an Eating Disorders; hair pulling in the presence of Trichotillomania; concern with appearance in the presence of Body Dysmorphic Disorder; preoccupation with drugs in the presence of a Substance Use Disorder; preoccupation with having a serious illness in the presence of Hypochondriasis; preoccupation with sexual urges or fantasies in the presence of a Paraphilia; or guilty ruminations in the presence of Major Depressive Disorder).

E The disturbance is not due to the direct physiological effects of a substance (eg, a drug of abuse, a medication) or a general medical condition.

Reprinted with permission from the *Diagnostic and Statistical Manual of Mental Disorders, Text Revision, Fourth Edition.* (© 2000). American Psychiatric Association.

Issues in the diagnosis of anxiety disorders

Phobias and OCD both have distinct sets of easily observable symptoms so we would expect their diagnosis to have quite good reliability. This is in fact largely the case, at least in comparison with some other disorders. Brown *et al.* (2001) assessed 362 outpatients at an American centre for mood and anxiety disorders. The Kappa score (see p191 for an explanation) was 0.86 for specific phobias and 0.85 for OCD. Social phobia came out a little worse at 0.77, but these are still amongst the best reliability figures for diagnosis of mental disorders. However, studies that have looked at long-term reliability of diagnosis of OCD have found less impressive results. Baca-Garcia *et al.* (2007) looked at 157 patients assessed at a Spanish psychiatric hospital between 1992 and 2004 with OCD. All patients in this study were assessed at least 10 times. The PPV for OCD was a less impressive 46.4 per cent (Kappa = 0.4). In other words, just under half the patients retained the same diagnosis.

▶ **Figure 9.29** Because the symptoms of phobias are so visible and distinctive, the reliability of diagnosis is relatively good

Smoller (2007) has discussed the construct validity (see p191) of phobias. He points out that there are overlaps between both symptoms of and genes affecting phobias and other mental disorders normally classified separately. For example, social phobia and avoidant personality disorder overlap considerably. This calls into question the existence of social phobia as a distinct disorder. The classification of OCD as an anxiety disorder has also been called into question. Mataix-Cols *et al.* (2007) surveyed 108 psychiatrists, 69 psychologists and 10 other specialists in OCD, asking them whether they believed it should be classed as an anxiety disorder. Seventy-five per cent of psychiatrists and 40–45 per cent of the other professionals agreed that OCD should be removed from the anxiety disorders category. This is because OCD shares some features of disorders like Tourette's syndrome, which are classified as different types of disorder. Although anxiety is part of OCD it may not be its defining feature in the same way as it is for phobias.

Biological explanations for anxiety disorders

Genetic vulnerability

It seems unlikely that a single gene or a particular set of genes directly causes phobia or OCD. However, it does seem likely that some people are more vulnerable than others to acquiring anxiety conditions because of the inherited characteristics of their nervous system. For example, twin studies suggest that phobias are more likely to be shared by identical than non-identical twins. In one study Skre *et al.* (2000) compared the frequency of sharing phobia in 23 pairs of identical twins and 38 pairs of same-sex non-identical twins. The identical twins were significantly more likely to share a diagnosis of phobia (particularly specific phobias) than non-identical twins. Looking more broadly at the role of genetic vulnerability in anxiety disorders, Hetterna *et al.* (2001) reviewed the results of twin and family studies concerned with a range of anxiety problems including generalised anxiety, panic

disorder, phobias and OCD. Overall, family members of a patient with an anxiety disorder were four to six times as likely as others to develop an anxiety condition themselves.

Recent research has moved well beyond the tendency for OCD to run in families to look at the role of particular genes. In one recent study, for example, Stewart *et al.* (2007) found that variations in a gene called OLIG-2 were particularly common in OCD patients and their families. OLIG-2 is involved with the genetic coding for the production of myelin, the material that covers nerve cells. It is not known what the connection might be between this and the symptoms of OCD, but it does provide evidence to suggest that people with particular genetic variations may be particularly vulnerable to OCD.

Thinking critically about psychology

Just because a disorder is shared by family members, to what extent does this indicate that it is genetic in origin? What other factors apart from genes are shared within families?.

M E D I A   W A T C H : genetics and anxiety disorders

The missing grey cells that help to create an obsessive

The Times, 26 November 2007

Scientists at Cambridge have found changes in the brain that are linked to obsessive-compulsive disorder.

OCD tends to run in families, but the gene responsible has not so far been found. A team from the Brain Mapping Unit at the University of Cambridge decided to look not for the gene, but for effects of the gene on brain structure that might be detectable in patients and in unaffected relations.

To explore this, the team led by Ed Bullmore used magnetic resonance scanning of the brain and measures of individuals' ability to perform simple tasks involving brain and hand. They scanned the brains of 31 OCD patients, comparing them with 31 first-degree relations who were unaffected by OCD – sisters, brothers, parents, and children – and 31 unrelated healthy people.

The volunteers also completed computerised tests designed to assess their ability, once they had become established in a pattern of repetitive behaviours, to stop performing them.

Both the OCD patients and their close relations did worse on the computer task than the control group, the team reports in the journal Brain. Earlier research has shown similar results, suggesting that

when a pattern of actions is established, people with OCD find it hard to stop them.

When the performance on this test was compared with MRI scans, it was found that performing poorly was associated with decreases of grey matter in brain regions important in suppressing responses and habits.

But this was the case both in actual OCD cases, and in close relations who did not suffer the disease, suggesting that there must be additional factors that determine what triggers the condition in susceptible people.

Lara Menzies, the lead author of the paper, said: "Impaired brain function in the areas of the brain associated with stopping motor responses may contribute to the compulsive and repetitive behaviours that are characteristic of OCD.

"These brain changes appear to run in families and may represent a genetic risk factor for developing the condition. The current diagnosis of OCD is subjective and therefore knowledge of the underlying causes may lead to better diagnosis and ultimately improved treatments."

1 How clear do you think the links are between this sort of evidence and the authors' conclusions?

Biochemical factors in anxiety disorders

Few if any professionals believe that anxiety disorders are entirely the result of abnormal chemical levels. However, they may play an important role in individual vulnerability to and symptoms of anxiety problems. We know for example that the normal experience of anxiety is regulated in the brain by an amino acid called GABA. GABA operates a feedback loop, helping arousal levels to return to normal after a fright. It is possible that some people have a problem with their GABA system and so cannot control their anxiety as easily.

There is also some evidence linking OCD to abnormalities related to low levels of the neurotransmitter serotonin. The main evidence for this comes from the effects of SSRIs (Aouizerate *et al.*, 2005). These drugs are best known for treating depression but they also reduce symptoms of OCD. They work by preventing the breakdown of serotonin, increasing its levels in the brain. In addition, studies such as Hollander *et al.* (1992) have found that drugs like M-CCP, which reduces levels of serotonin, make OCD symptoms worse. However, De Silva (2000) has challenged the evidence for a serotonin basis to OCD on several grounds. Psychological treatments work without altering serotonin levels, serotonin levels in OCD patients are no different from those in several other anxiety and mood disorders, and there is no relationship between SSRI dose and relief from symptoms.

The sort of evidence linking serotonin to OCD can be just as well applied to phobias. Studies such as Stein *et al.* (1998) show that the symptoms of social phobia are reduced by SSRIs and other antidepressants, suggesting a role for serotonin. Specific phobias are normally treated psychologically rather than with drugs, although Benjamin *et al.* (2000) tested the antidepressant paroxetine on patients suffering specific phobias and found that symptoms were sharply reduced in 60 per cent of patients as opposed to 20 per cent of a control group. This suggests that the symptoms of specific phobias are serotonin-related. This does not mean that phobias are acquired simply as a result of low serotonin levels; however, low serotonin levels may make some people more vulnerable than others or they may be important in the experience of phobic anxiety.

Biological treatments for anxiety

Drug treatment

Various types of drugs can be used to reduce anxiety. Severe anxiety can be treated in the short term by benzodiazepines such as diazepam (Valium). These work by increasing the effectiveness of the GABA system. Benzodiazepines are quite effective at tackling the symptoms of anxiety, although they are addictive and when patients stop taking them after some time they often experience a sharp rise in anxiety. In the 1960s and 1970s, benzodiazepines were commonly prescribed long term for anxiety problems, but it is now generally agreed that this was a serious error, leaving large numbers of people addicted and suffering further anxiety problems when they tried to stop their medication.

Thinking critically about psychology

Think about the link between the effects of antidepressants on anxiety, the possible role of serotonin and the possible origins of the disorders. How strong are the logical links? What other sorts of evidence might you look for?

An alternative class of anti-anxiety drugs is beta-blockers. These counter the action of neurochemicals like adrenaline and noradrenaline that increase the body's arousal levels. This means that they tackle the rises in blood pressure and heart rate associated with anxiety and so are effective in reducing its physical symptoms.

Recently attention has turned to the use of antidepressants to treat anxiety. These work by preventing the breakdown of serotonin and so causing its levels to build up in the brain. Antidepressants are currently the most common biological treatment for social phobias and OCD.

Surgery

Psychosurgery, or neurosurgery for mental disorder (NMD) as it is now usually called, is a last resort for the treatment of patients suffering from particularly severe cases of various mental disorders, including OCD. It has been defined as 'a surgical procedure for the destruction of brain tissue for the purposes of alleviating specific mental disorders' (Royal College of Psychiatrists, 2000). Patients normally have to meet four conditions before undergoing neurosurgery for OCD:

- a formal DSM diagnosis of OCD
- severe symptoms that are interfering with living a happy, fulfilling life
- other treatments including drugs and psychological therapies have failed
- patients fully understand the procedure and its risks.

There is a number of NMD procedures. Two in particular are used for OCD. These are cingulotomy and capsulotomy. The areas of brain lesioned in each procedure are shown in Figure 9.30.

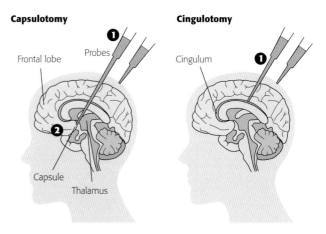

▲ **Figure 9.30** The areas of brain lesioned in capsulotomy and cingulotomy

In both procedures, holes are drilled in the skull and probes inserted. The tips are heated to around 85°C for about a minute and a half, allowing surgeons to burn away small areas of brain. In capsulotomy a small area of a region of the brain called the capsule is targeted, whilst in cingulotomy the target is the cingulate gyrus (see Figure 9.30).

Evaluation of biological treatments for anxiety

Biological treatments can be effective in reducing the symptoms of anxiety disorders. We have already looked at studies by Stein *et al.* (1998) and Benjamin *et al.* (2000) showing that antidepressants are effective in the treatment of social and specific phobias. There is also evidence to suggest that antidepressants help in the treatment of OCD. Hammad (2007) undertook a systematic review of six studies of antidepressants used to treat a total of 718 patients with OCD and found that there was significant overall reduction in symptoms. Neurosurgery also has supporting evidence. We can look at a study by Doughty *et al.* in detail.

Other studies have also found positive results for NMD. Rück *et al.* (2003) followed up 26 patients who had capsulotomy for treatment-resistant anxiety disorders including five suffering from severe social phobia. Overall there were significant reductions in anxiety. Anderson & Booker (2006) estimate that cingulotomy and capsulotomy have a success rate of 50 per cent for OCD. This figure is a little higher in other anxiety disorders, showing that OCD is slightly harder to treat successfully with surgery.

The appropriateness of biological treatments for anxiety disorders is a more complex question. Antidepressants have side effects. In the Hammad (2007) review it was concluded that antidepressants led to a small but detectable increase in suicidal thinking. For specific phobias it is well established that psychological therapies are very effective treatments that do not have the side effects of biological treatments. It is thus very questionable whether drug treatments should ever be used. OCD and social phobias can be treated with psychological therapies, but people vary as to which sort of

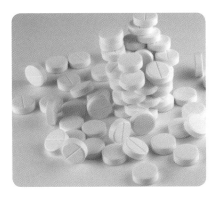

▲ **Figure 9.31** Some people with OCD and social phobias respond better to drugs

treatment works best for them. It is therefore important to have a range of treatments available.

The conditions under which NMD is generally considered appropriate are stated on p216. NMD is very much a last resort as it is associated with serious side effects. In the Ruck *et al.* (2003) study, seven of the 26 patients suffered serious side effects including apathy and reduced IQ. One patient, Mr N, was pleased with the results as he reported immediate relief from anxiety symptoms but he then sat in the same chair reading the same book about cats for several years. He neglected personal hygiene and did not respond to his wife's concern. Kullberg (1977) compared outcomes for cingulotomy and capsulotomy for 10 patients with OCD and 14 with other anxiety disorders. Capsulotomy was more effective at reducing symptoms but most patients who had that procedure suffered some lasting personality change.

Thinking creatively about psychology

Modern studies of NMD typically show better outcomes and fewer side effects than those conducted decades ago. Suggest three possible reasons for this.

RESEARCH NOW

Doughty DD, Baer L, Rees Cosgrove G, Cassem EH, Price BH, Nierenberg AA, Jenike MA & Rauch SL (2002) Prospective long-term follow-up of 44 patients who received cingulotomy for treatment-refractory obsessive-compulsive disorder. *American Journal of Psychiatry* **159**, 269–77

Aim: To assess the success of the cingulotomy procedure for the treatment of OCD patients for whom other treatments had failed.

Procedure: 44 patients (28 men and 16 women) were assessed before and after having cingulotomy for treatment-resistant OCD using standard measures of the severity of OCD symptoms and general functioning. They were followed up for 32 months and assessed regularly.

Findings: For patients who had a single cingulotomy, 15 per cent were judged as improved and 8 per cent partially improved immediately after the procedure. At the most recent follow-up this had improved to 35 per cent and 15 per cent, respectively. For those having two or more operations the outcomes were less good, with 6 per cent judged improved and 11 per cent partially improved immediately after the procedure, rising to 28 per cent and 11 per cent at the latest assessment.

Conclusion: Cingulotomy is moderately effective in treating OCD when all other treatments have failed.

Psychological explanations for anxiety

Behavioural (learning) theory

Although behavioural theory is one of the older approaches to psychology, it is still important in explaining anxiety disorders. You may recall hearing about classical conditioning and phobias at AS level, in particular the case of Little Albert. Recall that classical conditioning takes place when we come to associate something that initially does not produce any response (a neutral stimulus) with something that already produces a response (like anxiety). We now need to consider another type of learning. Operant conditioning takes place when we learn to repeat a behaviour if it has a good consequence and not repeat it if it has a bad result.

Avoidance conditioning

The simplest idea about how people can learn anxiety disorders is the avoidance-conditioning model, based on classical conditioning. In avoidance conditioning, the phobic-stimulus-to-be is paired with another stimulus that already leads to anxiety. What was a neutral stimulus becomes a conditioned stimulus. This is almost certainly how some specific phobias are learnt. The classic study of avoidance conditioning was the case of Little Albert. Early behaviourists Watson & Rayner (1920) paired the neutral stimulus of a white rat with the unconditioned stimulus of a loud noise to make the rat a conditioned stimulus producing a fear response. This study is described in detail in *Exploring Psychology for AS Level*.

The avoidance-conditioning model can also be applied to social phobias. One of the most common social phobias concerns public toilets. A common experience is paruresis – not being able to wee because of the presence of others. Someone who experiences paruresis once and suffers the resulting anxiety may become conditioned to avoid the situation of being in a public toilet. If other people notice and laugh this can be intensified – being laughed at is an unconditioned stimulus and if it is paired with public toilets then toilets will produce the same anxiety response as laughter.

◀ **Figure 9.32**
Public toilets can produce anxiety responses for quite different reasons in sufferers of OCD and social phobias

Avoidance learning is a well-documented phenomenon. However, what is not clear is how commonly it takes place or how many cases of phobia it can account for. Menzies (1996) surveyed patients on the origins of their phobias and the majority cited other reasons. Also, we can develop phobias of things we have never had experiences with (such as snakes). Presumably we cannot have a classical conditioning experience without directly encountering the stimulus.

Operant conditioning

Although classical conditioning remains the most common learning explanation for acquiring phobias, operant conditioning may be important in keeping them going. Every time we persuade someone else to put a spider out for us or manage to get out of a social situation that provokes anxiety, our anxiety levels go down. This reduction of anxiety rewards or reinforces the avoidance behaviour. When we reinforce a behaviour we increase the likelihood of it being repeated, and so the phobic response continues.

OCD can also be explained in terms of operant conditioning. Meyer & Chesser (1970) explained compulsive hand-washing as a way to reduce the anxiety associated with dirt or germs. When the person has a rush of anxiety in relation to dirt or germs and they respond by washing, their anxiety temporarily declines. This reinforces the washing behaviour and so the washing continues. Because in the short term washing is quite effective at reducing anxiety the habit is very hard to break. There is experimental support for this explanation of compulsive behaviour. Hodgson & Rachman (1972) monitored the anxiety levels of a group of OCD sufferers with washing compulsions, then introduced them to some dirty objects, then allowed them to wash. Anxiety rose sharply when the objects were presented but quickly declined once patients were allowed to wash. This shows that compulsive washing is indeed reinforced by a decline in anxiety.

Cognitive theory

A problem with learning theory as an explanation for anxiety disorders is that it doesn't explain why some people are more prone to acquiring anxiety problems than others. This can be explained from a cognitive perspective. The cognitive process of visual attention appears to work somewhat differently in people prone to acquiring phobias. Eysenck (1992) proposed that anxiety disorders are caused or at least maintained by a form of attentional bias. Phobic patients tend to focus their attention more on threatening stimuli than the rest of us do.

Kindt & Brosschot (1997) tested for attentional bias in arachnophobic patients using the Stroop task. In the Stroop procedure, participants have to name the ink colour of each word in a multicoloured word-list. The time taken to name the ink colours of whole lists or individual items is recorded. If people take a particularly long time to name the ink colour of particular words this shows that they could not disengage their attention from that word, and thus shows cognitive bias. In this study arachnophobics took significantly longer to name the ink colours for spider-related words and pictures. This showed that arachnophobia is associated with cognitive bias.

Another cognitive factor is the sort of beliefs people have about phobic stimuli. In an experimental procedure Armfield (2007) manipulated people's beliefs about the danger, predictability and controllability of a spider before asking them to imagine putting their hand in an aquarium with a spider. All the beliefs affected how afraid of spiders the participants were; high levels of danger, unpredictability and uncontrollability were associated with spider phobia. This study is described in detail in *Exploring Psychology for AS Level*.

Psychological treatments for anxiety disorders

Systematic desensitisation

Systematic desensitisation is a behavioural therapy based on the principles of classical conditioning. The aim of systematic desensitisation is to unlearn conditioned responses like phobias. An early example of systematic desensitisation comes from Mary Jones (1924), a student of John Watson (who led the Little Albert study). We can look at this study in *Classic Research*.

Modern desensitisation is slightly more sophisticated than the Jones procedure. It depends on the idea that we cannot be relaxed and afraid at the same time – by definition fear involves a high level of physical arousal. If we can stay relaxed in the presence of the thing we fear, we will no longer fear it. Patients learn in desensitisation that they can remain relaxed in the presence of the thing they fear. Relaxation can be achieved by hypnosis or meditation, or by anxiolytic drugs like Valium. Patients are then exposed to the thing they fear, working

through an anxiety hierarchy. This starts with a form of exposure they feel reasonably comfortable with and building up to the one they most fear. Arachnophobic patients may thus start by being exposed to a small picture of a spider and end up with a Venezuelan tarantula on their face. Once patients successfully remain relaxed with this sort of intense exposure to the object of their phobia they will have learnt not to fear it.

◀ **Figure 9.33**
We can learn to tolerate frightening things if we work up to them

Evaluation of desensitisation

There is plenty of evidence to support the idea that desensitisation helps reduce phobic anxiety. Brosnan & Thorpe (2006) used a 10-week desensitisation programme to help 16 technophobic students (who were afraid of computers) on an information technology course. As compared with a control

---

Jones MC (1924) A laboratory study of fear: the case of Peter. *Pedagogical Seminary* **31, 308–15**

Aim: To apply the work of John Watson on classical conditioning of phobias to treating a phobia of small furry animals in a two-year 10-month-old boy.

Procedure: Peter was described as 'almost Albert gown older' (1924, p30). Like Little Albert, Little Peter feared white rats and rabbits and other white fluffy objects such as a fur coat and cotton wool. He was most afraid of a rabbit so this was used as the phobic stimulus in the study. Initially having the rabbit anywhere in Peter's view would trigger extreme anxiety. When he could tolerate it being in the room it was gradually moved closer (12ft, 4ft, 3ft, touching distance, on his highchair tray). At one point the treatment had to be stopped for a few weeks when Peter suffered scarlet fever. It resumed afterwards. From this point on Peter was given foods he particularly liked when the rabbit was in the room in order to develop a positive association with the rabbit. At the end of the procedure Peter was assessed for fear of other animals.

Findings: Peter's fear at the start of the procedure was extreme but he became able to tolerate the rabbit at increasingly close distances. Following his scarlet fever Peter's level of fear returned to the baseline but on resuming treatment he continued to tolerate the rabbit at increasingly close proximity. At the end of the treatment Peter expressed affection for the rabbit. He was also able to tolerate other animals such as a white rat.

Conclusion: Exposure and association with positive stimuli can be used to desensitise patients from phobic stimuli.

group who had no desensitisation their anxiety levels were significantly lower at the end of the course. Desensitisation has also been applied to social phobia, but with more mixed results. Duff (2007) treated students on a public speaking course with systematic desensitisation, no treatment or a mixed programme of treatments. Although anxiety about public speaking declined throughout the course, there was no advantage to having formal therapy of either type. The participants' anxiety declined with experience anyway.

Thinking critically about psychology

Think about the Duff (2007) study of desensitisation. Why might the findings be described as a two-edged sword for systematic desensitisation?

The appropriateness of systematic desensitisation depends on the trade-off between effectiveness and ethical acceptability. Desensitisation is fairly effective and involves only minimal distress for patients. However, there is a more effective but far more brutal alternative treatment available. In flooding, patients are exposed immediately to an extreme form of the thing they fear. This is more effective than desensitisation and can work in a single session. However, it is traumatic and many patients leave rather than completing the session.

Cognitive behaviour therapy

We introduced cognitive behavioural therapies or CBT in your AS level. In this section we are specifically concerned with the use of CBT to treat phobias and OCD. CBT is now the most commonly used form of psychological therapy, in particular amongst clinical psychologists. It usually takes place once a week or fortnight for between five and 20 sessions. CBT involves helping patients identify irrational and unhelpful thoughts and trying to change them. This may involve drawing diagrams for patients to show them the links between their thinking, behaviour and emotions. The rationale of CBT is that our thoughts affect our feelings and behaviour, so by changing our thoughts we can make ourselves feel better. Some forms of CBT also focus on directly encouraging changes to behaviour.

The aim of CBT in treating anxiety is to challenge and help patients overcome the cognitions that are involved in their symptoms. To treat a spider phobia, for example, a cognitive behavioural therapist might first explore exactly what beliefs patients have about spiders. They might then challenge these beliefs by argument. They might also set patients reality-testing tasks like confronting a spider and showing themselves that they could touch it without harm. Patients might be encouraged to record successful encounters with spiders in a diary so they could be reminded afterwards if they felt negative about their progress. Similar techniques can be applied to treating OCD. Irrational beliefs about the dangers posed by dirt, for example, can be explored and challenged.

Thinking practically about psychology

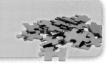

What short of irrational beliefs do you think people might have about dirt and/or spiders? How do you think a therapist might go about challenging such beliefs?

Evaluation of CBT for anxiety

There is considerable support for CBT as an effective treatment for anxiety disorders. For example Butler et al. (2006) reviewed meta-analytic studies of CBT and concluded that it was effective for a range of anxiety disorders including social phobias. Gould et al. (1997) compared the effectiveness of CBT versus drugs for social phobia by putting studies of each into a meta-analysis. They concluded based on this that CBT was significantly more effective. A fascinating recent study suggests that CBT has significant effects on brain functioning. Paquette et al. (2003) scanned the brains of 12 arachnophobic patients when exposed to spiders and found increased activity in three key areas of the brain. They were scanned again following CBT and it was found that all three regions were functioning normally.

CBT is also one of the major treatments for OCD. Van Oppen et al. (2005) compared the effectiveness of CBT alone or with exposure and that of antidepressants. A total of 102 patients who had taken part in random control trials of the three treatments were followed up after five years. All three treatments were associated with long-term reduction in symptoms.

CBT is not associated with the same ethical issues as drugs as it has no biochemical side effects. Nor does it raise the same issues as behavioural treatments like desensitisation do as it does not lead to the same degree of distress. Therefore, for social phobias and OCD, CBT can be seen as an appropriate first line of treatment. For specific phobias, exposure therapies are probably at least as effective and can be quicker. There have been more fundamental objections to CBT, however. Holmes (2002) points out that there are relatively few long-term studies of CBT's effectiveness and that most studies have involved highly selected patients with single symptoms or very simple sets of symptoms. The findings may not generalise well to most real-life settings where patients present with complex sets of symptoms.

KEY TERMS

random control trial a procedure in which patients are randomly allocated to a treatment or control condition and the outcomes compared

LOOKING FURTHER Using specialist search engines like Google Scholar and databases like PubMed, find studies of CBT for the treatment of anxiety disorders. Overall, how effective and appropriate is CBT?

Chapter summary

Classification and diagnosis
- It is customary to classify psychopathology into various categories of mental disorder. Classification forms the basis of diagnosis. The best-known system for classifying and diagnosing mental disorder is the Diagnostic and Statistical Manual of Mental Disorder (DSM).
- Systems for classifying and diagnosing mental disorder need to be reliable (that is, they consistently measure the same thing) and valid (that is, they measure what they set out to measure).

Depression
- Depression is a relatively common set of mental disorders characterised by disruption to mood. Reliability and validity of the diagnosis are reasonably good.
- There is strong evidence of some role for genetic vulnerability and biochemical abnormality in explaining depression.
- Biological treatments include antidepressant drugs and ECT. These are reasonably effective.
- There is also considerable evidence for the importance of psychological factors such as faulty cognition and disrupted early relationships in depression.
- Psychological treatments include CBT and psychodynamic therapies. These are probably at least as effective as biological treatments and do not have the same problems of side effects.

Schizophrenia
- Schizophrenia is a less common condition, affecting around 1 per cent of the population. Reliability of diagnosis is good but there are serious questions around its construct validity.
- There is strong evidence for the role of genetic and biochemical factors in schizophrenia.
- Biological treatments for schizophrenia include antipsychotic drugs and ECT. These are reasonably effective.
- There is also considerable evidence for the role of psychological factors in schizophrenia, including faulty cognition and childhood trauma.
- Schizophrenia can be treated by CBT or psychodynamic therapies, usually alongside biological treatment. There is currently more evidence to support the effectiveness of CBT.

Phobias and OCD
- Anxiety disorders are very common. Reliability of diagnosis is relatively good but some people question whether OCD should be classified as an anxiety problem.
- There is evidence to suggest that genetic factors make some people more vulnerable than others to developing anxiety problems. Genetic factors may impact on biochemical systems in the brain, for example that of the neurotransmitter serotonin.
- Learning experiences and distinctive cognitions including attentional bias and irrational thinking are also associated with anxiety disorders.
- Both biological and psychological treatments are used for anxiety. For simple phobias, exposure such as by systematic desensitisation or flooding are particularly appropriate. For social phobias and OCD, drugs and occasionally even surgery are needed.

 What do I know?

1 (a) Outline the clinical characteristics of schizophrenia, depression or one anxiety disorder. (5 marks)
   (b) Explain the issues associated with the classification and diagnosis of your chosen disorder. (10 marks)
   (c) Outline and evaluate one biological explanation for your chosen disorder. (10 marks)

2 (a) Describe one or more psychological explanations for schizophrenia, depression or one anxiety disorder. (10 marks)
   (b) Outline and evaluate one psychological explanation for your chosen disorder. (15 marks)

3 Outline and evaluate one biological treatment for a mental disorder of your choice. (25 marks)

4 (a) Outline biological explanations of depression, schizophrenia or OCD. (10 marks)
   (b) Outline and evaluate one psychological treatment for the disorder you described in part (a). (15 marks)

CHAPTER 10
Media Psychology

Thinking ahead

By the end of this chapter you should be able to:

- define pro- and antisocial behaviour and briefly outline research into their possible links with the media

- understand alternative explanations for the alleged impact of the media on pro- and antisocial behaviour

- outline and evaluate research into the possible effects of video games and computers on young people

- explain what is meant by persuasion and attitude change, with particular reference to the Hovland-Yale and elaboration likelihood models

- understand the role of attitudes in decision making with particular reference to cognitive dissonance and self-perception

- outline and evaluate explanations for the effectiveness of television as an agent of persuasion

- understand social-psychological and evolutionary explanations for the attraction of celebrity

- outline and evaluate research into intense fandom

Before starting this chapter it is important to be clear what we are talking about. Although we hear about 'the media' everyday, we are generally not particularly precise or consistent in how we use the term. Technically media (the plural of medium) are all the ways in which information can be stored and delivered, including paper, film and digital formats. When we talk of 'the media', however, we usually mean the *mass media*. Mass media can be defined as the use of any medium to communicate information or ideas to the public. The mass media include newspapers, magazines, television, radio, computer games and the internet. In this chapter we are concerned with the social rather than technical aspects of the media so we use 'the media' and 'mass media' interchangeably.

We are an increasingly media-rich society, and for many of us much of our relaxation involves mass media of one sort or another. For some time, watching television has been the main leisure activity in the western world (Kubey *et al.*, 2002). There is, however, also considerable concern that some aspects of the media have quite an unhealthy influence on our social behaviour and even our mental health. It is alleged that the antisocial behaviour shown in some film, television and computer games leads to antisocial behaviour in young people. It is also widely believed that the mass media influence public opinion so strongly that democracy itself is an illusion; that our voting habits are manipulated by those who control the mass media. The high profile of celebrities and the public portrayal of the contrast between their standard of living and that of ordinary people has been linked to the current high rates of depression. It is with issues like these that we are concerned in this chapter.

Pro- and antisocial behaviour

Some of the most important debates in media psychology concern the power of mass media to alter social behaviour, in particular amongst children and young people. It has been suggested that both pro- and antisocial behaviour are subject to media influence. By *'pro-social' behaviour* we mean any action that benefits someone else but which does not lead to an obvious reward to the actor. Pro-social acts include helping others in need, comforting those in distress, sharing resources and including others in group activities. *Antisocial behaviour* is very much the reverse. In everyday speech antisocial behaviour is used loosely to include littering, graffiti etc. Usually when we speak of antisocial behaviour in psychology we mean aggressive behaviour – that is, any action designed to harm another person or people.

The media and antisocial behaviour

The vast majority of studies of the effects of media-viewing on behaviour have concerned antisocial behaviour. Specifically, many psychologists as well as politicians and the controllers of the mass media themselves worry that children may become more aggressive as a consequence of witnessing aggression. Concern about media violence is nothing new. However, at present there are perhaps particularly good reasons to worry. Films and

television are getting more violent, including that intended for an audience of children. Wilson *et al.* (2002) counted 14 violent acts an hour in children's television as opposed to fewer than four in adult TV. Children are also increasingly exposed to violent programmes designed for an adult audience. For example, *The Professionals*, which was shown after the 9pm watershed when it was made 30 years ago, is now shown in the morning,

▲ **Figure 10.1** *The Professionals* was intended for after the 9pm watershed but is now part of daytime TV

including the school holidays! Films like *Saw* and *Hostel*, which feature graphic and extended torture, are highly fashionable. Consider as well the fact that children are spending more time indoors than those of any previous generation (largely due to parents' fears for their safety) and they therefore tend to watch more television.

Research into the possible effect of witnessing aggression in the mass media on antisocial behaviour in viewers began in the early 1960s. In a series of experiments Albert Bandura and colleagues showed that under certain circumstances children tend to imitate aggression displayed by an adult. In one study in particular the effect of witnessing filmed aggression was tested. We examine this in detail in *Classic Research*.

Thinking critically about psychology

Consider the Bandura, Ross & Ross (1963) study. In particular:

1 How were the four conditions matched to control for confounding variables?
2 How good is the sample size once we take into account the number of conditions?
3 How well was cartoon violence simulated in the third experimental condition?
4 Why was an independent measures design used and what problems can this cause?

CLASSIC RESEARCH

Bandura A, Ross D & Ross S (1963) Imitation of film-mediated aggressive models. *Journal of Abnormal and Social Psychology 66, 3–11*

Aim: To test whether observing a model behaving aggressively on film would have the same effect on children's aggressive behaviour as observing the same behaviour by a live adult.

Procedure: 48 boys and 48 girls aged 35–69 months were divided into four groups, each containing 12 boys and 12 girls. One group served as a control group and did not witness aggression. The other three groups witnessed aggressive behaviour. One group joined an adult in a play room and watched them attack an inflatable 'Bobo' doll. The second experimental group watched a film in which the same adults performed the same violent actions towards the inflatable doll. The third condition was meant to simulate cartoon violence. A film of the same female adult displaying the same aggressive behaviour was shown, but this time she wore a catsuit and the background contained brightly coloured artificial grass, trees, birds etc. After watching the aggressive behaviour the children were individually frustrated by being introduced to attractive toys then having them removed. They were then left with a selection of toys including the Bobo doll. Their aggression towards the Bobo doll was rated by observers watching through a two-way mirror.

Findings: The mean number of total aggressive acts against the Bobo doll was higher in the three experimental conditions (83, 92 and 99 respectively) than in the control condition (54 acts). Aggression was actually slightly higher in the filmed conditions, although children who had watched the live aggression imitated the precise nature of the violence more closely.

Conclusions: Children imitate filmed aggression in a similar way to that in which they imitate aggression witnessed live.

▲ **Figure 10.2** Bandura *et al.*'s model displaying aggression and children imitating it

The major problem of course with laboratory experiments like Bandura *et al.*'s is that they only demonstrate short-term effects in artificial environments. On their own they tell us little about long-term effects in real life. We would therefore be unwise to accept as fact the link between media violence and children's aggression based on this evidence alone. Bandura *et al.*'s research into the effects of media violence has given rise to a number of lines of research. Interestingly, much but not all of this has supported the conclusion that children are influenced by witnessing media violence.

A way to get around the short-term outcomes in laboratory experiments is to conduct longitudinal studies which follow up children over long periods. Eron & Huesmann (1986) followed up 875 children from seven to eight years old until the age of 30, looking at the relationship between violence in programmes watched in middle childhood and probability of conviction for a violent crime by 30. Indeed a positive correlation was found, supporting the idea that watching violent television is associated with a long-term increase in physical aggression. However, there are problems with studies like this. First, many of the original participants were no longer part of the study by the end, and we don't know how representative those that were left were. Also, it is possible that the children who watched lots of violent television at the start of the study were already different in some way from those who did not. Remember this was not set up as an experiment so there was no way of setting up matched high and low violent television groups. We should be cautious therefore about saying that the violent TV watching in childhood *caused* the adult violent crime.

◀ **Figure 10.3** Adult violent criminals tend to have watched violent media as children but this does not necessarily mean that one caused the other

Other researchers have aimed to get around the artificial nature of laboratory research by conducting studies in real-life situations. Charlton *et al.* (2000) followed up the introduction of television to the island of St Helena in 1995. This was an excellent opportunity to observe any changes in behaviour resulting from television because the island went overnight from having no television at all to having multiple satellite channels showing a variety of programmes – including more violence than we see in the UK. Video cameras were set up in school playgrounds and children aged three to eight were filmed before and after the introduction of the television. No change in children's behaviour was recorded. This type of study poses a serious challenge to the assumption that violent television has an effect on children's aggression.

LOOKING FURTHER Do some internet research using both your favourite search engine and some of the specialist tools we have already recommended, perhaps *Google Scholar* or *PubMed*. Save or bookmark all the studies you can find investigating the link between media violence and aggression.

1 Do the bulk of studies support the media violence–aggression link?
2 How convincing do you personally find the studies on each side of the debate?
3 What biases do you have in this matter and what biases do you think might affect researchers?

The media and pro-social behaviour

A much smaller body of research has supported the idea that children can be influenced to show increased pro-social behaviour by the media. Although clearly the mass media contain many instances of antisocial behaviour, pro-social behaviour is also shown fairly frequently. Smith *et al.* (2006) analysed the content of 18 American television channels for one week. They found that 73 per cent of programmes featured some pro-social behaviour. Some children's programmes, notably *Sesame Street*, feature storylines explicitly designed to foster pro-social behaviour linked to current events such as floods or earthquakes (Wilson, 2008).

▲ **Figure 10.4** *Sesame Street* demonstrates pro-social behaviour

But how do children respond to pro-social messages? Calvert & Kotler (2003) asked primary school children to visit their website and report what they had learned from watching their favourite television programmes. Children, in particular girls, tended to report more social-emotional learning than factual learning. For example, they identified learning about respect, sharing and overcoming fears. Although this study does not directly measure the children's social behaviour it at least shows that children can learn *about* pro-social behaviour from the mass media. Other studies have looked at television viewing and various measures of pro-social behaviour. Mares & Woodard (2005) carried out a *meta-analysis* of 34 studies attempting to link television viewing and development of pro-social behaviour. They found a weak overall positive effect. The strongest link was with helping behaviour.

An example of an experiment demonstrating increased helping behaviour comes from Sprafkin *et al.* (1975). They showed infant school children either an of *Lassie* in which a main character rescues a puppy, a neutral *Lassie* episode or a neutral programme. They then presented the children with distressed puppies and those children who had seen the puppy-rescue episode were rated by observers as more helpful to the puppies themselves. Like physical aggression, helping behaviour is clearly observable behaviour and so it is readily imitated. This is consistent with a social learning explanation for acquiring pro-social behaviour.

◀ **Figure 10.5** Lassie's puppies. Modelling the rescuing of puppies led to children being more helpful to distressed puppies

Explanations for the link between the media and pro- and antisocial behaviour

There is clearly some evidence to suggest a link between what children watch and their later pro- and antisocial behaviour. Setting aside for a moment the limitations of this evidence and the arguments against it, let us look at why such a link might exist.

Social learning theory

Bandura (1977) proposed social learning theory (or SLT) to explain how social behaviour, including aggression, is acquired. The essential principle of social learning theory is that children learn social behaviours by imitating other individuals. However, children do not imitate everything they see. According to SLT ,children imitate behaviour when four conditions are met. First they must observe another individual, called a *model*, carry it out. Second, they then have to remember the behaviour and, third, they need the opportunity to reproduce it. Finally, there must be a motivation to reproduce the behaviour. This motive can be supplied when the model is observed being rewarded in some way. For example, the behaviour may be observed to help the model achieve a goal. This sort of observed reward is known as *vicarious reinforcement*.

Children are also selective about *whose* behaviour they imitate. Models can be parents, siblings, peers or media characters, but regardless of their relationship with the child, children are more likely to imitate those with whom they identify – people who they would like to become like. This means that models who are attractive, have high status and who are the same sex as the observer are most likely to be imitated.

Social learning and antisocial behaviour

SLT predicts that children will imitate attractive, high-status media characters of the same sex who are seen to be rewarded for their behaviour. This is certainly supported by studies like those of Bandura and colleagues. Boys imitated men more than they did women, and girls imitated women more than they did men. In variations on their procedure,

Bandura's team showed that aggression was enhanced when the *model* was visibly rewarded for attacking the Bobo doll.

SLT is also helpful in predicting when media violence is *not* likely to cause problems. In 1983 the Margaret Thatcher government banned a number of 'video nasties'. One scene of particular concern featured a woman (possessed at the time by a demon) stabbing a friend in the ankle with a pencil.

Actually there were no copycat ankle stabbings, and in the light of social learning theory this should come as no surprise! Boys, who account for most physical aggression, would be unlikely to imitate a female model. Also, she didn't have a happy time for the rest of the film following the stabbing, so there was no vicarious reinforcement.

◀ **Figure 10.6** *Evil Dead was banned as a 'video nasty'*

Social learning and pro-social behaviour

Children certainly reproduce pro-social behaviour they have seen in the same way as they do antisocial behaviour. Recall the meta-analysis by Mares & Woodard (2005). The strongest link between observed pro-social behaviour and repeating of that behaviour was in helping. Recall also the Sprafkin *et al.* (1975) *Lassie* study. The simplest explanation for their results is that the children imitated the modelled behaviour.

There is also evidence to show that children selectively imitate pro-social behaviour in same-sex models. Ostrov *et al.* (2006) assessed violent and educational TV viewing in 76 three- to four-year-old children by questioning their parents. They followed them up for two years measuring both pro- and antisocial behaviour by means of observations. Viewing violent programmes was associated with later physical aggression. Viewing educational media designed to demonstrate pro-social behaviour was associated with higher frequency of pro-social behaviour. The fact that children selectively imitated same-sex models in this study is also very much in line with social learning theory.

KEY TERMS

model someone whose behaviour is observed and imitated

vicarious reinforcement witnessing a model being rewarded for a behaviour

meta-analysis a mathematical procedure in which the results of several studies are combined and analysed together

Sensitisation and desensitisation

An alternative explanation for the link between viewing pro- and antisocial behaviour and repeating it lies in the effect of viewing on our sensitivity to the suffering of others. It has been suggested that repeated exposure to violence leaves us less sensitive to the state of victims. It has also been suggested that exposure to pro-social behaviour towards people who are suffering has the reverse effect – to make us more sensitive to human suffering.

Desensitisation and antisocial behaviour

Anderson *et al.* (2003) define desensitisation as 'a reduction in distress-related physiological reactivity to observations or thoughts of violence' (2003, p96). One of the reasons we are not more aggressive than we are is because we experience an unpleasant emotional response to seeing people hurt. This is part of our capacity for empathy, the ability to pick up and respond to the emotional states of others. Our empathy for people in pain inhibits us from acting aggressively. In other words, if you were to punch me on the nose you would probably feel really bad about it and not want to do it again. You might even not be able to hit me in the first place, anticipating your own negative emotional response. However, if you had seen enough bleeding noses (either in the flesh or on television), this response would probable have become dulled and you wouldn't feel inhibited in the same way. Films like *Saw* and *Hostel*, which feature extended and graphic torture scenes, may cause particular problems of desensitisation.

◀ **Figure** 10.7
A sexualised torture scene from *Hostel Part II*

The effects of viewing media violence on response to witnessing violence have been investigated in a number of laboratory experiments. Cline *et al.* (1973) exposed children and adults to mild scenes of violence and measured their arousal level. Arousal declined over time, and the more violence participants watched the less arousal response they showed when presented with a new scene of violence. In another experiment by Drabman & Thomas (1974), children aged eight to 10 years were shown a video then placed in a situation where they saw younger children apparently fighting. Those who had seen a violent video took significantly longer to break up the fight. Both these studies, one measuring sensitivity by physiological arousal and the other by behaviour, suggest that children were desensitised by viewing violent material.

Another line of research into the desensitising effect of media violence on adults involves exposure to violent

Thinking creatively about psychology

Design a study to assess whether a sadistic film of your choice leads to desensitisation (but for ethical reasons don't carry it out). You will need to think in particular about how you will assess desensitisation.

pornography – that is, sexually explicit material with themes of violence, rape and torture. Mullin & Linz (1995) questioned adult males about their response to sexual and domestic violence, and then showed them violent pornography. Three days later their attitudes were assessed again and they showed significantly less empathy with female victims of violence. However, two days later their attitudes had returned to the same level as at the start of the study. Studies like this suggest that desensitisation does occur but leave it unclear whether it can have a long-term effect.

Thinking critically about psychology

Studies like that of Mullin & Linz (1995) are often cited as evidence to suggest that pornography should be banned. How strong do you think this argument is?

LOOKING FURTHER Go to www.pubmed.gov **only** (do not use a search engine for this!). Input 'pornography' as a search term and you will find a number of studies into the link between viewing pornography and sexual aggression. What conclusions can you reach?

Sensitisation and pro-social behaviour

Wilson (2008) suggests that the development of empathy is a fundamental part of children's social-emotional development, and that children have numerous opportunities for such learning in media viewing (Smith *et al.*, 2006). Highly empathic children are known to engage in more frequent pro-social acts. We also know that children can empathise with characters portrayed on television, particularly if they are the same sex and if the story is realistic (Wilson, 2008). Putting these facts together it is logical to propose that watching well portrayed emotions and pro-social behaviour in response to them may help develop children's empathy – that is, to sensitise them. Sensitisation provides an alternative explanation for the results of Sprafkin *et al.*'s (1975) *Lassie* study. Rather than imitating the helping behaviour seen in the episode, the children may have been sensitised to the suffering of puppies by watching it. They then felt more empathy when presented with suffering puppies themselves.

The main limitation of sensitisation as an explanation for the impact of the media on pro-social behaviour is that it lacks direct evidence. There is a lack of studies demonstrating that exposure to pro-social behaviour in the media directly leads to higher levels of empathy in children. However, there is some evidence to suggest such an effect in adults. Shelton & Rogers (2006) showed participants video of industrial whaling and footage of (pro-social) anti-whaling environmental action. They found that this had the effect of enhancing empathy for whales. However, studies like this are quite far removed from the situation psychologists are most concerned with – whether the media can be used to develop long-term patterns of pro-social behaviour in children and young people.

▲ **Figure 10.8** Images like this may enhance our empathy for whales

The effects of video games and computers on young people

In the past decade 'the media' has ceased to mean just film, television and radio and increasingly also means computer technology. Computer use may have slightly different effects on human behaviour because it is a much more active process than simply viewing, as is often the case with film and television. Psychologists have turned their attention to studying the effects of computer use, in particular on the social development of young people.

Computer games and antisocial behaviour

If there is good reason to be concerned about the effects of violent film and television on antisocial behaviour then this is perhaps more the case for violent computer games. Most non-gamers would probably be surprised by just how violent some popular games now are. Haninger & Thompson (2004) analysed the content of computer games rated as suitable for teenagers in the USA. Ninety-eight per cent of games sampled required the player to be violent; 90 per cent required them to injure and 69 per cent to kill, while 42 per cent showed victims' blood. A glance at the best-selling games for X-Box in the week of writing this chapter (November 2008) shows that seven of the top 10 games have overtly violent themes. Apart from the sheer level of violence depicted in many video games, a further problem is the active role players take. Rather than simply watching, gamers actually participate in violent acts, albeit in virtual space.

▶ **Figure 10.9**

At first, the evidence linking violent game-playing with real-life violence was in the form of informal case examples. For instance, many commentators were quick to point out that the two teenage boys who carried out the Columbine High School massacre in the USA in 1999 had spent many hours playing violent video games. This type of evidence on its own is a very limited basis for linking gaming and aggression.

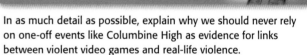

Thinking critically about psychology

In as much detail as possible, explain why we should never rely on one-off events like Columbine High as evidence for links between violent video games and real-life violence.

Although the volume of research into the effects of violent games is much smaller than that concerned with film and television, the existing studies paint a worrying picture. Hopf *et al.* (2008) carried out a two-year longitudinal study on German teenagers, looking at both watching of violent films and playing violent games as predictors of violent crime at age 14. Both factors did predict involvement in violent crime but the stronger relationship was with violent video games. Research also supports a role for both social learning and desensitisation in the link between playing violent games and aggressive behaviours. Konijn *et al.* (2007) demonstrated the role of identification with character, see *Research Now*, p229.

If identification and imitation have a role in explaining how violent video games link to real-life aggression then so might desensitisation. Staude-Muller *et al.* (2008) conducted an experiment in which 42 men played either a high- or low-violence version of a 'first-person shooter' game – that is, one in which the player takes the role of shooter. Participants then watched aggressive and generally unpleasant images whilst their heart rate and galvanic skin response were monitored. Those who had played the violent version of the game reacted

no points. Of the 24 people who had played the non-violent *Doom* only one chose not to co-operate but seven people in the violent condition did so. This suggests strongly that the participation in the violent game reduced the tendency to co-operate and share rewards.

Thinking practically about psychology

What do these studies of identification and desensitisation suggest we should do about violent video games?

Carry out a content analysis on one or more violent video games. You will need to draw up a list of aggressive behaviours, decide on a sampling procedure and record the frequency of the aggressive acts you are concerned with.

▲ **Figure 10.10** Eric Harris and Dylan Klebold carried out the Columbine High School massacre after playing violent games. But is this really evidence to suggest that games *cause* violence?

less to the pictures, showing that, at least in the short term, they had been desensitised.

Violent video games also appear to reduce pro-social behaviour. Sheese & Graziano (2005) randomly allocated undergraduate students to either a violent or non-violent version of *Doom* (a multi-user game) in pairs. They were told they were competing with other participants but not each other. After the game the pairs were separated and each person was given a choice of whether to pool scores with their partner or keep them separate. If both partners opted to co-operate their combined score was multiplied by 1.5. If both chose to separate each lost half their points. If one opted to separate while the former partner opted to co-operate they would have their score doubled and the partner would receive

◀ **Figure 10.11** Fighting in *Doom* reduces co-operation, at least in the short term

---

RESEARCH NOW

Konijn EA, Bijvank MN & Bushman BJ (2007) I wish I were a warrior: the role of wishful identification in the effects of violent video games on aggression in adolescent boys. *Developmental Psychology* 43, 1038–44

Aim: To test whether aggression following playing violent video games was greater when the player identified strongly with the game aggressor.

Procedure: 112 Dutch boys aged 12–16 years were randomly allocated to three conditions. In one condition they played a realistic violent video game (*America's Army*, *Killzone* or *Max Paine*). In a second condition they played a violent fantasy game. In a control condition they played a non-violent game. After 20 minutes of playing they took part in a reaction-time procedure and were told they were playing against an unseen partner. They were also told that the winner of this competition would get to deliver a blast of noise on a 1–10 scale where 8–10 risked permanent damage to hearing. There was no opponent and all were told they had won. Aggression was measured by the noise level they chose to give. To measure how strongly the boys identified with the game character they were asked to rate on a four-point scale their response to the statement 'I wish I were a character such as the one in the game'.

Findings: As expected, boys who had taken part in the realistic violent games averaged the highest level of noise. Within this group the boys who had identified most strongly with the aggressor gave significantly higher noise levels than less identified individuals.

Conclusion: Young people who play violent video games and who identify strongly with violent characters are more aggressive following the game.

Thinking practically about psychology

Explain how social learning and desensitisation could explain the effects of violent video games.

Thinking creatively about psychology

Put together a leaflet or web page to communicate to parents the potential dangers of letting children play violent video games.

LOOKING FURTHER Using resources like *PubMed* or *Google Scholar* find more studies of the effects of violent games. Do they paint the same negative picture as the studies featured here?

Social interaction by computer

Wilson (2008) has estimated that for the first time children and young people are now having *most* of their social experiences via electronic media rather than face to face. Between texting, email, instant messaging and use of social networking sites we can now have rich communication without face-to-face meeting. There is perhaps the potential for all this electronic communication to have both positive and negative effects on the development of children and young people. On the positive side Meskin *et al.* (1997) report that electronic communication has opened up a much richer social life to young people who are limited in their physical communication by disability. In addition, vulnerable groups can take advantage of online peer support without exposing themselves as they would disclosing details about themselves in conventional social interaction. Moreover, the sheer number of social contacts one can have and the frequency of communication is greater than in conventional face-to-face communication. On the other hand, electronic communication does not allow the same degree of non-verbal communication as does face-to-face communication, and there is so much opportunity to control what impressions others have of us in cyberspace that a degree of honesty is perhaps lost (Kramer, 2008). Also (to old farts like us anyway) it is unclear whether electronic communication can satisfy human social needs in the same way as face-to-face communication does.

Recent research into the nature and possible downsides of social interaction via a computer has centred on the use of social networking websites. Raacke & Raacke (2008) surveyed American university students to get an idea of just how popular electronic social networking is. They found that the vast majority of students spend substantial time every day using networking sites, both to make new friends and keep in touch with existing ones. No gender differences were found and a wide range of ethnic groups appeared to use social networking in the same way. There is thus no question of the importance of social networking, but can it cause problems?

◀ **Figure 10.12** Can Facebook satisfy human social needs?

OVER TO YOU Carry out a survey of social networking in your school or college. Test a specific hypothesis. You might, for example, be interested in whether boys and girls use networking sites in the same way, or you could test how popular different sites are and why people choose a particular site.

One limitation of online social networking may be that it primarily benefits those who are already extrovert and skilled at impression management. This is in contrast to early findings from the 1990s showing that vulnerable groups made particularly good use of the internet for social support. It may now be that 'cool' people dominate online networking in the same way as they do face-to-face social life. Sheldon (2008) surveyed 172 American university students about their use of Facebook. It emerged that those who were inhibited in face-to-face contact due to shyness or introversion did use Facebook but in a slightly different way from more outgoing students. They had fewer Facebook friends and were less likely to form relationships online. In contrast, other students in this group were more likely to use Facebook just to pass time or to stave off feelings of loneliness.

A particularly worrying phenomenon that may be linked to social networking is *suicide contagion*. Suicide contagion was identified long before online social networking. The US Center for Disease Control and Prevention defined suicide contagion as 'a process by which exposure to the suicide or suicidal behaviour of one or more persons influences others to commit or attempt suicide' (CDCP, 1994). Adolescents are believed to be particularly vulnerable to suicide contagion. Factors including media attention, imitation of role models and glorification of the deceased may all contribute to suicide contagion. All of these can take place via social networking sites (Hacker, 2008).

KEY TERM

suicide contagion the phenomenon in which one suicide increases the chances of more suicides in the same area

Suicide: a teen's way to instant fame

Kathy Brewis, *The Sunday Times*, **27 January 2008**

Suicide is far from painless, both for the people who do it and for the ones they leave behind. The cluster of seven suicides in Bridgend, south Wales, has left scores of grieving relatives and friends and the rest of us stunned at the thought that these young people – some pictured partying just days earlier – could take their own lives.

Already two other teenagers have tried to end their lives and 12 pupils at a comprehensive school are on suicide watch. Danielle, a 16-year-old in a white tracksuit, says: 'Kids round here have been drinking, smoking dope, taking ecstasy and having sex since they were 13 or 14. By the time they reach my age they've done everything. The combination of booze, drugs and the boredom of living around here screws young people up so much that they think killing themselves will be exciting.'

What makes a teenager turn to suicide? There are no easy answers and cases vary – one youngster might kill himself apparently out of the blue while another talks about it obsessively for months beforehand. But there are common factors. 'A suicidal teenager feels hopeless. They often feel no one cares about them, perhaps even that it would be better for everybody if they weren't there. If a young person is feeling suicidal they must confront that head-on and seek help.'

Even the general social networking sites like Bebo – which millions of British teenagers use – can play a part. Three of the Bridgend suicides – Zachary Barnes, Liam Clarke and Natasha Randall – all shared friends on Bebo. Randall posted a message to Liam following his death whose almost jokey tone reflects the slight unreality that often attaches to online behaviour: 'RIP Clarky boy!! gonna miss ya! allways remember the good times! love ya x'. Randall's site – perhaps typical of many teenagers' – featured sex quizzes and pictures of herself in revealing outfits.

Online 'memorials', eerily reminiscent of the flowers and cards left at roadside accident sites by friends and strangers alike, are now commonplace. Randall's suicide attracted hundreds of comments before her profile was taken down on Wednesday, most of which made reference to her looks and praised her. Even the negative comments alluded to the attention she was receiving after her death. 'Chrissie' wrote: 'R.I.P Like … But why? … Isit Tru She Wanted More Bebo Views? Hope Your Lookin Down On Your Family and Friends. They Must Be In Peices Because Of Youu … No Need Too Do Somethin Soo Selfish.'

It's too simple to blame the internet for a phenomenon that, according to Loren Coleman, author of the book *Suicide Clusters*, has ebbed and flowed throughout the centuries and is often linked to complex social factors. In the depression of the 1930s, he points out, Americans blamed comic books for suicides plainly linked to economic deprivation. Today, says Coleman, 'it's not video games, it's not the media, it's not television. It's part of the human condition'.

It is an unpalatable but undeniable fact that death attracts attention. 'Reality TV means young people are constantly bombarded with instant fame and instant success. A young person in a deprived area sees this and it's psychologically destructive. They think: if I'm a nobody but I commit suicide, I'll be a somebody. I'll get my photo in the papers, I'll have a memorial on the internet. How can I be a celebrity? Well, if I don't get onto *Big Brother*, an alternative is death. My friends are doing it.'

1 How credible do you think the link between social networking and suicide contagion is?

2 What other aspect of the media may play a role here?

Persuasion, attitude and change

Numerous people and organisations use the media to persuade us to do things and to try to change our attitudes, opinions and behaviours. Most obviously, advertisers try to influence us to choose their products, whilst politicians seek to influence our voting patterns. Many groups, including the religious and the political, try to influence our social and moral behaviour. Others focus on changing our health-related behaviour. It is important to understand how these processes work, in order to make important campaigns, such as those promoting public health, more effective. Ultimately, if the mass media become successful enough at manipulating our attitudes and persuading us to alter our behaviour, then democracy and even our free will will disappear. It is therefore also important to understand the role of media in persuasion and attitude change to clarify the limits we should place on the media.

◀ **Figure 10.13** The mass media certainly believe in their power to persuade!

Understanding the terms

Aronson *et al.* (1994) has defined an attitude as 'an enduring evaluation – positive or negative – of people, objects and ideas' (1994, p287). We can pick out a couple of important features of attitudes from this definition. First, attitudes tend to remain the same unless something happens to change them. Once we have a firm attitude we are likely to stick with it. Second, attitudes involve making judgements. Our attitudes towards anything thus tend to be positive or negative rather than neutral. Persuasion is the process of actively and deliberately guiding people towards adopting a particular attitude or behaviour. It may involve changing an existing attitude or simply instilling an attitude in someone who was once neutral on an issue. Persuasion can be described as *manipulation* where it is judged to be unfair and purely for the benefit of the persuader and at a cost to the persuaded.

The Hovland–Yale model of persuasive communication

In the 1950s Carl Hovland and colleagues at Yale University proposed a model for changing attitudes by means of persuasion. This involves five stages of persuasion and five factors affecting the effectiveness of persuasion. The stages can be seen in Figure 10.14.

▼ **Figure 10.14** The stages of the original Hovland-Yale model

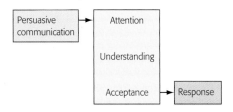

Before we can be persuaded there must first be a message. This can be in the form of an advert, article, party political broadcast or a rant by a media personality. Before it can have any effect on us it must grab our attention. Highly visual media such as television and the internet are at an advantage here because vision is our dominant sense. We must then understand the message. Finally it must be accepted. Acceptance of the message is not the same as attitude change but is a necessary part of it. Following television adverts to save energy, for example, we might first accept that we are required to turn lights out, then perhaps later change our attitude to wasted energy. A later version of the model (McGuire, 1968) changed the later stages as follows:

▼ **Figure 10.15** The stages of the later Hovland-Yale model

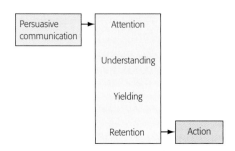

Initially we yield to persuasion (that is, we are persuaded) and retention (the persuasion leads to a long-term change in belief). A change in behaviour (action) requires retention.

The Hovland-Yale model also addresses what factors influence the acceptance of persuasive messages.

1   The **communicator** – the role and intentions of the person doing the persuading. An expert without an obvious agenda or arguing against their own interests has more credibility than an obvious salesperson. Attractive and likeable people may also be more persuasive.

2   The **content** – the appeals and arguments used. Fear can be persuasive provided that there is a credible case for an unpleasant event really being avoided if the argument is acted on. One-sided arguments work best where there is no opposing argument, but where the arguments are obvious it can be more persuasive to acknowledge both sides of the argument.

3   The **media characteristics** – whether the message is verbal or in the form of images, song etc. If the message is simple (for example, buy Matt's dodgy washing powder) a visual medium might be best; however if the message is complex and the main difficulty is at the understanding stage, a written medium is perhaps best.

4   The **situational surroundings** – pleasant or unpleasant aspects of the physical and social environment. Messages can be most persuasive when there are enough distractions to prevent us working out counter-arguments (such as when the door-to-door salesman catches us at a busy moment).

5   The **characteristics of the person** receiving the message – how easy the individual is to persuade. Self-esteem may be important here, people with lower self-esteem being easier to persuade.

▲ **Figure 10.16** Because estate agents clearly have a vested interest in selling houses, people tend to be distrustful and so they need to appear expert and likeable

Discussion of the Hovland-Yale model

The Hovland-Yale model was based on sound experimental research and there is plenty of evidence from the time to support several aspects of the model. Perhaps the most basic idea in the model is that people must attend to a message before they can be persuaded by it. Andreoli & Worchel (1978) compared the effectiveness of radio vs television adverts and found that people paid more attention to TV adverts; presumably having images as well as words is more effective at grabbing our attention. The model also has much to teach us in practical terms about how to go about persuading people. However, later research has identified some additional factors not mentioned in the model.

Kenton (1989) pointed out that even when matched for expertise and trustworthiness male speakers are judged as more persuasive than female. Howard (1997) found that the familiarity of messages is an important characteristic affecting the persuasiveness of an argument. Participants found familiar phrases like 'don't bury your head in the sand' more persuasive than unfamiliar ones conveying the same message, for example 'don't pretend a problem doesn't exist'. Later research has not generally supported the idea that people with lower self-esteem are easier to persuade; however another personality characteristic, self-monitoring, may be important. Those high in self-monitoring (that is, people who monitor their own behaviour very closely in relation to the social situation) appear to be especially impressed when the person delivering a message has status, attractiveness and popularity.

Thinking practically about psychology

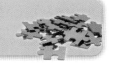

Imagine you are running for the role of student president at your school, college or university. Put together some strategies to impress your public and gain votes based on the Hovland-Yale model.

The elaboration likelihood model

Although the Hovland-Yale model has proved useful in identifying some of the factors and processes involved in persuasion, it is incomplete. In particular it leaves us with a question: under what circumstances should we stress the argument itself, and when should we go to more effort to get the credibility and attractiveness of the persuader just right? These are called central factors (the logic and power of the argument) and peripheral factors (all the other factors affecting whether the argument is accepted). Petty & Cacioppo (1986) tried to answer this question with their elaboration likelihood model.

The central idea behind the elaboration likelihood model is that there are two ways in which persuasion can lead to attitude change:

- The **central route** – people can be persuaded by the logic of an argument.
- The **peripheral route** – people can also be more persuaded by peripheral details such as the nature of the communicator.

The central route involves *elaborating* the argument. By this we mean listening carefully to and thinking deeply about the argument, in other words deeply processing it. This is how we respond to arguments under perfect conditions – that is, when we are motivated to think deeply about the details of the argument and when we have time to pay careful attention. When we are not so interested in the argument, or when we are distracted, we become less concerned with the argument itself and whether we are persuaded or not depends more on peripheral factors.

Discussion of the elaboration likelihood model

There is evidence to support the model. Petty *et al.* (1981) carried out an experiment on undergraduate students in order to test the idea that people will be influenced more by the argument when they are motivated to pay close attention to it – that is, when it is directly relevant to them. Participants listened to a speech on the case for a new exam that all students had to pass. Half the participants heard strong logical arguments, for example that the quality of teaching was improved by such exams. The remainder heard much weaker arguments, for example that students would enjoy the challenge of risking failure. Half the students heard the speech from a high school student and half from an eminent professor. Half were told that the exam might be implemented in their year (high motivation) and half were told it was being considered for some time in the future (low motivation). In keeping with the model, the students in the high motivation condition made their judgements based on the argument whereas those in the low motivation condition were more persuaded by who gave the talk. Yang *et al.* (2006) have applied the elaboration likelihood model to internet shopping. Internet traders have particular problems gaining trust from shoppers. The elaboration likelihood model may give 'e-tailers' a way to persuade shoppers to trust them. We can look at a study of this in *Research Now*.

RESEARCH NOW

Yang S, Hung W, Sung K & Farn C (2006) Investigating initial trust towards e-tailers from the elaboration likelihood model perspective. *Psychology and Marketing* **23,** 429–45

Aim: To test whether participants' trust of websites could be explained in terms of central and peripheral routes to persuasion. Specifically it was hypothesised that participants highly involved with the product and low in anxiety would take a central route whereas more anxious and less involved people would be more persuaded by peripheral factors.

Procedure: 160 participants took part in a laboratory procedure. They were assessed for general levels of anxiety and interest in webcams and told they were evaluating a website selling webcams. In different conditions they saw slightly different versions of the website in which the quality of information about the cameras was high or low (the central route) and peripheral information about the trustworthiness of the site was also either high or low (the peripheral route), manipulated by the presence or absence of a range of certificates on the site. After viewing the site, participants were given a questionnaire to assess how persuasive they found the website.

Findings: Participants low in anxiety and highly interested in webcams were most influenced by the quality of information on the website – that is, they took the central route to persuasion. Those high in anxiety and low in product-interest were less persuaded by this central route to trust the site but were more influenced by the presence of certificates guaranteeing the trustworthiness of the site (the peripheral route).

Conclusion: The elaboration likelihood model provides a way of understanding what sort of customers will be influenced to trust commercial websites by particular types of information.

▼ **Figure 10.17** Students think much harder about debates on exams when they might be taking them!

Theories of attitudes and decision-making

Cognitive dissonance

Cognitive dissonance is the unpleasant sensation we experience when an attitude we already have comes into conflict with a new situation or information. For example, we might believe that our current level of alcohol consumption is safe, or that our current shampoo is great at getting rid of dandruff. We might then encounter a media campaign by the authorities to highlight the risks of drinking too much or an advertising campaign by a different shampoo manufacturer. The existing attitude and behaviour and the cognitions brought about by the new information are not compatible, and so we would probably experience dissonance. We can deal with this dissonance in one of two ways. We could change our attitude and behaviour, for example cut down on the beer or change our brand of shampoo. We might, however, use one of a number of possible *rationalisations* to avoid changing our attitude. We could for example tell ourselves that cutting down our alcohol intake would be too difficult or that the stress of doing so would harm us more than drinking a little more than the ideal amount of alcohol.

Cognitive dissonance theory shows us one way in which the mass media may change our attitudes and decision-making behaviour – by giving us information that conflicts with existing attitudes and pushing us to change our attitude and make a decision to change our behaviour. It also explains why we have a tendency to resist such messages and not change. There is evidence to show that cognitive dissonance does in fact take place. We can look at one such study in *Classic Research*, p235.

Self-perception theory

Bem (1967) suggested an alternative to cognitive dissonance theory. Bem believed that our ability to perceive our internal states is actually quite weak, meaning that cognitive dissonance simply would not be a powerful enough sensation to have an effect on our decision-making. Instead Bem proposed that we judge our attitudes by observing our own behaviour. This is why we say things like 'I must have been hungrier than I thought' when we eat a lot. We judge our state of hunger from our behaviour – how much we eat. *Self-perception* theory provides an alternative interpretation of studies like that of Festinger & Carlsmith. Bem (1972) proposes that participants in the Festinger & Carlsmith study observed their own behaviour in each condition and made judgements accordingly. Those who saw themselves say nice things about the study in the absence of an incentive (that is, the $1 condition) changed their attitude and made a decision to rate the experiment positively in response to this observation.

CLASSIC RESEARCH

Festinger L & Carlsmith JM (1959) Cognitive consequences of forced compliance. *Journal of Abnormal and Social Psychology 58, 203–210*

Aim: To test whether people who had been led to behave in a way that contradicted their attitudes would experience cognitive dissonance and resolve this by changing their attitude.

Procedure: 71 male psychology students took part in the experiment. They were told that as part of the course they would have to take part in a study on 'measures of performance'. They individually attended an appointment with the experimenter who set them two boring half-hour tasks (putting spools on a tray then emptying it and turning pegs on a board). They were then asked to introduce the task to the next participant. In a control condition they were neither paid nor asked to say anything particular to the next participant. In the two experimental conditions they were paid $1 or $20 and asked to tell the next participant that the procedure was fun and interesting. They were then asked four questions:

- Were the tasks interesting and enjoyable?
- Did the experiment give you an opportunity to learn about your own ability to perform these tasks?
- Would you say the experiment was measuring anything important?
- Would you have any desire to participate in any similar experiments?

Participants had to respond to each of these on an 11-point scale from –5 to +5.

Findings: For all questions participants were more positive when they had been paid to speak positively about the experiment to the next participant. For question 1 the mean rating in the control condition was –4.5 but this rose to +1.35 in the $1 condition and –0.62 in the $20 condition.

Conclusion: These findings support the idea of cognitive dissonance. In the control condition nothing took place to alter the participants' opinion that the experiment was boring and pointless. When a large incentive was offered there was no need to change opinion dramatically because there was a clear logical reason to speak positively about the experiment for the $20. However, the $1 condition produced dissonance and the participants responded by changing their attitudes in favour of the experiment.

Thinking critically about psychology

Evaluate the Festinger & Carlsmith (1959) study. In particular:

1 How well might the findings generalise to the modern population in general?
2 How natural were the environment and the tasks given to participants?
3 How strongly do the findings point to cognitive dissonance? Can you think of any other explanation for the findings?

Thinking practically about psychology

An advertising company has asked you to explain why its advertising campaign for tennis coaching by Julia is having no impact on people's tennis-related behaviour. Explain why this might be, using cognitive dissonance and self-perception theories.

KEY TERMS

cognitive dissonance   the discomfort we experience when we encounter new information that is not compatible with our current beliefs and behaviours

self-perception   the process in which we judge our attitudes by looking at our own behaviour

The effectiveness of television in persuasion

Given the importance of television in the leisure activities of most people it is potentially a very powerful way of altering attitudes and persuading people to alter their behaviour. Millions of pounds are spent every year to use television to change attitudes towards politicians, commercial products, health and 'good' causes (Petty *et al.* 2002). Around a third of all advertising budgets are spent on television advertising in the belief that it is more effective than other forms of advertising (Beattie & Shovelton, 2005). There has long been concern that powerful individuals who either control the media directly or can afford to sponsor programmes can exert an unhealthy influence over public opinion. We can apply the models looked at in this section to explain why television can be a powerful persuader.

Applying models of persuasive communication to television

In the early days of television it was widely believed that messages put across this way would have almost complete influence over viewers. This is clearly not the case: people are free to ignore or challenge the messages put across on television. The Hovland-Yale model is useful in identifying the factors that might make messages put across on television effective in persuasion. The elaboration-likelihood model has been particularly useful in understanding the influence of television because it explains *when* different strategies are likely to be effective in persuading us.

An important factor identified in both models is the characteristics of the person doing the persuading. As a visual medium television makes good use of people's appearance. The physical attractiveness of the person delivering a message may be one visual factor. Apparent trustworthiness may be another. Priester & Petty (2003) point out that when the persuader appears untrustworthy people elaborate more – which may be a good or bad thing. This is counter to common sense which would suggest that trustworthiness is always a good thing. In fact when people question the trustworthiness of a persuader they think more about the argument or product. It is important to avoid this sort of critical thinking when advertisers are putting across a dubious message! On the other hand, it can be a positive thing when we want people to engage in thinking about a serious issue. One way in which trustworthiness has been used to make television adverts more effective is the 'science bit' often used to push cosmetics. Consider the famous L'Oréal advert with Jennifer Aniston (you can watch it here: **http://www.youtube.com/watch?v=Yz4AiiN0mVQ**).

▶ **Figure 10.18** L'Oréal have benefitted from the 'science bit' approach

In terms of models of persuasive communication this was a very sophisticated advert. Clearly the persuader is very attractive but the really clever part is the way this is combined with the trustworthy-sounding scientific explanation for the effectiveness of the product. Crucially, because the 'science bit' sounds so credible and trustworthy, we pay less attention to it and more to the peripheral aspect of the message – namely, Jennifer Aniston. The advert is thus effective, not because we are persuaded by the science bit, but because the science bit makes us pay more attention to the attractive persuader!

For a lot of product advertising, where there is actually little to tell between rival brands or little to justify differences in prices, it is important to move people towards the peripheral route to persuasion; the logic of the central route just doesn't hold up. However, some television persuasion is concerned with more serious issues such as politics. Here the situation is more complex as there are some circumstances where the details of policy are central to voting decisions and others where politicians' charisma and attractiveness are more important. The elaboration-likelihood model can explain this in terms of the personal relevance of the message. When political debates appear to not impact directly on the individual, he or she is more likely to be persuaded by the peripheral route and so look for attractiveness, trustworthiness and charisma. When the debates have direct relevance to us, however, we are more likely to be persuaded by the central route.

Some television advertising campaigns are aimed at altering health-related attitudes and behaviour. Agostinella & Grube (2002) have analysed the success of alcohol counter-advertising in the light of the elaboration-likelihood model. They point out that as drinkers are at best only moderately interested in anti-drinking messages and campaigns, therefore attempts to use the central route to

▲ **Figure 10.19** Tony Blair's charisma was persuasive in economic good times when politics had less personal relevance. Gordon Brown's emphasis on policy may be more suitable for harder times where political decisions have clear and direct effects on people's lives

persuasion are likely to be ineffective. Unfortunately most advertising campaigns have attempted to use the central route. Agostinella & Grube conclude that the most effective anti-drinking campaigns in the USA have made use of the peripheral route by using celebrities. Interestingly, campaigns sponsored by the alcohol industry were regarded suspiciously: people questioned the motives of the industry, who clearly have a vested interest in people drinking lots.

Applying theories of attitude change

Cognitive dissonance and self-perception theories (p234) both suggest that attitudes can be altered by information. According to cognitive dissonance theory, information provided in advertisements can conflict with our existing behaviour, leading

MEDIA WATCH: SCIENCE AND ADVERTISING

Here comes the (pseudo)science bit

Joe Humphreys, *The Irish Times*, 4 October 2008

Science and advertising have always had something of a fraught relationship. Explaining complex technology is not easy at the best of times. But what if you have only 20 seconds to get your message across, and are also trying to sell a product on the back of it?

Faced with this dilemma, most advertisers plump for style over substance. Audi, for instance, does not waste its time explaining its new anti-lock braking system, or advances in power-steering. Instead, it shows us a bald, spectacled man in a lab coat carrying a clipboard (ie your stereotypical boffin) performing tests at an assembly plant before a sole voice-over line is delivered: '*Vorsprung durch Technik.*'

Food, cosmetics and pharmaceutical companies often plump for super-realistic graphics. Bad bugs are dressed in black (boo!), and good bugs white (hurrah!) as they do battle in an animated digestive tract. Hair ends are split open to reveal a secret world of bubbly molecules, and outlandishly out-of-scale lumps of dandruff. 'Now for the science bit,' proclaims L'Oréal Elvive, as it leads us by hand into such dizzying, fantastical graphics.

Part of the problem is that few scientific claims can be made without qualification, and advertising watchdogs are today quick to clamp down on exaggerated claims.

Some years ago, cat-food company Whiskas could get away with a line like 'eight out of 10 cats prefer it'. Now, however, advertising-standards authorities would ask: 'Prefer Whiskas to what exactly?' and 'How precisely did you consult the cats?'

Note that Whiskas dropped its famous slogan in 2004 for the altogether less emphatic: 'Whiskas: be happy.'

One advertiser that has pushed the boundaries out more than others in this area is the French food giant Danone. Not only is it branding its products with the logo 'scientifically proven' (complete with a natty image of a microscope), it has incorporated scientific graphics in its advertising to further convey the impression that it is a company that doesn't mess with the truth.

The 'scientifically proven' stamp is a risky one in that it implies the claims that are made for its products are a cut above the claims made for other products in advertising. The message is: our competitors' goods are supported by 'clinical tests' or 'widespread research' but ours are (cue trumpet blast) 'scientifically proven' to do what they say they will do.

1 Explain in terms of models of persuasive communication how each of these adverts aims to be effective

---

us to alter our behaviour in favour of that which is compatible with the message in the advertisement. Actually it may well be that on television most persuasion is via peripheral routes and so information is rarely processed deeply enough to change behaviour. However, cognitive dissonance theory is useful in understanding why some television campaigns do *not* persuade us to change behaviour. When new information conflicts with existing attitudes and behaviour, causing dissonance, we may change our behaviour or we might respond defensively, rejecting the new information. Freeman *et al.* (2001) suggest that cognitive dissonance can explain why anti-smoking campaigns have been unsuccessful. They questioned young smokers about their responses to anti-smoking messages and found considerable defensiveness, particularly in those who strongly identified themselves as smokers. This suggests that cognitive dissonance contributed to their rejection of anti-smoking campaigns.

Self-perception theory has also been applied to explaining the effectiveness of television in persuasion. According to self-perception theory, our attitudes are at least in part a response to our behaviour. Like cognitive dissonance this principle can be used to explain why it is quite hard to persuade us to change

our attitudes and behaviour. According to self-perception theory I (Matt) know I like beer because I drink it and I know I don't like the Conservative Party because I don't vote for it. In the face of this evidence I will take a lot of persuading not to drink beer or to vote Tory! Self-perception theory also explains the related phenomenon that people are most receptive to adverts that confirm their existing behaviour. Thus Austin *et al.* (1999) found a positive correlation between how much alcohol students drank and how positively they rated alcohol adverts.

Thinking critically about psychology

A limitation of correlations is that they don't necessarily tell us which variable affects what. Looking at the Austin *et al.* study, there is a correlation between alcohol consumption and positive ratings of alcohol adverts. Self-perception theory would interpret this as meaning that students looked at their own consumption of alcohol for evidence of how much they liked the adverts. Suggest two other possible interpretations of the findings.

The psychology of celebrity

North *et al.* (2005) have defined a celebrity as someone who is well known but who produces little or nothing with a lasting impact on society. According to this definition a celebrity is quite different from a 'great person' whose contributions have a lasting impact on the world. Celebrities are thus by definition not particularly special people, yet they are regarded as extremely 'important' individuals. Why celebrity should have such importance to us as a society is the sort of mystery psychologists can be called on to investigate.

◀ **Figure 10.21**
One type of attraction to celebrity is celebrity gossip

◀ **Figure 10.20**
Chantelle Houghton. By definition a celebrity contributes little of lasting worth

We can be attracted to celebrity in a number of ways. We might, for example, want to become a celebrity. 'Desire for fame' is such an important factor in young people that it is becoming accepted as a real aspect of the human personality. When Johnson & McSmith (2006) surveyed British children under the age of 10 about what they would most like for Christmas, to be made a celebrity came out as the most popular wish! We are also fascinated by the lives of celebrities. Celebrity gossip is now a multimillion pound international industry. We might also be influenced by celebrities, seeing them as role models. Because of this, celebrities are extensively used in advertising to influence consumer choice of products (Pringle, 2004).

Although celebrity culture is very much a current topic of discussion, it is not an entirely new phenomenon. Gountas & Gountas (2007) point out that over the past century entertainers and sports personalities have gradually replaced military, religious and political leaders as those regarded as the most important individuals. So why should we be so attracted to celebrity?

Social comparison theory – a social psychological explanation

Social comparison theory (Festinger, 1954) suggests that we are all driven to evaluate ourselves in order to have a realistic view of our strengths and weaknesses. One way we evaluate ourselves is to compare ourselves to other people. We make different comparisons for different purposes. For a highly realistic perception of ourselves we tend to compare ourselves with people very similar to us. However, we also make downward comparisons with people who have lower status than us to make ourselves feel better, and upward comparisons in order to establish what we should aspire to. Celebrities are obvious people with whom to make upward comparisons because they represent the ideals of our culture. Certainly studies have found that young people consider celebrities their ideal selves (Caughey, 1994).

Social comparison with celebrities may be associated with a range of problems. One problem is materialism – the attitude that happiness can only be achieved by owning more expensive possessions. Chan & Zhang (2007) looked at the relationship between social comparison with celebrities and materialism in 299 Chinese students. Those who engaged in the most social comparison with celebrities tended to be the most materialistic in their outlook, with a correlation coefficient of +0.33. They reported, for example, that they would be happier if they could afford more things and that they admired people who owned expensive houses and cars. Social comparison with celebrity body types may also be associated with eating problems. We can look at one study of this in *Research Now*.

▼ **Table 10.1 The desire for fame scale**

		SA	A	?	D	SD
1	One day I would like to be famous.					
2	If I were famous I would be happier.					
3	I would like to be a famous celebrity because it would give me a higher social status.					
4	I would like to be famous because other people would perceive me as having more power and influence.					
5	The lifestyle of famous celebrities appeals to me a lot.					
6	I love the idea of becoming a famous person.					

SA Stongly agree   A Agree   ? Don't know   D Disagree   SD Strongly disagree

RESEARCH NOW

Shorter L, Brown SL, Quinton SJ & Hinton L (2008) Relationships between body shape discrepancies with favoured celebrities and disordered eating in young women. *Journal of Applied Social Psychology* **38**, 1364–77

Aim: To examine the relationship between having a different body shape from that of one's favourite celebrity and having psychological problems relating to eating.

Procedure: 159 female students aged 18–27 took part in the study. They were asked to name a favourite celebrity of the same sex and similar age. They were then asked to identify their own and the celebrity's body shape by choosing from seven pictures of women in swimsuits. A measure of difference between self and celebrity shape was calculated by subtracting one size from the other. Eating problems were measured with a standard 26-item questionnaire called the Eating Attitudes Test (EAT-26). Correlations were calculated between the self–celebrity size difference and dieting, bulimia symptoms and anorexia symptoms as measured by EAT-26.

Findings: Strong positive correlations were found between the three EAT-26 scales and the self–celebrity size difference (+0.39 for dieting, +0.5 for bulimic symptoms and +0.51 for anorexia symptoms)[1].

1 Details of bulimic and anorexic symptoms can be found on p113

Conclusions: Results suggest that social comparison with celebrities in terms of body shape contributes to eating problems by giving people an unrealistic perception of what their body shape should be.

Thinking creatively about psychology

It is important to know how reliable a test like EAT-26 is before using it in research. Read up on reliability (p191 and p316), then design your own study to test the reliability of EAT-26.

Evolutionary theory

Evolutionary approaches to psychology aim to explain how human social behaviour has been influenced by evolution. The basic idea is that particular patterns of social behaviour are adaptive – that is, they increase the probability of survival. Natural selection means that they are passed on to future generations and they become part of human nature. Unlike social theories like social comparison theory, evolutionary theories explain *why* rather than *how* social phenomena like the attraction of celebrity happen.

McAndrew & Milenkovic (2002) have applied this principle to explaining the popularity of celebrity gossip. Gossip is important in all human societies. According to McAndrew & Milenkovic, one reason for this is that gossip gives us a fairly non-threatening way to make upward social comparisons. Imagine for a moment that you meet and directly compare yourself to Brad Pitt or Angelina Jolie. Let's face it, unless you are a lot cooler than us the results would be pretty depressing. Celebrity gossip allows us to identify high-status people to use for upward comparison without the sort of direct comparisons that would damage our self-esteem.

◀ **Figure 10.22** Gossiping about Brad Pitt and Angelina Jolie allows us to compare ourselves with them indirectly without it being too threatening

In our evolutionary past, say a million years or so ago, humans lived in small communities. For these communities to survive and grow into larger and more complex societies it was important to develop social behaviours to help find a mate and manage friendships, alliances and family relationships. Upward social comparison and gossip about high-status members in the community may both have been adaptive for these early humans. For example, gossip may have helped us form friendships. Gossiping about high-status individuals might also have helped early humans learn to be more like them, so improving their attractiveness and chances of finding a mate and reproducing.

▲ **Figure 10.23** People probably enjoyed a good gossip about cave-celebrities a million years ago

Clearly a million years ago there were no *OK!* or *Hello!* magazines and no celebrities as such. So how well does the evolutionary perspective explain modern celebrity gossip? The approach actually works quite well as an explanation because, through modern mass media, we see our favourite celebrities almost as frequently as cave-people would have seen their neighbours. We thus respond to them as if they are part of our community. It is quite hard, however, to test ideas directly from evolutionary psychology. This is a problem for a scientific theory – testability is one of the main characteristics of a good theory.

Intense fandom

Most of us can identify a favourite celebrity, and most psychologists would say that there is nothing unusual or unhealthy about paying attention to celebrities. However, most people spend a fairly limited amount of time thinking about them! A minority of celebrity fans take things a stage further and their behaviour is classified as intense fandom. Intense fandom is obsessive behaviour directed toward celebrities. It can range from *celebrity worship* to celebrity *stalking*. We can look at research into both of these.

KEY TERMS

celebrity worship obsessive attachment to one or more celebrities

erotomania sexual obsession

stalking harassment of a particular person, usually in the form of following them

Celebrity worship

Maltby *et al.* (2003) define celebrity worship as the 'seemingly abnormal phenomenon whereby persons with assumed intact identities become virtually obsessed with one or more celebrities' (2003, p25). It is entirely normal in childhood and adolescence to have a strong attachment to adult celebrities (how many children's bedrooms don't have posters of boy/girl bands or premiership footballers?). However, on occasion this attachment can become extreme enough to be thought of as a mental disorder. Haynes & Rich (2002) give an example of a 16-year-old girl who was hospitalised after cutting her arms and neck after hearing that a musician whom she worshipped was getting married. There have been various approaches to researching the phenomenon of celebrity worship, for example focusing on the personality, mental health, religiosity and self-perception of those engaged in celebrity worship.

Celebrity worship is often assessed using the Celebrity Attitude Scale (CAS) (see Table 10.2). The CAS measures three aspects of celebrity worship. The entertainment-social subscale includes items like 'My friends and I like to discuss what my favourite celebrity has done' and measures the extent to which the person is entertained directly by the celebrity or by talking about them. The intense-personal subscale measures the extent to which we are emotionally attached to our favourite celebrities, for example with the item 'I have frequent thoughts about my favourite celebrity even when I don't want to'. The borderline-pathological subscale measures irrational beliefs and attitudes, for example 'My favorite celebrity and I have our own code so we can communicate with each other secretly (such as over the TV or special words on the radio)'.

Thinking creatively about psychology

Read up on the concept of validity (p317). How could you go about testing the validity of the Celebrity Attitude Scale?

Maltby *et al.* (2003) investigated whether those with particular personalities are more at risk of celebrity worship. They used the Eysenck Personality Questionnaire (EPQ) to measure three aspects of personality. Extroversion is liveliness, impulsiveness and sociability. Neuroticism is anxiety and moodiness. Psychoticism is tough-mindedness, the lack of empathy for others. There were some significant correlations between personality traits and celebrity worship. Extroversion correlated (+0.297) with entertainment-social celebrity worship. As extroverts are particularly interested in other people it is not surprising that extroversion should be associated with interest in high-profile people or that they should enjoy discussing celebrities with other people. Neuroticism correlated positively (0.267) with intense personal celebrity worship as did psychoticism with borderline pathological worship (0.208). High levels of neuroticism and psychoticism are associated with vulnerability to mental health problems. We might expect therefore that they would be associated with the less healthy aspects of celebrity worship.

▼ Table 10.2 **The Celebrity Attitude Scale**

		SA	A	?	D	SD
1	If I were to meet my favourite celebrity in person, he/she would already somehow know that I am his/her biggest fan					
2	I share with my favourite celebrity a special bond that cannot be described in words					
3	I am obsessed by details of my favourite celebrity's life					
4	I would gladly die in order to save the life of my favourite celebrity					
5	My friends and I like to discuss what my favourite celebrity has done					
6	When something good happens to my favourite celebrity I feel like it happened to me					
7	My favourite celebrity and I have our own code so we can communicate with each other secretly (such as over the TV or special words on the radio)					
8	One of the main reasons I maintain an interest in my favourite celebrity is that doing so gives me a temporary escape from life's problems					
9	I have pictures and/or souvenirs of my favourite celebrity which I always keep in exactly the same place					
10	If my favourite celebrity endorsed a legal but possibly unsafe drug designed to make someone feel good, I would try it					
11	My favourite celebrity is practically perfect in every way					
12	The successes of my favourite celebrity are my successes also					
13	I enjoy watching, reading, or listening to my favourite celebrity because it means a good time					
14	I consider my favourite celebrity to be my soulmate					
15	I have frequent thoughts about my favourite celebrity, even when I don't want to					
16	When my favourite celebrity dies (or died) I will feel (or I felt) like dying too					
17	I love to talk with others who admire my favourite celebrity					
18	When something bad happens to my favourite celebrity I feel like it happened to me					
19	Learning the life story of my favourite celebrity is a lot of fun					
20	My favourite celebrity would immediately come to my rescue if I needed help					
21	I often feel compelled to learn the personal habits of my favourite celebrity					
22	If I were lucky enough to meet my favourite celebrity, and he/she asked me to do something illegal as a favour, I would probably do it					
23	It is enjoyable just to be with others who like my favourite celebrity					
24	When my favourite celebrity fails or loses at something I feel like a failure myself					
25	If I walked through the door of my favourite celebrity's home without an invitation she or he would be happy to see me					
26	If my favourite celebrity saw me in a restaurant he/she would ask me to sit down and talk					
27	If my favourite celebrity found me sitting in his/her car he or she would be upset					
28	If someone gave me several thousand dollars to do with as I please, I would consider spending it on a personal possession (like a napkin or paper plate) once used by my favourite celebrity					
29	I like watching and hearing about my favourite celebrity when I am in a large group of people					
30	If my favourite celebrity was accused of committing a crime that accusation would have to be false					
31	Keeping up with news about my favourite celebrity is an entertaining pastime					
32	News about my favourite celebrity is a pleasant break from a harsh world					
33	To know my favourite celebrity is to love him/her					
34	It would be great if my favourite celebrity and I were locked in a room for a few days					

SA Stongly agree   A Agree   ? Don't know   D Disagree   SD Strongly disagree

LOOKING FURTHER

Using a standard search engine, read up further about personality traits and think about how they might be linked to celebrity worship.

Earlier in this chapter we looked at a study (Shorter *et al.*, 2008) showing that the perceived difference between our own and our favourite celebrity's body shape was associated with eating problems. Celebrity worship is particularly associated with such dysfunctional attitudes. Maltby *et al.* (2005) surveyed adolescents, university students and adults using the Celebrity Attitude Scale and two standard measures of body image. In adolescent girls, but not in older samples, intense personal celebrity worship was associated with poor body image. This does not necessarily mean that the celebrity worship *caused* the poor self-perception of body shape. It does, however, suggest that intense personal celebrity worship is psychologically unhealthy.

The relationship between celebrity worship and religious belief has also been investigated. This is interesting because common sense might lead us to predict two opposite findings. On the one hand, all major monotheistic religions demand that believers should not worship anything other

▲ **Figure 10.24**
Celebrity worshippers who attach to skinny celebrities like Victoria Beckham tend to have a poor image of their own body shape

than their god – therefore we might expect religious people to indulge in less celebrity worship than non-religious people. On the other hand, religious people may have more of a tendency to worship in general than non-religious people; this would suggest that religious people should engage in *more* celebrity worship. This was investigated by Maltby *et al.* (2002). They asked 307 British adults to complete the Celebrity Attitude Scale and standard measures of religious belief. Moderate negative correlations (up to around –0.3) were found between the three subscales of the CAS. This suggests that, in general, religious people are slightly less likely to be involved in all three types of celebrity worship. However, a number of individuals were found who were highly religious and who engaged in celebrity worship. This suggests that there may be a 'worshipful personality'.

Thinking creatively about psychology

How might you go about investigating the existence of a 'worshipful personality'?

Celebrity stalking

Stalking has been defined by Meloy & Gothard (1995) as 'wilful, malicious, and repeated following or harassing of another person that threatens his or her safety' (1995, p258). Celebrity stalking can be regarded as an extreme variation on celebrity worship. Celebrities are often stalked; high-profile examples have included Madge, both Beckhams and Jodie Foster (who ironically later played Clarice Starling in the Hannibal Lecter films). The (fairly) good news for celebrities is that this type of stalking is less likely to result in violence than stalking of someone with whom the stalker has a personal relationship (Palarea *et al.*, 1999). However, this is not always the case. John Hinckley, obsessed by Jodie Foster after the 1981 film *Taxi Driver*, attempted to assassinate US President Reagan in order to get her attention. In 1993 Gunther Parche stabbed tennis star Monica Seles in order to please her rival Steffi Graf, with whom he had an *erotomaniac* obsession.

Zona (1993) has identified three types of stalker. The first is the stereotypical stalker who is sexually obsessed with their victim (known as erotomania). The erotomaniac (usually but not exclusively a heterosexual woman) suffers the delusion that a member of their target sex, usually older and of higher social status, is in love with them. This category of stalker was vividly portrayed in the film *Fatal Attraction*, in which a stalker kills and cooks her victim's child's pet rabbit. An interesting piece of trivia is that this is the origin of the term 'bunny boiler'. Zona's second category of stalker is most directly relevant here: the celebrity stalker, who often suffers from a

▼ **Figure 10.25** Monica Seles was stabbed by the stalker of rival tennis player Steffi Graf

serious category of mental disorder called psychosis, which includes delusions such as erotomania. Zona's third category is the rejected stalker who seeks revenge or a reconciliation following a failed relationship.

An interesting line of research has been psychiatric in nature, looking at the diagnoses of celebrity stalkers. Kamphuis & Emmelkamp (2000) reviewed research and concluded that celebrity stalkers suffer a range of psychotic conditions characterised by erotomaniac delusions. Disorders that can include such delusions include schizophrenia, bipolar disorder and serious cases of depression. Mullen (2008) conducted an archival study into over 20,000 incidents of stalking involving the British Royal Family, looking at police records. In over 80 per cent of cases the stalker was diagnosed as having a psychotic disorder. This suggests that celebrity stalkers are quite distinct from those who stalk people they know and supports Zona's classification of stalkers.

Thinking critically about psychology

Identify strengths and potential weaknesses of the Mullen (2008) study. Think in particular about the use of archived data from police records.

Chapter summary

Media influences on social behaviour

- There is a large body of evidence linking antisocial behaviour to viewing violent media and a smaller body of research suggesting that pro-social behaviour can also be influenced by viewing positive behaviour towards others.
- One explanation for the effects of the media on social behaviour is social learning theory. This suggests that people, children in particular, learn social behaviour by observing and imitating the behaviour of people whom they wish to be like.
- An alternative explanation for the link between viewing and social behaviour is that viewers are desensitised to suffering by viewing antisocial behaviour and sensitised by viewing pro-social behaviour.
- There is some recent evidence to suggest that playing violent video games can have a similar effect on the development of aggressive behaviour.
- Frequent computer use may have additional effects on children's development. The use of social networking sites is a particular topic of current research. Of particular concern is the possible link between networking sites and suicide contagion.

Persuasion, attitudes and change

- The mass media are widely used as agents of persuasion for commercial and political purposes. A range of theories casts light on how and when these can be effective. It appears that there is a range of factors affecting how persuasive the media are at persuading and different routes to persuasion.

- Theories of attitude change such as cognitive dissonance and self-perception are helpful in explaining why sometimes we are so resistant to media persuasion.
- Both theories of persuasive communication and theories of attitude change can be applied to explain the apparent influence of television as an agent of persuasion.

Psychology and celebrity

- A current phenomenon receiving a lot of attention is celebrity. Celebrities such as entertainers and sports personalities have gradually taken over from politicians, religious leaders etc as the most 'important' individuals.
- Social comparison theory suggests that we are attracted to celebrity because we are driven to compare ourselves with high-status individuals to get an idea of our ideal self.
- Evolutionary theory suggests that celebrity gossip is adaptive because it improves our chances of surviving and reproducing by helping us identify and describe socially successful characteristics in others so that we can imitate them.
- Celebrity worship is obsessive interest in celebrities. There are different types of celebrity worship, ranging from the normal entertainment-social interest to the more extreme and unhealthy borderline-pathological type.
- Celebrity stalking is perhaps the most extreme form of celebrity worship. Typically, celebrity stalkers are suffering from psychotic conditions like schizophrenia.

What do I know?

1 (a) Explain one way in which the media might affect antisocial behaviour. (10 marks)
  (b) Outline and evaluate research into the effects of computer use on young people. (15 marks)

2 (a) Outline the effects of playing violent video games on young people. (10 marks)
  (b) Explain why television might be such an effective agent of persuasion. (25 marks)

3 (a) Explain what is meant by the term 'cognitive dissonance' (5 marks)
  (b) Outline social comparison theory as an explanation of the attraction of celebrity. (10 marks)
  (c) Evaluate explanations of the attraction of celebrity. (10 marks)

4 (a) Explain what is meant by pro- and antisocial behaviour. (5 marks)
  (b) Outline and evaluate explanations of the link between watching violent media and antisocial behaviour. (20 marks)

5 (a) Outline the Hovland-Yale model of persuasion. (10 marks)
  (b) Outline and evaluate research into intense fandom. (15 marks)

CHAPTER 11
The Psychology of Addictive Behaviour

Thinking ahead

By the end of this chapter you should be able to:

- describe and critically evaluate biological, cognitive and learning models of addiction
- apply these explanations to specific addictions including smoking and gambling
- assess factors affecting vulnerability to addiction including self-esteem, attributions and social context
- critically consider the role of the media in addictive behaviour
- describe, evaluate and apply models of prevention including the theory of reasoned action and the theory of planned behaviour
- describe and evaluate strategies for reducing addictive behaviour including biological, psychological, public health and legislative interventions

I n your AS level you learned about drugs used to help people to cope with stress and the treatment of mental disorders. Here we will discuss the biological action of drugs again, focusing particularly on those drugs that cause addiction. We will also consider other types of addiction and explore explanations other than biological ones. At AS you also learned about different influences on our behaviour, such as social and cognitive factors. We will look at the ways in which such factors affect addiction. Finally we will explore ways to prevent and reduce addiction, drawing on both biological and psychological ideas.

Explaining addictive behaviour

In Chapter 10 we referred to the *DSM*, a manual for the diagnosis of mental disorders. This is also used to diagnose addictions. Two important addictions are:

- substance misuse
- gambling.

Both of these appear in *DSM-IV-TR* (for gambling, see p257).

■ **Box 11.1 The *Diagnostic and Statistical Manual (DSM-IV)***

Criteria for disorders of substance misuse

For a diagnosis of the chronic problem of **substance dependence** an individual must show three of the following at any time in a 12-month period:

- tolerance
- withdrawal symptoms
- increasing doses
- unsuccessful attempts to cut down intake
- considerable time spent obtaining, using or recovering from the use of the substance
- important social, occupational or recreational activities are given up (eg being too hung over to turn up for work)
- continuation of use despite recognition that this causes physical or psychological problems.

For a diagnosis of the acute or episodic problem of **substance abuse** an individual must experience one or more of the following in a 12-month period:

- interference with obligations in their major role eg at work, home or school (eg missing lessons)
- recurrent use in potentially hazardous situations (eg drink-driving)
- legal problems related to drug use
- continued use despite social or interpersonal problems caused by substance use.

Reprinted with permission from the *Diagnostic and Statistical Manual of Mental Disorders, Text Revision, Fourth Edition.* (© 2000). American Psychiatric Association.

Drugs and synapses

▼ **Figure 11.1a** How a synapse works

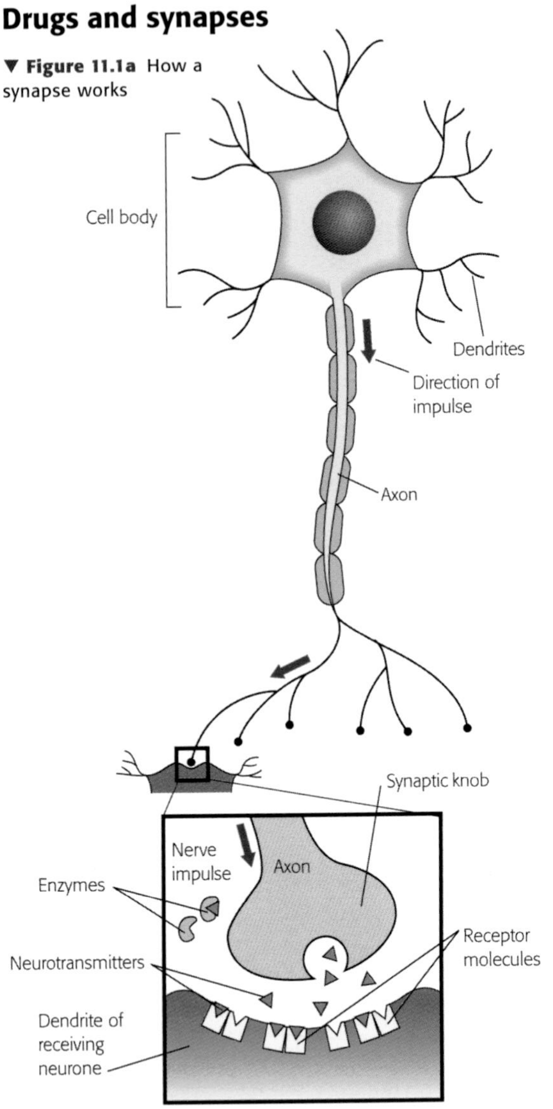

Cell body

Dendrites

Direction of impulse

Axon

Synaptic knob

Nerve impulse

Axon

Enzymes

Neurotransmitters

Receptor molecules

Dendrite of receiving neurone

Biological models of addiction

To understand biological models of drug addiction you will need to recall how a synapse works. A nerve impulse travels along the axon and causes the release of neurotransmitters into the synapse. When enough neurotransmitters attach to receptor sites on the post-synaptic membrane they cause another nerve impulse. There are specific receptor sites for specific neurotransmitters.

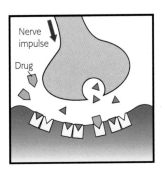

Nerve impulse

Drug

◀ **Figure 11.1b** The action of drugs at a synapse

Drugs can interfere with the synapse in several ways. They can:

- block the receptors so that neurotransmitters cannot fit into them
- attach to the receptors and have the same effect as a neurotransmitter
- prevent the recycling of neurotransmitters so that they stay in the synapse and can reattach to receptor sites.

Drug users often need greater doses of the drug over time in order to achieve the same effects as they did at first. This is called *tolerance*. There are several explanations for this. Each drug type attaches to a particular type of receptor. When drug molecules are present in addition to the normal neurotransmitters the body adapts. The number of receptor sites (or their sensitivity) is reduced – a process called *down regulation*. Larger doses of the drug are then needed to reach the same level of stimulation.

Another explanation for tolerance is related to the way that drugs are disposed of by the body. Drugs molecules are broken down by enzymes in the liver. In response to some drugs, the liver produces more of the enzymes responsible for removing that drug. A body that has been repeatedly exposed to a drug can therefore break it down more quickly than one that has not. This is because the user's liver is more efficient at processing the drug molecules so the user needs more of the drug to reach the same level in the body.

KEY TERMS

tolerance the development of a need for greater amounts of a drug with repeated use in order to achieve the same effect. It occurs with many drugs, such as alcohol, heroin and cocaine

down regulation the reduction in the sensitivity or number of receptor sites on the post-synaptic membrane in response to long-term exposure to a drug

Family patterns of addictive behaviour

If addiction is a biologically controlled behaviour, we would expect that families would show similar patterns of addiction. This idea is supported in several ways. For example, children of smokers are also more likely to smoke. Of course, this could be explained by environmental factors (see p261), although evidence from both animal and human research suggests that such similarities are at least partly genetic.

Nielsen *et al.* (2008) compared samples of DNA from 104 former heroin addicts and 101 controls. They found significant associations between heroin addiction and several gene variants. One genotype pattern was associated with heroin addition and accounted for 27 per cent of the risk for the individuals in the experimental group. Another genotype pattern protected individuals against developing heroin addiction.

By looking at patterns of drug misuse, researchers can attempt to separate the risk factors of genetics and upbringing using twin, adoption studies and family studies. If an individual whose parents took drugs is also drug-dependent this might be due to aspects of their environment or a genetic predisposition. Fowler *et al.* (2007) looked at possible causal factors of problem drinking

The findings of Overstreet *et al.* suggest that risk of alcoholism could be predicted by testing liking for sweet drinks. To what extent could this knowledge be helpful to people who are at risk, and to what extent might it lead to even higher levels of alcoholism amongst those found to have a 'sweet tooth'?

in 862 twin pairs aged 11–17 years in England and Wales. Although they found that genes were important, environmental factors, such as best friends' alcohol use, mattered too. However, as Fowler *et al.* observe, even choice of friends may have some genetic component so it is likely that the two influences, of genes and the environment, do not act independently.

▲ **Figure 11.2** Twins tend to share addictions, but is this similarity genetic or environmental?

Maes *et al.* (1999) investigated the genetic component of risk in tobacco, alcohol and other drug use by adolescents. They studied 1412 monozygotic (MZ) and dizygotic (DZ) twin pairs aged 8–16 and found a significant genetic influence in the use of all three drugs. However, from a comparison of 327 MZ and 174 same-sex DZ twins, Han *et al.* (1999) concluded that the environment was the major contributor to risk of alcohol abuse. Using a different technique, Kendler *et al.* (2000) compared tobacco use in reared-together and reared-apart twins. They found a gender difference: for men, genes played a large part in tobacco use; for women, the pattern changed with social factors over time. Few women born before 1925 used tobacco and twin similarity was environmental in origin. For women born after 1940, tobacco use and the importance of genetic factors increased, resembling those of males. Kendler *et al.* concluded that, as social restrictions relaxed, the influence of genetic factors became apparent in women.

Studies such as Maes *et al.* and Han *et al.* that compare MZ and DZ twins can be criticised as the relative differences in environments between the two twin types is difficult to ascertain. Although separated twin studies overcome this particular problem, they are not without flaws. For example, Kendler *et al.* treated twins as 'reared apart' if they were separated by age 11 years (although most had been separated by age two years). Clearly this means the environment could have affected both individuals in the same way.

Evidence also suggests that addictions tend to cluster: individuals with one problem are often at risk from other addictive behaviours. For example, studies of different rat strains have shown that those who readily become addicted to alcohol also prefer sweeter drinks (Overstreet *et al.*, 1993). The same pattern seems to be evident in twins. Kampov-Polevoyetal (2003) found that alcoholic male twins also shared a liking for sweet-tasting things. Furthermore, Pepino & Mennella (2007) found that women with a history of alcoholism in the family craved sweets more often.

▼ **Figure 11.3** People with one addiction are at greater risk from other addictions

Button *et al.* (2007) found a correlation between alcohol dependence and illicit drug dependence in adolescent twins. Similarly, cigarette smoking and alcohol use was found to be related in a study of Chinese male twins (Lessov-Schlaggar *et al.*, 2006). Links have also been found between drug-related and non-drug addictions. For example, Kessler *et al.* (2008) found that pathological gambling and substance abuse were related.

Evaluating biological models of addiction

Clearly, the biological model of addiction, at least for drugs, is well supported by evidence from studies of genetics in both animals and humans. In human research, evidence from both twin and family studies supports the idea that a tendency towards drug addiction is inherited. These patterns suggest that there is an underlying biological predisposition for dependence in some individuals.

Other evidence supports the biological model. There are different groups of drugs, based on their chemical structure and properties, such as the opiates (eg heroin and morphine) or hallucinogens (eg LSD). Prolonged use of one drug in a group results in the development of tolerance to the others – called *cross-tolerance*. It occurs because the drug molecules are very similar and supports the down regulation explanation of tolerance. Since all the related drugs in a chemical group attach to the same receptors, tolerance to one drug will affect sensitivity to related drugs.

Clearly, biological models more obviously account for drug addictions than other addictions, such as to food, exercise or gambling. However, one brain area, called the nucleus accumbens, is thought to be important in many addictions. This area seems to be linked to the rewarding properties of addictive behaviours and is part of the 'brain reward system'.

Learning theory models of addiction

Three aspects of learning theory can help to explain drug use:

- positive reinforcement
- negative reinforcement
- social learning theory.

Positive and negative reinforcement are mechanisms in operant conditioning, which we will consider first.

Operant conditioning

Operant conditioning occurs when the frequency of a behaviour is affected by its consequences. Pleasant consequences increase the frequency of a behaviour and this is more likely if the reward closely follows the behaviour. You may remember this idea as an explanation for attachment from your AS level.

There are two kinds of 'reward': positive reinforcement and negative reinforcement.

- A *positive reinforcer* increases the frequency of a behaviour because its effects are pleasant, eg nice food.
- A *negative reinforcer* also increases the frequency of a behaviour because its effects are pleasant. In this case, however, the pleasant effect is the removal of something nasty, eg the stopping of an annoying sound.

◄ **Figure 11.4** Animals such as rats and monkeys will learn to self-administer drugs in a Skinner box

Positive reinforcement and drug use

Skinner box experiments have shown that many laboratory animals, such as rats and monkeys, will self-administer drugs. For example, rats will press the bar for a dose of cocaine. As immediate reinforcers are more effective than delayed ones, drugs that pass quickly into the brain are powerful reinforcers: a rat will learn more quickly to press a bar for an intravenous dose of cocaine than for a sip of alcohol. This is because alcohol is slower to have an effect. The relative speed of reinforcement helps us to understand how a user can become addicted to a drug that has unpleasant or even life-threatening effects. Such risks are long term, whereas positive reinforcement is short term. Immediate rewards are thus more powerful than the delayed consequences of withdrawal, imprisonment or death.

KEY TERMS

extinction the disappearance of a behaviour in the absence of reinforcement

reinforcement schedule the pattern of rewards, which may be continuous (a reinforcement for every behaviour) or partial (for only some)

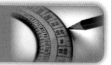

Schedules of reinforcement

A strange aspect of operant conditioning is the effect of infrequent rewards. Imagine a rat in a Skinner box pressing the bar for food pellets. Given a reward for every bar press (continuous reinforcement), the rat presses infrequently and, in the absence of food, quickly stops altogether. This is called *extinction*. Surprisingly, if it has to press the bar, say, four times before receiving its reward, it will press more often and will be less likely to stop.

The harder an animal has to work for the reward, and the less predictable that reward is, the more frequently and persistently it presses the bar. Reinforcers can be provided on partial rather than continuous *reinforcement schedules*. These are where a reinforcer is given after a number of responses (eg every four, called 'fixed ratio 4' or FR4). Partial reinforcement schedules can also be variable. Here, the reinforcement is random, arriving after an average rather than exact number of bar presses. For example, on 'variable ratio 4' (VR4) a rat might receive a pellet for food after one, four, five, six and three bar presses.

Variable ratio schedules lead to very high rates of response and are highly resistant to extinction. This is one reason that gamblers persist even when they are losing. They have learnt that wins come intermittently and unpredictably, so they have been reinforced on a variable ratio schedule and keep responding.

KEY TERMS

relapse the return to drug use by a previously dependent user after a period of abstinence

self-medication the use of a non-prescribed drug to reduce pre-existing psychological symptoms (such as depression, anxiety or low self-esteem)

Negative reinforcement and drug use

The effects of withdrawal are negative reinforcers so provide a reason for the maintenance of drug use. Dependent users may continue drug use to avoid unpleasant effects such as nausea, anxiety and depression which they experience in the absence of the drug. Negative reinforcement can also explain why dependent users who no longer experience the positively reinforcing effects continue their drug use. A dependent heroin user feels little of the euphoria or well-being that a non-dependent user would experience. They do, however, need to continue to take the drug to ward off withdrawal and the effects of craving.

So far we have only considered the maintenance of drug use. Negative reinforcement may also be able to explain the initiation of drug use. Imagine an individual who tries an illicit drug in order to reduce some pre-existing psychological symptom. This idea, referred to as '*self-medication*', would

Thinking critically about psychology

Imagine a gambler at a fruit machine. It hasn't paid out for ages. Why, according to learning theory, do they keep feeding money into it?

explain why an anxious person might misuse alcohol, or someone suffering low self-esteem might take cocaine: the user is seeking to remove unpleasant feelings.

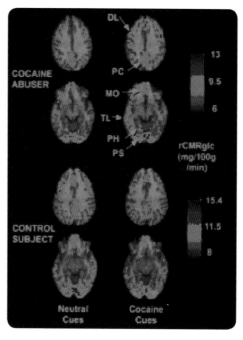

▼ **Figure 11.5** PET scanning shows more activation in cocaine users' brains in a situation designed to induce craving than in non-users'. From Grant *et al.* (1996)

A physiological correlate of craving has been illustrated using PET scans of the brains of cocaine users and non-users. Grant *et al.* (1996) showed that users', but not non-users', brains showed increased activity in an area called the amygdala in response to cocaine-related stimuli such as a mirror, a straw and some cocaine itself.

Social learning theory

The idea of social learning suggests that behaviours may be acquired by observation and imitation. Some individuals are more likely to be observed than others, such as members of the family who are seen often. The individual who is copied is called a model and is more likely to be imitated if they are familiar, the same gender and seen to be of high status or to gain from the behaviour (see also p75). Adults, especially parents,

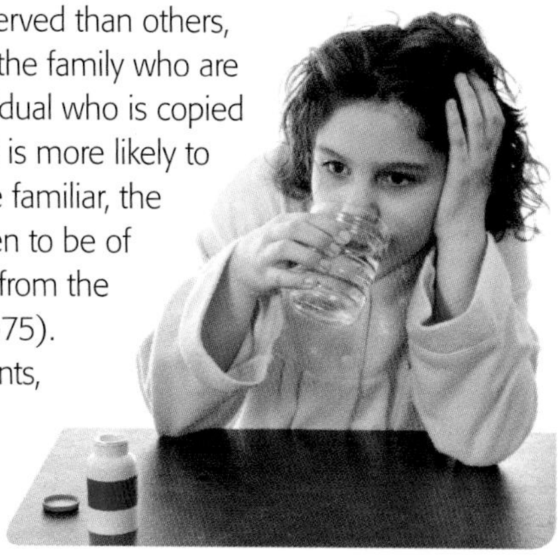

▶ **Figure 11.6** Parents may be role models for addictive behaviours

CLASSIC RESEARCH

Morgan & Grube (1991) Smoking and drinking with friends.

Aim: To investigate how peers affect the initiation and continuation of cigarette smoking, drinking alcohol and the use of other drugs.

Procedure: Anonymous questionnaires were given to secondary school children in Dublin on two occasions. The sample was stratified for gender and for size and type of school. The number of males and females was approximately equal and the mean age was 15.8 years. The initial sample of 5709 participants fell to 2057 at follow-up, largely due to students leaving school. Those who left the sample were more likely to smoke, drink and use drugs, but only very slightly.

The self-report questionnaire asked (at each test time):

- whether they had ever smoked a cigarette, drunk alcohol or taken any of a list of 12 illicit substances
- how many cigarettes they smoked a day
- how many times during the previous month they consumed alcohol
- how many times during the previous month they used illicit drugs.

At the initial testing, participants were also asked about drug use of:

- their current best friend
- other good friends
- most young people of their age.

For the best friend and other good friends the participants were also asked to rate how likely they would be to approve of the respondent's substance use.

Questionnaires were administered in the students' normal classroom without the teacher present (except in one school where several classes were brought together and another where disciplinary problems were anticipated so the teacher was present but interacted very little). Each individual's questionnaire was matched across testing sessions using a code based on information including gender, date of birth and number of older brothers and sisters. Seventy-seven per cent of the questionnaires were matched at follow-up and there were no significant differences in substance abuse between matched and unmatched participants. The internal reliability of items measuring substance abuse was high (0.7 to 0.91). The test-retest reliability between the two initial testing sessions was 0.83 for smoking, 0.72 for drinking and 0.59 for substance abuse.

Findings: The influence of a best friend was stronger and remained more influential than that of other friends. Perceived use by friends was more important than perceived approval (for both best and other friends). Whilst the best friend was most important in the maintenance of drug use the wider friendship group was influential in the initial use of drugs, through both example and approval.

Conclusion: Friends play an important role in drug use throughout the teenage years, being important in both the initiation and continuation of drug use.

---

are familiar and are powerful within the family so are likely to be imitated. Observers may see the model benefiting from drug use, which also increases the likelihood of imitation and is called *vicarious reinforcement*. For example, a child may be aware that a parent is more relaxed after smoking a cigarette. They may be exposed to family gatherings at which adults enjoy themselves more the more they drink. They may see the euphoria of a parent who uses heroin. These are sources of vicarious reinforcement for the observing children which will raise their motivation to copy the behaviours they have seen.

Lucchini (1985) observes of the 'drug scene' for heroin or cocaine users that young people may see some addicts as

having high status – a key characteristic for an effective model. But is there any evidence for the effect of such models? Bahr *et al.* (2005) showed that peer drug use had a strong effect in a sample of 4230 American adolescents and concluded that their findings were consistent with a social learning explanation. Dielman *et al.* (1991) found peer norms to be more important than parental norms as predictors of alcohol use, and Best (2005), in a study of 2078 14–16-year-olds in London, found that those who spent more of their free time with friends who smoked, drank alcohol and used illicit drugs were more likely to use cannabis themselves.

▲ **Figure 11.7** When starting drug use, close friends matter but the best friend has a more lasting effect

Why was it critical that the participants who left Morgan & Grube's sample early were similar in their drug use to those who stayed?

Why was their use of a code-based system for matching questionnaires ethically important?

Evaluating learning theory models of addiction

Positive reinforcement can clearly explain initial drug use, since effects such as hallucinations or euphoria act as rewards. However, due to tolerance, these effects will lessen unless the dose is increased and this carries costs: higher doses are more expensive and more debilitating. Positive reinforcement cannot explain continued use by dependent users when the reinforcement of, for example, euphoria can no longer be obtained (although it can explain increasing doses).

Negative reinforcement *can* account for continued use even in the absence of the initial effects: the user is reinforced by the removal of unpleasant withdrawal symptoms. However, this explanation is also incomplete. Following abstinence, withdrawal symptoms subside yet ex-users often feel compelled to resume their drug use. Indeed, when their habit becomes too costly some dependent heroin users deliberately abstain to reduce the dosage they need. They wouldn't to do this if avoiding withdrawal was maintaining their habit.

Craving is important in both continued use and *relapse*. It can be induced, in animals or humans, by giving users a 'taste' of the drug or exposing them to something associated with it (see Grant *et al.*, 1996, p249). For example, a rat that has learned to self-administer cocaine will bar-press for more of the drug if it is given a small 'priming' dose. This provides indirect support for the negative reinforcement explanation.

Recovered alcoholics are warned of the risks associated with even a single drink. How does the idea of priming explain this risk?

Cognitive models of addiction

If you are in hospital, and in pain, you may be given an opiate such as morphine – but you won't feel euphoric and are unlikely to become dependent. If biological explanations alone accounted for drug dependence, this is not what we would expect. So other processes, such as cognitive ones, must be involved.

Imagine a businessman needs to wind down after work. He goes to the pub, has a drink and relaxes. If his business begins to fail, he drinks more often. But this produces problems of its own: his drinking escalates, he is less effective at work, and begins to destroy his previously supportive family relationships. As his addiction grows, so does his need for the escape provided by alcohol – he is in a vicious circle. The more he fears the loss of his business and family, the more he drinks, thus making the problem worse. This cycle can be represented in a triangle (see Figure 11.8).

This pattern persists because of users' dysfunctional beliefs. They attribute their problems to external causes such as 'the market' for business problems or 'their partner' for relationship problems. By doing this, they avoid the reality that their drug dependence plays a critical role in the ongoing problems.

▼ **Figure 11.8** The path to addiction

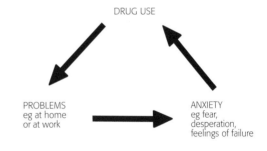

Taking the example of a dependent drug user, their dysfunctional beliefs about drug-taking could include expectations that:

- there is a psychological or emotional *need* for it
- social or intellectual functioning is better with it
- it will provide excitement or pleasure
- it will energise the individual or make them more powerful
- it will have a soothing effect
- it will relieve boredom, anxiety, depression or tension
- that without it the craving and distress will get worse.

So, one reason users are unable to abstain is because of their distorted thinking. You have already encountered this idea in

Chapter 9. A dependent user faced with the logic of abstinence may say 'I can't do without it because ...':

- 'I'll feel down all the time.'
- 'I'm only good company when I've had a drink.'

These are dysfunctional beliefs about mood. Users believe that without the drug they will be unable to feel happy or useful.

Other dysfunctional beliefs surround distress and deprivation. The user may say 'I can't stop because ...:

- 'I won't be able to cope with people.'
- 'I won't have anything to live for.'

Dysfunctional beliefs may be self-fulfilling. Individuals who believe they are unable to stop taking drugs will find it hard to do so, and their difficulty supports their belief that they cannot abstain. The user's helplessness may be indicated by saying:

- 'I don't have the willpower to stop.'
- 'I've stopped before but I just start all over again.'

The craving individuals experience supports their belief that it is impossible for them to give up, so they keep using. The dysfunctional belief that they are incapable of controlling the urge to take a drug confirms the belief that they are unable to help their own addiction.

▲ **Figure 11.9** Shopping addicts cannot drag themselves away from a tempting window display

Hester & Garavan (2005) suggest that, because thoughts of the addiction are in working memory, this makes redirecting attention away from important environmental cues very difficult. Attention to those cues, in turn, maintains addiction-related thoughts in working memory. This approach helps to explain how rumination (persistent thoughts) and craving become cyclical and self-perpetuating.

The importance of rumination in gambling addiction is supported by the findings of Ratelle *et al.* (2004): 412 casino gamblers were given a questionnaire to assess whether they had an 'obsessive' or 'harmonious' passion for gambling as well as dependence on, and consequences of, gambling. The researchers found that those individuals with an obsessive passion showed greater rumination (and poorer concentration on daily tasks) and were more likely to be problem gamblers.

Thinking creatively about psychology

If you used *Exploring Psychology* for AS level you may remember a study on the working memory model that suggested that visual distraction (by tracking the tapping of a finger across the forehead) helps to reduce food craving (McClelland *et al.*, 2006). The idea was that filling the visuo-spatial sketchpad with the tracking task would prevent the visualisation of tempting foods.

How might a similar task be used to reduce cravings in smokers or gamblers?

Evaluating cognitive models of addiction

Cognitive models of addiction have led to effective therapies (see p259). This suggests that the cognitive problems identified and explained by the theory are, indeed, important factors in addiction. By breaking the self-fulfilling cycle in drug use, for example, therapists are able to enhance self-belief and help clients to abstain.

Cognitive theory can readily account for individual differences in addiction: both differences in life experiences and personality can lead to differences in vulnerability. Beck *et al.* (2001) identified some of the factors that make people more vulnerable to addiction:

- high sensitivity to unpleasant emotions (eg being less tolerant of normal mood changes)
- low motivation to control behaviour (so more likely to seek short-term satisfaction than resist)
- poor strategies for self-control and coping (so the desire to exert control cannot be followed through)
- automatic responses to urges (so unlikely to reflect on consequences and exert control)
- low tolerance for boredom (so likely to seek stimulation and excitement)
- low tolerance for frustration (so likely to become angry when other goals cannot be reached, leading to the urge to reduce tension through the addiction)
- attention focused on the present (so short-term satisfaction is more important than long-term goals).

Imagine an addict who can't find something they've lost. They may become frustrated very quickly, feel the loss is highly significant, blame someone else for moving it and get angry. Since none of these help to find the lost object, the addict becomes tense and experiences a greater need to satisfy themselves (eg by giving in to the craving) than would an individual with a higher tolerance for frustration. This illustrates an effect of individual differences in personality or 'disposition'.

Thinking creatively about psychology

Imagine a gambler who is trying to resist his addiction and cannot pass his driving test. Explain how his personality might lead him to surrender to the urge to gamble.

Thinking critically about psychology

On the basis of Beck *et al.*'s list of predispositional factors leading to addiction, what other characteristics would you predict in obsessive internet users?

RESEARCH NOW

Ko CH, Yen JY, Yen CF, Chen CS & Wang SY (2008) The association between Internet addiction and belief of frustration intolerance: the gender difference. *Cyberpsychology and Behavior* 11(3), 273–8

Aim: To investigate the relationship between frustration tolerance and internet addiction.

Procedure: 2114 students (1204 male, 910 female) were assessed using two questionnaires: the Chen Internet Addiction Scale (CIAS) and a frustration discomfort scale. The CIAS, a self-report measure of internet use, has 26 items, each scored on a four-point Likert scale. It assesses five dimensions relating to internet use: compulsion, withdrawal, tolerance, interpersonal and health problems and time management problems.

Findings: Females were generally more intolerant of frustration than males. There was a relationship between frustration and internet addiction in both genders, being strongest in males. In general, individuals with internet addiction were less tolerant of frustration.

Conclusion: The prevalence of low frustration-tolerance amongst individuals who were more highly addicted to using the internet shows that the inability to tolerate frustration can lead to a redirection of the resulting tension to addictive behaviour.

From a review of research, Toneatto (1999) identified typical cognitive distortions in gamblers including:

- magnification of their own gambling skills
- minimisation of other gamblers' skills
- superstitious beliefs
- interpretive biases, including internal and external attributions (see p261), *gambler's fallacy* and chasing
- selective memory
- illusion of control over luck.

These suggest that there are many false beliefs associated with addiction to gambling and that, although different from those associated with substance abuse, they are also dysfunctional. This suggests that Beck's model could account for a range of addictive behaviours.

Joukhador *et al.* (2003) assessed gambling beliefs in problem and social gamblers. They found that the problem gamblers held more irrational beliefs, such as illusions of control, superstitious beliefs and selective memory. They did not, however, differ in terms of denial as would be predicted by the cognitive model.

Ariyabuddhiphongs & Phengphol (2008) investigated the gambler's fallacy in two groups of 200 players of the Thai lottery. One group simply bought their tickets from lottery stalls, the other used superstitious methods to search for lottery numbers to bet. The superstitious group showed higher levels of near-miss, gambler's fallacy and entrapment. These results confirm that cognitive distortions are typical in problem gamblers.

▲ **Figure 11.10** The gambler's fallacy: if there's been a run of blacks, there will be a run of reds

KEY TERM

gambler's fallacy this is the belief that if random events have been going one way (eg a run of blacks on a roulette wheel) then they will even out (ie a run of reds will follow). This is not so, simply because random events are just that – random

M E D I A W A T C H : COMPUTER-BASED THERAPY

Computer-based CBT shows promise in substance abuse treatment

http://pn.psychiatryonline.org/cgi/content/full/43/14/21-a

Cognitive-behavioral therapy [CBT] delivered via computer-based training appears to be a successful adjunct to treatment of substance use disorders, according to a report in the June *American Journal of Psychiatry*.

Patients receiving biweekly access to computer-based training in cognitive-behavioral therapy (CBT4CBT) skills in addition to standard treatment submitted significantly more urine specimens that were negative for any type of drugs than did patients who did not receive CBT4CBT. There was also a trend toward longer continuous periods of abstinence.

'This study points to a means of delivering this form of CBT much more broadly and inexpensively, and with improved consistency, potentially 24/7 with remote access,' lead author Kathleen Carroll, PhD, told *Psychiatric News*.

77 individuals seeking treatment for substance dependence at an outpatient community setting were randomly assigned to standard treatment or standard treatment with biweekly access to CBT4CBT. CBT4CBT consisted of six lessons, or modules, covering the following core concepts: understanding and changing patterns of substance use, coping with craving, refusing offers of drugs and alcohol, problem-solving skills, identifying and changing thoughts about drugs and alcohol, and improving decision-making skills.

The concepts were depicted in 'movies' using actors and realistic settings in which an individual was offered drugs or had to cope with a challenging situation in which substance use was likely. Then the movie was repeated with a different ending to demonstrate the use of skills required to change the outcome.

Each module included an interactive assessment followed by a short vignette with an actor explaining how use of each skill had helped him or her avoid substance use and how each CBT principle could be applied to other problems. Finally, a narrator reviewed key points, and participants were given a practice assignment.

The participants assigned to CBT4CBT submitted significantly fewer urine specimens that were positive for any drug and a lower proportion that were positive for any drug. This was most marked for cocaine (28 per cent for patients in the CBT4CBT group versus 44 per cent for those in the treatment-as-usual group). Patients in the CBT4CBT group had an average of 22 days of continuous abstinence during treatment compared with 15 days for those in the treatment-as-usual group.

The investigators also found that outcome in the CBT4CBT was strongly related to treatment adherence—indicated by the number of days retained in the treatment program, the number of individual and group sessions attended, and homework completion.

Mark Moran, *Psychiatry News*, 18 July 2008, Vol 43, No 14, p21. [edited]

Reprinted with permission from *Psychiatric News*, (copyright 2008). American Psychiatric Association.

1 Identify two ways in which CBT4CBT is preferable to face-to-face therapy, other than its efficacy.

2 The participants were randomly assigned to treatment groups. What ethical issues does this raise?

Thinking critically about psychology

If a gambler has had a losing streak, getting all low cards, they may continue to bet on the basis of the gambler's fallacy. Why would they do this?

Search the internet for 'Gamblers Anonymous' and find out about the process. Which approach(es) to therapy do you think it employs?

Addictive behaviours

Smoking as an addiction

The 2006 General Household Survey (GHS) showed that 22 per cent of British adults (over 16 years old) are smokers – 23 per cent of men and 21 per cent of women. Men also smoke more cigarettes – on average 15 cigarettes a day for men compared with 13 for women. However, this is the lowest ever recorded level, down from 27 per cent in the second half of the 1990s. Sixty-eight per cent of the respondents said they wanted to give up, 59 per cent said it would be difficult to last a whole day without a cigarette and 16 per cent said they would have had their first cigarette of the day within five minutes of waking up – suggesting they are addicted.

▼ **Figure 11.11** Prevalence of smoking in Great Britain, 1974–2006. From Eileen Goddard (2006) *Smoking and Drinking among Adults*. Cardiff: Office for National Statistics, p5

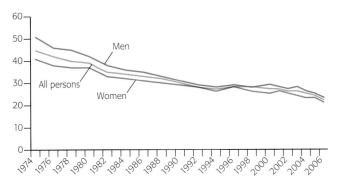

Even though the number of smokers is falling, smoking represents a major health threat. A report from the Royal College of Physicians (RCP) estimates that, in 1997, 117,400 of the total of 628,000 deaths in the UK could be attributed to smoking – that's one in every five.

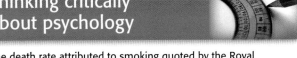

Thinking critically about psychology

The death rate attributed to smoking quoted by the Royal College of Physicians equates to an average of 2300 people killed by smoking every week in the UK. Work out the number this represents each day, and every hour.

Thinking practically about psychology

The *DSM* criteria for substance dependence are used to diagnose addiction to smoking. However, several of the criteria do not apply, even to heavy smokers. Look back to p246. Which criteria do you think are most helpful in diagnosing nicotine dependence?

▲ **Figure 11.12** Sigmund Freud: addicted to nicotine

LOOKING FURTHER You can use the 'research' link from a *Guardian* newspaper article to find both a 2008 summary of findings on cigarette and alcohol use in Great Britain and the 2006 General Household Survey results:

http://www.guardian.co.uk/society/2008/jan/22/health.smoking

You can also read the Royal College of Physicians' report at:
http://www.rcplondon.ac.uk/pubs/books/nicotine/1-overview.htm

The biological approach

In the 2006 GHS survey, dependence was reported to be greater in heavier smokers – they were more likely to say it would be hard to give up (82 per cent of those smoking more than 20 a day compared with only 26 per cent of those smoking less than 10 a day). A similar pattern was seen in the need for a cigarette. Thirty-six per cent of the heavy smokers had their first cigarette within five minutes of waking. The urgency for those smoking less than 10 a day was much less marked, with only 2 per cent reporting an early-morning need. These figures suggest that dependent smokers experience considerable craving and that this perpetuates their addiction. This can be explained using the biological approach.

A cigarette contains approximately 0.5–2mg of the drug nicotine, most of which is either not inhaled or is rapidly broken down by enzymes in the liver. The exact dose received by the smoker can be controlled by the frequency and depth of inhalations as well as the time the smoke is held in the lungs and the number of cigarettes smoked.

As nicotine is removed from the bloodstream so quickly, the dependent user needs to smoke frequently to satisfy their craving and avoid withdrawal. The urgency for a morning cigarette is caused by the fall in blood-nicotine level overnight (approximately 2.5 nanograms/ml). Sometimes two cigarettes in quick succession are needed to raise the blood-nicotine level enough to feel comfortable (that is, to approximately 20–40 nanograms/ml).

Nicotine readily enters the brain and affects movement, thinking, perception, attention and memory. One important brain area that it affects is the nucleus accumbens – the 'brain reward centre'. Initially, nicotine has a positively reinforcing effect. This accounts for initiation and early maintenance of smoking. However, tolerance to this effect develops, and long-term dependent users lose this effect so maintenance is largely determined by avoidance of withdrawal.

Dependence on nicotine is largely psychological, in that there does not appear to be a marked change in nicotinic receptors that would characterise biological tolerance. Nevertheless, the withdrawal symptoms and craving are severe and prolonged. The observation that biological therapies for nicotine addiction (see pp268–9) are effective supports the biological explanation of compulsive smoking.

Finally, children of smokers are more likely to smoke. This could be due to their environment but inheritance also plays a part. Pergadia *et al.* (2006) conducted genetic analyses of nicotine dependence in a large sample of twins (3026 women and 2553 men). Their results suggested that, even taking into account the influence of genetic factors on the incidence of experimentation with cigarettes and the number smoked, there was a significant heritability effect for nicotine withdrawal. This suggests that vulnerability to the problems of abstinence once dependent is another important biological factor.

The cognitive approach

On pp251–3 we considered Beck *et al.*'s cognitive explanation of addiction. This can be readily applied to the problems experienced by dependent smokers. Dysfunctional beliefs could include expectations that:

- they *need* a cigarette
- cigarettes contribute to cognitive functioning
- a cigarette will provide an immediate sensation of pleasure
- cigarettes have a stimulant effect
- cigarettes help to calm nerves
- cigarettes help to reduce appetite
- without a cigarette, craving will worsen.

Dependent smokers may therefore be unable to abstain because their distorted thinking makes them believe that they cannot. These dysfunctional beliefs may be self-fulfilling: smokers who think they will feel anxious unless

they can have a cigarette are likely to experience this effect. Furthermore, the craving that smokers experience confirms their belief that they cannot give up. This is an example of Beck *et al.*'s 'vicious circle'. The smoker believes that he or she cannot control the urge to smoke and each time they surrender to the craving to have a cigarette, this confirms their dysfunctional belief about being incapable of controlling their addiction.

▲ **Figure 11.13** According to the cognitive model, salient cues make abstinence difficult

Cues may also be important in the maintenance of smoking. If smokers can't turn their attention away from their need to smoke, this will perpetuate their addiction. There may be many salient cues in the home, such as ashtrays, cigarette packets and the lingering smell of smoke. With these potential triggers present, taking control and avoiding the urge to smoke is very difficult.

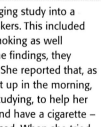

Thinking critically about psychology

Giarelli *et al.* (2004) conducted a wide-ranging study into a target population of American women smokers. This included investigating the prevalence and risks of smoking as well as educational interventions. To illustrate the findings, they described a case study of a typical smoker. She reported that, as a student, she had a cigarette when she got up in the morning, after meals and when she was writing or studying, to help her concentrate. She would finish a good job and have a cigarette – for pleasure – but also when she was stressed. When she tried to quit she recognised the need to change her self-image as a smoker – feeling trapped in a cycle of thinking about when she could have another cigarette. Even deterrents such as restricted access, prohibition, negative public attitude and her husband's dislike of her habit did not stop her smoking.

Identify all the aspects of this case that illustrate dysfunctional beliefs or cognitive distortions.

The learning theory approach

For relatively new or infrequent smokers, nicotine is positively reinforcing: it produces a 'rush'. This effect, caused by a high concentration of nicotine reaching the brain, is one of the reasons for the initiation of smoking as well as its maintenance in the early stages of addiction. It may be sufficiently reinforcing to outweigh the unpleasant effects that nicotine has, such as stimulating the brain's 'vomit centre'.

▼ **Figure 11.14** Changes in blood nicotine level with different sources of nicotine after overnight abstinence from cigarettes. Data adapted from Russell MAH 'Nicotine intake and its regulation by smokers'. In Martin WR, Loon GRV, Iwamoto ET, Davis L (eds) (1987) *Tobacco Smoking and Nicotine: a Neurobiological Approach*. New York: Plenum Publishing Corporation, pp25–50

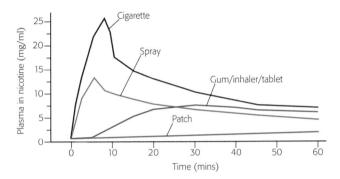

Many animals, such as monkeys, dogs, rats and mice, will self-administer nicotine. Indeed, a monkey will press a lever for nicotine in a Skinner box almost as often as to receive cocaine (Goldberg *et al.*, 1981). And when dogs learned to press a pedal, they would give several hundred responses to get a single injection of nicotine (Risner *et al.*, 1983). Studies such as these demonstrate the powerful reinforcing properties of nicotine.

Over continued use, unpleasant effects such as nausea and vomiting disappear but so too does the positively reinforcing 'rush'. Instead, smoking in dependent users is maintained by negative reinforcement. The rapid breakdown of nicotine by the liver means that smokers need to smoke frequently to maintain a high enough blood-nicotine level to avoid craving and withdrawal symptoms.

Gambling as an addiction

The British Gambling Prevalence Survey (2007) gave questionnaires to over 9000 people aged 16 and above. The findings show that approximately 68 per cent of the population – about 32 million adults – participate in some kind of gambling. This is a decrease from the estimated 72 per cent in 1999 – mainly because fewer people are doing the National Lottery (although for many people this is their only gambling activity). Of the remainder, 48 per cent said they had participated in another form of gambling in the past year. This is an increase from 1999 (46 per cent). The most popular forms of gambling were:

- the National Lottery (57 per cent)
- scratchcards (20 per cent)
- betting on horse races (17 per cent)
- slot machines (14 per cent).

The British Gambling Prevalence Survey (BGPS) found some differences in the incidence of gambling, for example men gamble somewhat more than women (71 per cent and 65 per cent, respectively).

▲ **Figure 11.15** The most common kind of gambling in the UK is buying tickets for the National Lottery

> ■ **Box 11.2**
>
> ## *The Diagnostic and Statistical Manual (DSM-IV) criteria for pathological gambling*
>
> For a diagnosis of persistent and recurrent maladaptive gambling behaviour, the individual must show five (or more) of the following (and their behaviour must not be better explained by a manic episode):
>
> - **preoccupation**: eg reliving past gambling experiences, planning the next one or thinking of ways to get money with which to gamble
> - **tolerance**: needs to gamble with larger amounts of money or more frequently to achieve the desired excitement
> - **loss of control**: repeated attempts to cut back or stop gambling are unsuccessful
> - **withdrawal**: restless or irritable if trying to cut down or stop gambling
> - **escape**: gambles as a way to avoid problems or improve mood (eg to reduce feelings of helplessness, guilt, anxiety, depression)
> - **chasing**: tries to get even after losing by gambling more
> - **lying**: attempts to hide involvement with gambling from family members, therapist etc.
> - **law breaking**: commits illegal acts eg fraud or theft to fund gambling
> - **damage to relationships**: risks losing or has lost a significant relationship, job or educational opportunity because of gambling
> - **bailout**: relies on others (eg friends or family) for money to cope financially as a result of gambling.
>
> Reprinted with permission from the *Diagnostic and Statistical Manual of Mental Disorders, Text Revision, Fourth Edition.* (© 2000). American Psychiatric Association.

Problem gambling was assessed for the BGPS in two ways: using *DSM-IV* and a Canadian screening tool called the Problem Gambling Severity Index (PGSI). As the two techniques produced very similar estimates, the researchers could be sure that their measures were reliable. The *DSM-IV* screening found that the rate of problem gambling in the adult population was about 0.6 per cent (about 284,000 adults in Great Britain) – the same percentage as was found in 1999. The PGSI screen identified 0.5 per cent of the adult population with a gambling problem.

▼ **Figure 11.16** According to the BGPS, on average problem gamblers engage in more than six types of gambling such as betting machines, casinos, online gambling and dog racing

LOOKING FURTHER To find out details of the British Gambling Prevalence Survey (2007), look at:

http://www.gamblingcommission.gov.uk/Client/detail.asp?ContentId=311

LOOKING FURTHER This online quiz assesses problem gambling. Following the answers given, it provides advice about possible problems reported by the respondent, such as believing in 'lucky numbers' or being able to predict outcomes.

http://problemgambling.checkyourgambling.net/cyg/CYGScreenerP1.aspx

On the same site, the page below provides many useful links about the signs and consequences of pathological gambling:

http://www.problemgambling.ca/EN/AboutGamblingand ProblemGambling/Pages/InformationAboutProblemGambling. aspx

The biological approach

Earlier in the chapter we noted that Kessler *et al.* (2008) found a relationship between pathological gambling and substance abuse. This suggests that both may be affected by some underlying predisposition to addictive behaviour. If so, this would suggest that there was an important biological risk factor in addiction.

Kim (1998) has found biochemical evidence that suggests gambling may activate the brain's reward system. This would explain the excitement and craving associated with gambling. The biochemical system involved could offer possible routes to treatment. Following on from this research, Kim & Grant (2001) tested naltrexone (an opioid antagonistic) as a treatment for pathological gamblers and found that it was effective. It reduced the intensity of urges to gamble, thoughts about gambling and actual gambling behaviour when given in sufficiently high doses.

An alternative way to explore evidence for the role of biological factors in addiction is to consider genetics. Eisen *et al.* (2001) investigated pathological gambling in twins and found they were similar in the occurrence and severity of gambling problems. Pathological gambling also co-occurred with alcohol misuse. This supports both the genetic and physiological aspects of the biological approach to explaining gambling addiction.

RESEARCH NOW

Bonnaire C, Varescon I & Bungener C (2007) Sensation seeking in a French population of horse betting gamblers: comparison between pathological and regular. *Encephale* 33(5), 798–804

Aim: To investigate whether French pathological gamblers who bet on horses at the racetrack are higher sensation-seekers than non-pathological gamblers.

Method: Gamblers were recruited from five different race tracks. These were divided using *DSM-IV* and another screening tool (the South Oaks Gambling Screen or SOGS) into regular gamblers (72 participants) and pathological gamblers (42 participants). Sensation-seeking was assessed using Zuckerman's sensation-seeking scale.

Results: Pathological gamblers had significantly higher sensation-seeking scores than regular gamblers. Specifically, they had higher overall scores for sensation-seeking and also for the factors of disinhibition and boredom susceptibility. No correlation was found between sensation-seeking score and the number of ordinary games played.

Conclusion: The personality trait of sensation-seeking discriminates between pathological and regular gamblers, at least for those who bet on horses at the race track.

If an individual's genes put him or her at greater risk of becoming addicted to gambling, how could this arise? One suggestion is that pathological gamblers, like people with other addictions, have certain personality traits that predispose them to risk-taking. Zuckerman (1979) proposed the personality characteristic of 'sensation-seeking'. This is a tendency to look for opportunities that raise arousal, for example by engaging in high-risk behaviours. Such activities include sports like white-water rafting, jobs such as being a pilot, pastimes that provide high levels of excitement such as gambling and the tendency to try consciousness-changing drugs. Recent research by Bonnaire *et al.* (2007) supports this idea (see *Research Now*).

▼ **Figure 11.17** Pathological gamblers who go to the races are higher 'sensation-seekers' than non-problem gamblers

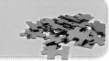

Thinking practically about psychology

If measurable personality factors such as sensation-seeking can indicate high-risk individuals, perhaps psychologists are duty-bound to act to reduce risk for those individuals. What ethical issues would surround any attempt to identify and help individuals who might be at risk of addiction to gambling later in life?

The cognitive approach

On pp251–3 we explored the cognitive factors that predispose individuals to addictions. For gamblers, dysfunctional thinking distorts their perception of their own skills and luck, as well of the skill of others. They hold superstitious beliefs and tend to interpret and remember situations in a biased way (eg Joukhador *et al.*, 2003, and Ariyabuddhiphongs & Phengphol, 2008 – see p253). These cognitive distortions lead pathological gamblers to take greater risks and persist with gambling for longer.

Wohl *et al.* (2007) tested 82 young adult gamblers at the University of Windsor for symptoms of pathological gambling, perception of dispositional luck (belief that they were 'lucky')

and enjoyment of gambling. The participants were divided into recreational gamblers and disordered gamblers. The latter group enjoyed gambling more and saw themselves as more lucky – illustrating another cognitive bias in high-risk gamblers.

A different approach was taken by Marazziti *et al.* (2008) who assessed pathological gamblers on a range of standard cognitive tests, such as the Wisconsin card-sorting task. In this test, the participant must find different strategies for sorting cards into groups as the rules for the sorting task are intermittently changed. The gamblers had difficulty finding alternative ways to solve the card-sorting problem. Their efficiency decreased, rather than increasing, as they progressed through the test, suggesting that they couldn't learn from their mistakes. Such cognitive rigidity may predispose individuals to develop impulsive or compulsive behaviours such as pathological gambling.

The learning theory approach

Both of the explanations we have considered so far suggest that the reason someone becomes a gambler is, at least in part, internal: it is a characteristic of them as an individual – either biological or cognitive. Learning theory takes a different view: that it is an individual's experiences that put them at risk and determine their behaviour.

On p248, we described the concept of positive reinforcement. Early research showed that, contrary to what you might expect, animals work harder, and keep trying longer, in the absence of rewards. Skinner (1953) suggested that winning, for a gambler, provides intermittent and unpredictable reinforcement – a variable ratio schedule of reinforcement. This results in the learning of a pattern of behaviour with a high response rate that is very resistant to extinction. This can explain why a gambler will persist in playing even when they are losing. However, everyone who tries gambling experiences the random positive reinforcement of occasional wins – but not everyone becomes addicted. This is clearly a problem for a simplistic learning theory explanation.

▲ **Figure 11.18** Not everyone who tries gambling becomes addicted

Custer (1984) suggested that the difference between those who go on to become problem gamblers and those who do not lies in their initial experiences with gambling. He proposed that an early winning streak and big win might predispose individuals to addiction. This explanation was tested by Christopher (1988) using pigeons in a Skinner box. The pigeons were initially trained on a fixed ratio schedule to 'work' for their food. They had to peck a disc (when it lit up) 50 times to earn three seconds' access to the food tray, ie FR50. This enabled the birds to maintain their body weight by 'working' for about half an hour each day.

Access to food was then changed. Although they could still work for food, a 'gamblers' disc' was introduced. When this lit up food rewards were variable – with occasional 'big wins' eg 15 seconds' access to the tray. This simulated a novice gambler's experience of 'getting lucky'. In the first three days of this arrangement, the birds could gain much more access to food by gambling than working. The advantage of gambling was then removed – the birds could gain longer access to the food tray by working than gambling. Did they revert to working?

No! The pigeons, just like gamblers, were addicted. They continued to peck the gamblers' disc even though it provided less access to food. The birds spent so long, and expended so much energy, pecking the unproductive gamblers' disc that they lost weight. To avoid the pigeons starving themselves, Christopher prevented them from gambling. The pigeons resumed 'working' for food and gained weight. However, when the gamblers' disc was reinstated, the pigeons hadn't lost their addiction – they just pecked the unsuccessful gambling disc and lost weight again.

So, one difference between people who become addicted to gambling and those who do not might be their early experience of big wins. This could explain some of the strategies of a 'pool hustler'. In competitive pool halls, where bets are placed on the outcomes of games, experienced players may

Thinking practically about psychology

Why might a casino provide free chips for new customers? What other strategies might they use to entice inexperienced gamblers?

use strategies to give inexperienced players early successes, thus tricking them. For example, a pool hustler may:

* intentionally miss simple shots
* pretend to be drunk
* use a cheap cue to look less experienced
* play erratically so their good shots look like luck.

The hustler lets the novice win early on. The stakes are then raised and the hustler plays 'for real' so the novice loses the game – and significant amounts of money.

When this was tested in a casino environment, rather than on rats in a laboratory, the findings were not as expected (Weatherly et al., 2004). Participants playing on a computer-simulated slot machine earned credits that could be exchanged for cash. The game outcomes were fixed, with different groups experiencing:

* a big win on the first game
* a big win on the fifth game
* two small wins, on the second and fifth games
* no wins.

If early wins were important in triggering addiction, the first group should persist with playing longer than the others. Weatherly et al. found instead that this group quit playing earlier than the participants who did not win until game five. This resistance to extinction when rewards are intermittent is, of course, consistent with a simple learning theory explanation.

Factors affecting addiction

Regardless of the possible cause of addiction, or the substance or behaviour involved, various factors can influence an individual's level of risk. Some are internal to the individual, such as aspects of their personality. Others are external, such as the social context and the effect of the media.

The effect of self-esteem

Self-esteem is an aspect of our self-concept. It reflects the difference between how we see ourselves (our self-image) and what we would like to be (our ideal self). If these two are similar, our self-esteem is high. If, however, we judge ourselves to fall short of our expectations, our self-esteem will be low. Individuals with low self-esteem may be at greater risk of developing addictive behaviours.

Fieldman et al. (1995) found that heroin and cocaine addicts typically had low self-esteem. In a longitudinal study, Friedman et al. (2004) followed up 431 children though to adulthood. In the final assessment, at age 37 years, drug use was associated with a negative self-perception, especially in women. Of course, such findings may be flawed as drug use, and other addictions, may affect self-perceptions.

Taylor et al. (2006) investigated the relationship between childhood self-esteem and drug use and whether this predicted drug dependency at age 20. Self-esteem was assessed in a questionnaire asking the participants to rate the truthfulness of statements such as 'I don't like myself as much as I used to' and 'In general I feel I am a failure'. An analysis of data collected over nine years from a multi-ethnic sample of 872 boys showed that low self-esteem at age 11 was linked to childhood drug use. Boys who were disappointed with themselves were also more likely to use drugs in adulthood. Those with low self-esteem at 11 were 1.6 times more likely to meet the criteria for drug dependence at 20 than those with higher self-esteem. Importantly, this relationship held regardless of early drug use. This finding is especially important as it could enable at-risk individuals to be identified and helped before they develop addiction problems.

▲ **Figure 11.19** Boys with low self-esteem are at greater risk of drug dependence as adults

Of course, this study only looked at boys, and it is likely that findings for girls would be different. Typically, girls with low self-esteem suffer depression or eating disorders rather than substance abuse.

Not all evidence supports the relationship between self-esteem and drug use. Greenberg *et al.* (1999), in common with other studies, found evidence for multiple addictions, such as to alcohol, caffeine, chocolate, cigarettes, exercise, gambling, internet use, television and video games. However, they did not find a link between self-esteem and any of these activities except exercise – people with lower self-esteem exercised less.

Attributions for addiction

An attribution is a judgement an individual makes to explain behaviours. These attributions may be external or internal.

- *External attributions* – we judge a behaviour to be caused by some factor in the situation, eg 'I take drugs because I grew up in a rough area'.
- *Internal attributions* – we judge a behaviour to be caused by some individual characteristic or 'disposition', eg 'He is addicted to gambling because he is too weak to resist the urge'.

These examples illustrate an important bias in the way we make attributions. For socially undesirable behaviours, like addictions, we tend to make external or *situational attributions* for our own behaviour, but internal or *dispositional* ones for the behaviour of others. For example, Seneviratne & Saunders (2000) found that alcohol-dependent patients blamed situational factors for their own relapses but those of other patients on their personality, ie their disposition.

  Look at a description of Seneviratne & Saunders' study at: http://www.basisonline.org/2004/03/the-wager-vol-9.html. Find at least two criticisms of the findings.

KEY TERMS

situational attribution using external causes to explain a behaviour

dispositional attribution using internal causes to explain a behaviour

This attributional bias is called the *actor–observer effect*. The 'actor' or person performing a behaviour – smoking, for example – tends to make situational attributions when the behaviour is socially undesirable. 'Observers', in contrast, tend to make dispositional judgements. Thus an individual might say 'I smoke because I have a stressful job but she smokes because she hasn't the willpower to stop.'

Feigin & Sapir (2005) investigated the attributions made by addicts coping with abstinence from drugs. Two groups of 128 short-term and 40 long-term abstinent patients were asked about possible solutions for their problem. Both groups attributed the responsibility for their recovery to themselves, ie they made internal attributions. This differs from the nature of attributions for the addiction itself as abstinence is socially desirable.

The social context and addiction

The social world can have both positive and negative influences on addiction risk – we have seen how parents, peers and attitudes in society can influence the risk of substance abuse. Parental norms for alcohol and cannabis use were shown to affect adolescent use (Dielman *et al.*, 1991; Courtois *et al.*, 2007), though less so than norms among friends. Morgan & Grube (1991) showed that peers affected both the initiation and maintenance of smoking and Simons-Morton *et al.* (2005) found that adolescents who spent more time with deviant peers were more likely to drink. Kendler *et al.* (2000) suggested that attitudes towards women smokers changed over time, as did the incidence of women smoking. These findings all illustrate how the social context increases risk, although this is not always the case. Simons-Morton *et al.* (2001) showed that more involved parenting and higher expectations of children were linked to a *lower* risk of drug use.

Other people may not only provide social norms for addictive behaviours, but may increase risk more directly. Consider how meeting with dealers who supply cannabis might expose someone to other drugs. Wagner & Anthony (2002) found that tobacco and alcohol users were more likely to have tried cannabis and were then more likely to continue this use. Similarly, individuals with prior cannabis use were more likely to try cocaine if it was available than those who had not previously used cannabis. This 'gateway' or 'stepping stones' sequence of drug use is more likely to arise in social contexts where opportunities to experience drugs are available.

▲ **Figure 11.20** High parental involvement and expectations may reduce a child's risk of later drug use

Other social variables also increase risk. Recent evidence from Lund (2007) has shown that single and divorced people are at greater risk of gambling addiction than married people. In relation to substance abuse, Stein *et al.* (2008) found that homeless people and those in poor housing had a high risk of alcohol and intravenous drug abuse, and alcohol use is also linked to low self-esteem (see p260). Conversely, good social support reduced distress and increased coping. This suggests that the effects of social context are complex.

▲ **Figure 11.21** Homelessness and poor housing increase the risk of addiction to drugs or alcohol

A more direct effect of social context was illustrated experimentally by Rockloff & Dyer (2007). Using a computer-simulated gaming machine, participants played games with predetermined outcomes (a winning sequence followed only by losses). One group of participants received

false feedback about players in adjacent rooms who were sometimes winning – indicated by instant messages (visual) and bells (auditory). When participants received both visual and auditory information about the wins of these fake players they placed more bets and lost more money than participants given less information.

Whilst other people's behaviour can increase gambling, social desirability causes gamblers to under-report their behaviour. Kuentzel *et al.* (2008) studied samples of problem and non-problem gambling students. In both groups, the more gambling problems an individual had, the more susceptible they were to impression management – reducing the gambling problems they reported (but not behaviour) to more socially acceptable levels. So, although the frequency of gambling, amount of time spent gambling and money spent may be reasonably accurate in self-reports, the accuracy of gambling-related problems reported may not be. This aspect of social influence brings into question the validity of studies based on self-reported data about gambling problems.

In both cognitive and learning theory explanations of drug use, salient cues are important in priming or triggering craving in dependent users. Since a social context can act as a cue, some contexts present a risk. A problem gambler will find it much harder to resist the urge to gamble in a casino or at a race track than at home.

The role of the media in addictive behaviour

Role models such as parents and peers are important in drug use. Are models in the media influential too? Since media personalities have characteristics such as being high status, powerful or likeable they could be highly effective models. These features may apply to celebrities, characters in films or TV programmes, people in advertisements and in behaviours depicted in songs.

Advertising promotes legal drugs such as alcohol (and, previously, tobacco). Charlton (1986) found that British children aged 9–13 who could name a favourite cigarette advert were more likely to claim that smoking led to looking grown up, calmed the nerves, gave confidence or was useful in controlling weight. However, these children were no more likely to smoke the brand they preferred. Similarly Atkin & Block (1981) found little relationship between exposure to television advertising of alcohol and teenagers' consumption of alcohol.

Thinking creatively about psychology

Many products, such as new sweets, with incessant advertising directed at children do not succeed in the market (Smith & Sweeny, 1984). Suggest a list of factors that might be more important than mere exposure and devise a TV advert.

Television programmes may also affect children's behaviour. In a correlational study of 400 adolescent boys, Tucker (1985) found that those who watched more television also consumed more alcohol. However, not all studies have demonstrated this relationship. Hanssen (1988) found no indication that TV viewing was linked to higher alcohol consumption.

Since the evidence is contradictory, direct experimentation is useful. Rychtarik *et al.* (1983) investigated the influence of television on children aged 8–11 years. Each child did one of the following: viewed an episode of *M*A*S*H*, viewed the same episode with the drinking scenes deleted or did not see the programme. The children who had seen the full programme were more likely to choose alcohol than water to serve to a 'parched' adult. This, of course, does not tell us about the children's own drinking habits.

Some of the most potentially influential models in the media are celebrities. Boon & Lomore (2001) found that 75 per cent of young adults reported that they had, at some time, had a strong attachment to a celebrity and 59 per cent reported that these idols affected their attitudes and beliefs. When numerous celebrities are reported to use illicit drugs, and this is often glorified in the press, such observations suggest that celebrities may influence drug-taking. Gunsekera *et al.* (2005) investigated the way drugs were represented in 200 high-earning films. Whilst the drug use depicted did not included injected illicit drugs, the portrayal of drug use was very positive and without negative consequences. The drugs used were primarily tobacco (68 per cent of films included at least one character smoking), alcohol (32 per cent included intoxication) and cannabis (8 per cent of films), the latter typically being used by a background character.

In an experimental investigation of the power of celebrity endorsement, Ross *et al.* (1984) studied children's views about advertisements. When a famous presenter endorsed a toy racing car, children believed that they were experts and preferred the product. So, if celebrities are seen as better informed, as well as high in status, they are likely to be influential. Since Gunsekera *et al.* found that drug use was positively portrayed in film media – providing a source of vicarious reinforcement – these two effects could combine to produce highly effective role models.

▲ **Figure 11.22** Do celebrities such as Kate Moss act as role models for drug use?

Another possible source of powerful models for young people is popular music. Roberts *et al.* (2002) surveyed 300 music videos. Images of illicit drugs and references to them in lyrics were rare (appearing in nine and 51 videos, respectively) although references to alcohol and smoking were more common (37 per cent and 21 per cent of videos, respectively). Unlike Boon and Lomore's findings with respect to films, Roberts *et al.* argue that drugs in music are depicted in a neutral manner, being common elements of everyday life. Whilst this could be seen as better than presenting drugs as highly desirable, it could equally be argued that this makes drug use acceptable, promoting a social norm of drug use rather than non-use.

The overall influence of exposure to the media is difficult to interpret. The effects on behaviour are typically small and other factors, such as the individual's vulnerability or the attitudes of their peers or friends, are probably more important.

Reducing addictive behaviour: models of prevention

There are several theories that can guide the development of interventions to reduce addiction. The two we will explore are the theory of reasoned action and the theory of planned behaviour.

The theory of reasoned action

The theory of reasoned action (TRA) was proposed by Ajzen & Fishbein (1980). It aims to explain the decision-making behind an individual's behaviour. It suggests that people make judgements about their actions – so behaviours such as drug use are not the inevitable consequence of a set of predisposing factors but the result of reasoning. A person's intention to act, and the factors that influence that intention, are therefore important in determining abstinence or relapse in addiction.

People behave in certain ways because they decide they can, or that it is desirable. In relation to addictions, individuals can continue with the addictive behaviour, cut down or abstain. Each of these would, according to the TRA, be a reasoned decision. The TRA says that people make rational judgements about these options using two types of information: how they feel and what they believe.

- *Attitudes – a person's feelings and beliefs about a behaviour.* If an individual believes that anti-smoking propaganda is all hype, this is likely to lead to a decision not to quit smoking because they have a pro-smoking attitude.
- *Subjective norms – a person's beliefs about what is expected of them by other individuals or society in general.* As society became more accepting of women smoking, more did so. This is an example of a change in the subjective norm.

Together, attitudes and norms affect whether an individual thinks they are going to break their addiction or not, ie it determines their *behavioural intention*.

Attitudes are made up of two parts:

- *beliefs:* the individual's own opinion about what will happen depending on the way they behave, eg 'giving up smoking will make me feel healthier' or 'only gambling can make me happy'
- *evaluation:* whether those outcomes are worth having, eg 'If I give up smoking I'll be healthier but more stressed' or 'having fewer debts if I stop gambling would make me less stressed'.

Norms are also made up of two parts:

- *externally driven component*: what the person thinks specific individuals and society in general expect from them, eg 'everyone at work is giving up so I suppose I should too' or 'my children want me to stop'
- *internally driven component*: how motivated they are to comply with these expectations, eg 'I feel ridiculous outside in the rain on my own having a cigarette so I want to give up' or 'being a better parent is important to me so I ought to stop'.

The relationship between these factors is illustrated in Figure 11.24.

▲ **Figure 11.23** If smoking is the norm, are you more likely to smoke?

Applying the theory of reasoned action to addictive behaviour

The TRA helps us to understand why people continue with addictive behaviours. It can also explain why some people recover from addictions and others find this impossibly difficult and yet others relapse. When an individual's attitudes and norms support quitting, their behavioural intention will be to do so. This requires:

- beliefs about the effects of the behaviour (eg drug taking) and the outcome of abstinence
- an evaluation of whether the consequences of those behaviours are worthwhile
- an expectation from others that the behaviour, or abstinence, is important
- personal motivation to satisfy those expectations.

Each of these can be a reason to continue use or a potential stumbling block for an individual aiming to resolve their addiction, but is also a potential route for intervention.

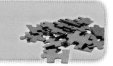

Thinking practically about psychology

1 Consider the four bullet points above in relation to a problem gambler. What reasoning might be applied in each case?

Beliefs
- What positive beliefs might they have about gambling or abstinence?
- What negative beliefs might they have about gambling or abstinence?
- How might an intervention increase positive expectations/ opinions about abstinence?

Evaluation
- Why might the outcomes of gambling or abstinence be perceived as worthwhile?
- Why might the outcomes of gambling or abstinence be perceived as pointless?
- How might an intervention help to make evaluations of abstinence more positive?

External factors
- What subjective norms might support abstinence?
- What subjective norms might encourage continuation of gambling?
- How might an intervention help to make an individual aware of subjective norms that discourage gambling?

Internal factors
- Why might an individual be personally motivated to abstain from gambling?
- Why might an individual be personally motivated to continue gambling?
- How might an intervention help to raise personal motivation to stop gambling?

2 Repeat this exercise for an addicted smoker.

Evaluating the theory of reasoned action

In a test of the TRA, Morrison *et al.* (2002) investigated drug use by teenage mothers. They found that intention to use marijuana was mainly predicted by attitudes but that norms were also related to intention. Furthermore, intention was related to actual marijuana use six months later, showing that the elements of the TRA do relate to behaviour.

Wood & Griffiths (2004) investigated the factors affecting lottery playing and scratchcard use by adolescents. A questionnaire given to over 1000 11–15-year-olds showed that their attitudes accurately predicted their gambling behaviour. Again this supports the theory of reasoned action.

However, many addictive behaviours may not be volitional, ie not 'reasoned', at all. Schlegel *et al.* (1992) investigated whether the TRA could predict intention and behaviour in problem drinkers. As the TRA assumes that the behaviour being predicted is volitional, they anticipated that the model would become less predictive as drinking became heavier. This was indeed the case. Although these findings do not contradict the TRA, they also show that there are aspects of addictive behaviour that are not reasoned. This seems likely as we know that some dependent users are well aware that their behaviour is irrational. Most smokers want to give up, but even when intention, attitudes and norms predict that they will, they don't.

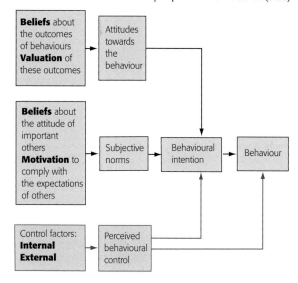

▼ **Figure 11.24** The theory of reasoned action (in green) and the additional elements of the theory of planned behaviour in (blue)

Sheeran & Orbell (1999) investigated the role of intentions in lottery play. They found that intention did predict lottery use, supporting the TRA. However, they also found that anticipated regret was important. Gambling behaviour was greatest when participants intended to play the lottery and anticipated that they would regret *not* playing. So regret is another factor in addiction that the TRA cannot explain.

M E D I A   W A T C H : 3 MINUTE WONDERS

Help tackle drugs: 3 Minute Wonders songwriting competition

http://www.westyorkshire.police.uk/section-item.
asp?sid=12andiid=4383

Teenagers in West Yorkshire are being urged to help tackle the problem of drugs on their streets, whilst also uncovering a possible hidden talent.

West Yorkshire Police have teamed up with Northern Rail, and its NorthernTrax initiative, to launch a song-writing competition – '3 Minute Wonders'. It encourages all people under 19 to write a three-minute song about the fight against drugs.

The competition is being backed by singer Corinne Bailey Rae – who comes from Leeds. She hopes it will raise awareness amongst teenagers about the negative effects of drug-taking. She said: 'Helping raise awareness amongst teenagers about the danger of drugs is vital, and combining this with the chance to showcase local song-writing talent is a great idea. The impact of drugs in our local communities cannot be underestimated, so I'm happy to be supporting West Yorkshire Police's "3 Minute Wonders". All you budding song-writers have got until February 2008 to get your entries in – you just never know who might be listening.'

West Yorkshire Police's Inspector Janet Ballance said: 'West Yorkshire Police see the effects of drugs on young people day in day out, so we're always looking for new ways to help educate them about the dangers. We are looking for a song approximately three minutes long, that will give positive messages about the danger of drugs. It can be any style from rap to reggae, from ballad to bhangra.'

Malcolm Brown, Area Director, Northern Rail said: 'We're delighted to be supporting this competition. NorthernTrax gives young people the opportunity to showcase their musical talent and this competition will enable them to deliver vital safety messages to their peers.'

1 How would the TRA or TPB explain the reasoning behind this campaign?

2 To what extent could the success of such a campaign also be explained by social learning theory?

The theory of planned behaviour

The theory of planned behaviour (TPB) was proposed by Ajzen (1985) and attempts to explain some of the factors influencing behaviour that the TRA cannot. It differs from the TRA in that it also includes the role of *perceived behavioural control*. This is whether an individual believes they can or cannot perform a behaviour – how difficult or easy they think they will find it. This can be governed by internal factors, such as knowing that you can force yourself to avoid going to the shops so you can't buy any more cigarettes, and by external factors, such as whether someone you live with smokes too. In all other respects it is like the TRA (see Figure 11.24).

Applying the theory of planned behaviour to addiction

The TPB considers an individual's reasons for continuing with their behaviour *and* their belief in their determination to abstain. This is important in taking the first steps to giving up and in resisting the effects of withdrawal and craving. The individual's perceived behavioural control must lead them to expect to be able to overcome each of these hurdles. Imagine someone trying to quit smoking: they must believe they will be able to avoid buying cigarettes, going to places where they might be given

cigarettes and smoking one if it is offered to them. These are all aspects of behavioural control. If the individual believes they can do these things, the TPB would predict that they would succeed in abstaining. Conversely, the more difficult the individual expects abstinence to be, the less likely they are to quit.

Thinking critically about psychology

One reason that teenagers' lottery behaviour cannot be predicted by the TPB is that they have been widely exposed to the lottery from childhood. This may result in little cognition or reasoning being applied to the purchase of tickets.

If this is the case, how can the TPB account for the variables predicting intention but not behaviour? Look back to Figure 11.24 and think about the stage at which other possible variables, not accounted for by TPB, must be acting.

Being able to predict health behaviour is clearly useful in planning interventions to help reduce addictive behaviours. However, the effectiveness of a strategy depends on the factors most important in the decision-making process for that individual or behaviour.

RESEARCH NOW

Miller R & Howell G (2005) A test of the theory of planned behavior in underage lottery gambling. *Broadening the Boundaries – Proceedings of the 8th Australia and New Zealand Marketing Academy (ANZMAC) Conference, Fremantle, 5–7 December*

Aim: To investigate whether the TPB could predict gambling by underage teens.

Procedure: 170 participants were obtained by opportunity sampling from three Australian secondary schools. Ordinal data were collected using seven-point Likert scales (from 1=strongly disagree to 7=strongly agree). Some information was also collected using closed questions requiring yes/no answers or a number (*). Some statements are reproduced below:

Attitudes

I would find playing lotto a very satisfying experience.
I would find playing lotto very exciting.
Thinking about playing lotto makes me happy.

Norms

I frequently gather information from family about a product before I buy.
If I have little experience about a product, I ask friends about the product.

Perceived behavioural control

One day my lucky numbers will win lotto.
Anyone can win lotto.
Selecting winning lotto numbers requires skill.

Intention

Number of lotto tickets you intend to play in the next two weeks (*).
It is easy to collect lotto prizes.

Findings: Two students self-reported excessive and unlikely levels of lottery use and their results were removed as they were not representative of the population. Analysis of the data suggested that the variables measured could predict intentions to buy lotto tickets but not actual behaviour.

Conclusion: Although attitudes, norms and perceived behavioural control can predict intentions, they are not good predictors of actual lottery behaviour in young people.

Evaluating the theory of planned behaviour

Just because an individual has the intention to perform a behaviour does not necessarily mean they will do it. A smoker may be convinced that they will quit, make a New Year's resolution to do so and be very determined, but still may not actually do so.

We are more likely to fulfil an intention if it is specific; 'I will not buy any more cigarettes' is more likely to be successful than 'I will cut down the number I smoke'. Latency also affects the link between intention and behaviour. We are more likely to follow an intention through if we do it immediately after making the decision. So deciding to quit smoking today is more likely to work than having a New Year's resolution. The theory of planned behaviour can therefore account for the effects of the individual's self-belief as well as attitudes, social norms and intentions.

One interesting finding in relation to perceived control is the extent to which this differs between individuals who are addicted and those who are not. Goodie (2005) investigated the role of perceived control in problem and non-problem gamblers. Two hundred students who were frequent gamblers were assessed for gambling problems. They answered questions and judged their confidence in each answer. They then considered bets on their answers. These were rigged so they were fair if their own judgements were good, but unfavourable if their judgements were overconfident. In a second study, each individual's control was manipulated and the bets were fixed. Overall, problem gamblers showed greater overconfidence and greater acceptance of bets. This suggested that they were less affected by their level of control in betting decisions than non-problem gamblers.

Walker *et al.* (2006) investigated whether the TPB could explain why people play the lottery. Using a telephone interview conducted in English, Cantonese and Mandarin, intention to play the lottery was measured in over 500 British and Chinese-Canadians. Some aspects of attitudes and norms were found to be important supporting both the TRA and TPB. Self-efficacy was not an important predictor for any group and controllability was only an important predictor for Chinese-Canadian females. These results suggest that perceived behavioural control is not an important factor in determining intention. In a questionnaire sent to participants a month later, self-reports of actual lottery play were obtained from over 200 of the original participants. In relation to gambling behaviour, intention was found to be an important predictor for both British-Canadian and Chinese-Canadian males and females. These findings support the TRA and TPB in relation to the role of intention but contradict the TPB, in that self-efficacy and controllability – aspects of behavioural control – were found to be less important. Similar problems were identified by Miller & Howell – see *Research Now*.

Being able to predict health behaviour is clearly useful in planning interventions to help reduce addictive behaviours. However, the effectiveness of a strategy depends on the factors most important in the decision-making process for that individial or behaviour.

Practical strategies for reducing addictive behaviour

On pp246–53 we explored biological, cognitive and learning approaches to explaining addiction. Each of the approaches provides ideas that can contribute to the reduction of addictive behaviours. If you have already studied psychopathology (Chapter 9) you will have considered some of these ideas before.

Biological strategies for reducing addictive behaviour: drug intervention

In *Exploring Psychology for AS Level,* and in Chapter 9, we have discussed biological strategies for coping with stress and reducing the symptoms of mental disorder. One of these biological strategies is the use of drugs, which we will now apply to the reduction of addictive behaviours.

Drug action

At the beginning of this chapter we described the different ways that drugs, by mimicking neurotransmitters, can affect brain function (see p246). These effects fall into two broad groups:

- *agonistic effects*: drugs having the *same* effect as the neurotransmitter
- *antagonistic effects*: drugs having the *opposite* effect from the neurotransmitter.

Drugs used medicinally are generally quite specific in the receptors they attach to. So drugs are manufactured which, say, act as agonists at receptors for the neurotransmitter serotonin or antagonists at receptors for the neurotransmitter dopamine. The neurotransmitters for addictive behaviours include:

- serotonin
- dopamine
- acetylcholine
- endorphins (opioids).

In the treatment of addiction to drugs such as heroin, two approaches to drug intervention are possible. In one, a similar but less harmful drug (methadone) is used (sometimes with additional drugs to reduce withdrawal symptoms). This is an agonist but does not produce the same 'high' that heroin does. It is therefore possible for users to achieve abstinence slowly by reducing the amount of methadone used. An alternative approach is to detoxify very quickly using large doses of an antagonist such as naloxone. Because this induces withdrawal symptoms immediately, it is often done under anaesthetic.

One recent approach to therapy is to prescribe heroin itself. Blättler *et al.* (2002) investigated the use of prescribed heroin for poly-drug-users (people abusing more than one drug). The participants, who used both heroin and cocaine (and other drugs), had all made unsuccessful attempts to treat their addiction. They attended counselling and received health care in addition to being given maintenance doses of heroin which was self-injected under supervision. Patients typically attended two to three times a day. The programme reduced illicit heroin and cocaine use. This suggests that heroin maintenance in a high-monitoring situation can help poly-drug-users.

Drug interventions to reduce smoking

Nicotine, the addictive drug in cigarettes, acts on 'nicotinic receptors' that normally respond to the neurotransmitter acetylcholine. These receptors offer one possible way for drug interventions to act, but are not the only possibility. Nicotine itself, whilst addictive, is much less damaging to the body than the other components of cigarettes (such as the carcinogenic tars). One strategy for reducing smoking is therefore to replace the nicotine obtained through smoking with a safer nicotine source. Nicotine replacement therapy is available in a range of forms, including:

- patches
- gum
- nasal spray
- inhalers.

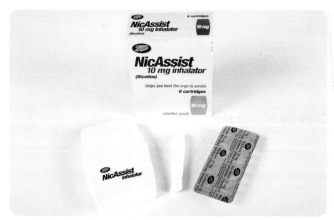

▲ **Figure 11.25** Sources of nicotine replacement therapy

All of these methods are effective in assisting abstinence in smokers: nicotine replacement therapy roughly doubles the rate of quitting. Although the inhaler mimics the action of smoking a cigarette so might seem more likely to work, this is not the case. Patches are believed to be more effective as compliance is higher – because they are easy to use, people follow the instructions correctly.

An alternative to actual nicotine is to use a drug that acts as an agonist at nicotinic receptors. Varenicline (Champix) acts in

this way. It is a partial agonist, meaning that, like acetylcholine, it attaches to nicotinic receptors, but has slightly different effects from nicotine itself. When it binds to acetylcholine receptors, varenicline alleviates the symptoms of craving and withdrawal experienced by abstinent smokers (just as nicotine replacement therapy does). However, varenicline also reduces the rewarding and reinforcing effects of smoking by preventing nicotine binding to the receptors. This makes smoking less appealing and helps to maintain abstinence.

Thinking practically about psychology

Look up nicotine replacement therapy (NRT) on the internet. Identify all the specific benefits that are attributed to using NRT and decide how each helps quitting.

LOOKING FURTHER You can read the full National Institute for Health and Clinical Excellence (NICE) report on Champix (*Varenicline for smoking cessation*, 2007) at www.nice.org.uk/TA123. In addition to the report itself, there are several links to other useful websites about the drug.

Research has shown that varenicline is very effective in assisting with smoking cessation. Nakamura *et al.* (2007) recorded the continuous abstinence rate (CAR) – the length of time over which participants did not smoke *at all*. This was compared in groups taking varenicline (at different strengths) or a placebo. The participants took the drug for 12 weeks and were followed up for a further 40 weeks. The CAR for participants receiving all doses of varenicline was higher than for the placebo group during the initial period (weeks nine to 12), with participants taking the highest dose showing the greatest resistance to smoking (65 per cent CAR compared with 40 per cent for the placebo group). The CARs were also significantly better for the highest dose varenicline group at the end of the follow-up period compared with the placebo group (34.6 per cent compared with 23.3 per cent). However, more side effects were also reported by the varenicline group compared with the placebo group, including nausea and headaches.

As smokers have a higher than average rate of depression, it has also been suggested that smoking may be an attempt to self-medicate for this problem. An alternative drug intervention is thus to treat smokers with antidepressants. Two examples include:

- nortriptyline
- bupropion hydrochloride.

Hall *et al.* (1998) found that nortriptyline was effective in assisting quitting and that this advantage was increased if the drug was used alongside cognitive behavioural therapy (see p269). Hurt *et al.* (1997) found that bupropion doubled the quit-rate compared with a placebo. Interestingly, the efficacy of bupropion was not markedly improved in combination with nicotine patches (Jorenby, 1999) and was no more effective in people who had symptoms of clinical depression and those who did not (Hayford *et al.*, 1999). This suggests that the effect of bupropion on cigarette cessation is not simply a function of its antidepressant effect.

Thinking critically about psychology

One infrequently reported side effect of varenicline is an increased risk of suicide. Consider the withdrawal symptoms of smoking cessation and the mental health of typical smokers. Why is this potentially a serious issue? Why might it be prescribed anyway?

Drug interventions and gambling

The possibility of using one drug to counteract the effects of another is understandable in terms of the action of neurotransmitters. Using drugs to reduce gambling is possible but less obvious. However, if you think of gambling as a symptom of a mental disorder, the efficacy of drug intervention is less surprising.

Grant & Kim (2006) observed that pathological gambling, whilst as prevalent as schizophrenia or bipolar disorder, receives less attention from clinicians and researchers. In a review of drug interventions with pathological gamblers, they identified three key approaches involving the use of:

- opioid antagonists – eg naloxone
- antidepressants – eg selective serotonin reuptake inhibitors (SSRIs)
- mood stabilisers.

In relation to opioid use, Grant & Kim observe that gamblers experience a 'rush' of excitement akin to that of opiate drug users. Logically, countering the gambling-related excitement and craving should help to control the behaviour.

In one study, Kim & Grant (2001) showed that naloxone reduced thoughts about gambling, the urge to gamble and – at relatively high doses – gambling behaviour itself. Kim *et al.* (2001) also demonstrated that, over a 12-week period, naloxone was more effective than a placebo at controlling the frequency and intensity of urges to gamble as well as the behaviour.

Evidence indicates that the neurotransmitter serotonin may be related to pathological gambling. First, the level of a breakdown product of serotonin found in the fluid around the brain is low in pathological gamblers. This pattern is associated with impulsiveness and sensation-seeking behaviour. If this arises because the level of serotonin itself is too low, SSRIs should be effective as they raise serotonin levels.

Using the SSRI fluvoxamine, Kim *et al.* (2002) found a reduction in gambling symptoms and an improvement in mood in the drug group compared with the placebo condition, but this advantage was not apparent in a larger, 16-week replication (Grant *et al.* 2003), nor in a similar study using the

SSRI sertraline was an advantage found in using the SSRI over a placebo (Saiz-Ruiz *et al.*, 2005).

Mood stabilisers are drugs used to control mood fluctuations for people with mental illnesses such as bipolar disorder. Hollander *et al.* (2005) tested the effectiveness of lithium carbonate compared with a placebo in 40 pathological gamblers who also had bipolar spectrum disorders. They found that, over 10 weeks, the drug reduced thoughts and urges related to gambling. However, the drug group did not lose less money, or gamble less often, or for less time, than the placebo group.

Evaluating biological strategies

Some drug interventions, such as using prescribed heroin for heroin addicts, are still at a relatively exploratory stage; others are well supported by evidence. Nicotine replacement therapy (NRT), bupropion and varenicline for smoking are all effective. One risk with NRT is that smokers may continue to smoke in addition to the intervention. Side effects are also problematic with both bupropion and varenicline. Indeed, whilst bupropion is an antidepressant, used in part because smokers have a higher incidence of depression, varenicline has been associated with increasing depression. Clearly there is a need for careful monitoring of patients.

Tønnesen (2006) suggests that NRT should be used in the first instance as it is highly effective and produces fewest side effects. Varenicline is also highly effective, although the side effects are greater. Bupropion is recommended for those individuals at risk from depression or for whom other treatments have been unsuccessful.

Drug treatments for pathological gambling are still at a relatively experimental stage, although the use of opioid antagonists is showing some promise.

Psychological strategies for reducing addictive behaviour

Cognitive and behavioural approaches offer strategies for intervention with addictive behaviours.

Cognitive therapy

In Chapter 9 (p201) we described the use of cognitive behaviour therapy for depression. This technique can also be used for addiction. Beck *et al.* (2001) observed that, precisely because addicts' cravings make them feel 'out of control', they are likely to seek help. Although many addicts will deny that they have a problem, repeatedly failing to stop their own habit can encourage them to turn to professional help.

The cognitive therapist aims to build a trusting relationship with his or her clients. This facilitates the use of an active, focused approach to identifying and challenging their false beliefs about their addiction. Cognitive therapy (CT) can help in several ways, by:

- confronting dysfunctional beliefs
- reducing craving
- establishing control.

In common with the treatment of depression, CT for addiction involves identifying the triggers – in the case of an addict, the sources of craving. Strategies are then developed to help the individual to assert control. In reality, addicts do not satisfy every craving immediately, so they do have some level of resistance. The purpose of CT is to enable them to achieve a better balance between their craving (a bodily state in the case of drug users) and their willpower (a psychological factor). To overcome the addiction successfully, help is needed to shift the balance so that the strength of self-control exceeds the strength of the urge.

▲ **Figure 11.26** Cognitive therapy helps with addictions by helping the individual to resist cravings – like walking past a betting shop

Increasing control is achieved through therapy by creating situations that induce craving, then rehearsing control. For example, a gambler might be asked to imagine walking up to the door of a betting shop. They then picture their alternative behaviours: eg walking past and going to visit a friend or to see a film at the cinema that will absorb them. Another option is to carry flashcards with rational explanations of the craving and read them – this counters the false belief that the gambler cannot resist the urge to walk through the door.

Thinking creatively about psychology

Consider the example of a drug addict in therapy imagining how they could respond to being offered a line of cocaine at a party. Suggest three ways they could respond to reduce their urge.

The therapist can also help the addict to re-evaluate their permission-giving thoughts that lead to loss of control. The therapist asks the client to describe out loud thoughts relating to the 'permission' they give themselves to indulge. The therapist then engages in a debate with them to counter these reasons. To enable the client to reduce their craving, the therapist must help them to solve any underlying social or psychological problems that 'justify' permission-giving, such as relationship problems or being frustrated.

Although addicts may express a strong conviction that they will resist the urge, when presented with a situation that induces craving, they may fail. This is described as the degree of *commitment*. The extent to which individuals commit in the face of temptation is affected by their self-beliefs (see p266). Feeling helpless leads to being unable to resist so the therapist needs to help the individual to develop a positive self-image.

Thinking critically about psychology

Relate the ideas about commitment and self-belief in addiction to the theory of planned behaviour.

In making decisions to resist, the individual may make irrational judgements about costs versus benefits. For an addict, short-term gains are more important than long-term costs. A smoker may have a cigarette because the threats to health are too far in the future to consider. A gambler may deny that the financial risk they are taking is real. This imbalance can also be addressed in therapy, for example though advantages–disadvantages analysis (see Table 11.3).

▼ **Table 11.1** Using an advantages-disadvantages analysis, the therapist can challenge the client's belief that it is 'better' not to quit

	Advantages	Disadvantages
Quitting smoking	• Better-smelling breath • Not having dirty-looking fingers and a smelly car • Having more money	• Getting withdrawal headaches • Not knowing what to do with my hands when I'm out • Won't cope with stress
Not quitting	• No withdrawal to deal with • Avoid all the hassle of trying	• I'll be smelly with yellow teeth • It'll kill me • I'll feel lousy because I've failed

▼ **Figure 11.27** Thinking about the advantages of not smoking can help quitting

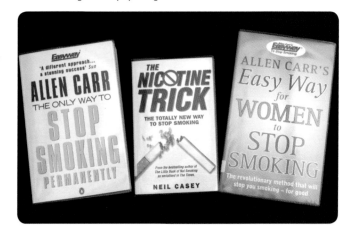

Create an advantages–disadvantages analysis for a gambler. Suggest how the therapist might counter a false belief about one advantage (of not stopping) and one disadvantage (of stopping).

Therapists set 'homework' for clients. This is designed between the client and therapist and allows the client to identify triggers or practise strategies for self-control. In follow-up sessions, the client identifies automatic thoughts that have prevented them from resisting their urge. Succeeding at a homework task allows the therapist to provide the client with valuable positive feedback.

Thinking practically about psychology

Design a homework task for a smoker and suggest what a therapist might say in response to the client succeeding or failing the task.

Cognitive–behavioural therapy is effective in reducing addictive behaviour for both gamblers and people with a drug addiction. Floyd *et al.* (2006) attempted to modify the beliefs and gambling behaviour of students who were playing computerised roulette games with imaginary money. Of three groups, one heard a discussion of irrational beliefs held by gamblers and saw 'warning messages' during play, one saw brief warning messages about these beliefs, and the third just heard a discussion about the history of roulette. Although the first two groups were both motivated by being allowed to exchange the 'imaginary' winnings for prize draw tickets, the warning message group engaged in less risky gambling behaviour and reported fewer irrational beliefs about gambling than the control group. This demonstrates that simple psychological interventions can affect both beliefs and behaviour, at least in non-clinical samples.

▼ **Figure 11.28** Does knowing the odds cut the risk?

However, cognitive interventions are not always successful. Williams & Connolly (2006) taught students about probability theory either using examples from gambling or not. Those who received the intervention relating to gambling were better at calculating gambling odds and more resistant to gambling fallacies six months later. This did not, however, produce a decrease in actual gambling, suggesting that knowledge alone is not sufficient to change gambling behaviour.

Thinking critically about psychology

Turner *et al.* (2008) described a school-based intervention designed to raise students' awareness of gambling problems and their own self-monitoring skills. The programme increased knowledge of random events, of the problems that gamblers experience and their own behaviour-monitoring. To what extent would you expect such an intervention to alter the students' gambling behaviour?

Behavioural therapy and addictive behaviours

The token economy approach to therapy uses the operant conditioning principles of positive reinforcement and *shaping* – the rewarding of successive approximations to the desired behaviour. For dependent users, the goal is to be drug-free, so longer and longer abstinences are rewarded. Token economies can be used in institutions or operated from outreach centres. Abstinence is positively reinforced with tokens that are saved to exchange for 'treats'.

Olmstead *et al.* (2007) collected data from stimulant abusers on token economy programmes at eight clinics. Four hundred and fifteen participants abusing cocaine, amphetamine or methamphetamine were randomly assigned to 'usual care' or 'usual care plus abstinence-based incentives'. The latter group received positive reinforcers in the form of prize draw entries (tokens taken from a fishbowl). Of the 500 tokens, 250 said 'good job', 209 were for items worth about $1, 40 were for $20 prizes and there was one worth $100. The number of entries increased with the length of their drug-free period. Compared with the control group, participants in the prize draw group had significantly longer periods of abstinence. Although effective, the programme was costly.

Sindelar *et al.* (2007) demonstrated similar success using the same programme with 120 cocaine abusers on a 12-week programme. When payouts were bigger ($240 rather than $80) the participants provided a higher percentage of drug-free urine samples, stayed clean for longer and were more likely to complete the treatment programme. Even though the prizes were bigger, the overall cost-effectiveness was better. One problem with token economies is that they may lead to a different kind of dependency. For example, drug users may expect to be rewarded simply for staying drug-free, which would make coping without the system difficult.

M E D I A   W A T C H : US ADDICTION PROGRAMMES

Scientists put price on addicts' treatment

Della Fok, yaledailynews.com, 11 October 2006

Yale scientists have put a price on incentive-based treatments for drugs abusers, helping to clarify the programs' costs and benefits.

Researchers from the Yale Department of Epidemiology and Public Health and the University of Connecticut Health Center found that it costs an additional $258 per patient to use prize-based incentives, which past research has shown can encourage patients to remain drug-free. The study, conducted by Yale research scientist Todd Olmstead and professor Jody Sindelar, along with University of Connecticut researcher Nancy Petry, was recently published in the September issue of *Drug and Alcohol Dependence*.

The researchers gathered data from eight clinics serving a variety of patients across the country, focusing on treatment for addiction to cocaine, amphetamine and methamphetamine. The incentive method they explored was a supplemental program used alongside traditional treatment.

If the patients submitted drug-free urine samples, they earned chances to draw from a fishbowl with 500 chips, representing different levels of prizes. Out of 500 chips, 250 said 'Good job,' 209 were for small items worth about $1, 40 were for larger prizes worth $20, and one was for the jumbo prize worth $100. The longer the patients remained drug-free, the more draws they earned.

'The incentive is to have continuous days of abstinence, which encourages long periods of abstinence,' Sindelar said. 'This escalates the number of consecutive days and weeks patients stay clean, which mimics getting out of the habit.'

Petry, who designed the prize-based incentive technique, compared it to traditional behavior modification methods such as giving children allowances to encourage them to do a particular task more often.

Previous studies have proven that these types of treatment supplements are effective in helping substance abuse patients stay abstinent for longer periods of time, Olmstead said.

Although he said he wasn't surprised by the effectiveness of the method, he was surprised by the amount of money required for the administration. Including inventory, restocking and shopping for the items, the cost of the administration totaled almost as much as that of the prizes themselves.

'The next question is how to improve cost-effectiveness, streamline administration and improve efficiency,' Olmstead said.

While the researchers said it remains to be proven whether or not this strategy makes financial sense, they said they believe spending the extra $258 will cut back on some of the negative consequences of drug use, including crime and lost work days.

'Substance abuse treatment is becoming less punitive,' Petry said. 'It's becoming more of a positive experience, so the patients now like going to treatment because they get prizes and stay clean longer. It changes the atmosphere of the whole treatment.'

1 Identify two advantages of the treatment programme mentioned in the text.

2 Suggest two disadvantages of this programme.

Evaluating psychological strategies

Psychological interventions based on two different approaches have been considered: cognitive and behavioural strategies. Cognitive interventions aim to change beliefs and hence behaviours. Although they are typically effective at changing thinking, this does not always result in a reduction in the addictive behaviour (eg Williams & Connolly, 2006). However, CBT combines the cognitive approach with active behaviour therapy and, as studies such as Floyd *et al.* (2006), Petry *et al.* (2006) and Carroll *et al.* (2008) (see *Media Watch*) demonstrate, this can be effective in reducing addictive behaviour in people with gambling and drug addictions.

Behavioural therapy, based on operant conditioning alone, has also been successfully employed for substance abuse, eg

Olmstead *et al.* (2007) and Sindelar *et al.* (2007). However, such an approach is less likely to be suitable for a gambling addiction as the token economy is, itself, a lottery-type programme.

Thinking critically about psychology

Why would a token economy programme such as that employed by Sindelar *et al.* be unsuitable for use with gamblers?

Thinking creatively about psychology

Professor Bordnick is investigating a novel line of research into addiction using virtual reality to simulate environments for addicts that create cravings. 'Virtual world therapeutic for addicts: study shows impact of environment to addiction cravings' can be found at: http://www.sciencedaily.com/releases/2008/04/080428175336.htm

Consider how such a system could be used as part of a therapeutic intervention.

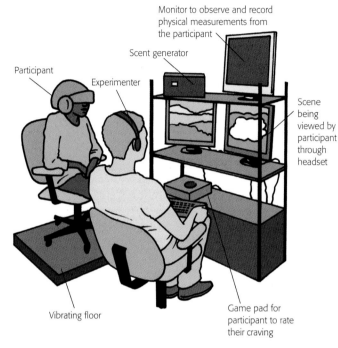

Monitor to observe and record physical measurements from the participant

Scent generator

Participant

Experimenter

Scene being viewed by participant through headset

Vibrating floor

Game pad for participant to rate their craving

▲ **Figure 11.29** Virtual reality can help to investigate the problems of craving

Public health interventions to reduce addictive behaviour

Public health interventions tackle a range of addictive behaviours and use a variety of strategies. Some target a wide population, such as the televised drink-driving campaigns seen at Christmas. Others are aimed at those who are already addicted, such as warnings on cigarette packets, and yet others try to avoid addictions developing, such as the '3 Minute Wonder' campaign aimed at encouraging young people to resist drug use (see p265).

NICE (2007) has published guidelines to advise on public health interventions to reduce smoking in young people. Suggested mass media strategies for reaching large numbers of people included television, radio, newspapers, billboards, posters, leaflets and booklets. The document identifies other areas including family-based, community-based and school-based interventions that could also be used. Many of these techniques are already employed in the NHS Go smokefree campaign (see *Looking Further*).

LOOKING FURTHER Look at details of the NHS Go smokefree campaign here: http://gosmokefree.nhs.uk/?WT.mc_id=ilevel_search_08. Look especially at the 'Quit tools' section.

▶ **Figure 11.30** The NHS Go Smokefree campaign helps smokers to quit

A long-running national campaign to reduce smoking is the charity-run 'No Smoking Day'. This achieves consistently high levels of public awareness and participation, and so has the potential to be a highly effective health intervention. Using local organisers and events, the day gains significant media coverage, expanding its sphere of influence.

In 2008, No Smoking Day was on Wednesday 12 March. The charity worked with both national and local organisations and set up 307 promotional events. In addition to these, resources included a website, text messaging, posters, leaflets, press articles, outdoor advertising and 'quit packs' which contained a leaflet, a sponsorship form, a window sticker, a badge and a wristband.

Evaluating public health interventions

A total of 1.2 million smokers stopped smoking on No Smoking Day 2008 and 20 per cent of smokers who were aware of No Smoking Day made an attempt to quit.

The campaign measures its success every few years. An evaluation of the 2004 campaign reported that 70 per cent

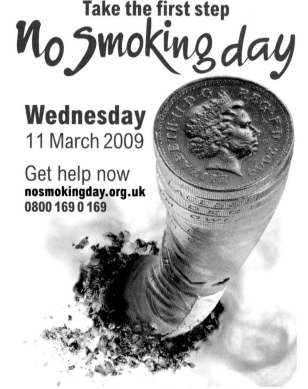

Take the first step

No Smoking day

Wednesday 11 March 2009

Get help now **nosmokingday.org.uk** 0800 169 0 169

▲ **Figure 11.31** No Smoking Day is a highly effective health intervention

of all smokers were aware of No Smoking Day. Of those who attempted to quit, 11 per cent were still not smoking more than three months later (Owen & Youdan, 2006). This equates to approximately 1.84 million smokers taking part in the day and 85,000 still abstaining after three months. These findings suggest that No Smoking Day is successful both in providing smokers with information and in helping them to quit.

Thinking critically about psychology

Sharpe *et al.* (2005) assessed an experimental intervention that aimed to minimise harm in problem gamblers. Eight electronic gaming machines (like ones in hotels and clubs) were altered to accept only smaller notes and smaller bets and to reduce the reel spin. They found that the problem gamblers used higher denomination notes and placed larger bets. The modified machines were beneficial as they reduced the bet levels and the losses. In addition, the modified machines were associated with lower levels of smoking and alcohol consumption.

A summary of this study can be found at: http://www.ncbi. nlm.nih.gov/pubmed/16311879.

▼ **Figure 11.32** Could this evidence be used to provide support for a public health intervention or the introduction of legislation?

Legislation to reduce addictive behaviour

Legislation controls the sale and use of many drugs and access to gambling facilities. Despite this, many people gain access and develop addictive behaviours. For example, even though heroin is a grade A drug, with severe penalties for supplying and using it, the incidence of heroin addiction in Britain is high. The British Crime Survey 2007–8 reported that 0.1 per cent of adults had used heroin in the previous year. This looks like a small percentage but represents a huge number of people countrywide. Figures from the Home Office for 2005–6 estimated that there were in excess of 280,000 problem opiate users aged 15–64 in England alone (Hay *et al.*, 2007).

In the UK, various pieces of legislation have attempted to reduce smoking. In February 2003 cigarette advertising on billboards and in the press and magazines was banned. Further restrictions on advertising at the point of sale were introduced in December 2004. Bans on smoking in enclosed public places came into force in Scotland in the spring of 2006, in Wales in April 2007 and in England in July 2007. To what extent are such bans effective?

Thinking critically about psychology

There is also a need for legislation on gambling, since, like smoking, it damages the lives of a great many people. However, in common with cigarette sales, income for the government (through tax) is also generated by gambling. Andreson (2006) discusses this issue in relation to the Canadian government. She reports that gambling-related activities contributed 5.1 per cent or $11.8 billion to provincial revenues in 2003. It is estimated that 35 per cent of that comes from problem gamblers, especially from video lottery terminal slots – the main income-generating activity and the chosen activity of most problem gamblers.

To what extent could legislation be effective in controlling gambling addiction?

The smoking ban

As the smoking bans in the UK are relatively recent, most research assessing efficacy has been conducted in other countries (but see *Research Now*).

Following the imposition of a smoking ban in Italy (in 2005), Gorini *et al.* (2007) reported several benefits. Measuring physical consequences, they tested the air quality in 50 locations such as pubs and discos and found that the concentration of particulates from smoke fell by 70–97 per cent. The total sales of cigarettes also fell by 6.1 per cent compared with 2004, although this rose again by 1.1 per cent in 2006 due to the increased availability of outdoor smoking areas (eg in bars and restaurants). However, the overall prevalence of smoking fell by 7.3 per cent from 2004 to 2006, and the ban is generally respected. Furthermore, Gorini *et al.* report that support for the ban amongst Italians has increased since it was imposed.

The Canadian city of Saskatoon enforced a public smoking ban in 2004, whilst the city of Saskatchewan did not. Using a telephone survey to compare smoking prevalence in 2003 and 2005, Lemstra *et al.* (2008) reported that smoking fell in Saskatoon from 24.1 per cent to 18.2 per cent but remained constant in Saskatchewan (at 23.8 per cent). Seventy-nine per cent of Saskatoon residents were in favour of the smoking ban. Furthermore, the imposition of the ban was associated with a reduced rate of hospital admissions for heart attacks (from 176.1 to 152.4 cases per 100,000 population) so there were immediate health benefits.

Jiménez-Ruiz *et al.* (2008) investigated the impact of a partial smoking ban in Spain, introduced in 2005, which restricted smoking in public places such as bars and restaurants without completely prohibiting it. They used a

Thinking critically about psychology

The post-ban survey was conducted three months after the ban. Consider the reasons why this is a good, and a poor, time interval.

computer-assisted telephone interview administered prior to and one year after the ban. In the first survey, of 6533 people, 59.8 per cent were non-smokers. In the second survey, of 3289 people, 65 per cent were non-smokers. Observations of environmental tobacco smoke also showed decreases, especially in work places (down 58.8 per cent) but also in homes (27 per cent decrease) and recreation venues (8 per cent decrease). This suggests partial bans do have some effect on smoking prevalence.

Legislation to control smoking can be specifically designed to reduce the likelihood of people taking up smoking by restricting the age at which cigarettes can be bought. Alternatively, restrictions can be imposed on the opportunity young people have to smoke. However, the success of such attempts to control smoking in young people depends on their co-operation. How likely are those who smoke, or want to smoke, to support a ban?

The Global Youth Tobacco Survey (GYTS) is a worldwide assessment of smoking among young people. Warren *et al.* (2008) reported on the GYTS findings from 2000–2007, which assessed 140 World Health Organization member states. It is a school-based survey of 13–15-year-olds whose participation is voluntary and anonymous. The survey found that 9.5 per cent of students currently smoked cigarettes, 70 per cent of whom wanted to quit. In most areas, the level of cigarette smoking in boys and girls is similar and the susceptibility to initiate smoking among never-smokers is also similar among boys and girls. Approximately 80 per cent favoured a smoking ban in public places. Warren *et al.* conclude that interventions such as increasing taxes, media campaigns, school programmes and reducing access to tobacco must focus on boys and girls and have components directed toward prevention and cessation.

Evaluating legislative interventions

Legislation in a number of different countries has attempted to restrict smoking. Where bans are more extensive, they seem to be more successful. Support for such legislation is generally positive and bans are typically adhered to. In general, they lead to a decrease in the number of smokers and corresponding improvements in air quality in public places and in health. However, this improvement is not consistent. Where bans allow exclusions, they are less effective in reducing exposure to smoke. Where, for example, smoking is permitted outdoors, some of the initial reduction in smoking may be eradicated as ways are found to smoke outside.

Those smokers who resist the imposition of legislation are typically those who are most dependent on nicotine even though they may express a desire to quit. These individuals may gain most from smoking bans. Lotrean (2008) reviewed the impact of smoking bans in many countries (including Norway, Malta, Italy, Sweden, Scotland, Wales, England, Ireland, France, Finland and Estonia). One benefit was to strengthen social norms against smoking. This can help smokers as predicted by the theory of reasoned action. Limiting opportunities for smoking reinforces the impact of social norms by physically segregating smokers. Attitudes of smokers may also be affected as their beliefs, and evaluations of those beliefs, change as they endure increased 'costs' of smoking through the inconvenience or discomfort of having to smoke outdoors.

 LOOKING FURTHER Read about the methods used in the Global Youth Tobacco Survey and its findings at: http://www.cdc.gov/mmwr/preview/mmwrhtml/ss5701a1.htm

---

RESEARCH NOW

Elton & Campbell (2008): What does banning smoking do?

Aim: To investigate the impact of the English smoking ban on smoking in the English town of Bury.

Procedure: A questionnaire was distributed by post prior to the change in the law to determine the prevalence of smoking. The survey was then repeated three months after the smoking ban was imposed and the level of smoking was compared. Participants were randomly selected using a database of people registered with general practitioners. Three thousand five hundred questionnaires were sent out in the baseline and second surveys.

Findings: The response rates were 59.5 per cent in the baseline survey and 56.3 per cent in the second survey. Results were standardised to age and gender bands from Bury's population. Although the prevalence of smoking showed little difference (22.4 per cent in the baseline survey and 22.6 per cent in the follow-up), the proportion of smokers reporting smoking 20 cigarettes a day or more fell from 27.6 to 21.8 per cent.

Conclusions: The smoking ban did not appear to affect smoking prevalence but did reduce the proportion of heavy smokers.

No smoking
It is against the law to smoke in these premises

◄ **Figure 11.33** Smoking bans do help to reduce smoking

Chapter summary

Explaining addictive behaviour

- The biological approach to drug addiction suggests that drug use affects receptor sites for neurotransmitters, causing a greater need for the drug with greater use.
- Twin and family resemblances and DNA studies show that a disposition for addictive behaviours may be partially inherited. Multiple additions also suggest a genetic component to risk.
- Family similarities in drug use might alternatively be explained by environmental factors such as social learning.
- The learning approach includes operant conditioning (positive and negative reinforcement) and social learning.
- Operant conditioning theory suggests that drug effects like euphoria are positively reinforcing and this can account for initiation and maintenance of drug use, although the rewarding effects of drugs diminish with increasing dependence.
- Gambling wins are unpredictable: they follow a variable ratio schedule of positive reinforcement. This leads to the behaviour being repeated frequently and being highly resistant to extinction.
- Negative reinforcement can account for the maintenance of drug taking. The user continues to take the drug to avoid withdrawal and, more importantly, to reduce craving.
- Social learning theory suggests that addictions may be acquired by observing and imitating models such as peers and, to a lesser extent, parents, especially if they are vicariously reinforced.
- The cognitive approach to addiction suggests that a there is a cycle of low self-esteem or anxiety that causes drug use and that this has consequences (such as loss of money or ill health) that exacerbate the emotional problems and perpetuate the addictive behaviour.
- This cycle persists because the individual has irrational beliefs about their addiction and its role in their life. This distorted thinking makes abstinence difficult.
- This theory readily explains individual differences as people differ in life experiences and personality, both of which contribute to vulnerability.

Smoking as an addictive behaviour

- Smoking is highly prevalent and damaging. It results in an addiction that is hard to break.
- Biological explanations of smoking identify withdrawal, craving, tolerance and genetic effects as important.
- Cognitive explanations of smoking suggest that smokers develop dysfunctional beliefs that permit and perpetuate smoking. Salient cues such as seeing an ashtray can induce the urge to smoke as the smoker cannot redirect their attention.

- Learning explanations of smoking suggest that the use of nicotine initially provides a 'rush' that acts as a positive reinforcer, and that negative reinforcement maintains smoking in order to avoid withdrawal and craving.

Gambling as an addictive behaviour

- Many people gamble but only some become addicted. Those who do risk debt, crime and damage to their social relationships.
- Biological explanations of gambling suggest that, like drugs, gambling activates the brain reward system. Problem gamblers exhibit craving, and genetic risks have been identified, such as sensation-seeking personalities.
- Cognitive explanations of gambling suggest that gamblers have dysfunctional beliefs in relation to their luck and skill. Gamblers find it difficult to learn from their mistakes so repeatedly take risks.
- Learning explanations of gambling suggest that early wins, especially if they are big, may predispose individuals to problem gambling and that the partial reinforcement schedule maintains the behaviour.

Factors affecting addiction

- Low self-esteem may put people at greater risk of developing an addictive behaviour, but not all evidence supports this.
- People with addictions tend to make external attributions for their addictive behaviour but internal ones for the success of their abstinence.
- Social context can increase or decrease the risk of addiction. Having drug-taking peers makes drug use more likely; single and divorced people gamble more; homeless people are at risk of alcoholism. Involved parenting, in contrast, lowers the risk of drug use in children.
- Models in the media are high status, likeable and often provide vicarious reinforcement for addictions. This makes them powerful role models so imitation is likely.
- Television advertisements and celebrities do provide models, although the extent of their impact on addiction is unclear.

Reducing addictive behaviour

- The theory of reasoned action suggests that addictive behaviours could be reduced by changing attitudes and norms, which in turn would affect the intention to abstain.
- Although people with addictive behaviours may express the intention to change, this does not necessarily lead to abstinence.
- The theory of planned behaviour suggests that people with addictive behaviours also need to believe that they are *able* to abstain.

- Individuals are more likely to be able to control their urge to relapse if their goals are specific and implemented immediately.
- A biological strategy for reducing addictive behaviours is drug intervention. This can either replace the effect of the addictive behaviour, eg treating heroin addicts with methadone, or attempt to minimise the unpleasantness of abstinence, eg treating heroin addicts with naloxone to speed up and pass through the withdrawal stage.
- For smokers, nicotine replacement therapy, drugs that act like nicotine to reduce craving, and antidepressants are all effective although some produce side effects.
- For gamblers opiate drugs, antidepressants and mood stabilisers are being tested. As yet there are few conclusive results.
- A psychological strategy for reducing addictive behaviours is cognitive therapy. This aims to build the individual's ability to resist the urge to relapse.
- Commitment is raised though exercises such as challenging the individual's irrational beliefs about the advantages of their addictive behaviour and the disadvantages of abstinence.

- Strategies for coping are developed and homework is set to enable the individual to identify triggers and test self-control.
- A learning theory strategy for reducing addictive behaviours is the token economy. This provides positive reinforcement for abstinence.
- This system is effective for drug addictions but dependency on the system itself may develop. Because it is a 'prize'-based system, it is unsuitable for use with gamblers.
- Public health interventions to reduce addictive behaviours include mass media campaigns using TV, posters and school- or community-based projects.
- 'No Smoking Day' is highly effective at reducing smoking and strategies such as '3 Minute Wonder' are based on TRA principles.
- Legislation to reduce addictive behaviour includes making the supply and use of drugs such as heroin illegal, bans on smoking and age limits on drug use.
- Smoking bans have been shown to reduce the prevalence of smoking in many countries. Age limits, however, appear to be less effective.

What do I know?

1 (a) Describe how learning explanations account for addictive behaviours. (10 marks)
  (b) Evaluate learning explanations of addiction. (15 marks)

2 (a) Outline **one** cognitive explanation of addictive behaviour. (5 marks)
  (b) Apply this model to smoking as an addiction. (10 marks)
  (c) Apply this model to gambling as an addiction. (10 marks)

3 (a) Describe biological explanations of addiction. (10 marks)
  (b) Explain how biological explanations underlie biological strategies for reducing addictions. (5 marks)
  (c) Evaluate biological strategies for reducing addictions. (10 marks)

4 Describe and evaluate the role of the media in addictive behaviour. (25 marks)

5 (a) Describe **either** the theory of reasoned action **or** the theory of planned behaviour and how it is used to plan strategies to reduce addictive behaviours. (10 marks)
  (b) Evaluate the model you have described in part (a) (15 marks)

CHAPTER 12

Anomalistic Psychology

Thinking ahead

By the end of this chapter you should be able to:

- define key terms in anomalistic psychology including anomalous experience, the paranormal and parapsychology
- explain the role of fraud and pseudoscience in the history of investigating and explaining anomalous experience
- outline the Ganzfeld procedure and controversies surrounding its use
- outline research into psychokinesis and the controversies surrounding it
- understand some of the cognitive, personality and biological factors that can underlie anomalous experience
- explain the functions for the individual of belief in the paranormal, including its cultural significance
- be familiar with the psychology of deception, self-deception, superstition and coincidence
- describe research into belief in unexplained experiences, with particular regard to psychic healing, out-of-body and near-death experiences and mediumship

Anomalistic psychology involves the study of human experiences that cannot easily be explained by conventional science. An anomaly is something highly unexpected and unusual. Anomalous experiences range from contact with ghosts and aliens to telepathy and future-telling. Such experiences are sometimes collectively called 'paranormal'. However, this is a biased term, assuming that anomalous experiences are the result of a real paranormal; that ghosts, aliens and demons in some form really exist. 'Anomalous experience' is a better term because it allows us to study people's unusual experiences without making any assumptions other than that the *experience* was real to the individual. In other words, if you have the experience of being abducted by aliens that is a genuine anomalous experience and worthy of study by psychologists regardless of whether the experience was the result of genuine contact with aliens.

Anomalistic psychology and parapsychology

Anomalous experiences were studied long before the existence of psychology. As psychology emerged as a science many psychologists became interested in anomalous experiences. In the early twentieth century many of the pioneers of psychology, including William James (who is widely regarded as the father of modern psychology), Sigmund Freud and William McDougall (who founded the British Psychological Society) were keen members of the Society for Psychical Research. However, it soon became clear that some anomalous experiences were much harder to study scientifically than others. The Society for Psychical Research took a very broad approach to research. However, some researchers, notably Joseph Rhine (1895–1980), wanted to take anomalistic psychology into the laboratory in order to make it more scientifically respectable. This approach became known as experimental psychical research or *parapsychology*. Parapsychology largely focuses on the sort of anomalous experiences that lend themselves to laboratory experiments, in particular *extrasensory perception* and *psychokinesis*. Anomalistic psychology is a broader field, tackling the complete range of anomalous human experiences.

◀ **Figure 12.1** It is important for psychologists to study people's experience of alien abduction regardless of whether we believe in aliens

Anomalistic psychology and psychological thinking

You may be wondering why a topic like this should end up on an A-level specification. The reason is that studying anomalistic psychology is a unique opportunity to learn how to think like a psychologist. In this chapter we will look at the role of fraud and sloppy scientific thinking in much of the literature surrounding anomalous experience. We look at the logic of debates between believers and sceptics and we give a chance to offer your own explanations and design studies to investigate allegedly paranormal phenomena. What makes anomalistic psychology so fascinating is that the debates over the existence of paranormal phenomena still go on. As procedures for investigating anomalous experiences have become more sophisticated, many but by no means all have been explained by coincidence, fraud or very ordinary psychological mechanisms. There *may* be a real paranormal, but it might equally be true that we just have a way to go yet to fully understand the role of fraud, coincidence and ordinary psychological mechanisms, in particular the latter.

KEY TERMS

parapsychology the laboratory study of anomalous experience

extrasensory perception awareness of things outside the range of our senses

psychokinesis the ability to influence matter by power of the mind

---

Theoretical and methodological issues

Science and pseudoscience

With a few notable exceptions psychologists generally regard psychology as a science. By this we mean that psychologists attempt to gather data (information) on real phenomena (things that exist or happen) and explain them with theories which can be tested by means of research. Good science allows us to make and test predictions. Good science also changes over time as we discover new phenomena, offer new theories to explain them and conduct new research to test these theories.

The term 'pseudoscience' literally means 'false science'. It is used to describe any discipline that appears on the surface to be scientific and makes scientific claims (for example 'we have discovered that …'), but which does not stick to the rules of good science. The term 'pseudoscience' goes back to at least 1843 when the French biologist François Magendie applied it to the practice of phrenology, which claims to be able to test personality using bumps on the head.

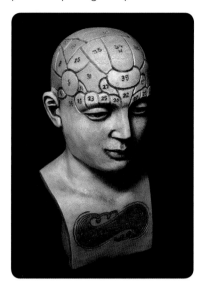

◀ **Figure 12.2**
A phrenology head; phrenology is a classic example of a pseudoscience

It is important to realise that not everyone draws the line between science and pseudoscience in precisely the same place. Randi (2001) suggests six hallmarks of a pseudoscience.

- It is illogical, ie it doesn't make sense. Randi gives the example of homeopathy, in which the more diluted a medicine the more powerful it is considered to be.
- It is inconsistent, ie it does not hang together logically with what we already know. For example, astrology is not consistent with astronomy.
- It requires that we suspend belief in well established scientific principles.
- It is based on the interpretation of a single charismatic leader or sacred text.
- It is fixed and does not change in response to new findings.
- It cannot be used to make predictions about the future.

Dutch (2006) identifies five types of pseudoscience.

- Authoritarian pseudoscience exists to validate an assumed truth. For example, creationism exists to validate Christianity.
- Mystical pseudoscience exists to explain an experience. For example, astrology explains apparently unlikely coincidences.
- Tabloid pseudoscience exists to excite us. For example, strange animals like Bigfoot make good news and exciting campfire stories.
- Junk science exists to support vested interests. For example, research that questions the existence of global warming or the link between smoking and cancer exists to support big business.
- Ignored science exists to support dated ideas in the face of modern evidence. For example, the Shroud of Turin has been dated as less than 1000 years old; however, this is simply ignored by people who insist it goes back to the death of Christ.

▶ **Figure 12.3**
Bigfoot legends certainly add some excitement to camping! This may be an example of tabloid pseudoscience

BIG FOOT XING

Occam's razor

Occam's razor is a logical rule sometimes used to define good science. It reportedly dates back to William of Ockham, a fourteenth-century Franciscan monk. Put simply it states that any theory should make as few assumptions as possible. In other words the simplest explanation is usually the best. One way of identifying pseudoscience is that it proposes complex explanations when there is a simpler one available. For example, *cryptozoologists* study the possible existence of strange creatures like the Loch Ness monster. According to Occam's razor the likeliest explanations for Nessie are fraud and misperception of ordinary objects in the loch, because we know that both these phenomena occur. No additional assumptions have to be made. However, to accept the idea of a real monster requires a new assumption: that monsters exist.

KEY TERM

cryptozoology the study of animal species such as Big Foot and Nessie for which we have no firm evidence

Pseudoscience and anomalous psychology

Some commentators have suggested that all study of anomalous experience is pseudoscience. However, this is a little unfair; psychologists study anomalous *experiences*. These experiences are real, regardless of their cause, and are therefore a valid topic for scientific research. Psychologists use scientific methods to gather data about these anomalous experiences and most are extremely cautious about offering explanations for them. It is true, however, that some explanations for anomalous experiences stray into the realm of pseudoscience. The existence of poltergeists, for example, is difficult to reconcile with what we know about kinetic energy (the sort of energy that enables movement).

Thinking critically about psychology

Consider the Loch Ness monster in the light of Randi's criteria for pseudoscience. In particular, think about the following:

1. Is the existence of an unknown animal in a large muddy loch theoretically possible?
2. Is the existence of such an animal consistent with what we know about evolution?
3. Does the existence of Nessie require suspending belief in any scientific principles?
4. Can we make any predictions based on the existence of Nessie?

◄ **Figure 12.4** Loch Ness. Is Nessie a pseudoscientific idea?

Thinking practically about psychology

Dutch's five categories of pseudoscience can all be related to anomalous experiences. Outline how each could help explain the reports of alien abduction experiences.

So what about Occam's razor? Although this is a popular scientific principle it is not universally accepted. Fox Mulder in the *X-Files* once famously called it 'Occam's principle of limited imagination'. It is always worth considering whether what we are observing can be accounted for by a simple explanation before going looking for aliens or ghosts, but just because we *can* explain something using a mundane explanation does not necessarily mean that this is the *correct* explanation.

▼ **Figure 12.5** Fox Mulder despised Occam's razor

The role of fraud

A major problem in the history of anomalistic psychology has been fraud. It is often quite straightforward to fake evidence for anomalous experience, for example photographs. A classic case of this sort of fraud was the Cottingley Fairies. Fraud complicates life for psychologists studying anomalous experience. Although the credibility of the Griffiths sisters is greatly undermined by their admission that four of the photographs were faked, they always maintained that their contact with fairies was real. They also had corroborating testimony from a clairvoyant, although some would say that his claim of clairvoyance took away all his credibility as a witness!

▲ **Figures 12.6a & b** Two of the faked pictures of the Cottingley fairies

CLASSIC RESEARCH

Cooper J (1982) Cottingley: the truth at last. *The Unexplained* 117, 2338–40

Case history: In 1916 and 1917, 16-year-old Frances Griffiths and her 10-year-old sister Elsie were on holiday in Cottingley, near Bradford. They claimed to have befriended a group of fairies that lived by the stream at the bottom of their garden. In August 1917 they borrowed their father's camera and produced two photographs, one of Frances with fairies and one of Elsie with a gnome. Their father believed the pictures were fakes and confiscated the camera. However, two years later their mother showed them to an occult conference at Harrogate. In 1920 they were published in the *Strand* magazine and attracted considerable public attention. In 1921 Elsie and Frances took three more photographs. Photographic experts examined these and could find no evidence of forgery. Sir Arthur Conan Doyle (the author of the Sherlock Holmes stories) took up the case and publicly supported the existence of the fairies. In 1921 a leading clairvoyant, Jeffrey Hodson, went to try to photograph the fairies. He failed to do so but claimed to have seen them. In 1966 the *Daily Express* followed up the story and Frances and Elsie were interviewed several times through the 1970s. In 1981 and 1982 they were interviewed by researcher Joe Cooper and both admitted that at least the first four pictures were faked. The fairies were simply cardboard cutouts held up with hat pins. Interestingly, however, both women insisted that although the pictures were forged the story of the fairies was entirely true. Frances also claimed that the fifth photograph was genuine.

Interpretation: This case illustrates clearly how easy it is to produce convincing but false photographic evidence for paranormal phenomena. The other significant aspect of the case is the fact that both women insisted until their deaths that they really had had contact with fairies.

Thinking creatively about psychology

Imagine that a neighbour has claimed to have seen elves in your local park. How could you go about investigating the claim in a scientific manner?

Former stage magician James Randi is an investigator specialising in exposing fraud. With his knowledge of conjuring he has exposed numerous instances of fraud and replicated many supposed psychic feats. Famously (Randi, 1983) he took on a leading parapsychology laboratory in much the same way as Rosenhan (1973) took on the psychiatry establishment with his 'On being sane in insane places' (p204). Randi trained two boys, aged 17 and 18, and had them present themselves to a parapsychologist at Washington University reporting that they could perform psychokinesis. Over three years they underwent a total of 16 hours of study. Under Randi's instruction they manipulated the experimenters, refusing to co-operate with strict laboratory protocols and deciding how and when they would demonstrate their 'powers'. Apparently very impressive results were reported, then Randi revealed that he had been mentoring the boys in how to fake results.

◀ **Figure 12.7**
James Randi

LOOKING FURTHER To read more about James Randi visit his website here: http://www.randi.org/. You can see footage here of James Randi testing James Hydrick, who claimed to be able to move objects with the power of the mind: http://blog.wired.com/tableofmalcontents/2007/03/james_randi_bob.html

The Ganzfeld procedure

We have seen that both pseudoscience and fraud can lead to the illusion of paranormal experience. A logical response to this is to set up a procedure that is so tightly controlled that fraud is difficult and any mundane reason for what takes place should be observable. The anomalous experiences that lend themselves best to tight control are the *psi* phenomena,

anomalous human abilities such as extrasensory perception and psychokinesis. The Ganzfeld procedure is an example of a well controlled laboratory procedure used to investigate extrasensory perception (ESP). There are three broad categories of ESP:

* clairvoyance – visually perceiving an object outside the visual field
* telepathy – transmission and receiving of thoughts between two people
* precognition – perceiving events before they take place.

The aim of the Ganzfeld procedure is to induce mild sensory deprivation in the hope that the reason we do not normally experience ESP is simply because of interference from information from our other senses. Participants sit in a comfortable chair in a soundproof room wearing ping-pong balls over their eyes and have a red light shone on them. They also listen to white noise through headphones. This eliminates distracting visual and auditory information, whilst the soundproofing helps eliminate *sensory leakage*. Stranger participants are brought together for the experiment to eliminate the possibility of collaboration. In the most common procedure, used to test telepathy, one participant takes the role of sender and the other receiver.

In another soundproof room the sender sees randomised images (pictures or video) and consciously tries to send them to the receiver. The receiver has to choose which of four images were sent. By chance we would expect a success rate of 25 per cent, so anything more than this suggests that telepathy is taking place.

▲ **Figure 12.8** The receiver in the Ganzfeld procedure experiences mild sensory deprivation

Since the mid-1980s researchers have favoured the *autoganzfeld* procedure. This improves experimental control by having a computer randomise the pictures, present them to the sender and collect the data from the receiver. In the standard procedure 80 still pictures and 80 segments of video are presented.

Controversies surrounding the Ganzfeld

Does it work?

That's really controversial! Much of the evidence suggests yes, but sceptics have found plenty to criticise. Bem & Honorton (1994) performed a meta-analysis of autoganzfeld studies and concluded that there was a reliable effect – see *Classic Research*.

CLASSIC RESEARCH

Bem D & Honorton C (1994) Does psi exist? Replicable evidence for an anomalous process of information transfer. *Psychological Bulletin* **115, 4–18**

Aim: To review studies of the autoganzfeld procedure and mathematically combine their results in order to draw conclusions about the existence of telepathy.

Procedure: 11 autoganzfeld studies were selected on the basis that they stuck to a very strict set of experimental procedures including computer administration and soundproof, electrically shielded rooms with one-way intercom communication. The total number of participants was 240, and the total number of trials was 354. Results were combined using the mathematical procedure of meta-analysis. This allowed not only the overall success rate to be measured but also the effect of other variables such as experience of participants and whether they were working with film or static images.

Findings: We would expect a 25 per cent 'hit rate' according to chance as receivers were selecting one image or video from four. Hit rates across the 11 studies ranged from 24 per cent to 54 per cent. The overall percentage was 32.5 per cent. The probability of this figure being arrived at by chance factors alone was less than 1 per cent. Experienced participants tended to do better than newbies and they scored better using video than static images.

Conclusion: The combined results of autoganzfeld studies suggest that telepathy does exist.

Bem & Honorton observe themselves that most psychologists have strong views on psi phenomena such as telepathy, and that prior views are the main factor affecting their response to findings like this. Unsurprisingly then, these results have been hotly debated. Milton & Wiseman (1999) point out that there were methodological flaws in some of the studies included in the Bem & Honorton research such as low-level sensory leakage. This meant that receivers might have heard background sounds to the videos, unconsciously helping them to identify the correct film. Milton & Wiseman conducted their own meta-analysis of 30 Ganzfeld studies and found almost no deviation from the combined results we would expect according to chance (the probability of arriving at these results by chance factors alone is 24 per cent). However, Storm & Ertel (2001) challenged the Milton & Wiseman study and published their own meta-analysis of 79 Ganzfeld studies, supporting Bem & Honorton's findings. The debate over whether telepathy really takes place in the Ganzfeld procedure is thus not resolved.

 Try to set up a Ganzfeld procedure yourself, or as close to it as you can given the facilities at your school or college. You may be able to use a soundproofed music practice room. White noise can be obtained by recording static from an untuned radio. Consider the following design issues.

1 Be really aware of ethics here. How can you avoid offending participants' religious principles or frightening participants if they have significant results?
2 What controls will you put in place to minimise the probability of sensory leakage and unconsciously passing information to participants about their success during the trial?
3 How many trials will you conduct before putting results together and analysing them?

KEY TERMS

sensory leakage a problem in ESP studies, in which participants hear background noise that gives a clue as to what they are meant to pick up by ESP

psi anomalous human abilities including ESP and psychokinesis

Thinking creatively about psychology

1 Based on what you have read so far, identify two reasons why the hit rate might have been better for video than static images in the Bem & Honorton study. Try to suggest one reason that would support the existence of telepathy and one that would explain the finding without the need for telepathy.
2 Bem & Honorton suggest that in science it is a far greater sin to suggest that a phenomenon is real when it isn't than to suggest it isn't real when it is. Do you agree?

Do some groups do better than others in the Ganzfeld?

We would expect chance variations to mean that some people will score more highly than others in Ganzfeld trials. However, there is some evidence that certain groups of people do better than others. In the Bem & Honorton meta-analysis, for example, believers in psi, extroverts and participants experienced in practising telepathy or a mental discipline like yoga or meditation did better than sceptics, introverts and newbies. If this is a reliable effect then it poses quite a tricky challenge for sceptics: if telepathy is not real, why should you get better scores with practice? In the Milton

& Wiseman study, most of these effects were not supported, with the exception that participants who had studied yoga or meditation scored consistently higher than those who had not. This leaves us with something of a problem. There is disagreement about how reliable these group differences in Ganzfeld scores are, yet *any* difference between groups that crops up consistently suggests that there is something to the Ganzfeld procedure and telepathy.

Thinking creatively about psychology

It does seem that in the Ganzfeld procedure, people who have studied meditation or yoga tend to get higher scores than others. This appears to support the existence of telepathy.

1 Based on the criticisms you have read of the Ganzfeld procedure, suggest a 'killjoy argument', in other words an alternative explanation for why those with training in a mental discipline requiring deep concentration might do well in the procedure.

2 How could you go about finding evidence for this explanation?

Psychokinesis

The other psi ability is psychokinesis (PK). Henry (2005) defines PK as 'paranormal action, that is, the mind's ability to affect or move an object at a distance by intention alone' (2005, p125). She distinguishes between four types of possible PK phenomenon:

- macro-PK: affecting by intention large enough objects to see the effect, eg spoon-bending
- recurrent spontaneous PK: *poltergeist* activity
- micro-PK: affecting very small objects, for example random numbers generated by computer
- DMILS: direct mental interaction with living systems, for example 'spiritual healing'.

◀ **Figure 12.9** Spoon-bending is an example of macro-PK

Controversies in the study of PK

All the PK phenomena are controversial. Looking back to Randi's criteria for pseudoscience we would have to say that PK doesn't really make sense and that it is inconsistent with what we know about the science of kinetic energy. That said, there *is* evidence for the existence of PK. We revisit the phenomenon of psychic healing later in this chapter, but for now we can look at two very different controversies: whether humans can influence random events by intention alone and whether poltergeist phenomena are real.

Can we influence random numbers?

PK can be studied in both natural and controlled surroundings. There is rather stronger evidence for the existence of micro-PK than for other effects. Micro-PK is usually studied by attempting to influence what numbers are generated by a random number generator. One standard protocol is to try to influence the generator to produce a number higher or lower than the last. We would expect by chance factors alone to achieve this 50 per cent of the time. A meta-analysis by Nelson & Radin (1987) showed that in fact we can do this between 50 and 51 per cent of the time. That does not sound impressive but given the number of participants and consistency of the effect, the odds against that data being due to chance alone are trillions to one (Henry, 2005). That said, when Bosch *et al.* (2006) carried out their own meta-analysis they found some additional effects that may call into question the existence of micro-PK. See *Research Now*, p285.

There are many 'random number' generators available on the internet. However, many are not random at all and tables of pregenerated random numbers are no use for this procedure. We recommend going to this page: http://www.random. org/integers/. Set the number to one integer (whole number) and click 'get numbers'. Try to influence the site to make the next number higher or lower. Keep trying and record the percentage of trials in which you get the result you are trying for. You may wish to conduct an experiment into one of the following:

- gender differences in micro-PK (some research has found that men do better)

- believers vs sceptics

- practice effects.

KEY TERMS

poltergeist unexplained phenomena involving kinetic energy, for example objects moving or knocking sounds

RESEARCH NOW

Bosch H, Steinkamp F & Boller E (2006) Examining psychokinesis: the interaction of human intention and random number generators – a meta-analysis. *Psychological Bulletin* **132, 497–523**

Aim: To combine the results of previous studies of micro-PK to determine whether overall it appears that we can influence random number generation and to look for patterns in the data that might suggest other reasons for apparent evidence for PK.

Procedure: 380 studies were included in the analysis: 372 were published studies and the remainder were obtained by requesting unpublished data from the Parapsychology Research Forum. Information about the number of trials, the behaviour of the experimenter, the setting and the quality of controls used to eliminate bias was included in the analysis.

Findings: Overall the results were highly significant: there was a small but consistent effect of intention on random number generation. However, there was massive variation between the findings of different studies. Older, smaller and less well controlled studies demonstrated greater effects than newer, larger and better controlled studies.

Conclusion: There is evidence for the ability to affect random number generation by intention, although it may be possible to account for this finding by poor research methodology in published studies.

Do poltergeist phenomena exist?

If micro-PK studies investigate very small events under tightly controlled conditions, the investigation of poltergeist phenomena is very much at the opposite end of the spectrum, involving field studies of reportedly dramatic events. Poltergeist phenomena have been reported for at least 500 years. A typical event involves unexplained noises such as knocking and the movement of objects such as furniture. Traditionally such events have been interpreted as hauntings by mischievous or malicious entities. However, the observation that many cases are in households with disturbed teenagers has led to an alternative hypothesis: that poltergeist phenomena are the result of recurrent spontaneous PK, ie a person is regularly and unconsciously moving objects by PK. Unlike micro-PK, poltergeist phenomena are impossible to study in the laboratory. To investigate the question of whether poltergeist phenomena really occur, researchers are forced to conduct field studies.

A classic example of a field study of poltergeist phenomena took place in Enfield, North London, in 1977. The events began in August when one evening a chest of drawers reportedly slid across a bedroom floor. For the next few months objects appeared, disappeared and moved around the house in the presence of numerous witnesses including police officers. Two researchers from the Psychical Research Society investigated the phenomenon in the presence of a sceptical barrister to ensure lack of bias. For 14 months the researchers recorded hard-to-explain events such as a 60lb fireplace being ripped out of a wall. Objects were photographed apparently levitating in mid-air in a bedroom. The picture is shown in Figure 12.10a. Such pictures are, however, easy to fake, as demonstrated by Figure 12.10b.

◄ **Figure 12.10b** A demonstration of how easily levitation photographs can be faked

▼ **Figure 12.10a** A pillow being apparently levitated by an unseen force

This case was unusually dramatic, but it illustrates well the controversy of poltergeist phenomena. We cannot investigate such events under controlled conditions and we know that it is possible to fake such events in natural surroundings. On the other hand, the family in this case had no professional experience of magic or fraud, and the investigating police and professional researchers were completely convinced that the case was genuine.

Thinking critically about psychology

Consider the Enfield poltergeist.

1 What arguments might you make for this case being good evidence for poltergeists?
2 What are the limitations of cases like this as evidence?

LOOKING FURTHER You can see footage here of interviews with several witnesses to the Enfield haunting including police officers, researchers and BBC journalists. How credible is their testimony and how convincing do you find this type of evidence? http://uk.youtube.com/watch?v=LQQj4dXJaZ8

Factors underlying anomalous experiences

Whilst staying neutral on the actual existence of psi abilities, aliens, ghosts, fairies etc, it is safe to say that psychological factors underlie at least some anomalous experiences. Such factors range from the cognitive to the cultural.

Cognitive factors

False memories of anomalous experiences

Several cognitive factors may be important when it comes to anomalous experiences. One is the development of false memories. Cognitive psychologists have found that it is surprisingly common for people to develop memories of events that have not in fact taken place. This is known as false memory syndrome. It seems that the phenomenon of false memory syndrome can lead to inaccurate accounts of anomalous experience. Clancy et al. (2002) investigated the role of false memory syndrome in anomalous experience by testing whether people who report experiences of alien abduction are particularly prone to false memories They recruited participants by advertising for volunteers who had had contact with aliens. Participants were divided into three groups: those who recalled having been abducted by aliens (n=11); those who had no memory as such but who nonetheless believed they had been abducted (n=9); and a control group who denied having been abducted by aliens (n=13). The hypothesis tested was that the group who recalled alien abduction experiences would make the most errors on tests designed to produce false memories. One such test for false memory involves showing groups of related words then testing for recognition with an additional 'lure' related word inserted (eg 'sweet' in a list including 'sour,' 'candy' and 'sugar.' A false memory is recorded when the 'lure' is wrongly

◀ **Figure 12.11** People who report having been abducted by aliens tend to be those most likely to generate false memories

identified as having been part of the list. As predicted, people who reported alien abduction did significantly worse on tests like this, supporting the idea that dodgy memory – specifically the tendency to produce false memories – may underlie alien abduction experiences.

Thinking critically about psychology

Consider the Clancy et al. (2002) study with particular regard to the following:

1 Comment on the sample size and sampling procedure.
2 How realistic are false word recognition tasks in relation to the real life situation being investigated?

Misattribution

Another cognitive factor affecting our interpretation of anomalous experience is attribution. Attribution is the cognitive process in which we decide why an event has happened. The misattribution hypothesis states that we have anomalistic experiences because we misattribute normal events to paranormal phenomena. Wiseman & Watt (2006) suggest four factors underlying misattribution:

- *General cognitive ability*: there is some evidence that believers tend to score lower than sceptics on tests of IQ and critical thinking.
- *Probability misjudgement*: people are inclined to attribute events to the paranormal when they underestimate the probability that such events could take place by chance or for mundane reasons.
- *Tendency to link distantly related material*: there is evidence to suggest that people are more likely to see their experiences as paranormal if they tend to make connections between unrelated or slightly related events (for example identifying non-existent pictures in random patterns of dots).
- *Fantasy-proneness*: there is some evidence to suggest that people who become so highly involved in fantasies that they become unclear where fantasy ends and reality begins are more likely to attribute experience to paranormal explanations.

Another way of looking at misattribution comes from Lindeman & Saher (2007). They looked at the similarity between typical children's beliefs about the role of intention and purpose in reality (lungs want to breathe, lions exist to be watched in zoos) and adult superstitious beliefs. They tested the idea that superstition is the result of childlike reasoning in a study of superstition (see *Research Now*).

RESEARCH NOW

Lindeman M & Saher M (2007) Vitalism, purpose and superstition. *British Journal of Psychology* **98, 33–44**

Aim: To test the hypothesis that superstitious adults are more likely than sceptics to attribute purpose, intention and lifelike qualities to objects in the way that children do.

Procedure: 239 Finnish volunteers took part in the study, 184 females and 55 males aged between 16 and 47 years; 123 were sceptics and 116 were superstitious, defined by being in the bottom and top 10 per cent respectively of a sample surveyed in an earlier study. All participants were emailed a link to an online survey. The survey measured three types of attribution:

- attribution of purpose, using a 1–5 scale of agreement (where 1 indicates no purpose and 5 clearly has a purpose), to a range of stimuli ranging from a pocket to a cloud
- attribution of intention to biological processes, choosing between alternative explanations including intention for animate processes, eg 'a cut finger wants to get better' as opposed to valid biological explanations, eg 'finger tissue and veins start growing'
- beliefs about energy, using a 1–5 scale of agreement to statements including the scientifically valid, eg 'energy can manifest itself as heat' and the dodgy 'energy can die'.

Findings: The differences between superstitious people and sceptics were significant on all three measures. Superstitious people were more likely to believe that a range of living and non-living objects had purpose, that biological processes had intentions and that inanimate objects had lifelike qualities.

Conclusions: Superstitious people show a lack of adult logical reasoning, thinking about the world in a childlike way.

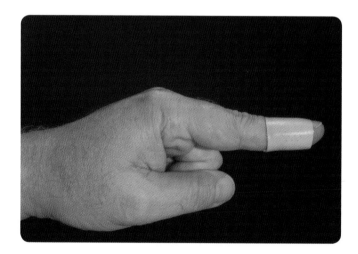

▲ **Figure 12.12** Superstitious people are more likely to believe that cut fingers get better because they want to

Personality factors

There is evidence to support the idea that belief in paranormal explanations of anomalous experience is associated with particular dimensions of personality.

A model of personality commonly used in anomalistic psychology research is Eysenck's three factor model. Eysenck & Eysenck (1991) suggest that personality can be understood as consisting of three independent traits:

- extroversion: lively sociable behaviour as opposed to quiet solitary behaviour
- neuroticism: anxious moody behaviour as opposed to emotional stability
- psychoticism: emotional tough-mindedness.

There has been particular interest into the link between neuroticism and paranormal beliefs. Wiseman & Watt (2004) surveyed 4339 people for neuroticism and paranormal beliefs, assessing neuroticism by a single item: a five-point scale of agreement (strongly agree to strongly disagree) to the statement 'I tend to worry about life' (yes=neurotic, no=stable). They also tested 116 people using Eysenck's personality test, the Eysenck Personality Questionnaire (EPQ). In both studies they found that highly neurotic individuals were more likely to hold paranormal beliefs. In another study Williams *et al.* (2007) tested personality and paranormal beliefs in adolescents – see *Research Now*.

RESEARCH NOW

Williams E, Francis LJ & Robbins M (2007) Personality and paranormal belief: a study among adolescents. *Pastoral Psychology* **56,** 9–14

Aim: To establish how common paranormal beliefs are amongst teenagers and to investigate relationships between paranormal beliefs and Eysenck's personality traits.

Procedure: 293 participants aged 13–16 years took part in the study. All were students at a single Welsh state secondary school; 56 per cent were male and 44 per cent female. All were offered the option to decline a place in the study but none did so. Personality was measured by the short-form Revised Junior Eysenck Personality Inventory. Paranormal beliefs were measured by the Index of Paranormal Belief (see Table 12.1).

Findings: There was considerable support for the existence of the paranormal, with 52.7 per cent believing in ghosts, 49.9 per cent believing in fate, 42.7 per cent believing in contact with the dead, 40.8 per cent believing in their horoscope, 27.7 per cent believing in tarot cards and 29.7 per cent believing their future was predetermined. There was no correlation between paranormal beliefs and extroversion or psychoticism. However, there was a significant correlation (+0.32) between paranormal beliefs and neuroticism.

Conclusion: Paranormal beliefs are common, and they are related to neuroticism.

▼ **Table 12.1 The Index of Paranormal Belief**

	SA	A	?	D	SD
I believe in ghosts					
I believe in fate					
I believe in my horoscope					
I believe it is possible to contact the spirits of the dead					
I believe that tarot cards can tell the future					
I believe my future is already decided for me					

SA Strongly agree   A Agree   ? Don't know   D Disagree   SD Strongly disagree

Thinking critically about psychology

Consider the Williams *et al.* (2007) study. In particular, think about the following:

1   How representative was the sample?
2   Only one personality test was used. Why might this be a problem?
3   What would you want to know about the Index of Paranormal Belief before accepting the results of a study like this?

Neuroticism is associated with paranormal belief, although it also appears that extroversion may be associated with psi abilities. Honorton *et al.* (1998) meta-analysed studies of the relationship between extroversion and psi and concluded that extroverts have a small but consistent advantage over introverts. Watt (2005) suggests two possible explanations for the extroversion–psi link. First, extroverts, being more sociable, are more relaxed in the potentially intimidating parapsychology laboratory. Alternatively, extroverts have lower arousal levels in the brain cortex and this may help their psi abilities.

There are other lines of research into personality variables and anomalous experience. One looks at defensiveness. Defensiveness can be defined as resistance to perceiving threatening information. There is evidence to suggest that highly defensive people score lower on tests of psi abilities. Haraldsson & Houtkooper (1992) combined results of 10 Icelandic studies of the relationship between psi and defensiveness, finding an overall correlation of –0.086. This does not sound impressive but it is statistically significant. If defensive people block out threatening information they may feel threatened by psi awareness and block this. Of course, if the positive results of psi studies are due to sensory leakage it is quite possible that defensive people block out this information. Exactly how well studies of defensiveness and ESP support the existence of the latter is thus debatable.

Biological factors

It is possible that special systems in the brain underlie real psi abilities. If this is true then we currently have very little idea what those systems might be. On the other hand, there is quite a lot of evidence to suggest that many anomalous experiences that do *not* have a paranormal basis are associated with particular neurological systems.

Temporal lobe lability and anomalous experience

The *temporal lobes* (see Figure 12.13) are lower sections of the cortex. They are known to be associated with speech, memory and hearing. We also know that some people have much greater consistency in the electrical activity of the temporal lobes than others, in extreme cases resulting in epileptic seizures. Highly inconsistent temporal lobe activity is called temporal lobe *lability*.

Persinger (1983) explains anomalous experience as the result of temporal lobe lability. He proposed that mystical experience is similar to the common experience of auditory and visual hallucination in the run-up to an epileptic seizure. Essentially there is a spectrum of temporal lobe lability, with sufferers of *epilepsy* at one end, those who report mystical experiences in the middle, and people without epilepsy or mystical experience at the stable end.

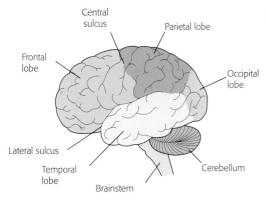

▲ **Figure 12.13** Side view of the brain showing the temporal lobe

Persinger (1985) has used the temporal lobe hypothesis to explain UFO sightings. Geological disturbance such as tectonic plates rubbing together produces weak, fluctuating magnetic fields. Persinger suggests that these magnetic fields could act on the temporal lobes to produce hallucinations. Persinger (1995) supported this argument by demonstrating that applying weak fluctuating magnetic fields to the temporal lobes induces a range of anomalous experiences, including the sense of a presence and hallucinations of lights, common to UFO experiences. There are also strong statistical associations between UFO 'hotspots' and sites of geological disturbance (Persinger, 1985).

The serotonin system and spiritual experience

Some people are more prone to spiritual experiences than others. This may show itself dramatically as religious visions or simply as an overwhelming sense of self-transcendence – giving priority to religious or spiritual beliefs over material concerns. We know that drugs such as LSD that give rise to hallucinations and sometimes spiritual experiences act on the serotonin system. We also know that the system is important in regulating mood, so may be important in the euphoria associated with spiritual experience.

Borg *et al.* (2003) set out to test the idea that people prone to mystical experiences have a distinctive serotonin system. Fifteen male Swedish participants were assessed for a range of personality traits including spiritual acceptance, an aspect of self-transcendence, using a standard test called the

Temperament and Character Inventory. Serotonin receptor density (the number of sites where serotonin is reabsorbed after crossing a synapse) was measured in three areas of the brain by radioactively labelling a chemical used for serotonin production and watching its reabsorbtion using a PET scan. The correlations between spiritual acceptance and serotonin receptor density were dramatic: −0.62 in the neocortex, −0.78 in the hippocampus and −0.79 in the raphe. Receptor density did not correlate with any other personality traits.

▼ **Figure 12.14** The areas of the brain associated with spiritual experience in the Borg *et al.* study

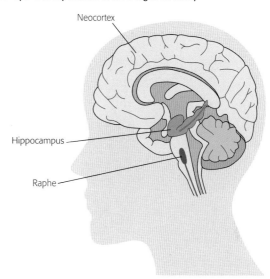

This study suggests strongly that the fewer serotonin receptors we have, the more inclined we are to have spiritual experiences. This may be because the serotonin system regulates perception: the weaker the serotonin system, the less accurately we perceive reality. This interpretation of Borg's results ties in neatly with other psychological factors affecting anomalous experiences. For example, think back to Wiseman & Watt's factors in misattribution (p286). Fantasy-proneness and tendency to connect distantly related items could both be explained on a neurological level by a weak perceptual system characterised by low serotonin receptor density. Low levels of serotonin are also associated with emotional instability; serotonin receptor density could therefore explain why paranormal beliefs are associated with high levels of neuroticism (p287).

Functions of paranormal and related belief

Paranormal belief as a coping strategy

One reason why people may hold strong views in favour of the existence of the paranormal is as a coping strategy for dealing with emotional trauma. In particular, people with a history of child abuse often experience a sense of powerlessness. Paranormal beliefs can perhaps be a strategy for feeling greater personal power. If witchcraft or psychokinesis really work, then an individual who feels helpless can take great comfort from the possibility of gaining power through acquiring such abilities.

Irwin (2005) proposed that childhood trauma leads to a sense of helplessness, which in turn leads to a coping mechanism of fantasies of personal power. This would explain the link between being fantasy-prone (p289) and having strong beliefs in the paranormal.

◀ **Figure 12.15** Powerless-feeling young people may be drawn to a belief in witchcraft as a coping strategy

This idea was investigated by Perkins & Allen (2006). They surveyed 107 university students, comparing paranormal beliefs in those who had suffered physical abuse with a control group who had not. If paranormal beliefs were related to a feeling of powerlessness we would expect that the physical abuse group would have greater belief in aspects of the paranormal associated with enhanced power, whilst there should be no motive to believe in paranormal phenomena not associated with personal power. This was in fact the case: students who had suffered physical abuse were more likely to believe in witchcraft and psi abilities but no more likely to believe in UFOs or superstition.

Cultural significance of paranormal beliefs

Paranormal beliefs vary between cultures. It might even be that some anomalous experiences are entirely the product of cultural beliefs. Hufford (1982) tested this with regard to the 'old hag' phenomenon, often reported in Newfoundland. 'Old hag' is believed to be experienced during sleep paralysis, a hybrid sleep–wake state in which people half wake but remain paralysed. In this state it is common to experience a malevolent presence. In Newfoundland people often report the presence as a witch which sits on their chest crushing them while they are paralysed. Hufford's study is reported in *Classic Research*.

CLASSIC RESEARCH

Hufford DJ (1982) *The terror that comes in the night: an experience-centered study of supernatural assault traditions.* **Philadelphia: Pennsylvania State University Press**

Aim: To investigate whether the 'old hag' phenomenon is only reported by people familiar with the cultural tradition. If only people familiar with 'old hag' experienced her this would suggest that the phenomenon is entirely a product of culture.

Procedure: 43 male and 50 female Canadian university students who had grown up in Newfoundland were surveyed about their experiences of 'old hag' and the experiences of anyone they knew. They answered a 14-question questionnaire, which asked about experiences of sleep paralysis and about the names they had for it. They were asked to define 'old hag'.

Findings: 23 per cent of respondents (12 males and nine females) accurately described at least one 'old hag' attack. Of these, 16.5 per cent were familiar with the cultural tradition of 'old hag' but 6.5 per cent were not. It is thus possible to have an 'old hag' attack without knowing about her, but awareness of her increased the probability.

Conclusion: 'Old hag' is not simply a product of a cultural tradition, but can be experienced by anyone. This is consistent with the idea that 'old hag' is a cultural explanation for a biological phenomenon.

◀ **Figure 12.16** If you come from Newfoundland, you may have woken in the night, paralysed, with this sitting on your chest. Nice!

It seems then that culture influences paranormal experience as well as belief in the paranormal. It may be that particular paranormal beliefs serve particular functions for the culture.

- Paranormal beliefs can make a hard-to-understand phenomenon possible to explain. For example, in Newfoundland the 'old hag' experience is made easier to cope with by the cultural belief that it results from a witch's curse.
- Paranormal beliefs can be used to enforce cultural rules. Thus American children are frightened into

obedience by threats that the 'boogeyman' will get them and fundamentalist Christians believe in Hell as a consequence of sin.

- Paranormal beliefs can be used to make the environment safer. For example, cultures living near major natural hazards often have legends of monsters associated with that hazard. These serve the function of keeping people away from the hazard or at least making them cautious in its vicinity. Thus in rainforest, children might become blasé about the dangers of crocodiles, big cats and venomous snakes and insects, but they will always be very careful if they believe that a forest demon lurks in wait.

Deception and self-deception

As we have already said, a huge problem in the scientific study of anomalous experience has been the amount of deception practised by so-called psychics. One simple way to deceive people is to deliberately distort their memory of an event. Recall from your study of eyewitness testimony at AS level the idea that memory for events is often altered after the event. Wiseman & Greening (2005) demonstrated how this principle can be used to alter the recall of witnesses of apparently paranormal events. They showed participants a videoclip of a magician pretending to be a psychic bending a key. In one condition the magician said that the key was continuing to bend after he had put it down. The camera then zoomed in on the key. In a control condition he put the key down and said nothing. Of course the key did not continue to bend but 40 per cent of participants who had heard him say that it did later recalled having seen it do so, as opposed to approximately 4 per cent (one participant) in the control condition. This shows that making verbal suggestions about possible paranormal events can be an effective way to deceive witnesses.

There are, of course, simpler ways of faking psychic metal-bending. A spoon that has been repeatedly bent back and forth in the 'psychic's' hand immediately before a demonstration will be very soft and warm, allowing a fraudster to claim to have melted it. An easy way to expose this scam is to make them use your spoon! Alternatively the 'psychic' can distract observers' attention momentarily by coughing or adjusting their chair and bend the spoon against a table top. Filming the event and looking for this kind of distraction in playback can generally identify this deception strategy. A previously bent key can be presented to observers at an angle that prevents the bend showing. When the key appears to bend it is simply being turned.

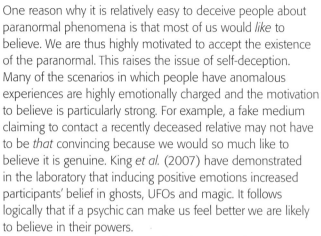

▶ **Figure 12.17**
Does this key look bent? It depends on the angle

LOOKING FURTHER James Randi is an expert on the psychology of deception. You can see him demonstrate some techniques including the faked bending of spoons and keys here: http://www.youtube.com/watch?v=vJQBljC5RIo

One reason why it is relatively easy to deceive people about paranormal phenomena is that most of us would *like* to believe. We are thus highly motivated to accept the existence of the paranormal. This raises the issue of self-deception. Many of the scenarios in which people have anomalous experiences are highly emotionally charged and the motivation to believe is particularly strong. For example, a fake medium claiming to contact a recently deceased relative may not have to be *that* convincing because we would so much like to believe it is genuine. King *et al.* (2007) have demonstrated in the laboratory that inducing positive emotions increased participants' belief in ghosts, UFOs and magic. It follows logically that if a psychic can make us feel better we are likely to believe in their powers.

Interestingly, psychics as well as clients may be prone to self-deception. In a case study, Rose & Blackmore (2002) investigated a psychic, DS. Eight experiments were carried out over a two-year period, involving predicting the results in computer-simulated horse races. The results were precisely what would be expected by chance – 21 correct predictions in 210 10-horse races. However, when interviewed, DS was convinced that he had proved his psychic abilities. This suggests that his belief in his abilities was a matter of self-deception. It also suggests that in the case of at least some professional psychics without real ability there is no deliberate attempt to deceive clients.

Superstition

Superstition can be defined as a belief not based on reason or knowledge. In other words it is an irrational belief. Different cultures have different superstitions. In the UK, for example, it is considered unlucky to walk under a ladder or on the cracks in the pavement. In rural Ireland certain trees are left in otherwise cultivated fields out of fear of revenge by homeless fairies. So why do we have superstition? Clearly cultural factors are important: we are brought up exposed to a set of cultural beliefs, some of which are more founded on reason and knowledge than others. There may also be a grain of truth in some superstitious beliefs. If you walk under ladders you probably do increase the chances of having something fall on your head! One factor in superstition that has been investigated by psychologists is the role of operant conditioning. Operant conditioning involves learning to repeat behaviour because it results in a favourable consequence. This type of learning is not unique to humans but occurs in many species. Its role in superstition was demonstrated by Skinner in a classic study involving pigeons.

CLASSIC RESEARCH

Skinner BF (1948) Superstition in the pigeon. *Journal of Experimental Psychology* **38**, 168–172

Aim: To test whether pigeons could acquire superstitious behaviour by operant conditioning.

Procedure: Eight pigeons were put on diets to reduce their weight and ensure they were hungry for the experiment. When each was down to 75 per cent of its normal body weight it was placed in a Skinner box containing a food dispenser. All had spent time in a Skinner box previously so they were familiar with having to learn how to obtain food. For several days the dispenser produced food every 15 seconds regardless of what the birds were doing. The time between food was then increased from 15 seconds to one minute. Independent observers rated the pigeons' behaviour.

Findings: Six of the eight pigeons developed repetitive behaviours during the period in the Skinner box. One hopped continually, one spun in circles and another bobbed its head. When the frequency of the food dropped the birds frantically increased the rate of their repetitive behaviours.

Conclusion: The birds had acquired the 'superstitious' belief that whatever they were doing when they received food led to the food being dispensed.

This phenomenon where superstitious behaviour is acquired by operant conditioning is called uncontrollable reinforcement (reinforcement meaning a behaviour is strengthened or reinforced by the response, and uncontrollable because the response is not really controlled by the behaviour). There is evidence to suggest that superstitious behaviour in humans as well as animals can be acquired by uncontrollable reinforcement. Matute (1996) set up an experiment in a library in which computers made loud noises. The people using them tried pressing various buttons to stop the noise. Although none of the buttons actually stopped the noise, when it was repeated they were observed to frantically press whatever button they had been pressing when the noise had stopped previously. They had acquired the superstitious belief about the button. Uncontrollable reinforcement probably plays a role in the development of some superstitions. Every time we don't walk under a ladder and nothing goes wrong our ladder-avoidance is reinforced. Every time we walk backwards round a well chanting and wait two weeks for our cold to go away, which it does, the superstitious belief that the chanting got rid of the cold is similarly reinforced.

Thinking practically about psychology

A common superstition in the UK is based around the rhyme 'step on a crack, break your mother's back'. Explain how uncontrollable reinforcement can lead to avoiding stepping on cracks in the pavement.

Coincidence

I (Matt) was once teaching when I heard my iPod playing in my jacket pocket and went to turn it off. I noticed that the band playing was the very one I had been to see the previous night. My class and I agreed that this was a spooky coincidence. Actually it wasn't! I had been listening to the band the previous day in anticipation of seeing them, so when the iPod received a knock and switched on, that's what you'd expect it to play. This is obvious once you look at the sequence of events, but it illustrates how bad most of us are at making sense of coincidences.

Matthews & Blackmore (1995) have attempted to explain why we are so impressed by coincidences using the Birthday Paradox. The Birthday Paradox involves asking people to estimate how many people have to be in a group before the probability that two will share the same birthday reaches 50 per cent. Actually (bizarrely you might think) the number is 23. By the time we have 40 people together the probability of two or more sharing a birthday rises to around 90 per cent. However, people usually estimate the required group number to be much higher. Put simply, coincidence is much more common and likely than we realise.

Thinking creatively about psychology

Design a study to find out whether age or gender affects the accuracy of our ability to judge the probability of coincidence.

▲ **Figure 12.18** Irrational as it seems, most of us avoid the cracks in the pavement

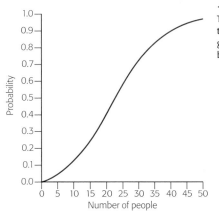

◀ **Figure 12.19** The probability of two people in a group sharing a birthday

▼ **Figure 12.20** The chances are around 3:1 that two or more of these people share a birthday

▼ **Table 12.2 The statements used in the Blackmore (1997) study**

1	There is someone called Jack in my family
2	I have a scar on my left knee
3	Last night I dreamed of someone I haven't seen for many years
4	I travel regularly in a white car
5	I once broke my arm
6	My back is giving me pain at the moment
7	I am one of three children
8	I own a CD or tape of Handel's *Water Music*
9	I have a cat
10	I have been to France in the past year

Taking this line of thinking a stage further, it may be that one factor affecting people's belief in the paranormal is their ability to estimate probability. Believers may be simply more impressed by coincidence than non-believers because they are poorer at estimating the probability of coincidence, and therefore more likely to attribute coincidence to non-chance factors like the paranormal. This was tested in a study by Blackmore (1997). A questionnaire was published in the *Daily Telegraph* asking people whether 10 statements were true of them and to estimate the probability of a number of statements being true for other people. They were also asked about their beliefs in the paranormal. The statements are shown in Table 12.2.

A total of 6238 replies were received. There was no difference between believers and non-believers in their probability judgements. This study does *not* therefore support the idea that believers are particularly bad at estimating probability and coincidence. However, it remains quite likely that our generally poor probability judgements are a factor in the general tendency to accept paranormal phenomena.

Thinking practically about psychology

This is a true story. In the 1990s an American woman tried to commit suicide by jumping out of her flat because she had found out her husband was having an affair. She landed on him, killing him, but survived herself. At first sight this seems like an incredible coincidence. Think of all the factors that might make the event more probable than it first appears.

Belief in exceptional experience

We have already discussed a number of factors that impact on people's beliefs in exceptional experiences, ranging from the biological to the cultural. In this section we examine some particular exceptional experiences, looking both at people's beliefs and the likelihood of those beliefs having a basis in fact.

Psychic healing

Psychic healing is defined by Benor (2005) as 'the systematic intentional interaction by one or more persons to alter the condition of another living being or beings (person, animal, plant or other living system), by means of focused intention, hand contact or 'passes', without apparently producing the influence through known conventional physical or energetic means' (2005, p137). Benor suggests four sets of beliefs that underlie people's experience of psychic healing:

◀ **Figure 12.21** Faith healers claim to use the power of God to heal

- the influence of God or spirit
- healing energies in the healer
- psychokinesis
- self-healing powers in the patient.

LOOKING FURTHER Before we look at the evidence for psychic healing, have a look for yourself. YouTube has some excellent footage, for example here: http://uk.youtube.com/watch?v=w1NZYaFvgWw What is your first impression?

Thinking practically about psychology

Think back to the last section of this chapter. Consider how beliefs in psychic healing *could* be the result of misattribution, neuroticism, serotonin receptor density, cultural tradition and probability misjudgement.

Healers may explain their practice in any of the above ways, most commonly in terms of the first two. Faith healers, for example, claim to channel the power of God.

Just because we *can* explain belief in psychic healing in terms of psychological factors, this does *not* necessarily mean it isn't a real phenomenon. Be aware of the limitations of Occam's razor and the assumption that the killjoy argument is always the respectable one! Unlike conventional medical professions, healers do not keep records of their success that we can audit, although there is a number of controlled studies that do provide some support for healing. Sicher *et al.* (1998) set up a trial with 20 matched pairs of patients suffering from Aids. One of each pair received healing at a distance for 10 weeks from an experienced healer as well as their usual treatment. Both the patients and the medical staff seeing them during the trial were unaware of which patients were receiving healing. After six months, the group receiving the distance healing had significantly fewer symptoms, made significantly fewer visits to their doctor and spent significantly less time in hospital.

Thinking critically about psychology

Consider the Sicher *et al.* study. In particular:

1 Why was it important that patients were unaware they were receiving healing?
2 Why was it important that those working directly with the patients were also unaware?
3 What was the advantage of the healing being conducted at a distance?
4 Why was it important to match the patients in the healing and no healing groups?
5 Why was it important to have several measures of how well the patients were doing?

Generally, published reviews of healing have led to cautiously optimistic conclusions. Astin *et al.* (2000) carried out a meta-analysis of 23 studies into the effectiveness of healing. These included five of healing by prayer, 11 of non-contact therapeutic touch and the rest miscellaneous. All these different approaches to healing were beneficial, with non-contact therapeutic touch emerging as the most effective and prayer the least.

Of course we must remember that, just because healing appears to be of benefit to some patients, this does not necessarily mean that it works for the reason the healer claims. One factor in many cases is likely to be the placebo effect. People undergoing healing experience attention, warmth, good will and perhaps new hope. These factors certainly make people feel better and in some cases this is probably all they do. That said, double blind studies like that of Sicher *et al.* should eliminate the placebo effect and they still show benefits to healing. As with studies supporting the existence of telepathy and psychokinesis, it may be that very subtle bias or methodological flaws cause studies to indicate an effect that is not really there.

Out-of-body (OOB) and near-death experiences (NDEs)

Although OOB experiences and NDEs can occur independently of one another they often take place together so are often treated as closely related exceptional experiences. Blackmore (2005a) defines OOB as 'an experience in which a person seems to see the world from a location outside the physical body' (2005, p188). This is an unusual experience but in itself it is not 'psychic'. According to Blackmore (1996), 15–20 per cent of people have an OOB experience at some point. Belief in OOB experiences is not a controversy; the OOB experience clearly takes place. What *causes* the experience is another matter. Several cultural traditions have described the existence of a second body (sometimes called the astral body), which can exist for short periods independent of the physical body. There is, however, no direct evidence for the existence of such a body.

Many, though not all, OOB experiences occur in acute medical emergencies where a patient's life is in danger, hence they form part of what are commonly called NDEs. Recent studies of the occurrence of NDEs have found that they occur in 6–12 per cent of cardiac arrests (Van Lommel *et al.*, 2001). NDEs occur in a number of cultures and have some common features. These include a sense of peace, OOB experiences and the presence of a bright light. Nelson KR *et al.* (2006) looked in detail at the frequency of the common features of NDEs in 55 cases of NDE. The results are shown in Table 12.3.

Thinking creatively about psychology

Design an experiment to test the idea that people having OOB experiences can perceive things beyond the range of their senses.

**Table 12.3 The frequency of different features of NDE.
From Nelson KR et al. (2006)**

	n 55 (%)
Cognitive	
Altered sense of time	34 (62)
Accelerated thought processes	24 (44)
Life review	20 (36)
Sense of sudden understanding	33 (60)
Affective	
Feeling of peace	48 (87)
Feeling of joy	35 (64)
Feeling of cosmic unity	37 (67)
Seeing/feeling surrounded by light	43 (78)
Purportedly paranormal	
Vivid senses	42 (76)
Purported extrasensory perception	17 (31)
Purported precognitive vision	16 (29)
Sense of being out of physical body	44 (80)
Apparent transcendental	
Sense of an 'other-worldly' environment	41 (75)
Sense of a mystical entity	30 (55)
Sense of deceased/religious spirits	26 (47)
Sense of a border/'point of no return'	37 (67)

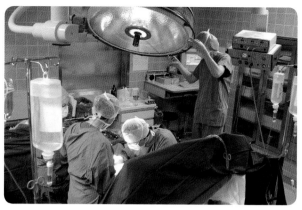

▲ **Figure 12.22** People in medical emergencies sometimes report an out-of-body experience

Most people who have had OOB and ND experiences believe that something paranormal has occurred (Blackmore, 2005a,b). This is perhaps not surprising as both are very intense and emotional, as well as unusual, experiences. In addition, both can have tremendous cultural and religious significance. Christians tend to report seeing Jesus during NDEs whilst Hindus tend to see messengers from Yamraj. The most common belief about OOB and NDE is thus that an aspect of consciousness (thought of as spirit, soul or atman in different cultural traditions) actually leaves the body. Looked at from the viewpoint of parapsychology, OOB and NDEs may be a form of extrasensory perception. This would suggest that people having OOB experiences should be able to perceive things not within the range of their senses.

As scientists we have to accept the existence of OOB and NDE *as experiences*. However, we also have to look at a range of possible explanations for such experiences. There are clearly cultural influences on the details of NDEs but the basics of the the experience remain the same across cultures. This means that it is unlikely that OOB and NDE are purely cultural in origin. Because NDEs generally occur when the body is under extreme stress, physiological explanations have been especially important. Nelson KR et al. (2006) have examined the possibility that NDEs are related to dream experiences. More specifically, people who have NDEs are distinctive in that they experience the intrusion of REM sleep into conscious states. REM intrusion causes a range of symptoms including sleep paralysis, cataplexy (limb weakness or paralysis) and hallucinations just before falling asleep or just after waking.

RESEARCH NOW

Nelson KR, Mattingley M, Sherman AL & Schmitt FA (2006) Does the arousal system contribute to near death experience? *Neurology* 66, 1003–9

Aim: To test the idea that people who have had NDEs are more likely than the general population to have suffered REM intrusion.

Procedure: 446 on a database of those who had reported NDEs were contacted. Sixty-four volunteered to take part in the study and 55 of these were selected as having had 'typical' NDEs. They were matched against a control group of 55 people who had not had an NDE. All participants had a structured interview designed to establish whether they had suffered from REM intrusion. They were asked about experiences of sleep paralysis, cataplexy and hypnogogic (just before sleep) and hypnopompic (just after waking) auditory and visual hallucinations.

Findings: For three of the four indicators of REM intrusion, the NDE group scored much higher than the control group; 36 per cent of the NDE group and 7 per cent of the control group had hypnogogic or hypnopompic auditory hallucinations. For visual hallucinations this rose to 42 per cent for the NDE group (7 per cent for the controls). Forty-six per cent of the NDE group as opposed to 13 per cent of the controls had suffered sleep paralysis. The difference in the incidence of cataplexy (7–0 per cent) was not statistically significant.

Conclusion: People who had NDEs were much more likely to have experienced REM intrusion. This suggests that NDEs may be the result of a problem with the brain's arousal system that regulates the sleep cycle.

In this case the 'killjoy argument' appears to be quite convincing, ie NDEs can be explained by means of brain physiology. However, the possibility that consciousness, or at least a form of extrasensory perception, can briefly be separated from the body remains an open debate. Studies are currently being carried out that may cast more light on OOB and NDEs, in the future. For example, stimuli such as images and number sequences are being placed on top of strip lights in operating theatres and intensive care units. If patients who have NDEs in which they look down on themselves from the ceiling *actually* look down from the ceiling (as opposed to hallucinating it) they should be able to tell us what was on the strip lights.

Mediumship

Mediums are defined by Gauld (2005) as 'individuals through whose agency or through whose organisms there are ostensibly received communications from deceased human beings or other supposed disembodied or remote entities' (2005, p215). Put more simply, mediums claim to be able to communicate with dead people and other spirits. Mediums can work in a range of ways. A common distinction is between mental and physical mediumship. Mental mediumship involves the medium communicating for the spirit, for example by automatic writing or automatic speaking. In physical mediumship, the spirit communicates directly in the presence of the medium. Some but not all mediums enter a trance state when communicating with the spirits.

A huge number of people believe in psychic mediumship. A Gallup poll (Newport & Strausberg, 2001) revealed that almost 30 per cent of Americans believed that mediums can communicate with the dead. According to Roe (1998), around 10 per cent of people in Great Britain visit mediums for advice. Such belief in mediumship, is not confined to Great Britain and the USA but is widespread across a wide range of cultures (Gauld, 2005). So is this belief justified?

Thinking practically about psychology

Thinking back to what you have read in this chapter so far, suggest some reasons why so many people might believe in communication with spirits and accept what mediums tell them? Consider cognitive, cultural, biological and motivational factors.

Since the 1880s there have been attempts to test whether what mediums say or write is accurate or whether their apparent success is a combination of clever guesswork and making very general statements like those you find in magazine horoscopes. There are, however, serious methodological problems with most studies. O'Keefe & Wiseman (2005) identify three particular issues that have made tests of mediumship so difficult.

- How to eliminate the possibility of sensory leakage. It is sometimes possible that the medium can obtain information about clients through non-paranormal means (particularly easy in the age of the internet). This allows them to 'cheat'.
- A way to judge whether statements are specific enough. People are often easily impressed by very general statements, especially those containing compliments (eg 'you have hidden talents'). Obviously these are easy to throw into a 'reading' with any client.
- The need for 'blind' judgement of the accuracy of the medium's statements. For obvious reasons the clients of mediums tend to find it very hard to judge objectively how specific and accurate the statements made by the mediums are.

OVER TO YOU For ethical reasons it is not possible for you as students to study mediums. However, you can test the idea that people are highly susceptible to believing that very generalised statements are specific to them. Draw up five very broad statements that could apply to most people. Present them to some people and ask them to rate how true they are of them. If your statements are quite general and fairly complimentary you will probably find that people readily accept the statements as specific to them.

O'Keefe & Wiseman devised a procedure to test mediums that took account of these three problems. Five mediums were recruited through the Spiritualist Nationalist Union. Five male 'sitters', as mediums' clients are called, were recruited from among the staff and students of a British university. All were aged 25–30 and did not know each other. Mediums and sitters did not meet but sat in adjacent rooms. Each medium was instructed to contact the spirits and give each of the five sitters a reading. The accuracy of each medium's statements were rated by the sitters. The results did not support the idea that the mediums had any psychic ability. The most accurate of the five mediums made the most general statements whilst the only one that made highly specific statements was judged to be the least accurate.

It is highly unlikely that mediums are all deliberately defrauding their clients. Many must believe that their statements are accurate and represent genuine communications with the spirits. Of course they may be correct, although evidence from well controlled studies like that of O'Keefe & Wiseman (2005) suggests that this is not the case. Assuming then for a moment that mediums are well meaning but mistaken, how can we explain their belief? To begin with there is nothing unusual about believing in contact with spirits. In the Williams *et al.* study (p288), over 40 per cent of respondents believed that it is possible to contact the dead. However, actually experiencing contact *may* be a symptom of mental disorder. Moreira-Almeida *et al.* (2008) investigated this idea by assessing the mental health of Brazilian mediums. Some similarities were found with the symptoms of dissociative disorders, although the mediums were found to be generally well adjusted and have little history of mental health problems. They also reported fewer childhood traumas than is typical of patients with dissociation problems. This suggests that mediums are not suffering from mental disorder.

Thinking critically about psychology

The findings of O'Keefe & Wiseman suggest that mediums are not in fact privy to any special information about their clients. However, there may be weaknesses to their procedure. For a moment take the mediums' side and identify these methodological weaknesses.

Chapter summary

Theoretical and methodological issues

- Anomalistic psychology is important because it investigates human experiences that are of profound importance to the individuals that have them, and because it presents great opportunities to develop critical thinking and understanding of research methods.
- A problem with the study of anomalistic psychology has been pseudoscience. Some people believe that all anomalistic psychology is pseudoscience, although we believe that sound scientific principles and methods can be applied to understand unusual experiences better.
- Fraud has also been a huge problem in this field. Over the years many people claiming to have anomalous experiences, in particular psychic powers, have turned out to be fraudsters.
- An attempt to overcome fraud and bias has been the Ganzfeld, a completely controlled procedure for testing telepathy. There is an ongoing debate about whether the Ganzfeld really demonstrates telepathic abilities.
- Other highly controlled procedures exist to test the possibility of psychokinetic abilities. Once again there is some evidence for such abilities but arguments remain about the credibility of the evidence.

Factors underlying anomalous experience

- Regardless of whether psychic abilities are genuine, psychologists have learned a lot about the factors that can explain some anomalous experiences without reference to a paranormal or psi abilities.
- Cognitive factors include misattribution of ordinary events to the paranormal and false memories for

paranormal events that never took place. There is also some evidence to suggest that some aspects of personality are particularly associated with beliefs in the paranormal. Neurological factors including temporal lobe lability and serotonin receptor density are also associated with having anomalous experiences.

- There are a number of other reasons why we might believe in phenomena that do not actually exist. Paranormal beliefs form part of our general cultural beliefs. They may also be a coping mechanism against feelings of powerlessness. We are also generally quite bad at judging the probability of coincidence and quick to make associations between unrelated events. We also tend to deceive ourselves when we have a motive for doing so.

Belief in exceptional experience

- Many people believe in psychic healing. Evidence is fairly supportive of the effectiveness of healing, although this does not mean we should take healers' understanding of how it works at face value.
- Many people report out-of-body and near-death experiences. These are closely tied up with cultural and religious beliefs but there is little concrete evidence to suggest that they are anything other than dream-related hallucinations.
- The situation is similar with mediumship. A huge number of people believe in spirit contact and use mediums, although mediums tested under controlled conditions tend not to be able to offer accurate and specific information to their clients.

What do I know?

1 (a) Explain how pseudoscience and fraud have caused problems for the study of anomalous experience. (10 marks)
(b) Outline and evaluate studies of the Ganzfeld procedure. (15 marks)

2 (a) Describe **one** cognitive factor that might underlie anomalous experience. (10 marks)
(b) Explain how belief in anomalous experiences could have psychological functions. (15 marks)

3 (a) Outline the issue of fraud in relation to anomalistic psychology. (5 marks)
(b) Describe research into psychokinesis. (10 marks)
(c) Evaluate research into psychokinesis. (10 marks)

4 (a) Explain what is meant by psychic healing. (5 marks)
(b) Outline research into belief in exceptional experience. (10 marks)
(c) Evaluate research into psychic mediumship. (10 marks)

5 (a) Describe and evaluate research into biological factors underlying anomalous experience. (15 marks)
(b) Explain the psychology of coincidence. (10 marks)

CHAPTER 13

Psychological Research and Scientific Method

Thinking ahead

By the end of this chapter you should be able to:

- describe the application of the scientific method in psychology, including:
  - **features of science such as replicability and objectivity**
  - **the scientific process including theory construction, hypothesis testing, empirical methods and developing general principles**
  - **validating knowledge and peer review**
- design psychological investigations, including:
  - **selecting and applying research methods**
  - **sampling strategies and issues with sampling**
  - **types of reliability and how to assess and improve them**
  - **internal and external validity and how they can be assessed and improved**
  - **ethical issues to consider in designing and conducting research**

- understand how to analyse and interpret data from psychological investigations, including:
  - **selecting appropriate graphs**
  - **probability and significance including type 1 and 2 errors**
  - **levels of measurement**
  - **choosing statistical tests**
  - **using inferential statistics: Spearman's Rho, Mann-Whitney, Wilcoxon and Chi-squared**
  - **analysis and interpretation of qualitative data**
- in addition, you should:
  - **have carried out, analysed and written up psychological investigations so that you have put these concepts and processes into practice**

I n your AS level you learned about writing hypotheses, how to conduct research to test those hypotheses using a range of different methods and about some of the issues, such as reliability and validity, that arise in studies in psychology. We will explore these topics further in this chapter, looking at why we conduct research the way we do, how we can improve the way we conduct research and how we can use statistics to be more confident about the conclusions we draw.

The scientific method in psychology

What is a science?

Science is about 'knowing' rather than just 'believing'. This leads to two ideas: that scientific knowledge is somehow different from non-scientific information and that it is obtained through a different, ie 'scientific', process. This process, called the *scientific method*, is important and, confusingly, can again mean two things. 'Scientific *methods*' are ways of collecting data, like experiments for example. The 'scientific *method*' is the process of making an observation and developing an explanation for it which is tested and refined (see Figure 13.1).

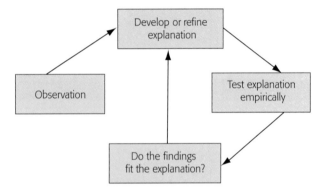

▲ **Figure 13.1** The scientific method

The body of information built up using the scientific method constitutes science in the sense of scientific knowledge. We will explore each of these meanings, and some related ideas, in a little more detail.

Evidence in science

For science to be based on knowledge, rather than belief, evidence is needed. What makes evidence 'scientific'?

RESEARCH IN ACTION

Klimek *et al.* (1997) (p197)

Klimek *et al.* (1997) investigated the size of a brain region called the locus coerulus in depressed and non-depressed individuals after death. Most of the depressed individuals had committed suicide. To find out about the previous mental state, interviewers talked to the individuals' next-of-kin. The measurement of locus coerulus volume was highly **objective**. The data obtained by interview would have been more **subjective**.

Subjectivity and objectivity

One important consideration is whether the evidence is *objective*, that is, whether it has been obtained without reference to the observer. To increase objectivity in their research, psychologists use standardised instructions, operational definitions of variables they are observing and physical measures of performance such as reaction time. These ensure that the researcher is not affecting the outcome of the study. If a researcher knows which condition of an experiment a participant is in they may respond to them in a particular way. This could influence their results.

A personally biased perspective is described as being *subjective*. For example, interviewers may be affected by a participant's emotions. If this biases their choice of questions or their interpretation they are being subjective.

KEY TERMS

subjective a personal viewpoint that is likely to be biased as it is not independent of the situation

objective being unbiased in conducting a study, so that the data collected are independent of the researcher's individual perspective

replicability being able to repeat a study and obtain the same results

Replicability

When a study can be repeated in exactly the same way, it is *replicable*. This matters as scientific evidence needs to be consistent. If the investigation produces the same results when replicated it is likely to be valid and reliable (see pp316–8).

The scientific process: Popper and Kuhn

Although many philosophers of science have influenced the development and understanding of the scientific method, Karl Popper (Figure 13.2) and Thomas Kuhn (Figure 13.3) are especially important. Both have written key works discussing the scientific method including *The Logic of Scientific Discovery* (Popper, 1959) and *The Structure of Scientific Revolutions* (Kuhn, 1962).

▶ **Figure 13.2** Sir Karl Popper

Popper was concerned with the difference between whether a theory was scientific and whether it was true. He suggested that science involves proposing explanations and testing them against experience, that is, by observation and experiment. These methods are described as *empirical* because they are based on experiences with the world. They allow scientists to move from observations and experiments to theories by *inductive* generalisations. However, Popper was concerned that the scientific theories developed must make *specific* predictions: when tested they must risk being contradicted. It must be possible to show that they are wrong – this is called *falsifiability*. So, according to Popper, what separates science from non-science is not the ability to verify but to falsify. Scientists propose explanations, test them and reject those that are disproved. They can then tentatively accept those that are not – although we cannot be certain that they will not be falsified in the future, so science cannot establish truths.

Kuhn suggested that science 'cycles', with new sets of beliefs about science replacing old ones. The sets of beliefs – or the *paradigm* – are the underpinning assumptions of a scientific approach. The paradigm is used to explain and predict the world but also defines the way in which research is conducted. As progress is made, and theories are improved and applied, new evidence ultimately results in the old paradigm being replaced. This is called a *paradigm shift* or 'scientific revolution'. Not only do the beliefs (or theories) change, but the standards and measures, ie the methods, change too. In Kuhn's view, this means that science does not result in progress, merely change. He concludes that science is what the scientific community accepts as scientific. This is one reason for the importance of peer review (see p303) – to maintain scientific credibility.

Constructing a theory

A theory is developed in order to explain observation about a phenomenon in the world, such as the behaviours or beliefs exhibited in a particular situation. An effective theory should be able to account for the range of possible responses that occur and to predict which response will arise under a specified set

of circumstances. Think back to the topic of memory you studied at AS. A useful theory of memory should be able to explain what will be remembered and what will not. It should also be able to predict sets of circumstances that will cause us to remember or will cause us to forget.

▶ **Figure 13.3**
Thomas Kuhn

K E Y   T E R M S

empirical   information that has been gained through methods based on direct experience, such as experiments and observation (and those methods themselves)

induction   reasoning that works from specific cases to general ones, for example, findings from experiments on particular behaviours or participants can be used to produce general laws or explanations

falsifiable   a hypothesis or theory that can be tested and could be shown to be wrong by the evidence

Thinking critically about psychology

Table 13.1 demonstrates the application of scientific criteria to a study from your AS course. Select a study from your A2 course. To what extent do you think the study you have chosen counts as 'scientific'?

Table 13.1 An experiment on eyewitness testimony: is it science?

What characterises a science?	Loftus & Palmer (1974)
Isolating a single variable and measuring it to see what happens, ie science focuses on **objective** measures	They studied EWT by deliberately manipulating verbs (contacted, bumped, hit, collided, smashed) and measured the participants' estimates of speed
Generating a **hypothesis** that is testable	They predicted that changing a single word in the question would cause estimates of speed to change
Employing **controls** so that changes in the variable being measured should only occur because of the researcher's manipulation as it is isolated from other features of the situation	They controlled the setting (a laboratory) and stimuli (eg the crash scenes on film) and changed only the verb to be sure that differences in estimates of speed were due to the leading questions
The intention to **falsify** rather than confirm hypotheses	Similar estimates for all verbs would have falsified the hypothesis. Also, as the study was well controlled it could be replicated so the findings could be refuted
The development of **general laws** from the evidence of rigorous studies	This study and others like it formed the basis of ideas about reconstructive memory; the findings support the common assumptions that memory is not a static structure but a fluid process
Having a single **paradigm** – a common set of general laws or principles that are used to explain and predict the world and which define the way that research is conducted	The findings support the cognitive paradigm – that information flows through a system and is processed along the way (so it is open to change)

Thinking critically about psychology

Theories help us to predict. Name a theory of memory and use it to imagine a situation that would cause a person to remember a piece of information. Now imagine a situation that would cause the person to forget a piece of information.

▶ **Figure 13.4** Ewald Hering developed a hypothesis about colour vision

Hypothesis testing

If you recall Popper from p301, you can see why we need to test hypotheses. First, they make predictions. When the variables are operationally defined, those predictions are very specific. When we state an alternative hypothesis, we are accepting that it could be falsified – the evidence we find might show that the alternative hypothesis is wrong. This is why we need a null hypothesis – it states the conclusion we must draw if the evidence fails to confirm the alternative hypothesis. Sometimes it is obvious that our alternative hypothesis is incorrect, for example, if we predict that people will concentrate better when they have eaten than when they are hungry, but we find that hungry people concentrate the best. However, deciding which hypothesis to accept is not always that easy, which is why we use statistical tests (see p324).

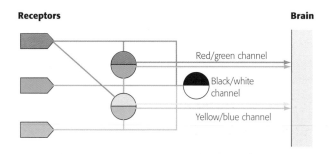

▲ **Figure 13.5** The conflict between Hering and Helmholtz was resolved by Ladd Franklin (1932). She was the first to suggest that the information from the three types of cones was combined to create an opponent process

When the evidence we find fails to confirm our alternative hypothesis we assume that it is false. However, this may be a misassumption. A failure to confirm our prediction could be due to other factors, such as errors in the procedure or bias in the sample. If this is the case, a theory may be rejected for the wrong reasons. This is a risk in hypothesis testing and we will return to it at the end of the chapter. By using falsification, we may discard or change a theory unnecessarily. For example, an early researcher into vision, Ewald Hering, suggested that we detect colour using 'opponent processing', that is, with pairs of 'opposite' colours: yellow/blue and red/green (and black/white). However, for many years this theory was rejected because evidence could only be found for red, green and blue colour detectors in the retina (supporting a theory proposed by Helmholtz). Ultimately, evidence showed that opponent processing happened not in the light-detecting neurones themselves, but further along the chain of neurones carrying visual information. It could then be concluded that both Hering and Helmholtz were correct. The evidence did not, in fact, falsify either theory.

Thinking critically about psychology

Recall the theories of memory you learned about for your AS. In what ways did the working memory model and the evidence supporting it falsify the simple view of short-term memory proposed by the multi-store model?

RESEARCH IN ACTION

Koster *et al.* (2005) (p200)

Koster *et al.* gave their participants a computerised test of attention. The **standardised instructions** for the test appeared on the screen, which was exactly 60 cm away from the participant, and all participants performed a practice task to ensure they understood.

The precise **controls** in this procedure allowed Koster *et al.* to **replicate** their experiment. Although the results partially replicated those of the first test, there were some differences. Koster *et al.* attributed this to differences in the instructions and the sample size.

▶ **Figure 13.6** Using computers to present instructions and stimuli helps to reduce experimenter effects

Empirical methods

As we explained on p301, empirical evidence comes from our observations and experiments. Some philosophers of science argue that we can never experience the world as it really is. Nevertheless, we should aspire to do so. This means using direct observation and recording of data. However, making direct observations can, in itself, be problematic.

We can make data collection more objective by introducing controls and limiting or removing the human element from the process of recording results. The Skinner box (see p151) automatically counts the frequency of an animal's responses so there can be no subjective influence on the scoring of a 'bar press' as there might be if a person were keeping count. This would be an example of observer bias – and is avoided altogether by using electronic recording.

In order to investigate the world 'as it really is' we need to limit the influence of people in research. To this end, researchers use strategies such as standardised instructions and blind procedures. These help to ensure that the findings are the consequence of the variables being investigated and not the result of investigator effects or demand characteristics.

RESEARCH IN ACTION

Klimek *et al.* (1997) (p197 and 320)

Klimek *et al.* investigated the brains of depressed and non-depressed individuals after death. They used a **blind procedure** so the experimenters assessing the brain samples were unaware of which participant group each individual belonged to.

Schooler *et al.* (2005) (p207)

Schooler *et al.* used a **double blind procedure**. In a test of drug treatments for schizophrenia, the patients themselves did not know which drug they were receiving (risperidone or haloperidol) and neither did the researchers assessing their mental health.

Human observers are used in many studies, for example in recording the responses of a child in the 'Strange Situation' (a test of attachment that you learned about at AS). In this instance, the accuracy of observations can be improved by using operational definitions for the various possible responses (such as showing fear). This helps to ensure that the records of one observer are consistent over time and are similar to those of other observers watching the same behaviours, that is, they show good inter-observer reliability (see also p316).

You have already encountered a range of empirical methods, and we will revisit them later in the chapter. Such methods include laboratory, field and natural experiments, correlational analyses, observational studies, self-report methods (including questionnaires and interviews) and case studies.

Thinking critically about psychology

Pick a study you have learned about – either one from A2 so far or one you can recall from AS. Identify the aspects of the design that present risks to objectivity and what the researchers did – or could have done – to reduce those risks.

The development of general laws or principles

According to Kuhn (see p301) a science has a single paradigm – shared assumptions that are used to explain and predict the world and which define the way that research is conducted. Central to any paradigm, therefore, should be a unified set of general laws or principles. Whether psychology has such a unifying thread is open to debate.

If you think back to your AS and to topics such as psychopathology, you will have noticed that psychology encompasses a number of different approaches such as the biological, psychodynamic and cognitive perspectives. Each is different in its underlying principles and, correspondingly, in its methods. For example, biological explanations rely on general principles about the function of neurones and genes. The psychodynamic approach, in contrast, is based on ideas about the unconscious mind and the effect of early experiences. Both can be applied to the same phenomena, such as explaining mental illness, but in different ways. This suggests that psychology has not yet reached the stage of a true science as it does not have a single paradigm, but has several simultaneously. This is reflected in the use of different research methods. Biological and cognitive psychologists use laboratory experiments as their predominant methods, whereas psychodynamic psychologists use case studies.

Within each of the psychological perspectives, however, there are general laws and principles. To an extent, the major paradigm has shifted over time. Early psychologists used a method called 'introspection' – they obtained evidence by studying their own conscious experience. This was replaced by more objective experimentation, for example by behaviourists who focused on observable responses in learning experiments using Skinner boxes. The general laws for behaviourists were based on relationships between stimuli and responses, such as in operant conditioning. The paradigm for the cognitive psychologists who followed them returned to the study of events that could not be directly observed, but this time using more rigorous methods such as experiments to test the way information is processed. In these changes you can see how Kuhn's idea of science being cyclical applies to psychology.

Validating knowledge

The role of peer review

When psychologists develop theories, or test them, they publish their findings in peer-reviewed journals. This has two important functions. First, it disseminates information

Thinking critically about psychology

Consider two contrasting approaches to psychology, such as cognitive and psychodynamic, and compare the central ideas on which they are based and the methods they use. You could make comparisons using a particular phenomenon, such as schizophrenia or addictive behaviour.

– it provides a way for psychologists to find out about the thinking and findings of other researchers. Second, it provides a forum for critical appraisal. This can happen in three ways:

- potential articles for publication are vetted by an editorial board – individuals who are knowledgeable in the field
- some journals invite comments from readers, and replies to them from the original authors, which are published in response to articles appearing in earlier issues
- other researchers can replicate research to verify findings.

▲ **Figure 13.7** By publishing their work, psychologists allow other researchers to comment on their methods and findings

Thinking critically about psychology

Use the internet to find examples of whole journal articles. If you want to look at a specific article, try typing in the name of the author plus 'university' and see if you can find their home page. This may have links to free text whole articles. Alternatively, use the American medical publications site: http://www.ncbi.nlm.nih.gov/sites/entrez?db=pubmed and type in some search terms that you think will identify an area you are interested in. Articles relating to your terms will appear in a list. Look down the list for ones that have either a green bar or both orange and green bars at the top of the icon to the left of the article title. These are available to download as free full text.

The views of peers within the academic community are essential to the validity and progress of research. Alternative views may offer insight into aspects of an explanation that a researcher has overlooked, can provide different solutions to problems

encountered in the design of studies and can, by adding more evidence, help to either confirm or refute current explanations.

Writing up psychological investigations

Throughout this book we have referred to studies. These research studies are generally presented to the scientific community as a journal article. Most journal articles follow a standard format. This is similar to the way you may have written up experiments in science and any studies you conduct in your psychology lessons. In a research report there are usually six sub-sections.

- *Abstract*: this is a brief summary of the aim, method, results and conclusion. It appears at the front of the article. The abstracts of many psychology articles can be found on the internet.
- *Introduction*: this presents the aims of the research and sets them in the context of relevant background research. This can include theories and other similar empirical work. The introduction may report hypotheses explicitly, although this is not standard.
- *Method*: this may be subdivided but, even if it is not, it will contain information about the sample (the sampling method and details about participants such as number and gender ratio), materials used, procedure and controls. There may also be a section on ethics.
- *Results*: full results are rarely presented so summary results are provided using tables (eg displaying measures of central tendency and spread), graphs and the conclusions of inferential statistics. In the case of statistics, it is normal to quote the test used, the number of participants, the observed value and the significance level.
- *Discussion*: this section reviews the relationship of the findings to the previous research that was presented in the introduction. On the basis of this, conclusions are drawn about the contribution of the research to the scientific area being investigated.
- *References*: this provides the details of other research that is referred to. The references can be presented in a number of different standard forms. One style of referencing can be seen on pp355–81 of this book.

 Use the internet to find examples of abstracts on one topic and see how they relate to one another. You can do this by entering very specific search terms into a search engine and scrolling through the results. Here are two alternative ways to search:

- Access *Google Scholar*: http://scholar.google.co.uk/schhp?hl=en&tab=ws. Enter some search terms and a list of articles will be presented.

- Access the American medical publications site: http://www.ncbi.nlm.nih.gov/sites/entrez?db=pubmed and type in some search terms. Articles relating to your terms will appear in a list. If you click on one that looks interesting, the abstract will be displayed and, on the right, some related articles will be listed.

Think of a question you want to answer, such as: Are people who become easily absorbed in a story more likely to believe they have been abducted by aliens?

Decide what you would put in the introduction for a study to investigate your question. Search in books or on the internet for suitable studies. Write approximately a side of prose that sets your idea in the context of other research.

▲ **Figure 13.8** It is important to put new research into context

In an analysis of the effectiveness of a smoking-cessation programme, the COMMIT research group (1995) compared 22 communities. Each of the 11 communities in the programme was matched with a community that was not involved in the smoking-cessation intervention. They were matched for geographic location (state or province), size and general sociodemographic factors.

Identify why geographic location and community size was an important factor for matching and suggest at least three other sociodemographic factors that may have been considered.

Design an experiment that you can conduct. Write out the method (including details of the participants, procedure and ethics) and check it with your teacher. Make or collect the materials you need and write instructions for your participants. Think about how you will reduce demand characteristics and possible experimenter effects. Make sure that you consider the ethical issues your study could raise. Conduct the experiment and write a results section. Include a table, a graph and the results of an inferential test.

Designing psychological investigations

Selecting and applying a research method

At AS, you learned about different research methods including:

- laboratory experiments
- field experiments
- natural experiments
- correlational analyses
- observational studies
- questionnaires
- interviews
- case studies.

In this section we will remind you about these and explore how an appropriate technique is selected and applied to a research problem. The most commonly used method is the experiment. This is a study in which an independent variable (IV) is manipulated and consequent changes in a dependent variable (DV) are measured in order to establish a cause and effect relationship. Different experimental designs may be used in which participants are allocated to levels of the IV in different ways. These include:

- *independent groups design* – different groups of participants are used for each level of the IV
- *repeated measures design* – each participant performs in every level of the IV
- *matched pairs design* – participants are arranged into pairs, each pair is similar in ways that are important to the study and the members of each pair perform in the two different levels of the IV.

In Table 13.2, a range of research methods is briefly described to remind you about how they can be used.

RESEARCH IN ACTION

Lindstroem *et al.* (1999) (p206)

Lindstroem *et al.* conducted an experiment using an **independent groups design**, comparing people with schizophrenia with a control group who did not have a diagnosis of schizophrenia. Brain scans showed that the schizophrenics produced more dopamine.

Adams (1967)

One of the studies reviewed by Tharyan & Adams was Abrams (1967). He compared performance on a memory task before and after ECT was administered to patients with schizophrenia using a **repeated measures design**. No impairment was found following treatment.

Lubman *et al.* (2000)

Lubman *et al.* investigated the role of cues in triggering craving. They used a **matched pairs design** to compare the reaction time of 16 opiate addicts and 16 control participants. Each addict was age-matched with a control participant. They found that the addicts had an attentional bias for drug-related cues. They were faster than control participants to respond to a stimulus preceded by a drug-related picture compared to a neutral picture. This suggested that the addicts' attention was biased toward salient, drug-related cues.

▼ Table 13.2 **Research methods**

Research method	Description of the method	When is the method used?
Laboratory experiment	A true experiment, conducted in an artificial environment, in which the experimenter manipulates an IV and measures the consequent changes in a DV whilst carefully controlling extraneous variables. Participants are allocated to conditions by the experimenter.	When looking for differences, comparisons or cause and effect relationships. It must be possible to actively change the levels of the IV and record the DV accurately. It is important that the behaviour is likely to be relatively unaffected by a contrived environment.
Field experiment	A true experiment in which the researcher manipulates an IV and measures a DV in the natural setting of the participants. Participants are allocated to conditions by the experimenter.	When looking for differences, comparisons or cause and effect relationships. It must be possible to actively change the levels of the IV and record the DV accurately. It is preferable when it is likely that behaviour could be affected by a contrived environment.
Natural experiment	A study in which an experimenter makes use of an existing change or difference in situations to provide levels of an IV and then measures the DV in each condition. Participants cannot be allocated to conditions so it is not a true experiment.	When looking for differences or comparisons between variables that cannot be artificially controlled or manipulated.
Correlational analysis	A technique used to investigate a link between two measured variables.	When looking for relationships between variables. Can be used when it is unethical or impractical to control or manipulate variables artificially. There must be two variables that can be measured.
Controlled observation	A technique in which the researcher watches and records the behaviour of participants in a situation that has been set up by the researcher for the purpose of observing specific behaviours that have been decided in advance. The participants are generally aware that they are being observed although this is not necessarily the case. The observer is generally not a member of the group or activity being observed.	When seeking to record behaviours under different situations or changes in behaviour that require an artificially controlled situation, eg when they are unlikely to arise spontaneously. The recording units must be observable behaviours rather than inferred states, but may be variables that cannot be measured by asking questions.
Naturalistic observation	A technique in which the researcher watches and records the behaviour of participants in their own environment, ie in the normal place for the activity being observed. The participants may or may not be aware of the presence of the observer and the observer may or may not be a member of the group or activity being observed.	When seeking to record behaviours or changes in behaviour that are unlikely to be observable in an artificial situation, eg which are only likely to arise in real-life settings and/or social situations. The recording units must be observable behaviours as above.
Questionnaire	A self-report method used to obtain data by asking participants to provide information about themselves using written questions.	When aiming to collect data about opinions or attitudes from a large sample and when the questions to be asked are largely straightforward and the same for every participant. Also if face-to-face contact might reduce the response rate or honesty.

Interview	A self-report method used to obtain data by asking participants to provide information about themselves by replying verbally to questions asked by an interviewer.	When aiming to collect data from individuals using questions that may require explanation or when the questions may need to vary between participants.
Case study	A method that focuses on a single instance – eg one person or one family or institution – which is explored in detail. Other methods are used to gain a range of information, eg observations, questionnaires and interviews. A history of the participant is obtained and this is related to their subsequent development.	When varied, detailed data is required from one participant, especially if they are a rare or particularly interesting case. The aim of a case study may be to report on, investigate or help someone, so the outcomes are also varied.

When any of the research methods listed above and in Table 13.2 are employed, a number of different design decisions need to be considered.

Design decisions in experiments

Laboratory, field or natural?

The first decision is whether the IV can be manipulated at all. If the IV will change during the experiment, but this is not under the control of the researcher, then it is a natural experiment – that is one in which the researcher does not control the IV or allocate participants to conditions. It does not necessarily have to be conducted in the participants' 'natural' environment, although this is likely to be so. The only thing that is natural is the changing of the experimental conditions. This method tends to be used when it is unethical or impractical to manipulate the IV.

Here is an example of a natural experiment. A researcher believes that high stress levels will lead to a greater incidence of depression. It would clearly be unethical to increase stress deliberately with the intention of inducing depression. However, the researcher could measure the incidence of

> **RESEARCH IN ACTION**
>
> **Koster *et al*. (2005)** (p200)
>
> Koster *et al*. conducted a **laboratory experiment**. They found that depressed people were slower to move their attention away from negative words than non-depressed people, supporting the cognitive explanation of depression.

> **KEY TERMS**
>
> **demand characteristics** aspects of an experimental setting that accidentally tell the participants the aim of the study. They can cause the participants' behaviour to change. They can be reduced by deception and using an independent groups design
>
> **investigator effects** any unwitting influence a researcher has on the participants. These include experimenter bias and the effects of researchers in non-experimental investigations such as in interviews

> **RESEARCH IN ACTION**
>
> **Charlton *et al*. (2000)** (p77)
>
> Charlton *et al*. conducted a **naturalistic experiment** on the children in an isolated community on St Helena island. They found that levels of aggression did not change when satellite TV was introduced.
>
>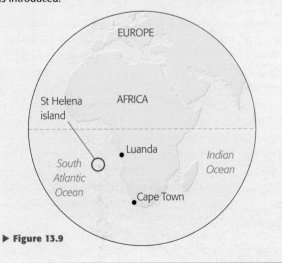
>
> ▶ **Figure 13.9**

depression in students immediately before their exams and sometime afterwards.

In true experiments the researcher actively allocates participants to conditions or manipulates the situation to create different conditions. These conditions may be set up either in a contrived environment – a laboratory experiment – or in the participants' normal surroundings for the activity being tested – a field experiment. A laboratory environment offers high levels of control over the situation, accurate measurement of the DV and the potential to use specific apparatus, for example:

- presenting stimuli at a fixed distance or for a specific length of time can only practically be achieved in laboratory conditions
- timing participants' reactions requires precision that can only be achieved in the laboratory
- using a brain scanner requires a laboratory.

A laboratory experiment is therefore chosen when practicality or the need for experimental rigour exceeds the importance of reducing *investigator effects* and *demand characteristics*. When, however, it is more important that the participant is responding without the influence of an artificial setting, or in cases where they may even be unaware that they are participating in an experiment at all, a field experiment would be chosen if this were possible.

If a researcher conducts a laboratory experiment they have the advantages of rigorous control over the situation and their participants. They can control precisely the nature and presentation of stimuli, sources of distraction and the order of conditions (see counterbalancing, p309). However, they also have some hurdles. Demand characteristics can be a risk as they indicate to the participants the aims of the study which, in turn, affects the participants' behaviour. Clearly this should be avoided. A researcher can minimise the effects of demand characteristics by disguising the purpose of the experiment, for example by using 'filler' questions between the critical ones in a questionnaire. Such distractions make it harder for the participants to guess the experimental aims correctly. Alternatively, participants can be deliberately deceived about the aims. This is likely to be effective but also raises ethical issues (see p319).

Another risk in laboratory studies is that of investigator effects, for example the distortions that arise because the experimenter responds differently to participants in the different levels of the IV. This response may be unconscious but can subtly alter responses, creating or hiding patterns in the results. Imagine a researcher looking for differences between participants with and without an eating disorder who acts in a kindlier way to the participants with mental health problems. This might make them feel more confident or positive about completing the experimental task so they try harder or persist for longer. Any differences in the results could be caused by experimenter bias so would be erroneous.

Which experimental design?

Thinking critically about psychology

The following studies all included experiments. Was each one a laboratory, field or natural experiment?

- **Lindstroem et al. (1999)**, (p206)
- **Bandura et al.**, (p75 and p224)
- **Lubman et al.** (2000), (p307)
- **Calvert & Kotler (2003)**, (p225)
- **Sprafkin et al. (1975)**, (p227)
- **Konijn et al. (2007)**, (p229)

One important decision to be made about an experiment is the allocation of participants to levels of the IV. Sometimes the experimenter must simply allocate different individuals to different levels of the IV because that is determined by the experiment – if they are looking for differences between men and women or people with schizophrenia and those without, for example. In this case the only possible experimental design is independent groups.

However, there are other reasons for choosing this design. By having different participants in each level of the IV, the researcher avoids *order effects* – the possibility that performance will improve or worsen when an individual repeats the experimental task. An additional advantage of this design is that the participants have less opportunity to become aware of the experimental aims so will be less likely to exhibit demand characteristics.

Finally, when conducting an experiment using an independent groups design, it is possible for all conditions to be tested simultaneously. This may not always be desirable or possible, but in some instances it is an advantage. Imagine a field experiment comparing attention in recovered-depressives and never-depressed participants that relies on a particular social context such as a staged distraction. As there may be many variables that *could* affect attention, it might be better to have all the participants, from both levels of the IV, together.

Thinking creatively about psychology

In the example of a comparison between recovered-depressives and never-depressed participants, what possible variables could affect attention?

If an experimenter wanted to compare attention in a real-life situation for people with depression who were undergoing treatment and those who were untreated, why might it be better to conduct a laboratory experiment than a field experiment?

Sometimes a repeated measures design is preferable as it overcomes the problems presented by individual differences. If there are different participants in each level of the IV, any differences found between these conditions could be due to the people rather than the variable being manipulated. In a repeated measures design each individual acts as their own 'baseline'. Any differences between their performance in each level of the IV should be due to the experimenter's manipulation. However, there is a problem here. It is possible that differences may arise because an individual experiences the same (or similar) tasks more than once, ie the risk of order effects.

KEY TERMS

counterbalancing a way to overcome order effects in a repeated measures design. Each possible order of levels of the IV is performed by a different sub-group of participants. This can be described as an ABBA design as half the participants do condition A then B and half do B then A

Order effects cannot be avoided in a repeated measures design but their influence can be cancelled out using *counterbalancing*. Let's say participants will get bored and perform worse the second time they do a task. All we need to do is ensure that, for half the participants, the 'second' task is one level of the IV and for the remaining participants, it is the other level of the IV. This will even out the influence of being the 'first' task in the experiment compared with the second. Consider a researcher who wants to test memory for familiar and unfamiliar lists of words in people with schizophrenia. The participants might improve as they get practised at the task or used to the experimental setting. Alternatively, their performance might decline on the second task as the words from the first list become muddled with those from the second. Using counterbalancing, the experimenter could have some participants recalling the familiar list followed by the unfamiliar one, and others performing these two conditions in the opposite order.

▼ **Figure 13.10** A repeated measures design runs the risk of a fatigue effect

Ideally, researchers would like to avoid the problems of both individual differences and order effects. This is, to an extent, possible with a matched pairs design. To set up a study using matched pairs the researcher decides on the important ways in which participants could differ. Consider a study about eating disorders that is investigating the influence of a big meal on body image. What design would be best? In repeated measures the aim would be obvious so demand characteristics would be a problem. Using two groups of participants, one who ate a large meal and one who did not, in an independent groups design would be possible but variables other than the meal size could influence the individuals. Age, gender, educational level or socio-economic group could all affect vulnerability to eating disorders. In a matched pairs design, participants are identified that share

important characteristics so that one of each similar pair can be placed into each level of the IV. So, in this case, if two 25-year-old female students from the same socio-economic group were found, one would be allocated to each group. As you can imagine, this procedure is very time consuming and is not without risk – it relies on the assumption that the criteria being used for matching are those that are most important, but this may not be the case. Nevertheless, once established, the two matched groups have all the advantages of an independent measures design.

Thinking creatively about psychology

If you were a researcher trying to answer each of these questions, which would you choose – a laboratory, field or natural experiment – and which design would you use?

- Do depressed and non-depressed people respond differently to compliments?
- Are eating disorders more prevalent in a school population after a tragedy such as a mass shooting?
- Do problem gamblers behave in more risky ways in their everyday life than non-problem gamblers?
- Does watching a physically violent TV programme lead to immediate increases in verbally aggressive behaviour?
- Are people who believe they have been abducted by aliens more likely to be fantasy-prone?

Design decisions in correlational studies

Remember that a correlational study looks for relationships between two variables. Both variables must exist over a range and it must be possible to measure them numerically. This means that the participants' scores cannot just be in named categories, they must be on a scale that is, or can be converted to, numbers. These types of data are called ordinal, interval or ratio levels of measurement (see p322).

Researchers are likely to choose to conduct a correlational study when the variables they are investigating cannot be manipulated for practical or ethical reasons. Consider variables such as the length of time a person has had schizophrenia, the depth of an individual's depression, the severity of the parenting strategies used with a child or the number of negative life events an individual has experienced.

RESEARCH IN ACTION

Pontizovsky *et al*. (2006) (p194)

Pontizovsky *et al*. assessed the relationship between diagnosis on admission to hospital and on release in depressed patients. They obtained a Kappa value of 0.62, a fairly strong **correlation**.

Baca-Garcia *et al*. (2007) compared the same measures for patients with bipolar disorder. Their Kappa value of 0.3 indicated a weak **correlation**.

▼ **Figure 13.11** A correlation can be used to demonstrate the extent of similarity between identical twin pairs compared with non-identical pairs

A correlational design is also used when the similarity between individuals is being assessed, such as in a twin study. For example, McGuffin *et al.* (1996) found a stronger positive correlation for major depression between identical twin pairs than non-identical pairs (p195). A similar pattern was found by Gottesman (1991) in relation to schizophrenia (p205).

Another occasion when correlations are used is to assess reliability. If participants are assessed on the same variable twice, the two sets of scores should correlate. This means the measures are consistent or reliable (see p316). For example Baca-Garcia *et al.* (2007) found a stronger correlation for the reliability of diagnoses of schizophrenia than of depression (p194).

Thinking practically about psychology

Why do you think the following studies were conducted as correlations rather than any other design?

- **Eron & Huesmann (1986)**, (p186)
- **McGuffin *et al.* (1996)**, (p195)
- **Button *et al.* (2007)**, (p248)
- **Tucker (1985)**, (p263)

Design decisions in observations

As with other research methods, there are several factors affecting the decision to conduct an observation. In general, observations will be chosen when records are needed of actual behaviours rather than, say, what people *think* they would do, which they would report in a questionnaire. Having access to physical responses rather than verbal ones, scores on tests or performance on experimental tasks, means that researchers can investigate participants who cannot follow instructions or give spoken responses, for example, very young children or non-verbal participants with schizophrenia.

One ethical concern in designing an observation is the need to ensure that privacy is being safeguarded. Participants should either give their consent to being observed or observations should only take place in situations where the individuals would reasonably expect to be watched by others.

Mezulis *et al.* (2006) (p199)

Mezulis *et al.* conducted a **controlled observation**. They videotaped children doing a maths task on a laptop at home. The task was designed to be hard and all the children were given computerised feedback saying they had done poorly (regardless of how they had performed). The mother's reaction to this feedback was observed and showed that the child's cognitive vulnerability was linked to maternal anger, supporting the cognitive model of depression.

▲ **Figure 13.12**

Naturalistic or controlled?

A researcher has to decide whether to observe in a naturalistic or a contrived situation. If the behaviour is very infrequent and is dependent on a certain set of circumstances appearing, a controlled observation is likely to be chosen. Note that this does not have to be in a laboratory. Controlled observations simply employ deliberate manipulation of the setting. You may recall the 'Strange Situation' test of attachment from AS. This was a controlled observation because it used a specific set of people and events. This ensured that the separation and reuniting of mother and infant, and the infant's response to a stranger, were all seen. Furthermore, it assisted consistency. A controlled observation would be preferred in circumstances such as recording the responses of gamblers to winning and losing, or scoring changes in aggressive behaviour following pro- or antisocial television programmes.

Charlton *et al.* (2000) (p77)

Charlton *et al.* conducted **naturalistic observations** as part of their experiment on the effect of television on aggression in children. They used a researcher with a video recorder on view to the children in the school playground. Recording began when the children stopped taking any notice of the camera operator who was a **disclosed observer**. The recordings were then scored by pairs of observers watching together to test **inter-observer reliability**.

Chapter 13 Psychological Research and Scientific Method **311**

The responses elicited in the strange situation *could* be observed in a naturalistic way but this could take a very long time. The observer would have to wait for the mother to come and go spontaneously and for a stranger to turn up! Nevertheless, this may be the preferred technique if the researcher is more interested in the normal frequency of a behaviour, for example, how often a depressed child cries.

Disclosed or non-disclosed, participant or non-participant?

If the researcher knows that their participants will be affected by being observed they may conduct a *non-disclosed observation*. This is where the participants are unaware that they are being observed and is useful if their expectations or beliefs would affect their behaviour. We are more likely to obtain representative information about the behaviour of gamblers by observing them covertly than if they are aware of our role as they may change their behaviour, eg gamblers may 'play safe' or take even bigger risks.

▼ **Figure 13.13** Participant observers become part of the social situation being observed

Clearly, non-disclosed observations raise both ethical and practical issues. In general, a non-disclosed observer is physically hidden, eg is far away. However, this can also be achieved by being within the observed group so that their role is disguised. This is called a *participant observation* because the real participants believe the observer is a member of the group. In the gambling situation, the observer could appear to be another gambler or the croupier. This is advantageous for researchers as they can more easily conduct a controlled observation, for example, changing their betting strategy to observe the effect on the participant.

Participants can be made aware that they are going to be observed. This is a *disclosed observation*. This raises fewer ethical issues. Participants can be asked for their informed consent and so can be observed in a greater range of environments.

Rosenhan (1973) (p204)

Rosenhan conducted a **non-disclosed observation** of the reactions of hospital staff to pseudopatients who initially reported hearing voices. Each pseudopatient was a **participant observer** and described the behaviours of doctors and nurses towards them – which was mainly to ignore them.

▶ **Figure 13.14** Rosenhan conducted a non-disclosed observation

In either disclosed or non-disclosed designs, the observer may either be a participant or a *non-participant observer*. In the latter, the observer is not included within the activities being studied. Non-participant disclosed observations are readily achieved using a video recorder or one-way screen. This design is ideal when the behaviour being observed is likely to be affected by the knowledge that one is being observed since, even with a non-disclosed participant observer, their role may become apparent and affect the individual's behaviour.

A non-participant design helps observers to concentrate on the behaviours of interest as they do not have to pay attention to maintaining their role in the social situation. It is also easier for the non-participant observer to remain objective, so when subjective bias is a potential risk this is preferable. In contrast, participant observation may be more useful for exactly the opposite reason – by becoming involved in the social situation the observer may gain greater insight into the participants' feelings or motives than a non-participant observer.

Thinking critically about psychology

The two experiments below used observations to measure the DV. Was each procedure controlled or naturalistic?

- **Bandura, Ross & Ross (1963)** (p224)
- **Leibert & Poulos (1975)** (p227)

Preparing to collect data

In an observation, design decisions also have to be made as to how data will be collected. These include:

- the sampling strategy
- behavioural categories.

In *event sampling* the observer uses a checklist and tallies each occurrence of a behaviour. Alternatively, records may be taken at fixed time intervals, such as every 10 seconds; this is called *time sampling*.

Each behaviour or '*behavioural category*' should be operationally defined. This ensures that observers are consistent in their recording of each type of event and that the records of different observers are also consistent (see inter-observer reliability, p316). It is important at the design stage that each behavioural category is independent and observable, that is, that they can be readily separated from the continuous stream of events and are reliably identifiable – they must be directly observable and not inferred. For example, recording a gambler 'getting excited' would not be a valid category as 'excitement' itself cannot be seen, whereas an observable product of excitement, such as tapping the fingers, would be a valid category.

Design decisions in self-report studies

Self-report studies are those in which participants report their beliefs, thoughts or feelings to the researcher. They include questionnaires and interviews. In both techniques the researcher presents the participant with questions.

◀ **Figure 13.15**
If people are likely to clam up under the scrutiny of an interviewer, a questionnaire is a better choice

Interview or questionnaire?

The first decision to be made here is whether to collect data face to face – by *interview* – or on paper, using a *questionnaire*. If the nature of the investigation is socially sensitive, a questionnaire may be preferable. Respondents are less likely to be affected by social desirability, and lie or omit answers, if they do not feel judged because they are not face to face with a researcher. For example, interviewees may under-report childhood abuse because they are embarrassed. Conversely, spending time building up a trusting relationship may help an interviewer to elicit *more* information.

Structured, semi-structured or unstructured?

Although different questions *can* be given to different individuals in a questionnaire, in general everyone's is identical. This is an example of a *structured* design because the structure remains the same for every participant. In a *semi-structured* design, the same questions are used for each respondent, but additional questions can be used, so there is some tailoring of the questions to the individual on the basis of the answers given. Interviews can alternatively be *unstructured* – these are entirely variable so the interviewer can respond to the answers a participant gives with different questions. This adaptable technique is more likely to gain useful, detailed information when this is difficult to obtain. For example, with a reticent participant with mental health problems, more is likely to be learned using a flexible approach than by sticking rigidly to a set of predetermined questions.

▼ **Figure 13.16** Interviews tend to be more flexible than questionnaires as they can be unstructured

RESEARCH IN ACTION

Wilhelm *et al.* (2006) (p195)

Wilhelm *et al.* used **interviews** to measure depression and life events. They found a strong association between negative life events and depression.

Open or closed questions?

There are a number of different ways to ask questions, and decisions must be taken about how these will be employed. Both open and closed questions can be used in either questionnaires or interviews. A *closed question* gives the participant little choice and typically requires just one of a small number of alternative answers, such as a cross or tick in a box or saying 'yes' or 'no'. A researcher may choose to use closed questions as the results are easy to analyse because they generate simple numbers. For example, we could ask 'Do you believe in the power of mediums?' using a yes/no format. Alternatively, we could ask a forced choice question: 'Which of the following have you experienced: psychokinesis, alien abduction, contact with a dead person, seeing a ghost?' This would allow us to say that *x*% of participants reported particular anomalistic experiences. Another kind of closed question is the Likert-style question. This is used to elicit opinions, offering the participant a range of responses:

> strongly agree ☐, agree ☐, don't know ☐, disagree ☐, strongly disagree ☐.

Questions like this can be used to find out people's views, for example in relation to ECT as a treatment for depression. Participants would indicate their response on the scale above to statements such as:

> - I feel the risks are worthwhile as ECT works when other treatments have failed
> - I think ECT is unsafe
> - I believe that a patient would benefit from ECT
> - It is wrong to administer ECT to patients when they may not understand what will happen

When using Likert-style scales some of the statements must be 'reversed' so that the 'positive' or socially acceptable response is not always at the same side of the page.

Another question type is the *semantic differential*. This elicits feelings about a topic or situation and can be used to generate quantitative data. It is useful when the researcher wants to obtain data on a scale rather than simple yes/no answers. Participants with and without depression could be asked:

> Do thoughts about your future make you feel:
> | | | |
> |---|---|---|
> | confident | _____ | doubtful |
> | powerful | _____ | weak |
> | sad | _____ | excited |
> | tense | _____ | calm |

When writing scales for semantic differentials it is important to ensure that some have the positive emotion on the left, others on the right.

Closed questions, including Likert-style and semantic differentials, all produce results that are numerical or 'quantitative' (see p321). If, however, the nature of the research requires detailed, in depth answers then *open questions* are more appropriate as they can elicit an extended answer. An open question, eg 'How do you feel when you have the urge to

---

RESEARCH IN ACTION

Swaffer & Hollin (2001) (p200)

Hollin used a **questionnaire** to assess anger in young offenders. Those who suppressed their anger were more likely to suffer depression, supporting the psychodynamic model.

▶ **Figure 13.17**

gamble?', will supply much more information than ticking boxes about excitement or desperation. Unlike the numbers produced by closed questions, the results generated by open questions are qualitative, that is, they are detailed and descriptive. This data is more difficult to analyse, and this would be a consideration for researchers who wanted to collect a wide range of information from a large sample of participants.

Both qualitative and quantitative data can be collected using either questionnaires or interviews. In practice, researchers would generally choose questionnaires to gather specific, quantitative information and interviews to gather more indepth, qualitative data.

Thinking creatively about psychology

Eranti *et al*. (2007) (p198) used many different ways to assess patients following ECT for depression. These included the Hamilton Depression Rating Scale (a structured interview), questionnaires including the Beck Depression Inventory and visual analogue mood scales. In a questionnaire to assess any side effects from treatment, patients were asked five questions: 'Have you had trouble recalling people's names?' 'Have you felt confused or disoriented?' 'Have you had any memory problems?' 'Have you had trouble concentrating?' and 'Have you had trouble holding in your memory new things you have learned?'

- Why do you think they used both interviews and questionnaires to assess the effectiveness of the treatment?
- Were the questions about side effects open or closed?
- Suggest two more questions they could have asked to reveal possible effects on memory.

Visual-analogue scales for mood are like semantic differentials; they consist of a line with opposing mood descriptions at either end along which the participant makes a mark. The position of the mark along the line is then measured.

- Will this generate quantitative or qualitative data?
- Draw two possible visual-analogue scales that could have been used to assess mood in this study.

Wilhelm *et al*. (2006) (p195) interviewed participants every five years about positive and negative life events such as bereavement and unemployment.

- Why do you think they chose an interview rather than a questionnaire to assess these life events?

Design decisions in case studies

The primary decision in a case study is who will be investigated, such as an interesting individual in therapy. The aims of the case study must then be considered. Is the objective to help the individual or to find things out? This will determine the methods used within the case study. Another factor affecting the choice of methods is the theoretical perspective taken by the researcher. Consider a psychodynamic theorist helping a patient with depression, versus a biological or cognitive psychologist investigating unusual brain patterns in a person with auditory hallucinations. The former is likely to use interviews, perhaps aiming to build up a relationship with the client that allows catharsis and transference to occur (see p202). The latter would use more objective techniques, perhaps conducting a single-participant experiment using a brain scanner.

RESEARCH IN ACTION

Cooper (1982) (p281)

Cooper reports a **case study** from anomalous psychology that explored the belief of two sisters who claimed to have seen, and photographed, fairies.

▲ **Figure 13.18** The fifth photograph taken by the sisters, which they always insisted was not a fake

Other techniques are used within a case study, such as controlled or naturalistic observations and questionnaires (eg to members of the individual's family). Which techniques will be used, and how often, are important design decisions as well as a consideration of the time span over which the case will be explored.

Since case studies by their very nature look in depth into one individual, especial care must be taken to ensure that the investigation is ethical. Privacy, confidentiality, the right to withdraw and real informed consent are all important here. This is even more crucial when the individual has mental health problems – they may be more vulnerable or less able to give informed consent.

Thinking critically about psychology

Bhowmick (1991) reports a case study of an elderly man who repeatedly had near-death experiences.

Why is this the most likely research method for this kind of investigation?

Giarelli *et al*. (2004) (p256) conducted a case study of a 51-year-old adult female former smoker with a 30-year habit to support their investigation into the incidence of smoking in American women. This was important because the personal experiences of smokers provide a deeper and richer understanding of habitual use than statistics. The participant mirrored the demographic profile of a typical smoker. Data was obtained through a tape-recorded semi-structured interview. The transcribed responses were read by the four researchers and condensed into a description covering the participant's experiences relating to tobacco from her earliest use to the interview.

Why was this particular individual an ideal choice for a case study in this instance?

Developing a plan

When designing a study researchers need to work through several important steps to plan effectively. They should:

- decide on their aim and, if appropriate, develop hypotheses to test
- select the most appropriate research method
- identify and operationalise the variables
- make design decisions (including considering what controls are necessary)
- ensure the design is ethically sound
- devise appropriate materials or apparatus
- use a pilot study to resolve any practical issues
- identify the target population
- decide which sampling method to use and the sample size they will need.

These decisions are all explored in the next section. Finally, researchers should decide how the results will be analysed, choosing which descriptive and – if appropriate – inferential statistics they will use once the data have been collected (see p324–31).

Sampling strategies

The participants in a study are called the *sample* and are selected from the *target population*. The sample should be representative of the wider group so needs to contain individuals with all the important characteristics that appear in the population. However, not all samples represent the population equally well.

Opportunity sampling

Researchers often choose a sample simply by using those people who are around at the time, such as the first people to walk past the laboratory door. This is *opportunity sampling* and is unlikely to represent the population fairly.

People who are available in the same place at the same time are likely to be similar so the sample won't include the variety that exists in the population from which they come. This means it may be biased. Consider a department that offers psychology students extra credits for participating in research (a procedure that is common in universities). This may not matter for some studies, ones on perception or memory for example, but where age is important, educational level, or prior knowledge of the topic, the predominance of young, well educated psychology students may influence the results.

▲ **Figure 13.19** University psychology students are often used as participants for studies. How representative is such an opportunity sample?

Volunteer sampling

An alternative strategy to asking people directly is to request volunteers, for example using a notice in a shop window or a post on the internet. The respondents are a *volunteer sample*. This sampling technique may also be unrepresentative of the population. Volunteers are likely to have more free time than average and, apart from being willing, tend to have other characteristics in common, such as being better educated.

However, it is a very useful technique when looking for participants who are unusual in some way. For example, people with mental illnesses who are willing to contribute to a study that requires them to have a brain scan would be difficult to find, but volunteers might be recruited via doctors' surgeries.

Random sampling

Participants obtained by *random sampling* are more likely to be representative of the population. This is because the sampling strategy ensures that each person in the population has an equal chance of being chosen. If a researcher in a university were to place an advert for volunteers on the library noticeboard, students who never go to the library could not be selected – the sample would be biased. However, if they started with a numbered list of all the students and used a random number generator to identify a sample, any individual is equally likely to be chosen. For a small population this can be done by allocating each person a number, putting numbered pieces of paper in a hat, and drawing out numbers until the sample is big enough.

Even with random sampling there are potential problems. It may not be possible to access all members of the population, so sampling biases can still arise. Consider a study that randomly selects people diagnosed with depression from doctors' records. The potential participants are then contacted by phone or post. The most severely depressed individuals may also be those least likely to keep their contact information up to date so the sample may be biased towards those whose symptoms are less severe.

Furthermore, a random sample is exactly that – random. Did you ever play snakes and ladders with someone who rolled a six nearly every go? Just because the process is unbiased does not mean the outcome necessarily is. The smaller the sample the greater the risk that it will be unrepresentative. To extend the snakes and ladders analogy, if you played enough games, the random throws of the die would even out and you and your opponent would enjoy about the same level of 'lucky throws' overall. The sample size in a study is therefore very important.

Thinking critically about psychology

Explain the sampling choices made in each of the following studies. Consider the sampling method, the sample size and how representative you feel they would have been.

● **Kurtz *et al.* (2007)** (p209 and p320) compared 25 patients with schizophrenia and 18 healthy controls. The participants with schizophrenia were an opportunity sample of patients who already had a diagnosis. The healthy controls were a volunteer sample recruited using local advertisements.
● **Miller & Howell (2005)** (p266) used opportunity sampling to recruit 170 students from three Australian secondary schools. The sample was used to investigate the theory of planned behaviour in relation to underage lottery gambling.
● **Mezulius *et al.* (2005)** (p199) investigated the relationship between negative thinking (relating to depression) and parenting style. Two hundred and eighty-nine child participants and their parents were studied. The sample was found by recruiting pregnant women who were already part of an ongoing research project in Wisconsin. Seventy-eight per cent were from the Milwaukee area and 22 per cent from the Madison area. The criteria for inclusion in the project were: over 18 years old; 12–21 weeks pregnant; living with the baby's father; at least one member of the couple in paid employment; not a student; not unemployed and seeking work; having a telephone; English sufficiently to understand an interviewer; literacy sufficient to complete self-report questionnaires.

What sampling method would it be best to use in each of the following studies?

- An investigation into depression that requires participants to keep a diary of their feelings over two months.
- A questionnaire-based study looking at the incidence and nature of everyday phenomena that are similar to 'hearing voices in your head'.
- An experiment comparing experiences of craving in compulsive shoppers and problem gamblers.
- An interview with parents designed to find out whether those with children who have been excluded from school allow them to watch television in a less restricted way than children who have not been excluded.

Reliability

Psychologists need to measure variables consistently. This aspect of accuracy is called *reliability*. If you are a reliable student you regularly turn up at to your lessons or hand in your homework. A reliable psychological test or measure has consistency as it will always produce the same results in the same situation. Reliability is used to assess both experimental procedures and 'tools' such as tests, interviews and behavioural categories in observations.

Types of reliability

There are two broad types of reliability:

- *Internal reliability* – the consistency of a measure within itself. For example, the items on a questionnaire or questions in an interview should all be testing the same phenomenon.
- *External reliability* – the consistency of a procedure from one occasion to another. For example, an experiment performed on two different days, in different laboratories, or by different researchers should produce similar results. *Inter-rater* or *inter-observer reliability* is an aspect of this. Two researchers using the same interview format, equipment, observational schedule or test should obtain the same results.

Assessing reliability

Internal and external reliability are assessed in different ways.

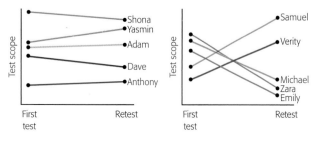

▲ **Figure 13.20 (a) good reliability (b) poor reliability** If test–retest reliability is high, individuals achieve similar scores on both occasions

Internal reliability can be assessed by:

- *Split-half procedure* – participants' scores on a test are divided into two halves. For example, a single test or questionnaire can be divided into 'even-numbered questions' and 'odd-numbered questions'. Participants' scores on the two halves should correlate strongly if the test is reliable.
- *Equivalent forms* – two tests, questionnaires or structured interviews of the same type are given to the same participants. Participants' results on the two forms of the test should correlate strongly if the tests are reliable.

External reliability can be assessed by:

- *Test-retest procedure* – participants take the same test twice, at different times. If the results for the two occasions correlate, the test is reliable. This can identify individual items that generate inconsistent results or other factors that cause variation, such as different settings or researchers. This is typically used to test the reliability of structured interviews and questionnaires (see Figure 13.20).
- *Simultaneous observation* – to assess inter-observer reliability, two (or more) observers watch the same behavioural sequence (eg on video). Equipped with the same behavioural categories they should achieve identical records. A similar process can be used to assess the reliability of interviewers.
- *Replication* – experimental studies can be tested for reliability by repeating them exactly, using a standardised procedure. The results should be the same if the procedure is reliable.

Improving reliability

Tests of internal reliability (split-half and equivalent forms) allow the researcher to identify individual unreliable items, for example particular questions on a questionnaire that fail to produce consistent results. These can then be removed or replaced. If this results in an improvement, then a stronger correlation will be found when reliability is checked again.

If external reliability is low, this may be caused by low internal reliability so improvements as above may help. If inter-observer reliability is low, this can be improved by discussing and agreeing on operational definitions of behaviours and through common practice sessions where recorded behavioural sequences are watched, scored and then discussed until agreement is reached.

Mezulius *et al.* (2006) (p199)

Mezulius *et al.* videotaped interactions between mothers and their children. These were transcribed and coded by undergraduate research assistants into standardised categories and ratings. There were many hours of training and rating of pilot tapes. After group training, the raters had to demonstrate **reliability**, reaching a criterion of 0.80 agreement on categories with the trainer. After training **inter-rater reliability** for the various different types of category was between 0.82 and 0.99.

Charlton *et al.* (2000) (p77)

Charlton *et al.* videotaped children's behaviour on the island of St Helena before and after the introduction of satellite TV. The observers worked in pairs, making separate records of the behaviours in each 60 seconds of tape. **Reliability** was ensured by keeping records they agreed on and, where they disagreed, the segment was replayed and recoded to reach agreement.

▶ **Figure 13.21**

Validity

Validity is the extent to which a technique is capable of achieving the intended purpose. For example, if a score on an experimental task is a valid indicator of the DV, it measures the variable under scrutiny rather than varying because of the influence of demand characteristics, fatigue or the effect of the experimenter. Like reliability, validity assesses not only experimental procedures but tools such as tests, questionnaires and behavioural categories in observations.

Types of validity

In an experiment, *internal validity* refers to whether changes in the DV can be attributed to the manipulation of the IV rather than sources of error. In other research methods, internal validity also relates to the extent to which the tool is measuring the variables it was designed to. There are several kinds of internal validity, including:

- *Face validity* – whether a measure appears, at face value, to test what it claims to. For example, does an interview about addiction to alcohol genuinely measure drinking habits or does it simply elicit socially desirable responses?
- *Content validity* – whether the measure is appropriate for investigating the aims in terms of its academic relevance. For example, measures of addictive gambling might be expected to include questions about the frequency of the behaviour, the types of gambling, the

amount of money lost, whether lost money is 'chased' and the experience of craving and withdrawal.
- *Concurrent validity* – whether a new test produces a similar measure of a variable as existing and useful tests of the same phenomenon. For example, a new questionnaire that identifies risk factors in drug abuse should find many of the same factors as an existing questionnaire.
- *Predictive validity* – whether the measure can accurately forecast future consequences. For example, a test or measure should be able to indicate relevant outcomes such as performance, mental health or recovery.

External validity, in contrast, relates to issues beyond the investigation. For example, whether the findings are representative of:

- other settings – *ecological validity*
- different periods in time – *historical validity*
- other groups of people – *population validity*.

Ecological validity is the extent to which findings from one environmental setting generalise to other settings. One important example of this is whether results from laboratory experiments apply outside the laboratory, that is, whether they *generalise* to 'real life'. Ecological validity also includes the extent to which an experimental task is representative of the real world; this is its *mundane realism*. This takes into account factors such as whether the task required of participants is a plausible one or if the stimuli used are things that they might genuinely encounter. So, findings from experiments that are realistic representations of the real world and which are likely to generalise to other settings have high ecological validity.

▲ **Figure 13.22** Are high sensation-seekers more likely to be at risk of substance abuse?

Thinking creatively about psychology

Design a study to test one of the following hypotheses. Be sure that you can justify the decisions you have made to ensure that your study is valid and reliable.

- People with schizophrenia are less able to recognise a picture they have drawn than control participants.
- There is a difference between the speed that people with and without depression respond to positive and negative facial expressions.
- Children who are read pro-social stories are more likely to help another child than those who are read neutral stories.
- High sensation-seekers will abuse a wider range of drugs than low sensation-seekers.
- People who have consulted a medium are more likely to attribute the cause of missing objects to poltergeists than those who have not consulted a medium.

Assessing validity

Internal validity

To assess face validity researchers must consider the test, questionnaire, interview or experimental procedure they are using. For example, if an interview about addiction to alcohol includes leading questions that might trigger socially desirable responses it is unlikely to be valid.

Content validity is similar to face validity, but assessment is based on the opinions of experts in the field. For example, a group of clinical psychologists could read and comment on a structured interview about eating disorders to decide whether it is asking relevant and appropriate questions that will reveal useful indicators.

Assessing concurrent validity requires a comparison between the tool in question and one known to be valid. If the new tool produces similar results to the existing one, it is valid.

For example, a new structured interview schedule for assessing vulnerability to an eating disorder should identify many of the same individuals as an existing interview.

As predictive validity relates to the ability of a tool to forecast future consequences, it can only be assessed in relation to actual outcomes. A longitudinal design is used in which baseline measures are taken of the variable in question (eg current drinking behaviour and risk factors for later alcohol abuse such as parental behaviour, peer group behaviour and personality). From these measures predictions are made. The validity of those predictions is assessed by retesting the drinking behaviour of the sample at a later date. If validity is high, those individuals identified as having more risk factors will be more likely to exhibit signs of alcohol abuse.

External validity

External validity relates to the generalisibility of findings so is assessed by replication. Demonstrating historical validity requires performing an experiment or using a questionnaire or other research instrument again and showing that it still produces similar results years or decades later. This would show that the test is resistant to changes over time, for example that the tasks used are still relevant and understandable. Similarly, population validity is demonstrated by repeating a study on different cultural or sub-cultural groups to show that the findings generalise from one group to another.

Demonstrating ecological validity is slightly different. Here it is necessary to show that findings from one context apply in another. The results of an experiment that found that people with schizophrenia more often generated word associations in a laboratory setting would need to show that the same individuals also demonstrated more stimulus-driven behaviour in their day-to-day environments.

Improving validity

In experiments, internal validity is improved using controls such as standardised instructions and blind or double blind procedures. These help to reduce experimenter bias and demand characteristics. The effect of individual differences can be reduced by randomisation or counterbalancing in repeated measures designs, and by random allocation of participants to conditions in independent groups designs.

Standardisation can also help to improve internal validity in other methods such as interviews and questionnaires where greater structure is possible. Individual items in tests, questionnaires or interviews that have been identified as lacking validity should be replaced.

Historical and population validity can be improved by taking larger, more varied samples, for example including a wider age group or geographical area. A sampling method called *stratified sampling* allows researchers to identify the different sub-groups within the population and build a sample that represents each sub-group in proportion to their existence in the population. This can improve external validity in this respect.

RESEARCH IN ACTION

Eranti *et al.* (2007) (p198 and p313)

Eranti *et al.* (2007) used a **single blind procedure**, standardised instructions and random allocation to ECT or rTMS conditions for the treatment of depression. Furthermore, it was ensured that patients from each of the two participating hospitals were represented in each treatment condition, ie allocation was stratified. To check that the raters were indeed blind to the participants' condition, they were asked to guess the allocated treatments after the end-of-treatment assessments.

In terms of ecological validity in experiments, a balance must be sought between improvements achieved by introducing more controls (so that internal validity is increased) and making the situation or task more realistic (so that ecological validity and hence generalisibility is increased).

Finally, in order to have high validity the experiment or tool must have high reliability.

Ethical issues

You will already have encountered ethical issues raised in earlier chapters. Here we will look at a range of ethical dilemmas that psychologists face and how they can deal with them effectively.

BPS guidelines

To help psychologists to deal with ethical issues arising in research and professional practice, the British Psychological Society (BPS) regularly updates its ethical guidelines. Since psychologists are concerned with people's welfare, it is important that these guidelines are followed. They are summarised in Table 13.3. When research is conducted at institutions such as universities, the planned study must be approved by an ethical committee. This ensures that these guidelines are being followed. Whilst the primary concern is for the welfare of individuals, another issue is the perception of psychology in society. Participants who are deceived or distressed may not want to participate again, may portray psychology in a poor light to others, and are unlikely to trust the findings of psychological research. These are all outcomes we would want to avoid.

Thinking critically about psychology

Eranti *et al.* (2007) (p198 and p313) studied the treatment of depression. Those invited to participate had been referred for ECT for depression by a psychiatrist and were at least 18 years old. Possible participants were excluded if they were unable to have rTMS because of metallic implants, history of seizures, recent substance misuse, were unable to have a general anaesthetic or ECT or had received ECT or rTMS recently. People who were unable to give informed consent or refused to do so were also excluded. Patients received their usual medical care and medications during the study and the study was approved by local ethical committees. Potential participants received a complete description of the study, written informed consent was obtained and the patients were not blind to their allocated treatment. In addition to receiving ECT or rTMS, participants were given cognitive tests and measures of depression. They were asked about side effects (such as scalp discomfort or hearing loss) and asked several questions (look at these on p313). Of the 260 patients referred for ECT, 107 were eligible. Many were excluded because they did not consent to ECT. Of the remainder, 46 consented to participate in the study. Five patients in the rTMS group terminated treatment early because they felt they were not improving, and one patient could not attend a session. All but one agreed to being assessed following treatment.

What ethical dilemmas were being faced and how were they dealt with in this study?

Thinking creatively about psychology

Design two experiments to investigate whether depressed people have poor memories. One should have high mundane realism and the other should have rigorous controls.

▼ **Table 13.3 British Psychological Society Code of Ethics (2006) in summary**

1	**Introduction:** the public needs to have confidence in psychology, so the way that researchers treat participants is important as it affects public perception of all psychologists.
2	**General:** psychologists must always consider the ethical implications of their research. Foreseeable threats to the well-being, dignity, health and values of participants should be eliminated. They should only conduct research in areas where they are competent.
3	**Consent:** researchers must take reasonable steps to obtain real consent from participants. *Real* consent can only be given by participants who fully understand what they are agreeing to. Researchers should not use payment or their position of power over participants to persuade them to consent to activities.
4	**Deception:** deceiving participants should be avoided whenever possible. Participants should be told about the aim of the investigation as soon as possible. Deception should not be used when it is likely that participants will object or become distressed when debriefed.
5	**Debriefing:** whenever participants are aware that they have taken part in a study they should be given a full explanation of the research as soon as possible. Researchers should also ensure that the participants' experiences were not distressing and that they leave the study in at least as positive a mood as they entered it.
6	**Withdrawal:** participants should be made aware of their right to withdraw from a study at any point and that payment does not affect this right. When debriefed, participants have the right to withdraw their data.
7	**Confidentiality:** unless agreed with participants in advance, their individual results and any personal information about them should be completely confidential.
8	**Protection:** participants should be protected from physical and psychological harm, including stress. They should not be exposed to any more risk than they would encounter in their usual lifestyle.
9	**Observation:** observational studies risk invading privacy. If participants are unaware they are being observed this should only be done in places and situations where they would expect people to watch them.
10	**Advice:** if researchers see signs of a physical or psychological problem that participants are unaware of, but which might be a threat, they should inform them about it. Where participants seek professional advice, researchers should be cautious.
11	**Colleagues:** if colleagues are seen to break any of these principles, it is important to tell them and to try to persuade them to alter their conduct.

> ### RESEARCH IN ACTION
>
> **Baker *et al.* (2006) / Kurtz *et al.* (2007)** (p209 and p323)
>
> Baker *et al.* / Kurtz *et al.* investigated schizophrenia using virtual reality. All the participants gave their written **informed consent**, the procedures met institutional ethical approval and all participants were paid $20 per hour for participation.
>
> **Wilhelm *et al.* (2006)** (p195)
>
> Wilhelm *et al.* investigated life events, genetics and depression. They obtained **informed consent** for the collection of both psychological and physiological data. The participants were followed up every five years. At the 20-year point, 149 of the original 165 participants remained. Some could not be located or had died and four exercised their **right to withdraw**.

Designing and conducting ethical research

Consent and deception

As we saw on p318, it is important in experiments to hide the aims from participants, or even deceive them, in order to reduce demand characteristics. However, potential participants also have the right to know what is going to happen so they can give their *informed consent*. These two opposing needs mean that it may be hard to get genuine consent. Ideally, researchers should obtain full and informed consent from participants by giving them sufficient information about the procedure to decide whether they want to participate.

However, in some situations the researcher cannot ask for consent. This is often (but not always) the case in naturalistic observations and field experiments and in laboratory experiments where *deception* is essential to the aims. In these situations, a researcher can attempt to decide whether participants in the sample would be likely to object by asking other people. Using a group of people similar to those who will become participants, the researcher can ask whether they would find the study acceptable if they were involved. This is called *presumptive consent* because it allows the researcher to *presume* that the actual participants would also be happy to participate.

> ### RESEARCH IN ACTION
>
> **Rosenhan (1973)** (p207)
>
> Rosenhan investigated the behaviour of hospital staff towards patients who had a diagnosis of schizophrenia based on pretend symptoms. In this study **deception** was necessary in order to achieve the aims.

Right to withdraw

Participants have the right to leave a study at any time if they wish. This is their *right to withdraw* and it must be observed even if this means data are lost. Whilst participants can be offered incentives to join a study, these cannot be taken back if they leave – so that they do not feel compelled to continue. Nor should researchers use their position of authority to encourage participants to continue beyond the point where they want to stop. In practice, this means that researchers must make the right to withdraw explicit to participants and be prepared to relinquish data if a participant chooses to withdraw. So if, in a repeated measures design, a participant leaves between the first and second testing, their data from the first condition cannot be used.

Protection from harm

Studies have the potential to cause participants psychological harm (eg distress) or physical harm (eg engaging in risky behaviours such as taking drugs). In these situations, participants have the right to be protected and should not be exposed to any greater risk than they would be in their normal life. If participants have been negatively affected by a study, the researcher has a responsibility to return them to their previous condition. This is one of the functions of the debrief but is not an alternative to designing an ethical study. It is therefore important to consider all the ways in which a study could cause distress and to minimise them.

> ### RESEARCH IN ACTION
>
> **Eranti *et al.* (2007)** (p198 and p313)
>
> Eranti *et al.* excluded possible participants from their study on ECT and rTMS for their own safety if they had metallic implants or foreign bodies. This ensured the participants were **protected from physical harm**.
>
> **Turkington *et al.* (2004)** (p211)
>
> Turkington *et al.* investigated the effectiveness of different treatments for schizophrenia. To satisfy the right of participants to be **protected from psychological harm**, all were offered CBT as part of the experiment or immediately following it if they were part of the control group.

Thinking practically about psychology

Klimek *et al.* (1997) (p197) interviewed the next-of-kin of suicide victims (and of control participants) whose bodies were to be used in an investigation on brain abnormalities and depression.

Koster *et al.* (2005) (p200) tested depressed and non-depressed participants using lists of words that included the following: worthless, loser, failure, inferior, rejected, lonely, desperate, useless, vulnerable, incompetent, unwanted, hopeless, lost.

What special ethical care would need to be taken in these instances?

Privacy and confidentiality

Studies that ask for personal information or observe people risk invading privacy. A researcher should make clear to participants their right to ignore questions they do not want to answer, thus protecting their privacy. When completing a questionnaire in a laboratory situation, participants should be given an individual space and assured of the confidentiality and security of their data. Participants' identities can be protected by allocating each person a number and using this to identify them. In experiments with an independent groups design this helps to identify and keep a record of which condition each participant was in. In repeated measures designs, participant numbers are essential for pairing up an individual's scores in each condition.

Thinking creatively about psychology

Plan a study to investigate whether people with depression are less likely to find positive words in anagrams than negative ones. Include in your design variables that you will control and steps you will take to make sure that the study is ethical.

Which words would a person with depression find?

frae	**acres**
dandes	**idm**
rathet	**veil**
spedres	**orels**
gwonr	**brad**

Answers on next page

RESEARCH IN ACTION

Bhowmick (1991) (p314) reported a case of an out-of-body experience. The participant was referred to as Mr TA, a 67-year-old Caucasian male. Even though report gives Bhowmick's place of work (the Department for Health Care of the Elderly, HM Stanley Hospital in St Asaph, north Wales) it would be impossible to identify Mr TA from this information. This protected the participant's identity thus satisfying the guideline of **confidentiality**.

In observations, people should only be watched in situations where they would expect to be on public display. When conducting a case study, including those of larger groups such as institutions, confidentiality is still important and identities must be hidden. For example, the identities of schools or hospitals should be concealed.

The only exceptions to this general principle are that personally identifiable information can be communicated when the individual gives their informed consent to do so or in exceptional circumstances when the safety or interests of the individual or others may be at risk.

▼ **Figure 13.23** Privacy and confidentiality should still be maintained even when consent cannot be obtained

Thinking practically about psychology

How did **Morgan & Grube (1991)** (p250) ensure the confidentiality of their participants' data?

Analysing and interpreting data

The findings of research need to be presented so that other people can readily understand what has been found. To do this the results are often summarised and presented using tables and charts. This is only possible when the results are numerical, ie for *quantitative data*. Quantitative data can also be analysed mathematically, eg using measures of central tendency (averages), measures of spread (eg the range or standard deviation) or correlations. If the results are descriptive, ie *qualitative data*, different methods are used. These either allow the descriptive detail in the data to be preserved, or

extract numerical data, thus converting qualitative data to quantitative data so that it can be analysed and interpreted.

KEY TERMS

quantitative data numerical data collected as totals in named categories or on linear scales

qualitative data descriptive data providing depth and detail

Levels of measurement

When quantitative data is collected, there will be one or more 'scores' or numerical values for each participant. These can be summarised using measures of central tendency (averages) and measures of spread, represented on graphs and analysed using inferential statistics. There are several different ways to do this in each case. One key factor that will help you to decide how to analyse data is the *level of measurement*.

There are four different types of numerical data, referred to as different levels of measurement. These are:

- Nominal
- Ordinal
- Interval
- Ratio.

Note that their initial letters spell 'NOIR', a helpful way to remember them.

Nominal data

Results that are just totals in two or more named categories that are unrelated are called *nominal data*. This includes simple alternatives, such as whether a symptom of schizophrenia is positive or negative. It is possible for there to be more than two categories, eg the main drug a user takes could be cocaine, heroin, cannabis, LSD etc. The important idea is that these groups are not related in a way that would allow them to lie along the same scale. Closed questions in interviews or on questionnaires often generate nominal data. To help you remember that nominal data is in *named* categories, think '*nom*', the French for 'name'. When analysing nominal data the mode is the only possible measure of central tendency.

Ordinal data

In *ordinal data*, the results are points from a scale. The results themselves may be numbers or words but the points relate to one another so they could be put in order. The value of points increases along the scale but the size of each increase does not have to be equal, ie the gaps between the points do not have to be the same. For example, we could ask participants to rate how likely they think it is that the Loch Ness monster exists on a scale that reads: 'very likely', 'fairly likely', 'quite unlikely', 'very unlikely'. We could give these points numbers: 'very likely'=4, 'fairly likely'=3, 'quite unlikely'=2, 'very unlikely'=1 and we would know that people who rated the chances as 'very likely' (4) were reasonably convinced. However, we would not know if they were precisely twice as sure as people who said it was 'quite unlikely' (2) because the numbers themselves are not exact.

> ### RESEARCH IN ACTION
>
> **Miller & Howell (2005)** (p266) used a questionnaire with Likert scales to collect information in relation to participants' beliefs about gambling. These produced **ordinal data**.

Numerical scales can also produce ordinal data. Gamblers could say how certain they felt that they would avoid gambling again on a scale of 1–10. Because the participants are only estimating, we cannot be sure that one person's interpretation of the scale is the same as another's, so the absolute value of each point may not be the same. To help you to remember that **ord**inal data is points in **ord**er along a scale, look at the first three letters.

Two measures of central tendency can be used on ordinal data, the mode and the median. Two measures of spread can also be used, the range and the interquartile range.

Answers to anagrams on p321

frae	fear	fare
acres	scare	cares/races
dandes	sadden	sanded
idm	dim	mid
rathet	threat	hatter
veil	vile/evil	live
spedres	depress	pressed
orels	loser	roles
gwonr	wrong	grown
brad	drab	bard

Interval data

Like ordinal data, *interval data* has scores on a linear scale – the points increase in value. However, on an interval scale, the divisions between the points are equal. For example, if participants in a parapsychology experiment were required to identify unseen playing cards, such as the nine of spades, six of hearts etc, each one is equally difficult (consisting of a number and a suit). This would be an interval scale. However, if the 'court' cards (jack, queen, king) or the joker were included, which are less equivalent, the gaps between the points on the scale of 'the number of unseen cards correctly identified' would not all be equal. This would mean that the scale could not be described as an interval level of measurement. In psychology, commonly used interval scales include measures of intelligence and personality. To help you to remember interval scales remember that there are equal *intervals* between the points.

Three measures of central tendency can be used on interval data: the mode, the median and the mean. Three measures of spread can also be used, the range, the interquartile range and standard deviation.

Ratio data

Ratio data, like interval data, has equal intervals between the points. They differ because a ratio scale also has a real zero. It might not be possible for participants to score zero, but this is where measurements on the scale start. In an experiment on arousal in gamblers we might measure pulse rate. Even the most relaxed people wouldn't score zero for their pulse rate, but the scale of 'beats per minute' would be measured from this baseline. All physical measures, such as centimetres, kilograms and degrees Centigrade are ratio scales. To help you remember that ratio scales are often mathematical units, think of working out *ratios* in maths.

RESEARCH IN ACTION

Koster et al. (2005) (p200 and p302) used a **ratio** measure – reaction time – to assess depression.

As with interval data, three measures of central tendency can be used on ratio data: the mode, the median and the mean. Three measures of spread can also be used: the range, the interquartile range and standard deviation.

Graphical representation

Graphs are used to illustrate the findings of studies that are in the form of frequencies, percentages and any of the measures of central tendency or measures of spread. Different graphs are used for different types of data.

RESEARCH IN ACTION

Kurtz et al. (2007) (p209 and p320)

The results of this study can be illustrated using a **bar chart**. This shows that participants with schizophrenia made more errors and checked the clock more frequently than control participants.

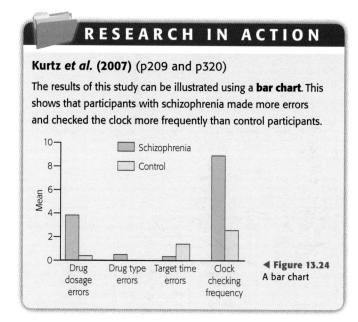

◀ **Figure 13.24** A bar chart

Bar charts

A bar chart is used when the data are in discrete categories, that is, for nominal data, totals or measures of central tendency. The bars on a bar chart must be separate because the *x* axis represents distinct groups not a linear scale. When the results of an experiment are plotted, the levels of the IV go along the bottom (on the *x* axis – think 'X is a cross') and the DV goes on the *y* axis.

A bar and whiskers plot is a type of bar chart. It shows the median (or mean) as the top of the bar and the upper and lower quartiles (or standard deviation) as short horizontal lines with a vertical line between them. This forms a pair of 'whiskers' sticking out above and below the top of the bar to indicate the spread of scores. For example, a researcher might collect scores on a scale measuring aggressive verbalisations after playing a video game that produced an ordinal score from 1–10.

	Aggressiveness of verbalisations									
Participant number	1	2	3	4	5	6	7	8	9	10
Violent video game	9	6	2	4	8	7	4	6	9	1
Non-violent video game	3	4	2	1	8	3	5	2	7	6

To draw a bar and whiskers chart we need to work out the medians and interquartiles for each condition:

Violent video game: 1, 2, 4, 4, 6, 6, 7, 8, 9, 9

Median $= \dfrac{6+6}{2} = 6$, lower quartile $= 4$, upper quartile $= 8$

Non-violent video game: 1, 2, 2, 3, 3, 4, 5, 6, 7, 8

Median $= \dfrac{3+4}{2} = 3.5$, lower quartile $= 2$, upper quartile $= 6$

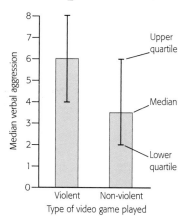

◀ **Figure 13.25** A bar and whiskers chart showing measures of central tendency and spread from an experiment on the effect of playing video games on verbal aggression

From this graph we can see several things. Participants who played violent video games were more verbally aggressive than participants who played non-violent games. However, there is some overlap between the aggression levels of participants in both groups.

This type of graph can be drawn in a number of different ways. For example, the whiskers can represent the standard deviation or the range.

Histograms and frequency distributions

Histograms are used to illustrate continuous data, eg to show the distribution of a set of scores. The scale of the DV is plotted along the *x* axis and the frequency of each score is plotted up the *y* axis. The scores along the *x* axis may be grouped into categories. Because the scale being represented is continuous the bars are drawn next to each other. An alternative way to present frequency data is on a line graph. This uses similar axes but a point is marked at the height of frequency of each score. These points are then joined to form a line making a frequency distribution curve.

Scattergrams

Scattergrams are used to display the findings of correlational studies. To construct a scattergram, a dot is plotted at the point where the individual's score on each variable crosses. A line of best fit is then drawn at an angle so that it comes close to as many points as possible. In a strong correlation, all the data points lie close to the line, in a weak correlation they are more spread out. Where there is no correlation, the points do not form a clear line at all.

▼ **Figure 13.26** Scattergrams and the strength of correlations

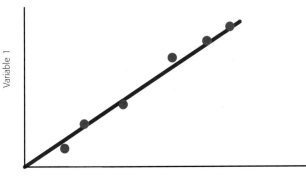

▲ **Figure 13.26a** A strong positive correlation

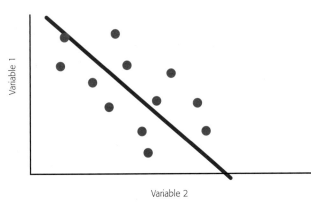

▲ **Figure 13.26b** A weak negative correlation

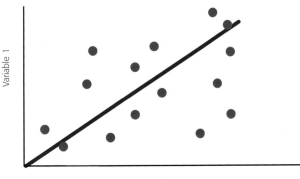

▲ **Figure 13.26c** A very weak positive correlation

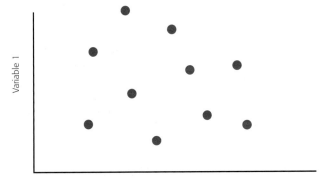

▲ **Figure 13.26d** A zero correlation

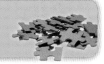

Thinking practically about psychology

Which graph would be suitable for the results of each of the following studies?

- **Koster *et al.* (2005)**, (p200)
- **Gottesman (1991)**, (p205)
- **Konijn *et al.* (2007)**, (p229)
- **Eron & Huesmann (1986)**, (p186)
- **Ko *et al.* (2008)**, (p253)
- **Elton & Campbell (2008)**, (p275)
- **Lindeman & Saher (2007)**, (p287)
- **Skinner (1948)**, (p292)

KEY TERMS

alternative hypothesis (H_1) a testable statement that predicts, in general terms, the anticipated outcome of a study such as a difference in an experimental study or a relationship in a correlational study

null hypothesis (H_0) a testable statement that predicts that any difference or correlation is due to chance, ie that no pattern in the results will arise from the variable(s) being studied

non-directional hypothesis an alternative hypothesis that states there will be a difference or relationship but not the nature of that pattern

directional hypothesis an alternative hypothesis that states the nature of the anticipated difference or relationship, ie which condition will produce 'higher' results or whether a correlation will be positive or negative

Inferential analysis

Inferential analysis helps us to make *inferences* about our data, that is, to draw meaningful conclusions from numbers. Only quantitative data can be used in statistical tests so they tend to be used on the results of experimental and correlational studies. Where questionnaires, interviews or observations are used to generate numerical data in experimental or correlational designs, these data can be analysed statistically. Different inferential tests are used in different situations, for example with different levels of measurement and experimental designs.

Hypotheses in inferential analysis

You may recall writing hypotheses in your AS. An experimental hypothesis formally states the prediction that we are investigating in our research. When we test our findings using inferential statistics, we use two other hypotheses. The experimental hypothesis is replaced by the *alternative hypothesis*. This makes the same prediction but, rather than referring to the findings of one specific investigation based on a small sample, it makes a more general statement about the whole population. In this respect, the alternative and the null hypothesis are opposites. The *null hypothesis* refers to the non-existence of a pattern in the general population.

Consider an investigation into the effects of cannabis on memory. An experimenter might use the null hypothesis 'Any difference between the recall of people who have and have not used cannabis is due to chance'. The general form of a null hypothesis in an experiment is 'Any difference between the *scores on the DV* for people in *different levels of the IV* is due to chance'. In a correlational study, a researcher might ask participants to say how long they have used cannabis and to estimate how often they have lapses of memory. The null hypothesis might be 'Any relationship between the duration of cannabis use and number of lapses of memory is due to chance'. The general form of a null hypothesis in a correlation is 'Any relationship between *the scores on the one variable* and *scores on the other variable* is due to chance'.

In statistical testing we are aiming to *reject* the null hypothesis. This is what we will do if our results fit the expected pattern. If we can show that it is *unlikely* that the pattern we have found could have arisen by chance, then we can confidently reject the null hypothesis. In this case we would then be able to accept the alternative hypothesis. This is important because it means that we can satisfy the falsifiability requirement of the scientific method (see p301).

Directional and non-directional hypotheses

An alternative hypothesis may be quite general, predicting that there will be an effect but not its direction, in which case it is a *non-directional hypothesis*. In an experiment this states that 'there will be a difference' but does not say which level of the IV will be 'better' or produce 'higher' scores. In a correlational study, a non-directional hypothesis predicts that there will be a relationship between the two measured variables.

A non-directional hypothesis for the experimental example above would be: 'There will be a difference between the recall of people who have and have not used cannabis.' For the correlation, a non-directional hypothesis would be 'There will be a relationship between the duration of cannabis use and number of lapses of memory.'

When there is evidence to suggest the direction of the effect, researchers may choose to use a *directional hypothesis*. This states the nature of the anticipated difference or relationship. In an experiment it will state which level of the IV will be 'better' or produce 'higher' scores. In a correlational study, a directional hypothesis predicts whether the correlation will be positive or negative.

A directional hypothesis for the experimental example above would be: 'Recall by people who have not used cannabis will be better than recall by people who have used cannabis.' For the correlation, a directional hypothesis would be 'There will be a positive correlation between the duration of cannabis use and the number of lapses of memory'.

Probability and significance

Statistical tests aim to find out whether it is likely that any pattern in the data could have arisen by chance or is more likely to be due to the variable(s) under investigation. If the test shows that the pattern is likely to be due to the variable(s) being investigated it is described as *significant*. A statistical

Thinking practically about psychology

Look back at the studies that appear in the *Research in Action* boxes in this chapter. Choose an experimental study and a correlational study. For each write:

- a non-directional hypothesis
- a directional hypothesis
- a null hypothesis.

test therefore compares the mathematical probability of any pattern in our results arising by *chance*.

Each test calculates a single number, called the *observed value*, from the scores *observed* in the study. A comparison between this value and a *critical value* from a table tells us whether the pattern is significant or non-significant. However, the key to this comparison is the *significance level*. This is the *probability*, set by the researchers (and reflected in the critical value tables), at which they are prepared to accept the risk that a pattern could have occurred by chance. In most psychological research this is set at $p \leq 0.05$, which means there is a less than or equal to 5 per cent probability that a pattern could simply have arisen by chance. Conversely, if the test says the pattern in our results is significant, we can be 95 per cent sure that this could not have arisen by chance.

If psychologists wanted to be more sure than this, they could set the significance level at a probability of 1 per cent ($p \leq 0.01$) or even 0.1 per cent ($p \leq 0.001$). In fact, $p \leq 0.05$ is generally chosen when there is evidence, such as previous research, to suggest that the predicted difference or correlation will arise. More stringent significance levels are used in studies requiring greater certainty (eg where errors could have dangerous implications) or in replications to verify the findings of previous research. The significance level therefore represents how confident we are about the pattern in our results and indicates the level of risk that we will tolerate. At any significance level there is a possibility that our conclusion could be wrong – we will discuss this on p330.

KEY TERMS

significance level the probability that a pattern in the results (a difference in an experiment or relationship in a correlation) could have arisen by chance. It is usually set at $p \leq 0.05$

observed value the single number calculated by a statistical test from the scores *observed* in the study. It is compared with a critical value to determine whether the pattern in the results is significant

critical value a value from a table for the appropriate statistical test to which an observed value is compared. This indicates whether the pattern in the results is significant

Choosing and using a statistical test

You need to know when to use four different inferential tests and how to interpret their results. Several factors affect your choice:

- *research method*: correlation or experiment (ie test of difference)
- *design of an experimental study*: if it was repeated measures (or matched pairs) or independent groups
- *level of measurement*: nominal or ordinal/interval/ratio data.

▼ **Table 13.4 Choosing an inferential test**
Each test produces a single number, the observed value. This is given a 'name' (eg χ^2 for Chi-squared). To be significant, the observed value must be greater than or equal to the critical value for tests in purple, and smaller than or equal to the critical value for tests in black

Method/design	Nominal data	Ordinal/interval/ratio data
Correlation		Spearman's rho (r or r_s)
Experiment: independent groups	Chi-squared (χ^2)	Mann Whitney (U)
Experiment: repeated measures or matched pairs		Wilcoxon (T)

Use Table 13.4 to decide which test to use or, alternatively, follow the flowchart in Figure 13.27.

As we said on p325, significance is judged by comparing the *observed value* (from the test) to a *critical value* (from a table). To look up a critical value you need to know three pieces of information:

- whether the *hypothesis* is directional (in which case we do a one-tailed test) or non-directional (so we do a two-tailed test)
- *significance level*: eg $p \leq 0.05$
- the *number of participants* in the sample, which is generally written as 'N =' then a number. However:
  - for the Mann Whitney, the two samples may have different number of participants, so N_1 and N_2 may be used to distinguish them
  - for the Chi-squared test, '*degrees of freedom*' is used instead of N.

▼ **Figure 13.27 Choosing a statistical test**

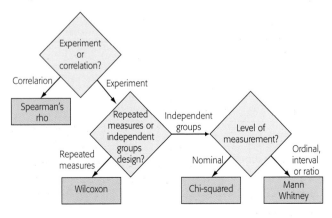

KEY TERMS

degrees of freedom (*df*) in the Chi-squared test this is used instead of N. It is the number of categories of data minus one and is calculated using the formula: (number of rows in the table −1) × (number of columns in the table −1).

Using this information and the correct table for the test, you can find the relevant critical value. For some tests (indicated in purple on Table 13.4) the observed value must be greater than or equal to the critical value to be significant; for the remainder it is the other way round. If the difference or correlation is significant then we can reject the H_0 and accept the H_1. However, even if the test indicates significance, a directional H_1 can only be accepted if the difference or correlation is in the predicted direction.

Chi-squared

When is the Chi-squared test used?
The Chi-squared test is a test of association. It looks for patterns in nominal data. This is the only test you will learn about that can be used with nominal data. It tests whether the distribution of results in an experiment differs from what would be expected on the basis of chance alone. It does this by comparing the data actually collected with a data set based on the null hypothesis.

The criteria for using the chi-squared test are:

- dependent variable has *nominal* level of measurement
- design of the research is *independent groups*
- looking for an *association* between the independent variable and the dependent variable.

How is the Chi-squared test used?
To enter data into a Chi-squared test, a table of totals is needed.

Table 13.5 Example of a table of totals

	£ lost in last week	number of games abandoned on a losing streak	number of games won
problem gamblers	61	15	24
non-problem gamblers	27	25	38

The data in the table is used in the formula:

$$\chi^2 = \frac{\Sigma(O - E)^2}{E}$$

You would not be asked to calculate χ^2 in an exam, but you might want to use the test on real data. When psychologists conduct statistical tests, they use computers to work out the observed value. You can see how to do this in the *Thinking Practically* box.

The formula produces the observed value for this test, called χ^2. To compare this with a critical value, you need the following information:

- *degrees of freedom (df)* – this is calculated using the formula: (number of rows in the table −1) × (number of columns in the table −1)
- *alternative hypothesis* – directional or non-directional
- *level of significance* – the 'p-value' eg $p \leq 0.05$.

If the observed value is greater than the critical value, then the association is significant so the null hypothesis is rejected and the alternative hypothesis is accepted. If the observed value is less than the critical value, then the association is not significant so the null hypothesis is accepted and the alternative hypothesis is rejected.

If the data collected consist of only one row of data, for example comparing the number of aggressive acts in four different TV programmes, a χ^2 'goodness of fit' test is performed. In this case the degrees of freedom are calculated by subtracting 1 from the number of categories present. So, in the TV example, the degrees of freedom would be $4 - 1 = 3$. The critical values are read from the table as for the χ^2 test of association.

Thinking practically about psychology

To run a Chi-squared test online, go to http://faculty.vassar.edu/lowry/VassarStats.html. Follow the link to 'frequency data' on the navigation bar, scroll down to 'Chi-squared, Cramer's V, and Lambda' and click on it. The first thing you will have to do is select the number of rows and columns. If you wanted to enter the data in Table 13.5, you would click on two rows and three columns, then enter the data into the rows provided. You then click on 'Calculate' and look for the Chi-squared box. The figure here is your observed value for Chi-squared, which should be 18.32 if you have used the data opposite. So, in this case, we would say that the observed value of $\chi^2 = 18.32$. You also need to find the figure labelled 'df' which you will need to look up the critical value. In this case, it is $(2-1) \times (3-1) = 2$. The table below contains an extract from a table of critical values for Chi-squared. Let's assume that $p \leq 0.05$ as we have evidence to suggest what will happen in studies such as this, ie that there will be differences between problem and non-problem gamblers. The researchers would also have a null hypothesis and an alternative hypothesis, which could be directional or non-directional. Let's assume in this case it was directional. We now have all the information we need to look up the critical value:

- $df = 2$
- $p \leq 0.05$
- one-tailed test.

To look up the correct critical value for our test, we need to find the row corresponding to $df = 2$, then the column for a two-tailed test at $p \leq 0.05$.

	Level of significance for a two-tailed test				
	0.2	0.1	0.05	0.02	0.001
	Level of significance for a one-tailed test				
df	0.1	**0.05**	0.025	0.01	0.0005
1	2.706	3.841	5.024	6.635	7.879
2	4.605	**5.991**	7.378	9.210	10.597
3	6.251	7.815	9.348	11.345	12.838
4	7.779	9.488	11.143	13.277	14.860

The critical value is 5.991. In order to decide what the results mean, this must be compared with the observed value. If the observed value is greater than or equal to the critical value, then the pattern in the results is significant. Since the observed Chi-squared value, $\chi^2 = 18.32$, is greater than the critical value (5.991), we can conclude that there is a significant pattern. This means that the null hypothesis can be rejected and the alternative hypothesis can be accepted.

Mann-Whitney

When is the Mann-Whitney test used?
The Mann-Whitney test is used to find out whether there is a significant difference between two sets of data. The test uses several pieces of information, including the number of participants in each of the two levels of the IV, which may be the same or different.

The criteria for using the Mann Whitney test are:

- dependent variable has an *ordinal*, *interval* or *ratio* level of measurement
- design of the research is *independent groups*
- looking for a *difference* between the effect each level of the independent variable has on the dependent variable.

How is the Mann-Whitney test used?
Two sets of data are assembled, one for each level of the independent variable. The Mann–Whitney U-test then involves ranking the data set and examining how the ranks are spread across the two levels of the independent variable. To retain the null hypothesis, which states that any difference is due to chance, we would expect the ranks to be randomly distributed between the two levels of independent variable. If the distribution of ranks is predominantly in one direction (eg participants in condition A generally score higher than those in condition B), the Mann-Whitney test will detect a significant difference between the two conditions.

This calculation produces two values, the smaller of which is the observed value of U. To compare this with a critical value, you need the following information:

- N_a and N_b – the number of participants (ie scores) in each of the two levels of the IV
- *alternative hypothesis* – directional or non-directional
- *level of significance* – the 'p-value' eg $p \leq 0.05$.

If the observed value is less than or equal to the critical value, then the difference between the sets of scores is significant so the null hypothesis is rejected and the alternative hypothesis is accepted. If the observed value is greater than the critical value then the difference is non-significant so the null hypothesis is accepted and the alternative hypothesis is rejected. You can see an example of the Mann-Whitney test in action in the *Thinking Practically* box.

RESEARCH IN ACTION

Bandura *et al.* (1963) (p224) investigated imitation of aggression. They compared the imitation by boys and girls. This is a comparison between independent groups so they used a **Mann Whitney test**

Thinking critically about psychology

Kurtz *et al.* (2007) (see also **Baker *et al.*, 2006**, p209) compared 25 patients with schizophrenia and 18 healthy controls on their ability to follow accurately a prescription for different medication in virtual reality. They tested the difference in performance using a Mann-Whitney test.

Their average results were:

variable \ group	mean (standard deviation)	
	schizophrenia	healthy controls
dosage: taking the wrong number of pills or at the wrong time	4 (3.7)	0.67 (1.6)
type: taking the wrong colour pills	0.4 (0.6)	0.1 (0.3)

They found a significant difference between the accuracy of the two groups in terms of dosage but a non-significant difference in their accuracy with regard to pill type.

Thinking practically about psychology

To calculate a Mann-Whitney test you will first need to work out the mean for each group. To calculate the observed value online, go to http://faculty.vassar.edu/lowry/VassarStats.html. Follow the link to 'Ordinal Data' on the navigation bar, scroll down to 'Mann-Whitney test' and click on it. You should then see an extra box asking for the number of participants in group A (n_a): type in 10. A second box should then appear asking for the number of participants in group B (n_b): type in 10 again. (If this doesn't happen, you need to go back and do a browser check on the home page and allow your computer to accept browser windows.) Once you've entered the number of participants in each group you will arrive at the main Mann-Whitney page. Don't be put off by the formulae – just scroll down to the page until you come to 'Data Entry'. In the right-hand columns labelled 'Raw Data for' enter the data for 'Sample A' and 'Sample B'. Then click on 'Calculate from Raw Data'. The observed value (U) will appear in the box labelled '$U_a =$'.

Here is an example. Galynker *et al.* (2000) used a brain scan to test the brain activity of people with a history of drug abuse. They used a Mann-Whitney test to see whether there was a significant difference in brain activity between the two groups:

- Group 1: the control group (who did not have a history of opiate abuse)

- Group 2: the experimental group (who had abused opiates but had been drug free for four years).

The amount of activity in the anterior cingulate gyrus was greater in the ex-users than in the controls – but was the difference small enough to have just arisen by chance?

The Mann-Whitney test produced a U value of 2. This is compared with a critical value found from the table. To look up the critical value we need to know:

- the level of significance ($p \leq 0.05$)
- whether the test is comparing a directional or non-directional prediction (directional – so we use a one-tailed test)
- the number of participants (n) in each group ($n_a = 5$, $n_b = 4$)

Table of critical values for Mann-Whitney U:
One-tailed tests at $p \leq 0.05$ and two-tailed tests at $p \leq 0.1$

n_b \ n_a	3	4	5	6
3	0	0	1	2
4	0	1	2	3
5	1	2	4	5
6	2	3	5	7

The critical value is 2.

For the Mann-Witney test to be significant, the observed value must be smaller than or equal to the critical value.

Since the observed value of 2 is the same as the critical value of 2, we can conclude that there is a significant difference between the activity recorded in the brains of the control (non-user) and ex-user participants. Before we can decide whether to accept the alternative hypothesis, we must be sure that this difference is in the predicted direction. The mean rate of glucose use was higher for the ex-users than for the controls so Galynker *et al.* could reject their null hypothesis and accept their alternative hypothesis so could conclude that opiate users do, even after prolonged abstinence, show increased activity in one brain area (the anterior cingulate gyrus).

Wilcoxon

When is the Wilcoxon test used?

The Wilcoxon test is used to find out whether there is a significant difference between two sets of data. These must come from the same participants (or from matched pairs).

The criteria for using the Wilcoxon test are:

- dependent variable has an *ordinal, interval* or *ratio* level of measurement
- design of the research is either *repeated measures* or *matched pairs*
- looking for a *difference* between the effect each level of the independent variable has on the dependent variable.

How is the Wilcoxon test used?

Two sets of data are assembled, one for each level of the independent variable. As with the Mann-Whitney test, the formula involves ranking the data. To retain the null hypothesis, which states that any difference is due to chance, we would expect the ranks to be randomly distributed between the two levels of independent variable. If the distribution of ranks is predominantly in one direction (eg participants generally score higher in condition A than condition B), the Wilcoxon test will detect a significant difference between the two conditions.

The number of ranks relating to the least direction of difference generates an observed value for the test, called 'W-' (or 'T'). It is compared with a critical value, which is found using the following information:

- *N* – the number of participants (or the number of matched pairs if it is being used for an experiment with a matched pairs design)
- *alternative hypothesis* – directional or non-directional
- *level of significance* – the 'p-value', eg $p \leq 0.05$.

If the observed value is less than or equal to the critical value then the difference between the sets of scores is significant so the null hypothesis is rejected and the alternative hypothesis accepted. If the observed value is greater than the critical value then the difference is significant so the null hypothesis is accepted and the alternative hypothesis is rejected. You can see an example of the Wilcoxon test in action in the *Thinking Practically* box.

RESEARCH IN ACTION

Bandura *et al.* (1963) investigated imitation of aggression. They matched children between groups seeing different models. To compare the effect of different models they used a **Wilcoxon test**.

Thinking practically about psychology

To run a Wilcoxon test online, go to http://www.fon.hum.uva.nl/Service/Statistics/Signed_Rank_Test.html. You will see a box labelled 'The observation pairs'. Enter the pairs of scores, each pair along one line with a single space between the two numbers. Then click on 'Submit'. Above the box four numbers will appear. 'W-' is your observed value. (Ignore 'W+', this is an alternative way of expressing the observed value.) There will also be a value for N, the number of participants or paired scores. This will be the same as the number of rows in the table, unless there are any pairs in which both numbers are identical – these will have been excluded.

If you enter the numbers in the table below, you should obtain the following four figures: W+ = 68, W− = 10, N = 12, $p \leq 0.021$.

participant number	1	2	3	4	5	6	7	8	9	10	11	12
Correct selection of images												
with autoganzfeld procedure	28	18	17	14	7	18	17	22	34	14	14	23
without autoganzfeld procedure	26	14	19	3	6	14	16	21	32	11	15	22

The table below contains an extract from a table of critical values for Wilcoxon. Let's assume that $p \leq 0.05$ and that there will be differences between the ability of participants to receive telepathic images with and without autoganzfeld apparatus but we are not sure which will be better so the alternative hypothesis would be non-directional. We now have all the information we need to look up the critical value:

- N = 12
- $p \leq 0.05$
- two-tailed test.

To look up the correct critical value for our test, we need to find the row corresponding to N = 12, then the column for a two-tailed test at $p \leq 0.05$.

	Level of significance for a two-tailed test			
	0.1	0.05	**0.02**	**0.01**
	Level of significance for a one-tailed test			
N	**0.05**	**0.025**	**0.01**	**0.005**
9	8	6	3	2
10	11	8	5	3
11	14	11	7	5
12	17	14	10	7
13	21	17	13	10

The critical value is 14. In order to decide what the results mean, this must be compared with the observed value. If the observed value is less than or equal to the critical value, then the difference is significant. Since the observed Wilcoxon value, W− = 10, is less than or equal to the critical value (14), we can conclude that there is a significant difference. This means that the null hypothesis can be rejected and the alternative hypothesis can be accepted.

Spearman's rho

When is Spearman's rho used?

Spearman's rho is used to find out whether there is a relationship between two variables.

The criteria for using the Spearman's rho test are:

- two variables with an *ordinal*, *interval* or *ratio* level of measurement
- design of the research is a *correlation*
- looking for a *relationship* between the two variables.

Two sets of paired scores are used. These are usually two scores from every participant gathered from two different scales. Alternatively, they can be pairs of scores on the same scale, one from each twin, for example to compare intelligence or severity of a mental illness. When a Spearman's rho is used to test for reliability, the pairs of scores come from different researchers, eg interviewers or observers, or from different versions of a test.

How is Spearman's rho used?

The Spearman's rho test initially rank-orders each variable separately. If the rank orders for each variable are very similar then a positive correlation is expected. If the rank orders appear to be a mirror image of one another, then a negative correlation is expected. If the rank orders appear to be randomly distributed and there are large differences in rank for each participant's scores, then no correlation is expected.

The formula for the Spearman's rho produces an observed value for the test (the *correlation coefficient*), which is given the term rho (r or r_s). It is compared with a critical value, which is found using the following information:

- N – the number of participants (or pairs of scores)
- *alternative hypothesis* – directional or non-directional
- *level of significance* – the '*p*-value', eg $p \leq 0.05$.

If the observed value is greater than the critical value then the relationship is significant so the null hypothesis is rejected and the alternative hypothesis accepted. If the observed value is less than the critical value then the relationship is not significant so the null hypothesis is accepted and the alternative hypothesis is rejected. You can see an example of the Spearman test in action in the *Thinking Practically* box.

A correlation coefficient is always a number between +1 and −1. A zero correlation has $r = 0$. A perfect positive correlation is $r = +1$ and a perfect negative correlation is $r = −1$. The closer the correlation coefficient is to plus or minus 1, the stronger the correlation. For example, a strong positive correlation would be $r = 0.85$; a weak negative correlation is $r = −0.4$.

Type 1 and Type 2 errors

As we observed on p325, even if we conclude from an inferential test that the pattern in the results is significant, we cannot be certain that this conclusion is correct. This is because the tests are only calculating the *probability* that the distribution of scores could have arisen by chance. This is not a certainty. There are two possible problems here.

Thinking practically about psychology

To run a Spearman test online, go to http://faculty.vassar.edu/lowry/VassarStats.html. Follow the link to 'Correlation and Regression' on the navigation bar, scroll down to 'Rank Order Correlation' and click on it. The first thing you will have to do is say how many participants you wish to enter data for. Enter 10 and scroll down the page until you come to 'Data Entry'. In the 'Raw Data' columns enter the following data:

Participant	1 2 3 4 5 6 7 8 9 10
Frequency of childhood TV viewing	6 9 2 8 5 7 6 4 2 6
Criminality in adulthood	23 30 12 30 20 26 26 15 10 25

Click on 'Calculate from Raw Data' and look for the r_s box. The figure here is your correlation coefficient, in this case 0.97. Being almost +1, this is a very strong positive correlation. The critical value for N = 10, for a one-tailed test at $p \leq 0.05$, is 0.56. Since the observed value of 0.97 is greater than the critical value of 0.56, this is a significant relationship.

Thinking practically about psychology

Explain which statistical test you would use on the data from each of the following studies. Note that it may not be possible to analyse *all* the data from one study with a single test.

- **Baker *et al.* (2006)**, p209
- **Gottesman (1991)**, p205
- **Konijn *et al.* (2007)**, p229
- **Eron & Huesmann (1986)**, p186
- **Bonnaire *et al.* (2007)**, p258
- **Maes *et al.* (1999)**, p247
- **Williams *et al.* (2007)**, p288

If the alternative hypothesis is accepted when, in fact, the distribution of results *is* due to chance, we have made an 'optimistic' error. We have concluded that there is a difference or correlation between variables when there is not. This is called a *type one error*. It might help you to remember that both '*optimistic*' and '*one*' begin with the letter 'O'. Type 1 errors are more likely at higher (less stringent) significance levels. For example, we are more likely to make a type one error at $p \leq 0.05$ than at $p \leq 0.01$. This is because there is a greater margin for generous errors – it is easier to accept the alternative hypothesis at $p \leq 0.05$ than at $p \leq 0.01$.

Conversely, we may accept the null hypothesis when, in fact, the distribution of results is *not* due to chance. In this case we would be making a 'pessimistic' error, that is, erring on the safe side by *not* accepting results that might be right. We will conclude that there is not a difference or correlation between variables when there is one. This is called a *type 2 error*. To help you to remember this, think of '*It is better 2 be safe than 2 be sorry'*. Type 2 errors are more likely at lower (more stringent) significance levels. For example, we are more likely to make a type 1 error at $p \leq 0.01$ than at $p \leq 0.05$. This is because there is a smaller margin of error – it is harder to accept the alternative hypothesis at $p \leq 0.01$ than at $p \leq 0.05$.

It is important to note that if we try to cut the risk of making a type 1 error, by reducing the significance level from $p \leq 0.05$ to $p \leq 0.01$, then we *increase* the risk of making a type 2 error.

▲ **Figure 13.28** If we raise the significance level we increase the risk of a type 1 error (rejecting the H_0 when it is true), but if we lower the significance level, we risk making a type 2 error (accepting the H_0 when it is false) – we have to find a balance

Thinking practically about psychology

1 A researcher is replicating a study on the effectiveness of an antidepressant for use with suicidal patients. Which significance level should they use and why?

2 Which would give greater certainty, $p \leq 0.01$ or $p \leq 0.001$?

3 Justify a choice of test for each situation below:
   (a) a repeated measures design with ordinal data
   (b) an independent groups design with nominal data
   (c) an experiment with an independent groups design and ratio data
   (d) a correlational study.

4 Use this Wilcoxon test table extract to answer the question below. (Remember, for a Wilcoxon test to be significant, the observed value must be less than or equal to the critical value.)

	one-tailed		two-tailed	
	$p \leq 0.05$	$p \leq 0.01$	$p \leq 0.05$	$p \leq 0.01$
N				
20	60	43	52	37
25	101	77	90	68

Which of these possibilities would be significant?

	observed value of T	N	hypothesis	significance level
a	35	20	one-tailed	$p \leq 0.01$
b	65	25	one-tailed	$p \leq 0.05$
c	55	25	two-tailed	$p \leq 0.05$
d	72	20	two-tailed	$p \leq 0.01$

Analysis and interpretation of qualitative data

Descriptive statistics such as averages and inferential statistics can only be used with quantitative data. Much data generated in psychological research is non-numerical. The findings of case studies, open questions in questionnaires and unstructured interviews are qualitative and cannot be analysed in this way. Such data *can* be simplified and changed into numerical data and analysed as we have described in the previous section. Alternatively, the detail can be preserved and it can be analysed in ways that allow researchers to explore information such as the connections between ideas.

Qualitative studies produce rich, detailed data so analytical techniques must reflect this. There are several different techniques, each of which aims to preserve the diversity and depth of the data collected. We will look at thematic analysis as an example.

Thematic analysis

This technique can be used with qualitative data from sources such as questionnaires and interviews and also in material extracted from sources such as observations of television programmes or content analysis of newspapers.

Researchers begin by familiarising themselves with the range of ideas that are expressed in the data. The most important task is to identify the concepts or themes of interest so that the data can be organised within these themes preserving the diversity of the findings. This is different from purely putting the data into simple categories. Importantly, it can retain unusual but significant examples of responses. Imagine a parapsychology researcher reading questionnaire responses from mediums. In response to questions about their experiences, answers might include:

- 'I often feel as though I am in contact with someone who is no longer of this world'
- 'I know that I enter a trance when I am speaking with the other side'
- 'Sometimes I think I am almost part of the spirit world myself'
- 'I only have a talent for writing the words sent to me by The Dead'
- 'My clients can talk to the deceased directly through my connection.'

Some themes might include:

- *level of certainty*
  - certainty about the effect ('I know', 'My clients can talk …')
  - feelings rather than certainties ('I feel', 'Sometimes I think …')

- *nature of experience*
  - communication ('I am in contact with …', '…when I speak with …')
  - providing a service ('My clients can …')
  - automatic writing ('… a talent for writing the words sent to me …')

Thematic analysis, however, is more than just listing examples within themes. The researcher may identify comments which demonstrate each particular theme clearly, as well as retaining examples that are uncommon. If a respondent to the questionnaire reported 'I almost always know when I am about to receive an email, and can say who it will be from' and few other respondents mentioned this psychic ability, it could become an important theme even though it would be the only instance. This illustrates the capacity of qualitative data over quantitative data to preserve unique findings rather than obscuring them by averaging.

Thinking creatively about psychology

Sheldrake & Smart (2005) investigated telepathic communication in relation to emails. Design a study to test this phenomenon and identify possible themes that might be generated in observations during the study or subsequent interviews.

▼ **Figure 13.29**

Reflexive analysis and collaborative research

Two other techniques can enrich qualitative data and guide its analysis. In *reflexive analysis* the response of the researcher to the participant's behaviour is recorded. In a case study, the researcher can express opinions in the course of discussions with the participant. This increases insight into the case as it adds the dimension of an involved observer. Reflexive analysis allows for engaging in exchanges with the participant and facilitates genuine emotional responses to real situations. This additional information can be used to interpret and augment the data. Consider the experience of interviewing a participant with schizophrenia who is experiencing hallucinations and delusions. The extent of their fear or paranoia may be very apparent to the interviewer but could be lost in a simple transcript of what was said. In reflective analysis this can be preserved.

RESEARCH IN ACTION

Nelson KR *et al*. (2006) (p295) studied reports of near-death experiences and reported many **themes** in the participants' descriptions (see Box 13.00). This used qualitative reports which were then reduced to quantitative data. This was done by counting the number of reports in each theme and combining them into four categories.

Bhowmick (1991) (p314 and p321), in contrast, preserved the descriptive nature of his participant's report of an out-of-body experience, thus retaining the **qualitative data**.

Another technique for ensuring that appropriate detail is preserved in qualitative data is to involve the participants. In a case study, participants may read the researchers' report of their findings and comment on whether they think this fairly reflects their experiences or feelings. This is called *collaborative research*. It allows researchers to refine the detail of their findings in order to improve validity. Consider a study of a depressed adult who experienced privation as a child in which the transcript of the interview is interpreted by the researcher. When the participant reads the report they can correct any misinterpretations and add insights into the analysis. This ensures that the information is detailed and accurate.

Thinking critically about psychology

Giarelli *et al*. (2004) (p256) used a case study as part of a wider investigation into women smokers. The semi-structured interview was taped, transcribed and condensed by the researchers. The resulting description was reviewed by the participant so that she could verify that it was an accurate representation of her experiences.

Identify the advantages and disadvantages of this review process.

Chapter summary

The Scientific Method

- The scientific method is a process of observing and generating hypotheses to explain phenomena and testing those explanations empirically. The evidence is then used to build general laws.
- Scientific explanations should be falsifiable. Empirical evidence should be objective and replicable.
- Empirical methods used by psychologists aim to be scientific by avoiding investigator effects and demand characteristics. Standardised instructions and blind procedures help with this.
- According to Kuhn, a science has a single paradigm, although this can change over time. Psychology currently has several simultaneous paradigms – the different approaches such as biological, psychodynamic and cognitive.
- Peer review helps psychologists to be scientific. Other researchers can criticise or validate research which allows the building of an objective body of evidence.
- Peer-reviewed journals follow a standard format of an abstract, introduction, method (procedure, sample, materials, controls, ethics, etc), results, discussion and references.

Designing psychological investigations: methods and sampling

- There is a range of research methods. Different factors affect the choice of research method as do the advantages and disadvantages of each technique.
- In a true experiment the IV is changed by the experimenter and causes an effect on a DV. This change is measured.
- There are three experimental designs. Independent groups uses different participants in each condition and repeated measures uses the same participants in every condition. In matched pairs, participants who are similar on key variables are paired up and one member of each pair is put in each condition.
- Independent groups designs avoid order effects and reduce the effect of demand characteristics but participant variables are a problem. These can be minimised by random allocation of participants to conditions and a single blind design. In repeated measures designs order effects are avoided using counterbalancing. Using a matched pairs design solves most of these problems but finding similar pairs of people can be difficult.
- Investigator effects can cause bias. This can be avoided by using a double blind procedure.
- A natural experiment is not a true experiment. The IV is not manipulated by the experimenter, instead they use a naturally occurring difference to provide experimental

conditions. Participants cannot therefore be randomly allocated to levels of the IV, which lowers validity.
- In a correlational analysis, two variables are measured to look for a link between them. A single correlation cannot indicate whether the relationship between variables is causal – changes in both variables could be being caused by another factor. Correlations allow researchers to investigate variables that could not be manipulated for practical or ethical reasons.
- Observational techniques can be used either as a research method or as a measure of a DV in an experiment. An observer may be disclosed or non-disclosed and participant or non-participant. Non-disclosed observers cannot affect the behaviour of the participants and non-participant observers are less likely to become subjective. The observation can take place in an artificial situation or can be naturalistic. The latter is harder to control but produces valid data as the situation is real.
- When conducting an observation, the researcher operationalises behavioural categories. Multiple observers should agree definitions and practise using them to raise inter-observer reliability.
- Questionnaire and interview studies can use closed or open questions. Questionnaires are written whereas interviews are conducted verbally. Questionnaires tend to be highly structured whereas interviews can be unstructured. Unstructured interviews are more flexible but differences between questions for different participants make the answers hard to compare. Closed questions limit the possible answers but produce numerical data that is easy to analyse using quantitative techniques. Open questions produce longer, descriptive answers that take longer to analyse.
- A case study investigates one person in detail, eg using interviews, observation and tests. It can be done in rare instances that could not be created artificially but can provide useful information. The findings are very thorough and come directly from real situations, which increases validity but the results may not generalise to other people as each case is unique. The researcher may lose objectivity as they get to know the participant and unstructured interviewing can reduce objectivity further.
- The sample of participants should be representative of the population they came from. An opportunity sample is taken on the basis of availability and is commonly used, although it is unrepresentative. In volunteer sampling, the participants offer themselves and it is a good way to get an unusual group, but the sample is likely to be biased. Random sampling is more representative as every member of the population has an equal chance of being chosen.

Designing psychological investigations: reliability and validity

- Reliability refers to the consistency. This includes internal reliability (within the measure) and external reliability (consistency between occasions or researchers).
- Internal reliability can be assessed by split-half or equivalent forms procedures and external reliability can be assessed through test-retest procedures, simultaneous observation or replication.
- Reliability can be improved by identifying and removing individual items that are not consistent and improving consistency between researchers by agreeing definitions and practising their use.
- Validity is about measuring what you set out to and whether your results apply outside the population your sample was taken from.
- Internal validity is about being certain you are measuring what you claim to and can be judged as face, content, concurrent or predictive validity.
- External validity is about being sure that your findings will generalise and can be judged as historical, population and ecological validity.
- Ecological validity includes both mundane realism (whether tasks are like real life) and generalisibility (whether findings in one situation apply to other situations).
- Issues of validity create a conflict because experiments need to be well controlled but also need to be realistic in terms of the task and setting.
- Assessing internal validity: content validity can be assessed by experts, concurrent validity can be assessed by comparing a new measure to an existing one, and predictive validity can be assessed using a longitudinal design.
- Assessing external validity: replication over time (historical validity), social groups (population validity) and settings (ecological validity) all demonstrate whether the findings from one situation generalise to others.
- Internal validity can be improved by reducing errors caused by investigator effects and demand characteristics by using controls, standardised instructions, blind procedures, randomisation, counterbalancing, etc.
- External validity can be improved by improving reliability and by using larger and more varied samples and more realistic tasks and experimental settings.

Designing psychological investigations: ethics

- Ethical issues are guided by the British Psychological Society Code of Ethics. This identifies some important ethical issues: consent, the right to withdraw, protection from physical and psychological harm, privacy and confidentiality.
- Issues of consent are resolved by avoiding deception and providing participants with enough information to allow them to decide whether they want to participate and, if this is not possible, to debrief them and allow them to withdraw their data, having obtained presumptive consent from a different group of people.
- The right to withdraw must be explained to participants and should not be affected by payment or the authority of the researcher.
- As studies could cause psychological or physical harm psychologists must ensure that participants leave their studies in the same or a better condition than they entered. Effective debriefing is important in this.
- Participants must be certain that their information is safe. They should not be identified by name and the data should be kept secure. Observations should not be carried out in situations that people would expect to be private.

Analysing and interpreting data

- Quantitative data is numerical and can be scored on a nominal, ordinal, interval or ratio level. These levels of measurement refer respectively to data in named categories, points in order, points on a scale with equal intervals and points on a scale that has a real zero.
- Measures of central tendency, the mode, median and mean, summarise whole data sets. Only the mode can be used with nominal data. Only the mode and median can be used with ordinal data. Any measure of central tendency can be used with interval or ratio data.
- Measures of spread include the range, interquartile range and standard deviation.
- Graphs are used to present data. Bar charts are used for data in discrete categories, eg nominal data or averages. A histogram is used for continuous data, eg for showing frequency distributions.
- Scattergrams are used to show the findings of a correlational study. In a positive correlation the line of best fit runs diagonally from the origin; in a negative correlation it runs downwards from left to right. The closer the points are to the line of best fit the stronger the correlation.
- An alternative hypothesis predicts a general pattern in the results. It can be directional (saying which level of the IV will be 'better' or whether a correlation will be positive or negative) or non-directional (just predicting a difference or relationship).
- A null hypothesis predicts that any pattern in the results is due to chance.
- In a statistical test, the pattern in the results is analysed to see whether it is likely to have arisen by chance. The significance level is the probability at which it is *unlikely* that the distribution of results could have arisen by chance. This is usually $p \leq 0.05$.
- There are different statistical tests. The choice depends on the research methods, experimental design and level of measurement.
- Chi-squared: experiment, nominal data, independent groups.
- Mann-Whitney: experiment, ordinal, interval or ratio data, independent groups.

- Wilcoxon: experiment, ordinal, interval or ratio data, repeated measures or matched pairs.
- Spearman's rho: correlation, ordinal, interval or ratio data.
- Each statistical test generates an observed value that is compared with a critical value from a table in order to decide whether the distribution of results is significant.
- Qualitative data can be obtained from interviews, questionnaires, observations or case studies. The detailed data, eg as answers to open questions or descriptions of behaviour, are used to illustrate important, repeating themes. This is thematic analysis.
- Qualitative research may also use reflexive analysis – the researcher's response to the participant provides additional information.
- In collaborative research, input from participants themselves guides interpretation to improve validity.

What do I know?

1 A research group wanted to know whether people with schizophrenia who had auditory hallucinations found it harder to recognise their own voice than those who did not have hallucinations. They recruited participants from the mental health outpatients department at a local hospital. Ten participants from each group were tested individually in a room at the hospital on two occasions. On the first they were recorded saying 'Mary had a little lamb'. All 20 recordings were put together in a random order, with a gap between each. On the second occasion the participants listened to the recording twice and watched a screen. A new number (increasing from one to 20) appeared for each voice. They had to press a key when they heard their own voice on the second run-through.

Total number of participants identifying correct or incorrect voices

		schizophrenia without auditory hallucinations	schizophrenia with auditory hallucinations
Number of participants making each response	other voice identified	3	7
	own voice identified	6	2
	unable to decide on own voice	1	1

(a) This study was an experiment. Name the experimental design used. (1 mark)
(b) Identify the independent variable and dependent variable in this experiment. (2 marks)
(c) Identify the sampling method used in this study and describe one advantage and one disadvantage of this sampling method. (4 marks)
(d) Name an appropriate statistical test for analysing these data. Justify your choice of test. (4 marks)
(e) Explain what is meant by the term 'significance level'. (2 marks)
(f) Using the data in the table, describe and discuss the findings of this investigation. (10 marks)
(g) The researchers thought that there might be a pattern in the severity of visual hallucinations in schizophrenia. They wanted to investigate whether people with more severe visual hallucinations also had worse problems with auditory hallucinations. Design a study to investigate the relationship between the severity of visual and auditory hallucinations. Write a plan that includes enough detail for a researcher to follow. You could include a hypothesis, variables, the design, details of the procedure, sampling and ethical considerations. (12 marks)

2 Some students were interested in how much attention people pay to drug use on television and whether it affects behaviour, and conducted a correlational study. They designed a questionnaire asking people to describe all the scenes on television they could remember from the last week in which people were using legal or illegal (but not prescription) drugs. There was also a question asking how many cigarettes the respondent smoked per day. The questionnaire was given out to 120 people and 100 returned it. The students counted up the number of scenes each individual recalled and how many cigarettes they smoked. The results can be seen in the figure on the right.

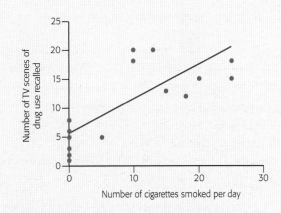

(a) Write a suitable hypothesis for this study. (1 mark)

(b) Many of the participants did not return the questionnaire. Describe two problems that could arise as a result of this. (2 marks)

(c) Identify **one** question from the questionnaire that would produce qualitative data and **one** question that would produce quantitative data. Outline one advantage and one disadvantage of qualitative data. (6 marks)

(d) Identify the type of graph shown in the figure. (1 mark)

(e) Name an appropriate statistical test for analysing these data. Justify your choice of test. (4 marks)

(f) Explain what is meant by a 'type 1 error'. (1 mark)

(g) Using the data in the figure, describe and discuss the findings of this investigation. You may also refer to your answer to 2(a). (8 marks)

(h) The students thought it would be interesting to conduct an experiment to see whether watching characters using drugs on television gave people a more positive attitude towards smoking. Design a laboratory experiment to test this idea. Write a plan that includes enough detail for a researcher to follow. You could include variables, the design, details of the procedure, controls, sampling and ethical considerations. (12 marks)

CHAPTER 14

Your Examinations

Thinking ahead

By the end of this chapter you should be able to:

- understand the requirements of your A2 examinations
- know how and what to write
- understand what is good and bad examination practice
- develop strategies to improve your examination performance
- apply your learning to examination-style questions
- enter the examination process with motivation and confidence

Difﬀerent people have different opinions on what is the best way to assess a student's worth. However, whichever opinion you support, the fact remains that formal examinations will form the basis on which you will be assessed. For many of us examinations can seem a daunting progress, regardless of how much work you have done during your psychology course. Remember, though, that the very nature of formal assessments poses difficulties for all types of students. How well any of you do will depend solely upon your individual performance on questions that you have never encountered before and on one particular day. Therefore the secret to success in formal examinations is quite simple: be well prepared.

The prospect of sitting examinations may depress you so much that your first thought is to just walk away and give up. There are students who welcome the challenge of examinations, but they are rare beasts indeed. However, the rest of you should not despair; help is at hand, for there are ways and methods of dealing with the stresses and strains of examinations. A tremendous amount of work goes into preparing examination papers in order to make them a fair process, and if you can comprehend what the exams require from you and revise thoroughly, then there is every chance that you will succeed.

The AS examinations

You will be required to sit two A2 examinations that will thoroughly test your knowledge and understanding of the material covered in the specification. The Unit 3 (PSYA3) examination paper lasts one hour and 30 minutes, whilst the Unit 4 (PSYA4) examination paper lasts two hours.

Unit 3: PSYA3 Topics in Psychology

The Unit 3 paper will be divided into eight sections: Biological Rhythms and Sleep; Perception; Relationships; Aggression; Eating Behaviour; Gender; Intelligence and Learning; and Cognition and Development. The topics that these sections cover are those featured in Chapters 2–9 of this book.

This paper will account for 50 per cent of the total A2 marks and 25 per cent of the total A level (AS + A2).

There will be one question on each of the eight topics. You must answer three of these questions.

Each question will be worth 25 marks, comprising nine AO1 marks, 12 AO2 marks and four AO3 marks.

This means that there will 75 marks available in total for this paper, comprising 27 AO1 marks, 36 AO2 marks and 12 AO3 marks.

You may sit this paper in either January or June.

Unit 4: PSYA4 Psychopathology, Psychology in Action and Research Methods

The Unit 4 paper will be divided into three sections, the first covering Psychopathology, the second covering Psychology in Action and the third covering Research Methods.

This paper will account for 50 per cent of the total A2 marks and 25 per cent of the total A level (AS + A2). The three sections that it covers are those featured in Chapters 10–14 of this book.

The first section, covering questions on the Psychopathology section, will contain three questions, one on each of the three sub-sections: Schizophrenia, Depression and Anxiety Disorders, of which you must answer one question. This section will total 25 marks, comprising nine AO1 marks, 12 AO2 marks and four AO3 marks.

The second section, covering questions on Psychology in Action, will contain three questions, one on each of the three sub-sections: Media Psychology, The Psychology of Addictive Behaviour and Anomalistic Psychology, of which you must answer one question. This section will total 25 marks, comprising nine AO1 marks, 12 AO2 marks and four AO3 marks.

The third section, covering questions on the Research Methods section, will contain one structured question divided into sub-questions, based upon some stimulus material. All parts of this question must be answered. This section will total 35 marks, comprising three AO1 marks, four AO2 marks and 28 AO3 marks.

This means that there will be 85 marks available in total for this paper, comprising 21 AO1 marks, 28 AO2 marks and 36 AO3 marks.

You may sit this paper in either January or June.

ASSESSMENT OBJECTIVES

Both the A2 examinations, Unit 3 and Unit 4, are designed to test your knowledge of three assessment objectives. Each of these assessment objectives tests a different skill.

AO1 (Assessment Objective 1) involves questions designed to test your knowledge and understanding. Candidates should be able to:

- recognise, recall and show understanding of knowledge
- select, organise and communicate relevant information in a variety of forms.

AO2 (Assessment Objective 2) involves questions designed to test your application of knowledge and understanding. Candidates should be able to:

- analyse and evaluate knowledge and processes
- apply knowledge and processes to unfamiliar situations, including those relating to issues
- assess the validity, reliability and credibility of information.

AO3 (Assessment Objective 3) involves questions designed to test your knowledge and application of knowledge and understanding of how psychology as a science works. Candidates should be able to:

- describe ethical, safe and skilful practical techniques and processes, selecting appropriate qualitative and quantitative methods
- know how to make, record and communicate reliable and valid observations and measurements with appropriate accuracy and precision, through using primary and secondary sources
- analyse, interpret, explain and evaluate the methodology, results and impact of their own and others' experimental and investigative activities in a variety of ways.

Examination questions

A number of different types of questions will make up your Unit 3 and Unit 4 A2 examination papers.

- On both Unit 3 and Unit 4 there can be essay questions worth 25 marks that will assess AO1, AO2 and AO3 skills.
- On both Unit 3 and Unit 4 there can be parted essay questions, worth an overall 25 marks, that will assess AO1, AO2 and AO3 skills.

- On Unit 4 there will be one compulsory Research Methods question worth 35 marks divided into parted sub-questions that will be based on some stimulus material.

Examples of all these types of questions, with sample answers, examination guidance and examiner's comments will be featured later on in this chapter.

Revision strategies

There is no 'magic method' of successful revision; there are many useful forms of revision, and some of these methods suit some students well but not others. You will probably need to indulge in a process of trial and error to find which methods are the ones that suit you best and which ones do not.

You may be inclined to use methods of revision that have served you well in the past, but just as your GCSE examinations tended to have a greater emphasis on knowledge than did your AS examinations, which also tested your ability to use knowledge in an analytical and evaluative way, you will find that A2 examinations tend to be more inclined towards the application of knowledge and understanding (an AO2 skill) than was the case in your AS examinations. Therefore revision strategies that you use for your A2 examinations should be geared towards their specific requirements.

Traditionally, many students leave revision until very late on in the learning process, and for the vast majority of students this is not to be advised. Apart from being very stressful it will not lead to you performing to the best of your abilities. A much more recommended method is one that incorporates regular revision into your studying regime.

- At the end of each week revise the material you have been looking at in order to assist your learning.

- The best way to achieve this is to do something with the material, for instance read through it and record the important points, maybe highlight them in some way.
- Use the relevant section of your textbook to aid your understanding and to further your knowledge of the topic.
- After you have done this it would be a good idea to attempt an examination-style question. There are examples of such questions at the end of each chapter of this book and later on in this chapter.
- Remember to practise not only AO1 questions that assess your knowledge and understanding, but also AO2 and AO3 questions that assess your ability to analyse and evaluate material and your knowledge and understanding of Research Methods.

When you first begin practising examination-type questions you will most probably need to have your learning materials immediately available to you, such as your notes and your textbook. Ensure that in the answer you prepare you have included enough detail to earn all the marks on offer. There is even a school of thought that advises including a little more than may be necessary to try and ensure the marks will be gained. However, do not include what is clearly far too much material in an answer: it will not gain extra credit and you will have wasted valuable time that could have been better spent on another question. This is also the case for material that is not relevant to the question, however interesting you feel that it is and however much time you have spent learning and revising it. Also do not include too little; for example, if a question asks for *two* extraneous variables that the investigator addressed, then make sure you have provided two and not just the one.

When you are comfortable and familiar with this method of regular revision, it will be time to advance on and practise answering questions without using notes. A good way to do this is to read through the relevant material first and then put it out of view and write down your answer. In this way you will be gradually creating the actual environment of the examination that you will sit. You can do this by first creating, from memory, a plan for your answer – maybe consisting of relevant bullet points in numbered order.

After you become accustomed to writing answers without the topic materials in front of you, you will be ready to put time constraints on yourself. It is difficult to assess exactly how much time should be spent on a particular question, but a general rule is that each Unit 3 question should have 30 minutes dedicated to it; this, remember, includes time for planning out your answer and reading through it when you've finished. If a Unit 3 question occurs as a parted question,

be sure to spend the majority of the time on the part of the question worth the most marks. For instance if a Unit 3 question is divided into two parts, part a) worth five marks and part b) worth 20 marks, then it stands to reason that you shouldn't spend too long on part a) and then discover that you have very little time left to address part b).

With the Unit 4 paper, you will answer one question from section A and one question from section B, and both these questions are worth 25 marks, whilst the compulsory question on section C is worth 35 marks. It is advisable therefore that you break down the two hours available in the examination to suit the allocation of marks. So you should spend around 35 minutes on each of the questions worth 25 marks and 50 minutes on the compulsory question worth 35 marks. There are those who believe that the compulsory Research Methods question can be successfully completed in less than 50 minutes, freeing up extra time to spend on the two essay-type questions. Only by practising Research Methods type questions, will you be able to find if this is true for you and, if so, how much extra time it frees up for you.

If you use the forms of revision detailed above on a regular basis, not only will it aid your learning, it will also prepare you well for your main revision period preceding the examination and will give you the confidence and motivation to do well.

Revising for the examination

You will not have studied all the topics that occur on the Unit 3 and Unit 4 specification. Decisions will have been made as to which individual topics will be studied. Therefore you are most probably going to have to revise all the topics you have studied in order to be able to answer sufficient questions on the Unit 3 and Unit 4 examination papers; this includes any topics you don't like or have struggled with as they could still in all probability occur on the examination paper.

It is also inadvisable to omit revising something on the basis that it was on the examination paper last time; it could be there again this time. Therefore when revising for your examinations ensure that you:

- have a copy of all the specification topics for each of the individual topics you have studied
- have all the necessary materials for revising each topic
- have created a realistic examination timetable; this needs to have all topics on it, with enough time dedicated to each separate topic to ensure each is revised thoroughly; try to ensure there are a couple of 'spare' slots on your timetable in case extra revision of a topic is needed, or if, through some unforeseeable circumstances, you lose a timetable slot.

Find somewhere you are comfortable to do your revision. For most of us this will be away from other people and possible distractions, but there are no hard and fast rules.

For instance, some people work well with background music, whilst for others it is a distraction. One distraction to be aware of is suddenly finding 'vitally necessary' tasks to do. It is quite easy to use up all of a planned revision session by tidying your bedroom, arranging your books in size order and then sharpening 25 different coloured pencils! Remember a revision session is for revising and nothing else. Make necessary preparations beforehand and not during revision sessions, such as ensuring you have enough pens and paper to revise with.

Remember that for a January examination you will need to revise over the Christmas period and over Easter for the summer examination. There will be a lot of distractions to avoid at these times.

Ensure you have a revision timetable and that you stick to it. Some students can work over protracted periods, but for most an hour to 90 minutes per session will be best. During that time it is advisable that you use the revision methods you have been practising regularly throughout the course.

- Read through the necessary materials for that topic.
- Record or highlight in some way the important points.
- Use previous examination questions and examination-style questions to construct practice answers. By this stage of your learning you should be used to doing these without having materials in front of you and to time constraints.

- At the end of each planned revision session, as long as you achieve your goal, for example writing a satisfactory practice answer, then reward yourself in some way. This will be different for each of us, but could take the form of a preferred TV programme. Such rewards can even be written into your revision timetable as a form of motivation.

Indeed motivation is very important, as is its close cousin confidence. If you have used revision techniques throughout the course and have prepared well for the examination revision period, then you will feel confident that you can succeed and therefore will be motivated to revise well.

Having a realistic revision timetable is very important to your confidence and motivational state of mind, as it allows you to see that everything can be covered in sufficient detail before the examination date rears its ugly head. There is no worse way of denting your confidence and motivation than feeling a blind sense of panic and despair that it is all too much and that there is not enough time, even if you knew where to begin. Feeling in control of the situation will help to keep you confident and motivated.

Another good way of ensuring confidence and motivational levels stay high is to remind yourself constantly why you are doing this, what your target is. This target should be important to you and not be one that someone else has imposed upon you.

▼ **Figure 14.1** Create a realistic revision timetable that will give you time to complete all the topics and have some free time!

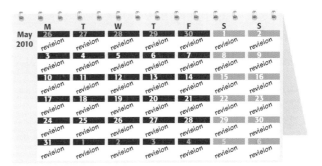

The examination

For a start, make sure you've not only got the date right, but the actual time of the examination too. Plan these details into your revision timetable. I have known students to miss examinations before now because they had medical appointments booked, or were away on holiday, and in one unique case a student missed an examination as she had a revision session for another subject planned for that particular time.

Make sure you take everything you need with you to the examination; it is advisable to prepare a little bag containing the essentials. The inclusion of a couple of spare pens is especially recommended. Remember that you are not allowed to use red pens in your examination, or correcting fluid.

If you have to take your mobile phone with you, ensure it is switched off: if it isn't, you can be excluded from the examination. One student was famously disqualified when her mother phoned her during the examination to see how she was getting on!

When you are told to begin, do not immediately start writing, but first of all read through the questions in order to ensure that you fully understand them and also as a way of mentally preparing yourself for the task at hand.

You may wish to begin with a question that immediately appeals to you, but remember to dedicate only the necessary amount of time to it and no longer. You can then attempt the less appealing questions when you have become more attuned to the examination.

You may wish to jot down a simple plan for an answer, possibly using numbered bullet points before you begin your answer, as a form of useful preparation. Such plans are also creditworthy.

If you do finish before the allotted time is up, do not sit there for the remainder of the time looking smug and sophisticated; instead use that time to read through what you've written. In my experience, you will usually discover some horrendous mistake you've made, or at least an answer you could add a little more to.

EXAMINATION INJUNCTIONS

Examination questions make use of examination injunctions. These are simply the words used in questions to instruct you what kind of answer is required. So by having an understanding of these terms you will be more able to compose examination answers that are in line with what each individual question requires in order to gain the maximum number of marks on offer.

The following is an explanatory list of the most common examination injunctions for the AO1, AO2 and AO3 assessment objectives that you will encounter in your A2 examinations.

◀ **Figure 14.2** Remember to switch off your mobile or, better still, leave it at home!

AO1

Identify = name
Name = identify
Define = what is meant by
Outline = give brief details without explanation
Describe = give a detailed account without explanation

AO2

Analyse = examine in detail
Give = show awareness of
Explain = give clear account of why and how something is so

Evaluate = assess the value or effectiveness
Discuss = give a reasoned, balanced account
Apply = explain how something can be used

AO3

Outline = give brief details without explanation
Give = show awareness of
Identify = name
Explain = give clear account of why and how something is so
Write = compose your own example

Exam-type questions

Throughout this book, at the end of each chapter, you will find examples of questions that relate to the material covered in that chapter. These types of questions are designed to facilitate your learning in that by preparing answers for them you will have to engage with the material covered. The actual questions that you will be set in your A2 examinations will be very much in the style of the questions included in this book, so by practising them you will not only be aiding your learning of the various topic areas, you will also be preparing yourself for the real examination.

Actual examination questions can only be asked about subject material that is named specifically on the specification. So, for example, it would not be possible for you to be asked a question about Duck's (1988) model of relationship dissolution, as it isn't directly named on the specification. However, you could get asked a question about Bruce and Young's theory of face-recognition as it is explicitly named on the specification.

There are a number of differently styled types of questions that you may be presented with under examination conditions and it would be a good idea to familiarise yourself with each of these. A good way to do this is to have a go at answering them in a manner that apes examination conditions as closely as possible, for example only allowing yourself the notional amount of time that you would have for each question in the actual examination. This means in practice that if a question is an essay-type question worth 25 marks, then you really ought to be giving about 30 minutes to writing your answer. Questions worth fewer marks should have less time dedicated to answering them. Probably the biggest mistake you can make is to spend too much time on some questions and then run out of time to complete the other questions. Only by practising examination-type questions under timed conditions can you really develop the ability to know how long to spend on each particular answer.

Also have a look at the sample answers that are presented with the questions in this chapter; they will allow you to see what is good practice and what is poor practice. If you can identify similar good and bad practices in your own work,

then this will help you to form strategies to maximise your performance. Simply by removing identified poor practices from your own work and accentuating and building upon identified good practices, you will provide yourself with a platform for self-improvement.

Generally speaking, there are fewer types of questions on the A2 examinations than you encountered in your AS examinations. For instance, there will not be selection-type questions, where you are given bits of information and asked to put them in the correct parts of a table.

We shall now have a look at the different types of questions that you may encounter in your actual A2 examinations. Each question will be explained in terms of what kind of answer is being asked for.

Provided with each question will be two sample answers: one of these will be of a moderate standard, whilst the other will be of a good standard. Both answers will include examiner's comments that identify good and bad practice and also comments on what would be needed to improve the answer. Therefore, whatever the current standard of your written work under examination-type conditions, you should, by studying these sample answers, be able to identify ways in which you can improve your own work and therefore gain higher marks.

Short answer, parted essay-type questions

On both the A2 examination papers there may be parted essay-type questions that are worth a few marks of the overall 25 marks available for that specific question. Exactly how many marks will always be stated in brackets after the wording of the question. We will now look at one such example of a question that requires AO1 material to answer it and then will follow with a similar question that requires AO2 material to answer it (though AO3 material would also be required in such an answer).

These short answer types of questions will generally be very specific in their requirements and orientated towards specific areas of the specification. Therefore, when answering these types of question care should always be taken that the material to be utilised is carefully chosen and is orientated towards the demands of the question; in other words make sure that you really are answering the question you have been set.

Let us now have a look at an example of a short answer question that requires AO1 content.

> Outline factors that may influence attitudes to food and eating behaviour. (5 marks)

Examination guidance

This question would occur in the 'Eating Behaviour' section of the Unit 3 examination paper. The instruction to 'outline' is an AO1 requirement and you would need to give brief details, without explanation, of material that displays your knowledge of this specific topic area. More common answers would probably be ones that include material on learning experiences, differences between cultures, mood concerns, health concerns and attitudes of peers and parents. The wording of the question asks for 'factors', so at least two must be offered.

Answers to this question would be marked using a specific mark band criteria (see below), and examiners would be sensitive to the depth/breadth trade-off. What this means in essence is that examiners would expect answers that focus on a small number of factors to have more depth to them than answers that focus on a larger number of factors.

AO1 mark bands (5 marks)

5–4 marks	Outline is reasonably thorough, coherent and accurate
3–2 marks	Outline is limited, reasonably coherent and generally accurate
1 mark	Outline is weak and muddled
0 marks	No creditworthy material is apparent

The overall mark for answers to this question would therefore be determined by which descriptor from the above mark bands the answer best fits.

Moderate answer by Rupert

One factor that influences attitudes to food and eating behaviour is bad parenting. Bruch gave a psychodynamic explanation that saw anorexia originating in early childhood when the mother fails to cope with her child's needs, such as only feeding it when it's anxious, and the child then fails to develop self-reliance. Anorexia then emerges during adolescence as a means of attaining self-control.

Another factor is that bad experiences can lead to having an eating disorder.

Examiner's comments

If the second part of this answer were as informative and clear as the first part, then Rupert would have scored more highly. As it is, Rupert explains the factor of parental attitudes in a reasonably thorough, accurate and coherent manner, matching the criteria for the top band of marks. However,

he then goes on to offer a second factor, that of learning experiences, in a weak and uninformative manner. Taking these points collectively and using the specific mark band criteria, the examiner would award three marks as overall the answer is limited, reasonably coherent and generally accurate. The answer scores three rather than two marks as the quality of the answer sits closer to the band above than the band below. Marks: 3/5

Good answer by Chardonay

One factor that influences attitudes to food and eating is the media. In western cultures the media portrays desirable women as being thin and displays negative attitudes to food. This is a culture-bound syndrome as not all cultures have a media that does this. In China for example the media does not transmit negative attitudes to food and anorexia is not common. In western cultures the media creates a social norm that being thin is desirable and people then imitate thin role models that the media portrays in a positive light.

Another factor might be disordered thinking, this cognitive approach believes anorexics perceive themselves as unattractive as they are fat. People with such faulty belief systems subsequently cannot perceive their excessive weight loss.

Examiner's comments

Chardonay offers two factors, which satisfies the requirements of the question and both of these can be seen to be relevant, accurate and coherent. The first factor offered cleverly mixes cultural and media influences, contains a decent amount of detail and provides an illuminating example, that of attitudes to food in China. The second factor offered concerns a cognitive approach; this is again clearly outlined with an appropriate amount of detail. All the information offered is relevant; at no point does Chardonay make the common mistake of offering material that does not answer the question. Marks: 5/5

Let us now have a look at an example of a short answer question that requires AO2 content.

> Evaluate the role of genetic factors in intelligence test performance. (16 marks)

Examination guidance

This question would occur in the 'Intelligence and Learning' section of the Unit 3 examination paper. The instruction to 'evaluate' is an AO2 one and basically means that you need to assess the role of genetic factors in intelligence test performance. One important thing to stress here is that only 12 of the 16 marks available are AO2 ones for analysis and evaluation. The other four marks available are AO3 marks for evaluation of the methodology of studies to investigate the role of genetics.

Answers to this question would be marked using a specific mark band criteria (see below) and this would assess AO2 and AO3 content collectively.

A popular approach to answering this question would probably focus on evaluation of evidence concerning twin studies and adoption studies. Material on environmental factors, for example enrichment studies such as the Headstart project, would only be creditworthy if offered as evaluation of the genetic argument.

A general commentary could be coherently formed around the interaction of genetic and environmental factors, but could also include references to historical debates, controversies surrounding the area and the complex nature of intelligence when considering attempts to measure it.

To move beyond the basic level and accrue more than eight marks would require some input of issues and debates into an answer, for example focusing on culture and gender bias and/or ethical issues and the nature/nurture debate.

Also, to gain access to the higher levels of marks there is a need to demonstrate substantial evidence of synopticity, ie material drawn from across the specification and not just from one area.

AO2/3 mark bands (16 marks)

16–13 marks. Effective
Evaluation shows sound analysis and understanding
A well focused answer that displays coherent elaboration and/or a clear line of argument is apparent
Effective use of issues/debates/approaches
There is substantial evidence of synopticity
Well structured ideas are expressed clearly and fluently
There is consistent effective use of psychological terminology and appropriate use of grammar, spelling and punctuation

12–9 marks. Reasonable
Evaluation shows reasonable analysis and evaluation
A generally focused answer that displays reasonable elaboration and/or the line of argument is apparent
A reasonably effective use of issues/debates/approaches
There is evidence of synopticity
Most ideas are appropriately structured and expressed clearly
There is appropriate use of psychological terminology and some minor errors of grammar; spelling and punctuation only occasionally compromise meaning

8–5 marks. Basic
Evaluation and analysis show basic, superficial understanding
An answer that is sometimes focused and has some evidence of elaboration
There is a superficial use of issues/debates/approaches
There is some evidence of synopticity
The expression of ideas lacks clarity
There is limited use of psychological terminology and errors of grammar, spelling and punctuation are intrusive

4–1 marks. Rudimentary
Evaluation and analysis are rudimentary, showing very limited understanding
A weak, muddled and incomplete answer
Material is not used effectively and may be mainly irrelevant
Any reference to issues/debates/approaches is muddled or inaccurate
There is little or no evidence of synopticity
The expression of ideas is deficient, demonstrating confusion and ambiguity
The answer lacks structure and may be just a series of unconnected points
There are errors in grammar, spelling and punctuation that are frequent and intrusive

0 marks
No creditworthy material is evident

◀ Figure 14.3 Higher band answers often require reference to issues and debates, such as gender bias

Moderate answer by Quinton

There is evidence that intelligence test performance is genetic. This evidences comes from twin studies, such as Shields (1962), which shows that MZ twins tend to score very similarly in IQ tests.

Other supporting evidence to suggest that intelligence test performance is genetic comes from adoption studies.

The environmental argument believes that intelligence test performance is dependent upon learning experiences. In America in the 1960s' children from disadvantaged backgrounds received enrichment to boost their intelligence. Lee et al. (1990) showed this had the effect of boosting not only children's cognitive performances but their social skills too. However, this positive effect proved only to be short-lived.

Some people have argued that IQ tests aren't very good at measuring intelligence.

Intelligence is something that seems to develop as you get older; Piaget thought that it developed in stages, but that some people didn't reach the last stage.

Examiner's comments

Quinton's answer has some relevant, decent material within it and could have been quite easily developed to form a reasonable answer. However, as it stands this is just a series of fairly unconnected points, not all of them made relevant to the question being asked.

Quinton begins quite promisingly; he correctly states that twin studies have suggested that genetic factors are indeed important. However, the fact that MZ twins tend to score similarly in IQ tests, though correct, is not explained in terms of its relevance to the question being asked. He should have explained that the fact that their genetic similarity is 100 per cent and that of DZ twins is only 50 per cent, and that MZ twins have much more highly correlated intelligence test scores than MZ twins, does indeed point towards genetic factors being important. This would then have presented an opportunity to discuss the methodology of twin studies, especially their limitations, such as MZ twins not only having similar genes, but also being raised in similar environments. This in turn would have presented the opportunity to discuss separated MZ and DZ twin studies, what their findings suggest and further discuss their limitations, such as separated MZ twins being raised in similar environments, or the accusation that the influential studies of Burt were based on fabricated evidence.

Quinton's point about adoption studies supporting the argument is correct and relevant, but is devoid of all explanation, evidence or evaluation. This area would have again been a ripe one for a discussion of methodological and ethical issues which could have accrued AO3 as well as AO2 marks.

The material concerning the environmental argument, centred on the Headstart project, is better related and contains relevant and accurate detail. However, it is not creditworthy, as it does not address the question. If such evidence had been used to evaluate the genetic argument, by way of comparison, then it would have been creditworthy.

The comment that intelligence tests may not measure intelligence is again a relevant comment that could have been made highly pertinent to the answer. However, it contains no detail or elaboration and just sits on its own as an unconnected point.

The final comment about intelligence developing in stages is not made relevant to the question and so again does not attract any credit. The rudimentary mark band descriptor seems to best fit this answer, though at the top end of the band. Marks: 4/16

Good answer by Tobias

The idea that genetic factors play a role in determining intelligence test performance is part of the nature/nurture debate and is supported by twin studies that compare genetically identical MZ twins with DZ twins who only have a 50 per cent genetic relationship. Therefore studies such as Shields (1962) and Burt (1966) suggest that as MZ twins have a higher concordance rate for intelligence, it is genetic factors that are most important.

The criticism has been levelled that MZ twins are similar in environmental influences as well as genetic ones and so twin studies have been done on separated twins and again the evidence strongly suggested a genetic factor at work. Burt found a concordance rate of 77.1 per cent for separated MZ twins, compared to 55.2 per cent for DZ twins raised together. However, such studies as these are also not without their critics. 'Separated' twins often turn out to have been separated at quite an advanced age or to have been adopted by different family members, therefore suggesting that environmental factors may also be playing a role. Burt, who was a very influential figure on other researchers, has been shown to have probably fabricated a lot of his evidence and Shields has been accused of experimenter bias.

There is other evidence too to suggest that it isn't only genetic factors that determine intelligence test performance. Enrichment programmes such as the Headstart programme in 1960s' America showed that IQ scores could be affected by environmental inputs. Lazar (1992) showed that disadvantaged children who had been on the pre-school programme were more likely to go to college, suggesting that environmental factors can have a long-term influence.

Evidence from adoption studies is contradictory; some studies suggest that children score more closely to their biological parents, indicating support for the genetic argument, whilst other studies like McGurk (1975) show that adoptive children move towards their adoptive parents in terms of IQ and score much better than their biological parents. This is support for the alternative environmental point of view.

It should also be noted that intelligence is measured by IQ and such tests have been heavily criticised for the theoretical basis upon which they are founded, which tends to have a biased orientation towards the genetic point of view, and for the fact that they have often been wrongly standardised and are biased in favour of the culture upon which they are based. Results from such possibly biased tests are then wrongly used as support for a genetic basis to intelligence test performance.

Examiner's comments

A highly creditworthy, well argued and wide-ranging answer. A lot of the points here are ones that Quinton tried to make, but on this occasion they are made in an effective, elaborated and coherent fashion.

Tobias begins with a clear, concise detailing of twin studies and what they entail for conclusions about the nature/nurture debate. He makes reference also to twin studies of separated twins and presents relevant evidence in an accurate fashion. Intertwined with this discussion are relevant criticisms of a methodological manner that help to form an effective commentary. His criticisms of Burt and Shields are again accurate and relevantly made, though they could possibly have been elaborated on a little more, though time constraints would have made this difficult.

The comments about environmental factors, centred on the Headstart programme, are made relevant as they are used as part of a discussion to evaluate the genetic argument. Again the points made here are coherent and well developed in a logical fashion.

The following comments about adoption studies, although brief, are clear and concise and make a good contribution to the discussion on the nature/nature debate as it affects this psychological area.

The concluding comments about the validity of IQ tests themselves and their universal relevance to all cultures again are accurate and contribute to the discussion in an illuminating manner.

The answer generally fits into the descriptors for the highest band of marks and so scores very highly. Marks: 15/16

▼ **Figure 14.4**
Cultural issues can help to earn the highest band marks. Some IQ tests contain items that are on the curriculum in some countries but not others

Research Methods question

Let us have a look now at an A2 paper Research Methods question. This type of question would occur on the Unit 4 examination paper. There will be one compulsory example of this type of question on the examination paper. It will consist of some stimulus material that will form the basis of the sub-questions asked. Twenty-eight of the possible 35 marks on offer will be AO3 marks, so a sound knowledge of research methodology will be required along with the ability to apply such knowledge to a given scenario.

Each sub-part of the Research Methods question should be answered by itself, with care being taken to ensure that the actual question asked is being addressed and that sufficient relevant and accurate material is provided to gain access to all the marks available. Only by thoroughly studying this important psychological area and practising your application of such knowledge on practice-type questions will you master the skills needed and gain the necessary confidence to do well on such questions.

▼ **Figure 14.5**
The Research Methods question presents you with a novel situation to understand, such as an experiment into the effect of body position on perception

Two parts of the following question, which involve a substantial amount of the overall marks, would be answered by reference to mark band descriptors (see below). It should be noted that in order to access the higher mark bands for question 1f), there is a requirement to present increased evidence of synopticity, where material drawn from across the specification rather than just one area is used. The remainder of the sub-questions, generally worth just a few marks each, can be gained by providing an accurate answer and then elaborating sufficiently upon this answer.

1f) AO2/AO3 mark band descriptors

10–9 marks. Effective
Discussion and application of knowledge to unfamiliar material is effective
Overall, the material shows coherent elaboration and/or a clean line of argument
There is substantial evidence of synopticity

8–6 marks. Reasonable
Discussion and application of knowledge to unfamiliar material is reasonably effective
Overall, the material shows reasonable elaboration and/or a line of argument is evident
There is evidence of synopticity

5–3 marks. Basic
Discussion and application of knowledge is basic
Overall, the material shows some evidence of elaboration
There is some evidence of synopticity

2–1 marks. Rudimentary
Discussion is rudimentary. It is weak, muddled and incomplete
Application of knowledge to unfamiliar material is rudimentary
The material presented may be mainly irrelevant
There is little or no evidence of synopticity

0 marks
No creditworthy material is presented

1g) AO3 mark band descriptors

12–10 marks. Thorough and well reasoned
Design is thorough. Design decisions are appropriate and well reasoned
There is sufficient detail provided for the study to be implemented

9–7 marks. Reasonable
Design is reasonable. Most design decisions are appropriate and some justification is provided
There is sufficient detail provided for most aspects of the plan to be implemented

6–4 marks. Basic
Design is basic. Some design decisions are appropriate. Justification provided is very limited
There is insufficient detail provided for the plan to be implemented

3–1 marks. Rudimentary
Design is rudimentary. Design decisions are muddled and incomplete and are not justified
The plan could not be implemented

0 marks
No creditworthy material is evident

Researchers have found that weightlifters can raise heavier weights when being watched by an audience than they can without an audience. A psychologist wanted to find out whether the same effect happened with other sports.

To test this idea he obtained 40 people who all regularly took part in competitive sports to participate in a study that involved running back and forth along the length of a sports hall six times.

Participants were randomly allocated to one of two groups. Twenty of them were asked to run on their own without an audience, the other 20 were asked to run whilst being watched by an audience present in the sports hall. Participants activated a stop-watch to start their run and stopped it to complete their run. The time taken by each participant to complete the run was recorded.

The psychologist used a statistical test to see if there was a significant difference in the times recorded by the participants running without an audience compared with the times recorded by the participants running with an audience. A significant difference was found at the 5 per cent level for a one-tailed test ($p \leq 0.05$).

▼ **Table 1** Average time recorded when running alone and when running with an audience

	Running alone (in seconds)	Running with an audience (in seconds)
Average time recorded	58	42
Standard deviation	1.86	2.99

1 a) Identify the type of experimental design used in this study. (1 mark)

Examination guidance

One AO3 mark is available here to correctly identify the independent groups design.

Naming the experimental method would not gain credit. There is no need to outline the design, as the question does not ask for it.

1 b) A random sampling method was used for this investigation.
  (i) Explain what is meant by a random sample. (2 marks)

Examination guidance

Two AO3 marks are available here and an accurate and full explanation is required to get both marks, for example stating that a random sample is an unbiased method of selecting participants whereby each member of a population has an equal chance of being selected for any of the testing groups.

The question does not ask you to describe how a random sample would be achieved and attempts to do so would attract no credit and would merely waste valuable time.

1 b) (ii) In the context of this investigation explain one limitation of using a random sample. (2 marks)

Examination guidance

Two more AO3 marks are available here and both would be earned if a valid limitation is provided and is made in the context of the investigation quoted, for example that a random sample doesn't guarantee the selection of a totally representative sample; it would be quite possible for one of the testing groups to have more participants familiar with competitive sports than the other testing group.

1 c) Name an appropriate statistical test for analysing these results and explain why it would be a suitable test. (4 marks)

Examination guidance

There is one AO1 mark available for correctly selecting the Mann-Whitney test and a further three AO3 marks available for explaining its suitability. Material concerning the ordinal level of data, the purpose of the test in looking for a difference and reference to the independent groups design would attract suitable credit.

1 d) Explain what is meant by 'a significant difference was found at the 5 per cent level'. (2 marks)

Examination guidance

Two AO1 marks are available here and to earn both an accurate and sufficiently elaborated explanation would be required; for example that the probability of the results occurring by chance is less than five times in 100.

1 e) Give one reason why a one-tailed test was used by the psychologist. (2 marks)

Examination guidance

Two AO3 marks are available here and a valid reason would have to be supplied with sufficient detail to earn both marks, for example that a one-tailed hypothesis was used due to previous research indicating that this was likely to be the outcome.

1 f) With reference to the data in Table 1, outline and discuss the findings of the investigation. (10 marks)

Examination guidance

Four AO2 marks are on offer for a description of the overall results that could make reference to the average scores for the two conditions, the range or the standard deviations of the two conditions.

There are additionally six AO3 marks up for grabs for analysis, evaluation and interpretation of the methodology and the impact of the findings. Answers could make reference to what the findings indicate, the reliability of stopping and starting the stop-watch and the appropriateness of both the task and the audience present.

Total marks here though would be determined by reference to mark band descriptors (see above).

▶ **Figure 14.6** Remember that you still need to think critically in research methods questions

> 1 g) The psychologist noticed that the fastest running times with an audience present were achieved by those participants who had been taking part in competitive sports for the longest. Design a study to investigate the relationship between running time (with an audience) and time involved in competitive sports.
>
> You should include sufficient details to permit replication, for example a hypothesis, variables, detail of design and procedure and sampling. (12 marks)

Examination guidance

Twelve AO3 marks are available here and the number of marks gained would be determined by reference to mark band descriptors (see above).

Answers would need to make possible reference to operationalisation of an appropriate correlational hypothesis, detailing of methodology, co-variables, sampling method and size, step by step procedure permitting replication and consideration of ethical issues.

Moderate answer by Petronella

1a) The type of experimental design used is the laboratory experiment method.

Examiner's comments

This is quite a common type of mistake, but naming the research method is not creditworthy. Marks: 0/1

1b) (i) A random sample is where participants are selected without bias.

Examiner's comments

This is an incomplete answer. It is true that random sampling involves selecting participants without bias from the researcher, but this is not fully explained. Petronella would need to go on and give more detail as to what random sampling involves. Marks: 1/2

1b) (ii) One limitation of a random sample is that not all members of a population may be available for selection.

Examiner's comments

This is an accurate and clear answer to the question, but doesn't attract full credit as the candidate fails to address that part of the question that requires the answer to be made in the context of the investigation quoted. Petronella would explicitly need to do this to gain the second mark available Marks: 1/2

1c) Mann-Whitney would be used, as it's a test of difference.

Examiner's comments

Again, an accurate and clear answer, but one that isn't informative enough to gain full credit. There is one AO1 mark available for naming the statistical test and Petronella gets this mark for correctly naming the Mann-Whitney test. However, there are three AO3 marks available for explaining why it would be a suitable test and simply correctly stating that it's a test of difference would only be good enough to gain one of those marks. Petronella could have referred to the ordinal level of the data and the use of the independent groups design to gain the other marks available. Marks: 2/4

1d) When an investigation is done the results are subjected to a statistical test, in this case the Mann-Whitney test, to see if the results are significantly different.

Examiner's comments

What Petronella writes is true: statistical tests are used to see if results are significant or not, that is their purpose. However, the question isn't asking what the purpose of statistical tests is and so the answer provided here is irrelevant and not creditworthy. What should have been written about was establishing whether differences in results fall inside or outside the boundaries of chance. Marks: 0/2

1e) One reason a one-tailed test was used was because the hypothesis was directional.

Examiner's comments

Again an accurate answer is supplied, showing that Petronella does have a good working knowledge of research methods. However, as is common with many students, Petronella is not going on to elaborate her answers sufficiently to gain the extra marks that evidently should be within her capabilities. This is a weakness that will limit the overall grade attained unless it is addressed by practising answering these types of questions on a regular basis. To gain the additional credit on offer Petronella could have gone on to explain that a one-tailed hypothesis is used when previous research gives some indication as to the outcome of the present research. Marks: 1/2

1f) Averages show us what the mathematical middle number is when all scores are added together and divided by the number of participants. The findings here show that participants run quicker with an audience on average by 16 seconds.

Standard deviation is a measure of variability; it shows the typical deviation of a given sample of scores from its mean. In this case it shows us that there was more average deviation in the scores from the participants running with an audience than those running without an audience, 2.99 as opposed to 1.86.

Examiner's comments

A sound and clear knowledge of the mean and standard deviation is conveyed here and is linked to an explanation of the findings in this particular instance. So as such Petronella scores all four AO1 marks available for the part of the question that asks for an outline of the findings. The other six marks available are AO3 marks for a discussion of the findings. This would be achieved by analysis, evaluation and interpretation of the findings, but as Petronella does not address this part of the question she accrues no further credit. Marks: 4/10

1g) A correlational study would be used. One co-variable would be how fast in seconds it took each participant to complete the running task with an audience and the second co-variable would be how long each participant had been involved in competitive sports. This could be measured by the number of years they had been involved.

The hypothesis would be one-tailed as the previous research is suggesting those more familiar with competitive sports will perform best with an audience.

About 20 participants would be needed to make the findings representative and they would need to be gathered from a population of competitive sports players.

Examiner's comments

Petronella has correctly identified the correlational method and goes on to describe the two co-variables in a clear and accurate fashion that demonstrates a good knowledge of how correlational studies work; these co-variables are both operationalised. Also pleasingly, Petronella identifies the need for a one-tailed hypothesis and includes the reasoning behind this decision. Therefore it is quite disappointing, having done the hard work so to speak, that she doesn't include an actual hypothesis for her proposed study. This would have attracted extra credit.

Petronella also shows some understanding of the number of participants needed to make the results generalisable, but doesn't go on to explain what type of sampling method it would be useful to employ. She could also have included brief details of the procedure, including ethical considerations, for example gaining informed consent, as well as showing the need for a step-by-step procedure to permit replication.

As it stands, her answer fits the top end of the basic mark band descriptor, but with a few additions, such as those suggested earlier, she could quite easily have scored a lot better. Marks: 6/12

Examiner's overall comments

Petronella actually gave correct answers to most of the questions. She demonstrated that she has a sound knowledge of this important area of the specification and can apply it to the research quoted. So it is a real shame, and one that is only too common with a lot of students, that she isn't accumulating the overall mark that she is clearly capable of. By utilising the revision practice of regularly attempting these types of questions and concentrating on elaborating answers fully so that she can gain access to the whole range of marks available, Petronella would surely improve her achievements.
Overall mark: 15/35

▼ **Figure 14.7** As with most things, in research methods questions, practice makes perfect

Good answer by Dorothea

1a) The design being used is the independent groups design.

Examiner's comments

The correct answer is supplied and no irrelevant material is apparent, such as a description of the design. Marks: 1/1

1b) (i) A random sample is one where every member of a population has an equal chance of being selected for any of the testing groups. All the names within a population could be entered into a computer and then a random selection programme used to select the names without any form of bias.

Examiner's comments

An accurate answer sufficiently elaborated to gain both marks available is apparent. The second sentence, which explains how such a sample would be determined, is not creditworthy, as the question does not ask for this, apart from the final comment about random sampling occurring without selection bias. Marks: 2/2

1b) (ii) There is no guarantee that random selection will create two testing groups of equal running ability. It is quite possible that more gifted runners could end up in one group than the other. Also not all members of the target population may be available for selection.

Examiner's comments

A clear, accurate and sufficiently elaborated answer that makes reference to the context of the investigation being used earns both the AO3 marks on offer. The reference to running ability puts the answer in context, though Dorothea also provides a second limitation that would not gain credit. With Research Methods questions, if one limitation is asked for then only the first one supplied is marked. Marks: 2/2

1c) The Mann-Whitney test would be most appropriate because it's a test of difference and the data level is at least ordinal.

Examiner's comments

The AO1 for correctly naming the statistical test is gained, as are two of the three AO3 marks on offer for explaining why it's the appropriate test. Dorothea could have gone on to explain that, as it was an independent groups design, the Mann-Whitney test was also appropriate, to gain the third mark. Marks: 3/4

1d) When a significant difference is found at the 5 per cent level it means that the likelihood that the difference found is due to chance and not the influence of the IV on the DV, is less than five times in 100.

Examiner's comments

An accurate, clear and thorough explanation is provided that shows a sound understanding of what is meant by the term 'significant difference'. Therefore both AO1 marks on offer are easily captured. Marks: 2/2

1e) One-tailed tests are used when previous research indicates that the results will lie in a certain direction. For instance that participants will perform better with an audience.

Examiner's comments

Both marks are gained here as the question is accurately and fully answered. There was no actual requirement for Dorothea to put her answer into context, but by doing so it did add relevant elaboration to her answer. Marks: 2/2

1f) The participants in the with-audience condition ran, on average, faster than the non-audience condition, 42 seconds compared to 58 seconds, a difference of 16 seconds on average. Also the standard deviation gives us extra information that tells us the typical deviation of a sample of scores from the mean, in this case there was less standard deviation in the running alone condition (1.86 seconds) than the with-audience condition (2.99 seconds). This suggests that the presence of an audience improves performance and that there is more variation in individual scores with participants in the audience condition.

There is a potential problem with the reliability of the scores as there may have been differences in when participants stopped and started the stop-watch and this could affect the findings.

Also the make-up of the audience could affect performances, if the audience is known to some participants this may affect them differently than if they didn't know the audience. The same is true for how similar the audience might be to the participants, for example in terms of gender, age and cultural background.

The nature of the task may have an effect too: running is fairly easy, would there have been a different effect if the activity had been complex?

Examiner's comments

A good answer that addresses both the 'outline' and 'discuss' parts of the question. The findings are fully outlined and there is an indication of what the findings may indicate.

Dorothea also has a grasp of reliability issues concerning the use of the stop-watch, as well as realising that the make-up of the audience and the nature of the task being tested could also be influential.

Overall, the answer is effective, coherent elaboration is provided and a clear line of argument is provided. There is also evidence of synopticity. This places the answer in the top mark band descriptor, but there is a slight lack of explanation in the answer at times, which ultimately places the answer at the lower end of the mark band. Marks: 9/10

1g) A correlational study would be needed as it would establish the degree of relationship between running time and time involved in competitive sports. It would be best to have a one-tailed directional hypothesis as the previous research is indicating the expected result. The hypothesis would be that there will be a negative relationship between time spent running six lengths of the sports hall and amount of time involved in competitive sports.

The first co-variable would be time spent running in seconds and the second co-variable would be time spent involved in competitive sports measured in years.

It would be best to use a volunteer sample of competitive sports folk, as they'd be keen to do it, you could put up a poster to get them; about 20 would be needed to get a good result.

Standardised instructions would be read to the participants giving them full information to allow them to give informed consent. They should be reminded of the right to withdraw at any time and no one should be referred to by name, but instead by number to guarantee anonymity.

The participant running order would be determined by random selection and they would, in turn, activate the stop-watch, perform their run in front of the audience and then stop the stop-watch.

Examiner's comments

The correlational method is correctly identified and the reason why is given. The hypothesis is clearly provided in an operationalised form and the co-variables are clearly stated. Details of the sample and procedure are also well documented permitting reasonable replication, and relevant ethical considerations are also provided. Overall, the answer fits the criteria for the highest mark band, but occasionally the answer could be a little better explained, for example what is meant by a 'good result'? This places the quality of the answer at the lower end of the mark band. Marks: 10/12

Examiner's overall comments

A high quality is maintained by Dorothea throughout her answer. She fully answers the questions set, though occasionally offers irrelevant material too, which can waste valuable time. Dorothea demonstrates that she has a very sound knowledge of research methods and, more importantly, that she can apply this knowledge in a coherent, accurate and incisive manner. A good quality answer that accumulates the good quality marks it deserves. Overall mark: 31/35

Long-essay type questions

A lot of the questions on both the Unit 3 and Unit 4 examination papers will consist of the 'traditional' long-essay type questions. These questions will be worth 25 marks each, of which there will be nine AO1 marks for knowledge and understanding, 12 AO2 marks for the application of knowledge and understanding and four AO3 marks for how science works. We have already looked at examples of parted long-answer questions, where the requirement is to present different aspects of your answer in separate sections. However, in the long-essay type questions you will be required to present the AO1, AO2 and AO3 material for your answer in a continuous piece of prose writing. You will have come across this type of question in your AS examinations, but they are much more a feature of the A2 examination and your ability to master this type of question could be crucial to how well you will ultimately perform. It will not be possible to know beforehand or to predict precisely which topics the questions will be set on. This means therefore that you must be prepared to answer such a question on any topic and, as this type of question will form a large part of those on the examination papers, it would be a good idea to have a look at and practise quite a few of this type of questions.

The marks for AO1 and AO2/AO3 content will be determined by the use of mark band descriptors that remain fairly similar for all of these questions. This is to your advantage, for it will therefore be possible to familiarise yourself with the requirements needed to gain access to the higher band descriptors and to practise satisfying these requirements by attempting practice answers to such questions. It must be remembered that the content requirement for these types of questions is weighted in favour of the AO2/AO3 material. Previously examiners have commented on a general student trend to concentrate on the AO1 part of this type of question at the expense of the AO2/AO3 content. It is therefore highly recommended that you practise constructing answers to this type of question until you get it right.

There are two general strategies that can be employed to answer this type of question. The initial one is to first provide all your AO1 material, followed by your AO2/AO3 material. The trick is in knowing when you have provided sufficient AO1 material to be able to move on to the AO2/AO3 requirement. Remember there are only nine marks available for AO1 and if you provide material that is worth more than these nine marks you will not be awarded extra AO1 credit and, of course, you will have wasted valuable examination time that could have been spent on providing relevant AO2/AO3 material.

Second, you could adopt the strategy of providing an AO1 comment followed by a relevant AO2 comment. This is a strategy that needs to be thoroughly practised to be useful to a student, but can be a highly effective method of maximising performance when mastered.

▼ **Figure 14.8** To achieve a balance of AO1, AO2 and AO3 you can either think of AO1 as a 'starter' followed by a 'main course' of AO2 and AO3, or imagine a multi-layered sandwich of AO1 slices of bread and AO2 or AO3 filling

Let us now have a look at one such question concerning theories of cognitive development. Such a question would appear on the Unit 3 examination paper in the Cognition and Development sub-section.

> Outline and evaluate **one** theory of cognitive development. (25 marks)

Examination guidance

This question focuses in particular on the subject area of theories of cognitive development. Your AO1 material is therefore going to be a description of one such theory of cognitive development; Piaget and Vygotsky will probably prove the most popular choices. If you were to provide a description of more than one theory, then each theoretical description would be marked separately and the best one credited. This would mean that a lot of your AO1 material, however relevant, accurate and detailed, would not gain credit and you would have wasted valuable time. Also if you were to provide AO1 material that describes anything other than a theory of cognitive development, then that too would not attract any credit, as it would fall outside of what the question is asking for.

If you are to gain high AO1 credit for this question, then you need to satisfy the demands of the higher mark band descriptors. (These are provided later on.) Therefore to earn all nine AO1 marks on offer you would need to describe a theory of cognitive development, showing knowledge and understanding that was accurate and well detailed. The organisation and structure of your answer would need to be coherent and there would need to be substantial evidence of breadth/depth.

If you are to also earn high AO2 credit for this question, then you will need once more to satisfy the demands of higher mark band descriptors. So to earn all 12 AO2 marks and all four AO3 marks on offer would require an effective evaluation. In order to achieve this, your evaluation should demonstrate sound analysis and understanding, with your answer being well focused and showing coherent elaboration and a sound line of argument. Also issues/debates approaches would need to be used in an effective manner with substantial evidence of synopticity being given. To gain access to the highest mark band would also necessitate appropriate use of grammar, punctuation and spelling and consistently effective use of psychological terminology. To develop the skills to be able to bring all these required threads together will take regular and patient practice of these types of questions.

Research studies will probably form the main basis of AO2 material. Alternatively, the general explanatory power of your chosen theory in explaining cognitive development would be an effective way of accessing AO2 credit. Alternative theories could be introduced as a means of comparison, but would have to be used explicitly as evaluative material to earn AO2 marks. AO3 credit could be earned through a methodological analysis of research studies. Issues/debates/approaches relevant to this question could include the nature–nurture debate, ethical issues involved in working with children and the cognitive approach.

AO1 mark bands

9–8 marks. Sound

Knowledge and understanding are accurate and well detailed
A good range of relevant material has been presented
There is substantial evidence of breadth/depth.
Organisation and structure of the answer are coherent

7–5 marks. Reasonable

Knowledge and understanding are generally accurate and reasonably detailed
A range of relevant material has been presented
There is evidence of breadth and/or depth
Organisation and structure of the answer are reasonably coherent

4–3 marks. Basic

Knowledge and understanding are basic/relatively superficial
A restricted range of material has been presented
Organisation and structure of the answer are basic

2–1 marks. Rudimentary

Knowledge and understanding are rudimentary and may be muddled and/or inaccurate
The material presented may be brief or largely irrelevant
The answer lacks organisation and structure

0 marks

No creditworthy material is apparent

AO2 mark bands

16–13 marks. Effective

Evaluation demonstrates sound analysis and understanding
The answer is well focused and shows coherent elaboration and/or a clear line of argument
Issues/debates/approaches are used effectively
There is substantial evidence of synopticity
Ideas are well structured and expressed clearly and fluently
There is consistent effective use of psychological terminology
There is appropriate use of grammar, punctuation and spelling

12–9 marks. Reasonable

Evaluation demonstrates reasonable analysis and understanding
The answer is reasonably focused and shows reasonable elaboration and/or a clear line of argument
Issues/debates/approaches are used in a reasonably effective manner
There is evidence of synopticity
Most ideas are appropriately expressed and expressed clearly
There is appropriate use of psychological terminology
Minor errors of grammar, punctuation and spelling only occasionally compromise meaning

8–5 marks. Basic

Analysis and evaluation demonstrates basic, superficial understanding
The answer is sometimes focused and shows some evidence of elaboration
Superficial reference may be made to issues/debates/approaches
There is some evidence of synopticity
The expression of ideas lacks clarity and there is limited use of psychological terminology
Errors of grammar, punctuation and spelling are intrusive

4–1 marks. Rudimentary

Analysis and evaluation are rudimentary, demonstrating very little understanding
The answer is weak, muddled and incomplete and the material is not used effectively and may be mainly irrelevant
Any reference to issues/debates/approaches is muddled or inaccurate
There is little or no evidence of synopticity
Deficiency in expression of ideas results in confusion and ambiguity
The answer lacks structure and is often no more than a series of unconnected assertions
Errors of grammar, punctuation and spelling are frequent and intrusive

0 marks

No creditworthy material is apparent

Moderate answer by Octavia

Jean Piaget was interested in how children develop and so constructed his stage theory of cognitive development that describes the cognitive changes children go through in each stage.

The first stage was the sensori-motor stage from birth to two years of age. In this stage children develop object permanence, realising objects still exist even when they can't be seen. The second stage is the pre-operational stage from two to seven years of age. In this stage children are egotistic and can't see the world through another's perspective. Children in this stage use rules, but ones that are not based on logic. The third stage is the concrete operational stage from seven to 11 years of age where logical rules appear. Children now develop the ability to conserve and realise that quantity doesn't change when an object is transformed. The final stage is the formal operations stage from 11 years onwards. This is where children become capable of abstract and hypothetical thought.

Dasen has claimed that a third of adults never achieve formal operations so maybe this stage isn't universal.

There is a lot of research evidence which Piaget and others did which backs up his theory. However, other researchers have found evidence to contradict Piaget's theory.

The theory has a lot of use in child rearing and educational purposes.

Examiner's comments

This is actually a very representative essay answer, because examiners see a lot of answers that are similar to this one. It is not a particularly awful answer, everything in it being accurate and relevant, but there is a huge scope for improvement that revision of study topics and examination techniques would help with considerably.

Octavia begins with a pure description of Piaget's stages of cognitive development. This material is all exclusively AO1 material. She names the stages correctly, gives the correct approximate ages and provides a sparse description of each stage. The impression is never gained, however, that Octavia fully understands what she is writing about; the detail is lacking that would have removed this suspicion. Although Octavia ultimately earns reasonable AO1 marks, it would have been relatively simple for her to have increased this mark. She could have explained the mechanics of the theory in terms of how schemas develop, for example the role of assimilation and accommodation. The role of equilibration behind the process of adaptation would also have attracted similar AO1 credit. Octavia mentions very briefly the research that Piaget performed and description of this could also have attracted AO1 credit.

There is AO2 material present, but it is basic at best, bordering on rudimentary. The comment about Dasen stating that formal operations is maybe not universal provides a promising start, but after that the AO2 material consists of a general comment that research evidence is contradictory in its support of the theory and that the theory has practical applications for child rearing and education in particular. Evidently Octavia has some understanding of the evaluative worth of the theory, but has failed to elaborate or develop these points in a way that would have increased her overall mark. As was stated earlier, description of relevant research accrues AO1 credit, but evaluation and analysis of such studies as to whether they provide support or not for the theory would have gained suitable AO2 marks. It would not have been difficult to present some of the studies that Piaget used to support his theory, for example the Swiss Mountain study that was used to back up his claims about the ages at which children can conserve, alongside other research that challenges such claims, for example Hughes' (1975) police doll study. An evaluation of Piaget's theory in education would have also been relatively easy to construct and could have focused on research that has attempted to assess the viability of Piagetian ideas in schools.

There is a total lack of AO3 material in Octavia's answer, which could have been quite easily attained by a methodological analysis of research studies, for instance that shortcomings in his research methodology led to Piaget underestimating what children can do at particular ages. Finally, material on issues/debates and approaches is highly intrinsic at best and there would be a need for Octavia to provide more explicitly some material on these areas if she is to improve the quality of her answer. It would not have been difficult, for example, to highlight the ethical concerns of working with children, for instance the difficulties in attaining informed consent and the high risk of psychological harm.

Overall the descriptive content is easily better than the evaluative material and by reference to the mark band descriptors Octavia's AO1 content is probably just a little better than basic and thus scrapes into the bottom reaches of the reasonable mark band descriptor, earning five out of nine possible marks. However, the AO2/AO3 material taken collectively fits into the rudimentary mark band descriptor, though at the top end of the mark band as it is closer to basic than the band below. Therefore Octavia gains four out of the possible 16 marks here. Overall mark: 9/25

Good answer by Gregor

Piaget worked on some of the earliest IQ tests and so had a long-term interest in the development of intelligence. Piaget believed intelligence was a process of biological adaptation that allowed a child increasingly to interact efficiently with its environment. He used the idea of a schema, a psychological structure representing everything a child knew about something, and how such schemas developed as a child interacted with its environment. He saw the process of adaptation as having two parts to it; firstly assimilation where new information is fitted into existing schemas and secondly accommodation where schemas

are changed when new information can't be assimilated. This ongoing process of cognitive development occurs in four different stages and different kinds of thinking occur in the different stages.

In the sensori-motor stage, from 0 to two years, object permanence is gained where a child comes to learn that objects still exist even when they cannot be seen. The next stage is the pre-operational stage from two to seven years; children here learn increasingly to use mental symbols to represent objects and events. Children are egocentric and can't see the world from another's point of view. In the concrete operational stage from seven to 11 years of age children develop complex mental schema that allow them to reach logical conclusions. In this stage children learn conservation skills that enable them to realise that quantity doesn't change when an object is transformed.

The final stage, which may not be universal, as not all people seem to achieve it, is the formal operations stage; in this stage children develop the ability to indulge in abstract and hypothetical thought.

Piaget's theory was important as it was groundbreaking, had practical applications, especially in education, and generated lots of interest and research in this important area. However, he is not without criticism, due often to the impaired methodology of his research. For instance Piaget often underestimated what children could do at certain ages because he presented them with tasks that were unfamiliar to them. In his Swiss Mountain experiment children had to choose a picture that represented the view a doll would be able to see and from this Piaget claimed that children below the age of seven years couldn't do it because they were egocentric. However, Donaldson (1978) used children's familiarity with hide and seek to challenge children to hide a doll where a police doll couldn't see it and children much younger than Piaget would have believed could do it.

Piaget also often used a question and answer technique, such as in his conservation experiments; this involved asking the same question twice and critics such as Samuel and Bryant have claimed children give a different answer the second time due to demand characteristics. When they changed this aspect of similar research they found children could conserve a lot earlier than Piaget claimed.

Cross-cultural evidence does seem to back up Piaget's claim that the stages are invariant and so are probably biological in origin. Many believe that Piaget under-emphasised the role of language and social development in cognitive development and Vygotsky believed that cultural experiences were necessary to transform intellect into higher mental functions.

Piaget's theory has big implications for education, especially through his idea of discovery learning, where the

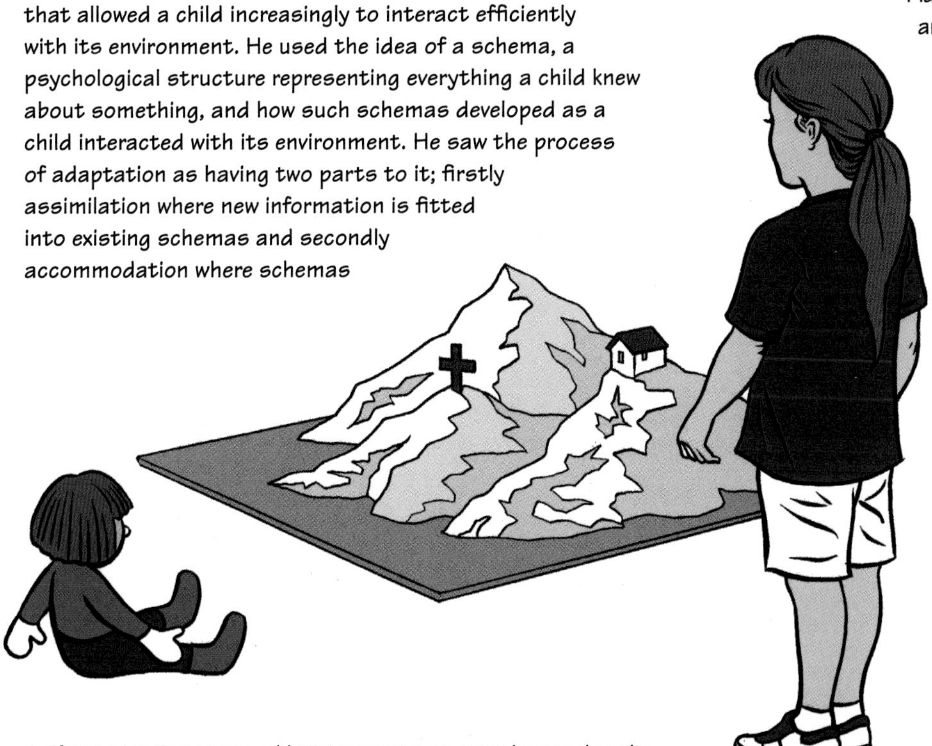

▲ **Figure 14.9** One way to add AO3 context to an essay is to analyse the methodology of the studies you have described

child constructs knowledge for itself through experience. The teacher's role is to push the child into disequilibrium so that it is motivated to accommodate the new information into its schemas. This approach has had success with some subjects such as mathematics where step-by-step learning is apparent, but not with more abstract subjects. Also some have argued, like Modgil (1983), that discovery learning hampers real learning as it reduces the amount of time that can be spent on learning basic skills such as reading and writing.

Lastly it should be remembered that research in this area involves very young children who are too young to give informed consent. Care should be given that such consent is gained not only from the relevant educational institutions, but also the children's parents or guardians.

▼ **Figure 14.10** Participants may find studies stressful. Relevant references to ethics can help to boost your essay mark

Examiner's comments

Gregor presents an excellent response to the question, not an easy task as this is such a wide-ranging area. Gregor has decided to present his AO1 material first; he does this by explaining the theoretical background of how children learn and detailing the major occurrences in each of the four stages of development. Gregor does not waste time, as he is able to present his material in an informative, yet concise style. There is a little more AO1 content later on too when Gregor explains the role of Piaget's theory in education.

Gregor's evaluation of the theory has several strands to it, always a good approach to take when trying to accumulate AO2 credit. He also includes AO3 material here by concentrating on Piaget's methodological deficiencies. This he does in a coherent and elaborated fashion, giving a couple of examples, notably from Donaldson and Samuel and Bryant, to further illuminate the points being made. After this, Gregor appears to take time-constraints into account and adopts a punchy, concise style to make several concluding points that centre on a breadth rather than depth approach. As there is such a wealth of material to choose from in this topic area this is a wise decision; there would not be enough time to cover every possible evaluative angle in a lot of detail. And so Gregor adds to his evaluation comments on the contribution of cross-cultural studies and the role of language and social development. He then contrasts Piaget's central beliefs with those of the Russian psychologist Vygotsky, before moving on to consider Piaget's contribution to education. Finally, there is a comment about the suitability of using children in research that conveys a sense that Gregor has an understanding of such considerations.

Overall, this is a balanced, relevant and informative answer that creates a coherent commentary around the topic area and thus accesses the higher reaches of the mark band descriptors. The AO1 material falls into the highest band, but at the lower end, as a little more detail would have been possible, for example detailing the important role of equilibration. The AO2 material is effective, and a clear line of argument is used, and there is evidence of synopticity. There is possibly a little more scope for analysis at times, but Gregor still scores very highly here. Overall marks: AO1 = 8/9 + AO2 = 14/16 = 22/25

References

Aarts H & Dijksterhuis A (2002) Category activation effects in judgement and behaviour. *British Journal of Social Psychology* **41**, 123–38

Abrams R (1967) Daily administration of unilateral ECT. *American Journal of Psychiatry* **124**, 384–86

Adam K (1977a) Body weight correlates with REM sleep. *British Medical Journal* **1**, 813

Adam K (1977b) Dietary habits and the effect of bedtime food drinks on sleep. *Proceedings of the Nutrition Society* **36**(1), 48A

Adityanjee M, Sajatovic M & Munshi K (2005) Neuropsychiatric sequelae of neuroleptic malignant syndrome. *Clinical Neuropharmacology* **28**, 197–203

Aggleton JP (1993) The contribution of the amygdala to normal and abnormal emotional states. *Trends in Neuroscience* **16**, 328–33

Agostinella G & Grube JW (2002) *Alcohol Counter-Advertising and the Media: A Review of Recent Research*. Bethesda: NIAAA

Alaez C, Lin L, Flores AH, Vazquez M, Munguia A, Mignot E, Haro R, Baker H & Gorodezky C (2008) Association of narcolepsy-cataplexy with HLA-DRB1 and DQB1 in Mexican patients: a relationship between HLA and gender is suggested. *BMC Medical Genetics* **15**(9), 79

Al-Ansari BM & Baroun KA (2005) Impact of anxiety and gender on perceiving the Müller–Lyer illusion. *Social Behavior and Personality* **33**(1), 33–42

Aldrich MS (1992) Narcolepsy. *Neurology*, 42: 34–3

Alexander GL, Davis WK, Yan AC & Fantone JC 3rd (2000) Following medical school graduates into practice: residency directors' assessments after the first year of residency. *Academic Medicine* **75**(10 Suppl.), S15–17

Allardyce J, Gaebel W, Zielasek J & Van Os J (2007) Deconstructing Psychosis conference, February 2006: The validity of schizophrenia and alternative approaches to the classification of psychosis. *Schizophrenia Bulletin* **33**, 863–67

Allcock CC & Grace DM (1988) Pathological gamblers are neither impulsive nor sensation-seekers. *Australian & New Zealand Journal of Psychiatry* **22**(3), 307–11

Allport G & Pettigrew T (1957) Cultural influences on the perception of movement: the trapezoid illusion among Zulus. *Journal of Abnormal and Social Psychology* **55**, 104–13

American Academy of Paediatrics. Committee on Nutrition, In RE Kleinman (ed.) *Pediatric Nutrition Handbook* 4th edn Elk Grove Village IL: American Academy of Pediatrics, 833.

Amir S & Stewart J (1996) quoted in 'Clocked off', *New Scientist*, 8 November 1997, 29

Anand BK & Brobeck JR (1951) Localization of a 'feeding centre' in the hypothalamus of the rat. *Proceedings Society for Experimental Biology and Medicine* **77**, 323–24

Anderson CA, Berkowitz L, Donnerstein E, Huesmann LR, Johnson JD, Linz D, Malamuth NM & Wartella E (2003) The influence of media violence on youth. *Psychological Science in the Public Interest* **4**, 81–110

Anderson JL, Crawford CB, Nadeau J & Lindberg T (1992) Was the Duchess of Windsor right? A cross-cultural review of the socioecology of body shape. *Ethology & Sociobiology* **13**, 197–227

Anderson SW & Booker MB (2006) Cognitive behavioral therapy versus psychosurgery for refractory obsessive-compulsive disorder. *Journal of Neuropsychiatry & Clinical Neuroscience* **18**, 129

Andreoli V & Worchel S (1978) Effects of media, communicator, and message position on attitude change. *Public Opinion Quarterly* **42**, 59–70

Andresen M (2006) Governments' conflict of interest in treating problem gamblers. *Canadian Medical Association Journal* **175**(10), 1191

Aouizerate B, Martin-Guehl C, Cuny E, Guehl D, Amieva H, Benazouz A, Fabrigoule C, Bioulac B, Tignol J & Burbaud P (2005) Deep brain stimulation for OCD and major depression. *American Journal of Psychiatry* **162**, 2192

Apostolou M (2008) Parent-child conflict over mating: the case of beauty. *Evolutionary Psychology* **6**, 303–15

Ariyabuddhiphongs V & Phengphol V (2008) Near miss, gambler's fallacy and entrapment: their influence on lottery gamblers in Thailand. *Journal of Gambling Studies* **24**(3), 295–305

Arkkelin D & O'Connor R (1992) The 'good' professional: effects of trait-profile gender type, androgyny, and likableness on impressions of incumbents of sex-typed occupations. *Sex Roles* **27**(9–10), 517–32

Armfield J (2007) Manipulating perceptions of spider characteristics and predicted spider fear: evidence for the cognitive vulnerability model of the etiology of fear. *Journal of Anxiety Disorders* **21**, 691–703

Aronfreed J, Messick S, Diggory J (1953). *Journal of Personality* **21**(4), 517–28

Aronoff J & Crano WD (1975) A re-examination of the cross-cultural principles of task segregation and sex role differentiation in the family. *American Sociological Review* **40**, 12–20

Aronson E, Wilson TD & Akert RM (1994) *Social Psychology*. New York: HarperCollins

Arroll B, Macgillivray S, Ogston S, Reid I, Sullivan F, Williams B & Crombie I (2005) Efficacy and tolerability of tricyclic antidepressants and SSRIs compared with placebo for treatment of depression in primary care: a meta-analysis. *Annals of Family Medicine* **3**, 449–56

Aserinsky E & Kleitman N (1953) Regularly occurring periods of eye motility, and concomitant phenomena, during sleep. *Science* **118**, 273–74

Ash JA & Gallup GG (2007) Brain size, intelligence and paleoclimatic variation. In G Geher & G Miller (2007) *Mating Intelligence: Theoretical and empirical insights into intimate relationships*. Mahwah NJ: Lawrence Erlbaum Associates

Astin JA, Harkness E & Ernst E (2000) The Efficacy of 'Distant Healing' A Systematic Review of Randomized Trials. *Annals of Internal Medicine* **132**, 903–10

Astington JW (1998) Theory of mind, Humpty Dumpty and the ice box. *Human Development* **41**, 30–39

Aubry S, Ruble DN & Silverman LB (1999) The role of gender knowledge in children's gender-typed preferences. In L Balter & CS Tamis-LeMonda (eds) *Child Psychology: A Handbook of Contemporary Issues*. Hove: Psychology Press, 363–90

Austin EW, Pinkleton B and Fujioka Y (1999) Assessing prosocial message effectiveness: effects of message quality, production quality, and persuasiveness. *Journal of Health Communication* **4**, 195–210

Baca-Garcia E, Perez-Rodriguez MM, Basurte-Villamor I, Fernandez del Moral AL, Jimenez-Arriero MA, Gonzalez de Rivera JL, Saiz-Ruiz J & Oquendo MA (2007) Diagnostic stability of psychiatric disorders in clinical practice. *British Journal of Psychiatry* **19**, 210–16

Badcock C (1994) *Psychodarwinism: a new synthesis of Darwin and Freud.* London: HarperCollins

Badcock, C (2000) *Evolutionary Psychology: A Critical Introduction*. Cambridge: Polity Press

Baeyens F, Crombez G, De Houwer J & Eelen P (1996) No evidence for modulation of evaluative flavour–flavour associations in humans. *Learning and Motivation* **27**

Bahr SJ, Hoffmann JP and Yang X (2005) Parental and peer influences on the risk of adolescent drug use. *Journal of Primary Prevention* **26**(6), 529–51

Bahrick H (1984) Memory for people. In Harris & Morris (1984) *Everyday Memory, Action and Absentmindedness*. London: Academic Press

Baic K, London ED, Monterosso J, Wong ML, Delibasi T, Sharma A & Licinio J (2007) Leptin replacement alters brain response to food cues in genetically leptin-deficient adults. *Proceedings of the National Academy of Sciences*, 6 Nov, 1798661

Baker RR (1984) *Bird navigation: the solution of a mystery.* London: Hodder & Stoughton

Baker EK, Kurtz MM & Astur RS (2006) Virtual reality assessment of medication compliance in patients with schizophrenia. *Cyberpsychology & Behaviour* **9**, 224–29

Balcetis E & Dunning D (2006) See what you want to see: motivational influences on visual perception. *Journal of Personality & Social Psychology* **91**(4), 612–625

Bandura A (1965) Influence of a model's reinforcement contingencies on the acquisition of imitative responses. *Journal of Personality & Social Psychology* **36**, 589–95

Bandura A (1977) *Social Learning Theory*. Englewood Cliffs NJ: Prentice-Hall

Bandura A, Ross D & Ross SA (1961) Transmission of aggression through imitation of aggressive models. *Journal of Abnormal & Social Psychology* **63**, 575–82

Bandura A, Ross D & Ross SA (1963) Imitation of film-mediated aggressive models. *Journal of Abnormal and Social Psychology* **66**, 3–11

Banse R (2004) Adult attachment and marital satisfaction: evidence for dyadic configuration effects. *Journal of Social & Personal Relationships* **21**, 273–82

Bard P (1929) The central representation of the sympathetic nervous system. *Archives of Neurology & Psychiatry* **22**, 230–46

Bardy BG, Marin L, Stoffregen TA & Bootsma, RJ (1999) Postural coordination modes considered as emergent phenomena. *Journal of Experimental Psychology: Human Perception and Performance* **25**, 1284–1301

Baron-Cohen S, Leslie AM & Frith U (1985) Does the autistic child have a theory of mind? *Cognition* **21**, 37–46

Barthomeuf L, Droit-Volet S & Rousset S (2009) Obesity and emotions: differentiation in emotions felt towards food in obese, overweight and normal-weight adolescents. *Food Quality and Preference* **20**(1), 62–68

Bartlett S (2003) Motivating patients towards weight loss. *The Physician and Sports Medicine* **31**(11)

Bartness TJ, Powers JB, Hastings MH, Bittman EL & Goldman BD (1993) The timed infusion paradigm for melatonin delivery: what has it taught us about the melatonin signal, its reception, and the photoperiodic control of seasonal responses. *Journal of Pineal Research* **15**, 161–90

Bartoshuk LM (1993) Distinctions between taste and smell relevant to the role of experience. In ED Capaldi & TL Powley (eds) *Taste, Experience and Feeding: Development and Learning*. Washington DC: American Psychological Association, 62–72

Baroun KA, & Alansari BM (2004) The Impact of Anxiety and Gender on Perceiving the Muller-Layer Illusion Perception. *Journal of Social behavior Personality* **33**(1), 33–42

Bauer R (1984) Automatic recognition of names and faces in prosopagnosia, neurological application. *Neuropsychology* **22**, 457–69

Baumeister AA & Bacharach VR (2000) Early generic educational intervention has no enduring effect on intelligence and does not prevent mental retardation. *Intelligence* **28**, 161–92

Beattie G & Shovelton S (2005) Why the spontaneous images created by the hands during talk can help make TV advertisements more effective. *British Journal of Psychology* **96**, 21–37

Beauchamp GK & Bartoshuk L (1997) *Tasting and Smelling. Handbook of Perception and Cognition*. San Diego CA: Academic Press

Beauchamp GK & Moran M (1982) Dietary experience and sweet taste preferences in human infants. *Appetite* **3**, 139–52

Beck AT (1976) *Cognitive Therapy and the Emotional Disorders*. New York: International Universities Press

Beck AT, Wright FD, Newman CF & Liese BS (2001) *Cognitive Therapy of Substance Abuse*. New York: Guilford Press

Beeman EA (1947) The effect of male hormone on aggressive behaviour in mice. *Physiological Zoology* **20**, 373–405

Behera SK (1989) Gender role biases on Indian television. *Media Asia* **16**(3), 119–24

Bem D (1967) Self-perception: an alternative interpretation of cognitive dissonance phenomena. *Psychological Review* **74**, 183–200

Bem D (1972) Self perception theory. *Advances in Experimental Social Psychology* **1**, 199–218

Bem D & Honorton C (1994) Does psi exist? Replicable evidence for an anomalous process of information transfer. *Psychological Bulletin* **115**, 4–18

Bem SL (1974) The measurement of psychological androgyny. *Journal of Consulting and Clinical Psychology* **42**, 155–62

Bem SL (1981) Gender schema theory: A cognitive account of sex typing. *Psychological Review* **88**, 354–64

Benedetti G (1987) *Psychotherapy of Schizophrenia*. New York: New York University Press

Benjamin J, Ben-Zion-IJ, Karbofski E & Dannon P (2000) Double-blind placebo-controlled pilot study of paroxetine for specific phobia. *Psychopharmacology* **149**, 194–6

Benor DJ (2005) Healing. In J Henry (ed.) *Parapsychology*. London: Routledge

Bentall R, Baker GA & Havers S (1991) Reality monitoring and psychotic hallucinations. *British Journal of Clinical Psychology* **30**, 213–22

Bergin C, Talley S & Hamer B (2003) *Journal of Adolescence* **26**, 13–32

Bernstein B (1971) *Class, Codes and Control, Vol 1*. London: Paladin

Bernstein B (1978) Learned taste aversions in children receiving chemotherapy. *Science* **200**, 1302–03

Best D, Gross S, Manning V, Gossop M, Witton J & Strang J (2005) Cannabis use in adolescents: the impact of risk and protective factors and social functioning. *Drug & Alcohol Review* **24**(6), 483–88

Bettencourt BA & Miller N (1996) Gender differences in aggression as a function of provocation: a meta-analysis. *Psychological Bulletin* **119**(3), 422–47

Bezinová V (1974) Effect of caffeine on sleep: EEG study in late middle age people. *British Journal of Clinical Pharmacology* **1**(3), 203–08

Bhowmick BK (1991) Recurrent near-death experience with post-vagotomy syndrome. *Journal of the Royal Society of Medicine* **84**, 311

Bigler RS (1995) The role of classification skill in moderating environmental influences on children's gender stereotyping: a study of the functional use of gender in the classroom. *Child Development* **66**, 1072–87

Bindon JR & Baker PT (1997) Bergman's rule and the thrifty genotype. *American Journal of Physical Anthropology* **124**, 201–10

Binet A (1905) In T Wolfe (1973) *Alfred Binet*. Chicago: University of Chicago Press

Bion WR (1967) *Second Thoughts*. London: William Heinemann

Birch LL, Gunder L, Grimm-Thomas K and Laing DG (1998) Infants' consumption of a new food enhances acceptance of similar foods. *Appetite* **30**, 283–95

Birch LL, Zimmerman SI and Hind H (1980) The influence of social-affective context on the formation of children's food preferences. *Child Development* **51**, 856–61

Birnholz JC (1981) The development of human fetal eye movement patterns. *Science* **213**, 679–81

Bitterman M & Kniffin C (1953) Manifest anxiety and perceptual defence. *Journal of Abnormal Social Psychology* **48**, 248–52

Bjorklund DF & Shackleford TD (1999) Differences in parental investment contribute to important differences between men and women. *Current Directions in Psychological Science* **8**, 86–89

Bjorntorp P & Rosmond R (2000) Obesity and cortisol. *Nutrition 2000* **16**(10), 924–36

Blackmore S (2005a) Out of body experiences. In J Henry (ed.) *Parapsychology*. London: Routledge

Blackmore S (2005b) Near death experiences. In J Henry (ed.) *Parapsychology*. London: Routledge

Blackmore S (1996) *In Search of the Light: The Adventures of a Parapsychologist*. New York: Prometheus Books

Blackmore S (1997) Probability misjudgement and belief in the paranormal: a newspaper survey. *British Journal of Psychology* **88**, 683–89

Bodamer J (1947) Prosopagnosia, a clinical, psychological and anatomical study of three patients. In *Journal of Neurology, Neurosurgery and Psychiatry* **40**, 395–403 (1977)

Boesche C & Boesche H (1992) Tool use and tool making in wild chimpanzees. *Folia Primatologica* **54**, 86–99

Bond A, Kamil A & Balda R (2003) Social complexity and transitive inference in corvids. *Animal Behaviour* **65**, 479–87

Bonnaire C, Varescon I & Bungener C (2007) Sensation seeking in a French population of horse betting gamblers: comparison between pathological and regular. *Encephale* **33**(5), 798–804

Borg J, Andree B, Soderstrom H & Farde L (2003) The serotonin system and spiritual experiences. *American Journal of Psychiatry* **160**, 1965–69

Bosch H, Steinkamp F & Boller E (2006) Examining psychokinesis: the interaction of human intention and random number generators – a meta-analysis. *Psychological Bulletin* **132**, 497–523

Bouchard T & McGue M (1981) Familial studies of intelligence. A review. *Science* **22**, 1055–59

Bouchard T, Lykken D, McGue M, Segal N & Tellegen A (1990) *Science* **250** (4978), 223

Bower T (1966) The visual world of infants. *Scientific American* **215**, 80–92

Bower T, Broughton J & Moore M (1970) Infant responses to approaching objects: An indicator of response to vistal variables. *Perception and Psychophysics* **9**, 193–96

Bowlby J (1969) *Attachment and Loss. Vol I*. London: Pimlico

Boxer P, Goldstein SE, Musher-Eizenman D, Dubow, E F & Heretick, D (2005) Developmental issues in school-based aggression prevention from a social-cognitive perspective. *Journal of Primary Prevention* **26**, 383–400

Bradfield P & Slocumb P (1997) Student performance in SOI model schools in the Lamar consolidated independent school district, Rosenberg TX. www.newhorizons.org/strategies/styles/tracey.htm. Accessed on 07/01/2009

Bradley SJ, Oliver GD, Chernick AB & Zucker KJ (1998) Experiment of nurture: ablatio penis at 2 months, sex reassignment at 7 months, and a psychosexual follow-up in young adulthood. *Pediatrics* **102**(1), e9

Bradmetz J (1999) Precursors of formal thought: a longitudinal study. *British Journal of Developmental Psychology* **17**, 61–81

Braet C & G Crombez (2001) Cognitive interference due to food cues in childhood obesity. *Journal of Clinical Child and Adolescent Psychology* **32**(1), 32–39

Bray GA (1998) Evolutionary explanations of overeating and overweight. *Appetite* **47**

Bray GA, Nielsen SJ & Popkin BM (2004) Consumption of high-fructose corn syrup in beverages may play a role in the epidemic of obesity. *American Journal of Clinical Nutrition* **79**, 537–43

Brédart S & Schweich M (1995) *Journal of the International Neuropsychological Society* **1**, 589–95

Breland K & Breland M (1961) The misbehaviour of organisms. *American Psychologist* **16**, 681–84

British Association for Behavioural & Cognitive Psychotherapies (BABCP) (2002)

British Psychological Society (2006) *Ethical Principles for Conducting Research with Human Participants: Introduction to the revised principles*. Leicester: BPS

Brobeck JR (1946) *Physiological Reviews* **25**, 541–59

Bronson G (1974) The postnatal growth of visual capacity. *Child Development* **45**, 873–90

Brooks-Gunn J, Klebanov P & Duncan G (1996) Ethnic differences in children's intelligence scores: role of economic deprivation, home environment, and maternal characteristics. *Child Development* **67**, 396–408

Brosnan MJ & Thorpe SJ (2006) An evaluation of two clinically-derived treatments for technophobia. *Computers in Human Behavior* **22**, 1080–95

Brown AS, Schaefer CS, Wyatt RJ & Susser E (2002) Paternal Age and Risk of Schizophrenia in Adult Offspring. *American Journal of Psychiatry* **159**, 1528–33

Brown T, Di Nardo P, Lehman CL & Campbell LA (2001) Reliability of DSM-IV anxiety & mood disorders: implications for the classification of emotional disorders. *Journal of Abnormal Psychology* **110**, 49–58

Brown WJ & Cody MJ (1991) Effects of a prosocial television soap opera in promoting women's status. *Human Communication Research* **18**(1), 114–42

Bruce V & Green PR (1990) *Visual Perception*. Hove and London: Lawrence Erlbaum Associates

Bruce V & Valentine T (1988) When a nod's as good as a wink. The role of dynamic information in facial recognition. In M Gruneberg, P Morris and R Sykes (1988) *Practical Aspects of Memory: Current Research and Issues Vol 1*. Chichester: Wiley

Bruce V & Young A (1986) Understanding face recognition. *British Journal of Psychology* **77**(3), 305–27

Bruner J & Goodman C (1947) *Journal of Abnormal and Social Psychology* **42**, 33–44

Bruner JS (1966) *Towards a Theory of Instruction*. New York: Norton

Bruner JS (1974) *Beyond the Information Given*. London: George Allen & Unwin

Bruner JS & Minturn AL (1955) Perceptual identification and perceptual organization. *Journal of General Psychology* **53**, 21–28

Brunner HG, Nelen M, Breakfield XO, Ropers HH & van Oost BA (1993) Abnormal behaviour associated with a point mutation in the structural gene for monoamine oxidase A. *Science* **262**, 578–80

Brunsdon R, Coltheart M, Nickels L & Joy P (2006) Developmental prosopagnosia: a case analysis and treatment study. *Cognitive Neuropsychology* **23**, 822–40

Bruyer R (1991) Covert face recognition in prosopagnosia. *Brain and Cognition* **15**, 223–35

Bruyer R, Laterre C, Seron X, Feyereisen P, Strypstein E, Pierrard E & Rectem D (1983) A case of prosopagnosia with some covert remembrance of familiar faces. *Brain and Cognition* **2**(3), 257–84

Buddeberg-Fischera B, Richard Klaghofera R, Abelb T & Buddeberga C (2003) The influence of gender and personality traits on the career planning of Swiss medical students. *Swiss Medical Weekly* **133**, 535–40

Buijzen M & Valkenburg PM (2008) Communication in retail environments: a developmental and socialisation perspective. *Human Communication Research* **34**, 50–69

Burchardt CJ & Serbin LA (1982). Psychological androgyny and personality adjustment in college and psychiatric populations. *Sex Roles* **8**, 835–51

Burt C (1955) The evidence for the concept of intelligence. *British Journal of Educational Psychology* **25**, 158–77

Buss D (1989) Sex differences in human mate preferences. *Behavioural & Brain Sciences* **12**, 1–49

Buss DM (1992) Manipulation in close relationships: five personality factors in interactional context. *Journal of Personality* **60**, 477–99

Buss DM, Larsen RJ, Westen D & Semmelroth J (1992) Sex differences in jealousy: evolution, physiology and psychology. *Psychological Science* **3**, 251–55

Bussey K & Bandura A (1984) Influence of gender constancy and social power on sex-linked modeling. *Journal of Personality & Social Psychology* **47**, 1292–1302

Bussey K & Bandura A (1992) Self-regulatory mechanisms governing gender development. *Child Development* **63**, 1236–50

Butler AC, Chapman JE, Forman EM & Beck AT (2006) The empirical status of cognitive-behavioral therapy: a review of meta-analyses. *Clinical Psychology Review* **26**, 17–31

Button TM, Rhee SH, Hewitt JK, Young SE, Corley RP & Stallings MC (2007) The role of conduct disorder in explaining the comorbidity between alcohol and illicit drug dependence in adolescence. *Drug & Alcohol Dependence* **87**(1), 46–53

Byrne R (1995) *The Thinking Ape. Evolutionary Elements of Intelligence*. Oxford: Oxford University Press

Cadoret RJ, Yates WR, Troughton E, Woodworth G & Stewart MA (1995) Genetic–environmental interaction in the genesis of aggressivity and conduct disorders. *Archives of General Psychiatry* **52**, 916–24

Calvert S and Kotler J (2003) Lessons from children's television: the impact of the Children's Television Act on children's learning. *Journal of Applied Developmental Psychology* **24**, 275–335

Calvert SL, Kotler JA, Zehnder SM & Shockey EM (2003) Gender stereotyping in children's reports about educational and informational television programs. *Media Psychology* **5**, 139–62

Camchong J, Goodie AS, McDowell JE, Gilmore CS & Clementz BA (2007) A cognitive neuroscience approach to studying the role of overconfidence in problem gambling. *Journal of Gambling Studies* **23**(2), 185–99

Campbell A, Shirley L, Heywood C & Crook C (2000) Infants' visual preference for sex-congruent babies, children, toys and activities: a longitudinal study. *British Journal of Developmental Psychology* **18**, 479–98

Campbell R, Brooks B, de Haan E & Roberts T (1996) Dissociating face processing skills: decision about lip-read speech, expression, and identity. *Quarterly Journal of Experimental Psychology* **49A**, 295–314

Campbell SS (1995) Effects of timed bright-light exposure on shift-work adaptation in middle-aged subjects. *Sleep* **18**, 408–16

Campos JJ, Langer A & Krowitz A (1970) Cardiac responses on the visual cliff in prelocomotor human infants. *Science* **170**(954), 196–97

Capaldi ED (1996) Conditioned food preferences. In ED Capaldi (ed.) *Why We Eat What We Eat: The Psychology of Eating*. Washington DC: American Psychological Association, 53–80

Capron C & Duyme M (1989) Assessment of effects of socioeconomic status on IQ in a full cross-fostering study. *Nature* **340**(6234), 552–53

Carroll KM, Ball SA, Martino S, Nich C, Babuscio TA, Nuro KF, Gordon MA, Portnoy GA & Rounsaville BJ (2008) Computer-assisted delivery of cognitive-behavioral therapy for addiction: a randomized trial of CBT4CBT. *American Journal of Psychiatry* **165**(7), 881–88

Case R (1985) *Intellectual from Birth to Adulthood*. New York: Academic Press

Cattell R (1963) Theory of fluid and crystallized intelligence: a critical experiment. *Journal of Experimental Psychology* **54**, 1–22

Cattell R (1997) An open letter to the American Psychological Association

Caughey JL (1994) Gina as Steven: the social and cultural dimensions of a media relationship. *Visual Anthropology* **10**, 126–35

CDCP (1994) Suicide contagion and the reporting of suicide: Recommendations from a national workshop. *Morbidity and Mortality Weekly* **43**, 9–18

Celec P, Ostatnikova D, Putz Z & Kudela M (2002) The circalunar cycle of salivary testosterone and the visual-spatial performance. *Bratislavské lekárske listy* **103**(2), 59–69

Ceulemans M & Fauconnier G (1979) *Mass Media: The Image, Role and Social Conditions of Women*. Paris: UNESCO

Champion L & Power M (2000) *Adult Psychological Problems*. Hove: Taylor & Francis

Chan K & Zhang C (2007) Living in a celebrity-mediated social world: the Chinese experience. *Young Consumers* **8**, 139–52

Charlton T & O'Bey S (1997) Links between television and behaviour: students' perceptions of TV's impact in St Helena, South Atlantic. *Support for Learning* **12**(3), 130–36

Charlton T, Gunter B & Hannan (2000) *Broadcast Television Effects in a Remote Community*. Mahwah NJ: Lawrence Erlbaum Associates

Charlton T, Panting C, Davie R, Coles D & Whitmarsh L (2000) Children's playground behaviour across five years of broadcast television: a naturalistic study in a remote community. *Emotional & Behavioural Difficulties* **5**, 4–12

Chemelli RM, Willie JT, Sinton CM, Elmquist JK, Scammell T, Lee C, Richardson JA, Williams SC, Xiong Y, Kisanuki Y, Fitch TE, Nakazato M, Hammer RE, Saper CB & Yanagisawa M (1999) Narcolepsy in orexin knockout mice: molecular genetics of sleep regulation. *Cell* **98**(4), 437–51

Chen C, Rainnie DG, Greene RW & Tonegawa S (1994) Abnormal fear response and aggressive behaviour in mutant mice deficient for alpha-calcium-calmodulin kinase II. *Science* **266**, 291–94

Cheney DL & Seyfarth RM (1988) Assessment of meaning and the detection of unreliable signals in Vervet monkeys. *Animal Behaviour* **36**, 477–86

Chi M (1978) Knowledge, structures and memory development. In RS Siegler (ed.) *Children's Thinking: What Develops?* Hillsdale NJ: Lawrence Erlbaum Associates, 73–96

Chien SH-L & Bronson-Castai KW (2003) Lightness constancy in four month old infants. *Vision Research* **46**(13), 2139–48

Chien S H-L, Palmer J & Teller DY (2006) Achromatic contrast effects in infants: adults and 4-month-old infants show similar deviations from Wallach's ratio rule. *Vision Research* **45**(22), 2854–61

Chrisler JC (1997) Adherence to weightloss and nutritional regimens. In DS Gochman (ed.) *Handbook of Health Behavior Research, Vol. 2: Provider Determinants*. New York: Plenum Press, 323–33

Christensen A, Atkins DC, Berns S, Wheeler J, Baucom DH & Simpson LE (2004) Traditional versus integrative behavioral couple therapy for significantly and chronically distressed married couples. *Journal of Consulting and Clinical Psychology* **72**, 176–91

Christopher AB (1988) *Predisposition versus experiential models of compulsive gambling: an experimental analysis using pigeons*. Unpublished PhD thesis, West Virginia University, Morgantown

Clancy SA, McNally RJ, Pitman RK, Schachter DL & Lenzenweger M (2002) Memory distortion in people reporting abduction by aliens. *Journal of Abnormal Psychology* **111**, 455–61

Cline VB, Croft RG & Courrier S (1973). Desensitization of children to television violence. *Journal of Personality and Social Psychology* **27**, 360–65

Cloninger CR, Sullivan S, Przybeck TR, Klein S (2007) Personality characteristics in obesity and relationship with successful weight loss. *Int J Obes* **31**, 667–74

Cohen W (1957) Uniform optic array. *American Journal of Psychology* **70**, 403–410

Cohen-Bendahan CC, van de Beek C & Berebaum SA (2005) Prenatal sex hormone effects on child and adult sex-typed behavior: methods and findings. *Neuroscience & Biobehavioral Reviews* **29**(2), 353–84

Cohen-Kettenis PT, van Goozen SH, Doorn CD & Gooren LJ (1998) Cognitive ability and cerebral lateralisation in transsexuals. *Psychoneuroendocrinology* **23**(6), 631–41

Coleman DL (1973) Effects of parabiosis of obese with diabetes and normal mice. *Diabetologia* **9**(4), 294–8

Collins J (1998) Seven kinds of smart. *Time* **152**(16), 94–97

Conner DB & Cross DR (2003) Longitudinal analysis of the presence, efficacy and stability of maternal scaffolding during informal problem-solving interactions. *British Journal of Developmental Psychology* **21**, 315–34

Cook EP (1985) *Psychological Androgyny.* New York: Pergamon Press

Cooper J (1982) Cottingley: the truth at last. *The Unexplained* **117**, 2338–40

Cordua GD, McGraw KO & Drabman RS (1979) Doctor or nurse: children's perception of sex-typed occupations. *Child Development* **50**(2), 590–93

Cosmides L & Tooby J (1997) *Evolutionary Psychology: A Primer*

Courage ML & Adams RJ (1996) Infant peripheral vision: the development of monocular visual acuity in the first three months of post-natal life. *Vision Research* **36**, 1207–15

Courtois R, Caudrelier N, Legay E, Lalande G, Halimi A & Jonas C (2007) Influence of parental tobacco dependence and parenting styles on adolescents' tobacco use. *Presse Médicale* **36**(10 Pt 1), 1341–49

Cowart BJ (1981) Development of taste perception in humans: sensitivity and preference throughout the life span. *Psychological Bulletin* **90**, 43–73

Cox MV (1992) Children's drawings of the human figure. *Child Development* **67**(6), 2743–62

Cronce JM, Corbin WR, Steinberg MA & Potenza MN (2007) Self-perception of gambling problems among adolescents identified as at-risk or problem gamblers. *Journal of Gambling Studies* **23**(4), 363–75

Cserjesi R, Molnar D, Luminet O & Lenard L (2007) Is there any relationship between obesity and mental flexibility in children? *Appetite* **49**(3), 675–78

Cuelbras A & Moore JT (1989) Magnetic resonance findings in REM sleep behaviour disorder. *Neurology* **39**, 1519–23

Cummings DE, Weigle DS, Frayo RS, Breen PA, Ma MK, Dellinger P, Purnell JQ (2002) Plasma ghrelin levels after diet-induced weight loss or gastric bypass surgery. *New English Journal of Medicine* **346**(21), 1623–30

Custer RL (1984) Profile of the pathological gambler. *Journal of Clinical Psychology* **45**, 35–38

Czeisler CA, Johnson MP, Duffy JF, Brown EN, Ronda JM & Kronauer RE (1990) Exposure to bright light and darkness to treat physiologic maladaptation to night work. *New England Journal of Medicine* **322**(18), 1253–59

Dabbs JM Jr & Hargrove MF (1997) Age, testosterone, and behavior among female prison inmates. *Psychosomatic Medicine* **59**(5), 477–80

Dabbs JM Jr, Bernieri FJ, Strong RK, Campo R & Milun R (2001) Going on stage: testosterone in greetings and meetings. *Journal of Research in Personality* **35**(1), 27–40

Dabbs JM Jr, Carr TS, Frady RL & Riad JK (1995) Testosterone, crime and misbehaviour among 692 male prison inmates. *Personality & Individual Differences* **18**, 627–33

Dailey M & Cottrell G (1999) Organization of face and object recognition in modular neural network models. *Neural Networks* **12**, 1053–73

Daly M & Wilson M (1988) *Homicide*. New York: Aldine de Gruyter

Daly M & Wilson M (1992) The man who mistook his wife for a chattel. In JH Barkow, L Cosmides & J Tooby (eds) *The Adapted Mind*. New York: Oxford University Press

Daly M & Wilson M (1994) Evolutionary psychology of male violence. In J Archer (ed.) *Male Violence*. London: Routledge

Daly M, Wilson M & Wehorst SJ (1982) Male sexual jealousy. *Ethology & Sociobiology* **3**, 11–27

D'Anci K, Taylor H & Kanarek R (2008) Low carbohydrate weight loss diets: effects on cognition and mood. *Appetite* **52**(1), 96–103

Dannemiller J & Hanko S (1987) A test of colour constancy in four month old infants. *Journal of Experimental Child Psychology* **44**(2), 255–67

Davidenko N (2007) Silhouetted face profiles: a new methodology for face perception research. *Journal of Vision* **7**(4), 6, 1–17. http://journalofvision.org/7/4/6/, doi:10.1167/7.4.6

Davis C (1939) Results of the self-selection diets of young children. *Canadian Medical Association Journal* **41**, 257–61

De Araujo IE, Oliveira-Maia AJ, Sotnikoa TD, Gainetdinov RR, Caron MG, Nicolelis MG & Simon SA (2008) No such thing as a sweet tooth. *Neuron* **57**

de Castro, JM (1991) Social facilitation of the spontaneous meal size of humans occurs on both weekdays and weekends. *Physiology and Behavior* **49**, 1289–91

Decety J & Keenan JP (2006) Introducing social neuroscience. *Social Neuroscience* **1**, 1–4

De Haan E & Campbell R (1991) A fifteen year follow up of a case of developmental prosopagnosia. *Cortex* **27**, 489–509

Demas GE, Kriegsfeld LJ, Blackshaw S, Huang P, Gammie SC, Nelson RJ & Snyder SH (1999) Elimination of aggressive behavior in male mice lacking endothelial nitric oxide synthase. *Journal of Neuroscience* **19**, RC30

Dement W & Kleitman N (1957) The relation of eye movements during sleep to dream activity: an objective method for the study of dreaming. *Journal of Experimental Psychology* **53**, 339–46

Dement WC (1960) The effect of dream deprivation. *Science* **15**, 1705–07

Dement WC (1965) Studies on the function of rapid eye movement (paradoxical) sleep in human subjects. In M Jouvet (ed.) *Aspects anatomo-fonctionnels de la physiologie du sommeil*. Paris: Editions du Centre Nationale de la Recherche Scientifique

De Munck VC (1996) Love and marriage in a Sri Lankan Moslem community: towards an evaluation of Dravidian marriage. *American Ethologist* **23**, 698–716

De Munck VC & Korotayev AV (2007) Wife husband intimacy and female status in cross-cultural perspective. *Cross-cultural Research* **41**, 307–35

Depatie L & Lal SL (2001) Apomorphine and the dopamine hypothesis of schizophrenia: a dilemma? *Journal of Psychiatry & Neuroscience* **26**, 203–220

Deregowski JB (1972) Pictorial perception and culture. *Scientific American* **227**, 82–88

de Silva P & Rachman S (1987) Human food aversions: nature and acquisition. *Behavior, Research and Therapy* **25**, 457–68

Deary IJ & Tait R (1987) Effects of sleep disruption on cognitive performance and mood in medical house officers. *British Medical Journal* **295**, 1513–1516

Desor JA, Maller O, Turner RE (1973) Taste in acceptance of sugars by human infants. *J Comp Physiol Psychol* **84**, 496–501

Devlin M & Yanovski N (1995) Role of behavioural therapy in the management of obesity. *Endocrine Practice* **1**(5), 340–45

Diamond LM (2002) Having a girlfriend without knowing it: intimate friendships among adolescent sexual minority women. In SM Rose (ed.) *Lesbian Love and Relationships*. Binghampton: Harrington Park Press

Diamond M & Sigmundson K (1997) Sex reassignment at birth: a long term review and clinical implications. *Archives of Pediatrics & Adolescent Medicine* **151**(3)

Diamond R & Carey S (1986) Why faces are not special: an effect of expertise. *Journal of Experimental Psychology General* **115**, 107–17

Dielman TE, Butchart AT, Shope JT & Miller M (1991) Environmental correlates of adolescent substance use and misuse: implications for prevention programs. *International Journal of the Addictions* **25**(7A–8A), 855–80

Diener E (1980) Deindividuation: the absence of self-awareness and self-regulation in group members. In PB Paulus (ed.) *The Psychology of Group Influence*. Hillsdale NJ: Lawrence Erlbaum Associates

Diener E, Suh EM, Lucas RE & Smith HE (1999) Subjective well-being: three decades of progress. In Paulus PB (ed.) *Psychology of Group Influence.* Hillsdale NJ: Lawrence Erlbaum Associates

DiMeglio DP & Mates RD (2000) Liquid versus solid carbohydrate. *International Journal of Obesity and Related Metabolic Disorders* **24**, 794–800

Donaldson M (1978) *Children's Minds*. London: Fontana

Doughty DD, Baer L, Rees Cosgrove G, Cassem EH, Price BH, Nierenberg AA, Jenike MA & Rauch SL (2002) Prospective long-term follow-up of 44 patients who received cingulotomy for treatment-refractory obsessive-compulsive disorder. *American Journal of Psychiatry* **159**, 269–77

Drabman RS & Thomas MH (1974). Does media violence increase children's tolerance for real-life aggression? *Developmental Psychology* **10**, 418–21

Drigotas SM & Rusbult CE (1992). Should I stay or should I go?: a dependence model of breakups. *Journal of Personality & Social Psychology* **62**, 62–87

Dudley R (2008) Ants prefer salt over sugar. *Proceedings of the National Academy of Sciences*, Dec

Duff DC, Levine TR, Beatty M, Woolbright J & Park HS (2007) Testing public anxiety treatments against a credible placebo control. *Communication Education* **56**, 72–88

Dugatkin l (2000) *The Imitation Factor: Beyond the Gene*. New York: Free Press

Dunbar R (1992) Neocortex size constraint on group size in primates. *Journal of Human Evolution* **20**, 469–93

Dunbar R, Barrett L & Lycett J (2005) *Evolutionary Psychology, A Beginner's Guide*. Oxford: One World Books

Dunn D (1999) Eating without killing, http://www.wordwiz72.com/veg.html. Accessed on 16/12/08

Durkin K (1995) *Developmental social psychology*. Melbourne, Blackwell

Dutch S (2006) *Science and Pseudoscience.* Madison WI: University of Wisconsin Press

Ehmer B, Reeve H & Hoy R (2001) Comparison of brain volumes between single and multiple foundresses in the paper wasp *Polistes dominulus*. *Brain, Behavior and Evolution* **57**(3), 161–68

Eisen SA, Slutske WS, Lyons MJ, Lassman J, Xian H, Toomey R, Chantarujikapong S & Tsuang MT (2001) The genetics of pathological gambling. *Seminars in Clinical Neuropsychiatry* **6**(3), 195–204

Eisenberg N (1986) *Altruistic Emotion: Cognition and Behaviour*. Hillsdale New Jersy: Lawrence Erlbaum Associates

Ellis H, Shepherd J & Davies G (1979) Identification of familiar and unfamiliar faces from internal and external features. Some implications for theories of face recognition. *Perception* **8**, 431–39

Elton PJ & Campbell P (2008) Smoking prevalence in a north-west town following the introduction of smoke-free England. *Journal of Public Health* **30**(4), 415–20

Ember CR & Levinson D (1991) The substantive contributions of worldwide cross-cultural studies using secondary data. *Behavior Science Research* **25**, 79–140

Empson J (1993) *Sleep and Dreaming*. Hemel Hempstead: Harvester Wheatsheaf

Engell D, Bordi P, Borja M, Lambert C and Rolls B (1998) Effects of information about fat content on food preferences in pre-adolescent children. *Appetite* **30**, 269–82

Epel E, Lapidus R, McEwan B & Brownell K (2001) Stress may add bite to appetite in women: a laboratory study of stress-induced cortisol and eating behaviour. *Psychoneuroendocrinology* **26**(1), 37–49

Epstein R, Lanza R & Skinner B (1981) Self-awareness in the pigeon. *Science* **212**, 695–96

Eranti S, Mogg A, Pluck G, Landau S, Purvis R, Brown RG, Howard R & Knapp M (2007) A randomized, controlled trial with 6-month follow-up of repetitive transcranial magnetic stimulation and electroconvulsive therapy for severe depression. *American Journal of Psychiatry* **164**, 73–81

Eron LD & Huesmann LR (1986) The role of television in the development of antisocial and prosocial behavior. In D Olweus, J Block & M Radke-Yarrom (eds) *Development of Antisocial and Prosocial Behaviour, Theories and Issues.* New York: Academic Press

Eron LD, Huesmann LR, Leftowitz MM & Walder LO (1972) Does television violence cause aggression? *American Psychologist* **27**, 253–63

Espie CA, Broomfield NM, MacMahon KM, Macphee LM & Taylor LM (2006) The attention-intention-effort pathway in the development of psychophysiologic insomnia: a theoretical review. *Sleep Medicine Reviews* **10**(4), 215–45

Evans L & Davies K (2000) No sissy boys here: a content analysis of the representation of masculinity in elementary school reading books. *Sex Roles* **42**, 255–70

Evans R & Rowe M (2002) For club and country: taking football disorder abroad. *Soccer & Society* **3**, 37–53

Eysenck MW (1992) *Anxiety*. Hove: Psychology Press

Eysenck MW & Keane MT (1990) *Cognitive Psychology*. Hove, East Sussex: Lawrence Erlbaum Associates

Fagot BI & Leinbach MD (1989) The young child's gender schema: environmental input, internal organization. *Child Development* **60**(3), 663–72

Fantz R (1961) The origin of form perception. *Scientific American* **204**(5), 66–72

Feigin R & Sapir Y (2005) The relationship between sense of coherence and attribution of responsibility for problems and their solutions, and cessation of substance abuse over time. *Journal of Psychoactive Drugs* **37**(1), 63–73

Feinberg I, Braun M & Koresko RL (1969) Vertical eye-movement during REM sleep: effects of age and electrode placement. *Psychophysiology* **5**(5), 556–61

Feingold A (1988) Matching for attractiveness in romantic partners and same-sex friends: a meta-analysis and theoretical critique. *Psychological Bulletin* **104**, 226–35

Felliti VJ (2001) Sleep-eating and the dynamics of morbid obesity, weight loss, and regain of weight in five patients. *Permanente Journal* **5**(2)

Fessler DMT (2003) An evolutionary explanation of the plasticity of salt preferences: prophylaxis versus dehydration. *Medical Hypotheses* **63**(3), 412–15

Festinger L (1952) Some consequences of deindividuation in a group. *Journal of Abnormal and Social Psychology* **47**, 382–389

Festinger L, Pepitone A & Newcombe T (1952) Some consequences of deindividuation in a group. *Journal of Abnormal Psychology* **47**, 382–9

Festinger L (1954) A theory of social comparison processes. *Human Relations* **1**, 117–40

Festinger L & Carlsmith JM (1959) Cognitive consequences of forced compliance. *Journal of Abnormal & Social Psychology* **58**, 203–10

Fieldman NP, Woolfolk RL & Allen LA (1995) Dimensions of self-concept: a comparison of heroin and cocaine addicts. *American Journal of Drug & Alcohol Abuse* **21**(3), 315–26

Finch CE & Stanford CB (2004) *Quarterly Review of Biology* **79**, 3–50

Fiore AT & Donath JS (2004) *Online Personals: an Overview.* CHI 24–29 April, Vienna

Fiore AT & Donath JS (2005) *Homophily in Online Dating: Do You Like Someone Like Yourself?* CHI np. 2–7 April, Portland

Fisher J & Hinde R (1949) The opening of milk bottles by birds. *British Birds* **42**, 347–57

Fichter MM & Pirke KM (1986) Effects of experimental and pathological weight loss on the hypothalamo-pituitaryadrenal axis. *Psychoneuroendocrinology* **11**, 295–305

Flapan, D (1968) *Children's Understanding of Social Interaction*. New York: Teachers College Press

Floyd K, Whelan JP & Meyers AW (2006) Use of warning messages to modify gambling beliefs and behavior in a laboratory investigation. *Psychology of Addictive Behaviors* **20**(1), 69–74

Foley RA & Lee PC (1991) Ecology and energetics of encephalization in hominid evolution. *Philosophical Transactions of the Royal Society of London* **B334**, 223–32

Folkard S (1996). Biological disruption in shiftworkers. In WP Colquhoun, G Costa, S Folkard & P Knauth (eds) (1996) *Shiftwork: Problems and Solutions*. Frankfurt am Main: Peter Lang

Foster GD (2006) Clinical implications for the treatment of obesity. *Obesity Research* **14**, S182–85

Freeman MA, Hennessey EV & Marzullo DM (2001). Defensive evaluation of antismoking messages among college-age smokers: the role of possible selves. *Health-Psychology* **20**, 424–33

Freud S (1917) *Mourning and Melancholia. Collected Works, Vol 14*. London: Hogarth

Freud S (1921) *The Psychology of Day-dreams*. London: Standard Edition 18, 271

Frey KS & Ruble DN (1992) Gender constancy and the 'cost' of sex-typed behavior: a test of the conflict hypothesis. *Developmental Psychology* **28**(4), 714–21

Friedman AS, Terras A, Zhu W & McCallum J (2004) Depression, negative self-image, and suicidal attempts as effects of substance use and substance dependence. *Journal of Addiction Disorders* **23**(4), 55–71

Friedman CK, Leaper C & Bigler RS (2007) Do mothers' gender-related attitudes or comments predict young children's gender beliefs? *Parenting* **7**(4), 357–66

Friedman J (2005) Wired to eat. *MIT Technology Review*

Friedman JM, Proenca R, Maffei M, Barone M, Leopold L & Zhang Y (1994) Positional cloning of the mouse obese gene and its human homologue. *Nature* **372**(6505), 425–32

Frith CD (1992) *The Cognitive Neuropsychology of Schizophrenia*. Hove: Psychology Press

Fromm-Reichmann F (1948) Notes on the development of treatment of schizophrenics by psychoanalytic psychotherapy. *Psychiatry* **11**, 263–73

Frueh T & McGhee PE (1975) Traditional sex-role development and amount of time spent watching television. *Developmental Psychology* **11**, 109

Gale C (2002) IQ in childhood and vegetarianism in adulthood: 1970 British cohort study. *British Journal of Medicine* **334**(7587), 245

Galef B Jr (1992) The question of animal culture. *Human Nature* **3**, 157–78

Gallese V & Goldman A (1998) Mirror neurons and the simulation theory of mind-reading. *Trends in Cognitive Science* **2**, 493–501

Gallup G (1971) Chimpanzees: self recognition. *Science* **167**, 86–87

Galynker II, Watras-Ganz S, Miner C, Rosenthal RN, Des Jarlais DC, Richman BL & London E (2000) Cerebral metabolism in opiate-dependent subjects: effects of methadone maintenance. *Mount Sinai Journal of Medicine* **67**(5–6), 381–87

Gammie SC, Huang PL, Nelson RJ (2000) Maternal aggression in endothelial nitric oxide synthase-deficient mice. *Hormones & Behavior* **38**(1), 13–20

Garcia J & Koelling R (1966) Relation of cue to consequences in avoidance learning. *Psychonomic Science* **4**, 123–24

Garcia J, Ervin FR, & Koelling RA (1966) Learning with prolonged delay of reinforcement. *Psychonomic Science* **5**, 121–22

Garcia J, Rusiniak K & Brett W (1977) Conditioning food illness in wild animals: caveant canonici. In H Davis & HMB Hurwitz (eds) *Operant-Pavlovian Interactions*. Hillsdale NJ: Lawrence Erlbaum Associates, 273–316

Garcia-Falgueras A & Swaab DF (2008) A sex difference in the hypothalamic uncinate nucleus: relationship to gender identity. *Brain* **131**(12), 3132–46

Gardner H (1983) *Frames of Mind. The Theory of Multiple Intelligences*. New York: Basic Books

Gauld A (2005) Survival. In J Henry (ed.) *Parapsychology*. London: Routledge

Gauthier I, Tarr M, Anderson A, Skudlarski P & Gore J (1999) Activation of the middle fusiform 'face area' increases with expertise in recognising novel objects. *Nature Neuroscience* **2**, 568–73

Gauthier IT, Moylan J, Skudlarski P, Gore J & Anderson A (2000) The fusiform 'face area' is part of a network that processes faces at the individual level. *Journal of Cognitive Neuroscience* **12**(3), 495–504

Gaver W (1996) Affordances for interaction: the social is material for design. *Ecological Psychology* **8**(2), 111–30

Gazzola V (2007) The anthropomorphic brain: the mirror neuron system responds to human and robotic actions. *Neuroimage* **35**, 1674–84

Geary DC (1998) *Male, female: the evolution of human sex differences*. Washington DC: American Psychological Association

Giarelli E, Ledbetter N, Mahon S & McElwain D (2004) 'Not Lighting Up': a case study of a woman who quit smoking. *Oncology Nursing Forum* **31**(3), E54

Gibson EJ & Walk RD (1960) The visual cliff. *Scientific American* **202**, 64–71

Gibson J (1950) Diagram of the optic flow. *Perception of the Visual World*. Boston: Houghton-Mifflin

Gibson J (1977) Theory of affordances. In Shaw & Brandsford (eds) *Perceiving, Acting and Knowing. Toward an Ecological Psychology*. Hillsdale NJ: Lawrence Erlbaum Associates, 67–82

Gibson J (1979) *The Ecological Approach to Visual Perception*. Hove: Psychology Press

Gibson J (1987) Cognition, brain size and the extraction of embedded food resources. In J Else & P Lee (eds) *Primate Ontogeny, Cognition and Social Behaviour*. Cambridge: Cambridge University Press

Gibson JJ & Bridgeman B (1987) The visual perception of surface texture in photos. *Psychological Research* **49**(1), 1–5

Gilligan C (1977) In a different voice: women's conceptions of self and morality. *Harvard Educational Review* **47**, 481–517

Gilligan C (1982) *In a Different Voice: Psychological Theory and Women's Development*. Cambridge MA: Harvard University Press

Glenberg AM, Brown M & Levin JR (2006) Enhancing comprehension in small reading groups using a manipulation strategy. *Contemporary Educational Psychology* **32**, 389–99

Go Y, Satta Y, Takenaka O and Takahata N (2005) Lineage-specific loss of function of bitter taste receptor genes in humans and nonhuman primates genetics, Vol. 170, 313-326, Copyright © 2005doi:10.1534/genetics.104.037523

Goddard E (2006) *Smoking and Drinking among Adults*. Cardiff: Office for National Statistics

Goldberg SR, Spealman RD & Goldberg DM (1981) Persistent behavior at high rates maintained by intravenous self-administration of nicotine. *Science* **214**, 573–75

Golombok S & Fivush R (1994) *Gender Development*. Cambridge: Cambridge University Press

Goodie AS (2005) The role of perceived control and overconfidence in pathological gambling. *Journal of Gambling Studies* **21**(4), 481–502

Goodwin R (2005) Why I study relationships. *The Psychologist* **18**, 614–15

Gorini G, Chellini E & Galeone D (2007) What happened in Italy? A brief summary of studies conducted in Italy to evaluate the impact of the smoking ban. *Annals of Oncology* **18**(10), 1620–22

Gosso F, De Geus M, Polderman T, Boomsma D, Posthuma D & Heutink P (2007) Exploring the functional role of the CHRM2 gene in human cognition: results from a dense genotyping and brain expression study. *BMC Medical Genetics* **8**, 66

Gottdiener WH (2006) Individual psychodynamic psychotherapy of schizophrenia: empirical evidence for the practising physician. *Psychoanalytic Psychology* **23**, 583–89

Gottdiener WH & Haslam N (2002) A critique of the methods and conclusions in the Patient Outcome Research Team (PORT) report on psychological treatments for schizophrenia. *Journal of the American Academy of Psychoanalysis & Dynamic Psychiatry* **31**, 191–208

Gottesman I (1963) Genetic aspects of intelligent behaviour. In N Ellis (ed.) *Handbook of Mental Deficiency. Psychological Theory and Research*. New York: McGraw-Hill

Gottesman I (1991) *Schizophrenia Genesis: The Origins of Madness*. New York: Freeman

Gottfredson LS (2003) Dissecting practical intelligence in theory: its claims and its evidence. *Intelligence* **31**, 343–97

Goudsblom J (1992) *Fire and Civilization*. London: Allen Lane

Gould S (1994) Curveball. *The New Yorker* http://www.prospect. org/archives/20/20gard.html. Accessed on 10/01/2009

Gountas J & Gountas S (2007). *Materialism and the Desire for Fame*. Egham: Academy of Marketing

Granrud CE (2006) Size constancy in infants. *Journal of Experimental Psychology* **32**(6), 1309–1404

Grant JE & Kim SW (2006) Medication management of pathological gambling. *Minnesota Medicine* **89**(9), 44–48

Grant JE, Potenza MN, Hollander E, Cunningham-Williams R, Numinen T, Smits G & Kallio A (2006) A multicenter investigation of the opioid antagonist nalmefene in the treatment of pathological gambling. *American Journal of Psychiatry* **163**(12), 303–312

Grant S, London ED, Newlin DB, Villemange VL, Lui X, Contoreggi C, Phillips RL, Kimes AS & Margolin A (1996) Activation of memory circuits during cue-elicited cocaine craving. *Proceedings of the National Academy of Sciences, USA* **93**, 12040–45

Greenberg JL, Lewis SE & Dodd DK (1999) Overlapping addictions and self-esteem among college men and women. *Addictive Behavior* **24**(4), 565–71

Greene LS, Desor JA & Maller O (1975) Heredity and experience: their relative importance in the development of the taste preference in man. *Journal of Comparative & Physiological Psychology* **89**, 279–84

Gregor A & McPherson D (1965) A study of susceptibility to geometric illusions among cultural outgroups of Australian aborigines. *Psychologist Africano* **11**, 1–11

Gregory R (1966) *Eye and Brain*. London: Weidenfield & Nicolson

Gregory R & Wallace J (1963) *Recovery from Early Blindness*. Cambridge: Heffer

Griskevicius V, Cialdini R & Kenrick DT (2006) Peacocks, Picasso and parental investment: the effects of romantic motives on creativity. *Journal of Personality & Social Psychology* **91**, 63–76

Groblewski TA, Nunez A & Gold RM (1980) Quoted in Carlson NR (1996) *Physiology of Behavior*. Boston: Allyn & Bacon

Gross R (1992) *Psychology – the Science of Mind and Behaviour*. London: Hodder & Stoughton

Guilford J (1950) Creativity. *American Psychologist* **5**, 444–54

Guilford J (1967) *The Nature of Human Intelligence*. New York: McGraw Hill

Gulevich G, Dement WC & Johnson L (1966) Psychiatric and EEG observations on a case of prolonged (264 hours) wakefulness. *Archives of General Psychiatry* **15**, 29–35

Hacker K, Collins J, Gross-Young L, Almeida S & Burke N (2008) Coping with youth suicide and overdose. *Crisis* **29**, 86–95

Hafeez ZH & Kalinowski CM (2007) Somnambulism induced by Quetiapine: two case reports and a review of the literature. *CNS Spectrums* **12**(12), 910–12

Hagell A & Newbury T (1994) *Young offenders and the media*. London: Policy Studies Institute

Hainline L (1998). In A Slater (ed.) *The Development of Basic Visual Abilities*. Hove: Psychology Press

Hall SM, Reus VI, Mu–oz RF, Sees KL, Humfleet G, Hartz DT, Frederick S & Triffleman E (1998) Nortriptyline and cognitive-behavioral therapy in the treatment of smoking. *Archives of General Psychiatry* **55**, 683–90

Hammad TA (2007) Benefits of anti-depressants outweigh risks of suicidal ideation and attempts in children and adolescents. *Evidence-based Mental Health* **10**, 108

Hammen C (1997) *Depression*. Hove: Psychology Press

Handscomb L (2006) Use of bedside sound generators by patients with tinnitus-related sleeping difficulty: which sounds are preferred and why? *Acta-Otolaryngologica Supplementum* **556**, 59–63

Haney C, Banks C & Zimbardo P (1973) Interpersonal dynamics in a simulated prison. *International Journal of Criminology & Penology* **1**, 69–97

Haninger K & Thompson KM (2004) Content and ratings of teen-rated video games. *Journal of the American Medical Association* **291**, 856–65

Haraldsson E & Houtkooper JM (1992) The effects of perceptual defensiveness, personality and belief on extrasensory perception tasks. *Personality & Individual Differences* **13**, 1085–96

Hardeman W, Griffin S, Johnston M, Kinmonth AL & Wareham NJ (2000) Interventions to prevent weight gain: a systematic review of psychological models and behaviour change methods. *International Journal of Obesity* **24**, 131–43

Hare L, Bernard P, Sánchez FJ, Baird PN, Vilain E, Kennedy T & Harley VR (2009) Androgen receptor repeat length polymorphism associated with male-to-female transsexualism. *Biological Psychiatry* **65**(1), 93–96

Harma M, Laitinen J, Partinen M & Suvanto S (1994a) The effect of four-day round trip flights over 10 time zones on the circadian variation of salivary melatonin and cortisol in airline flight attendants. *Ergonomics* **37**(9), 1479–89

Harma M, Suvanto S & Partinen M (1994b) The effect of four-day round trip flights over 10 time zones on the sleep-wakefulness of airline flight attendants. *Ergonomics* **37**(9), 1462–78

Harrell R, Woodyard E & Gates A (1955) *The Effects of Mothers' Diets*. Teachers College: Columbia University

Harris G, Tomas A & Booth DA (1990) Development of salt taste in infancy. *Developmental Psychology* **26**, 334–38

Hatcher PJ, Hulme C, Miles JNV, Carroll JM, Hatcher J, Gibbs S (2006). Efficacy of small group reading intervention for beginning readers with reading-delay: A randomized controlled trial. *Journal of Child Psychology and Psychiatry* **47**, 820–27

Hatgis C, Friedmann PD & Wiener M (2008) Attributions of responsibility for addiction: the effects of gender and type of substance. *Substance Use and Misuse* **43**(5), 700–08

Hayford KE, Patten CA, Rummans TA, Schroeder DR, Offord KP, Croghan IT, Glover ED, Sachs DP & Hurt RD (1999) Efficacy of bupropion for smoking cessation in smokers with a former history of major depression or alcoholism. *British Journal of Psychiatry* **174**, 173–8

Haynes E & Rich N (2002) Obsessed fans! *YM* [Your Magazine] **50**, 196–9

Hazan C & Shaver P (1987) Romantic love conceptualised as an attachment process. *Journal of Personality & Social Psychology* **52**, 511–24

Health Survey for England Obesity data. December 2008

Heather N (1976) *Radical Perspectives in Psychology*. London: Methuen

Heber R, Garber H, Harrington S, Hoffman C, & Falender C (1972) *Rehabilitation of Families At Risk for Mental Retardation*, University of Wisconsin Madison: Rehabilitation Research and Training Center in Mental Retardation

Held R (1985) Binocular vision: behavioural and neuronal development. In J Mehler & R Fox *Neonate Cognition: Beyond the Blooming, Buzzing Confusion*. Hillsdale NJ: Lawrence Erlbaum Associates

Henry J (ed.) (2005) Coincidence. *Parapsychology*. London: Routledge

Herman J & Roffwarg H (1983) Modifying oculomotor activity in awake subjects increases the amplitude of eye movement during REM sleep. *Science* **220**, 1074–76

Herrnstein R & Murray C (1994) *The Bell Curve: Intelligence and Class Structure in American Life*. New York: Free Press

Herxheimer A & Petrie KJ (2001) Melatonin for preventing and treating jet lag. *Cochrane Database for Systematic Reviews* **1**, CD001520

Hess E (1956) Space perception in the chick. *Scientific American*, July, 71–80

Hester R & Garavan H (2005) Working memory and executive function: the influence of content and load on the control of attention. *Memory & Cognition* **33**(2), 221–33

Hetherington A & Ranson SW (1940) Hypothalamic lesions and adiposity in the rat. *Anatomical Record* **78**, 149–72

Hetherington MM & Rolls BJ (1996) Sensory-specific satiety: theoretical frameworks and central characteristics. In ED Capaldi (ed.) *Why We Eat What We Eat: The Psychology of Eating*. Washington DC: American Psychological Association, 267–90

Hetterna JM, Neale MC & Kendler KS (2001) A review and meta-analysis of the genetic epidemiology of anxiety disorders. *American Journal of Psychiatry* **158**, 1568–78

Higley JD, Mehlman PT, Higley SB, Fernald B, Vickers J, Lindell SG, Taub DM, Suomi SJ & Linnoila M (1996) Excessive mortality in young free-ranging male nonhuman primates with low cerebrospinal fluid 5-hydroxyindolacetic acid concentrations. *Archives of General Psychiatry* **53**, 537–43

Ho Y, Cheung M-C & Chan A (2003) Music training improves verbal, but not visual memory. *Neuropsychology* **17**, 439–50

Hodgson R & Rachman S (1972) The treatment of chronic obsessive-compulsive neurosis: follow-up and further findings. *Behavioural Research & Therapy* **10**, 181–9

Holekamp K (2004) A view from the field: what the lives of wild animals can teach us about the care of laboratory animals. Proceedings of the International Workshop on Development of Science-Based Guidelines for Laboratory Animal Care. *ILAR Journal*. Washington DC: Institute for Laboratory Animal Research, National Research Council

Holekamp K & Engh A (2004) Uncovering the secret lives of hyenas. *Annual Science Encyclopaedia*. Chicago: World Book Publishing, 118–31

Hollander E, Decaria C & Nitescu A (1992) Serotonergic function in obsessive compulsive disorder: behavioural and neuroendocrine responses to oral-M-chlorophenylpiperazine and fenfluramine in patients and healthy volunteers. *Archives of General Psychiatry* **49**, 21–28

Hollander E, Pallanti S, Allen A, Sood E & Baldini Rossi N (2005) Does sustained-release lithium reduce impulsive gambling and affective instability versus placebo in pathological gamblers with bipolar spectrum disorders? *American Journal of Psychiatry* **162**(1), 137–45

Holmes J (2002) All you need is cognitive therapy? *British Medical Journal* **342**, 288–94

Honorton C , Bem DC & Ferrari DJ (1998) Extraversion & ESP performance: a meta-analysis and new confirmation. *Journal of Parapsychology* **62**, 255–76

Hopf WH, Huber GL & Wei RH (2008) Media violence and youth violence: a 2-year longitudinal study. *Journal of Media Psychology: Theories, Methods, & Applications* **20**, 79–96

Hopper K, Harrison G, Janca A & Sartorius N (2007) *Recovery From Schizophrenia: An International Perspective. A Report From the WHO Collaborative Project, the International Study of Schizophrenia*. Oxford: Oxford University Press

Horn J (1983) The Texas Adoption Project: adopted children and their intellectual resemblance to biological and adoptive parents. *Child Development* **54**, 268–75

Horne JA & Minard A (1985) Sleep and sleepiness following a behaviourally 'active' day. *Ergonomics* **28**, 567–75

Howard DJ (1997) Familiar phrases as peripheral persuasion cue. *Journal of Experimental Social Psychology* **33**, 231–43

http://flyfishingdevon.co.uk/salmon/year3/psy337/ EatingNeuralFactors/psy337/EatingNeuralFactors.htm. Accessed on 09/12/08

http://www.eurodiabesity.org/honours.htm. Accessed on 08/12/08

Hubel D & Wiesel T (1962) Receptive fields, binocular interaction and functional architecture in the cat's visual cortex. *Physiology* **109**, 106–54

Hudson W (1960) Pictorial depth perception in sub-cultural groups in Africa. *Journal of Social Psychology* **52**, 183–208

Hufford DJ (1982) *The Terror That Comes in the Night: an experience-centerd study of supernatural assault traditions*. Philadelphia: Pennsylvania State University Press

Humphrey N (1999) Why human grandmothers may need large brains. *Psycology* **10**(24)

Humphreys GW & Riddoch MJ (1987) *To See But Not to See: A Case Study of Visual Agnosia*. Hove: Psychology Press

Hunt DD, Carr JE & Hampson JL (1981) Cognitive correlates of biologic sex and gender identity in transsexualism. *Archives of Sexual Behavior* **10**(1), 65–77

Hunt E, Frost N & Lunneborg C (1973) Individual differences in cognition: a new approach to intelligence. In GH Bower (ed.) *The Psychology of Learning and Motivation: Advances in Research and Theory, Vol 7*. New York: Academic Press, 87–122

Hurt RD, Sachs DP, Glover ED, Offord KP, Johnston JA, Dale LC, Khayrallah MA, Schroeder DR, Glover PN, Sullivan CR, Croghan IT & Sullivan PM (1997) A comparison of sustained-release bupropion and placebo for smoking cessation. *New England Journal of Medicine* **337**(17), 1195–1202

Huttenlocher P (2002) *The Effects of Environment on the Development of the Cerebral Cortex*. Cambridge MA: Harvard University Press

Iacoboni M, Molnar-Szakacs I, Gallese V, Buccino G, Mazziotta JC & Rizzolatti G (2005) Grasping the intentions of others with one's own mirror neurons. *PLOS Biology* **3**, 530–35

Ickes W (1985) Sex-role influences on compatibility in relationships. In W Ickes (ed) *Compatible and incompatible relationships*, 187–208. New York: Springer-Verlag

Imura T, Yamaguchi MK, Kanazawa S, Shirai N, Otsuka Y, Tomonaga M, Yagi A (2007) Perception of shape from shading and line junctions in infants. *Perception* **36**

Ingalis AM, Dickie MM & Snell GD (1950) *J. Hered* **41**, 317–18

Inhelder B & Piaget J (1958) *The Growth of Logical Thinking from Childhood to Adolescence*. London: Routledge & Kegan Paul

Irwin HJ (2005). *The Psychology of Paranormal Belief*. New York: Parapsychology Foundation

Isaacs E, Gadian G & Sabatini S (2008) The effect of early human diet on caudate volumes and IQ. *Pediatric Research* **63**(3), 308–14

Jackson L (2008) Overweight and obesity are not your fault. http://hubpages.com/hub/Overweight-and-Obesity-are-NOT-your-fault. Accessed on 17/12/08

Jacobs DS & Blakemore C (1988) Factors limiting the postnatal development of visual acuity. *Vision Research* **28**, 947–58

Jacobsen NS & Margolin G (1979) *Marital Therapy: Strategies Based on Social Learning and Behaviour Exchange Principles.* New York: Brunner Mazel

Jahoda G & McGurk H (1974) The development of pictorial depth perception: the role of figural elevation. *Brithish Journal of Psychology* **65** 141–49

James W (1892) *A Text Book of Psychology.* London: Routledge & Kegan Paul

Jarvis M (2005) *The Psychology of Effective Learning and Teaching.* Cheltenham: Nelson Thornes

Jeffery RW (2000) Long-term maintenance of weight loss: current status. *Health Psychology* **19**(1)

Jerison H (1978) In Frost, *Brain and Intelligence in Whales, Volume II Whales and Whaling.* Canberra: Australian Government Publication Service, 159–97

Jilge B (1991) Restricted feeding: a nonphotic zeitgeber in the rabbit. *Physiology & Behavior* **51**, 157–66

Jiménez-Ruiz CA, Miranda JA, Hurt RD, Pinedo AR, Reina SS & Valero FC (2008) Study of impact of laws regulating tobacco consumption on the prevalence of passive smoking in Spain. *European Journal of Public Health* **18**(6), 622–25

Johansson G (1973) Visual perception of biological motion and a model for its analysis. *Perception and Psychophysics* **14**, 201–11

Johnson A & McSmith A (2006) Children say being famous is the best thing in the world. *The Independent* 18 December 2006

Johnson W & Bouchard T (2005) The structure of human intelligence: its verbal, perceptual and image rotation (VPR), not fluid crystallized. *Intelligence* **33**, 393–416

Johnston J & Ettema JS (1982) *Positive Images: Breaking Stereotypes with Children's Television.* Beverly Hills: Sage

Jones MC (1924) The elimination of children's fears. *Journal of Experimental Psychology* **7**, 382–90

Jorenby DE, Leischow SJ, Nides MA, Rennard SI, Johnston JA, Hughes AR, Smith SS, Muramoto ML, Daughton DM, Doan K, Fiore MC & Baker TB (1999) A controlled trial of sustained-release bupropion, a nicotine patch, or both for smoking cessation. *New England Journal of Medicine* **340**(9), 685–91

Jorgensen ME, Glumer C, Bjerregaard P, Gyntelberg F, Jorgensen T, Borch-Johnson K (2003) Obesity and central fat pattern among Greenland Innuit, relationship to metabolic risk factors. *International Journal of Obesity* **27**, 1507–15

Joukhador J, Maccallum F & Blaszczynski A (2003) Differences in cognitive distortions between problem and social gamblers. *Psychological Reports* **92**, 1203–14

Kähkönen P & Tuorila H (1998) Effects of reduced-fat information on expected and actual hedonic and sensory ratings of sausage. *Appetite* **30**, 13–23

Kahn A, Mozin MJ, Rebuffat E, Sottiaux M & Muller MF (1989) Milk intolerance in children with persistent sleeplessness: a prospective double-blind crossover evaluation. *Pediatrics* **84**(4), 595–603

Kahn BB & Flier JS (2000) Obesity and insulin resistance. *Journal of Clinical Investigation* **106**(4), 473–81

Kamphuis JH & Emmelkamp PMG (2000) Stalking: a challenge for contemporary forensic and clinical psychology. *British Journal of Psychiatry* **176**, 206–09

Kampov-Polevoy A, Garbutt JC & Janowsky D (1997) Evidence of preference for a high-concentration sucrose solution in alcoholic men. *American Journal of Psychiatry* **154**, 269–70

Kampov-Polevoy AB, Garbutt JC & Khalitov (2003) Family history of alcoholism and response to sweets. *Alcoholism, Clinical & Experimental Research* **27**(11), 1743–49

Kanwisher N, McDermott J, Marvin M & Chun M (1997) The fusiform face area: a module in human extrastriate cortex specialized for face perception. *Journal of Neuroscience* **17**(11), June, 4302–11

Katz SH (1982) Food, behaviour and biocultural evolution. In Barker L *The Psychobiology of Food Selection.* Westport CT: AVI

Katz SH (1987) Fava bean consumption: a case for the co-evolution of genes and culture. In M Harris & EB Ross *Food and Evolution.* Philadelphia: Temple University Press 133–59

Kawai M (1965) Newly-acquired pre-cultural behavior of the natural troop of Japanese monkeys on Koshima Islet. *Primates* **6**(1), 1–30

Kaye K & Bower T (1994) Learning and intermodal transfer of information in newborns. *Psychological Science* **5**, 286–88

Kendler KS, Thornton LM & Pederson NL (2000) Tobacco consumption in Swedish twins reared apart and reared together. *Archives of General Psychiatry* **57**, 886–92

Kendrick D (1980) Common factors towards longevity. Tutorial notes. Hull University Psychology Department, Hull, UK

Kenton, SB (1989) Speaker credibility in persuasive business communication: A model which explains gender differences. *The Journal of Business Communication* **26**, 143–57

Kessler RC, Hwang I, Labrie R, Petukhova M, Sampson NA, Winters KC & Shaffer HJ (2008) DSM-IV pathological gambling in the National Comorbidity Survey Replication. *Psychological Medicine* **38**(9), 1351–60

Kihlstrom JF (1998) The genetic and environmental relationship between general and specific cognitive abilities in twins. *Pychological Science* **9**, 183–89

Kim H, Roh S, Kwon HJ, Paik KC, Rhee MY, Jeong JY, Lim MH, Koo MJ, Kim CH, Kim HY, Lim JH & Kim DH (2008) Study on the health status of the residents near military airbases in Pyeongtaek City. *Journal of Preventative Medicine & Public Health* **41**(5), 307–14

Kim SW (1998) Opioid antagonists in the treatment of impulse control disorders. *Journal of Clinical Psychiatry* **59**(4), 159–62

Kim SW & Grant JE (2001) An open naltrexone treatment study in pathological gambling disorder. *International Clinical Psychopharmacology* **16**(5), 285–89

Kim SW, Grant JE, Adson DE & Shin YC (2001) Double-blind naltrexone and placebo comparison study in the treatment of pathological gambling. *Biological Psychiatry* **49**(11), 914–21

Kim SW, Grant JE, Adson DE, Shin YC & Zaninelli R (2002) A double-blind placebo-controlled study of the efficacy and safety of paroxetine in the treatment of pathological gambling. *Journal of Clinical Psychiatry* **63**(6), 501–07

Kindt M & Brosschot JF (1997) Phobia-related cognitive bias for pictorial and linguistic stimuli. *Journal of Abnormal Psychology* **106**, 644–48

King LA, Burton CM, Drigotas SM & Hicks JA (2007) Ghosts, UFOs, and magic: positive affect and the experiential system. *Journal of Personality & Social Psychology* **92**, 905–19

Kitazaki M & Shimizu A (2005) Visual-motor adaptation to stabilize perceptual world: its generality and specificity. *Proceedings of the Virtual Reality Society of Japan Annual Conference*

Kitcher P (1985) *Vaulting Ambition. Sociobiology and the Quest of Human Nature*. Cambridge MA: MIT Press

Klein M (1946) *Envy and Gratitude.* New York: Simon & Schuster

Kleinman PH, Kang SY, Lipton DS, Woody GE, Kemp J & Millman RB (1992) Retention of cocaine abusers in outpatient psychotherapy. *American Journal of Drug & Alcohol Abuse* **18**(1), 29–43

Kleitman N (1961) The nature of dreaming. In GEW Wolstenholme & M O'Connor (eds) *The Nature of Sleep*. London: J & A Churchill

Kleitman N (1963) *Sleep and Wakefulness.* Chicago: University of Chicago Press

Kleitman N (1969) Basic rest-activity cycle in relation to sleep and wakefulness. In A Kales (ed.) *Sleep: Physiology and Pathology.* Philadelphia: Lippincott

Kleitman N, Mullin FJ, Cooperman NR & Titelbaum S (1937) *Sleep Characteristics. How they Vary and React to Changing Conditions in the Group and the Individual*. Chicago: University of Chicago Press

Klimek V, Stockmeier C, Overholser J, Meltzer HY, Kalka S, Dilley G & Ordway GA (1997) Reduced levels of norepinephrine transporters in the locus coeruleus in major depression. *Journal of Neuroscience* **17**, 8451–58

Ko CH, Yen JY, Yen CF, Chen CS & Wang SY (2008) The association between Internet addiction and belief of frustration intolerance: the gender difference. *Cyberpsychology & Behavior* **11**(3), 273–78

Kohlberg L (1958) The Development of Modes of Thinking and Choices in Years 10 to 16. PhD Dissertation, University of Chicago

Kohlberg L (1966) A cognitive-developmental analysis of children's sex- role concepts and attitudes. In EE Maccoby (ed.) *The Development of Sex Differences*. Stanford CA: Stanford University Press, 95

Kohler W (1921, 1972) *The Task of Gestalt Psychology.* Princeton NJ: Princeton University Press

Konijn EA, Bijvank MN & Bushman BJ (2007) I wish I were a warrior: the role of wishful identification in the effects of violent video games on aggression in adolescent boys. *Developmental Psychology* **43**, 1038–44

Kornhaber ML (2001) Howard Gardner. In JA Palmer (ed.) *Fifty Modern Thinkers on Education. From Piaget to the Present.* London: Routledge

Kosslyn S (2006) Mental image. In Jones (ed.) *Sensorium: Embodied Experience, Technology and Contemporary Art*. Cambridge MA: MIT Press, 169–70

Koster EH, De Raedt R, Goeleven E, Franck E & Crombez G (2005) Mood-congruent attentional bias in dysphoria: maintained attention to and impaired disengagement from negative information. *Emotion* **5**, 446–55

Kozlowski L & Cutting J (1977) Recognizing the sex of a walker from a dynamic point light display. *Perception & Psychophysics* **21**, 575–80

Kramer N & Winter S (2008) Impression Management 2.0: The Relationship of Self-Esteem, Extraversion, Self-Efficacy, and Self-Presentation Within Social Networking Sites. *Journal of Media Psychology* **20**, 106–16

Kruijver FP, Zhou JN, Pool CW, Hofman MA, Gooren LJ & Swaab DF (2000) Male-to-female transsexuals have female neuron numbers in a limbic nucleus. *Journal of Clinical Endocrinology & Metabolism* **85**(5), 2034–41

Kubey, R & Czikszentmihalyi M (2002) Television addiction is no mere metaphor. *Scientific American* **286**(2): 74–80

Kuentzel JG, Henderson MJ & Melville CL (2008) The impact of social desirability biases on self-report among college student and problem gamblers. *Journal of Gambling Studies* **24**(3), 307–19

Kuhn TS (1962) *The Structure of Scientific Revolutions*. Chicago: Chicago University Press

Kujawski JH & Bower TGR (1993) Same-sex preferential looking during infancy as a function of abstract representation. *British Journal of Developmental Psychology* **11**(2), 201–09

Kula K & Słowikowska-Hilczer J (2000) Sexual differentiation of the human brain. *Przeglad Lekarski* **57**(1), 41–44

Kullberg G (1977) Differences in effect of capsulotomy and cingulotomy. In WH Sweet, S Obrador, JG Martín-Rodríguez, (eds) *Neurosurgical Treatment in Psychiatry, Pain, and Epilepsy*, pp 303–08. Baltimore: University Park Press.

Kummer H (1967) *Tripartite Relations in Hamadryas Baboons. Social Communication among Primates*. Chicago: University of Chicago Press

Kurdek LA & Siesky AE (1980) Sex role self-concepts of single divorced parents and their children. *Journal of Divorce* **3**(3), 249–61

Kurtz MM, Baker E, Pearlson GD & Astur RS (2007) A virtual reality apartment as a measure of medication management skills in patients with schizophrenia: a pilot study. *Schizophrenia Bulletin* **33**(5), 1160–72

Kurucz J & Feldmar G (1979) Prosop-affective agnosia as a symptom of cerebral organic disease. *Journal of the American Geriatric Society* **27**, 91–95

Kuttler AF & La Greca AM (2004) Linkages among adolescent girls' romantic relationships, best friendships, and peer networks. *Journal of Adolescence* **27**, 395–414

Labov W (1970) The logic of non-standard language. In Williams (ed.) *Language and Poverty*. Chicago: Markham

Lagerspetz K & Wuorinen K (1965) A cross-fostering experiment with mice selectively bred for aggressiveness and non-aggressiveness. *Reports of the Institute of Psychology of the University of Turku* **17**, 1–6

Lagerspetz KMJ (1979) Modification of aggressiveness in mice. In S Feshbach & A Fraçzek (eds) *Aggression and Behavior Change: Biological and Social Processes*. New York: Praeger Publishers

La Freniere P, Strayer FF & Gauthier R (1984) The emergence of same-sex affiliative preferences among preschool peers: a developmental/ethological perspective. *Child Development* **55**(5), 1958–65

Lahn BT, Evans PD, Anderson JR, Vallender EJ & Choi SS (2004) Reconstruction the evolutionary history of microcephalin, a gene controlling human brain size. *Human Molecular Genetics* **13** 1139–45

Lamy JB, Duclos C, Bar-Hen A, Patrick Ouvrard P & Venot A (2008) An iconic language for the graphical representation of medical concepts. *BMC Medical Informatics & Decision Making* **8**

Langer J, Gillette P & Ariaga RI (2003) Toddlers' cognition of adding and subtracting objects in action and in perception. *Cognitive Development* **18**, 233–46

Lavie P (1996) *The Enchanted World of Sleep*. New Haven: Yale University Press

Lazar (1992) Cited in S Merrick (1992) Multiple intelligences or multilevel intelligence. *Psychological Inquiry* **3**(4), 365–84

Lazar I & Darlington R (1982) Lasting effects of early education: a report from the Consortium for Longitudinal Studies. *Monographs of the Society for Research in Child Development* **47**(195). Chicago: University of Chicago Press

Lazarus R & McCleary R (1951) Automatic discrimination without awareness: a study of subception. *Psychological Review* **58**, 113–22

Leaper C, Breed L, Hoffman L & Perlman CA (2002) Variations in the gender-stereotyped content of children's television cartoons across genres. *Journal of Applied Social Psychology* **32**(8), 1653–62

Le Bon G (1895) *The Crowd: A Study of the Popular Mind*. London: Transaction Publishers

Lecendreux M, Bassetti C, Dauvilliers Y, Mayer G, Neidhart E & Tafti M (2003) HLA and genetic susceptibility to sleepwalking. *Molecular Psychiatry* **8**(1), 114–17

Leeper RW (1935) A study of a neglected portion of the field of learning – the development of sensory organization. *Journal of Genetic Psychology* **46**, 41–75

Leichsenring F, Rabung S & Leibing D (2004) The efficacy of short-term psychodynamic psychotherapy in specific psychiatric disorders. *Archives of General Psychiatry* **61**, 1208–16

Lemstra M, Neudorf C & Opondo J (2008) Implications of a public smoking ban. *Canadian Journal of Public Health* **99**(1), 62–65

Leslie AM (1994) ToMM, ToBy, and agency: core architecture and domain specificity. In L Hirschfeld & S Gelman (eds) *Mapping the Mind: Domain Specificity in Cognition and Culture.* New York: Cambridge University Press, 119–48

Lessov-Schlaggar CN, Pang Z, Swan GE, Guo Q, Wnag S, Cao W, Unger JB, Johnson A & Lee L (2006) Heritability of cigarette smoking and alcohol use in Chinese male twins: the Qingdao twin registry. *International Journal of Epidemiology* **35**, 1278–85

Levin M (1994) Comment on Minnesota Transracial Adoption Study. *Intelligence* **19**, 13–20

Lewis M (1990) Social knowledge and social development. *Merrill-Palmer Quarterly* **36**, 93–116

Lewis SE & Lewis JE (2007) Predicting at-risk students in general chemistry: comparing formal thought to a general achievement measure. *Chemistry Education Research & Practice* **8**, 32–51

Lichstein KL, Payne KL, Soeffing JP, Heith Durrence H, Taylor DJ, Riedel BW & Bush AJ (2007) Vitamins and sleep: an exploratory study. *Sleep Medicine* **9**(1), 27–32

Liddle HA, Dakof GA, Turner RM, Henderson CE & Greenbaum PE (2008) Treating adolescent drug abuse: a randomized trial comparing multidimensional family therapy and cognitive behavior therapy. *Addiction* **103**(10), 1660–70

Lieberman LS (2003) *Annual Review of Nutrition* **23**, 345–57

Lieberman MD (2007) Social cognitive neuroscience: a review of core processes. *Annual Review of Psychology* **58**, 259–89

Liem DG & Mennella JA (2003) Heightened sour preferences during childhood. *Chemical Senses* **28**, 173–80

Lin L, Faraco J, Li R, Kadotani H, Rogers W, Lin X, Qiu X, de Jong PJ, Nishino S & Mignot E (1999) The sleep disorder canine narcolepsy is caused by a mutation in the hypocretin (orexin) receptor 2 gene. *Cell* **98**(3), 365–76

Lindeman M & Saher M (2007) Vitalism, purpose and superstition. *British Journal of Psychology* **98**, 33–44

Lindsey EW & Mize J (2001) Contextual differences in parent-child play: implications for children's gender role development. *Sex Roles* **44**, 155–76

Lindstroem LH, Gefvert O, Hagberg G, Lundberg T, Bergstroem M, Harvig P & Langstroem B (1999) Increased dopamine synthesis rate in medial prefrontal cortex and striatum in schizophrenia indicated by L-DOPA and PET. *Biological Psychiatry* **46**, 681–8

Lisanby SH, Maddox JH, Prudic J, Devanand DP & Sackeim HA (2000) The effects of electroconvulsive therapy on memory of autobiographical and public events. *Archives of General Psychiatry* **57**, 581–90

Lloyd S (1994) *The Phonics Handbook*. Chigwell: Jolly Learning

Loftus EF & Palmer JC (1974) Reconstruction of automobile destruction: an example of the interaction between language and memory. *Journal of Verbal Learning and Verbal Behavior* **13**, 585–9

Logothetis NK & Pauls J (1995) Psychophysical and physiological evidence for viewer centred object representations in the primate. *Cerebral Cortex* **3**, 270–88

López HH, Bracha AS & Bracha HS (2002) Evidence based complementary intervention for insomnia. *Hawaii Medical Journal* **61**(9), 192–213

Lotrean LM (2008) Effects of comprehensive smoke-free legislation in Europe. *Salud Publica de Mexico* **50**(Suppl. 3), 292–98

Lowe et al. (2004) The effects of low-carbohydrate versus conventional weight loss diets in severely obese adults. *English Journal of Medicine* **348**, 2082–90

Lubman DI, Peters LA, Mogg K, Bradley BP, Deakin JF (2000) Attentional bias for drug cues in opiate dependence. *Psychological Medicine* **30**(1), 169–75.

Lucchelli F & De Renzi E (1992) Proper name anomia. *Cortex* **28**, 221–30

Lucchini R (1985) Young drug addicts and the drug scene. *Bulletin on Narcotics* **37**(2–3), 135–48

Luce GG & Segal J (1966) *Sleep*. New York: Coward-McCann

Lund I (2007) Lessons from the grey area: a closer inspection of at-risk gamblers. *Journal of Gambling Studies* **23**(4), 409–19

Lynn R (1989) The evolution of brain size and intelligence in man *Human Evolution* **5** (3), 241–42

Lynn R (2006) *Race Differences in Intelligence: An Evolutionary Analysis*. Augusta GA: Washington Summit Publishers

Lyons MJ, True WR, Eisen SA, Goldberg J, Meyer JM, Faraone SV, Eaves LJ & Tsuang MT (1995) Differential heritability of adult and juvenile antisocial traits. *Archives of General Psychiatry* **52**, 906–15

Lytton H & Romney DM (1991) Parents' differential socialization of boys and girls: a meta-analysis. *Psychological Bulletin* **109**, 267–96

Mackintosh N (1986) The biology of intelligence? *British Journal of Psychology* **77**, 1–18

MacMahon KM, Broomfield NM & Espie CA (2006) Attention bias for sleep-related stimuli in primary insomnia and delayed sleep phase syndrome using the dot-probe task. *Sleep* 1 **29**(11), 1420–27

Madden GJ, Ewan EE & Lagorio CH (2007) Toward an animal model of gambling: delay discounting and the allure of unpredictable outcomes. *Journal of Gambling Studies* **23**(1), 63–83

Maes HH, Woodard CE, Murrelle L, Meyer JM, Silberg JL, Hewitt JK, Rutter M, Simonoff E, Pickles A, Carbonneau R, Neale MC & Eaves LJ (1999) Tobacco, alcohol and drug use in eight- to sixteen-year-old twins: the Virginia Twin Study of Adolescent Behavioral Development. *Journal of Alcohol Studies* **60**(3), 293–305

Maestripieri D (2007) *Machiavellian Intelligence. How Rhesus Monkeys and Humans have Conquered the World*. Chicago: University of Chicago Press

Malone D, Morris H, Kay M & Levin H (1982). Prosopagnosia: a double dissociation between the recognition of familiar and unfamiliar faces. *Journal of Neurology, Neurosurgery & Psychiatry* **45**, 820–22

Maltby J, Giles DC, Barber L & McCutcheon LE (2005) Intense-personal celebrity worship and body image: evidence of a link among female adolescents. *British Journal of Health Psychology*, 1–17

Maltby J, Houran J & McCutcheon LE (2003) A clinical interpretation of attitudes and behaviours associated with celebrity worship. *Journal of Nervous & Mental Disease* 191, 1–25

Maltby J, Houran J, Lange R, Ashe D & McCutcheon LE (2002) Thou shalt worship no other gods unless they are celebrities: the relationship between celebrity worship and religious orientation. *Personality & Individual Differences* 32, 1157–72

Manning E (1975) An adventure in learning. In M Meeker (ed.) *Collected Readings, Vol I.* El Segundo CA: SOI Institute, 206–08

Maquet P, Degueldre C, Delfiore G, Aerts J, Péters JM, Luxen A & Franck G (1997) *Journal of Neuroscience* 17(8), 2807–12

Marazziti D, Catena Dell'osso M, Conversano C, Consoli G, Vivarelli L, Mungai F, Di Nasso E & Golia F (2008) Executive function abnormalities in pathological gamblers. *Clinical Practice & Epidemiology in Mental Health* 4, 7

Marchand T (2008) Negotiating tradition in practice: mud masons and meaning-making in contemporary Djenn. *British Journal of Educational Studies* 56(3), 245–71

Mares ML and Woodard E (2005) Positive effects of television on children's social interactions: a meta-analysis. *Media Psychology* 7, 301–22

Markowitz JC, Kocsis JH, Christos P, Bleiberg K & Carlin A (2008) Pilot study of interpersonal psychotherapy versus supportive psychotherapy for dysthymic patients with secondary alcohol abuse or dependence. *Journal of Nervous & Mental Disease* 196(6), 468–74

Marr D (1982) *A Computational Investigation into the Human Representation and Processing of Visual Information.* New York: Freeman

Marshall JF, Turner BH & Teitelbaum P (1971) Sensory neglect produced by lateral hypothalamic damage. *Nature* 174, 523–25

Martin CL & Halverson CF (1981) A schematic processing model of sex typing and stereotyping in children. *Child Development* 52, 1119–34

Martin CL & Little JK (1990) The relation of gender understanding to children's sex-typed preferences and gender stereotypes. *Child Development* 61, 1427–39

Martins Y, Pelchat ML & Pliner P (1997) Try it; it's good for you: effects of taste and nutrition information on willingness to try novel foods. *Appetite* 28, 89–102

Maslow AH (1950) Self-actualizing people: a study of psychological health. In *Personality Symposia: Symposium 1 11–34.* New York: Grune & Stratton

Mason DA & Frick PJ (1994) The heritability of antisocial behaviour: a meta-analysis of twin and adoption studies. *Journal of Psychopathology & Behavioral Assessment* 16, 301–323

Mataix-Cols D, Rosario-Campos MC & Leckman J (2005) A multidimensional model of obsessive-compulsive disorder. *American Journal of Psychiatry* 162, 228–38

Mather G & West S (1993) Evidence for second order motion detectors. *Vision Research* 33(8), 1109–12

Maton K & Muller J (2007) A sociology for the transmission of knowledges. In F Christie & J Martin (eds) *Language, Knowledge and Pedagogy.* London: Continuum, 14–33

Matthews M & Blackmore S (1995) Why are coincidences so impressive? *Perceptual & Motor Skills* 80, 1121–22

Matute H (1996) Illusion of control: detecting response-outcome in analytic but not in realistic conditions. *Psychological Science* 7, 289–93

Maxim PE & Storrie M (1979) Ultradian barpressing for rewarding brain stimulation in rhesus monkeys. *Physiology & Behavior* 22(4), 683–87

McAndrew FT & Milenkovic MA (2002) Of tabloids and family secrets: the evolutionary psychology of gossip. *Journal of Applied Social Psychology* 32, 1–20

McCarthy G (1999) Attachment style and adult love relationships and friendships: a study of a group of women at risk of experiencing relationship difficulties. *British Journal of Medical Psychology* 72, 305–21

McElhaney KB & Insabella GM (2000) The effects of autonomy vs. control in parent–adolescent relationships at age 16 on romantic relationships at age 18. Paper presented at the 2000 meeting of the Society for Research on Adolescence, Chicago

McFarlane T & Pliner P (1997) Increasing willingness to taste novel foods: effects of nutrition and taste information. *Appetite* 28, 227–38

McGarrigle J & Donaldson M (1974) Conservation accidents. *Cognition* 3, 341–50

McGinnies E (1949) Emotionality and perceptual defence. *Psychological Review* 56, 244–51

McGrew W (1992) *The Cultured Chimpanzee: Reflections on Cultural Primatology.* Cambridge: University of Cambridge Press

McGue M (1989) Nature–nurture and intelligence. *Nature* 340(6234), 507–08

McGuffin P, Katz R, Watkins S & Rutherford J (1996) A hospital-based twin register of the heritability of DSM-IV unipolar depression. *Archives of General Psychiatry* 53, 129–36

McGuire WJ (1968) Personality and attitude change. In G Lindsey & E Aronson (eds) *Handbook of Social Psychology.* Reading MA: Addison-Wesley

McKenna P & Warrington EK (1980) Testing for nominal dysphasia. *Journal of Neurology, Neurosurgery & Psychiatry* 43, 781–88

McNeal ET & Cimbolic P (1986) Antidepressants and biochemical theories of depression. *Psychological Bulletin* 99, 361–74

Meddis R (1977) *The Sleep Instinct.* London: Routledge & Kegan Paul

Meeker M (1969) *The Structure of Intellect.* Columbus OH: Merrill

Melican G & Feldt L (1980) An empirical study of the Zajonc-Markus hypothesis for achievement test score declines. *American Educational Research Journal* 17(1), 5–19

Meloy JR & Gothard S (1995) Demographic and clinical comparison between obsessional followers and offenders with mental disorders. *American Journal of Psychiatry* 152, 258–63

Meltzoff AN (1988) Infant imitation after a 1-week delay: long-term memory for novel acts and multiple stimuli. *Developmental Psychology* 24, 470–76

Mennella J (2008). 236th National Meeting of the American Chemical Society, Philadelphia, 21 August

Menzies RG (1996) The origins of specific phobias in a mixed clinical sample: classificatory differences between two origins instruments. *Journal of Anxiety Disorders* 10, 347–54

Merrick S (1992) Multiple intelligences or multilevel intelligence. *Psychological Inquiry* 3(4), 365–84

Merritt R, Bierwort L, Slatko B, Weiner M, Weiner E, Ingram J & Sciarra K (2008) Tasting phenylthiocarbamide (PTC): a new lab with an old flavour. *American Biology Teacher* online 70:4

Metcalf S (2007) Dissecting the IQ debate. http://www.slate.com/id/2179073/. Accessed on 10/01/2009

Meyer V & Chesser ES (1970) *Behaviour Therapy in Clinical Psychology*. Baltimore: Penguin

Mezulis AH, Hyde JS & Abramson LY (2006) The developmental origins of cognitive vulnerability to depression: temperament, parenting, and negative life events in childhood as contributors to negative cognitive style. *Developmental Psychology* **42**, 1012–25

Miell D (1995) Developing a sense of self. In P Barnes (ed.) *Personal, social and emotional development*. Milton Keanes: Open University Press

Milburn SS, Carney DR & Ramirez AM (2001) Even in modern media, the picture is still the same: a content analysis of clipart images. *Sex Roles* **44**, 277–94

Miles LE, Raynal DM & Wilson MA (1977) Blind man living in normal society has circadian rhythm of 24.9 hours. *Science* **198**, 421–23

Milgram S (1963) Behavioural study of obedience. *Journal of Abnormal & Social Psychology* **67**, 371–78

Miller R & Howell G (2005) A test of the theory of planned behavior in underage lottery gambling. *Broadening the Boundaries – Proceedings of the 8th Australia and New Zealand Marketing Academy (ANZMAC) Conference.* Fremantle, 5–7 December

Miller-Kovach K, Heshka S, Anderson JW, Atkinson RL, Greenway FL, Hill JO, Phinney SD, Kolotkin RL, Pi-Sunyer FX (2003) Weight loss with self-help compared with a structured commercial program. *Journal of the American Medical Association* **289**(14), 1792–98

Milton J & Wiseman R (1999) Does psi exist? Lack of replication of an anomalous process of information transfer. *Psychological Bulletin* **125**, 387–91

Milton K (1988) Foraging behaviour and the evolution of primate cognition. In A Whites & R Byrne (eds) *Machiavellian Intelligence: Social Expertise and the Evolution of Intellect in Monkeys, apes and Humans*. Oxford: Oxford University Press, 285–305

Mishima K, Fujiki N, Yoshida Y, Sakurai T, Honda M, Mignot E & Nishino S (2008) Hypocretin receptor expression in canine and murine narcolepsy models and in hypocretin-ligand deficient human narcolepsy. *Sleep* 1 **31**(8), 1119–26

Mistlberger RE (1991) Scheduled daily exercise of feeding alters the phase of photic entrainment in Syrian hamsters. *Physiology & Behavior* **50**, 1257–60

Mize KD, Shackelford TK & Weekes-Shackelford VA (2009) Hands-on killing of intimate partners as a function of sex and relationship status/state. *Journal of Family Violence*

Moeller FG, Dougherty DM, Swann AC, Collins D, Davis CM & Cherek DR (1992) Tryptophan depletion and aggressive responding in healthy males. *Psychopharmacology* **126**(2), 97–103

Moline ML, Salter CA & Hirsch E (1992) Age-related differences in recovery from simulated jet lag. *Sleep* **15**, 28–40

Money J (1975) Ablatio penis: normal male infant sex-reassignment as a girl. *Archives of Sexual Behavior* **4**(1), 65–71

Monneuse MO, Bellisle F & Louis-Sylvestre J (1991) Responses to an intense sweetener in humans: immediate preference and delayed effects on intake. *Physiology and Behavior* **49**, 325–30

Monsivais P, Perrigue MM & Drewnowski A (2007) Sugars and satiety: does the type of sweetener make a difference? *American Journal of Clinical Nutrition* **86**(1), 116–23

Montello DR (2006) *Spatial Information Theory*. Berlin/Heidelberg: Springer Verlag

Moreira-Almeida A, Neto, FL & Cardena E (2008) Comparison of Brazilian spiritist mediumship and dissociative identity disorder. *Journal of Nervous & Mental Disease* **196**, 420–24

Morgan M (1982) Television and adolescents' sex-role stereotypes: a longitudinal study. *Journal of Personality & Social Psychology* **43**(5), 947–55

Morgan M & Grube JW (1991) Closeness and peer group influence. *British Journal of Social Psychology* **30**(2), 159–69

Morgenstern M, Wiborg G & Hanewinkel R (2008) Acceptance of a total smoking ban in schools: students' attitudes. *Gesundheitswesen* **70**(6), 360–63

Morin CM, Koetter U, Bastien C, Ware JC & Wooten V (2005) Valerian-hops combination and diphenhydramine for treating insomnia: a randomised placebo-controlled clinical trial. *Sleep* **28**, 1465–71

Morrison AP, French P, Walford L, Lewis SW, Kilcommons A, Green J, Parker S & Bentall RP (2004) Cognitive therapy for prevention of psychosis in people of ultra-high risk: a random control trial. *British Journal of Psychiatry* **185**, 291–7

Morrison DM, Golder S, Keller TE & Gillmore MR (2002) The theory of reasoned action as a model of marijuana use: tests of implicit assumptions and applicability to high-risk young women. *Psychology of Addictive Behaviors* **16**(3), 212–24

Morton G (2007) Hypothalamic leptin regulation of energy homeostasis and glucose metabolism. *Journal of Physiology* **583**(2), 437–43

Morton LG (2007) MSM, the streets, and lockdown: sexual threat and social dominance in America. *Journal of African American Studies* **11**, 225–38

Moscovitch M, Winocur G & Behrmann M (1997). What is special about face recognition? Nineteen experiments on a person with visual object agnosia and dyslexia but normal face recognition. *Journal of Cognitive Neuroscience* **9**, 555–604

Mouras H, Stoléru S, Moulier V, Pélégrini-Issac M, Rouxel R, Grandjean BD, Glutron D & Bittoun J (2008) Activation of mirror-neuron system by erotic video clips predicts degree of induced erection: an fMRI study. *Neuroimage* **42**, 1142–50

Mrosovsky N (1988) Phase response curves for social entrainment. *Journal of Comparative Physiology* **162**, 35–46

Mullen PE (2008) *The psychopathology of those who stalk, threaten and attack public figures.* ANZFSS Symposium

Mullin CR & Linz D (1995) Desensitisation and resensitisation to violence against women: effects of exposure to sexually violent films. *Journal of Personality & Social Psychology* **69**, 449–59

Murch G (1973) *Visual and Auditory Perception*. Indianapolis IN: Bobbs-Merrill

Musani *et al.* (2008) Evidence for a strong genetic influence on childhood adiposity despite the force. *American Journal of Clinical Nutrition* **87**, 398–404

Nagell K, Olguin R & Tomasello M (1993) Processes of social learning in the tool use of chimpanzees and human children. *Journal of Comparative Psychology* **107**, 174–86

Nakamura M, Oshima A, Fujimoto Y, Maruyama N, Ishibashi T & Reeves KR (2007) Efficacy and tolerability of varenicline, an alpha4beta2 nicotinic acetylcholine receptor partial agonist, in a 12-week, randomized, placebo-controlled, dose-response study with 40-week follow-up for smoking cessation in Japanese smokers. *Clinical Therapy* **29**(6), 1040–56

Nakonezny PA & Denton WH (2008) Marital relationships: a social exchange theory perspective. *The American Journal of Family Therapy* **36**, 402–12

Narr K, Woods R, Thompson P, Szeszko P, Robinson D, Dimtcheva T, Gurbani M, Toga A & Bilder R (2006) Relationships between IQ and regional cortical grey matter thickness in healthy adults. *Cerebral Cortex* **17**(9), 2163–71

National Institute for Clinical Excellence (2002) *Schizophrenia: Core interventions in the treatment and management of schizophrenia in primary and secondary care.* London: NICE

National Institute for Clinical Excellence (2003) *The Clinical Management of Depression.* London: NICE

National Institute for Clinical Excellence (2004) *Depression: management of depression in primary and secondary care. Clinical Guideline 23.* London: NICE

National Institute for Health and Clinical Excellence (2007) *Public Health Intervention Guidance, Draft Scope: Preventing the Uptake of Smoking by Children and Young People, Including Point of Sale Measures*

Nefian A & Hayes H (1998) Hidden Markov models for face recognition. *Proceedings of the International Conference on Acoustics, Speech and Signal Processing.* http://users.ece.gatech.edu/~ara/icassp98.ps.Z. Accessed on 08/01/2009

Neisser U (1976) *Cognition and Reality.* San Fransisco: WH Freeman

Nelson KR, Mattingley M, Sherman AL & Schmitt FA (2006) Does the arousal system contribute to near death experience? *Neurology* **66**, 1003–09

Nelson RD & Radin DJ (1987) When immovable objects meet irresistible evidence. *Behavioural & Brain Sciences* **10**, 600–01

Nelson RJ, Demas GE, Huang PL, Fishman MC, Dawson VL, Dawson TM & Snyder SH (1995) Behavioural abnormalities in male mice lacking neuronal nitric acid synthase. *Nature* **378**, 383–86

Nelson RJ, Trainor BC, Chiavegatto S & Demas GE (2006) Pleiotropic contributions of nitric oxide to aggressive behavior. *Neuroscience & Biobehavioral Reviews* **30**(3), 346–55

Neuhaus Education Centre (2008). www.lapdavt.org/past-course/developing-metacognitive-skills-DSH-Cancelled. Accessed on 07/01/2009

Newman HH, Freeman FN, Holzinger KJ (1937) *Twins: a study of heredity and environment.* Chicago, IL: University of Chicago Press

Newport F & Strausberg M (2001) *Americans, belief in psychic and paranormal phenomena is up over last decade.* Princeton: Gallup News Service

Nishida T, Hasegawa T, Hayaki H, Takahata Y & Uehara S (1992) Meat-sharing as a coalition strategy by an alpha male chimpanzee? In *Topics in Primatology: Proceedings of Symposium. XIII Congress International Primatology Society*, Vol. 1

Nolen-Hoeksema S (2002) Gender differences in depression. In IH Gotlib & CL Hammen (eds) *Handbook of Depression.* New York: Guilford, 492–509

North AC, Bland V & Ellis C (2005) Distinguishing heroes from celebrities. *British Journal of Psychology* **96**, 39–52

Norton MI, Frost JH & Ariely D (2007) Less is more: the lure of ambiguity, or why familiarity breeds contempt. *Journal of Personality & Social Psychology* **92**, 97–102

Oberman LM, Edward T, Hubbard EM, McCleery JP, Altschuler EL, Ramachandran VS & Pineda JA (2005) EEG evidence for mirror neuron dysfunction in autism spectrum disorders. *Cognitive Brain Research* **24**, 190–98

O'Keefe C & Wiseman R (2005) Testing alleged mediumship: methods and results. *British Journal of Psychology* **96**, 165–79

Okwonko R (1997) Moral development and culture in Kohlberg's theory: a Nigerian (Igbo) evidence. *Ife Psychologia: an International Journal* **5**, 117–28

Oley N (2002) Extra credit and peer tutoring: impact on the quality of writing in introductory psychology in an open admissions college. In RA Griggs (ed.) *Handbook for Teaching Introductory Psychology. Vol 3.* Mahwah NJ: LEA

Olweus D, Mattsson A, Schalling D & Low H (1980) Testosterone, aggression, physical, and personality dimensions in normal adolescent males. *Psychosomatic Medicine* **42**(2), 253–69

Osborne J (2009) *Predicting need fulfillment and satisfaction in romantic relationships: defining and testing interpersonal need compatibility.* Paper presented at the annual meeting of the International Communication Association, New York

Ostrov JM, Gentile DA & Crick NR (2006) Media exposure, aggression and prosocial behavior during early childhood: a longitudinal study. *Social Development* **15**, 612–27

Oswald I (1969) Human brain protein, drugs and dreams. *Nature* **223**, 893–97

Oswald I (1980) *Sleep*. Harmondsworth: Penguin

Overstreet DH, Kampov-Polevoy AB, Rezvani AH, Murrelle L, Halikas JA & Janowsky DS (1993) Saccharin intake predicts ethanol intake in genetically heterogeneous rats as well as different rat strains. *Alcoholism, Clinical & Experimental Research* **17**(2), 366–69

Owen L & Youdan B (2006) 22 years on: the impact and relevance of the UK No Smoking Day. *Tobacco Control* **15**, 19–25

Pagano C (2008) Can invariant information be other than visual? *Industrial Ergonomics*, 1321–25

Palarea RE, Zona MA, Lane JC & Langhinrichsen-Rohling J (1999) The dangerous nature of intimate relationship stalking: threats, violence and associated risk factors. Conference of the American Psychology-Law Society, Redondo Beach CA

Paquette V, Levesque J, Mensour B, Leroux JM, Beaudoin G, Bourgouin P & Beauregard M (2003) Effects of cognitive behavioural therapy on the neural correlates of spider phobia. *Neuroimage* **18**, 401–9

Parker S & Gibson K (1979) A developmental model for the evolution of language and intelligence in early hominids. *Behavioural and Brain Sciences* **2**, 367–408

Pascalis O & Bachevalier J (1997) Face recognition in primates: a cross-species study. *Behavioural Processes* **43**, 87–96

Pavlov I (1927) *Conditioned Reflexes*. London: University Press

Pelchat ML & Rozin P (1982) The special role of nausea in the acquisition of food dislikes by humans. *Appetite* **3**, 341–51

Pengelly ET & Asmundson SJ (1974) Circannual rhythmicity in hibernating animals. In ET Pengelly (ed.) *Circannual Clocks.* New York: Academic Press

Pennington DC (1986*) Essential Social Psychology.* London: Edward Arnold

Pepino MY & Mennella JA (2007) Effects of cigarette smoking and family history of alcoholism on sweet taste perception and food cravings in women. *Alcoholism, Clinical & Experimental Research* **31**(11), 1891–99

Pereverzeva M & Teller D (2004) Infant colour vision: influence of surround chromocicity in spontaneous looking preferences. *Visual Neuroscience* **21**(3), 389–95

Pergadia ML, Heath AC, Martin NG & Madden PA (2006) Genetic analyses of DSM-IV nicotine withdrawal in adult twins. *Psychological Medicine* **36**(7), 963–72

Perkins SL & Allen R (2006) Childhood physical abuse and differential development of paranormal belief systems. *Journal of Nervous & Mental Disease* **194**, 349–55

Perner J, Stummer S, Sprung M & Doherty M (2002) Theory of mind finds its Piagetian perspective: why alternative naming comes with understanding belief. *Cognitive Development* **17**, 1451–72

Persinger MA (1983) Religious and mystical experiences as artefacts of temporal lobe function: a general hypothesis. *Perceptual & Motor Skills* **57**, 1255–62

Persinger MA (1985) Geophysical variables and behaviour: intense paranormal experiences occur during days of quiet global geomagnetic activity. *Perceptual & Motor Skills* **61**, 320–22

Persinger MA (1995) Sudden unexpected death in epileptics following sudden, intense increases in geomagnetic activity: prevalence of effect and potential mechanisms. *International Journal of Biometeorology* **38**, 180–87

Peters DK & Cantrell PJ (1993) Gender roles and role conflict in feminist lesbian and heterosexual women. *Sex Roles* **28**(7–8), 379–92

Petrill SA & Deater-Deckard K (2004) The heritability of general cognitive ability: a within family adoption design. *Intelligence* **32**(4), 403–09

Petry NM, Ammerman Y, Bohl J, Doersch A, Gay H, Kadden R, Molina C & Steinberg K (2006) Cognitive-behavioral therapy for pathological gamblers. *Journal of Consulting & Clinical Psychology* **74**(3), June, 555–67

Pettigrew et al. (1978) How cultural set affects perception. In T Malin (1994) *Cognitive Processes*. Basingstoke: Palgrave Macmillan

Petty RE & Cacioppo JT (1986) *Communication and Persuasion: Central and Peripheral Routes to Attitude Change.* New York: Springer Verlag

Petty RE, Cacioppo JT & Goldman R (1981). Personal involvement as a determinant of argument-based persuasion. *Journal of Personality & Social Psychology* **41**, 847–55

Petty RE, Priester JR & Brinol P (2002) Mass media attitude change: implications of the elaboration likelihood model of persuasion. In J Byant & D Zillmann (eds) *Media Effects: Advances in Theory and Research* (2nd edn). Hillsdale NJ: Lawrence Erlbaum Associates, 155–90

Pfeiffer JH, Lieberman MD & Dapretto M (2007) 'I know you are but what am I?!': neural bases of self- and social knowledge retrieval in children and adults. *Journal of Cognitive Neuroscience* **19**, 1323–37

Piaget J & Inhelder B (1956) *The Child's Conception of Space*. London: Routledge & Kegan Paul

Pilling S, Bebbington P, Kuipers E, Garety P, Geddes J, Orbach G & Morgan C (2002) Psychological treatments in schizophrenia: I. Meta-analysis of family intervention and cognitive behaviour therapy. *Psychological Medicine* **32**, 763–82

Pinel J (2000) *Biopsychology*. Allyn & Bacon, 260–01

Pinquart M, Duberstein PR & Lyness JM (2006) Treatments for later-life depressive conditions: a meta-analytic comparison of pharmacotherapy and psychotherapy. *American Journal of Psychiatry* **163**, 1493–1501

Pitt-Rivers J (1966) Honor and social status. In JG Persitiany (ed.) *Honour and Shame: The Values of Mediterranean Society*. Chicago: University of Chicago Press 19–78

Pliner P & Pelchat ML (1986) Similarities in food preferences between children and their siblings and parents. *Appetite* **7**, 333–42

Plomin R (2003) *Behavioural Genetics in the Post Genomic Era*. Washington DC: APA Books

Plomin R, Chorney MJ, Chorney K, Seese N, Owen MJ, Daniels J, McGuffin P, Thompson LA, Detterman DK, Benbow C, Lubinski D & Eley T (1998) A quantitative trait locus associated with cognitive ability in children. *Psychological Science*, **9**159–66

Politzia di stato. Photo identikit image. www.politziadistato.it/pds/chisiamo/territorio/reparti/scientifica/images/Identikit. Accessed on 6/1/2009

Polivy & Herman (1999) Distress and eating, why do dieters overeat? *International Journal of Eating Disorders* **26**, 153–64

Pollack R (1963) Contour detectability thresholds as a function of chronological age. *Perception & Motor Skills* **17**, 411–17

Pollack R & Silva S (1967) Magnitude of the Müller-Lyer illusion in children as a function of the pigmentation of the fundus oculi. *Psychonomic Science* **8**, 83–84

Pontizovsky AM, Grinshpoon A, Poogachev I, Ritsner M & Abramowitz MZ (2006) Changes in stability of first-admission psychiatric diagnoses over 14 years, based on cross-sectional data at three time points. *Israeli Journal of Psychiatry & Related Sciences* **43**, 34–39

Popper K (1959) *The Logic of Scientific Discovery*. London: Hutchinson

Postmes T & Spears R (1998) Deindividuation and antinormative behavior: a meta-analysis. *Psychological Bulletin* **123**, 238–59

Potegal M (1994) Aggressive arousal: the amygdale connection. In M Potegal & JF Knutson (eds) *The Dynamics of Aggression*. Hillsdale NJ: Lawrence Erlbaum Associates, 73–111

Potegal M, Ferris C, Herbert M, Meyerhoff JM & Skaredoff L (1996a) Attack priming in female Syrian golden hamsters is associated with a *c-fos* coupled process within the corticomedial amygdala. *Neuroscience* **75**, 869–80

Potegal M, Herbert M, DeCoster M & Meyerhoff JL (1996b) Brief, high-frequency stimulation of the corticomedial amygdale induces a delayed and prolonged increase of aggressiveness in male Syrian golden hamsters. *Behavioral Neuroscience* **110**, 410–12

Povinelli D, Nelson K & Boysen S (1990) Inferences about guessing and knowing by chimpanzees (pan troglodytes). *Journal of Comparative Psychology* **104**, 203–210

Prado-Lima PS, Cruz IBM, Schwanke CHA, Netto CA & Licinio J (2006) Human food preferences are associated with a 5-HT2A serotonergic receptor polymorphism. *Molecular Psychiatry* **11**(10), 889–91

Premack D (2007) Human and animal cognition: continuity and discontinuity. *Proceedings of the National Academy of Sciences of the USA* **104**(35)

Premack D & Woodruff G (1978) Does the chimp have a theory of mind? *Behaviour and Brain Sciences* **1**, 515–26

Priester JR & Petty RE (2003) The influence of spokesperson trustworthiness on message elaboration, attitude strength and advertising effectiveness. *Journal of Consumer Psychology* **13**, 408–21

Pringle H (2004) *Celebrity sells*. Bognor: Wiley

Prior H, SchwarzA & Güntürkün O (2008) Mirror-induced behaviour in the magpie. Evidence of self-recognition. *PLoS Biology* **6**(8), e202

Prior SM & Welling KA (2001) 'Read in your head.' A Vygotskian analysis of the transition from oral to silent reading. *Reading Psychology* **22**, 1–15

Prisidi (2008) Interdisciplines Enactive. www.interdisciplines.org/enaction/papers/8/1/1. Accessed on 25/11/2008

Provencio I, Rodriguez IR, Jiang G, Hayes WP, Moreira EF & Rollag MD (2000) A novel human opsin in the inner retina. *Journal of Neuroscience* **20**(2), 600–05

Raacke J & Raacke JB (2008) MySpace and Facebook: applying the uses and gratifications theory to exploring friend-networking sites. *Cyberpsychology & Behavior* **1**, 1169–74

Rabban M (1950) Sex-role identification in young children in two diverse social groups. *Genetic Psychology Monographs* **42**(1), 81–158

Radin DI & Nelson RD (1987) *Replication in Random Event Generator Experiments: A Meta-Analysis and Quality Assessment* (Technical Report 87001). Princeton, NJ: Princeton University Human Information Processing Group

Raine A, Buchsbaum M & LaCasse L (1997) Brain abnormalities in murderers indicated by positron emission tomography. *Biological Psychiatry* **42**, 495–508

Ralph MR, Foster TG, Davis FC & Menaker M (1990) Transplanted suprachiasmatic nucleus determines circadian rhythm. *Science* **247**, 975–78

Randi, J (1983) The Project Alpha experiment: Part 1. The first two years. *Skeptical Inquirer* **7**, 24–33

Randi J (2001) *Science and Pseudoscience.* Fort Lauderdale FL: The James Randi Educational Foundation

Randle J (2003) Experience before and throughout the nursing career: bullying in the nursing profession. *Journal of Advanced Nursing* **43**, 395–401

Ratelle CF, Vallerand RJ, Mageau GA, Rousseau FL & Provencher P (2004) When passion leads to problematic outcomes: a look at gambling. *Journal of Gambling Studies* **20**(2), 105–19

Rathod S & Turkington D (2005) Cognitive–behaviour therapy for schizophrenia: a review. *Current Opinion in Psychiatry* **18**, 159–63

Raven J, Raven JC & Court JH (2003) *Manual for Raven's Progressive Matrices and Vocabulary Scales. Section 1: General Overview.* San Antonio TX: Harcourt Assessment

Read J, Van Os J, Morrison AP & Ross CA (2005) Childhood trauma, psychosis and schizophrenia: a literature review with theoretical and clinical implications. *Acta Psychiatrica* **112**, 330–50

Rechtschaffen A, Gilliland MA, Bergmann BM & Winter JB (1983) Physiological correlates of prolonged sleep deprivation in rats. *Science* **221**, 182–84

Reed DR & McDaniel AH (2008) The human sweet tooth. http://www.pubmedcentral.nih.gov/articlerender.fcgi?artid=2147592. Accessed on 20/12/2008

Reeves AG & Plum F (1969) Hyperphagia, rage and dementia accompanying a ventromedial hypothalamic neoplasm. *Archives of Neurology* **20**, 616–24

Reif A, Jacob CP, Rujescu D, Herterich S, Lang S, Gutknecht L, Baehne CG, Strobel A, Freitag CM, Giegling I, Romanos M, Hartmann A, Rösler M, Renner TJ, Fallgatter AJ, Retz W, Ehlis AC & Lesch KP (2009) Influence of functional variant of neuronal nitric oxide synthase on impulsive behaviors in humans. *Archives of General Psychiatry* **66**(1), 41–50

Rendell L & Whitehead H (2001) Culture in whales and dolphins. *Behavioural Brain Sciences* **24**, 309–24

Retz W, Retz-Junginger P, Supprian T, Thome J & Rösler M (2004) Association of serotonin transporter promoter gene polymorphism with violence: relation with personality disorders, impulsivity, and childhood ADHD psychopathology. *Behavioral Sciences & the Law* **22**(3), 415–25

Rhodes G, Halberstadt J, Jeffrey L & Palermo R (2005) The attractiveness of average faces is not a generalized mere exposure effect. *Social Cognition* **23**, 205–17

Rideout B (1979) Non REM sleep as a source of learning deficients induced by REM deprivation. *Physiology & Behavior* **22**, 1043–47

Ridley M (2000) *The Autobiography of a Species.* New York: HarperCollins

Riesen A (1965) Effects of photic stimulation on early deprivation. In Oster & Cook *The Biosocial Basis of Mental Retardation.* Baltimore: Johns Hopkins University Press

Rigby K & Slee PT (1993) Dimensions of interpersonal relation among Australian children and implications for psychological well-being. *Journal of Social Psychology* **133**, 33–42

Righi G & Tarr M (2004) The neural substrates of chess expertise. 12th Annual Meeting of the Organization for Human Brain Mapping, Florence, Italy

Risner ME & Goldberg SR (1983) A comparison of nicotine and cocaine self-administration in the dog: fixed-ratio and progressive-ratio schedules of intravenous drug infusion. *Journal of Pharmacol Exp Ther* **224**, 319–26

Rizzolatti G, Fadiga L, Gallese V & Fogassi L (1996) Premotor cortex and the recognition of motor actions. *Cognitive Brain Research* **3**, 131–41

Roazzi, A & Bryant, P (1997) Explicitness and conservation: Social class differences. *International Journal of Behavioural Development* **21**(1), 51–70

Rockloff MJ & Dyer V (2007) An experiment on the social facilitation of gambling behavior. *Journal of Gambling Studies* **23**(1), 1–12

Roe CA (1998) Belief in the paranormal and attendance at psychic readings. *Journal of the American Society for Psychical Research* **90**, 25–51

Roffwarg HA, Muzio JN & Dement WC (1966) Ontogenetic development of human sleep-dream cycle. *Science* **152**, 604–19

Rogers C (1961) *On Becoming a Person: A Therapist's View of Psychotherapy.* Boston MA: Houghton-Mifflin

Rogers P (1988) The cognitive psychology of lottery gambling: a theoretical review. *Journal of Gambling Studies* **14**(2), 111–34

Rolls BJ, Rolls ET, Rowe EA & Sweeney K (1981) Sensory specific satiety in man. *Physiology & Behavior* **27**, 137–42

Rose H & Rose S (2000) *Alas Poor Darwin.* London: Harmony

Rose N & Blackmore S (2002) Horses for courses: tests of a psychic claimant. *Journal of the Society for Psychical Research* **66**, 29–40

Rose S, Lewontin R & Kamin L (1984). *Not in our Genes.* Harmondsworth: Penguin

Rosenhan DL (1973) On being sane in insane places. *Science* **179**, 250–58

Rosenthal RJ (2008) Psychodynamic psychotherapy and the treatment of pathological gambling. *Revista Brasileira de Psiquiatria* **30**(Supp. 1)

Ross L, Anderson DR & Wisocki PA (1982) Television viewing and adult sex-role attitudes. *Sex Roles* **896**, 589–92

Rossell SL, Bullmore ET, Williams SCT & David AS (2002) Sex differences in functional brain activation during a lexical visual field task. *Brain & Language* **80**, 97–105

Roth U & Dicke R (2005) Evolution of the brain and intelligence. *Trends in Cognitive Sciences* **9**(9), 411

Roth U and Dicke R (2008) Animal intelligence and the evolution of the human mind. *Mind & Brain.* http://www.sciam.com/article.cfm?id=intelligence-evolved. Accessed on 10/01/2008

Rowe *et al.* (2007) Genetics has key role in obesity. *International Journal of Bioinformatics Research and Applications* **3**(4), 504–22

Royal College of Psychiatrists (2000) Neurosurgery for Mental Disorder. *Report from the Neurosurgery Working Group of the Royal College of Psychiatrists* (Council Report CR89). London: Royal College of Psychiatrists

Rozin P (1990) Development in the food domain. *Developmental Psychology* **26**, 555–62

Rozin P, Fallon A & Mandell R (1984) Family resemblance in attitudes to foods. *Developmental Psychology* **20**, 309–14

Ruble DN, Taylor LJ, Cyphers L, Greulich FK, Lurye LE & Shrout PE (2007) The role of gender constancy in early gender development. *Child Development* **78**(4), 1121–36

Rück C, Andréewitch S, Flyckt K, Edman G, Nyman K, Meyerson BA, Lippitz BE, Hindmarsh T, Svanborg P, Mindus P & Asberg M (2003) Capsulotomy for refractory anxiety disorders: long-term follow-up of 26 patients. *American Journal of Psychiatry* **160**, 513–21

Runge TE, Frey D, Gollwitzer PM, Helmreich RL & Spence JT (1981) Masculine (instrumental) and feminine (expressive) traits: a comparison between students in the United States and West Germany. *Journal of Cross-Cultural Psychology* **12**(2), 142–62

Rusak B & Morin LP (1976) Testicular responses to photoperiod are blocked by lesions of the suprachiasmatic nuclei in golden hamsters. *Biology of Reproduction* **15**(3), 366–74

Ryback RS & Lewis OF (1971) Effects of prolonged bed rest on EEG sleep patterns in young, healthy volunteers. *Electroencephalography & Clinical Neurophysiology* **31**, 395–99

Sáez-Abad C & Bertol'n-Guillén JM (2008) Personality traits and disorders in pathological gamblers versus normal controls. *Journal of Addictive Diseases* **27**(1), 33–40

Sahley CL, Gelperin A & Rudy JW (1981) One-trial associative learning modifies food odor preferences of a terrestrial mollusc. *Proceedings of the National Academy of Sciences of the United States of America* **78**, 640–642

Saiz-Ruiz J, Blanco C, Ibá–ez A, Masramon X, Gómez MM, Madrigal M & D'ez T (2005) Sertraline treatment of pathological gambling: a pilot study. *Journal of Clinical Psychiatry* **66**(1), 28–33

Saltz R (1973) Effects of part time mothering on IQ and SQ of young institutionalised children. *Child Development* **44**(1), 166–70

Sanchez-Villegas A, Schlatter J, Ortuno F, Lahortiga F, Pla J, Benito S & Martinez-Gonzalez MA (2008) Validity of a self-reported diagnosis of depression among participants in a cohort study using the structured clinical interview for DSM-IV (SCID-I). *BMC Psychiatry* **8**, np

Sann C & Steri A (2007) Perception of object shape and texture in human newborns: evidence from cross-modal transfer tasks. *Developmental Science* **10**(3), 399–410

Sassaman E & Zartler A (1982). Mental retardation and head growth abnormalities. *Journal of Pediatric Psychology* **7**, 149–56

Sawaguchi T (1992) The size of the neocortex in relation to ecology and social structure in monkeys and apes. *Folia Primatologica* **58**, 131–45

Scarr S & Salapatek S (1975) The adopted child's IQ: a critical review. *Psychological Bulletin* **82**, 623–59

Scarr S & Weinberg R (1983) The Minnesota adoption studies: genetic differences and malleability. *Child Development* **54**, 260–67

Schenck CH, Garcia-Rill E, Segall M, Noreen H & Mahowald MW (1996) HLA Class II genes associated with REM sleep behavior disorder. *Annals of Neurology* **39**(2), 261–63

Schmitt DP (2003) Universal sex differences in the desire for sexual variety: tests from 52 nations, 6 continents, and 13 islands. *Journal of Personality & Social Psychology* **85**, 85–104

Schmitt DP (2005) Sociosexuality from Argentina to Zimbabwe: a 48-nation study of sex, culture, and strategies of human mating. *Behavioral & Brain Sciences* **28**(2), 247–75

Schneider A & Tarshis B (1995) *Elements of Physiological Psychology*. New York: McGraw Hill, 386–7

Schooler N, Rabinowitz J, Davidson M, Emsley R, Harvey PD, Kopala L, McGorry PD, Van Hove I, Eerdekens M, Swyzen W & De Smedt G (2005) Risperidone and Haloperidol in first-episode psychosis: a long-term randomized trial. *American Journal of Psychiatry* **162**, 947–53

Schutz W (1966) *The Interpersonal World*. Palo Alto CA: Science & Behavior Books

Schwarz A, Campos J & Baisel E, (1973) Cardiac and behavioural response on the deep and shallow side of the visual cliff at five and nine months. *Journal of Experimental Child Psychology* **15**

Sclafani A & Springer D (1976) Dietary obesity in rats. *Physiology and Behaviour* **17**, 467–71

Seamon J & Travis Q (1993) An ecological study of professors' memory for student names and faces: a replication and extension. *Memory* **1**, 191–202

Segall M (1990) *Human Behaviour in Global Perspective. An Introduction to Cross-cultural Psychology*. New York: Pergamon Press

Segall MH & DT Campbell (1963) Cultural differences in the perception of geometrical illusions. *Science* **139**, 769–71

Seiffge-Krenke I, Shulman S & Kiessinger N (2001) Adolescent precursors of romantic relationships in adulthood. *Journal of Social & Personal Relationships* **18**, 327–46

Seligman M (1970) On the generality of the laws of learning. *Psychological Review* **77**, 406–18

Seligman MEP & Hager JL (1972) Biological boundaries of learning. The sauce-bearnaise syndrome. *Psychology Today* (August), 59–61, 84–87

Selman RL (1976) Socio-cognitive understanding: a guide to educational and clinical practice. In T Lickona (ed.) *Moral Development and Behaviour; Theory, Research & Social Issues*. New York: Holt

Sen MG, Yonas A & Knill DC (2001) Development of infants' sensitivity to surface contour information for spatial lay-out. *Perception* **30**, 167–76

Seneviratne H & Saunders B (2000). An investigation of alcohol dependent respondents' attributions for their own and 'others' relapses. *Addiction Research & Theory* **8**(5), 439–53

Seo Y, Matsumoto K, Park Y, Shinkoda H & Noh T (2000) The relationship between sleep and shift system, age and chronotype in shift workers. *Biological Rhythm Research* **31**(5), 559–79

Serbin LA, Powlishta KK & Gulko J (1993) The development of sex typing in middle childhood. *Monographs of the Society for Research in Child Development* **58**(2), 1–99

Sergent J (1984) An investigation into component and configural processes underlying face perception. *British Journal of Psychology* **75**, 221–42

Shackelford TK, Goetz AT, Buss DM, Euler HA & Hoier S (2005) When we hurt the ones we love: predicting violence against women from men's mate retention. *Personal Relationships* **12**, 447–63

Sharkey KM & Eastman CI (2002) Melatonin phase shifts human circadian rhythms in a placebo-simulated night-work study. *American Journal of Physiological Regulatory, Intergrative and Comparative Physiology* **282**(2), R454–63

Sharkey KM, Fogg L & Eastman CI (2001) Effects of melatonin administration on daytime sleep after simulated night shift work. *Journal of Sleep Research* **10**(3), 181–92

Sharpe L, Walker M, Coughlan MJ, Enersen K & Blaszczynski A (2005) Structural changes to electronic gaming machines as effective harm minimization strategies for non-problem and problem gamblers. *Journal of Gambling Studies* **21**(4), 503–20

Shaungshoti S & Samranvej P (1975) Hypothalamic and pancreatic lesions with diabetes mellitus. *Journal of Neurology, Neurosurgery and Psychiatry* **38**, 1003–07

Shaw K, O'Rourke P, Del Mar C & Kenardy J (2008) Psychological interventions for overweight or obesity. Cochrane Database of Systematic Reviews 2005, **2**, CD003818. DOI: 10.1002/14651858. CD003818.pub2

Shee JC (1964) Pargyline and the cheese reaction. *British Medical Journal* **1**(5395), 1441

Sheeran P & Orbell S (1999) Augmenting the theory of planned behavior: roles for anticipated regret and descriptive norms. *Journal of Applied Social Psychology* **29**(10), 2107–42

Sheese BE & Graziano WG (2005) Deciding to defect the effects of video-game violence on cooperative behavior. *Psychological Science* **16**, 354–57

Sheldon P (2008) The relationship between unwillingness-to-communicate and students' Facebook use. *Journal of Media Psychology: Theories, Methods, & Applications* **20**, 67–75

Sheldrake P & Smart P (2005) Testing for telepathy in connection with e-mails. *Perception and Motor Skills* **101**(3), 771–86

Shepherd J, Davies G & Ellis H (1981) Studies of cue saliency. In *Perceiving and Remembering Faces.* London: Academic Press

Shields J (1962) *Monozygotic Twins Brought up Apart and Brought up Together.* London: Oxford University Press

Shintani M, Ogawa Y, Ebihara K, Aizawa-Abe M, Miyanaga F, Takaya K, Hayashi T, Inoue G, Hosoda K, Kojima M, Kangawa K, Nakao K (2001) Ghrelin a endogenous growth hormone secretagogue is a novel orexigenic peptide that antagonizes leptin action through the activation of hypothalamic neuropeptide Y/Y1 receptor pathway. *Diabetes* **50**(2), 227–32

Shorter L, Brown SL, Quinton SJ & Hinton L (2008) Relationships between body shape discrepancies with favoured celebrities and disordered eating in young women. *Journal of Applied Social Psychology* **38**, 1364–77

Sicher F, Targ E, Moore D & Smith HS (1998) A randomized double-blind study of the effect of distant healing in a population with advanced AIDS: Report of a small scale study. *Worldwide Journal of Medicine* **169**, 356–61

Sidanius J, Pratto F & Mitchell M (1994) In-group identification, social dominance orientation and differential intergroup social allocation. *Journal of Social Psychology* **134**, 151–67

Siegel A & Pott CB (1988) Neural substrates of aggression and flight in the cat. *Progress in Neurobiology* **31**(4), 261–83

Simmen B & Hladik CM (1998) Sweet and bitter taste discrimination in primates: scaling effects across species. *International Journal of Primatology* **69**(3)

Simons-Morton B, Haynie DL, Crump AD, Eitel SP & Saylor KE (2001) Peer and parent influences on smoking and drinking among early adolescents. *Health, Education & Behavior* **28**(1), 95–107

Simoons F (1974) Rejection of fish as human food in Africa: a problem in history and ecology. *Ecology of Food & Nutrition* **3**, 89–105

Simpson JA & Gangestad SW (1992) Individual differences in sociosexuality: evidence for convergent and discriminant validity. *Journal of Personality & Social Psychology* **60**(6), 870–83

Simpson JA & Gangestad SW (1992) Sociosexuality and romantic partner choice. *Journal of Personality* **60**(1), 31–51

Skinner BF (1938) *The Behavior of Organisms: An Experimental Analysis.* ISBN 1-58390-007-1

Skinner BF (1948) Superstition in the pigeon. *Journal of Experimental Psychology* **38**, 168–72

Skinner BF (1953) *Science and Human Behavior.* New York: Free Press

Skodak M & Skeels H (1949) A final follow up study of 100 adopted children. *Journal of Genetic Psychology* **75**, 85–125

Skoog G & Skoog I (1999) A 40-year follow up of patients with obsessive-compulsive disorder. *Archives of General Psychiatry* **56**, 121–27

Skre I, Onstad S, Torgersen S & Kringlen E (2000) The heritability of common phobic fear: a twin study of a clinical sample. *Journal of Anxiety Disorders* **14**, 549–62

Slaby RG & Frey KS (1975) Development of gender constancy and selective attention to same-sex models. *Child Development* **46**, 849–56

Slater A, Rose D & Morison V (1984) Newborn infants' perception of similarities and differences between two and three dimensional stimuli. *British Journal of Developmental Psychology* **2**, 287–94

Slater A, Mattock A & Browne E (1990) Size constancy at birth: newborn infants' response to retinal and real size. *Journal of Experimental Child Psychology* **49**, 314–22

Slater A & Morrison V (1985) Shape constancy and slant perception at birth. *Perception* **14**, 337–44

Slater A, Bremner G, Johnson S, Sherwood P, Hayes R & Brown E (1988) Newborn infants' preference for attractive faces: the role of internal and external facial features. *Infancy* **1**(2), 265–74

Smil V (2003) Eating meat, evolution patterns and consequences. http//:home.cc.umanitoba.ca~vsmil/pdf_/pubsPDR2003.pdf. Accessed on 15/12/08

Smith C (1995) Sleep states and memory processes. *Behavioral & Brain Research* **69**(1–2), 137–45

Smith C (1996) Sleep states, memory processes and synaptic plasticity. *Behavioral & Brain Research* **78**(1), 49–56

Smith PK, Cowie H & Blades M (1998) *Understanding Children's Development.* Oxford: Blackwell

Smoller JW (2007) Genetic boundary violations: phobic disorders and personality. *American Journal of Psychiatry* **164**, 1631–33

Snyder F & Pronko N (1952) *Vision with Spatial Inversion.* Wichita KA: University of Wichita Press

Solley C & Haigh G (1948) A note to Santa Claus. *Topek Research Papers, The Menninger Foundation* **18**, 4–5

Spearman C (1904) General intelligence, objectively determined and measured. *American Journal of Psychology* **15**, 201–93

Spence JT, Helmreich RL & Stapp J (1973). The Personal Attributes Questionnaire: a measure of sex-role stereotypes and masculinity-femininity. *JSAS Catalog of Selected Documents in Psychology* **4**, 43–44

Sperry R (1943) The effects of 180 degree rotation in the retinal field of visuo-motor co-ordination. *Journal of Experimental Zoology* **92**, 263–79

Sprafkin J, Liebert R & Poulos R (1975) Effect of a prosocial televised example on children's helping. *Journal of Experimental Child Psychology* **20**, 119–26

Sroufe LA, Bennett C, Englund M, Urban J & Shulman S (1993) The significance of gender boundaries in preadolescence: contemporary correlates and antecedents of boundary violation and maintenance. *Child Development* **64**(2), 455–66

Standford CB (1999) *The Hunting Apes: Meat Eating and Human Behaviour*. Princeton MA: Princeton University Press

Stapleton JA, Watson L, Spirling LI, Smith R, Milbrandt A, Ratcliffe M & Sutherland G (2008) Varenicline in the routine treatment of tobacco dependence: a pre-post comparison with nicotine replacement therapy and an evaluation in those with mental illness. *Addiction* **103**(1), 146–54

Staude-Muller F, Bliesener T & Luthman S (2008) Hostile and hardened? An experimental study on (de-)sensitization to violence and suffering through playing video games. *Swiss Journal of Psychology* **67**, 41–50

Steenbarger BN & Greenberg RP (1990) Sex roles, stress, and distress: a study of person by situation contingency. *Sex roles* **22**(1–2), 59–68

Stein JA, Dixon EL & Nyamathi AM (2008) Effects of psychosocial and situational variables on substance abuse among homeless adults. *Psychology of Addictive Behavior* **22**(3), 410–6

Stein M, Liebowitz M, Lydiard R, Pitts C, Bushnell W & Gergel I (1998) Paroxetine treatment of generalized social phobia (socialanxiety disorder): a randomized controlled trial. *Journal of the American Medical Association* **280**, 708–713

Steiner JE (1979) Oral and facial innate motor responses to gustatory and to some olfactory stimuli. In JHA Kroeze (ed.) *Preference Behaviour and Chemoreception*. London: Information Retrieval Ltd, 247–611

Stellar E (1989) Long term perspectives on the study of eating behaviour. *Annals of the New York Academy of Sciences* **575**, 478

Stephan FK & Zucker I (1972) Circadian rhythms in drinking behavior and locomotor activity of rats are eliminated by hypothalamic lesions. *Proceedings of the National Academy of Sciences of the USA* **69**(6), 1583–86

Steptoe A, Pollard TM & Wardle J (1995) Development of a measure of the motives underlying the selection of food: the Food Choice Questionnaire. *Appetite* **25**, 267–84

Stern W (1912). *Psychologische Methoden der Intelligenz-Prüfung*. Leipzig: Earth

Sternberg R (1977) *Intelligence, Information Processing and Analogical Reasoning*: *The componential analysis of human abilities.* Hillsdale NJ: Lawrence Erlbaum Associates

Stewart SE, Platko J, Fagerness J, Birns J, Jenike E, Smoller JW, Perlis R, Leboyer M, Delorme M, Chabane N, Rauch SL, Jenike ML & Pauls JL (2007) A genetic family-based association study of OLIG2 in obsessive-compulsive disorder. *Archives of General Psychiatry* **64**, 209–15

Stewart V (1973) Tests of carpentered world hypothesis by race and environmental in America and Zambia. *International Journal of Psychology* **8**, 83–94

Stice E, Spoor S, Bohon C & Small M (2008) Relation between obesity and blunted striatal response to food is moderated by TaqIA A1 Allele. *Science* **322**(5900), 449–52

Stirling LJ & Yeomans MR (2004) Effect of exposure to a forbidden food on eating in restrained and unrestrained women. *Appetite* **23**, 27–41

Stone LJ & Pangborn RM (1990) Preferences and intake measures of salt and sugar, and their relation to personality traits. *Appetite* **15**, 63–79

Storm L & Ertel S (2001) Does psi exist: comments on Milton & Wiseman's meta-analysis of Ganzfield research. *Psychological Bulletin* **127**, 424–33

Stratton G (1896) Some preliminary experiments on vision. *Psychological Review* **3**, 611–17

Streeter SA & Burney DH (2003) Waist–hip ratio and attractiveness: new evidence and a critique of 'a critical test'. **24**, 88–98

Stunkard AJ, Price RA, Ness R, Wadden T, Heshka S, Kanders B & Cormillot A (1990) Childhood onset (age less-than 10) obesity has high familial risk. *International Journal of Obesity* **14**(2), 185–195

Stunkard C, Sorensen TI & Hanis, TW Teasdale, R Chakraborty, WJ Schull & F Schulsinger (1986) An adoption study of human obesity. *The New England Journal of Medicine* v **314**(4), 93–198

Sullivan SA & Birch LL (1990) Pass the sugar, pass the salt: experience dictates preference. *Developmental Psychology* **26**, 546–51

Sumi S (1984) Upside down presentation of the Johansson moving light spot pattern. *Perception* **13**(3), 283–86

Surratt (2007) Snoring can be as harmful to a child's IQ as lead poisoning. http://blogswebmd.com/sleep-disorders/2007/03/snoring-can-be-as-harmful-to-childs-iq.html. Accessed on 10/01/2008

Suvanto S, Harma M, Ilmarinen J & Partinen M (1993) Effects of 10 hour time zone changes on female flight attendants' circadian rhythms of body temperature, alertness and visual search. *Ergonomics* **36**(6), 613–25

Swaffer T & Hollin C (2001) Anger and general health in young offenders. *Journal of Forensic Psychiatry* **12**, 90–103

Symons DK & Clark SE (2000) A longitudinal study of mother–child relationships and theory of mind in the preschool period. *Social Development* **9**, 3–23

Tanaka J & Farah M (1993) Parts and wholes in face recognition. *Quarterly Journal of Experimental Psychology*: *Human Experimental Psychology A* **46**, 225–45

Tanaka W, Kiefer M & Bukach C (2004) A holistic account of the own-race effect in face recognition: evidence from a cross-cultural study. *Cognition* **93**(1), B1–B9

Taylor J, Lloyd DA & Warheit GJ (2006) Self-derogation, peer factors, and drug dependence among a multiethnic sample of young adults. *Journal of Child & Adolescent Substance Abuse* **15**(2), 39–51

Teitelbaum P (1957) Random and food-directed activity in hyperphagic and normal rats. *J Camp Physiol Psychol* **50**, 486–90

Tenenbaum HR & Leaper C (2002) Are parents' gender schemas related to their children's gender-related cognitions? A meta-analysis. *Developmental Psychology* **38**(4), 615–30

Terzano MG, Parrino L, Fioriti G, Orofiamma B & Depoortere H (1990) Modifications of sleep structure induced by increasing levels of acoustic perturbation in normal subjects. *Electroencephalography & Clinical Neurophysiology* **76**(1), 29–38

Tharyan P & Adams CE (2005) Electroconvulsive therapy for schizophrenia. *Cochrane Database of Systematic Reviews* **2**, np

Thibault JW & Kelley HH (1959) *The Social Psychology of Groups*. New York: John Wiley

Thomas PR & Stern JS (eds) (1995) *Weighing the options: criteria for evaluating weight-management programs. Committee to Develop Criteria for Evaluating the Outcomes of Approaches to Prevent and Treat Obesity*. Washington DC: Institute of Medicine National Academies Press

Thompson P (1980) Margaret Thatcher: a new illusion. *Perception* **9**, 483–84

Thompson RF (2000) *The Brain: A Neuroscience Primer*. New York: Worth

Thompson SK (1975) Gender labels and early sex role development. *Child Development* **46**, 339–47

Thorndike E (1911) *Animal Intelligence*. New York: Macmillan

Thornhill R & Palmer CT (2000) *A natural history of rape*. Boston: MIT Press

Thornicroft G & Sartorius N (1993) The course and outcome of depression in different cultures: a 10 year follow-up of the WHO collaborative study on the assessment of depressive disorders. *Psychological Medicine* **23**, 1023–32

Thurstone L (1938) *Primary Mental Abilities*. Chicago: University of Chicago Press

Tobacco Advisory Group, Royal College of Physicians (2000) *Nicotine Addiction in Britain*. London: RCP

Tolman EC & Honzik CH (1930) Insight in Rats. *University of California Publications in Psychology* **4**, 215–32

Tomasello M, Davis-Dasilva M, Camak L & Bard K (1987) Observational learning of tool use by young chimpanzees. *Human Evolution* **2**, 175–83

Toneatto T (1999) Cognitive psychopathology of problem gambling. *Substance Use & Misuse* **34**(11), 1593–604

Tønnesen P (2008) Which drug to be used in smoking cessation? *Polskie Archiwu, Medycyny Wewnetrznej* **118**(6), 373–75

Traub J (1999) Howard Gardner debates James Traub on multiple intelligences. *Cerebrum: The Dana Forum on Brain Science* **1**(2), 13–36

Trivers RL (1971) The evolution of reciprocal altruism. *Quarterly Review of Biology* **46**, 35–56

Trivers RL (1972) Parental investment and sexual selection. In B Campbell (ed.) *Sexual Selection and the Descent of Man*. Chicago: Aldine-Atherton, 136–79

Trivers RL (1974) Parent–offspring conflict. *American Zoologist* **14**, 247–62

Troseth GL (2003) Two-year-old children learn to use video as a source of information. *Developmental Psychology* **39**(1), 140–50

Tucker LA (1985) Television's role regarding alcohol use among teenagers. *Adolescence* **20**(79), 593–8

Tulsky D (ed.) *Clinical Interpretation of the WAIS–111 and WMS–111*. San Diego: Academic Press

Tulving E & Schacter D (1994) *Memory systems*. Cambridge MA: MIT Press

Tuorila H & Pangborn RM (1988) Prediction of reported consumption of selected fat-containing foods. *Appetite* **11**, 81–95

Turkington D, Dudley R, Warman DM & Beck AT (2004) Cognitive-behavioral therapy for schizophrenia: a review. *Journal of Psychiatric Practice* **1**, 5–16

Turkington D, Kingdon D & Turner T (2002) Effectiveness of a brief cognitive-behavioural therapy intervention in the treatment of schizophrenia. *British Journal of Psychiatry* **180**, 523–27

Turnbull C (1961) *The Forest People*. New York: Simon & Schuster

Turner NE, Macdonald J & Somerset M (2008) Life skills, mathematical reasoning and critical thinking: a curriculum for the prevention of problem gambling. *Journal of Gambling Studies* **24**(3), 367–80

Turner T (2008) *Social Studies and the Young Learner* **21**(1), 11–14

Twemlow SW, Sacco FC & Williams P (1996) A clinical and interactionist perspective on the victim–bully–bystander relationship. *Bulletin of the Menninger Clinic* **60**, 296–313

Uddin MS (2006) Arranged marriage: a dilemma for young British Asians. *Diversity in Health & Social Care* **3**, 211–19

Ungerstedt U (1971) *Acta Physiol Scand* **82** Suppl. (367, 69–93)

Valzelli L (1973) The 'isolation syndrome' in mice. *Psychopharmacologia* **31**, 305–20

Valzelli L & Bernasconi S (1979) Aggressiveness by isolation and brain serotonin turnover changes in different strains of mice. *Neuropsychobiology* **5**, 129–35

van de Poll NE, Taminiau MS, Endert E & Louwerse AL (1988) Gonadal steroid influence upon sexual and aggressive behaviour of female rats. *International Journal of Neuroscience* **41**, 271–86

Vandello JA & Cohen D (2003) Male honor and female fidelity: implicit cultural scripts that perpetuate domestic violence. *Journal of Personality & Social Psychology* **84**, 997–1010

Van Lommel P, Van Wees R, Meyers V & Elferrich I (2001) Near-death experience in survivors of cardiac arrest: a prospective study in the Netherlands. *The Lancet* **358**, 2039–45

Van Oppen P, Van Balkom A, DeHaan E & Van Dyck R (2005) Cognitive therapy and exposure in vivo alone and in combination with fluvoxamine in obsessive-compulsive disorder: A 5-year follow-up. *Journal of Clinical Psychiatry* **66**, 1415–22

Vernon P (1960) *Intelligence and Attainment Tests*. New York: Philosophical Library Inc.

Vernon P (1969) *Intelligence and Cultural Environment*. London: Methuen

Virkkunen M, DeJong J, Bartko J, Goodwin FK & Linnoila M (1989) Relationship of psychobiological variables to recidivism in violent offenders and impulsive fire setters. *Archives of General Psychiatry* **46**, 600–03

Virkkunen M, Nuutila A, Goodwin FK & Linnoila M (1987) Cerebrospinal fluid monoamine metabolite levels in male arsonists. *Archives of General Psychiatry* **44**, 241–47

Von Helmholtz H (1909) In AGullstrand, J Von Kries & W Nagel (eds) Handbuch der Physiologischen Optic, 3rd edn Vol. 1. Hamburg: Goss

Von Senden M (1932, 1960) *Space and Sight: The Perception of Space and Shape in the Congenitally Blind Before and After Operations*. London: Methuen (original work published 1932)

Voracek M, Tran US & Formann AK (2008) Birthday and birthmate problems: misconceptions of probability among psychology undergraduates and casino visitors and personnel. *Perception & Motor Skills* **106**(1), 91–103

Vujovic S, Popovic S, Sbutega-Milosevic G, Djordjevic M & Gooren L (2008) Transsexualism in Serbia: a twenty-year follow-up study. *Journal of Sexual Medicine*, 4 March.

Wagner FA & Anthony JC (2002) Into the world of illegal drug use: exposure opportunity and other mechanisms linking the use of alcohol, tobacco, marijuana, and cocaine. *American Journal of Epidemiology* **155**(10), 918–25

Waldman I, Weinberg R & Scarr S (1994). Racial-group differences in IQ in the Minnesota Transracial Adoption Study: a reply to Levin and Lynn. *Intelligence* **19**, 29–44

Walker GJ, Courtneya KS & Jinyang D (2006) Ethnicity, gender, and the theory of planned behavior: the case of playing the lottery. *Journal of Leisure Research* **38**(2), 224–48

Wallien MS & Cohen-Kettenis PT (2008) Psychosexual outcome of gender-dysphoric children. *Journal of the American Academy of Child & Adolescent Psychiatry* **47**(12), 1413–23

Walster E, Aronson V, Abrahams D & Rottmann L (1966) Importance of physical attractiveness in dating behaviour. *Journal of Personality & Social Psychology* **4**, 508–16

Walster E & Walster GW (1969) *A New Look at Love*. Reading MA: Addison-Wesley

Wansink B, Garg N & Jeffrey J (2008) The sad are twice as likely to eat comfort food. *Journal of Marketing* **72**(1)

Warden D & Mackinnon S (2003) Prosocial children, bullies, victims and children. An investigation of their sociometric status, empathy and social competence. *British Journal of Developmental Psychology* **21**, 367–85

Wardle J, Carnell S, Haworth CMA & Plomin R (2008) Evidence for a strong genetic influence on childhood adiposity despite the force of the obesogenic environment. *American Journal of Clinical Nutrition* **87**, 398–404

Warren CW, Jones NR, Peruga A, Chauvin J, Baptiste JP, Costa de Silva V, el Awa F, Tsouros A, Rahman K, Fishburn B, Bettcher DW & Asma S (2008) Global youth tobacco surveillance, 2000–2007. *MMWR Surveillance Summaries* **57**(1), 1–28

Watson JB & Rayner R (1920) Conditioned emotional responses. *Journal of Experimental Psychology* **3**, 1–14

Watson RI (1973) Investigation into deindividuation using a cross-cultural survey technique. *Journal of Personality and Social Psychology* **25**, 342–45

Watt C (2005) Psychological factors. In J Henry (ed.) *Parapsychology*. London, Routledge

Weatherly JN, Sauter JM & King BM (2004) The 'big win' and resistance to extinction when gambling. *Journal of Psychology* **138**(6), 495–504

Weinraub M, Clemens LP, Sockloff A, Ethridge R, Gracely E & Myers B (1984) The development of sex role stereotypes in the third year: relationships to gender labelling, gender identity sex-typed toy preferences, and family characteristics. *Child Development* **55**, 1493–1503

Whiten A (1999) Culture in chimpanzees. *Nature* **399**, 682–85

Whiten A & Byrne RW (1988) *Machiavellian Intelligence: Social Expertise and the Evolution of Intellect in Monkeys, Apes, and Humans.* New York: Oxford University Press

Wiesel T & Hubel D (1982) Effects of visual deprivation on morphology and physiology of cells in the cat's visual cortex. *Nature* **299**, 583–91

Wilhelm K, Mitchell PB, Niven H, Finch A, Wedgewood L, Scimone A, Blair IP, Parker G & Schofield P (2006) Life events, first depression onset and the serotonin transporter gene. *British Journal of Psychiatry* **188**, 210–15

Willer CJ, Speliotes EK, Loos RJ, Li S, Lindgren CM, Heid IM, Berndt SI, Elliott AL *et al.* (2008) Six new loci associated with body mass index highlight a neuronal influence on body weight regulation. *Nature Genetics*

Willerman L, Rutledge A & Bigler G (1991) In vivo brain size and intelligence. *Intelligence* **15**, 223–28

Williams E, Francis LJ & Robbins M (2007) Personality & paranormal belief: a study among adolescents. *Pastoral Psychology* **56**, 9–14

Williams JE & Best DL (1990) *Measuring Sex Stereotypes: A Multi-Nation Study.* Newbury Park CA: Sage Publications

Williams JMG, Healy H, Eade JE, Windle G, Cowen PJ, Green MW & Durlach P (2002) Mood, eating behaviour and attention. *Psychological Medicine*, **32** 469–81

Williams RJ & Connolly D (2006) Does learning about the mathematics of gambling change gambling behavior? *Psychology of Addictive Behaviors* **20**(1), 62–68

Williams RL (1972) The B.I.T.C.H-100 — A culture specific test. At American Psychological Association Annual Convention

Williams TM (1981) How and what do children learn from television? *Human Communication Research* **7**(2), 180–92

Wilson BJ (2008) Media and children's aggression, fear, and altruism. *Future of Children* **18**, 87–118

Wilson BJ, Smith SL, Potter WJ, Kunkel D, Linz D, Colvin CM & Donnerstein E (2002) Violence in children's television programming: assessing the risks. *Journal of Communication* **52**, 5–35

Wilson P, Sharp C & Carr S (1999) The prevalence of gender dysphoria in Scotland: a primary care study. *British Journal of General Practice* **49**(449), 991–92

Wilson TW, Neuendorff DA, Lewis AW & Randel RD (2002) Effect of zeranol or melengestrol acetate (MGA) on testicular and antler development and aggression in farmed fallow bucks. *Journal of Animal Science* **80**, 1433–41

Wimmer H & Perner J (1983) Beliefs about beliefs: representation and constraining function of wrong beliefs in young children's understanding of deception. *Cognition* **13**, 103–28

Wing R & Hill J (2001) *Annual Review of Nutrition* **21**(1)

Wing RR (2002) Behavioral weight control. In TA Wadden & Stunkard AJ (eds) *Handbook of Obesity Treatment*. New York: Guilford 301–16

Winn *et al*. (1984) *Neuroscience* **12**, 225–40

Wisebeck G, Maurer C, Thome J, Jakob F & Boening J (1995) Neuroendocrine support for a relationship between 'novelty seeking' and dopaminergic function in alcohol-dependent men. *Psychoneuroendocrinology* **20**, 755–61 Wiseman R & Greening E (2005) 'It's still bending': verbal suggestion and alleged psychokinetic ability. *British Journal of Psychology* **96**, 115–27

Wiseman R & Watt C (2004) Measuring superstitious belief: Why lucky charms matter. *Proceedings of the 47th Annual Convention of the Parapsychological Association*. Vienna. 291–98

Wiseman R & Watt C (2006) Belief in psychic ability and the misattribution hypothesis: a qualitative review. *British Journal of Psychology* **97**, 323–38

Wohl MJ, Young MM & Hart KE (2007) Self-perceptions of dispositional luck: relationship to DSM gambling symptoms, subjective enjoyment of gambling and treatment readiness. *Substance Use & Misuse* **42**(1), 43–63

Wojciulik E, Kanwisher N & Driver J (1998) Specialized processing within the primate visual system. *Journal of Physiology* **79**, 1574–78

Wolff GE, Crosby RD, Roberts JA & Wittrock DA (2000) Differences in daily stress, mood, coping and eating behaviour in binge eating and non-binge eating college women. *Addictive Behaviour* **25**(2) 205–16

Wood DJ, Bruner JS & Ross G (1976) The role of tutoring in problem-solving. *Journal of Child Psychology and Psychiatry* **17**, 89–100

Wood RT & Griffiths MD (2004) Adolescent lottery and scratchcard players: do their attitudes influence their gambling behaviour? *Journal of Adolescence* **27**(4), 467–75

Wood W & Eagly AH (2002) A cross-cultural analysis of the behavior of women and men: implications for the origins of sex differences. *Psychological Bulletin* **128**(5), 699–727

Woody GE, McLellan AT, Luborsky L & O'Brien CP (1990) Psychotherapy and counseling for methadone-maintained opiate addicts: results of research studies. *NIDA Research Monograph* **104**, 9–23

World Health Organization (2006) 1.1. billion people are overweight. *Appetite* **47**

Xian H, Shah KR, Phillips SM, Scherrer JF, Volberg R & Eisen SA (2008) Association of cognitive distortions with problem and pathological gambling in adult male twins. *Psychiatry Research* **160**(3), 300–07

Xu B, Roos JL, Levy S, van Rensberg EJ, Gogos JA & Karayiorgou M (2008) Strong association of de novo copy number mutations with sporadic schizophrenia. *Nature Genetics* **40**, 880–85

Yamamura S, Morishima H, Kumano-go T, Suganuma N, Matsumoto H, Adachi H, Sigedo Y, Mikami A, Kai T, Masuyama A, Takano T, Sugita Y & Takeda M (2009) The effect of *Lactobacillus helveticus* fermented milk on sleep and health perception in elderly subjects. *European Journal of Clinical Nutrition* **63**(1), 100–05

Yang S, Hung W, Sung K & Farn C (2006) Investigating initial trust towards e-tailers from the elaboration likelihood model perspective. *Psychology & Marketing* **23**, 429–45

Yanowitz KL & Weathers KJ (2004) Do boys and girls act differently in the classroom? A content analysis of student characters in educational psychology textbooks. *Sex Roles: A Journal of Research* **51**, 101–07

Yerkes R (1915). In S Gould (1982) A nation of morons. *New Scientist*, May, 349–52

Yonas A, Cleaves WT & Pettersen L (1978) Development of sensitivity to pictorial depth. *Science* **200**, 77–79

Young AW, Hay DC & Ellis AW (1985) The faces that launched a thousand slips: everyday difficulties and errors in recognising people. *British Journal of Psychology* **76**, 495–523

Young AW, Hellawell D & Hay DC (1987) Configural information in face perception. *Perception* **16**, 747–59

Young AW, McWeeny KH, Hay DC & Ellis AW (1986) Matching familiar and unfamiliar faces on identity and expression. *Psychologische Forschung* **48**, 63–68

Young MM, Wohl MJ, Matheson K, Baumann S & Anisman H (2008) The desire to gamble: the influence of outcomes on the priming effects of a gambling episode. *Journal of Gambling Studies* **24**(3), 275–93

Zafirovski M (2005) Social exchange theory under scrutiny: a positive critique of its economic-behaviorist formulations. *Electronic Journal of Sociology*

Zahn-Waxler C (2000) The development of empathy, guilt, and internalization of distress: implications for gender differences in internalizing and externalizing habitually violent offenders. In R Davidson (ed.) *Wisconsin Symposium on Emotion: Vol 1. Anxiety, Depression, and Emotion*. Oxford: Oxford University Press

Zajonc RB (1968). Attitudinal effects of mere exposure. *Journal of Personality & Social Psychology Monographs* **9**(2, Pt 2), 1–27

Zajonc R & Markus H (1975) Birth order and intellectual development. *Psychological Review* **82**, 74–88

Zeller AC (1987) A role for children in hominid evolution. *Man* **22**, 528–57

Zepelin H & Rechtschaffen A (1974) Mammalian sleep, longevity and energy metabolism. *Brain, Behaviour and Evolution* **10**, 425

Zhao GQ, Zhang Y, Hoon MA, Chandrashekar J, Erlenbach I, Ryba NJP & Zuker CS (2008) Researchers define molecular basis of human 'sweet tooth' and umami taste. http://hum-molgen.org/NewsGen/11-2003/000011.html. Accessed on 19/12/2008

Zhou JN, Hofman MA, Gooren LJ & Swaab DF (1995) A sex difference in the human brain and its relation to transsexuality. *Nature* **378**(6552), 68–70

Zimbardo P (1969) The human choice: individuation, reason and order vs deindividuation, impulse and chaos. In WJ Arnold & D Levine (eds) *Nebraska Symposium on Motivation 17*. Lincoln: University of Nebraska Press

Zimbardo P (1970) The human choice: individuation, reason and order vs deindividuation, impulse and chaos. In WJ Arnold & D Levine (eds) *Nebraska Symposium on Motivation 18*. Lincoln: University of Nebraska Press

Zimbardo P (2004) A situationist perspective on the psychology of evil. In AG Miller (ed.) *The Social Psychology of Good and Evil*. New York: Guilford Press

Zinner (2002) Babies fond of salt have higher blood pressure and a granny with hypertension. *Journal of the American Heart Association*, August

Zona MA, Sharma KK & Lane J (1993) A comparative study of erotomanic and obsessional subjects in a forensic sample. *Journal of Forensic Science* **39**, 905–07

Index

Acknowledgements

The authors and publishers are grateful to the following for permissions to reproduce copyright material.

p1, © olly; p2, © cjpembertons; p3 (left), © Solovieva Ekaterina; p3 (right), © Margo Harrison; p4 (top), © Science Photo Library; p4(bottom), © Julia Russell; p4 (right), © Clivia; p5 (top), © Neil Borden/Science Photo Library; p5 (bottom), © Kurt De Bruyn; p6, © Mark Conlin/Alamy; p7, © Jean-Marc Strydom; p9, © Michael Chamberlin; p10, © Alan Novelli/Alamy; p12, © Greg Boiarsky; p13 (top), © Pirate!; p13 (bottom), © David Levenson/Alamy; p17, © Susan Stevenson; p19 (left), © NZG; p19 (right), © Paul Cowan; p21, © Christine Boyd; p24, © Victor Prikhodko; p25, © Pictorial Press Ltd/Alamy; p26 (left), © The Granger Collection, NYC/TopFoto; p26 (right), © Julia Russell; p26 (bottom), © The Granger Collection/TopFoto; p29 (both), Courtesy of Richard Gregory; p30 (top), Courtesy of Richard Gregory; p30 (bottom), © Stanislav Popov; p31, © Rainer Jahns/Alamy; p33, © Julia Russell; p34, © Andrey Filipskiy; p36 (left), © Cheryl Casey; p36 (right), © Julia Russell; p37, © nyul; p38, © 7artman; p39, © Science Source/Science Photo Library; p40, © Freddy Eliasson; p41, © Mary Evans Picture Library; p43, © Christine Osborne Pictures/Alamy; p49, © ImageState/Alamy; p51, © Thompson, 'Margaret Thatcher: a new illusion' Perception, 1980, 9, pp 483–4. Pion Limited, London; p52 (top), © AP/Press Association Images; p52 (bottom left and right), © NASA, Viking Project.; p56, © Monkey Business; p57, © sumos; p58, © robert mobley; p59 (top), © Andi Berger; p59 (bottom), © Hannamariah; p60, © ZTS; p61, © Yuri Arcurs; p62 (top), © Loke Yek Mang; p62 (bottom), © StudioNewmarket; p63, © Pictorial Press Ltd/Alamy; p64 (top), © Lazlo Inacio/Alamy; p64 (bottom), © Norman Reid; p65(left), © Kzenon; p65 (right), © Jason Stitt; p66, © Suprijono Suharjoto; p67, © Brebca; p68 (left), © memo; p68 (right), © Galina Barskaya; p69 (top), © Darren Baker; p69 (bottom), © Lisa F. Young; p73, © Shukaylov Roman; p74, © Getty Images; p75, © Albert Bandura; p76, © Photos 12/Alamy; p77 (top), © Doug Steley A/Alamy; p77 (bottom), © Content Mine International/Alamy; p78, © David Fisher/Rex Features; p79, © Viktors Neimanis; p80 (left, both), © Phillip Zimbardo; p80 (right), © David Hoffman Photo Library/Alamy; p81, © Monkey Business Images ; p82 (left), © Corbis 42-16590407; p82 (right), © Martine Oger; p84, © iofoto ; p85 (left), Eric Gevaert; p85 (right), © Wolfgang Amri ; p86, © MLA Photography; p87, © Alamy; p88, © Jason Maehl ; p90 (left), © Thomas M Perkins ; p90 (top right), © Muellek ; p90 (bottom), © imagebroker/Alamy; p91 (left), © IHLAS/Rex Features; p92, © Getty Images; p96, © Monkey Business; p97 (top), © Monkey Business Images; p97 (bottom), © Diego Cervo; p98 (left), © Lana K; p98 (right), © Ljupco Smokovski; p99, © Amy Walters; p100, © buzya kalapkina; p101, © Emilia Stasiak; p104 (top), © Kevin Renes; p104 (bottom), © Jan van der Hoeven; p105 (top), © gpalmer; p105 (bottom), © Bjorn Heller; p106 (left), © Max Earey; p106 (right), © Sergey Peterman; p107, © Ljupco Smokovski; p108, © Ivonne Wierink; p109, © Christian Darkin; p112, © Mark Aplet; p117, © amorando; p118, © Fotolia!; p119, © Pavel Losevsky; p121 (left), © Imagestate Media Partners Limited – Impact Photos/Alamy; p121 (right), © emin kuliyev; p122, © Pictorial Press Ltd/Alamy; p123, © Gelpi; p124, © Victor Fraile/Alamy; p125, © Karen Struthers;

p128, © Andrew Syred/Science Photo Library; p130 (left), © Julia Russell; p130 (right), © iofoto; p132, © Gianni Dagli Orti/Corbis; p133, © Sipa Press/Rex Features; p134, © Julia Russell; p135, Wallenrock; p136, © Pictorial Press Ltd/Alamy; p137 (left), © Diego Cervo/Shutterstock, © Vallentin Vassileff, © Lisa F. Young/ Shutterstock, © iofoto/Shutterstock, © Sudheer Sakthan/ Shutterstock, © Gelpi/Shutterstock,; p137 (right), © istock; p138 (top) © Julia Russell; p138 (bottom), © shutterstock/Todd Pierson; p140, © János Gehring; p142, © ktsdesign; p143 (left), © wizdata2; p143 (right), © Yong Hian Lim; p144, © kristian sekulic; p146, © Thomas Peter Voss; p147 (left), © Jonathan Larsen; p147 (right), © Olga Lyubkina; p149, © Szocs Jozsef; p151, © Adrian Hughes; p153, © Robyn Mackenzie; p153 (left), © Lee Torrens; p153 (right), © oksana.perkins; p154, © Marcin Perkowski; p155 (left), © Winthrop Brookhouse; p155 (right), © glen gaffney; p156 (top), © Trinity Mirror/Mirrorpix/Alamy; p156 (bottom), © Figure 1 from Prior H et al. (2008) Mirror-Induced Behavior in the Magpie (Pica pica): Evidence of Self-Recognition . PLoS Biol 6(8): e202 doi:10.1371/journal.pbio.0060202; p157, © William Attard McCarthy; p158, © Morgan Lane Photography; p159 (left), © Stefanie van der Vinden; p159 (right), © Zsolt Nyulaszi; p160, © iChip; p161, © Galina Barskaya; p162, © Rob Marmion; p163, © Linda Mattson; p166, © Kurhan; p167, © Dale A Stork; p168, © Doug Goodman/Science Photo Library; p170, © Monika Adamczyk; p171, © Trisha McCauley; p172, © Jose Manuel Gelpi; p173 (top), © Artyom Yefimov; p173 (bottom), © ChipPix; p174, © Neo Edmund; p175, © FutureDigitalDesign; p176, © Kelpfish; p178 (left), © bilderbox; p178 (right), © clearviewstock; p179, © Michael Wuelfrath; p180, © Edyta Pawlowska; p181, © Surkov Vladimir; p182, © Joanna Zielinska; p183, © Eline Spek; p184, © marilyn barbone; p185, © James Steidl; p186, © Marco Iacoboni1,2,3,4*, Istvan Molnar-Szakacs1,3,4, Vittorio Gallese5, Giovanni Buccino5, John C. Mazziotta1,3,6,7,8, Giacomo Rizzolatti5; p189, © Bruce Rolff; p182, © Anita Patterson Peppers; p194, © Marcin Balcerzak; p195, © karen roach; p197, © GARY MARSHALL; p198, © Will Mcintyre/Science Photo Library; p199, © Tracy Martinez; p200 (left), © Anton Novožilov; p200 (right), © Cheryl Casey; p201, © Gina Sanders; p202, © Dennis Cox; p203, © wrangler; p204, © RichG; p205, © Losevsky Pavel; p206, © Chad Littlejohn; p208, © alexandre zveiger; p209, © sint; p210, © Lisa F. Young; p211 (top), © Ella; p211 (bottom), © endostock; p212, © Alexander Gitlits; p213, © Elena Elisseeva; p214, © Tomasz Trojanowski; p217, © Stokato; p218, © viZualStudio; p219, © Ayesha Wilson; p222, © NiDerLander; p223, © ITV/Rex Features; p224, © Albert Bandura; p225 (left), © David Davis; p225 (right), © Reuters/ CORBIS; p226 (left) , © Bettmann/CORBIS; p226 (right), © New Line/Everett/Rex Features; p227, © Lions Gate/Everett/Rex Features; p228 (top), © netzfrisch.de; p228 (bottom), © GreenGate Publishing; p229 (left), © STEWART COOK/Rex Features; p229 (bottom), © GreenGate Publishing; p230, © PSL Images/Alamy; p232, © News Group Newspapers Ltd; p233, © PCmi; p234, © pst; p236 (left), © Chris Pearsall/Alamy; p236 (right), © Kirsty Wigglesworth/AP/PA Photos; p238 (left), © Entertainment Press; p238 (right), © Stewart Goldstein/Alamy; p239, © Entertainment Press; p240, © Duettographics; p242 (left), © Trinity Mirror/Mirrorpix/Alamy; p242 (right), © Phil Anthony;

p245, © Sergej Razvodovskij; p247, © franck camhi; p248 (left), © Monkey Business; p248 (right), © Courtesy of University of Texas; p249 (top), © (1996) National Academy of Sciences, U.S.A., p249 (bottom),© Glenda M Powers; p251, © Simone van den Berg; p252, © David Davis; p253, © cloki; p255, © Mary Evans Picture Library/Alamy; p256, © Horticulture; p257, © Ludovic LAN; p258, © EcoView; p259, © Kaspars Grinvalds; p259, © Yuri Arcurs; p261, © Leah-Anne Thompson; p262 (top), © Andresr; p262 (bottom), © Romain Letang; p263, © Anthony Devlin/PA Archive/PA Photos; p264, © iStock; p268, © Gustoimages/ Science Photo Library; p270 (left), © Helene Rogers/Alamy; p270 (right), © Helene Rogers/Alamy; p271, © Lukiyanova Natalia/ frenta; p273 (left), © Crown Copyright; p273 (right), © Courtesy of No Smoking Day; p274, © Shawn Talbot; p275, © jenny; p278, © Joel Calheiros; p279, © innovari; p280(left), © Stephen Coburn; p280 (right), © jay clark; p281 (left), © Gail Johnson; p281 (top right), © Photos 12/Alamy; p281(bottom left & right), © Science & Society; p282 (left), © Richard Gardner/Rex Features; p282 (right), © Jeremy Walker/Science Photo Library;

p284, © dragon_fang; p285 (left), © Mirrorpix; p285 (right), © Konstantin Sutyagin; p286, © Greg; p287, © Rob Byron; p290 (top), © Lev Dolgatshjov; p290 (bottom), © Katrina Brown; p291, © Franco Tinè; p292, © Jan Inberg; p293 (top), © Yuri Arcurs / Fotolia; p293 (bottom), © Patricia Marks; p295, © bilderbox; p299, © suravid; p300, © PA/PA Archive/PA Photos; p301, © Bill Pierce; p302 (bottom), © Vlad Mereuta; p304, © Editorial Image, LLC/Alamy; p305, © innovari; p309, © Ana Blazic; p310 (left), © Andresr; p310 (right), © Darren Baker; p311 (left), © Yuri Arcurs; p311 (right), © Leah-Anne Thompson; p312 (left), © Tomasz Trojanowski; p312 (right), © nsphotography; p313, © Riekephotos; p314, © Science & Society; p315, © Andresr; p317, © Angela Hampton pic library/alamy; p317, © Henrique Daniel Araujo; p321, © TTphoto; p331, © GOH SIOK HIAN; p332, © Konstantin Sutyagin; p337, © Tatiana Morozova; p341, © Yobidaba; p344, © Luc Ubaghs; p345, © Jani Bryson; p346, © Silvia Ottaviano; p347, © Anatoliy Samara; p349, © Julia Russell; p354, © Color and CopySpace™.